lonely planet

Bali, Lombok & Nusa Tenggara

Nusa Tenggara
p286

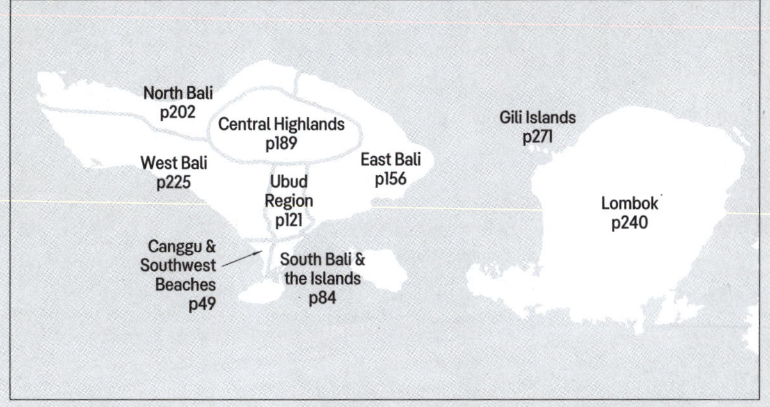

Sarah Reid, Jade Bremner, Mark Eveleigh,
Narina Exelby, Marco Ferrarese, Leyla Rose

OLENA ZN/SHUTTERSTOCK

Tirta Gangga (p176)

CONTENTS

Plan Your Trip

The Journey Begins Here....4
Bali, Lombok & Nusa Tenggara Map....6
Our Picks....8
Islands & Regions....22
Itineraries....24
When to Go....32
Get Prepared for Bali, Lombok & Nusa Tenggara....34
Where to Stay in South Bali....36
How to Navigate Bali's Traffic....37
The Food Scene....38
The Outdoors....42

The Guide

Canggu & Southwest Beaches....49
- Canggu Area....52
- Seminyak Area....63
- Kuta & Legian....73

South Bali & the Islands....84
- Sanur....88
- Denpasar....92
- Uluwatu....96
- Beyond Uluwatu....104
- Nusa Lembongan....109
- Beyond Nusa Lembongan....115

Ubud Region....121
- Ubud....124
- Beyond Ubud (North)....144
- Beyond Ubud (South)....149

East Bali....156
- Klungkung....160
- Beyond Klungkung....163
- Sidemen....166
- Beyond Sidemen....169
- Padangbai....172
- Beyond Padangbai....175
- Amed....180
- Beyond Amed....184

Central Highlands....189
- Munduk....192
- Beyond Munduk....198

North Bali....202
- Lovina....206
- Beyond Lovina....209
- Pemuteran....215
- Beyond Pemuteran....218

West Bali....225
- Tabanan & Mengwi....228
- Beyond Tabanan & Mengwi....231
- Jembrana Regency....235

Lombok....240
- Kuta....244
- Beyond Kuta....248
- Senggigi....251
- Beyond Senggigi....254
- Senaru....257
- Beyond Senaru....260
- Southwestern Peninsula & the Secret Gilis....264

Gili Islands....271
- Gili Trawangan....274
- Gili Meno....278
- Gili Air....281

Nusa Tenggara....286
- Flores....290
- Beyond Flores....301
- West Timor....306
- Beyond West Timor....315
- Sumba....318

Toolkit

Arriving....334
Getting Around....335
How to Hire a Car & Driver....336
Money....337
Accommodation....338
Family Travel....339
Health & Safe Travel....340
How to Travel Safely by Boat....341
Food, Drink & Nightlife....342
Responsible Travel....344
LGBTIQ+ Travellers....346
Accessible Travel....347
Bali's Temple Architecture....348
Women Travellers....350
Nuts & Bolts....351
Language....352

Storybook

A History of Bali, Lombok & Nusa Tenggara in 15 Places....356
Meet the Balinese....360
Threads of Tradition....362
Saving the 'Last Paradise'....364
Balinese Hinduism: A Spiritual Blend....366
In Indonesia, Contemporary Art Blooms & Booms....370

AUSCAPE/UNIVERSAL IMAGES GROUP/GETTY IMAGES

Diving, Pulau Menjangan (p220)

BALI, LOMBOK & NUSA TENGGARA

THE JOURNEY BEGINS HERE

I wasn't sure if Bali would be my kind of place. But there was something about the faded photo of my dad on a paradisiacal-looking Kuta street in 1976 that made me want to find out. In 2004, armed with a Lonely Planet guidebook, I visited Bali and Lombok for the first time. I was mesmerised by Balinese dance in Ubud. I rose with the roosters on Nusa Lembongan to surf uncrowded waves. I floated alongside turtles in the Gilis. I even scaled Gunung Agung after a big night out in Kuta. And I loved every minute.

Since then, I've criss-crossed Bali and Nusa Tenggara. Bali and other places have changed significantly over the years, but the region's endless opportunities for adventure continue to draw me back, again and again.

Sarah Reid

@sarahreidtravels

An award-winning travel writer, Sarah has contributed to over 40 Lonely Planet titles. Read her stories at sarahreid.com.au. Sarah researched Canggu & Southwest Beaches and North Bali.

My favourite experience is diving along the coral-encrusted walls surrounding **Pulau Menjangan** (p220) on the lookout for critters big and small.

WHO GOES WHERE

Our writers and experts choose the places that, for them, define Bali, Lombok and Nusa Tenggara.

CLOCKWISE FROM TOP LEFT: PATRICKWA/SHUTTERSTOCK, MONTICELLO/SHUTTERSTOCK, GORAN_SAFAREK/SHUTTERSTOCK, JAKOB FISCHER/SHUTTERSTOCK, DENIS MOSKVINOV/SHUTTERSTOCK

South Bali is a surfers' paradise with all the elements of an adventurous road trip. But I prefer to leave the mainland by boat to **Nusa Lembongan** (p109) for fewer crowds and truly spectacular waves.

Jade Bremner

𝕏 @jadebremner @jadeob

Jade has written more than 60 Lonely Planet books and specialises in adventure travel. She researched South Bali & the Islands.

I was astounded by the mountains that lie between Danau Tamblingan and the **Jatiluwih rice terraces** (p196). I hadn't expected to spend five hours trekking through such beautiful rainforest without seeing a single building or any other hikers.

Mark Eveleigh

Mark has authored several books on Bali, including Driftwood Chandeliers, *a magical realist novel. He researched the Central Highlands.*

I always find myself drawn back to **Sidemen** (p166). There are so many options for walking (the local guides know lots of trails), and the 3km-long community-managed Sidemen Rice Terrace trail is a good option for an independent walk.

Narina Exelby

ne-where.world

Narina is a roaming South African who has contributed to international titles for more than 25 years. She researched East Bali.

Bali has changed immensely since I first visited – so I was surprised to find a place like **Perancak** (p237), which still flies well under tourism's radar. Lined with colourful fishing boats moored in pairs like husbands and wives, Perancak feels untouristed and authentic.

Marco Ferrarese

@marcoferrarese

Marco is a Malaysia-based author who has travelled to dozens of Indonesian islands. He researched the Ubud Region and West Bali.

Tetebatu (p249) in the early morning is incredible – the first rays of sun illuminate the glistening fields, while the graceful Gunung Rinjani towers in the background. You'll feel as if you're the only person around, save for a few farmers getting a headstart to the day.

Leyla Rose

leylarosewrites.com

Leyla is a food and travel writer, and has written for publications around the world. She researched Lombok, the Gili Islands and Nusa Tenggara.

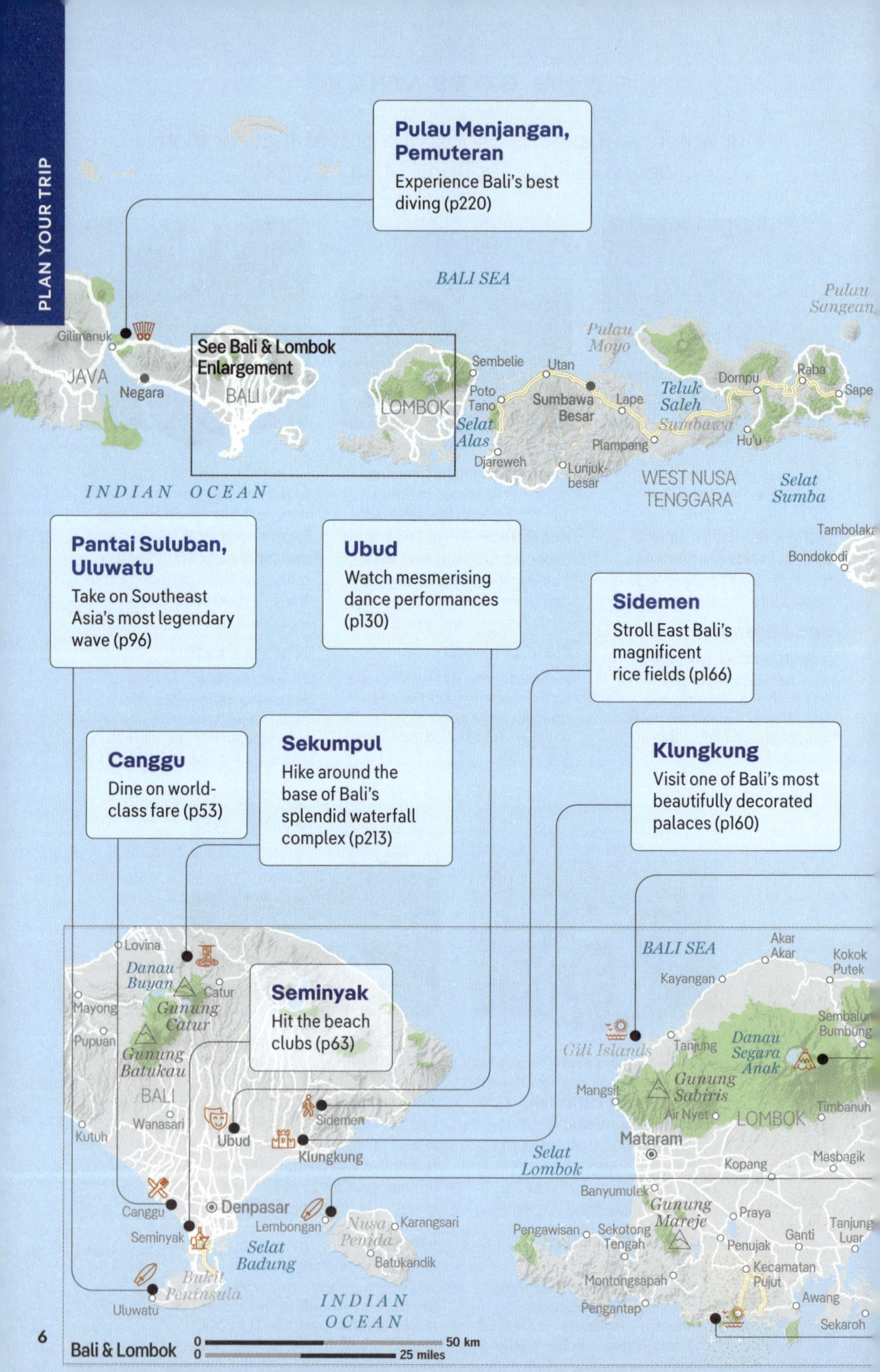

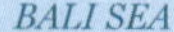

Pulau Menjangan, Pemuteran
Experience Bali's best diving (p220)
BALI SEA
Pulau Sangean
Gilimanuk
JAVA
Negara
See Bali & Lombok Enlargement
BALI
LOMBOK
Sembelie
Poto Tano
Selat Alas
Utan
Pulau Moyo
Sumbawa Besar
Lape
Teluk Saleh
Sumbawa
Dompu
Raba
Sape
Hu'u
Plampang
Djareweh
Lunjuk-besar
WEST NUSA TENGGARA
Selat Sumba
INDIAN OCEAN
Tambolaka
Bondokodi
Pantai Suluban, Uluwatu
Take on Southeast Asia's most legendary wave (p96)
Ubud
Watch mesmerising dance performances (p130)
Sidemen
Stroll East Bali's magnificent rice fields (p166)
Canggu
Dine on world-class fare (p53)
Sekumpul
Hike around the base of Bali's splendid waterfall complex (p213)
Klungkung
Visit one of Bali's most beautifully decorated palaces (p160)
Seminyak
Hit the beach clubs (p63)
Lovina
Danau Buyan
Catur
Mayong
Gunung Catur
Pupuan
Gunung Batukau
BALI
Wanasari
Kutuh
Ubud
Sidemen
Klungkung
Canggu
Denpasar
Seminyak
Lembongan
Nusa Penida
Karangsari
Batukandik
Selat Badung
Bukit Peninsula
Uluwatu
INDIAN OCEAN
BALI SEA
Akar Akar
Kokok Putek
Kayangan
Sembalun Bumbung
Gili Islands
Tanjung
Danau Segara Anak
Gunung Sabiris
Mangsit
Air Nyet
LOMBOK
Timbanuh
Mataram
Selat Lombok
Kopang
Masbagik
Banyumulek
Gunung Mareje
Praya
Pengawisan
Sekotong Tengah
Penujak
Ganti
Tanjung Luar
Kecamatan Pujut
Montongsapah
Awang
Pengantap
Sekaroh
Bali & Lombok
0 50 km
0 25 miles

Komodo National Park, Flores
Spot the world's largest lizard (p302)

Alor Archipelago
Go on a scuba-diving adventure (p315)

West Sumba
Witness Asia's most extravagant harvest festival (p323)

Gili Air
Kick back on a gorgeous beach (p281)

Gunung Rinjani, Senaru
Climb Indonesia's second-tallest volcano (p262)

Nusa Lembongan
Surf, snorkel and dine with your toes in the sand (p109)

Pantai Mawun, Kuta
Enjoy Kuta's sandy crescent of heaven (p246)

BEACH BLISS

Indonesia's 17,000-plus islands are blessed with countless beaches. Many of the very best can be found on Bali, Lombok and Nusa Tenggara. Pantai Kuta was the original lure for tourists to Bali. Since then, generations of travellers have discovered the endless diversity of beaches throughout the region. Pick your allure: buzzing parties or secluded isolation; mellow waves or pounding surf; gleaming white sand or elegant black. There's one for every whim.

Dreamy Sunsets

Any beach with a view west will likely enjoy one of Indonesia's famous technicolour sunsets; residents and visitors alike gather for the show.

Cool Down

At all but the most remote beaches, you'll likely find at least one drinks vendor nearby with an icy Bintang beer. Simple cafes are also common.

Cover Up

Nude and topless sunbathing are offensive to residents everywhere. And remember to cover up away from the sand, even on Bali.

FROM LEFT: COCOS.BOUNTY/SHUTTERSTOCK, YOEL INDRA/SHUTTERSTOCK, ARMAND JOSO/SHUTTERSTOCK

Pantai Kuta (p78)

BEST BEACH EXPERIENCES

Feel the energy of ❶ **Pantai Kuta** (p78) – the original magnet for visitors – that runs to Seminyak and beyond.

Descend 130 steps to isolated ❷ **Thomas Beach** (p96), the secluded pocket of white sand on Bali's Bukit Peninsula.

Follow the ring of powdery sand around the coast of ❸ **Gili Air** (p281) and try to decide on your favourite spot.

Shade your eyes at ❹ **Pantai Mawun** (p246), a gleaming crescent of white sand flanked by rolling hills, 20 minutes from Lombok's Kuta.

Luxuriate on the dreamy pink beaches of ❺ **Pulau Padar** (p302), the small island that's part of Komodo National Park.

MARE DE ZEE/SHUTTERSTOCK

Air Terjun Wai Marang (p322)

MAGNIFICENT NATURE

From towering cliffs and cerulean seas to astounding peaks and verdant terraces of jade, the natural beauty of Bali, Lombok and Nusa Tenggara knows no bounds. Witness gorgeous vistas, feel the cool mist of jungle waterfalls, amble through rice fields or leap out of your comfort zone and climb an active volcano.

Climb Every Volcano

Active volcanoes can be found on most major islands. Imposing icons such as Bali's Gunung Agung and Lombok's Gunung Rinjani are legendary and challenging climbs.

Discover Waterfalls

Waterfalls lace the mountains, their thundering white streaks plunging to green rainforests. In Bali, local communities permit access to previously hidden wonders.

BEST NATURE EXPERIENCES

Find new words for green when strolling the rice-fields of ❶ **Sidemen** (p166) in East Bali.

Trek through the rainforest surrounding Bali's ❷ **Danau Tamblingan** (p195), a source of plants for traditional medicine.

Summit ❸ **Gunung Kelimutu** (p300) in Flores to admire its three different-coloured lakes.

Hike down through jungle to ❹ **Air Terjun Wai Marang** (p322) in Sumba, which rewards the adventurous with a pristine swimming hole.

Explore the lush foothills of Lombok's ❺ **Gunung Rinjani** (p262), with its misty waterfalls and lush rice terraces.

SURFING THE CURL

In Bali, Lombok and Nusa Tenggara, you have dozens of great breaks on almost every island. You can spend a lifetime here riding the waves – and some do. Surfers buzz around the islands on motorbikes with board racks, looking for the next great wave and soaking up the surf vibe that permeates the beaches.

Bali's Surf Seasons

From September to December, go east; during the other months, go west. And most of the time, you can also go south.

Surf Schools & Gear

Board rental, repair and sales are found at popular breaks. Lessons for everyone, from enthusiastic kids to tentative adults, are easily arranged at the beaches.

Join the Search

In Nusa Tenggara's far east, remote Rote's consistent swells between March and November lure an increasing stream of intrepid surfers.

BEST SURFING EXPERIENCES

Learn to surf at ❶ **Pantai Batu Bolong** (p52), Canggu's version of Kuta's beginner-friendly beach break.

Find some of Southeast Asia's most legendary surfing at ❷ **Uluwatu** (p96). It's the climax of the breaks along the Bukit Peninsula.

Ride the waves past the reefs offshore of Nusa Lembongan's ❸ **Pantai Jungutbatu** (p111), or watch the action from beachside cafes.

Trek out to ❹ **Desert Point** (p267) on Lombok. It's a tough break, even for the experienced.

Paddle out alongside world-champ surfers at ❺ **Lakey Peak** (p301) in remote Sumbawa.

SACRED CULTURE

Bali's creative heritage is everywhere, and it is deeply tied to the culture and Hindu faith. Temples, or *pura*, are the epicentre of spiritual activity, featuring dance and musical performances that are the result of an ever-evolving culture with a centuries-long legacy. Precise choreography and discipline are hallmarks of the beautiful, captivating and ethereal Balinese dance. Balinese music is played by an ensemble called a gamelan, who create unforgettable melodies on various bamboo and bronze instruments.

FROM LEFT: BRESTER IRINA/SHUTTERSTOCK, CATWALKPHOTOS/SHUTTERSTOCK, CREATIVITY LOVER/SHUTTERSTOCK

Thousands of Temples

With over 10,000 temples (or possibly double that – no one counts), Bali has such varied temples that you can't even categorise them.

Bali's Daily Processions

With the peal of the gamelan, traffic halts for a temple procession that disappears as suddenly as it appeared, leaving only a trail of hibiscus petals in its wake.

Mesmerising Music & Dance

Balinese dance features mystical music, dancers with hypnotic grace and chants that tell stories rich with the essence of Hindu beliefs and lore.

Legong dance, Ubud (p131)

BEST CULTURAL EXPERIENCES

See nightly Balinese ❶ **dance performances** (p130) in a variety of styles in over half a dozen venues in Ubud.

Head to the ancient village of ❷ **Boti** (p312) on West Timor for ikat-weaving, traditional dance and royal rituals.

Learn the story of Nyepi at the ❸ **Saka Museum** (p106) in Jimbaran, with displays of extraordinary ogoh-ogoh – huge, cartoonish figurines crafted for Nyepi.

Catch the worm at Lombok's ❹ **Bau Nyale Festival** (p247), held each year during the harvest of the prized *nyale* (sea worm).

Witness ❺ **Pasola** (p323), the horseback-fighting festival in West Sumba that's one of Asia's most extravagant harvest festivals.

UNDERWATER WONDERS

Fringed by magnificent reefs, Bali, Lombok and Nusa Tenggara have oodles of places to slip on fins and a mask and enter beautiful underwater worlds. There's a huge variety of coral and colourful fish of all sizes in the azure waters that lap these islands. Scuba diving and snorkelling are big draws: for some, slipping beneath the waves is part of a larger trip; for others, it's the whole point.

FROM LEFT: KITJAPAT FILM/SHUTTERSTOCK, DUDAREV MIKHAIL/SHUTTERSTOCK, PURWANTO NUGROHO/SHUTTERSTOCK

Scuba Diving

Good dive operators are found throughout the region. Try out the sport on a discovery dive, get certified, join a fun dive or escape the crowds on a liveaboard.

Snorkelling

There is no shortage of places on Bali's coast to don mask and fins and explore the delights underwater, such as Pemuteran (pictured) with its pioneering artificial reef.

Freediving

Ready for something deeper? Plunge to depths of 20m and beyond on a single breath. Bali's Amed is a centre for freediving.

Diving, Pulau Menjangan (p220)

BEST UNDERWATER EXPERIENCES

Revel in Bali's best diving at 1 **Pulau Menjangan** (p220), lauded for its stunning walls festooned with corals and critters. Good snorkelling, too.

Don't just come for the dragons; 2 **Komodo National Park** (p302) is also famed for its dive sites, with liveaboard options aplenty.

Invest the time to reach the remote 3 **Alor Archipelago** (p315), where there's a serious dive culture, healthy reefs and large pelagics.

Experience epic shore diving in Bali's Tulamben, home to the 4 **Liberty** (p185), a sunken WWII cargo ship.

Brave the crowds for a dazzling day of snorkelling or diving around 5 **Nusa Lembongan** (p109) and Nusa Penida.

SOLARISYS/SHUTTERSTOCK

Nest (p278)

GREAT ESCAPES

From the serene corners of Bali, then east through Lombok and to Nusa Tenggara, sublime refuge awaits in quiet, often artful guesthouses and small resorts, replete with the gracious and convivial welcome for which the region is lauded. Untrodden beaches, thundering waterfalls and grand, green vistas are here.

Bali's Quiet Corners

Away from the frenzy of the south, you'll find plenty of blissful escapes on Bali. Consider Sidemen, Munduk, Medewi and Pemuteran, among many others.

Discovering Isolation

Relatively isolated and delightfully quirky resorts can be found in the quiet corners of Bali, and at sparse beaches and jungle-clad volcanoes further east.

BEST ESCAPIST EXPERIENCES

Head up into the hills of ❶ **Tanglad** (p118) in Nusa Penida to watch weavers at work.

Explore less-trodden beaches in ❷ **Sekaroh** (p250), Lombok's remote southwestern corner.

Explore the traditional Ngada village of ❸ **Bena** (p296), perched on the side of a forested volcano in Flores.

Jump on a scooter and follow the backstreets of ❹ **North Bali** (p210) to waterfalls, temples and other surprises.

Leave the world above the sand behind on Gili Meno as you snorkel to the surreal underwater sculpture, ❺ **Nest** (p278).

BALI'S GLORIOUS RESORTS

Whether you need to soothe your soul or desire a pampering stay, there's a luxurious Bali resort that fits the bill. Unplug at palatial retreats perched above dazzling white sands or in idyllic river valleys. The design and architecture win international acclaim, the service is world-class and the spas divine.

FROM LEFT: DICKADIPRTM/SHUTTERSTOCK, REVANZA_ALIF/SHUTTERSTOCK

Finding Bali's Best

Some of the world's top resort hotels can be found around Ubud and in the south, from Canggu and Seminyak to the Bukit Peninsula's south coast.

Yes, Sire

Set on a white crescent of sand that could almost be the fourth Gili, Sire (pictured) is a luxurious enclave on Lombok that's home to palatial resorts.

Lost in Sumba

Already far off the beaten path, Sumba is home to two noted and luxurious resorts: surfer-friendly NIHI Sumba and the Sanubari.

BEST BALI RESORT EXPERIENCES

Revel in sustainable luxury at Seminyak's ❶ **Desa Potato Head** (p66; pictured far left), and bounce between beach club, infinity pool and myriad restaurants.

Take in the phenomenal views at ❷ **Anantara Uluwatu** (p119), a lavish resort built on a cliff edge, in sight of legendary surf breaks.

Immerse in nature – and natural spring-fed pools – at ❸ **Bambu Indah** (p155), a bamboo oasis just outside Ubud.

Relax by the sea at ❹ **Como Uma Canggu** (p83), an ultra-luxurious resort with a superb spa.

Lose yourself in green at ❺ **Mandapa** (p155), a renowned resort set in Ubud's Sungai Valley.

FLORA & FAUNA

Bali, Lombok and Nusa Tenggara boast an array of creatures, from primeval dragons to some of the world's rarest birds. Off the coasts, the waters teem with myriad species, from colour-popping corals to leaping dolphins. Nesting on beaches, sea turtles bridge these worlds. And take time to smell the flowers, which grow everywhere in profusion.

BEST FLORA & FAUNA EXPERIENCES

Marvel at the world's largest lizard, and the star of ❶ **Komodo National Park** (p302).

Look for rare Bali starlings, ebony leaf monkeys and roaming deer in ❷ **West Bali National Park** (p218).

See fruit bats, fish and coral on a day trip to ❸ **Seventeen Islands Marine Park** (p298), off Flores.

In Bali's central highlands, wander the vast ❹ **Bali Botanic Garden** (p195), which celebrates the island's 2400 floral species.

Spot the Flores green pigeon and critically endangered Flores hawk-eagle on a bird-watching tour in ❺ **Flores** (p300).

FROM LEFT: DUDAREV MIKHAIL/SHUTTERSTOCK, BYPTY/SHUTTERSTOCK

Rich Waters

A rich variety of coral, seaweed, fish and other marine life thrive off the islands, and all of Indonesia is a manta ray sanctuary.

Turtle Power

Four of the world's seven sea turtle species (green, hawksbill, loggerhead and olive ridley) nest on Bali. The Bali Sea Turtle Society helps protect them.

Mind Your Banana

Troops of chattering, frolicking (and, yes, thieving) monkeys are found everywhere, from Bali temples to remote bends in the road deep in Nusa Tenggara.

LIU YU SHAN/SHUTTERSTOCK

Market, Ubud (p124)

SHOPPER'S DELIGHT

Some consider Bali a great shopping destination; for others, it's their destiny. The island draws creative designers from across Indonesia and the world, and inspires local talent. Major brands of today and the famous names of tomorrow are found in boutiques and shops. Across the region, markets are unmissable experiences.

BEST SHOPPING EXPERIENCES

Refresh your wardrobe in ❶ **Canggu** (p62), where boutiques pop with curated island wear and more.

Sumba is renowned for producing the finest ikat. Buy direct from weavers in ❷ **Prailiu** (p326) village.

Browse locally produced handicrafts, art and fashion in ❸ **Ubud** (p138) and nearby villages.

Buy a new outfit on Seminyak's Jl Kayu Aya, then shop for home decor in ❹ **Kerobokan** (p71).

Pick up more ikat in West Timor, where ❺ **Maubesi** (p313) is home to the region's best textile market.

Bargain Hunts

In markets, stalls and shops without fixed prices in Indonesia, bargaining is part of the purchasing process. Just don't stress about saving one last rupiah.

Local Markets

Residents bargain for flowers, baskets, fruit and ornaments at spirited, sprawling *pasars* (markets). Other stalls sell clothing, curios and daily essentials.

RADITYA/SHUTTERSTOCK

Potato Head Beach Club (p66)

ENDLESS PARTIES

It starts with beach cafes and clubs. Maybe mellow daytime cocktails at one and wild antics at the other. It segues to sunset drinks and continues through high-energy restaurants amid post-sunset glow and pulsing house beats. Later, world-class clubs draw you in, with international DJs spinning sets to packed dance floors.

Beach Clubs

Beach clubs have exploded across Bali, especially in the south, where they dot the beaches from Tabanan to the Bukit Peninsula,and draw big-name DJs.

Sandy Brews

If there's a beach and tourists, you'll find genial vendors dispensing Bintangs while you recline on loungers, cheap plastic chairs or right on the sand.

BEST PARTYING EXPERIENCES

Bring your A-game to ❶ **Finns Beach Club** (p58) in Canggu, where days and nights of hedonism await.

Join the adults-only sunset party at ❷ **El Kabron** (p105), one of the Bukit Peninsula's best beach clubs.

Dive into the frenetic scene at ❸ **Sama Sama** (p275) on Gili Trawangan – the Gilis' party island.

Play it cool at Seminyak's ❹ **Potato Head Beach Club** (p66), where artisan cocktails and cool tunes are de rigueur.

Begin with Bintangs on the beach and see where the night takes you in ❺ **Kuta** (p77), Bali's original party spot.

SENSATIONAL FOOD & DRINK

Bali excels at sublime eating and drinking. Canggu is bursting with excellent cafes, restaurants and bars; Seminyak's restaurant scene has something for everyone; Denpasar's eateries serve exceptional local fare in relaxed surroundings; while Ubud has a profusion of creative eateries, many healthy, all delicious.

FROM LEFT: CATWALKPHOTOS/SHUTTERSTOCK, MARIUS KARP/SHUTTERSTOCK

Brilliant Local Fare

Superb warungs (food stalls) serving exceptional Balinese and Indonesian cuisine are found across the island. Many are family-run affairs; peak opening hour is around midday.

Sizzling Street Food

At night markets like those in Sanur, Sayan and Gianyar, you can graze on exceptional street food. Find staples like *sate* (satay; pictured) and *pisang goreng* (fried banana).

Bali Booze

Bali's craft brews are excellent – sample some at Canggu's Black Sand Brewery. The burgeoning wine scene boasts Hatten and Sababay wineries, and artisan *arak* (distilled palm wine) is on the up.

BEST EATING & DRINKING EXPERIENCES

Taste the eponymous Balinese chef's passion for Indonesian cuisine at ❶ **Home by Chef Wayan** (p53) in Pererenan.

Tuck into a fresh seafood feast on ❷ **Pantai Jimbaran** (p103) with your toes in the sand.

Lean into Ubud's plant-based dining scene at ❸ **Sayuri Healing Food Cafe & Academy** (p141).

Drink in the sunset – and excellent cocktails – at ❹ **Rock Bar** (p105), which clings to the cliffs of the Bukit Peninsula.

Join Seminyak diners-in-the-know for excellent modern bistro fare at Balinese-run ❺ **Fed by Made** (p70).

ISLANDS & REGIONS

Find the places that tick all your boxes.

North Bali

ADVENTURE AND NATURE ALONG THE COAST

Far from the hubbub of Bali's south, the island's north encompasses history, culture, a national park, reef-protected beaches and sensational diving and snorkelling in Pemuteran and Pulau Menjangan. Singaraja has an array of museums, and nearby Lovina is popular for dolphin-watching. Hillside hikes lead to dozens of pounding waterfalls.

Central Highlands

VOLCANOES, FORESTS AND BEAUTIFUL MOUNTAIN VIEWS

Misty hikes to waterfalls and serene lodgings are highlights of Bali's central highlands, which include the unmissable Munduk area. Higher up the slopes, the evocative Pura Luhur Batukau attracts worshippers, and the sacred crater lakes of Danau Tamblingan and Danau Buyan shimmer amid their volcanic calderas to the awe of sunrise hikers.

West Bali

SURF BREAKS, BALINESE CULTURE AND FISHING BOATS

Seaside Pura Tanah Lot marks the end – for now – of Bali's wild development in the southwest. To the west are charcoal-sand beaches interspersed with the low-key surfing villages of Balian and Medewi. The region's main hub, Tabanan, is home to the incredible temple of Pura Taman Ayun rising from lush green lawns.

Ubud Region

TEMPLES, ARTS AND INDULGENCE

Bali's remarkable culture is celebrated in Ubud, where art, dance and religion bloom. Ever popular, the village of Ubud is a tantalising mix of chill cafes, yoga studios, creative shops, family-run guesthouses and memorable walks through lush rice fields. Nearby, ancient temples, artisans' studios, village markets, luxury resorts and white-water adventures beckon.

South Bali & the Islands

BLISSFUL BEACHES, FAMED WAVES AND ISLES OF FUN

Family-friendly Sanur is the gateway to the blissful islands of Nusa Lembongan and Nusa Penida. Both offer an escape from Bali's clamour and boast incredible beaches and good diving. Denpasar is Bali's commercial centre, while the Bukit Peninsula holds cloistered Nusa Dua and the popular beaches and surf spots of Uluwatu.

Canggu & Southwest Beaches

SUNSETS, SURF AND HOLIDAY VIBES

Bali's magnificent sweep of sand stretches in an arc across the southwest coast. These beaches lure the majority of Bali's visitors, from the original tourist town of Kuta through Legian, Seminyak and buzzing Canggu, all pulsing with cafes, clubs, restaurants, shops, surf and round-the-clock fun.

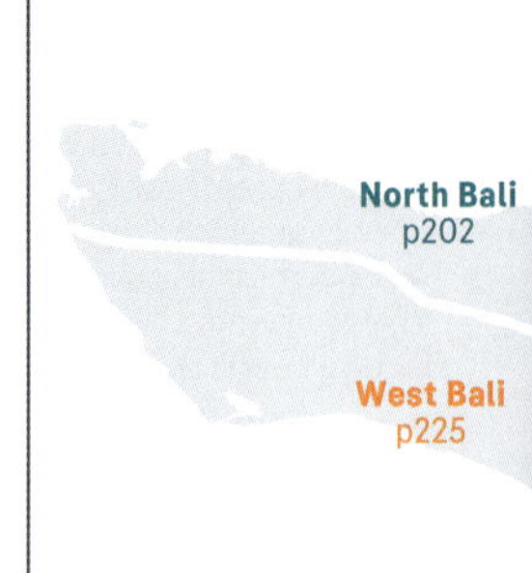

Nusa Tenggara

TIMELESS CULTURE, EPIC NATURE AND BIG WAVES

Nusa Tenggara is the great adventure east of Lombok. See dragons and dive teeming reefs in Komodo National Park, and relax in Labuan Bajo, the tourist centre for fascinating Flores. Other major islands include Sumbawa with its surf breaks, West Timor with its ancient villages and Sumba with its artisans and indigenous culture.

Gili Islands

CRYSTAL-CLEAR WATERS AND LAID-BACK LIVING

Just off Lombok are three islands with different personalities: Gili Trawangan is the largest, busiest and most popular with partiers. Gili Meno is the smallest, quietest and a haven for visitors seeking solitude. Gili Air melds the two in one family-friendly, enjoyable island. Offshore, snorkelling and diving await.

East Bali

ICONIC TEMPLES, EXHILARATING HIKES AND SPECTACULAR DIVING

Bali's east offers one delight after another. The ancient royal cities of Klungkung and Amlapura speak to the island's rich history. Bali's tallest volcano, sacred Gunung Agung, is the site of its holiest temple, Pura Besakih, while the coast boasts blissful beaches and good diving just offshore from Amed and Tulamben.

Lombok

BALI'S LESS-TRAVELLED NEIGHBOUR

Lombok has much to love. Surfers adore the southern coast and Kuta for its uncrowded breaks, while others laze away on the dozens of wide-open beaches. High above the waves, Gunung Rinjani – the iconic active volcano – is a draw for hikers. The island's Sasak culture infuses the main city of Mataram, a cultural melting pot.

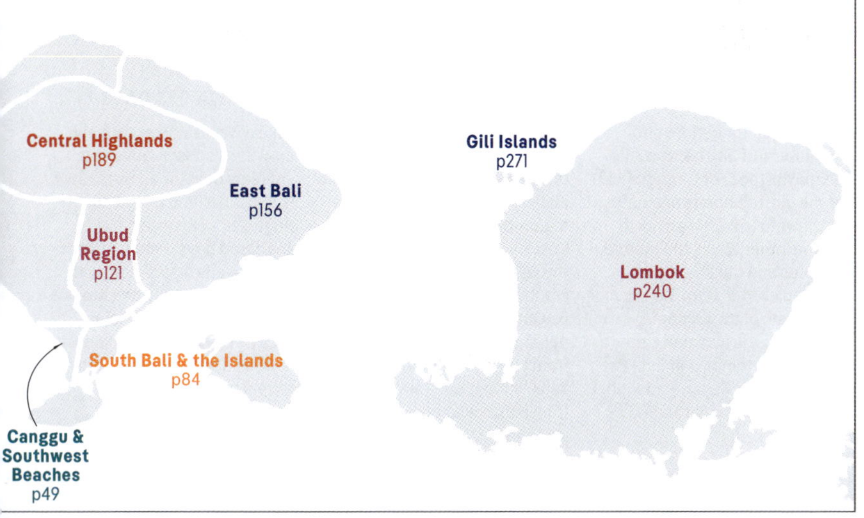

ITINERARIES

Bali to Nusa Tenggara

Allow 6 weeks **Distance** 1600km

Embark on an adventure across the region. Start in Indonesia's heart of tourism, Bali, before hitting the Gilis and Lombok. Then, it's the islands of Nusa Tenggara province: many travellers will know parts of Flores, but Sumbawa, Sumba, West Timor and others are little-visited and reward every day spent exploring.

1

BALI 8 DAYS

Start in **Bali** for culture and nightlife; surf and hang out in Seminyak (p63) or Canggu (p52) or the clifftop hotels and cafes of Uluwatu (p96). Head north for the 'other' Bali – the culture, temples and rich history of Ubud (pictured: Pura Taman Saraswati, p126). Immerse yourself in the lush natural beauty and temples in East Bali (p156) on your way to Padangbai to catch a fast boat to the Gilis.

2

GILIS & LOMBOK 1 WEEK

Bounce around the paradisaical beaches of the **Gilis** (p271). Join the parties on Gili Trawangan or chill on Gili Air. Take a fast boat to **Lombok** (p240) and enjoy Kuta's mellow vibes. Explore the wild beaches of South Lombok and consider a trek up Gunung Rinjani (pictured; p262). Keen surfer? Take a ferry from Labuhan Lombok to Poto Tano in West Sumbawa. Or fly from Lombok to Labuan Bajo in Flores.

3

SUMBAWA 3 DAYS

Chase waves and escape the crowds in conservative and sparsely developed **Sumbawa** (p301), an island of volcanic ridges, dry expanses and sheltered bays. Pantai Lakey is a relaxed surfers' hub, with cool guesthouses and cafes overlooking awesome surf: Lakey Peak and Lakey Pipe are hallowed names here. Catch a ferry from Sape to Flores.

FROM LEFT: ALEXANDRA LANDE/SHUTTERSTOCK, FARIZUN AMROD SAAD/SHUTTERSTOCK, ASIATRAVEL/SHUTTERSTOCK

4

FLORES ⏱ 9 DAYS

Flores (p290) is a rugged volcanic island with thriving ancient cultures and dramatic terrain. Labuan Bajo is the fast-growing hub in West Flores for seeing the dragons and teeming reefs of Komodo National Park. Visit Bajawa to explore the Ngada villages of Bena (pictured; p296) and Luba on the slopes of Gunung Inerie. At the old trading port of Ende, catch the ferry to Sumba.

5

SUMBA ⏱ 1 WEEK

Enter a different realm in **Sumba** (p318), which is filled with ancient villages, ancestral spirits and animist rituals. Tour the traditional villages of Waikabubak (pictured; p324) and Waibakul, where the peaked thatched roofs and ancient traditions will have you wide-eyed. Catch the waves on white-sand Pantai Marosi, one of Sumba's many superb beaches that is slowly attracting attention. Fly to West Timor.

6

WEST TIMOR ⏱ 1 WEEK

Ease into the off-the-grid feel of **West Timor** (p306) at Kupang. Visit entrancing ancient villages like None, where heads were still hunted just two generations ago. At Boti, see how residents follow their nine-day week, and in Tamkesi, climb a sacred mountain for a view back over a centuries-old village. Then jump over to Rote (pictured; p316) for powdery white-sand beaches and epic surf.

FROM LEFT: JON CHICA/SHUTTERSTOCK, HEINRICH DOMINGGUS DENGI/SHUTTERSTOCK, PAPANOAH/SHUTTERSTOCK

TORBEN KNAUER/SHUTTERSTOCK

Gili Meno (p278)

ITINERARIES

Best Beaches

Allow: 2 weeks **Distance:** 400km

You'll visit five islands and countless beaches on a trip that takes in the most interesting sandy shores and underwater places across Bali, the Gilis and Lombok. It's a mix of the famous, infamous and barely known, with something for every taste, from sublime snorkelling and long days lazing to perfect wave-riding.

1

CANGGU 2 DAYS

The charcoal-sand beaches of **Canggu** (p52) mightn't be Bali's finest, but the scene that unfolds around them is electric. Shred waves or watch the action from one of the many bars or beach clubs lining the sand. Sunsets are phenomenal.

***Detour:** Foray to the **Bukit Peninsula** (p102), where the waves are even better. Pocket-sized white-sand beaches here reward exploration.*

2

MENGWI 2 DAYS

Mengwi (p228) is the home of the surfing hotspot of Pantai Medewi and its much-vaunted long left-hand wave. The immediate beach is a stretch of large, smooth grey rocks interspersed among round black pebbles. Just west is the long swath of wide and sandy Pantai Yeh Sumbul, with a smattering of cool guesthouses – and no crowds.

3

PEMUTERAN 3 DAYS

On the northwest coast, low-key **Pemuteran** (p215) is the jumping-off point for Bali's best diving and snorkelling at Pulau Menjangan (pictured; p220), part of West Bali National Park. But there's also good snorkelling at an innovative artificial reef right off Pemuteran's calm, black-sand beach. With sunloungers for rent, Pemuteran Beach is an excellent spot to relax with a good book.

FROM LEFT: FIKACIKINI/SHUTTERSTOCK, VALERY BOCMAN/SHUTTERSTOCK, DUTA YONG/SHUTTERSTOCK

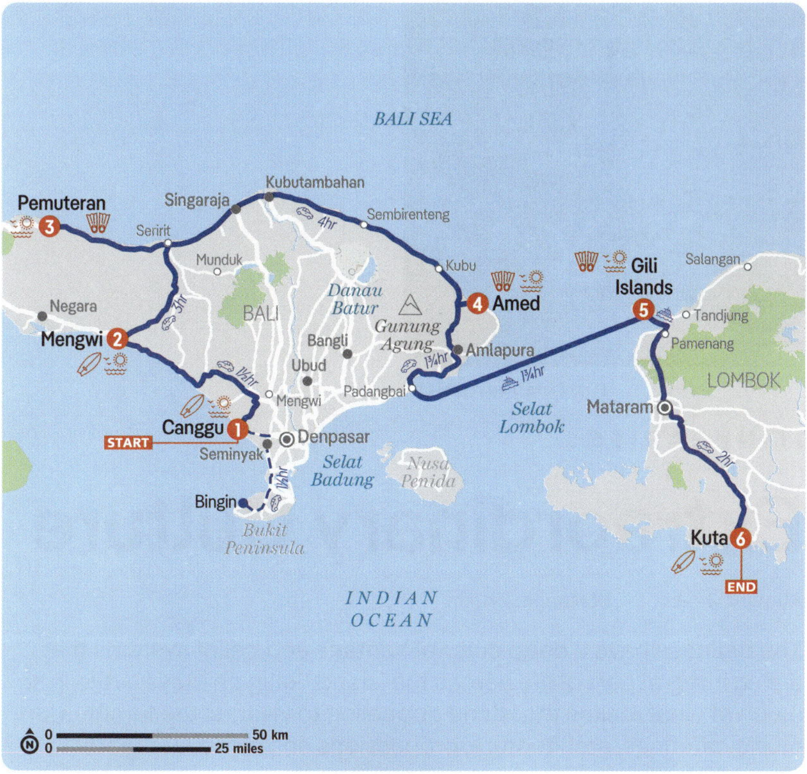

4

AMED 2 DAYS

Get all the beach time you need at the succession of scalloped bays on the east coast collectively known as **Amed** (p180). Little seaside villages such as Jemeluk and Lipah have boutique guesthouses where yoga seems to always be on offer. Just north is the diving and snorkelling centre of Tulamben, with a WWII shipwreck reached from the shore.

5

GILI ISLANDS 3 DAYS

Three little dots of white sand off Lombok, the **Gili Islands** (p271) could easily occupy your entire trip. Relax into island life on chill Gili Air (pictured; p281). Next up is Gili Trawangan, where there's more action (and parties). The perfect day here can include diving, napping, swimming, lazing and drinking – all before noon. Last is Gili Meno, where there's little to do except snorkel and ponder the peace.

6

KUTA 2 DAYS

The south coast near Lombok's **Kuta** (p244) has stunning beaches and surfing to reward the intrepid. Beaches just don't get much better than this: the water is warm, striped turquoise and curls into barrels; the sand is silky and snow white, framed by massive headlands and sheer cliffs. Typical is Pantai Selong Belanak (pictured; p248), which has the kind of beach you fly to Indonesia for.

FROM LEFT: ASIATRAVEL/SHUTTERSTOCK, GAGLIARDIPHOTOGRAPHY/SHUTTERSTOCK, KALAMA9/SHUTTERSTOCK

DOTMILLER1986/SHUTTERSTOCK

Pura Tirta Empul (p146)

ITINERARIES

Extraordinary Culture

Allow: 2 weeks **Distance:** 240km

The Balinese have a deep cultural heritage and belief systems that are an integral part of life across the island. Religion plays a role in so much of what makes the island appealing to visitors: the temples, art, music, offerings, architecture, processions and more. Get ready to dive right in.

1 TABANAN AREA 2 DAYS

Canggu makes a good base for visiting the important temples of **Tabanan** (p228). Hit the oceanfront Pura Tanah Lot (pictured; p233) early in the day to avoid the sunset crowds. Then make your way to the beautiful water temple of Pura Taman Ayun. Just west of the temple complex, the Ogoh Ogoh Bali Museum celebrates the papier-mâché monsters paraded at Nyepi celebrations.

2 UBUD 4 DAYS

Explore the temples in the heart of **Ubud** (p124) and attend Balinese dance performances. Then venture to nearby sites such as those in Pejeng, where treasures include one of Bali's oldest artefacts. Just south are the mysteries at Goa Gajah. To the north, Tegallalang has ancient sites like the wonderous Gunung Kawi (pictured; p147) and the rushing waters of Pura Tirta Empul.

3 KLUNGKUNG 1 DAY

Take a day trip from Ubud to **Klungkung** (p160) to marvel at the richly decorated pavilions of the Puri Agung Semarapura (often called Klungkung Palace; pictured; p161). Across the road, the Puputan Monument commemorates the last Balinese kingdom to succumb to the Dutch (1908) and the sacrifice of its royal family, who died by *puputan* (ritual suicide) rather than surrender.

FROM LEFT: LEMARET PIERRICK/SHUTTERSTOCK, EFIRED/SHUTTERSTOCK, GEKKO GALLERY/SHUTTERSTOCK

4

SIDEMEN 3 DAYS

The green cradle of **Sidemen** (p166) is an ideal base for visiting some of East Bali's holiest places. Looming to the north is Bali's mother volcano, Gunung Agung. On the slopes is the island's most sacred place, Pura Besakih (pictured; p171). Get your head above the clouds at Pura Pasar Agung Sebudi. In the foothills, the excellent Samsara Living Museum offers a window into Balinese culture and daily life.

5

TIRTA GANGGA 2 DAYS

Make your way to the exquisite water palace of **Tirta Gangga** (p176). Then head to the heavens of Pura Lempuyang, the series of mountaintop temples – marvel at the views on a magical uphill trek. It's only a short hop south to the tranquil former royal palace of Puri Agung Karangasem and the sprawling gardens of Taman Ujung, another beautiful water palace.

6

ULUWATU 2 DAYS

End your cultural adventure at clifftop **Uluwatu** (p96), home to the vital temple of Pura Luhur Ulu Watu (pictured; p100). Enjoy the views across the Indian Ocean by day, then return in the evening to witness the touristy but captivating Kecak (pronounced ke-chak) dance performed in the temple grounds, which has become one of the most iconic displays of Balinese culture.

FROM LEFT: JAN WEHNERT/SHUTTERSTOCK, SAIKO3P/SHUTTERSTOCK, COCOS.BOUNTY/SHUTTERSTOCK

SWUERFEL/SHUTTERSTOCK

Dream Beach (p114), Nusa Lembongan

ITINERARIES

Best of Bali

Allow: 1 week **Distance:** 115km

Short on time? This trip covers Bali's best in a week. You'll split your time between the incredibly popular south, with its nightlife, dining, shopping and beaches; and the hillside charms of Ubud, with its culture, cafes and natural beauty. Ubud is a good base for day trips to Central and East Bali if you're tempted to extend your trip.

1 CANGGU 1 DAY

Canggu (p52) is Southwest Bali's booming tourism hub, with hip restaurants, famous surf breaks and beach bars and clubs galore. Paddle out at Batu Bolong or watch from a seaside bar or club like Lawn. Inland amid a maze of too-narrow lanes, you'll find creative cafes, excellent restaurants, appealing boutiques and plenty of options for pampering.

2 UBUD 2 DAYS

Spend two full days in and around **Ubud** (p124). Spoil yourself and stay in one of Ubud's many hotels with views across rice fields. Visit a spa or yoga studio, then try one of the myriad great restaurants. At night, you'll be captivated by dance performances. Visit temples and walk along the rice fields.

FROM LEFT: THEDIRECTORART/SHUTTERSTOCK, HOWARD CHAPMAN/SHUTTERSTOCK

3

NUSA LEMBONGAN 2 DAYS

Take a fast boat from Sanur and arrive on the white-sand shores of **Nusa Lembongan** (p109) in just 30 minutes. Hang out on the sand at Pantai Jungutbatu, surf the breaks beyond, or sign up for a snorkelling or scuba-diving excursion.

Detour: *Consider adding on time at Lembongan's much larger neighbour, **Nusa Penida** (p115). Take in the amazing vistas from its cliffs and trek down to one of its hidden beaches.*

4

BUKIT PENINSULA 2 DAYS

Take your pick from the **Bukit Peninsula**'s (p102) lovely beaches stretching along the rocky coast from Jimbaran south to Uluwatu. Some fine coves such as Thomas Beach (pictured; p96) can be reached after climbing down steep staircases hugging a cliff face. The surfing is superb and the peninsula is flush with fancy resorts.

FROM LEFT: PETER116/SHUTTERSTOCK, TARIN C/SHUTTERSTOCK

WHEN TO GO

There's no bad time to visit Bali, Lombok and Nusa Tenggara – there's always a dry place in rainy season and a quiet place in high season.

Being tropical, when it rains in Indonesia the downfalls are usually only intense for a short while and are not typically widespread: if it's raining in Ubud, it may not be raining in Canggu.

Overall, the shoulder seasons in Bali (April–June; September–October) are wonderful times to travel. The months of May, June and September experience the best weather (drier, less humid). And don't write off the low seasons (January–April; October–November), as fewer crowds are a real plus.

Strategies for High Season

High season in Bali and the Gilis is July, August and the Christmas holidays. To a lesser extent, this also applies to the popular beach towns in Lombok, and Labuan Bajo in Flores. Accommodation rates increase and hotels are booked far ahead of time, as are the best restaurants. To beat the high costs, travel to other areas, make your plans as early as possible and shop around.

I LIVE HERE

THE DAY BALI STOPS

Tour guide Sika Purwita shares her passion for Balinese traditions on walking tours in Southwest Bali.

My favourite time of the year is Nyepi, the Balinese New Year (usually in March or April), when the whole island shuts down for 24 hours. It's not only a time for people to rest, but also for nature to take a break, even if it's only for one day.

Surfing, Uluwatu (p96)

FROM LEFT: MARIUS DOBILAS/SHUTTERSTOCK, CHRIS AND BRENDA/SHUTTERSTOCK

BALI'S SURF SEASONS

In the dry season, Bali's west coast has the best breaks; this is also when Nusa Lembongan is at its best. In the rainy season (October–March), surf the eastern side of the island, from Nusa Dua to Padang Bai.

Weather through the year

JANUARY	FEBRUARY	MARCH	APRIL	MAY	JUNE
Avg. daytime max: **33°C**	Avg. daytime max: **33°C**	Avg. daytime max: **34°C**	Avg. daytime max: **34°C**	Avg. daytime max: **33°C**	Avg. daytime max: **31°C**
Days of rainfall: **27**	Days of rainfall: **22**	Days of rainfall: **20**	Days of rainfall: **9**	Days of rainfall: **8**	Days of rainfall: **6**

WHERE IT'S COLD(ER)

There are no true 'cold' spots. However, it can get a bit less balmy as you ascend to higher elevations. In Ubud, that simply means you don't need air-con at night. On the volcanoes, that means dawn trekking requires layers.

Major Cultural Festivals

Nyepi (Day of Silence) (p369) Nyepi celebrates the Balinese new year. It's marked by inactivity – a strategy to convince evil spirits that Bali is uninhabited. The island shuts down completely, including the airport. **March or April**

Bau Nyale Festival (p247) The ritual harvesting of *nyale* (sea worms) takes place near Lombok's Kuta. Celebrations carry on until dawn. **February or March**

Pasola (p323) Held in West Sumbanese villages, this tournament between two teams of spear-wielding horsemen is an extravagant harvest festival. **February and March**

Galungan and Kuningan (p369) Galungan celebrates the death of the legendary tyrant Mayadenawa. Celebrations culminate with the Kuningan festival, when the Balinese thank the gods. Villages celebrate in grand style once or twice each year, depending on the 210-day Balinese calendar. **Dates vary**

The Biggest Events

Bali Arts Festival (p94) The premier event on Bali's cultural calendar. Held in Denpasar, the festival features traditional dances as the village-based groups compete for local pride. **Mid-June to mid-July**

BaliSpirit Festival (p136) A hugely popular yoga, dance and music festival in Ubud. There are more than 100 workshops, yoga classes and live music. **Usually May**

Ubud Writers & Readers Festival (p136) One of Asia's premier literary events, featuring authors from around the world in a celebration of writing – especially that which touches on Bali. **October**

Indonesian Independence Day Flags fly, traffic is snarled by processions, and fireworks light up the sky to celebrate Indonesia's independence from the Dutch, declared on 17 August 1945. **17 August**

I LIVE HERE

CALM AFTER THE RAIN

Gede Gusdarma, owner of Gede Transport, lives near Canggu and takes travellers on adventures all over Bali.

In May, at the end of the rainy season, the landscape is green and lush, the temperature is still a bit cooler and the sea is calm – perfect for fishing for calamari, grouper and sea bream. Melons are ripening and by the end of the season, mangoes are ready.

Nusa Penida (p115)

FOLLOW THE MANTAS

Hoping to snorkel or dive alongside a giant filter feeder? The peak season for mantas in Komodo National Park is from October to March. In Nusa Penida, manta high season runs from May to October.

JULY
Avg. daytime max: **30°C**
Days of rainfall: **4**

AUGUST
Avg. daytime max: **30°C**
Days of rainfall: **4**

SEPTEMBER
Avg. daytime max: **31°C**
Days of rainfall: **8**

OCTOBER
Avg. daytime max: **34°C**
Days of rainfall: **12**

NOVEMBER
Avg. daytime max: **33°C**
Days of rainfall: **16**

DECEMBER
Avg. daytime max: **33°C**
Days of rainfall: **22**

FROM LEFT: KHARISMA_ANU/SHUTTERSTOCK, MOVIESTORE COLLECTION LTD/ALAMY

Gunung Agung (p170)

GET PREPARED FOR BALI, LOMBOK & NUSA TENGGARA

Useful things to load in your bag, your ears and your brain.

Clothes

T-shirts and shorts To keep you cool in Bali and the Gilis.

Something stylish For nights out in South Bali.

Waterproof jacket Rain can fall anytime.

Small umbrella Never hurts to be prepared.

Warm layers For high-altitude hiking.

Hiking sandals For countryside walks.

Hiking boots For mountain and volcano treks.

Modest clothes For mosque visits (and in more conservative parts of Lombok and Nusa Tenggara) – wear long pants/skirts and shirts that fully cover shoulders. In Bali, temple attendants have sarongs available.

Modest swimwear Needed in parts of Lombok and Nusa Tenggara.

Post-beach cover-ups Bikinis and swimming trunks are never OK away from the sand, even in Bali.

Manners

Places of worship Remove shoes, and dress modestly when visiting mosques; wear a sash and sarong at Bali's temples.

Body language Don't display affection in public or talk with your hands on your hips.

Clothing Avoid showing a lot of skin. Don't go topless on the beach if you're a woman.

Photography Before taking photos of someone, ask – or mime – for approval.

READ

Ramayana (Valmiki; date unknown) This epic is central to Hinduism and underpins many Balinese temple and cultural traditions.

Island of Bali (Miguel Covarrubias; 1937) The classic work on Bali and its culture remains stunningly relevant today.

Secrets of Bali: Fresh Light on the Morning of the World (Jonathan Copeland & Ni Wayan Murni; 2010) About Bali, its people and its traditions.

Driftwood Chandeliers (Mark Eveleigh; 2023) The Lonely Planet writer's haunting tale of life and death in Bali is a top beach read.

Words

Bahasa Indonesia

Bahasa Indonesia is the national language of Indonesia. There are also myriad local dialects and languages.

'Salam' Hello.

'Selamat tinggal' Goodbye, if you're the one leaving.

'Selamat jalan' Goodbye, if you're the one staying.

'Apa kabar?' How are you?

'Kabar baik, Anda bagaimana?' I'm fine, and you?

'Permisi' Excuse me.

'Maaf' Sorry.

'Silahkan' Please.

'Terima kasih' Thank you.

'Kembali' You're welcome.

'Ya' Yes.

'Tidak' No.

'Bapak' Mr/Sir.

'Ibu' Ms/Mrs.

'Nona' Miss.

'Siapa nama Anda?' What's your name?

'Nama saya...' My name is...

'Bisa berbicara Bahasa Inggris?' Do you speak English?

'Saya tidak mengerti' I don't understand.

Balinese

Everyone on Bali speaks Bahasa Indonesia, but residents will respect you for trying the local language.

'Kenken kabare?' How are you?

'Matur suksma' Thank you.

'Sire wastene?' What's your name?

'Adan tiange...' My name is...

'Tiang sing ngerti' I don't understand.

'Bisa ngomong Bali sing?' Do you speak Balinese?

'Ne ape adane di Bali?' What do you call this in Balinese?

'Kije jalan lakar kel...?' Which is the way to...?

WATCH

Eat Pray Love (Ryan Murphy; 2010; pictured) The movie loses something in the adaptation, though the Ubud scenes are lovely.

The Act of Killing (Joshua Oppenheimer; 2013) Documentary about the 1965 slaughter of accused communist sympathisers.

Eat, Pray, Build (Foreign Correspondent; 2024) Explores the dark side of Bali's construction boom.

Cowboys in Paradise (Amit Virmani; 2011) Entertaining documentary about South Bali male gigolos.

Morning of the Earth (1972) The documentary that put Bali on the world surfing map.

LISTEN

NOW! Bali Podcast (Now! Bali; 2020–24) Excellent show that covers various aspects of Balinese culture, such as calendars, temples and dance.

Ancient Order of Bali (Damn Interesting; 2023) Absorbing and beautifully produced episode that explains Bali's *subak* system of rice-field irrigation.

Looking for Love in Wrong Places (Assia Keva; 2025) The Bali singing sensation's single hit one million Spotify streams in just a few months.

Sunset Di Tanah Anarki (Superman Is Dead; 2013) Song from the band that got their start in Kuta, now famous across Indonesia and the world.

TRIP PLANNER

WHERE TO STAY IN SOUTH BALI

When booking accommodation in South Bali, check the exact location. What looks good on a booking site may be located in an area you didn't want. Thankfully, it's easy to avoid this fate.

Kuta (p73)

The Lowdown

MISLEADING LOCATIONS

As tourist numbers in Bali have exploded, so have the number of chain hotels. The boom in the construction of large hotels in Kuta, Legian, Seminyak, Kerobokan and Canggu is changing the area's character in fundamental ways, especially as the many cheap and cheerful family-run spots are pushed out.

While some of these hotels are appearing in traditionally popular areas of South Bali, not far from the beaches and nightlife, scores more are opening far from the areas visitors consider desirable. Many chains have properties in both appealing and unappealing areas, and it's easy to get misled about their actual location, especially on booking websites. In the tradition of real estate agents everywhere, 'Seminyak' is now the address used for hotels deep in Denpasar. Note that most of these issues also apply to villas, which are being built *everywhere*.

DO YOUR RESEARCH

The good news is that with enlightened shopping, you can usually find good deals in the most appealing parts of South Bali, and often you can end up at a small or family-run guesthouse with oodles more charm and character than a generic cheap hotel. Or you may find yourself at some creative, charming boutique property or villa.

FINDING GREAT LOCATIONS IN SOUTH BALI

Carefully consider the following when choosing your accommodation:

Kuta–Kerobokan Strip

- Anything west of the Jl Legian–Jl Seminyak–Jl Kerobokan spine will be close to beaches and nightlife.
- East of the spine, things begin to get inconvenient fast: there will be less to walk to, beaches can be far and taxis hard to come by.
- Jl Ngurah Rai Bypass and Jl Sunset are both noisy, traffic-clogged streets that lack charm and are hard to cross – many chain hotels are located right on these unpleasant thoroughfares.
- East of Jl Ngurah Rai Bypass and Jl Sunset is Denpasar's uninteresting hinterland.

Canggu Area

- Watch out for accommodation far from beaches. Walking (and driving) can be a chore on roads hostile to pedestrians.

Bukit Peninsula

- Ensure there's beach access.
- A number of cliffside spots at Bingin were torn down by authorities in mid-2025, check online before planning to stay near there.

Sanur

- Jl Ngurah Rai Bypass should be the absolute western border of your room hunt.

Canggu (p52)

HOW TO... Navigate Bali's Traffic

Bali traffic can be horrendous in the south, with traffic jams stretching as far as Ubud to the north, Padang Bai to the east and Gilimanuk to the west. As bad as it is, there *are* ways to navigate it without worsening the problem.

Going Nowhere

A surfer sets out from her house in Canggu for a day on the breaks at Uluwatu – a 37km journey. Two hours later, she's barely halfway there. After a 10-hour flight, honeymooners thrilled to reach Bali end up stalled for an hour trying to drive the 5km to their hotel.

These are just two of the scenarios that bedevil residents and visitors to Bali every day. The Canggu area is ground zero for everything that's wrong – a lack of roads and public transport, too-narrow thoroughfares, a massive influx of travellers, and too many people trying to get around. As well as this, the millions of people who visit this small island every year often use their own wheels and taxis, only adding to the traffic filling the roads.

Difficult Remedies

Solutions are complicated: Bali's reverence for private property makes it difficult for the government to acquire it for road construction; ideas for tramways and subway systems are floated but have yet to materialise; a new toll road *is* being built between Denpasar and Gilimanuk but has encountered delays; rising numbers of travellers coming to Bali every year choke already-busy roads; and attempts at quick solutions mean pathways through rice fields get paved and are soon covered in traffic trying to navigate narrow byways.

In the meantime, the best strategies for dealing with Bali's traffic are to expect it, don't fret and try to be patient – remember that you only have to deal with the traffic for the duration of your trip, unlike the Balinese, for whom it's a little more long-term; live local, stay where you want to be, and visit what's within walking distance. Also try to keep travel to realistic timelines, maybe turning that day trip into an overnighter or weekender.

TOP TIPS

If you're going to Nusa Dua, Sanur or Ubud from the airport, ask your driver to use the toll road, bypassing the worst traffic. If they're reluctant to use the road because they don't want to pay the fare, offer to pay it yourself.

Traffic in Ubud centre can be unmoving, especially at lunchtime. Time trips outside the hours of 11am and 4pm, and try to get dropped off and picked up on the outskirts and walk in.

There's an unheralded pedestrian highway from Canggu south to Kuta: the beach. You can easily cover a long distance – and enjoy lovely views.

ARIYANI TEDJO/SHUTTERSTOCK

Nasi campur

THE FOOD SCENE

A great reason to travel to Bali, Lombok and Nusa Tenggara is the food: the variety and quality here are hard to beat.

Across the popular regions of Bali, you'll find every cuisine, in every style, and for every budget. In Lombok and Nusa Tenggara, the selection is narrower.

Bali caters to all taste buds. The culinary centres of Canggu and Ubud boast diverse eateries, including the hottest and best restaurants. Cafes and warungs (food stalls) across the island serve exceptional Balinese and Indonesian food in simple surroundings. There's also a profusion of creative, organic and healthful eateries. Balinese cuisine, whether truly Balinese or influenced by the rest of Indonesia and Asia, draws from the bounty of fresh local foods and is rich with spices and flavours. You can savour this fare at roadside eateries and top-end restaurants.

Food in Nusa Tenggara isn't quite as creative, but you'll have no trouble sourcing plenty of tasty meals, and more traditional options. In Lombok and the Gilis (which have their fair share of new-agey healthy-eating options), opt for simply prepared, freshly caught fish and seafood.

Flavours of Bali

Compared with elsewhere in Indonesia, Balinese food is more pungent and lively, with a multitude of layers making up a dish. A meal will contain six flavours (sweet, sour, spicy, salty, bitter and astringent), all of which stimulate the senses.

There's a predominance of ginger, chilli and coconut. The biting combination of fresh galangal (Thai ginger) and turmeric

Best Local Dishes

NASI CAMPUR
The great Balinese meal – centred on rice, with many small dishes.

NASI GORENG
Fried rice in a mix of meat and vegetables, topped with a fried egg.

MIE GORENG
Fried noodles in a mix of meat and vegetables, topped with a fried egg.

AYAM TALIWANG
Chicken roasted over coconut husks; with tomato, chilli and lime dip.

is matched by the heat of raw chillies; the complex sweetness of palm sugar, tamarind and shrimp paste; and the clean, fresh flavours of lemongrass, musk lime, kaffir lime leaves and coriander seeds.

Rice is the staple dish and is revered in Bali as a gift of life from the gods. It is served generously with every meal – anything not served with rice is considered a *jaja* (snack). Rice acts as the medium for the various fragrant, spiced foods – almost like condiments – that accompany it, with many ingredients chopped finely to complement the dry, fluffy grains.

Bali's Signature Dish

In Bali, food is not just about enjoyment and sustenance. Like everything here, it is an intrinsic part of the island's many daily rituals and a major aspect of ceremonies that honour the gods. The most revered dish is *babi guling,* presented during important ceremonies.

Babi guling is the quintessential Bali experience. A whole pig is stuffed with chilli, turmeric, ginger, galangal, shallots, garlic, coriander seeds and aromatic leaves, basted in more turmeric (and coconut oil), and skewered on a wooden spit over an open fire. You can enjoy *babi guling* at stands, warungs and cafes across Bali.

FROM LEFT: SRI WIDYOWATI/SHUTTERSTOCK, AHMET CIGSAR/SHUTTERSTOCK

Fried tempeh

Lombok's Sasak Cuisine

Lombok's Sasak people are predominantly Muslim, and their mains feature fish, chicken, vegetables and rice. The fact that *lombok* means 'chilli' in Bahasa Indonesia makes sense, because the Sasaks like their food spicy.

Indonesia's Meat-Free Fare

Tofu and tempeh are part of Indonesia's staple diet, and many of the tastiest dishes just happen to be vegetarian. In trendier parts of the region, there are numerous vegetarian, vegan and health-food cafes and restaurants.

MARKETS: FESTIVALS OF FOOD

Pasar (markets) are found in just about every town and offer a glimpse of the variety and freshness of local produce in the region, often brought from the mountains within a day or two of harvesting. The atmosphere is vibrant, with baskets loaded with fresh tropical fruits, vegetables, flowers, spices and varieties of red, black, yellow and white rice. There are cages of live chickens, trays of dead chickens, freshly slaughtered pigs, dried fish, eggs, cakes, offerings and stalls selling *es cendol* (a colourful iced coconut drink), *bubur* (rice porridge) and *nasi campur* (rice with side dishes).

There's no refrigeration, so it's best to purchase meat and fish earlier in the day. Bargaining is expected. Want a picnic? All sorts of pre-cooked foods are sold ready-to-go, often wrapped in banana leaves.

BABI GULING
Spiced, roasted pork is the quintessential Balinese food experience.

SATE LILIT
Fragrant combination of minced fish, chicken or pork with lemongrass.

SATE (AKA SATAY)
Marinated meat grilled on a skewer, served with sauces.

GADO GADO
Tofu, tempeh and steamed vegetables with boiled egg and peanut sauce.

PISANG GORENG
Fried bananas prepared myriad ways, served from breakfast to dessert.

Specialities

Sambal

Sambal, the ubiquitous spicy condiment, comes in endless variations. Below are the main ones (ignoring the generically sweet commercially bottled gloop):

Sambal bajak Fried tomato-based sauce filled with crushed chillies, palm sugar and shallots.

Sambal balado Sauteed chillis, shallots, garlic and tomatoes.

Sambal matah Raw Balinese sambal made from thinly sliced shallots, tiny chillies, shrimp paste and lemongrass. Divine.

Sambal pelecing A Lombok sambal with hot chillies in a tomato base.

Sambal taliwang Popular Lombok sambal made with peppers, garlic and shrimp paste.

Drinks

Jamu This ubiquitous health tonic was recognised by UNESCO as part of Indonesia's cultural heritage in 2023. No two versions are alike: ingredients range from tamarind to flowers to eggs.

Making sambal

Bintang Indonesia's national brand of lager is synonymous with beer. In Bali, craft breweries include Black Sand and South+East.

Wine In Bali, Hatten and Sababay wineries produce some nicely drinkable wines.

Arak At social gatherings and ceremonies, Balinese might enjoy traditional *arak* (colourless, distilled palm wine). It's lately had a renaissance.

Coffee Grown in Bali and elsewhere in Indonesia, coffee is widely served everywhere.

MEALS OF A LIFETIME

Nusantara (p133) Sample bold flavours from across the Indonesian archipelago in Ubud. By the team behind the lauded Locavore NXT.

Meimei (p57) Discover a love for refined Southeast Asian barbecue in Canggu.

Bali Asli (p179) Ultra-fresh *nasi campur* and spectacular views over rice terraces are on offer at this hybrid restaurant and cooking school in West Bali's Amlapura.

Dapur Bali Mula (p185) Fabulous Balinese lunches and dinners by famed Chef Yudi on Bali's northeast coast.

Kaum (p70) Desa Potato Head's signature Indonesian restaurant is a flavour fever dream with Seminyak sea views.

THE YEAR IN FOOD

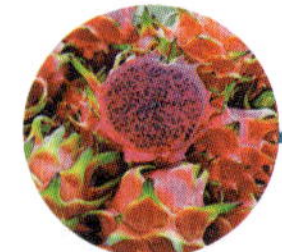

RAINY SEASON (OCTOBER–MARCH)

Tropical fruit delights – rambutan, dragon fruit (pictured), salak, mangosteen, pineapple, banana, mango, guava and lychee – are lush and abundant. In October, your nose will tell you that it's durian season as the huge, odoriferous (and beloved) fruit fills market stalls. Vendors hawk the nubby orbs in town centres and along roadsides.

DRY SEASON (APRIL–SEPTEMBER)

Enjoy year-round staples like papaya and coconut (pictured). April ushers in the Ubud Food Festival (p136). The end of the rice-harvesting season is celebrated in Bali from 1 May to 30 June, when *subak* (the complex system of rice-field irrigation) towns raise flags, erect shrines and prepare traditional regional dishes in honour of Dewi Sri, the goddess of rice and fertility.

AKARAT PHASURA/SHUTTERSTOCK

Night market, Gili Trawangan (p274)

HOW TO...

Eat & Drink

Meals in Indonesia don't have the same social role as meals elsewhere. On Bali, for instance, there are already so many reasons throughout the day for friends and family to gather that meals are simply a reason to eat as opposed to an opportunity to bring people to the same table.

Indonesians usually eat with their right hand, which is used to give and receive all good things. The left hand deals with unpleasant, sinister elements (such as ablutions). It's customary to wash your hands before eating, even if you use a spoon and fork; use the sinks outside the restrooms to do this.

When to Eat

Lunch is the big meal of the day, as it provides the chance to break up the day's toil. It's also when food is freshest. The day might start with a cup of rich, sweet black coffee and a few sweet *jajanan* at the market: colourful temple cakes, glutinous rice cakes, boiled bananas, *pisang goreng* (fried bananas) and *kelepon* (green rice-flour balls with a palm-sugar filling).

The famous *bubur injin* (black rice pudding with palm sugar, grated coconut and coconut milk), which is on most restaurant dessert menus, is actually a breakfast dish. A variation available at the morning market is the nutty *bubur kacang hijau* (green mung-bean pudding), fragrantly enriched with ginger and served warm with coconut milk.

The household or warung cook usually finishes preparing the day's dishes mid-morning, so lunch is served around 11am. Leftovers are eaten for dinner. Dessert is a rarity and mostly for special occasions; it usually consists of fresh fruit or delicious gelato-style coconut ice-cream.

Of course, for visitors there are few, if any, rules. Indonesians are used to the seemingly inexplicable habits of foreigners and handle most requests with aplomb. Traditional mealtimes are honoured, although you'll be hard-pressed to find many kitchens open late.

WHERE TO EAT

Restaurants Bali is a magnet for talented chefs, as the cost of doing business is low and the potential rewards are high. South Bali and Ubud are renowned for casual, innovative eateries.

Cafes There are Western-style cafes all over Bali, Lombok and the Gilis. Coffee is often made from local beans.

Warungs Local eateries serve great-tasting fare on a budget. In Nusa Tenggara, the terms warung and *rumah makan* are often interchangeable.

Fast-food vendors All residents gather round simple food stalls in *malam* (markets) and *pasar malam* (night markets). On village streets, wave down *pedagang* (mobile traders) for snacks.

FROM LEFT: WONDERFUL NATURE/SHUTTERSTOCK, SANATANA/SHUTTERSTOCK

Surfing, Uluwatu (p96)

THE OUTDOORS

This region is an incredible place to get outside and play: enjoy superb diving, surfing and hikes through rice fields or up volcanoes.

Powerful swells generated in the Southern Ocean send a conveyor belt of rollers towards Indonesia, so it's no surprise that the region's coastlines receive some truly spectacular waves. Scuba diving and snorkelling are huge draws in Bali and Nusa Tenggara, both of which are fringed by magnificent reefs that are easily accessed from the beach in many places. A walk or trek to one of the myriad waterfalls, verdant rice fields or rumbling volcanoes is a trip highlight for many.

Surfing

Surfing kick-started tourism in Bali in the 1960s. Many Balinese love to surf, and the grace of traditional dancing is said to influence their style. Surfers – local and visiting – buzz around on motorbikes with board racks, looking for the next great break. Waves blown out? Another spot is never far away.

Waves roll in from the Indian Ocean, so the best surf is generally on the islands' southwest coasts, particularly in the dry season (April to October). In the wet season, surf the eastern side of Bali, from Nusa Dua around to Padangbai.

Lombok also has some superb surfing and the breaks are generally less crowded. The giant bay at Gerupuk has multiple breaks, so there's always some wave action no matter the weather or tide.

In Nusa Tenggara, Sumbawa's southwest coast has white beaches with renowned surf, while the southeast waves are

Big Thrills

KITESURFING
Popular spots include **Ekas** (p250) in southwestern Lombok and **Pantai Lakey** (p301) in East Sumbawa.

WILDLIFE WATCHING
Spot deer, reptiles, monkeys and hundreds of bird species, including the striking Bali starling, at **West Bali National Park** (p222).

CYCLING
Coast downhill through the lush countryside amid the villages and rice terraces **north of Ubud** (p144).

FAMILY ADVENTURES

Hit the beach at **Kuta** (p76) where surf schools abound and at **Sanur** (p91) where reef-protected beaches are great for swimming.

Thrill underwater at **Pulau Menjangan** (p220) in North Bali for the best snorkelling in the region. Ideal for older kids.

Splash around at **Waterbom Bali** (p76) in Kuta, a huge aquatic playground with water slides and features.

Walk on water at the **Tirta Gangga** (p176) water palace in East Bali, where kids love to hop across the stepping-stone pond like frogs on lily pads.

Chase waterfalls in central Bali, where the **Red Coral Waterfall** (p195) is easy to access for travellers with young kids.

Play in the sand at **Gili Air** (p283), a delightful mix of laid-back vibes and fun-filled amenities.

year-round surf magnets. Directly south of Maluk is Supersuck, consistently rated among the best lefts in the world.

Stunning Pantai Nemberala on remote Rote island is home to the world-renowned T-Land break.

Diving & Snorkelling

With their warm water, extensive coral reefs and abundant marine life, Bali and Nusa Tenggara offer excellent diving and snorkelling adventures, especially during the dry season (April to October). Reliable dive schools and operators throughout the region (particularly at Pemuteran and Tulamben in Bali, in the Gilis, and in Labuan Bajo in Flores) can train complete beginners or arrange challenging trips that will satisfy the most experienced divers.

Snorkelling gear is available near all the most accessible spots; bring some along when you're out exploring the less-visited parts of the coasts. Dive operators can arrange trips (that include snorkellers) to the main dive sites in their regions.

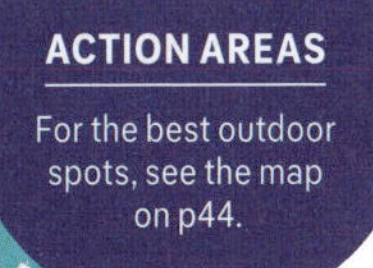

ACTION AREAS

For the best outdoor spots, see the map on p44.

Nest, Gili Meno (p278)

Walking & Hiking

You could travel through this region for a year and still not see all the islands have to offer. Day hikes and longer treks are easily arranged. Guides can help you summit volcanoes, while tour companies will take you to remote regions and emerald-green valleys.

Many trails are accessible on your own, especially those around Ubud, the Sidemen area and Munduk. In busy Seminyak or Canggu, you can walk onto the beach, choose a direction and just take off. Pack good boots for volcano and mountain treks, and non-slip hiking sandals or water shoes for waterfall walks. It's a good idea to use footwear on beach walks, too, as sharp marine debris can be hidden under the sand.

FREEDIVING
On Bali's far east coast, the **Amed region** (p182) is a base for freediving, with excellent operators and schools.

VOLCANO CLIMBS
Scramble up Bali's **Gunung Agung** (p170) Lombok's **Gunung Rinjani** (p262), Flores' **Gunung Inerie** (p295) and more.

YOGA
Ubud (p142) is yoga heaven, but you'll find wellness classes and gyms everywhere from **Canggu** (p57) to the **Gilis** (p283).

NATIONAL PARKS
East Nusa Tenggara's **Komodo National Park** wows with dragons, diving, pink beaches and superb viewpoints (p302).

ACTION AREAS

Where to find Bali, Lombok & Nusa Tenggara's best outdoor activities.

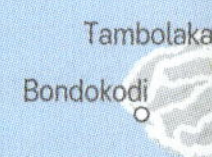

Volcano Climbs

1. Gunung Abang (p198)
2. Gunung Agung (p170)
3. Gunung Rinjani (p262)
4. Gunung Kelimutu (p300)
5. Gunung Inerie (p295)
6. Gunung Batur (p198)

Surfing

1. Canggu (p52)
2. Uluwatu (p96)
3. Kuta (p76)
4. Desert Point (p267)
5. Selong Belanak (p248)
6. Pantai Lakey (p301)
7. Nemberala (p316)

FLORES SEA
Labuan Bajo
Reo
Pota
Pangga
Ruteng
Seso
Olaja
Flores
Roa
Kolisia
Talibura
Tapowolo
Pulau Adonara
Sagu
Balauring
Pulau Pantar
Lewoleba
Pulau Marisa
Pulau Solor
Pulau Lembata
Gunung Sirung
Komodo National Park
Golo Mori
Repi
Bamo
Kotadirumali
Ende
EAST NUSA TENGGARA
TIMOR-LESTE
Naikliu
Kapan
Taemaman
WEST TIMOR
Oesao
SAWU SEA
Waibakul
Waingapu
Sumba
Melolo
Baing
Pulau Semau
Kupang
Akle
Pulau Sabu
Pulau Rote
Nemberala
INDIAN OCEAN

Walking/Hiking

1. Ubud (p127)
2. Danau Tamblingan (p195)
3. Munduk (p194)
4. Sidemen (p166)
5. Senaru (p258)
6. West Bali National Park (p218)

Snorkelling/Diving

1. Pulau Menjangan (p220)
2. Tulamben (p185)
3. Komodo National Park (p302)
4. Alor Archipelago (p315)
5. Nusa Lembongan (p109)
6. Seventeen Islands Marine Park (p298)
7. Gili Meno (p278)

Beaches

1. Thomas Beach (p96)
2. Pantai Jungutbatu (p111)
3. Pantai Pasir Putih (p175)
4. Gili Air (p283)
5. Pantai Mawun (p246)
6. Tanjung Aan (p244)
7. Pantai Nihiwatu (p326)

BALI, LOMBOK & NUSA TENGGARA

THE GUIDE

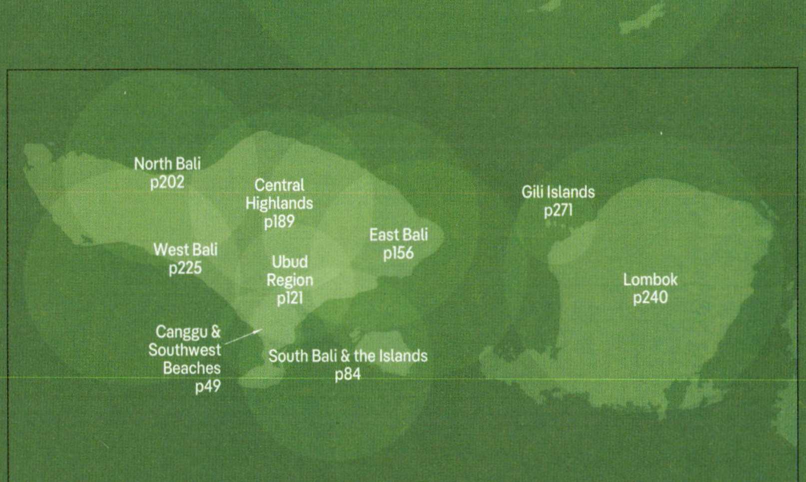

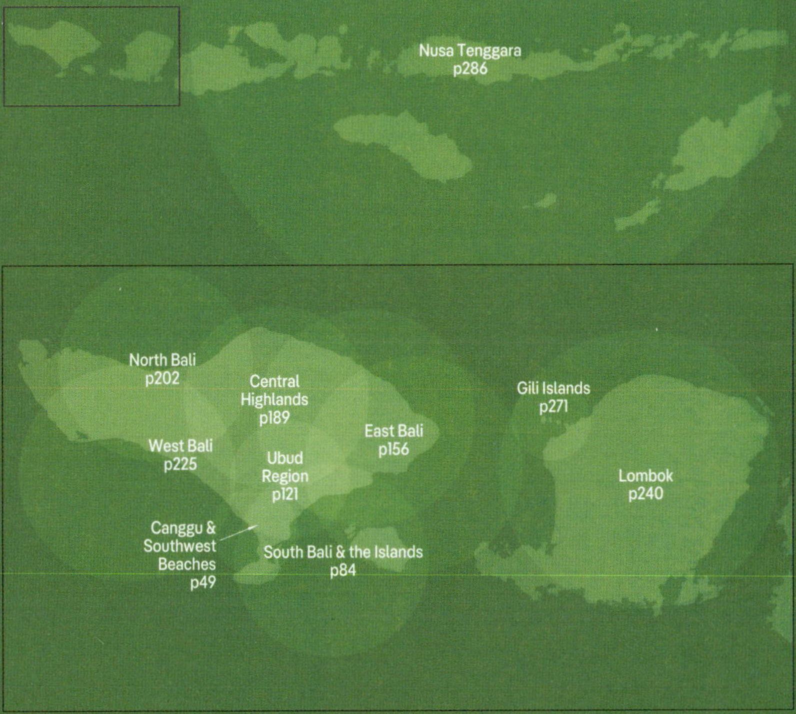

Chapters in this section are organised by hubs and their surrounding areas. We see the hub as your base in the destination, where you'll find unique experiences, local insights, insider tips and expert recommendations. It's also your gateway to the surrounding area, where you'll see what and how much you can do from there.

Pura Besakih (p171)

SUN_SHINE/SHUTTERSTOCK

For places to stay in Canggu & Southwest Beaches, see p83

KRIST SETYAWAN/SHUTTERSTOCK

Above: Pantai Batu Belig (p66); Right: Surfing, Kuta (p76)

Researched by
Sarah Reid

Canggu & Southwest Beaches

SUNSETS, SURF AND HOLIDAY VIBES

Bali's dynamic southwest coastline draws the crowds with exhilarating surf breaks, tranquil spas, cool cafes and world-class restaurants.

With a generous arc of wide sand sweeping up from the airport, the southwestern fringe of Bali's coastline is the island's original holiday playground – and still one of its most popular places to surf, party or simply bliss out. It's a region that never sleeps; where DJs at sprawling beach clubs spin beats late into the night, and surfers rise before dawn to ride some of Bali's most popular breaks. Freckled with umbrellas and sunloungers and lined by restaurants and bars, its beaches are the gateway to a carefree holiday traipsing between sand and spa, as well as an ever-expanding array of excellent places to eat.

IGNASIUS MADE/SHUTTERSTOCK

The region's western frontier, Canggu (pronounced *chan*-goo) beckons surfers, foodies and digital nomads who are drawn to a scene that is as alluring by day as it is by night, when crowds transition from the beach clubs, gyms and coworking cafes to trending restaurants and sultry cocktail bars. The black sands of Canggu transition to gold in the Seminyak area, known for its luxury resorts, laid-back beach bars, spa scene and shopping. Kuta and Legian, meanwhile, remain the casual beach hubs they've been for decades. Expect Bintang beers and plastic stools. A concrete jungle they may be, yet an easy-going spirit endures.

THE MAIN AREAS

CANGGU AREA
Cafes, cocktails, scenesters and surf. p52

SEMINYAK AREA
Sunsets, spas, shopping and resorts. p63

KUTA & LEGIAN
Beaches, Bintangs and an old-school atmosphere. p73

Find Your Way

The coastline of this area stretches only 12km from Bali's airport, but the roads around here are the island's most congested. Know that it could easily take an hour to travel less than 10km in a car.

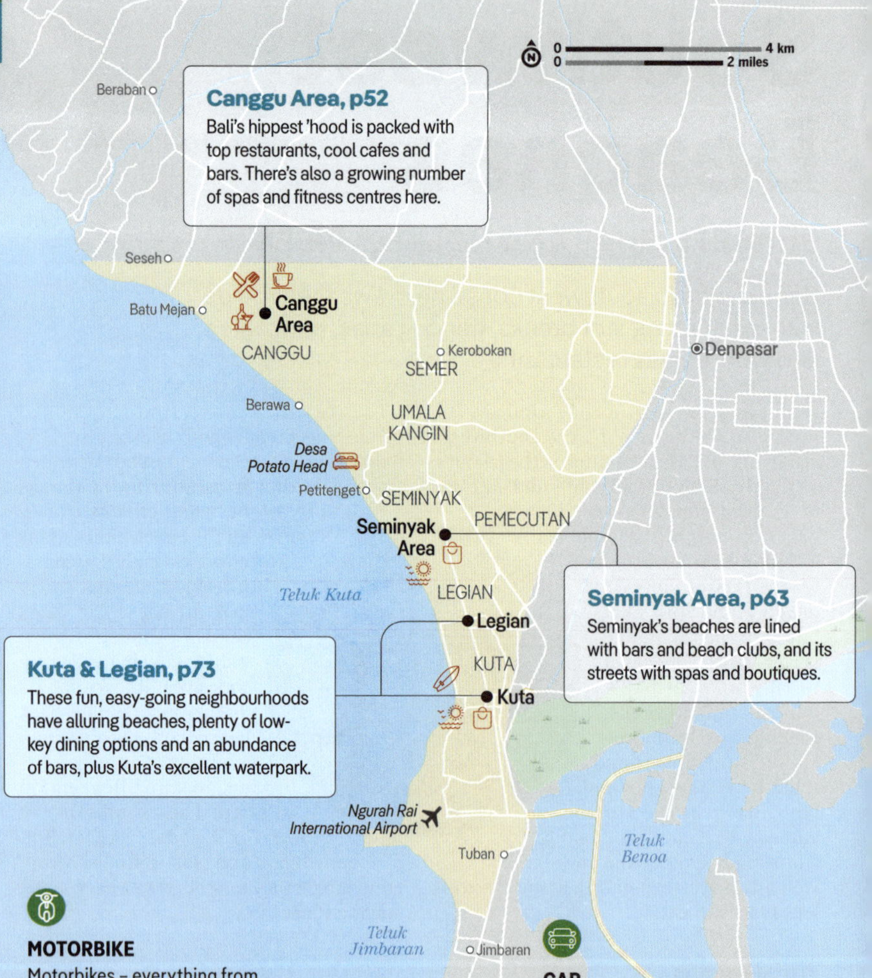

0 — 4 km
0 — 2 miles

Beraban
Seseh
Batu Mejan
Canggu Area
CANGGU
Kerobokan
SEMER
Denpasar
Berawa
UMALA KANGIN
Desa Potato Head
Petitenget
SEMINYAK
PEMECUTAN
Seminyak Area
Teluk Kuta
LEGIAN
Legian
KUTA
Kuta
Ngurah Rai International Airport
Tuban
Teluk Benoa
Teluk Jimbaran
Jimbaran
Bukit Peninsula

Canggu Area, p52

Bali's hippest 'hood is packed with top restaurants, cool cafes and bars. There's also a growing number of spas and fitness centres here.

Seminyak Area, p63

Seminyak's beaches are lined with bars and beach clubs, and its streets with spas and boutiques.

Kuta & Legian, p73

These fun, easy-going neighbourhoods have alluring beaches, plenty of low-key dining options and an abundance of bars, plus Kuta's excellent waterpark.

MOTORBIKE

Motorbikes – everything from small mopeds to retro cafe racers – are widely available for rent, but the congested roads can be overwhelming for inexperienced drivers. Ride-hailing apps Gojek and Grab make for a safer, affordable and convenient way to travel.

CAR

Taxis are common, and hotels will assist if you want to hire a car with a driver. Travel time is slow and only a worthwhile option if you plan to go beyond this coastal region.

EVGENY DRABLENKOV/SHUTTERSTOCK

Waterbom Bali (p76)

Plan Your Time

This is beach-holiday heaven, so get your dose of surf and sand and indulge at local cafes, restaurants and beach clubs before connecting with Bali's culture elsewhere on the island.

Pressed for Time

Begin your day with a **surf lesson at Pantai Kuta** (p76), then spend a thrilling afternoon at **Waterbom Bali** (p76), or at a **Seminyak spa** (p68). Afterwards, take a long **beach walk** (p79) before choosing a spot on the sand to watch the **sunset** (p78). Head out for dinner in Seminyak, then **party up a storm** (p76).

A Weeklong Stay

Lean into the Canggu lifestyle and fill your days with **surf sessions** (p52), **retail therapy** (p62), **massages** (p56) and **dining out** (p53). Work off the indulgence at a state-of-the-art **gym** (p57) or find the perfect **yoga class** (p57). And enjoy the Canggu sunsets just as much as the people-watching.

SEASONAL HIGHLIGHTS

JANUARY
Beach clubs organise huge New Year's Eve parties, and the weeks after the Christmas holidays bring fewer tourists.

MARCH
Some hotels and resorts have deals for Nyepi (Bali's Day of Silence; p81) – a special time to be on the island.

AUGUST
The height of the dry season is a lively time to immerse yourself in Canggu's party vibe and surf scene.

NOVEMBER
The start of the rainy season means fewer tourists and lower prices. Rain is normally short and sharp.

Canggu Area

SURFING | DINING OUT | HEALTH & WELLNESS

GETTING AROUND

The traffic around Canggu is notorious; on Jl Raya Canggu it can take over an hour to travel 10km in a car. Your quickest option to get from A to B in the Canggu area is to use a scooter from ride-hailing apps Grab or Gojek – and if you want to go further (say, to Ubud or Uluwatu), then book one of their cars. Your hotel can also help you source a private car and driver, if you prefer. Renting a standard scooter *(per day 100,000-120,000Rp)* isn't recommended for beginners.

TOP TIP

Beat the traffic (and work on your daily step count at the same time) by walking on the beach between Berawa, Canggu and Pererenan. You can then use Grab or Gojek to hail a scooter to take you to your destination.

Surfers put Canggu on the map, but during the last two decades this once-low-key stretch of Bali's coastline has evolved into the island's most cosmopolitan beach area, home to what may be the world's highest concentration of hip cafes and restaurants per capita.

Centred on Jl Batu Bolong, Canggu is also a catch-all term for the area between Seminyak and Cemagi, including Berawa and quieter but rapidly developing Pererenan, which flank Canggu to the east and west, respectively. Each of Canggu's three main areas houses a heady mix of bars and eateries, hotels and villas, boutiques and wellness offerings. There's also the surf, with breaks suitable for beginners to seasoned surfers, as well as a beach club for every mood.

While Canggu old-timers bemoan the continuing retreat of the area's once-abundant rice paddies – not to mention its ever-increasing traffic – travellers can't seem to get enough. Join the daily migration of gym-buffed bodies to the beach at sunset, and you'll begin to understand why.

Surf Canggu's Iconic Waves

Find your perfect break

Batu Bolong might fall short of Indonesia's finest surf breaks, but Canggu's main beach break is one of the most popular longboarding waves in the country. Also known as Old Man's (for the party venue just back from the beach), it's a beginner-friendly beach break that tends to break further out before reforming again.

Northwest of Batu Bolong is **Echo Beach**, home to several barrelling breaks better suited to intermediate and advanced surfers. Echo Beach Left or Stairs is a powerful left-hander breaking over a shallow reef, Sandbar is the middle section of the beach break, and River Mouth is a reef break.

Southeast of Old Man's, **Pantai Nelayan** is popular with kitesurfers (although not for beginners). Beginner surfers may also find some gentle waves here. Further southeast, **Berawa**

LILYROSEPHOTOS/SHUTTERSTOCK

Batu Bolong

has a beach break opposite Finns (p58) known as the Peak, which is suitable for beginners on small days. Further out, intermediate breaks called the Ledge and the Bommie work in bigger swells.

You can rent soft and hard boards on the beach from 50,000Rp for up to two hours and two-hour surf lessons are available from 350,000Rp. **Mojosurf** *(mojosurf.com)* also runs intense courses that can include accommodation at its Canggu Surf Camp.

A word of warning: a steady flow of stormwater onto Canggu's charcoal-sand beaches throughout the year means the water isn't the cleanest, especially during the wet season. Bacterial infections have been linked to polluted seawater.

CANGGU'S BEACHES

Pererenan: A giant statue of a mythical sea creature mounted by sea god Dewa Baruna marks the entrance to this black-sand beach that's better for surfing than swimming.

Echo Beach: Watch experienced surfers carve up the waves from the bars lining the beach. It's busy at sunset.

Batu Bolong: Board shacks, warungs (food stalls) and umbrellas line the beach between Jl Nelayan and Jl Batu Bolong.

Nelayan: Huts and fishing boats give relatively quiet Nelayan a distinctly local character.

Berawa: This wide, grey beach has surf spots for all levels along with its own collection of beach bars and clubs.

Dig Into Canggu's Dining Scene

Cafes and restaurants for every craving

World-class restaurants are now found across Bali, but no other region can compete with Canggu's density of cool cafes and international restaurants sporting fitouts as appealing as the menus.

Food quality (and, increasingly, hygiene) is high, and so are the prices – for Bali – especially when you factor in the 12% government tax and service charge (usually 5%to 10%) added to your bill. With an increasing number of venues also

continued on p56

EATING IN PERERENAN: OUR PICKS

Home by Chef Wayan: You haven't tasted Indonesian food until you've dined at the lauded Balinese chef's relaxed Pererenan restaurant. *11am-10pm* $$

Shelter: Superb Mediterranean fare served in an airy garden *bale* (open-side pavilion), with a special menu for vegans. *noon-midnight* $$

Arte: Dine on great wood-fired pizzas and homemade pasta while admiring the current exhibits by local artists (all for sale) adorning the walls. *8am-11pm* $$

Hippie Fish: Fancy Mediterranean-style fish with stellar Pererenan Beach views. What more could you want? *noon-11pm* $$

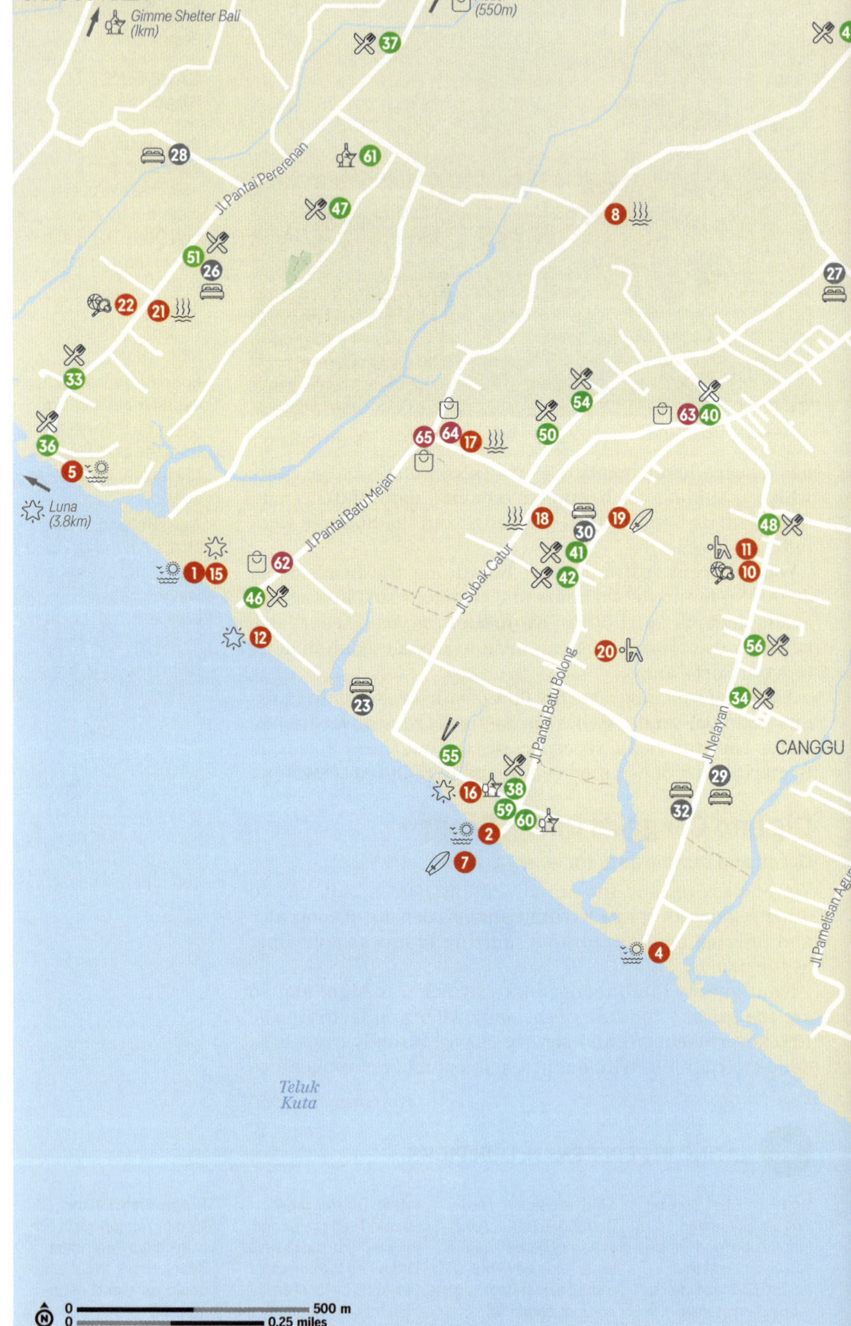
CANGGU AREA
Gimme Shelter Bali (1km)
Asasi (550m)
Jl Pantai Pererenan
Luna (3.8km)
Jl Pantai Batu Mejan
Jl Subak Catur
Jl Pantai Batu Bolong
Jl Nelayan
CANGGU
Jl Pamelisan Agung
Teluk Kuta
0 500 m
0 0.25 miles

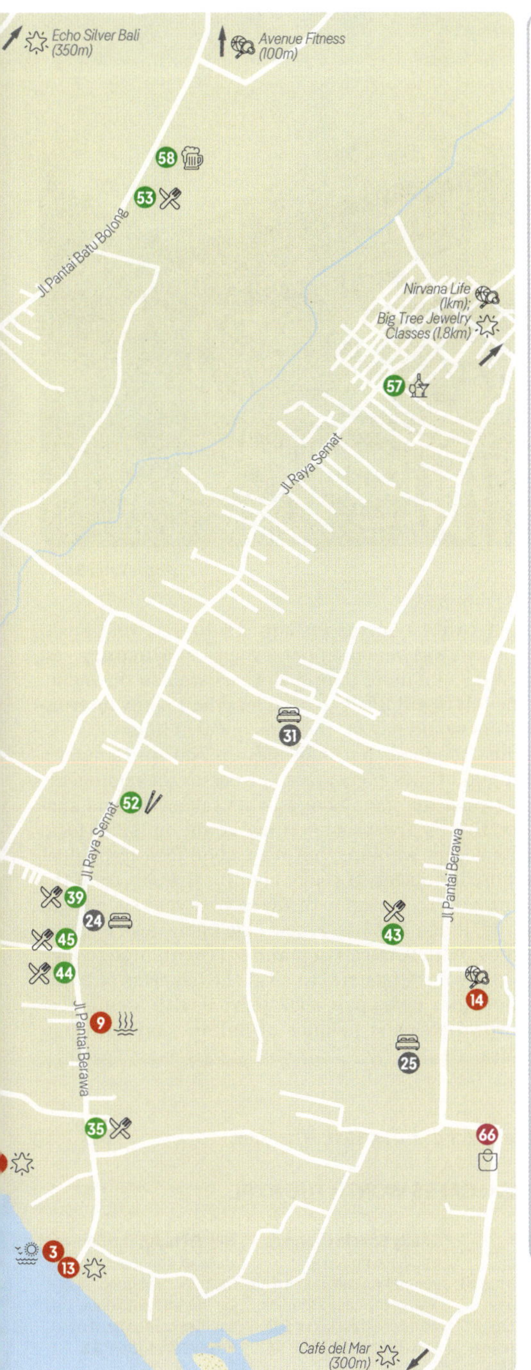

SIGHTS
1 Echo Beach
2 Pantai Batu Bolong
3 Pantai Berawa
4 Pantai Nelayan
5 Pererenan Beach

ACTIVITIES
6 Atlas Beach Club
7 Batu Bolong
8 Beach House by Tonic
9 Beautyful Spa
10 Body Factory Bali
11 BWork Yoga
12 Como Beach Club Canggu
see 23 Como Uma Shambhala Retreat
13 Finns Beach Club
14 Finns Recreation Centre
15 La Brisa
16 Lawn
17 Lotus Massage Therapy Echo
18 Marissa Spa
19 Mojosurf
20 Practice
21 Tyche Day Spa
22 Wrong Gym

SLEEPING
23 Como Uma Canggu
24 Dip & Doze
25 Guru Canggu
see 38 Hotel Tugu Bali
26 Kayu Village
27 Melati Bali Homestay
28 Noema
29 Serenity
30 Sunflower Stay and Surf
31 Wayang Retreat
32 Zin Canggu

EATING
33 Arte
34 Deli Canggu
35 Ghost Kitchen & Record Bar
36 Hippie Fish
37 Home by Chef Wayan
38 Kawisari Coffee Farm Shop & Eatery
39 Longtime
40 Luigi's Hot Pizza
41 Masonry
42 Meimei
43 Milk & Madu
44 Mosto
45 Neighbourhood
46 Numero Quattro
47 Openhouse Cafe
48 Revolver
49 Samadi Bali
50 Shady Shack
51 Shelter
52 Sista Dumpling
53 Warung Local
54 Warung Sika
55 Yuki
56 Yumei Noodles

DRINKING & NIGHTLIFE
57 Bar Souvenir
58 Black Sand Brewery
see 38 Ji Terrace
59 Motel Mexicola
60 Old Man's
61 Shady Fox

SHOPPING
62 Canggu Center
63 Deus Ex Machina
64 Island Traders
65 Luna & Rose
66 Ticket to the Moon
see 40 Tropicalife

AFFORDABLE MASSAGES IN CANGGU

Lotus Massage Therapy Echo: Good for couples, with private treatment rooms for two. Book at least a few hours ahead.

Tyche Day Spa: Sweet little Pererenan spot with consistently good massages for bargain prices *(1hr 190,000Rp)* with a choice of coconut, lemongrass or lavender oil.

Marissa Spa: A great find in central Canggu, with foot rubs and nails downstairs and full-body massages upstairs. Has another branch in Berawa.

Beach House Massage by Tonic: The sister venue of Palm Springs–styled Tonic down the road on Jl Padang Linjong has the same affordable massage prices.

Beautyful Spa: Peaceful, modern Berawa spa with Balinese massages *(1hr 190,000Rp)*.

ANITA EKA PERMATAWATY/SHUTTERSTOCK

Hotel Tugu Bali

continued from p53
charging for card payments (usually 2% to 3%), your sushi degustation at **Yuki** or contemporary feast at **Masonry** can end up costing a lot more than the price listed on the menu. And yet the bill is still likely to total less than many international visitors would pay for the same meal at home.

It's not just the food that makes dining out in Canggu a joy, but the good-times energy that permeates the photogenic venues. Between the happy hours, chef takeovers and special events, there's always something going on. Most local restaurants accept walk-ins, but it's a good idea to book at the most popular places. If you're coming straight from the beach, bring a chic cover-up to throw on over your swimwear.

Meanwhile, it can feel like a new cafe opens every day in Canggu, most with Australian-standard (read: high) coffee and decadently flaky pastries to rival the bakeries of Paris. The most popular cafes pair slick service with menus featuring a crowd-pleasing balance of Balinese and international dishes.

Great deals include 2-for-1 drinks from 4 to 7pm.

EATING IN THE CANGGU AREA: CAFES WORTH THE HYPE

Neighbourhood: An indoor-outdoor oasis in Berawa with a vast menu including a moreish kimchi toastie. *7.30am-10pm Tue-Sat, to 6pm Sun-Mon* $$

Openhouse Cafe: A somewhat hidden Pererenan location hasn't kept the crowds away from this leafy all-day cafe enlivened by house beats. *6am-10pm* $$

Shady Shack: Canggu's original wholefood vegetarian cafe is still a hit with plant-based foodies, with breakfast served all day. *7.30am-10.30pm* $$

Milk & Madu: The Berawa stalwart continues to nail the trifecta of good food, service and ambience. Has another branch on Jl Batu Bolong. *7am-10pm* $$

Begin (or Deepen) Your Yoga Practice

Find a class that suits your vibe

Ubud (p124) might be revered as Bali's yoga heartland but manic Canggu doesn't fall too far behind with its own growing offering of yoga studios. There is something for everyone here, from beginners to lifelong yogis, and hippies to hipsters. Near Pantai Nelayan, family-owned, permaculture-based **Serenity** *(serenitybali.com)* is a down-to-earth yoga resort offering nine 90-minute classes a day, including aerial yoga *(nonguest/guest 130,000/110,000Rp)*. Pop by for a class, workshop or wellness treatment (book all via the website), stay for a meal at Serenity's vegan restaurant, or check into the guesthouse and immerse yourself in yogic living.

You can't stay overnight at **Samadi Bali** *(samadibali.com)*, but you can spend all day there. This peaceful yoga and wellness centre (with a boutique, wholesome restaurant and eco-conscious supermarket) on busy Jl Padang Linjong provides an opportunity to embark on a comprehensive wellness journey that will nourish both your body and mind. Up to 15 classes ranging from 60 to 120 minutes *(155,000Rp)* are held throughout the day, and Samadi also offers a series of retreat packages for women. Different healers and therapists work from this dreamy, peaceful space.

In a breezy bamboo pavilion atop the BWork coworking hub on Jl Nelayan, **BWork Yoga** *(bwork.id/empoweredyoga; classes 165,000Rp)* specialises in power yoga, but there's also yin, Hatha and flow. Classes run from 60 to 75 minutes.

Another popular space is the **Practice** *(thepracticebali.com)*, on Jl Pantai Batu Bolong, where traditional Hatha yoga is king. It's a calm, powerful and very grounded space, with 75 to 90-minute classes *(150,000Rp)*.

Find Bali in Canggu

A slice of old Indonesia

Canggu is a cosmopolitan, ever-changing neighbourhood that nowadays feels distinctly un-Balinese, but there is one very special enclave that stands as a bastion of tradition and culture. **Hotel Tugu Bali** *(tuguhotels.com)*, a boutique hotel owned by an Indonesian art collector, offers a chance to connect with the history and traditions of the archipelago. Simply walking into the antique-filled property tucked behind Pantai Batu Bolong is an evocative journey into the Indonesia of old, and experiences like Balinese dance, cooking or *jamu*-making

continued on p60

CANGGU'S DESTINATION GYMS

Body Factory Bali: Sweat it out at a kickboxing class, then chill by the pool with a collagen shake. In Bewara.

Wrong Gym: The sleek Pererenan mega-gym comes complete with a 'Booty Room' dedicated to lower body building.

Nirvana Life: Takes a more holistic approach with its class schedule heroing movement and breathwork.

Finns Recreation Centre: A major renovation was underway in 2025, with the new centre set to include multiple training spaces, 25m indoor lap pool, recovery area and more.

Avenue Fitness: The cheapest of Canggu's full-service gyms has a limited class schedule and no pool, but there's an ice bath, sauna and hot tub.

EATING IN CANGGU: OUR PICKS

Deli Canggu: Great sandwiches aren't easy to come by in Bali, at least they weren't until this deli popped up in Canggu and Uluwatu. *6am-6pm* $$

Yumei Noodles: The umami-packed spicy beef noodle soup with Sichuan pepper is a solid choice at this Chinese noodle joint. *11am-2am* $$

Numero Quattro: Elevated neighbourhood Italian fare, with Echo Beach glimpses from the 1st-floor terrace. Try the spicy gin rigatoni. *5pm-midnight* $$

Meimei: The team behind excellent local Japanese restaurant Yuki are onto another winner with this sizzling Southeast Asian barbecue spot. *5pm-2am* $$$

Southwest Bali's Beach Clubs

Beach clubs have exploded across Bali, with more than 50 of these day-to-night party palaces dotting its coastlines at last count. Open year-round, Southwest Bali's best beach clubs are clustered in Canggu and Seminyak. Most are relatively relaxed – even family-friendly – during the day, with DJs typically hitting the decks from late afternoon. Most beach clubs also host regular big-name DJ events after dark, particularly during the dry season.

Where to Go If You Want...

To Chill in Style

La Brisa Resembling a sprawling bohemian castaway village overlooking Echo Beach, Bali's most Instagrammable beach club was built entirely from reclaimed wood from old fishing boats. Studded with palm trees (limiting sunbathing opportunities), La Brisa also hosts a popular 10am to 4pm Sunday Market. Free entry.

Potato Head Beach Club (p66) Part of Seminyak's Desa Potato Head complex, this horseshoe-shaped beach club encircling a seafront infinity pool has a cracking cocktail list featuring house-distilled spirits, with food and drink menus designed to minimise food waste. Redeemable cover charge from 4.30pm to 7pm *(250,000Rp)*.

BADASS ARTISTS/SHUTTERSTOCK

Lawn Its original grassy lawn is now paved, but it hasn't dulled the appeal of this compact Batu Bolong beach club founded by pro Kiwi surfer Tai 'Buddha' Graham. It has the requisite infinity pool, but most people come for the prime sunset viewing with a cocktail in hand (try the sunset margarita made with tequila, crème de cassis, agave, lemon and sparkling wine). Free entry.

To Party

Finns Beach Club This adults-only Berawa beach club bills itself as the world's best beach club, and if you're in the mood to let your hair down, you might agree. Bounce between its 11 bars and three pools, including a beachfront infinity pool, with multiple dining options available. The tempo (and rowdiness) increases as the evening progresses. Free entry.

Luna Technically in Tabanan, west of Pererenan, this newish beach club comes complete with a slippery slide from the more family-friendly upper pool down into the Utopia Cave Club, a Playboy Mansion–esque grotto for 21st-century revellers. Entrance to Nuanu Creative City, where Luna is located, is 50,000Rp.

A Family-Friendly Option

Ku De Ta With an infinity pool spilling onto Seminyak Beach, Bali's original beach club still holds its own, with family-friendly Sunday the best day to bring kids (or avoid for a more relaxed experience). Fans of a perfect steak won't want to miss SaltLick, above the beach club. Free entry.

Como Beach Club Canggu Attached to the luxurious Como Uma Hotel Canggu, this small beach club is popular with well-heeled families. A stylish surf-shack-style restaurant and bar opens onto an infinity pool. For non-guests a minimum spend of 1,500,000Rp is required to secure a daybed and use the pool.

ALI CHEHADE FARHAT/SHUTTERSTOCK

Finns Beach Club

HOW TO

Booking
Book in advance for a day bed, a prime sunset position, and for special events such as high-profile DJ shows and New Year's Eve.

Entrance fees
Entrance fees often include a credit towards food and beverage purchases. Sunlounger and daybed use typically requires a minimum spend.

Dress code
Most beach clubs have a minimum dress code; at least no alcohol-branded tops. Some clubs require footwear (not flip-flops) after 4pm.

Bag checks
Expect bags checks on entry; your own food and drinks, including bottled water, are generally not allowed. It's fine to BYO a towel, which isn't always included.

Best of the Rest

Mrs Sippy It mightn't have direct beach access, but Bali's largest pool club, in Seminyak, deserves an honourable mention. Saturdays are an all-day party with beats guaranteed to get you grooving. Good happy-hour deals most evenings and tasty wood-fired dishes. Entrance 150,000Rp.

Atlas Beach Club (pictured left) Next to Finns, Bali's biggest beach club can feel a bit empty. On the plus side, there's plenty of room to spread out, and it has family-friendly spaces and activities. Party on at the huge Atlas Super Club, behind the beach club. Entrance 100,000Rp.

Sunset Beach The Mrs Sippy team's newest Seminyak venue occupies a beachfront spot with a pool and sunlounger-dotted lawn. Food and drink menus feature well-executed classics along with signature tipples like the Golden Hour (vodka, Aperol, grilled pineapple, lime, pineapple juice). Free entry.

Azul Beach Club Legian's nicest beach club is anchored by an airy bamboo restaurant and bar rising up across the road from the sand. A food or beverage purchase secures free entry to the pools. The upper-floor tiki bar, infinity pool and hot tub are adults-only.

Café del Mar A slice of the Balearics in Berawa, this semi-circle venue is separated from the sand by a small river, but the views across the infinity pool are sensational and the tunes are on point. Free entry.

SURF 'N' ZOOM

Canggu has become one of the world's most popular hubs for digital nomads. While there are some positives – remote workers have created economic benefits for some locals, particularly hospitality businesses – the influx of digital nomads has partly driven a boom in villa construction that is contributing to the strain on Bali's infrastructure. There are nearly a dozen coworking spaces in Canggu alone. With a mission to create a sustainable future for the local community through its impact program, **Zin Canggu** *(zin.world)* resort offers a free coworking space next to its cafe, which fills up early. Note that Indonesian law prohibits travellers on standard tourist visas from conducting remote work.

CHAELINJANE/SHUTTERSTOCK

Nasi campur

continued from p57

classes (*jamu* is a turmeric-based elixir), ceremonial dinners, and spa treatments rooted in beauty traditions offer a chance to connect with Balinese culture. Balinese feasts fit for royals *(700,000Rp)* are served in the Bale Puputan, housing an extensive collection of artefacts from Bali's 1906 Puputan War with the Dutch (p160). Added in 2022, its street-level **Kawisari Coffee Farm Shop & Eatery** serves coffee from its own plantation, the oldest and largest certified organic coffee plantation in Java.

Hike 'Bali's Camino'

Uncover the real Bali

Need a break from the cacophony of Canggu? Slow down and connect with Bali's verdant ricescapes and ancient culture on the **Astungkara Way** *(astungkaraway.com)*, a 135km guided hiking experience crossing the island from south to north. Founded by former Bali Green School teacher Tim Fijal as a vehicle to support regenerative agriculture in Bali, the experience offers a meaningful opportunity to immerse in Balinese culture in an authentic, responsible way, with

This is a great spot to escape the sunset crowds.

DRINKING IN THE CANGGU AREA: BEST BARS

Ji Terrace: Sip classic and house cocktails (including a good pina colada) as you soak up the sunset views over Pantai Bolong Beach. *noon-11pm*

Bar Souvenir: The mid-century minimalist interior allows the cocktails and natural wine to shine. In Berawa. *7pm-midnight Mon-Sat*

Black Sand Brewery: Craft brews and pub grub in an airy, industrial-style space with a breezy beer garden and daily specials. *noon-midnight*

Motel Mexicola: Begin your night with tacos and happy hour margis at the colour-popping Canggu outpost of the Seminyak institution. *11am-1am*

several departures throughout the year. Beginning at Cemagi Beach, northwest of Pererenan, the full coast-to-coast experience *(15,900,000Rp)* takes 10 days and ends at Seririt in North Bali (p210). Everything is included, with wholesome meals showcasing farm-fresh produce, and camping accommodation in traditional Balinese family compounds and picturesque farms. With profits supporting free training, micro-financing and market access for regenerative rice farmers, it's an ultra-feel-good hike.

If you don't have the time (or the stamina), shorter four- and six-day sections of the trail are also offered *(4/6-day 6,100,000Rp/8,900,000Rp)* along with overnight experiences *(from 2,400,000Rp)*. The trails are suitable for kids aged 10 and above, while overnight experiences are suitable for kids as young as six. You'll need to get yourself to a start point, all of which are in the Central Highlands (p189). All experiences include transport back to Canggu or Ubud. Check the Facebook page *(facebook.com/astungkaraway)* for updates on spots on upcoming departures.

Feast on Traditional Indonesian Fare

Embrace Balinese-style *nasi campur*

Ubiquitous around Indonesia, *nasi campur* (rice with a choice of side dishes) is one of Bali's most beloved - and inexpensive - meals, with typical side dishes reflecting the island's rich culinary heritage. A traditional *nasi campur* warung will have bowls and plates stacked in the window displaying what's on offer, while larger eateries often have the food set out buffet-style behind a glass counter; there can be as many as 30 dishes to choose from, including beef rendang, spicy shredded chicken, grilled fish, fried eggs, corn fritters, crispy tempeh, *urap sayur* (steamed vegetables with shredded coconut), *sambal terong* (eggplant with sambal), *mie goreng* (fried noodles) and a variety of sambal. Many Balinese restaurants also offer a set-plate *nasi campur* on their menus, but it's more fun to choose the sides yourself. Often there will also be a choice of rice (try the Balinese red rice if available). Select your sides and the person behind the counter will make up a plate and charge you accordingly.

Simple warungs cook dishes before the lunch rush. Dishes are replenished throughout the day at busier *nasi campur* spots including **Warung Sika** on Jl Tanah Barak and **Warung Local** on Jl Pantai Batu Bolong.

BEYOND BEACH CLUBS: BEST FOR A NIGHT OUT

Revolver: Rev up for a night out during the daily happy hour (4pm to 7pm). Saturday is party night with DJs until 10pm.

Luigi's Hot Pizza: Start with a pizza, stay for the party, with DJs hitting the decks on Mondays and Thursdays.

Gimme Shelter: A rock'n'roll bar in Pererenan with a mini skatepark, open-mic Mondays and live music on Wednesdays and Saturdays.

Old Man's: Attracting a younger crowd, Canggu's original beach bar pumps until 1am. The party then moves to next-door Sandbar until 3am.

Shady Fox: From karaoke to live blues, there's always something going on at this clandestine Pererenan cocktail bar. DM the venue on Instagram *(instagram.com/theshadyfox__)* for the password.

EATING IN BERAWA: OUR PICKS

Ghost Kitchen: Simple dishes are supercharged with flavour at this neighbourhood bistro. Vinyl DJs on Fridays. *noon-midnight Fri-Sun, from 3pm Mon-Thu* $$

Sista Dumpling: A peaceful setting overlooking a rice paddy and spot-on *xiao long bao* (soup dumplings) make Sista a great lunch spot. *10am-11.30pm* $$

Longtime: Delicious mash-up of flavours from Indonesia, East Asia and beyond. Start with a beef rendang spring roll. *noon-midnight Tue-Sat, to 11pm Sun & Mon* $$

Mosto: Indonesia's first natural wine bar also turns out some of the most innovative dishes in Bali, combining local produce with international flavours. *5pm-12.30am* $$$

RIDER BEWARE

Many travellers affix smartphone holders to the handlebars of rented motorbikes to help navigate Southwest Bali's tangle of unplanned roads. Unfortunately, this has led to a rise in drive-by smartphone theft. Thieves snatch smartphones from the holders as they drive past you, with some robberies causing victims to crash and injure themselves. One way to avoid falling victim is to set your route on your phone and enable voice navigation, then secure your phone under the seat of your bike and follow the directions through your earphones. Thieves often target solo women and people riding along lonely roads late at night.

MARLON TROTTMANN/SHUTTERSTOCK

Jl Pantai Batu Bolong

Shop 'til You Drop

Hit the shops in Canggu

Canggu's retail game has never been stronger. With no main shopping strip in this neighbourhood, discovering boutiques tucked down unexpected alleys is half the fun.

While you'll find plenty of cheap-clothing emporiums like the **Canggu Center** and **Tropicalife**, Canggu's retail strength lies in its contemporary midrange fashion, lifestyle and jewellery boutiques, many of which feature products made on the island. Canggu is the spiritual home of Australian streetwear brand **Deus Ex Machina**; its on-site cafe often hosts live music and other events. In Berawa, **Ticket to the Moon** makes excellent foldable backpacks and hammocks from upcycled nylon parachute material. Fashion picks include **Island Traders** on Jl Batu Mejan Canggu for its curated islandwear for women and **Asasi** in Pererenan for stylish menswear designed in London and crafted in Bali. Also on Jl Batu Mejan Canggu, **Luna & Rose** is good for on-trend gold and silver jewellery.

Craft Your Own Souvenir

Take a jewellery-making course

Jewellery-making courses are a great rainy-day activity in Bali, and there's no shortage of them to choose from in Canggu. At most workshops, you'll make a small piece of silver jewellery with the option to have it gold-plated for an additional cost. In Berawa, north of Jl Raya Canggu, **Big Tree Jewelry Classes** *(bigtreejewelryclasses.com; classes from 450,000Rp)* runs popular classes in a comfortable, air-con workshop. Guided by an expert silversmith, a standard one to 2½-hour class will see you shape, hammer and solder 7g of silver (enough to make a ring pendant) to form your desired piece of jewellery, then sand and polish it for a professional finish. In Canggu, **Echo Silver Bali** *(echosilverbali.com; classes from 450,000Rp)* is also recommended.

Seminyak Area

BEACH BARS | SUMPTUOUS SPAS | SHOPPING

Seminyak effortlessly blends luxury with a laid-back beach vibe, and this busy neighbourhood is a magnet for those seeking a fusion of fun, style and relaxation. While its waves are no match for those of Canggu or Kuta, Seminyak's wide stretch of golden beach is arguably the region's nicest. Sunset is a busy time, when beanbags are hauled out and strings of lights are hung beneath umbrellas, ready for the revellers. Some of Bali's most-loved hotels and beach clubs are also found here.

Seminyak has long been an alluring destination for shoppers with its mix of designer boutiques, homewares emporiums and cheap and cheerful clothing shops. Northeast of Seminyak, more industrial Kerobokan is home decor heaven. The Seminyak area isn't short on dining options, either, with everything from Australian-style cafes to haute Indonesian fare served up by local and international chefs.

A Feast for the Senses

Learn to prepare Balinese cuisine

Bali's tropical climate and fertile volcanic soils yield an astounding range of fruits, vegetables, herbs and spices – and enrolling in a cooking class provides you with an excellent opportunity to explore not only how these ingredients shape Balinese cuisine, but also to be immersed in a multilayered experience that, as cliché as it sounds, really is a feast for the senses. Most cooking classes begin with a trip to a local market to shop for lemongrass, ginger, tamarind and other fresh ingredients, and they also provide an opportunity to catch a glimpse of authentic Balinese life. At **Nia Cooking Class** *(niacookingclass.com; adult/child 600,000/475,000Rp)*, which is based on the edge of the flea market on Jl Kayu Aya, the morning evolves as you set about making the various elements of iconic Balinese dishes, like spice pastes and the delicately flavoured minced fish mix for *sate lilit ikan* (minced fish satay). Throughout the class you will learn some of the methods used

continued on p66

GETTING AROUND

Seminyak's sidewalks are generally in decent condition, so walking is a great way to get around and explore the area, particularly if you have shopping on your mind. Much of Seminyak's beach is lined with a boardwalk and you can stroll along the paved walkway from here right through to Kuta. Scooters are readily available for rent, but it may be more convenient (or safer, if you're planning on a big night) to use the ride-hailing apps Grab or Gojek than to drive yourself. Allow an hour for airport transfers.

TOP TIP

With its lovely wide beach, decent footpaths and plentiful resorts, Seminyak has long been a popular option for families looking for a stylish stay within striking distance of the airport. Foodies will find the dining options a cut above those of Kuta and Legian.

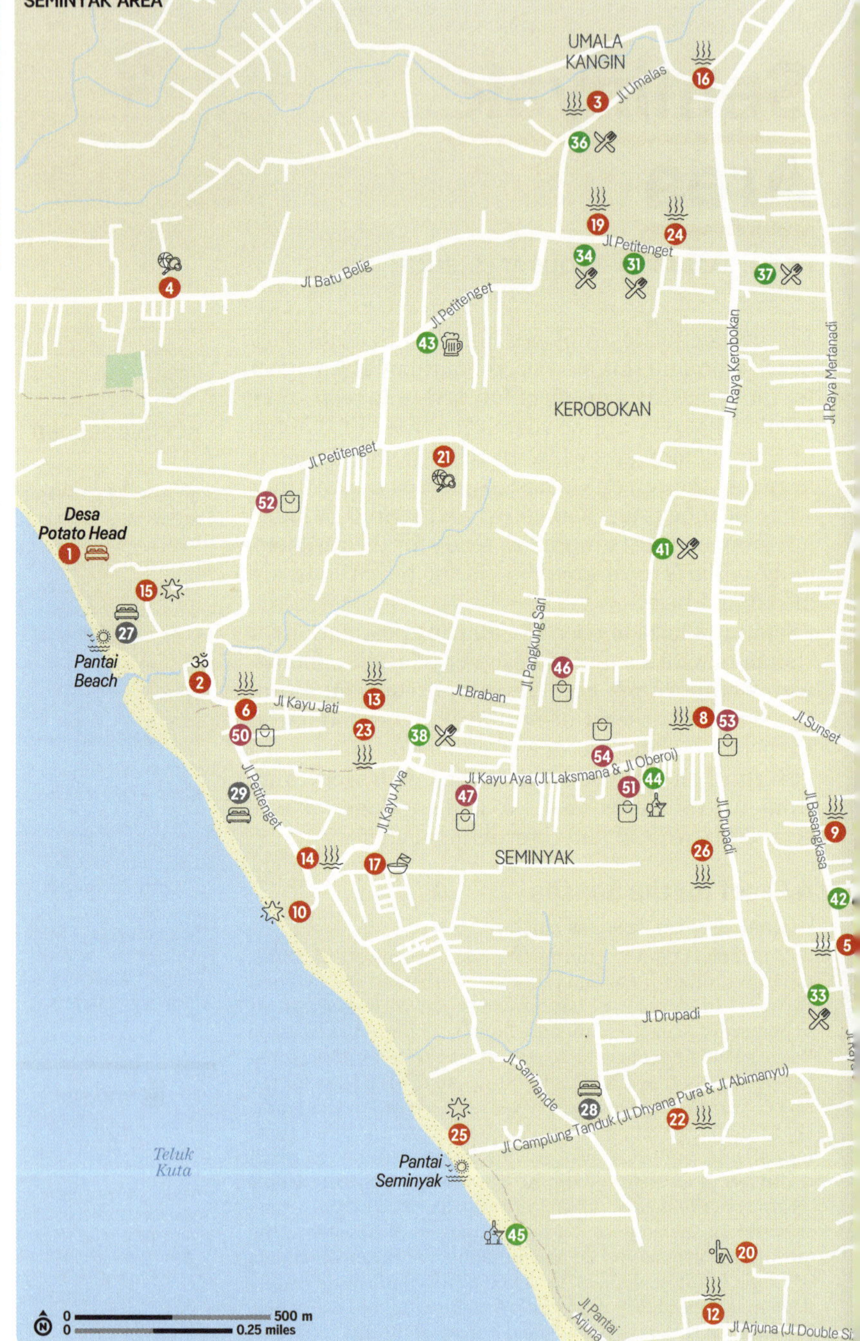
SEMINYAK AREA
UMALA KANGIN
KEROBOKAN
SEMINYAK
Desa Potato Head
Pantai Beach
Pantai Seminyak
Teluk Kuta
Jl Umalas
Jl Petitenget
Jl Batu Belig
Jl Raya Kerobokan
Jl Raya Mertanadi
Jl Pangkung Sari
Jl Braban
Jl Kayu Jati
Jl Kayu Aya
Jl Kayu Aya (Jl Laksmana & Jl Oberoi)
Jl Sunset
Jl Drupadi
Jl Basangkasa
Jl Sarinande
Jl Camplung Tanduk (Jl Dhyana Pura & Jl Abimanyu)
Jl Pantai Arjuna
Jl Arjuna (Jl Double Si
0 500 m
0 0.25 miles

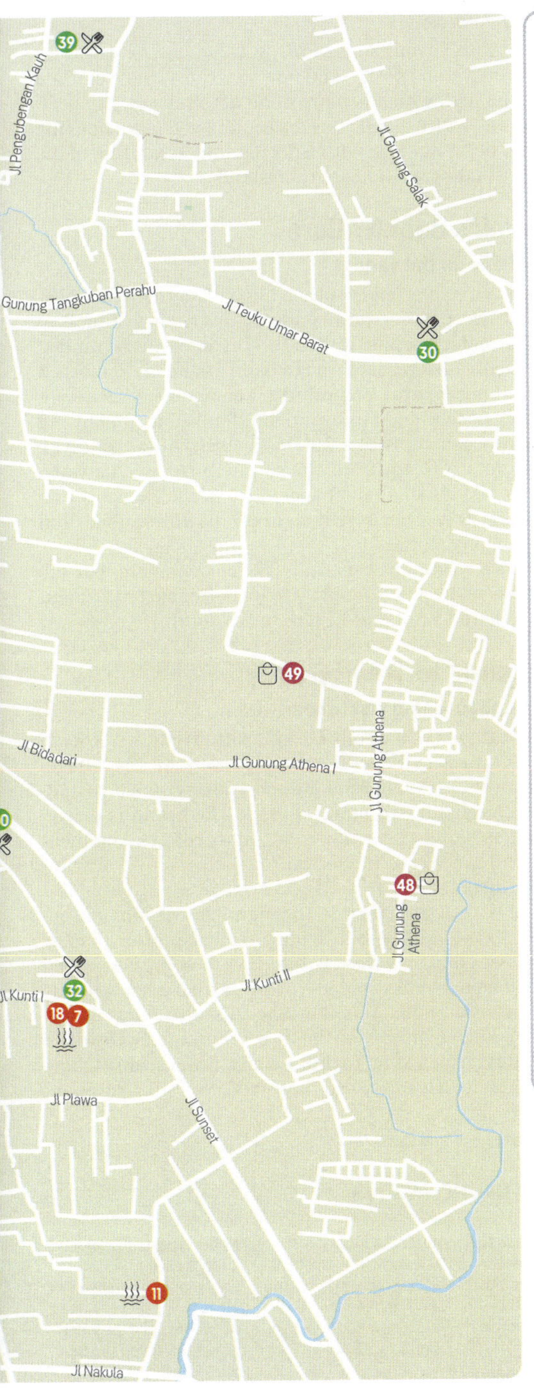

HIGHLIGHTS
1 Desa Potato Head

SIGHTS
2 Pura Petitenget

ACTIVITIES
3 Aliya Bali
4 Bali Pilates Plus
5 Body Lab Bali
6 Bodyworks
7 Chill Reflexology
see 4 F45 Seminyak
8 Glo Day Spa
9 Jari Menari
10 Ku De Ta
11 Lagoon Spa
12 Lamora Spa
13 Lotus Massage Therapy Seminyak
14 Mello Spa
15 Mrs Sippy
16 Natura Organics Spa
17 Nia Cooking Class
see 1 Potato Head Beach Club
18 Prana
19 Re Day Spa
20 Snana Yoga
21 Soham Wellness Center
22 Spa Bali Seminyak
23 Spring Spa
24 Sundari Wellness
25 Sunset Beach
26 Terra Spa

SLEEPING
27 Alila Seminyak
28 Grandmas Plus Hotel Seminyak
29 Legian

EATING
30 Babi Guling Sari Kembar 99
31 Da Maria
32 Fed by Made
33 Hut
see 1 Kaum
34 Livingstone Cafe & Bakery
35 Naughty Nuri's
36 Nook
37 Pasar Kerobokan
38 Sisterfields
39 T&T Chindo's Cuisine
40 Warung Babi Guling Pak Malen
41 Warung Balung Tianyar Mudah
see 17 Warung Nia

DRINKING & NIGHTLIFE
42 District 1
43 Forge Gastropub
44 La Favela
45 La Plancha

SHOPPING
46 Bali Tailor
47 Drifter Surf
48 Home Basket
49 Kara Home Living
50 Kim Soo
51 Lulu Yasmine
52 Magali Pascal
53 Mercredi
54 Uma and Leopold

SEMINYAK'S BALINESE FOOD SECRETS

Chef Wayan Kresna, who helms Desa Potato Head's Kaum, dishes on the dynamic local food scene. *@chefwayan*

Local chefs hang out at **T&T Chindo's Cuisine**, where Chef Renaldy makes an amazing pork noodle soup. Chef Made Danu at **Fed By Made** (p70) is also really talented; he uses local produce to create simple, modern dishes bursting with flavour. You can find *babi guling* (suckling pig) everywhere, but **Warung Balung Tianyar Mudah** is one of the few places you can find *babi balung* (braised pork-rib soup). **Pasar Kerobokan** is great for tropical fruit and *jaje Bali* (sweet snacks) and family-run **Warung Nia** makes an excellent Balinese *rijsttafel* (selection of Indonesian dishes served with rice).

continued from p63

to create these flavour sensations, such as how to grind ingredients on a stone pestle, and how to wrap a whole chicken in a banana leaf, which is more of an art than you'd expect. The class ends with a delicious feast – and you leave not only with a full belly, but also with a deeper understanding of the age-old culinary traditions of this island.

Seminyak's Beach Allure

Spend all day on the sand

Seminyak's stretch of golden beach lies halfway along the gentle arc that sweeps from the airport south of Kuta up almost to Tanah Lot, and it morphs from the umbrella-cluttered sand at Legian's Double-Six resort through more umbrellas and beach clubs to calmer **Pantai Batu Belig**. The northern section of Seminyak's beach tends to be quieter, flanked as it is by big hotels and beach clubs like Ku De Ta (p58), Alila Seminyak and Desa Potato Head, while the southern section, between Double Six and the small inlet near Noku Beach House, draws the crowds. Here, you can rent an umbrella and sunbed, and activate holiday mode.

Seminyak's waves are generally OK for beginners, but the shorebreak can be a bit dumpy. There's better surf in Canggu to the north and Kuta and Legian to the south.

Get Inspired to Tread Gently

Go on an enlightening waste tour

Much more than a beach club, **Desa Potato Head** *(seminyak.potatohead.co)* is a village-like complex (*desa* means village) integrating its **Potato Head Beach Club** with six restaurants and bars and two luxury hotels. The brand is driven by the ethos 'good times, do good', and from the moment you arrive here you're made aware of how your footprint will be reduced.

The pedestrian entrance is through 'the Womb', an enchanting 90m-long bamboo sculpture that houses display spaces showcasing how Desa Potato Head's waste is recycled and transformed into hip decor; there's also a sustainably designed radio studio. You can take this introduction further by signing up online for the free 90-minute **Follow the Waste Tour**, which starts at 11am daily. From seeing where and how Potato Head's waste is sorted, you'll learn about

Fashion, gifts and lifestyle items are also sold here.

EATING IN SEMINYAK: BEST BRUNCH SPOTS

Livingstone Cafe & Bakery: Prides itself on its croissants, but also serves a deliciously smoky carbonara. The light-filled dining area has air-con. *7am-10pm* $$

Sisterfields: Seminyak's OG brunch spot keeps pulling the crowds with its all-day brunch menu including a tasty Korean fried-chicken burger. *7am-9pm* $$

Hut: Lush rooftop hideaway with excellent all-day breakfast, pastries, sandwiches, bowls and more, all made in-house. *7am-5pm* $$

Nook: A peaceful garden outlook makes this sprawling cafe a relaxing place to linger over a meal; we recommend the local favourites. *8am-11pm* $$

Desa Potato Head

the steps taken to reduce waste through the supply chains, and how the plastic is recycled and shaped into furniture, beads and containers for Potato Head's amenities. You'll also see how hotel linen is given a new life as bags and clothing, and how waste cooking oil is turned into the candles the restaurants use. There's even a machine that shreds over 200kg of coconut shells used daily at the resort, with the fibres used to make hotel slippers. It's an incredibly inspiring tour that showcases what can be done when creativity meets responsibility, and at the end you get to make your own recycled waste item to keep.

Guardian Temple

Witness traditional architecture at a Hindu temple

Standing guard on Seminyak's busy beachfront is **Pura Petitenget** *(50,000Rp),* one of Bali's six sea temples built to protect the island from evil spirits. Its name translates loosely as 'magic chest' and relates back to the time, according to legend, the Hindu priest Dang Hyang Nirartha transformed Buto Ijo, a malicious beast, into the guardian of the nearby village. As Nirartha exorcised evil spirits from the area, he captured them in wooden chests, which were kept under the watch of Buto Ijo. With the iconic *candi bentar*

continued on p70

ALL ABOUT ARAK

Once considered backstreet hooch, *arak* (colourless, distilled palm wine) now features on many of Bali's trendy cocktail menus. Not to be confused with Middle Eastern *arak* (made from grapes and anise), Bali's *arak* can be tapped from more than a dozen different trees, most commonly the aren palm. Non-alcoholic *tuak* is the juice that is first collected; once fermented, the potent *arak* is around 40% alcohol content. You might also come across *brem* (sticky rice simmered with yeast, then fermented). *Arak* and *brem* are commonly used in the offerings placed on the ground for Bhuta Kala (the low spirits). Take care when consuming *arak* produced in village stills, as cases of methanol poisoning (leading to blindness and death) have been reported.

DRINKING IN SEMINYAK: OUR PICKS

La Plancha: Beanbags on the beach and lights strung under umbrellas make this one of Bali's most colourful sunset spots. A DJ plays from 5pm. *10am-11pm*

La Favela: A bohemian blend of Indonesia's jungles, Rio's underground bars and London's art scene. Cover charge 500,000Rp. *7pm-3am Sun-Thu, to 4am Fri & Sat*

District 1: Expertly crafted cocktails are the name of the game at this moody hidden speakeasy. *5.30pm-1am Mon-Sat, to midnight Sun*

Forge Gastropub: With sports on the telly and a trio of local craft beers on tap along with Bintang, plus Heineken and Guinness. *24hr*

HELP ME PICK

Seminyak Spas

Spas are to Seminyak as cafes are to Canggu (though Canggu also has a vast collection of spas), and you never need to walk far to find one. Seminyak's spa scene offers a harmonious fusion of traditional Balinese healing techniques and contemporary wellness practices, and there is something here for everyone – from budget salons, where a 60-minute massage costs under 200,000Rp, to ultra-luxurious destination day spas that are a sanctuary of indulgence and wellbeing.

Where to Go If You're Looking For...

Budget Spas

Lamora Spa Surrounded by a lovely garden, peaceful Lamora offers treatments with products like coconut or coffee scrubs made from local ingredients *(1hr massage from 175,000Rp).*

Lotus Massage Therapy Seminyak At 160,000Rp for an hour, the massages at this small parlour are cheaper (and arguably even better) than Lotus' Canggu branch.

Spa Bali Seminyak There's a vast array of treatments on offer, and the packages are brilliant value. The six-hour 'Ultimate' package (massage, body scrub, flower bath, facial, mani, pedi and hair cream bath) is 1,550,000Rp.

Day Spas

Spring Spa Located on the rooftop of Seminyak Village Mall, contemporary-style Spring offers urban views with many of its treatments. For a treat, book the 45-minute sunset package *(incl foot massage, shoulder massage and alcoholic drink 390,000Rp).*

Lagoon Spa A light and airy luxury day spa with facilities including a swimming pool, sauna and hot tub. Lagoon Spa has won multiple awards during the 20 years it has been operating.

Re Day Spa Sitting at the more affordable end of Seminyak's day spas *(1hr massage 310,000Rp)*, Re's treatments draw on Balinese traditions and local ingredients.

Sundari Wellness Modern Sundari is also one of the more affordable day spas. Massages here are from 90 minutes *(from 600,000Rp).* Also, book for scrubs, manis, pedis and fancy facials.

Natura Organics Spa This beautifully decorated tranquil oasis is an eco-friendly spa that works with natural products. Prices here are very affordable *(1hr massage from 235,000Rp).*

Terra Spa Minimalist and serene Terra offers divine massages, facials, scrubs, manis and pedis using locally sourced artisanal products.

Destination Spas

Bodyworks This incredibly dreamy spa is an Instagrammer's delight. You might be tempted to come just for the gorgeous Morocco-inspired design, but the luxurious treatments are even better.

Prana (pictured left) Also with a Moroccan touch, simply being at Prana is an experience in itself. Come for the Ayurvedic treatments, or indulge in a sublime three-hour 'Arabian Nights' package, which includes genuine pearl powder in one of the treatments and is set in an exotic room with thrones and red drapes.

Como Uma Shambhala Retreat The Como Uma Canggu's wonderfully serene spa focuses on Asian-inspired

SEACHELL/SHUTTERSTOCK

Bodyworks

HOW TO

Plan your time
You can walk into most budget spas and have a treatment straight away, but book ahead (sometimes a week in advance) for popular destination spas like Bodyworks and Prana.

What to wear
Most spas will give you disposable underwear to wear during your treatment. Consider keeping your own underwear on to minimise waste.

Tipping
Some of the larger spas might include a 10% service charge on your bill. At the smaller spas, a tip won't always be expected but it will be appreciated.

Etiquette
Massage treatment spaces in most budget spas are typically separated by curtains. Whisper to avoid disturbing others mid-massage.

therapies performed by some of the island's most highly trained therapists.

Spa Alila Seminyak The opulent menu here includes 'Wellness Escapes', consisting of three hours of spa treatments of your choice, followed by a three-course spa dinner. Some of the treatments conclude with a blissful Vichy shower.

Speciality Spas

Jari Menari Famous for its award-winning massages conducted only by men, Jari Menari's treatments – a unique blend of massage styles – are considered by many to be the island's best.

Glo Day Spa More on the beauty salon side of spas, Glo is revered for its tanning, tinting, waxing, lash and brow services, as well as a wide range of facials.

Chill Reflexology Specialising in reflexology and acupuncture, this peaceful contemporary spa has a brilliant reputation for its holistic treatments.

Mello Spa Newish on the local spa scene, Mellow dials up the sensory experience with temperature-controlled beds, a choice of scents and sounds during your treatment, and custom herbal tea.

Body Lab Bali This longstanding aesthetic clinic run by a trio of female doctors offers everything from Botox to retinol peels to cellulite treatments.

Aliya Bali While the spa has an extensive range of treatments for adults (from massages to pedis, waxing and even haircuts), it also offers many treatments for children, including nail art, body scrubs and lice treatment.

HEALTH & FITNESS IN SEMINYAK

Desa Potato Head: The resort's yoga, boxing, athletic training, qigong and meditation classes are available to non-guests *(per class 180,000Rp).*

Snana Yoga: Small, peaceful studio with a 9am class daily and a 4pm class Monday to Saturday. Both run for 90 minutes.

Bali Pilates Plus: Feel your abs burn in a good way at a group reformer class hosted by highly experienced teachers.

F45 Seminyak: Get your workout done in 45 minutes at the Seminyak outpost of this popular Australian fitness franchise.

Soham Wellness Center: Fitness classes span yoga to Muay Thai and there's a 25m pool, cold plunge, sauna and steam room. Plus a cafe and spa on-site.

continued from p67

(split gateway, see p349) flanked by *naga* (mythical snake-like creature) statues at its entrance, *meru* (a multitiered shrine) and the intricate stone carvings on the walls and around doorways, Pura Petitenget is a fantastic example of Balinese temple architecture. To enter you'll need to wear a sarong, which you can borrow when you pay the entrance fee at the southern side of the temple. Non-worshippers are limited to visiting the main courtyard, which offers a close-up of the trio of terracotta gates with gold-painted carved doors marking the entrance to the inner sanctum. Outside the northern corner of the temple and standing in a small, manicured garden is a large statue of Buto Ijo.

Sacred Ceremony

Observe a Melasti ceremony

One of the most important religious ceremonies in Bali – of which there are many – is **Melasti**, a purification ritual performed all around the island three days before Nyepi (the start of the new year, according to the Saka calendar; p106). It's the time for sacred temple objects, like masks and Barong and Rangda statues, to be cleansed and spiritually recharged, and they're carried in processions that lead down to the island's beaches. Seminyak is a spectacular place to be during this time, as entire village communities from the surrounding area – all dressed in white ceremonial clothing and carrying colourful, towering offerings and bright umbrellas – gather on the beach in front of Pura Petitenget (p67) for the ceremony.

Get It While It's Crispy

Get a taste for *babi guling*

Cafes in Bali's trendy traveller hubs are fast growing their offering of vegan dishes – but *babi guling* (spit-roasted suckling pig) remains an unapologetically carnivorous indulgence that sits as a firm favourite among the Balinese. It's an absolute delicacy on the island, prepared with infusions of coriander seeds, turmeric, lemongrass and other herbs and spices. Many warungs specialise in *babi guling* (you'll recognise them from the image of the skewered pig that hangs outside), but **Warung Babi Guling Pak Malen** on Jl Sunset is a great place to try it in Seminyak. The pork is served as would be

EATING IN SEMINYAK: BEST RESTAURANTS

Fed by Made: Three Bali-born, Melbourne-trained friends joined forces to open this excellent modern bistro. Go for the set menu. *6-11pm* $$

Naughty Nuri's: A long-time favourite on the island, this high-end warung is celebrated for its signature BBQ pork ribs. *11am-10pm* $$

Da Maria: Feast on Neapolitan pizzas in an OTT Amalfi Coast-inspired setting. *5pm-midnight Mon, Tue, Thu & Fri, to 3am Sat, Sun & Wed* $$

Kaum: Desa Potato Head's Indonesian restaurant is perhaps the island's best, showcasing little-known flavours from across the archipelago. *noon-10pm* $$$

Uma and Leopold

expected with a selection of meat from all parts of the pig. Crispy slices of liver and skin, some crunchy crackling, tender meat, and more meat minced and prepared as satay. They don't hold back on the chilli either, so be sure to order a fresh young coconut to wash it down. People also come from far and wide to feast on the Balinese delicacy at **Babi Guling Sari Kembar 99** in Kerobokan.

Retail Therapy

Shop up a storm in Seminyak

Seminyak is Bali's original shopping destination, and while an outpost of nearly every brand born here can now be found in Canggu and beyond, it's still a great place to shop.

The main shopping streets include Jl Raya Seminyak, Jl Kayu Aya and Jl Petitenget. The shops on Jl Raya Seminyak are generally a bit more old-school – think batik shops, homewares, cheap clothing and souvenirs. Jl Kayu Aya, on the other hand, houses the flagship stores of Bali brands including **Drifter Surf** *(driftersurf.com)* and womenswear label **Magali Pascal** *(magalipascal.com)* along with branches of womenswear labels **Uma and Leopold** *(umaandleopold.com)* and **Lulu Yasmine** *(luluyasmine.com)*. At the big bend in the road before it turns north, the 'flea market' is good for affordable clothing and souvenirs.

The retail cavalcade continues on Jl Petitenget with dozens of boutiques and shops including additional branches of Uma and Leopold and Magali Pascal. Other notable shops in the area include **Kim Soo** *(kimsoo.com)* and **Mercredi** *(@mercredi.home.bali)* for designer homewares, and the **Bali Tailor** *(balitailor.com)* for well-made leather footwear and jackets.

HOMEWARE & HANDICRAFT HEAVEN

Seminyak has plenty of home decor offerings, but many of the wares you'll find in its stores are crafted in neighbouring **Kerobokan**. Going straight to the source doesn't only offer better value, but also usually also more choice. Small-scale furniture factories, artisan workshops and retail stores are dotted all over this industrial neighbourhood; more established stores include **Kara Home Living** on Jl Gn Tangkuban Perahu, a one-stop home decorator's store stocking everything from palm-tree bottle openers to shell-encrusted mirrors; and **Home Basket** on Jl Persada with its myriad of styles, sizes and colours of baskets, as well as furniture and decorative tableware.

BALI'S SUBAK SYSTEM

Rice cultivation and irrigation is central to Balinese culture. Dating from the 9th century, the island's cooperative water management system of canals and weirs is known as the *subak* system. Reflecting the philosophical concept of Tri Hita Karana, which brings together the realms of the spirit, the human world and nature, the *subak* system is listed by UNESCO as part of Bali's unique cultural landscape. Sadly, this ancient system is increasingly under threat from tourism development and its demands on Bali's water supply - something to think about before you jump in the shower.

DARCY PERKINS/SHUTTERSTOCK

Rice field, Seminyak

Discover a Disappearing Tradition

Tour local rice fields

Looking around the urban jungle of Seminyak – and the entire southwest coast for that matter – today, it's hard to believe this landscape was a lush tangle of green just a few decades ago. Bulldozed along with the real jungle to make way for development were countless rice paddies tended by Balinese farmers for generations. Yet some determined farmers carry on. **Intrepid Travel**'s three-hour hidden rice terraces trek experience *(urbanadventures.com; per person US$39)* offers intriguing insights into this disappearing Balinese agricultural tradition – according to environmental organisation Walhi Bali, the island continues to lose 2000 hectares of rice fields each year. Meet your guide at Pasar Kerobokan (p66) for a crash course in locally farmed produce (and a chance to sample it) before setting off on foot to a pocket of rice fields that have outlasted the march of development (for now). Along the way you'll hear about Bali's complex World Heritage–listed *subak* irrigation system that's still in use today, and the importance of rice to Balinese culture. Meet local farmers tending their verdant fields, and learn about the role of the tiny temples dotting the surprisingly peaceful rice plots.

Kuta & Legian

BEACHES | LOW-KEY CROWD | GOOD SURF

Bali's original tourist hub may be dated, but Kuta still has its draws. If you've been lured to its golden beaches for sunshine, cocktails and cheap spas, you've come to the right place – and you'll find a dose of culture here too, among the shrines and temples (Buddhist and Hindu) and in the early morning market that has changed little over the last century. The once thronging Poppies I is more subdued these days, but Jl Legian is bustling. While Seminyak and Canggu sprawl quite widely, Kuta's long-established community has retained a town centre that is still walkable. The beach strip is lined with bars and a pleasant promenade, and a handful of newish hotels make the beachfront more appealing than ever.

Kuta merges into Legian at Jl Benesari. A hybrid of its neighbours, it blends the low-key vibe of Kuta with a touch of Seminyak style. The dining scene is a cut above Kuta's, and it's a short hop to Seminyak for a fancier night out.

TOP TIP

The sidewalks in Kuta and Legian are generally in good condition, which means they make convenient bypass routes for scooter drivers who're frustrated by slow-moving traffic. Be sure to look both ways before you step out from between stationary vehicles or onto the sidewalk as they are frequently used by scooters.

GETTING AROUND

The urban sprawl and traffic jams make walking the best (and often fastest) way to explore Kuta and Legian. Catching an *ojek* (motorbike taxi) is the nippiest way to get around when you're not burdened by bulky luggage (cheapest if booked through the Grab or Gojek apps). Taxis can also be booked through the apps. **Kura-Kura Bus** *(kura2bus.com)* runs a bus service between Kuta and Ubud.

Perama *(peramatour.com)*, which has an office on JL Legian, also runs shuttles to Ubud, Sanur, Amed, Lovina and other destinations. For longer trips across the island, consider hiring a car and driver. It's not wise to rent a motorbike unless you're experienced; generally you need to be licensed in your own country to be covered by travel insurance in the case of an accident.

SIGHTS
1 Kuta Beach Sea Turtle Conservation Center
2 Memorial Wall
3 Pantai Jerman
4 Pantai Kuta
5 Pantai Legian
6 Pantai Padma
7 Pantai Segara
8 Vihara Dharmayana Temple

ACTIVITIES
9 Azul Beach Club
10 Waterbom Bali

SLEEPING
11 Berlian Inn
12 De Puspa Residence
13 Hard Rock Hotel
14 Mamaka by Ovolo
15 Poppies Bali
16 Puri Damai

EATING
17 Coffee Cartel
18 Crumb & Coaster
19 Fat Chow
20 Gala More
21 Johnny Tacos
22 Lemongrass
23 Made's Warung
24 Mama's German Restaurant
25 Poppies Restaurant
26 Saikai 240 Izakaya
27 Warung Kampung
28 Warung Kubu Segara

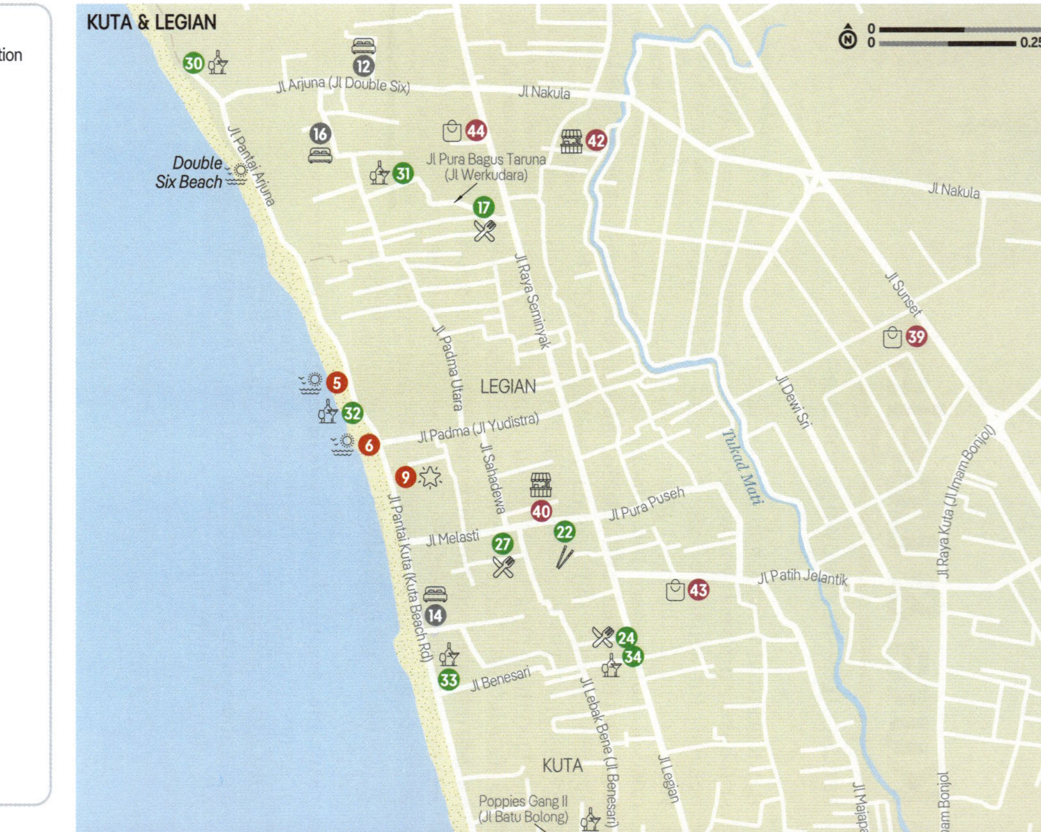

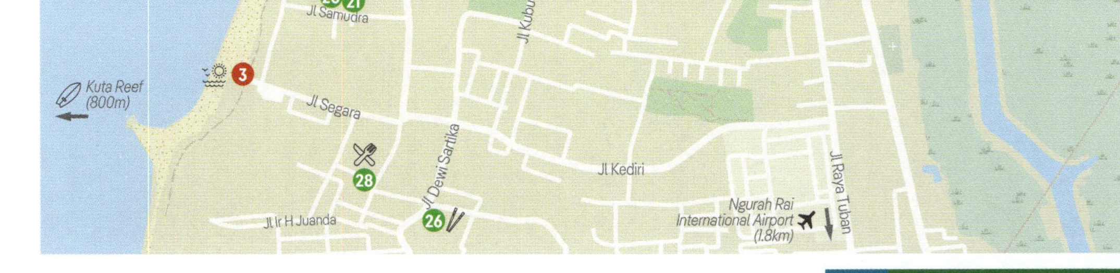

● **DRINKING & NIGHTLIFE**
29 Don Juan Mexican Restaurant & Bar
30 Double-Six Rooftop Sunset Bar
31 Goat Legian
32 Kanoa Bali
33 Kuta Social Club
34 The PaD Bar & Grill
35 Sky Garden Bali
36 Turtle Sports Bar

● **SHOPPING**
37 Beachwalk
38 Joger
39 Krisna Oleh-Oleh
40 Legian Art Market
41 Pasar Kuta
42 Pasar Pagi Desa Adat Legian
43 Syafruddin Patchwork Shop
44 Theater Art Gallery

● **TRANSPORT**
45 Kura-Kura Bus
46 Perama

KEEP BALI BEAUTIFUL

Bali (and Kuta in particular) often receives harsh media coverage because of the rubbish that washes up on the beaches. Some visitors assume that the beaches are permanently filthy, but they're like this particularly during the rainy season, when the rivers carry the trash accumulated along their banks during the dry months into the ocean. One of the organisations working hard to alleviate the island's plastic problem is **Sungai Watch** *(sungai.watch)*, which focuses on removing plastic from the island's rivers. There are permanent teams who clean the rivers daily, but Sungai Watch also organises river clean-ups for volunteers; the schedule is on its website. Another leader in the plastic war is **Desa Potato Head** (p66).

Wave of the Day

Where to surf around Kuta

Kuta has drawn surfers in ever-increasing numbers since Bob Koke – Kuta's first hotelier – had his boards shipped here from Hawaii in the early 1930s, and these days with rental boards available by the hundreds and surf instructors by the score, **Pantai Kuta** (Kuta Beach) is one of the best places in Bali to learn how to surf. You simply need to approach one of the board-rental kiosks on the beach to set up a lesson; expect to pay around 250,000Rp for a 60-minute private session. Or engage the expert coaches from the **Rip Curl School of Surf** *(ripcurlschoolofcurf.com; 2hr lessons from 722,500Rp)*, which has booths in Kuta (inside the Mamaka by Ovolo hotel) and Legian (on the boardwalk south of Jl Arjuna).

Although Kuta's waves are perennially busy, this area almost always has a wave to offer anyone who doesn't mind paddling away from the crowds or heading north to **Pantai Padma**. For less crowded waves, typically with less power, go to **Pantai Segara** on the far southern end of the beach.

Offshore winds combined with a decent swell see surfers with more experience beeline for breaks further out, including the left-hander at Kuta Reef, off **Pantai Jerman**, where you might think that you're out in open ocean if it weren't for the planes booming down just over your head. South of **Kuta Reef**, Airport Lefts and Airport Rights break either side of the rocky promontory at the end of the international runway. Between Kuta Reef and Airport Lefts is another left-hander, 'Middles', that's more suitable for intermediate surfers.

Boat operators can always be found on Pantai Jerman to shuttle you out to Kuta Reef, Middles and Airport Lefts *(return per person 100,000Rp)* and Airport Rights *(return per person 200,000Rp)*. The price drops if you buddy up with other surfers. Arrange a pickup time, then simply look for the boat when it's time to be collected. Boat operators also tout for business further up the beach, but it's a shorter (and typically cheaper) ride from Pantai Jerman.

A Wild Watery Adventure

Slip down the slides at Waterbom

One of the island's most popular family tourist attractions since the taps were first turned on in 1993, **Waterbom Bali** *(waterbom-bali.com; adult/child 325,000/370,000Rp)* is a seriously impressive waterpark. Spiralling, spinning, shooting and

Try the sweetcorn fritters.

EATING IN KUTA: OUR PICKS

Crumb & Coaster: Kuta's coolest cafe spills out of an industrial space, with brekkie served until 6pm. A wider menu is available from lunchtime. *7.30am-11pm* **$$**

Fat Chow: Delicious Asian fusion dishes include a refreshing caramelised pork-belly salad with shredded mango. On Jl Poppies II. *10am-10pm* **$$**

Made's Warung: Turning out some of Kuta's best Balinese food since 1969, with an additional location in Seminyak. *10am-9pm* **$$**

Poppies Restaurant: Soak up the old-school Kuta nostalgia at this longstanding international restaurant in a peaceful garden. *8am-11pm* **$$**

ZUL TRIONGGONO EDOARDO/SHUTTERSTOCK

Pantai Kuta

splashing across 5.1 hectares of carefully landscaped tropical gardens are 26 slides, and their names alone – Smashdown 2.0, Fast n Fierce, Constrictor and Climax – might convince you that Waterbom is for adrenaline junkies. But its strength lies in its appeal for 'kids of all ages'. There are several beautifully designed lagoon pools with sunbeds and VIP gazebos, and an enduringly popular 'Lazy River', which provides sufficient excitement in the form of bridges, cascades and water jets. In 2025 Waterbom opened Zuluu Hill, a new adventure zone just for kids with six slides across two levels. Those who prefer to relax can enjoy a massage or get their nails done, and there is a choice of seven bars and dining options when your energy needs replenishing. Run on 100% renewable energy, Waterbom has also implemented a number of water-saving initiatives including a closed-loop circulation system and recycling greywater for irrigation.

MEMORIAL WALL

The bombing attack of 12 October 2002 is regarded as one of the darkest days in Bali's modern history. Just after 11pm a bomb exploded at Paddy's Pub, a Kuta bar popular with backpackers, and as revellers fled to apparent safety on the street, another (bigger) bomb was detonated over the road, just outside Sari Club. The blasts killed 202 people, among them 38 Indonesians, 88 Australians and 23 Britons. There is now a **memorial wall** for those who lost their lives on Jl Legian, just metres from where Sari Club once stood. The victims' names are listed, and family and friends still bring flowers and photos to honour the memory of those who were killed.

The Long Flip-Flap to Freedom

Observe a baby-turtle release on Kuta Beach

A turtle hatchling making its bid for survival is an unforgettable sight, and the **Bali Sea Turtle Society** (BSTS; *baliseaturtle.org*) gives visitors an opportunity to play a hand in releasing these near-mythical creatures. Indonesia is home to six of the world's seven marine turtle species and, while attitudes are

DRINKING IN KUTA: OUR PICKS

Kuta Social Club: A relaxed rooftop pool club with Mediterranean-inspired dishes, colourful cocktails and views to the Bukit. *7am-11.30pm*

Don Juan Mexican Restaurant & Bar: The bar stools overlooking busy Jl Pantai Kuta are brilliant for people-watching while you sip margaritas. *8am-11.30pm*

Turtle Sports Bar: Crack an ice-cold Bintang and settle in for the game at this old-school sports bar, with drag show evenings Sunday to Thursday. *8am-11pm*

Sky Garden Bali: Kuta's only mega club pumps every night; reserve ahead for a semi-private party area. *9pm-4am*

BALI HEALTH HAZARDS

Stomach cramps, diarrhoea and vomiting do not a fun Bali trip make. Unfortunately, gastroenteritis, aka Bali Belly, remains a risk. Taking probiotics (start before your trip) can help to strengthen the gut's resistance to harmful bacteria in contaminated food and water, but it's not a guaranteed prevention. Practising good hygiene (make hand sanitiser your friend) is the best way to avoid falling ill. Other health hazards include rabies –13,000 cases and 25 deaths were reported between January and March 2025 alone – and dengue fever, transmitted by mosquitoes. Wearing insect repellent and avoiding contact with dogs and monkeys could literally save your life.

ELISABETH ALISIA/SHUTTERSTOCK

Pantai Legian

changing, the creatures are still threatened in many areas by collectors who harvest the eggs or kill mature turtles for meat.

Amid the urban development and light pollution in the Kuta and Legian area, it's incredible to think that turtles still come ashore here to lay their eggs between March and September. Eggs are collected from nests in insecure areas by the BSTS and relocated to the **Kuta Beach Sea Turtle Conservation Center** (KBSTCC) on Pantai Kuta. The hatching season is usually from April to October, with baby turtles generally released in the afternoons; this doesn't happen every day so keep an eye on KBSTCC's Instagram page *(instagram.com/baliseaturtlesociety)* for updates. KBSTCC is easy to find – simply look for the enormous fibreglass turtle off the beach just south of Jl Pantai Kuta. The event is free, but most visitors are happy to make a donation.

A Night to Remember

Watch the sunset on Kuta Beach

West-facing **Pantai Kuta** and **Pantai Legian** are famous for dramatic sunsets, and you could write an entire book about the activity that unfolds on this action-packed swatch of sand. Along here it's all about people-watching, so order a Bintang beer or a fresh coconut from a beachfront vendor and settle

DRINKING IN LEGIAN: OUR PICKS

Kanoa: The smartest beach bar on the Legian strip, with wine by the glass, local Island Brewing beers and spicy passionfruit margaritas. *7am-10pm*

Double-Six Rooftop Sunset Bar: Settle into a daybed surrounded by an infinity pond at one of Bali's largest rooftop bars. Chin-chin. *5-11pm*

Goat Legian: Catch all the big games at this modern sports bar with a Bintang in hand. Has two additional locations in Seminyak. *9am-1am*

The PaD Bar & Grill: Come for a cheap feed and stay for the party atmosphere, with drag shows Mon, Wed and Sat from 7.30pm. Also screens sports. *7.30am-11.30pm*

KUTA & LEGIAN'S BEACHES

Enjoy the seaside on a beachfront promenade stroll.

START	END	LENGTH
Pantai Jerman	La Plancha	5km; 2hr

Fringed by a paved promenade, Kuta and Legian's coastline was made for meandering. Start your walk at 1 **Pantai Jerman** (German Beach; p76) in the south, a sheltered cove where fishing boats double as surf taxis.

The promenade behind Discovery Mall Bali leads you to 2 **Pantai Segara** (p76). The southern end of this low-key stretch, before the coast guard tower, is the site of the Pura Dalem ('Death Temple') where Hindu cremations still take place.

After passing the 3 **Kuta Beach Sea Turtle Conservation Center** (p78) you'll reach Kuta's lively 4 **Pantai Kuta** (p78), where there are hawkers, surf schools and board-rental spots.

From here, the shaded promenade will lead you beyond the open-air 5 **Kuta Skate Park** (p80) to 6 **Pantai Padma** (p76), where plastic chairs and Bintang beers are supplanted by comfy beanbags and cocktails. Around sunset the bars here come to life with fairy lights and live music.

Next up is 7 **Double Six Beach** – named for the big resort, its wide beach is a favourite venue for playing beach soccer, volleyball and frisbee. At the northern edge of Double Six (where Legian was once separated from Seminyak by rice fields) is 8 **La Plancha** (p67). It's a popular bar at sunset, so arrive early to snag a beanbag and enjoy the sunset show.

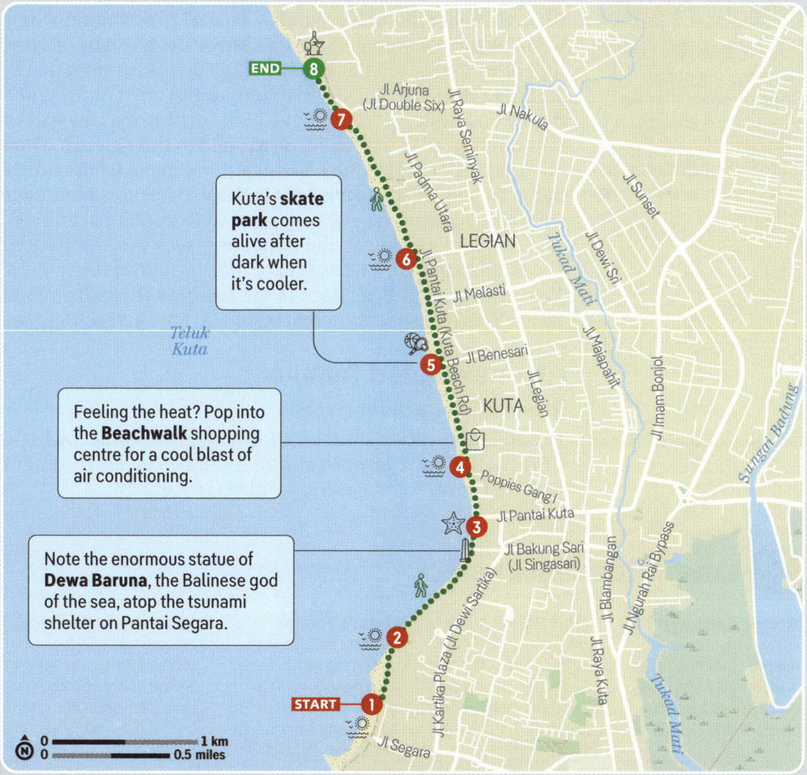

Kuta's **skate park** comes alive after dark when it's cooler.

Feeling the heat? Pop into the **Beachwalk** shopping centre for a cool blast of air conditioning.

Note the enormous statue of **Dewa Baruna**, the Balinese god of the sea, atop the tsunami shelter on Pantai Segara.

KUTA & LEGIAN FOR FAMILIES

Kuta and Legian have long been magnets for families. Family-friendly resorts abound, and the proximity to the airport means you can settle in quickly after a long flight. Popular children's activities include hair braiding, **surf lessons** (p76), splashing around at **Waterbom** (p76), and practising kick flips at Kuta's beachfront skate park. The beachfront boardwalk is pram-friendly, and the local dining scene couldn't be more relaxed. Resorts can arrange childcare, and drivers for family excursions, though many families prefer to stay put and avoid Bali's notorious traffic.

in for the show: there are talented surfers ripping the waves and beginners getting catapulted into the shore break, dogs and children race each other across the sand, honeymooners pose for selfies, and a medley of travellers and locals work on their TikTok game. Watching the sunset here can also become a static spa and shopping spree – without having to move from your seat, you could have your hair braided, get a fake tattoo, and enjoy a manicure and a back massage, all at the same time. From wandering hawkers you can buy kites, jewellery, sarongs, card games and bamboo blowpipes, and there's a never-ending procession of snacks and refreshments on offer. In Kuta, there's also a **skate park** *(8am-10pm)* that has become a favourite meeting place for kids of all ages, both locals and tourists, with skateboards available for hire *(per hr 50,000Rp)*. It's floodlit after dark.

Find the Perfect Souvenir

Look beyond the tat

The art markets of Kuta and Legian aren't what they used to be. While you can still find a few nice paintings and wood carvings at the **Legian Art Market** on Jl Melasti, the markets are better suited to picking up Bintang shirts and cheap, low-quality souvenirs. Unless prices are set, you'll be expected to bargain; be sure to take a friendly approach and don't drive the seller into the ground. A general rule of thumb: only begin to bargain if you're a serious buyer and begin by offering half of what the seller asks for. For set-price shopping there's **Krisna Oleh-Oleh**, a souvenir emporium on Jl Sunset, and **Joger** on Jl Raya Kuta. A handful of batik shops can still be found in the area, including **Syafruddin Patchwork Shop** on Jl Patih Jelantik, which sells clothing made from vintage batik. In Legian, **Theatre Art Gallery** specialises in vintage and reproduction *wayang* puppets used in traditional Balinese theatre. Just looking at the animated faces peering back at you is a delight. For high-street brands including H&M, Zara, Mango and Pull & Bear, head to the **Beachwalk** mall on Kuta Beach. There's also some decent boutique shopping on Jl Legian.

An Unexpected Temple

Reset at Vihara Dharmayana

Despite its location on busy Jl Blambangan, this colourful Chinese Buddhist **temple** dating from 1876 is quite possibly the most calm – and calming – place in Kuta.

EATING IN LEGIAN: OUR PICKS

Warung Kampung: This airy eatery serves all the popular Indonesian dishes. Tasty meals at very budget-friendly prices. *10am-10pm* $

Coffee Cartel: A contemporary cafe with an all-day breakfast menu plus burgers, bowls and salads for lunch. Good smoothies. *7.30am-5pm* $$

Mama's German Restaurant: Serving up German classics – from currywurst to pork knuckle – since 1985, Mamas is a Legian institution. *24hr* $$

Lemongrass: When you're craving some Thai comfort food, Lemongrass delivers with an authentically spicy kick. *11am-11pm* $$

GEKKO GALLERY/SHUTTERSTOCK

Vihara Dharmayana

A bright red-and-yellow entrance gate opens into the main courtyard where the **Baktisala** (main prayer hall) is strung with large Chinese lanterns and supported by giant crimson pillars that are wrapped by menacing dragons. A set of Chinese lion statues stand guard at the entrance to the prayer hall, its eclectic mosaic-tiled exterior wall adding to the colour-fest.

Incense swirls around the moodily lit interior. Several small shrines rise up behind the main altar, where devotees leave Balinese-style offerings. Opposite the Baktisala is a hexagonal temple featuring a four-faced Buddha on an altar. Ensure your shoulders and knees are covered before entering the complex.

Monster Parade

Witness a Nyepi tradition

The beginning of the Balinese year, according to the Saka calendar (p106), is **Nyepi**, a remarkable time to be on the island – a day when everything comes to a standstill and Bali descends into silence. Roads close, lights and even mobile networks are turned off, no fires can be lit and even the airport shuts. The night before, however, pandemonium reigns as enormous effigies of monsters and demons from Balinese mythology are paraded through the streets across Bali, and musical instruments are banged, clattered and beaten. The effigies, called ogoh-ogoh, are astounding pieces of art, often standing more than 3m tall before they're burned in a shower of sparks.

Kuta hosts one of the island's rowdiest and most impressive parades, with huge crowds converging in the evening to watch terrifying ogoh-ogoh paraded along Jl Legian. After the parades, the ogoh-ogoh are ritually burned, symbolising the destruction of evil and restoring the good energy for the year ahead. Nyepi typically falls in March.

BALI'S STRIKING SPLIT GATEWAYS

If you enter Pantai Legian from Jl Melasti, you'll walk through an ornate split gateway (called *candi bentar*) – the same sort of architectural structure you'll see at entrances to temples, palaces and other sacred sites around Bali. These traditional gateways serve as important cultural and spiritual symbols and consist of two symmetrically shaped pillars connected by a central opening, which creates a striking entryway. The gates are typically adorned with intricate carvings and decorative motifs, and represent the division between the profane world and the sacred realm, signifying the transition from the mundane to the divine. The inside edges of the gates are always smooth; some say to cleanse the mind upon entry.

THE FIRST HOTEL IN KUTA

Kuta's Hard Rock Hotel might seem like a world away from a quiet island paradise, but it was around there that in 1936 a bohemian couple, who had turned their backs on the Hollywood dream, built their Kuta Beach Hotel. The story is told in Louise Koke's excellent book, *Our Hotel in Bali*. Louise's husband Bob became a near-mythical character (an ex-CIA agent, according to some accounts) who was almost certainly Bali's first surfer. He'd shipped his redwood plank from Hawaii and showed the first Kuta Beach boys how to ride, and then to shape boards. However, the Kokes' dreams were shattered by WWII and, while Louise couldn't bear to return to Bali after the war, Bob eventually came back to see the hotel ruins.

AIKO_KONI/SHUTTERSTOCK

Pasar Pagi Kuta

To Market, to Market

Start your day in real Bali style

Kuta and Legian might feel like a long way from 'traditional' Bali, but a trip to a morning market will reveal a slice of life that's remained almost unchanged for generations; it's here where fruit, vegetables, meat and spices are traded. There are two morning markets in the area that are worth a visit: the popular Legian morning market (known officially as **Pasar Pagi Desa Adat Legian**) and the even more timeless **Pasar Pagi Kuta** (at the junction of Jl Raya Kuta and Jl Pantai Kuta). Legian's morning market is located in a large modern building, somewhat like a hangar inside, while Kuta's more colourful market is in a ramshackle shelter down an alleyway on the northern side of Jl Blambangan. If you're squeamish, it'll be best to avoid the butcher's section where pork, beef, chicken and a variety of fresh fish are carved up. The most lively sections of both markets are the fruit and vegetable stands, and the wonderfully colourful stalls that sell a mind-boggling selection of traditional offerings. Look out for the stalls where women sell *jamu* – this traditional elixir, a spicy turmeric-based drink, is a wonderful early morning pick-me-up. It is best to arrive early to see the markets at their most vibrant; Kuta's market opens at 4am and closes at 10am, while Legian's market opens and closes an hour later.

EATING & DRINKING IN KUTA: CHEAP EATS NEAR THE AIRPORT

Saikai 240 Izakaya: Flight delayed? Slurp ramen while you wait, just two blocks north of the terminal car park. *noon-9pm Sat-Thu* $

Warung Kubu Segara: This cheap and cheerful warung (*nasi goreng* costs 30,000Rp) is also an easy walk north from the terminal. *8am-10pm* $

Gala More: The Indo favourites are a cut above at this typical traveller restaurant. You can't go wrong with the beef rendang. *noon-10pm* $

Johnny Tacos: Cheap tacos and cold Bintangs are the go at this small, bright-yellow taco bar. No margaritas, unfortunately. *8am-11pm* $

Places We Love to Stay

$ Budget $$ Midrange $$$ Top End

Canggu

MAP p54

Serenity $ An eco-friendly guesthouse and yoga resort close to Pantai Nelayan, with a distinctly bohemian vibe. Rooms range from dorms to singles with shared bathrooms to more luxurious en-suite doubles. (p57)

Melati Bali Homestay $$ Lovely traditional wooden rooms are surrounded by a tropical garden. The property is small but private and full of character.

Sunflower Stay and Surf $$ Colourful mosaic tiles and sky-blue shutters give this cheerful guesthouse tucked off Jl Pantai Batu Bolong a distinctly Moroccan vibe. Rooms are spacious and there's a small pool.

Hotel Tugu Bali $$$ A hotel with lots of character and Indonesian antiques; it has many activities on offer, too. Tugu is a brilliant place to connect with Balinese culture. (p57)

Pererenan

Kayu Village $$ Twelve cosy but charming wooden bungalows face off in a lush garden. An excellent breakfast is served poolside.

Noema $$$ Pererenan's newest resort appeals to 'curious minds' but fans of modern design and a good lagoon pool (and gym) are bound to like it too. Great play area for kids.

Como Uma Canggu $$$ Sitting on a quiet stretch of beach between Canggu and Pererenan, Como is an elegant and ultra-luxurious resort. The spa here is exceptional.

Berawa

Dip & Doze $ Boutique hostel with clean, comfortable and more-spacious-than-usual eight-bed dorms and private rooms. There's a pool and shared kitchen.

Guru Canggu $$ This quiet boutique hotel has a small pool and garden. Each room is different, but there's a sweet tropical vibe and a guru 'theme' that connects them all.

Wayang Retreat $$ A real urban retreat featuring seven airy, traditional-style wooden villas – all with kitchen – in a peaceful garden with a pool.

Seminyak

MAP p64

Grandmas Plus Hotel Seminyak $$ A hop and a skip from the beach. Rooms here are compact and contemporary, and it's a convenient base from which to explore Seminyak.

Desa Potato Head $$$ Uberstylish sites and studios, and there's a huge and inspiring emphasis on minimising waste. There is always something happening here too, from sunrise yoga classes to DJ events. The infinity poolside breakfast is superb. (p66)

Legian $$$ Lap up the tropical elegance of this five-star beachfront sanctuary right on Seminyak Beach.

Kuta

MAP p74

Berlian Inn $ A good budget option (with a pool) 250m from the beach. Rooms at the back have private verandahs overlooking the tropical garden.

Mamaka by Ovolo $$$ Kuta's chicest hotel features a fantastic rooftop bar with a pool overlooking the beach, with included perks including a self-service laundry. (p76)

Poppies Bali $$$ This peaceful boutique hotel has been here for 50 years. It's an atmospheric tropical-oasis escape tucked into the very heart of built-up Kuta.

Legian

MAP p74

De Puspa Residence $$ This small homestay is tucked into a side street off Jl Arjuna. The location is excellent – on the doorstep of the beach, shops, spas and restaurants.

Puri Damai $$ Built around a garden of frangipani trees close to Double Six Beach, this well-cared-for accommodation has an old Balinese atmosphere and apartment-style rooms.

Researched by Jade Bremner

South Bali & the Islands

BLISSFUL BEACHES, FAMED WAVES AND ISLES OF FUN

From the marine-life-rich islands of Nusa Lembongan to the chic surf-havens of Uluwatu and sprawling beachfront hotels of Sanur – South Bali is all about laid-back life.

Thanks to its short distance from the airport (less than an hour's drive), and its easy access to dreamy beaches, South Bali is the island's premier holiday destination. Here wild trees, dramatic cliffs and white-sand coastlines collide. There are stylish hotels, world-class waves and reefs that make for extraordinary diving. Few reminders of rural Bali remain when passing from Sanur into Denpasar (the capital) or down the busy main highway to the Bukit Peninsula, but Bali's rich Hindu culture remains as strong here as it does elsewhere, and the coastal communities have a tradition of hospitality that runs deep.

To the southeast, on the Bukit Peninsula, Nusa Dua is more manicured, with its lawns and five-star hotels, while to the west Uluwatu has exceptional ocean views, chic boutiques and spas and legendary surfing breaks. Uluwatu is also increasingly popular with travellers who are drawn to the turquoise waters and growing collection of yoga studios, cafes, beach clubs and bars.

Some of Bali's longest-standing hotels are in Sanur and Denpasar. Sanur features powdery beaches fringed with well-established trees, and a boardwalk that threads past verdant resort gardens and a calm natural seawater lagoon, making it ideal for families.

As the crow flies, Nusa Lembongan is just 18km from Sanur, but the island is reached by ferry and it feels a world away from the bustle of mainland Bali. The pace of life slows down in Lembongan, where the diving is magnificent and there's a very good chance of spotting mantas, *Mola mola*, turtles and sharks.

ADI DHARMAWAN/SHUTTERSTOCK

THE MAIN AREAS

SANUR
A classic beach holiday destination with regal flair. p88

DENPASAR
Shopping and cultural sights in Bali's capital. p92

ULUWATU
Wild beaches, wonderful surf and chic cafes. p96

NUSA LEMBONGAN
Exceptional diving and a chilled island vibe. p109

For places to stay in South Bali & the Islands, see p119

BALNYES/SHUTTERSTOCK

Left: Paragliding, Gunung Payung (p105); Above: Kelingking (p116)

Find Your Way

Uluwatu sits at the southern tip of the Bukit Peninsula, the bulb that 'hangs off' mainland Bali, while Sanur is on the coast that fans northeast of the airport. Nusa Lembongan is an easy 40-minute fast-boat trip from Sanur.

RIDE-HAILING APPS

The Grab and Gojek apps are cheap and your best options for travelling shorter distances by car or scooter. For longer journeys consider hiring a car and private driver (most hotels can assist with this). On Nusa Lembongan the apps don't work.

MOTORBIKE

Scooters or motorcycles are widely available for rent and are an almost irresistible opportunity for independent exploration. South Bali's busy roads are not an ideal place to learn, accidents are common and traffic police have become stricter about licences and safety rules.

Sanur, p88

With a long promenade along a tranquil beach, Sanur is easy to navigate on foot and an ideal family holiday base. It has a range of accommodation options and great restaurants.

Uluwatu, p96

Dramatic rocky cliff-side beaches, trendy cafes and beach clubs, world-class waves and an iconic temple make Uluwatu one of Bali's most desirable holidays.

Nusa Lembongan, p109

It's rare to find a base that offers equal appeal for surfers and divers. Chilled-out Nusa Lembongan packs in this, plus empty beaches on its neighbouring isles.

IGOR LUSHCHAY/SHUTTERSTOCK

Pura Luhur Ulu Watu (p100)

Plan Your Time

It's the gorgeous beaches and ocean (for diving, snorkelling and surfing) that hold the big appeal around here, but don't miss the area's beautiful temples and viewpoints.

A Day to Experience the Bukit Peninsula

You can reach the Bukit Peninsula in under 30 minutes from Ngurah Rai airport. With a driver or scooter explore iconic beaches like **Balangan** (p102) and **Padang Padang** (p102), or visit **Rock Bar** (p105) or another celebrated beach club. In the afternoon head to **Pura Luhur Ulu Watu** (Uluwatu Temple; p100) for the enthralling sunset performance of the Kecak dance.

A Week to Explore the South

There are fantastic restaurants in Sanur, so work up an appetite with activities like **cycling** (p88), **SUP-ing**, **kayaking** (p91) or swimming in the sheltered beach. Transfer by boat to Nusa Lembongan, the perfect low-key base for anyone who wants to **dive** (p109) and **surf** (p111), before ending your trip among the **cafes** and **bars** (p98) around Uluwatu.

SEASONAL HIGHLIGHTS

MARCH

Many people avoid Nyepi (Bali's 'Day of Silence'; p106), yet it's a uniquely thrilling and poignant time to be on the island.

MAY

Uluwatu's waves tend to be well formed and consistent during the dry season (April to October).

JULY

The Bali Kite Festival (p91) takes place in the 'windy season' in Sanur and is usually held around July or August.

AUGUST

The ocean temperature drops from around late July until early November, the best time to see *Mola mola* (ocean sunfish) around Nusa Lembongan.

Sanur

SPACIOUS RESORTS | TRANQUIL BEACH | BEACHFRONT PROMENADE

GETTING AROUND

On Sanur's beachfront promenade, bikes can be the best way of getting around thanks to a dedicated cycle lane. For trips around the Sanur area use Gojek or Grab to hail a car or motorbike taxi. For travel beyond Sanur consider upgrading to a taxi – the speedy traffic on the fast-flowing Ngurah Rai Bypass can be unnerving for anyone unused to motorcycle transport. **Kura-Kura Bus** *(kura2bus.com)* services connect Sanur with Kuta and Ubud.

TOP TIP

Plan your beach activities according to the tide – since the reef-protected shoreline (blissfully tranquil in comparison with the wave-pounded coast elsewhere in the south) is almost dry at low tide. Surfers will need to get beyond the barrier reef, but boat rides are always available for a fee.

Sanur's waterfront promenade is noticeably laid-back compared to the beachfront bustle of Bali's southwest beaches, and draws a different crowd. Families and older travellers tend to prefer the luxury resorts or humble homestays here over the party vibes of Uluwatu. A peaceful, shaded walkway connects several kilometres of excellent bars, restaurants, shops and hotels – and some unexpectedly deserted sections of beach.

The area's refreshingly verdant and spacious resorts offer tropical gardens, big communal pools and lots of facilities. Off the beach, the ocean is protected by a reef, with waves breaking around half a kilometre out, meaning calm waters for watersports such as paddleboarding, wakeboarding and kayaking.

The area's intriguing history (a Chinese junk – a type of sailing ship – that was wrecked on the reef here ultimately brought about the ritual suicide of the entire royal family) has become barely a footnote in the ongoing tourism business. Still, traditional daily life is still evident among the villagers who harvest seafood from the reefs and in the traditional colourful *jukung* (outrigger fishing boats) with goggle-eyed swordfish faces decorating their bows.

Cycle the Coastline

Ride Sanur's beachfront promenade

Alongside **Sanur Beach** there is a paved, almost-6km-long promenade, and a leisurely cycle along it provides an idyllic opportunity to explore the coastline of one of Bali's most family-friendly beach towns. The bicycles available for rent are comfortable cruisers *(per hr 20,000Rp)*, most of which have baskets in front and a bell that should be gently pinged when you're approaching pedestrians from behind. The **Sanur beachfront promenade** has been designed with bicycles in mind, and along much of it there is a dedicated bike lane

HIGHLIGHTS
1 Rip Curl School of Surf
2 Sanur Beachfront Promenade

SIGHTS
3 Pantai Mertasari
4 Sanur Beach

ACTIVITIES
5 Baby Reef

SLEEPING
6 Kubu di Kayla's
7 Puri Mesari
8 Segara Village Hotel
9 Tandjung Sari Hotel
10 Villa Ivaya 8

EATING
11 Fisherman's Club
12 Laghawa Sea Side Bar
13 Seagrass by the Beach
14 Sindhu Night Market
15 Soul on the Beach
16 Titie's Warung

DRINKING & NIGHTLIFE
17 Byrd House Beach Club
18 Casablanca
19 Costa by Monsta
20 Shotgun Social

SHOPPING
21 Icon Bali Mall

TRANSPORT
22 Sanur Harbour

(cyclists must stick to the inland side of the path). On your ride, there are many places to stop for a coffee, massage, lunch or an ice cream, or even a spot of designer shopping. The chic **Icon Bali Mall** has an entrance right off the beach and houses designers from Calvin Klein to Ted Baker. The promenade runs from just south of **Sanur Harbour** to the parking lot at **Pantai Mertasari**, and there are pockets of bike-rental places all along here; many have small bikes for children, too. The bikes are usually available for rent from around 7am. The quieter early mornings make for the most carefree cycling.

EATING IN SANUR: ALONG THE BEACHFRONT

Tities Warung: A good budget option on the beach, Tities serves up Indonesian classics, as well as sandwiches and snacks. Cash only. *8am-6pm* $

Soul on the Beach: This breezy, laid-back cafe is a beachfront fave. It has an international menu with a focus on fresh, healthy meals. *7am-11pm* $$

Seagrass by the Beach: Laid-back beachfront restaurant with pizzas, tacos, seafood platters and superb Indonesian curries. *7am-11pm* $$

Fisherman's Club: A classy seafood resto on Sanur's promenade, with comfy seating on the shady beach. There's a kids menu, too. *11.30am-11pm* $$$

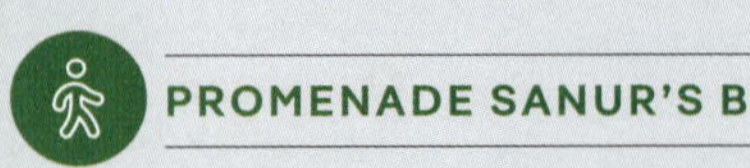

PROMENADE SANUR'S BEACH

Walk under the palms along Sanur's coastline with clear waters, golden beaches and traditional boats, passing resorts, restaurants and watersports outlets.

START	END	LENGTH
Le Mayeur Museum	Power of Now Oasis	6km; 2–3hr

Begin at the 'top' end of Sanur Beach admiring the architecture at ❶ **Le Mayeur Museum**, which houses some 90 works by acclaimed artist Adrien-Jean Le Mayeur. On the boardwalk there are shops, bicycle rental and vendors selling drinks. Around 1km south, just past ❷ **Byrd House** (p91; return for sunset cocktails) do some souvenir shopping at the entrance to ❸ **Sindhu Beach**, or stop for a smoothie at ❹ **Soul on the Beach** (p89).

An old coral wall fronts ❺ **Tandjung Sari**, an old hotel full of character, and shortly thereafter you'll reach the carved *candi bentar* (split gateway; see p 349) of ❻ **Pura Tandjung Sari**. Take time in the shade to admire the astounding craftsmanship of this carved temple entrance. Further along, at ❼ **Pantai Karang**, you'll reach a *bale* (a stilted shelter) on the path. Beside it is an unusual shrine made entirely from *karang* (coral).

By the time you reach Andaz Bali, you'll see colourful fishing boats. Notice the faces on the front, which are becoming rare these days. Pause at ❽ **Seagrass by the Beach** (p89) for a drink or to rent a kayak or SUP (see p91), or indulge in a treatment at the ❾ **Nest Beachside Spa**. Around 500m further on, you can get a beachfront massage beside the boardwalk. If, after this 6km walk, you're still up for some exercise, then continue to the ❿ **Rip Curl School of Surf** (p91) for a lesson, or take a yoga class at ⓫ **Power of Now Oasis**.

Le Mayeur Museum was under refurbishment at the time of research, but you can peer into the grounds to see the stunning architecture.

In the windy season (July and August), the annual Bali Kite Festival takes place on **Galak** or **Pantai Mertasari**.

Night Street-Food Sampling

Sampling tasty Indonesian dishes

Sanur's atmospheric **Sindhu Night Market** (sometimes called Senggol Market) might at first glance appear small, but its food stalls are a hive of activity in the evening and offer a fantastic opportunity to sample a wide variety of tasty traditional Indonesian fare from around 25,000Rp a dish. Many stalls are retro in appearance and are very photogenic; each specialises in something different, and most of the food is prepared while you wait. Try everything from *sate ayam* (chicken satay), *bakso* (meatball soup) and *lumpia* (similar to spring rolls) to *nasi campur* (rice with a choice of side dishes). The tables belong to the stalls near them; if you want to sit down, be sure to use one belonging to the stall you buy from. Leave some room for treats like doughnuts, *pisang goreng* (banana fritters) and *onde-onde* (sweet rice-cake balls filled with palm sugar), which are sold from a cart near the entrance to the market.

Sanur's Barrier Reef

Watersports off the beach

Sanur's tranquil coastline is protected by a barrier reef that stretches for 7km and creates a series of waveless beaches – a real novelty on Bali's south-facing coastline. Even at high tide the crystal-clear water in this 'lagoon' is rarely much over waist-level, making it an ideal playground for kayaking and stand-up paddleboarding (SUP). SUPs and kayaks can be rented from about 100,000Rp per hour all along the beachfront promenade. Those looking to surf will have a decent paddle (between 500m and 1km from shore) to get to the waves, but schools along the beach, including **Rip Curl School of Surf** *(ripcurlschoolofsurf.com; 2hr lessons 850,000Rp)*, offer boat rides with boards and lessons to the various reefs in the area, complete with insurance (a rarity in Bali). **Baby Reef** is suitable for beginners and intermediates. Boats are typically traditional outrigger *jukung* (unique in this part of the island), which are adorned with long swordfish 'noses' and staring eyes painted on the bows.

BALI KITE FESTIVAL

During the windy season Bali's sky is dominated by kites that are flown not only as a pastime, but also as a thanksgiving message to the gods for abundant harvests. For a few days, all eyes turn to Sanur (Galak or Pantai Mertasari), the hub of the **Bali Kite Festival**, as teams compete to get the most spectacular – and the most gigantic – kites soaring on the thermals. This colourful festival is usually held in July or August; the exact dates vary in order to capitalise on the favourable windy conditions that are needed to get the enormous kites (which sometimes measure more than 4m wide by 10m long) into the air. Check Bali Tourism's Instagram *(instagram.com/balitourismauthority)* for confirmed dates.

DRINKING IN SANUR: OUR PICKS

Byrd House Beach Club: This elegant 'beach house' sprawls beneath towering palms; there's a relaxed atmosphere and a view of Gunung Agung at sunset. *6.30am-11pm*

Shotgun Social: With 16 craft beers on tap, an extensive cocktail menu and a large garden and play area, this hip restaurant is great for families. *9am-11pm*

Costa by Monsta: Mediterranean vibes on the beach, with white linen seats, fairy lights at night and international wines and cocktails. *9am-10pm*

Casablanca: No-frills restaurant in the eve, vibey dive club later at night – with live music (usually cover bands), sports and happy-hour specials. *5pm-1am*

Denpasar

HISTORIC ARCHITECTURE | SHOPPING | CULTURAL HUB

GETTING AROUND

As the city can be hot and dusty it's quite unpleasant to travel by scooter; the most comfortable way to get around is in a car. It's very easy (and cheap) to use the ride-hailing apps Grab or Gojek as the rate is set and you don't need to explain your destination to the driver. You could also hire a car and driver for the day, which is best arranged through your accommodation.

To the west of the beach town of Sanur, Denpasar city has an entirely different feel; it's a vibrant cultural and economic hub with lively markets and historic monuments. Bali's busy capital city, which took over the helm from Singaraja just after WWII, is an intriguing place worth a visit, even if only for a few hours. Within the sprawling tangle of streets that form the hub of Bali's trade and commerce, there lies at Denpasar's centre a district of old tree-lined roads and manicured gardens that cluster around the bases of monuments built to honour the people and events that have shaped the island's history. From its vibrant markets and beautiful temples to a museum built more than nine decades ago, a dynamic arts festival and diverse culinary offerings, this cosmopolitan city offers an unexpected insight into Indonesian life.

Turtle Releasing

Preserving an iconic marine species

The well-run **Turtle Conservation and Education Centre** *(tcecserangan.jimdofree.com; by donation)* on Pulau Serangan is very active in rescuing and rehabilitating turtles. It allows visitors to get up close to various species, including baby turtles, and also offers the chance to play a hands-on part in preserving one of Indonesia's most iconic marine species. Here, you'll see heart-rending sights like green turtles that have lost flippers to sharks or boat engines, hawksbills that are recovering from operations to remove ingested plastic bags, and olive ridley turtles that were trapped in nets. You're also, however, likely to see dozens of newly hatched youngsters jostling in some of the centre's many pools.

The facility is free to visit, but you can pay 230,000Rp to 'adopt' a hatchling (during hatching season between April and September). You'll be given a coconut shell in which to transport your turtle, and then you'll be taken by boat to the edge of the bay where you can release it. Turtles are a protected species in Indonesia, but they are traditionally used in Hindu ceremonies as well as for food in fishing villages all over the

TOP TIP

Unlike the touristy spots, credit cards are not readily accepted at attractions. Take cash for visiting temples, museums and buying items from markets – the smaller the denomination the better.

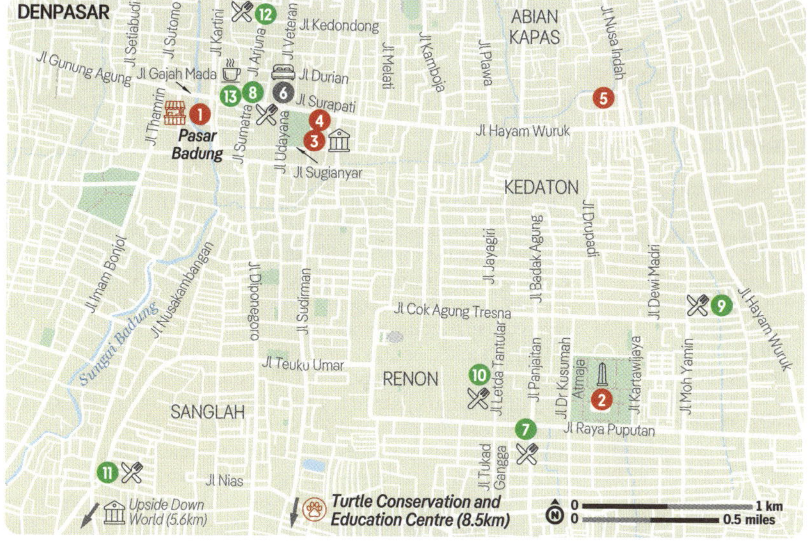

HIGHLIGHTS
1 Pasar Badung

SIGHTS
2 Bajra Sandhi Monument
3 Museum Negeri Propinsi Bali
4 Pura Jagatnatha
5 Taman Werdhi Budaya

SLEEPING
6 Inna Bali Heritage Hotel

EATING
7 Babi Guling Renon
see 7 Bali Buda Renon
8 FUKU
9 Gula Bali the Joglo
10 Kedai Emak
11 Mie Goreng Makassar Pelita
12 Warung Wardani

DRINKING & NIGHTLIFE
13 Bhineka Djaja

ENTERTAINMENT
see 5 Bali Arts Festival

island. The TCEC *(@tcecserangan)* plays a large part in educating the communities about turtle conservation, and on a busy day as many as 200 schoolchildren can pass through the facility. Scan the QR codes at the centre to listen to an audio guide about its work and the species it cares for.

Delving into Old Denpasar

Temples, museums and squares

Along the wide, tree-lined streets of central Denpasar are windows into the island's history and culture. There's the elaborate **Pura Jagatnatha** *(20,000Rp)*, a recently renovated temple dedicated to the supreme god Sanghyang Widhi. Nearby, Bali's first international-class hotel, the Bali Hotel, now called **Inna Bali Heritage Hotel** *(hig.id/hotels/inna-bali-heritage)*, was built in 1928. It has hosted a number of celebrities, including Queen Elizabeth II, Charlie Chaplin, Mahatma Gandhi and Indonesia's first president, Sukarno, and retains much of its original Art Deco charm and historic photos that can be perused inside. The restaurant still serves Sukarno's favourite meals: *betutu* chicken (stuffed with spices, wrapped in banana leaves and coconut husks and cooked in embers) and *rawon* (a strong black beef soup) with yellow rice.

Last but not least, the **Museum Negeri Propinsi Bali** *(adult/child 100,000/50,000Rp)*, or the Bali Museum, has a

MONUMENT TO THE STRUGGLE OF THE BALINESE PEOPLE

The imposing **Bajra Sandhi Monument**, in front of the Bali Governor's Office, stands to honour the resilience of the Balinese people and their struggle for independence from the Dutch colonisers. It rises from the centre of a peaceful, carefully manicured park, and the impressively ornate structure, completed in 1981, is laden with symbolism. Inside the monument are dioramas that trace Bali's history.

CELEBRATE BALI'S ARTISTIC HERITAGE

For one month every year Denpasar erupts into an extravaganza of colour and costumes as Bali's rich artistic heritage is celebrated. The **Bali Arts Festival** *(instagram.com/baliartsfestival)*, which is usually held around June and July, serves as a platform to showcase and preserve the island's vibrant traditional art forms. Dance, music, visual arts and literature take centre stage, and each day performances, competitions and workshops are held at the **Taman Werdhi Budaya Art Centre** *(03-6122 2776)*, the home of the festival. If you only see one thing, make it the opening-day parade, an absolute highlight of the festival when performers wearing intricate costumes and traditional dress take to the streets of Denpasar.

fascinating collection of relics, including daggers, religious objects, art, coins, effigies and more. These are housed throughout four striking pavilions in a building with pretty courtyards and gardens. The place is designed to showcase the different architectural styles from around the island. The **Tabanan Pavilion** is constructed from posts from the court of a nobleman from that regency, and the **Karangasem Pavilion** was built in the style of an audience hall at an East Bali palace. The **Buleleng Pavilion** was styled as a North Bali residence; it was originally built in 1914 for an event in Central Java and was then moved to Singaraja where it was a museum. Extra-special items in the pavilions include some from the Stone Age, such as a stone boulder-shaped sarcophagus and prehistoric human remains.

A pre-booked, knowledgeable local guide can help to put everything into perspective. The ones who approach offer very little value; instead try **Bali Walking Tours** *(WhatsApp +62 0895 3580 51932; prices vary by group size)*, which offers multihour walking tours of historic Denpasar, each with an introduction to Balinese culture and a history lesson of the city. Feel free to ask about the suicidal stand of Bali's royal family against the Dutch in 1906, Bali's caste system and the intricacies of the Balinese language. Schedule a time to do this at the beginning of your trip, as tours book up.

Bali's Biggest Traditional Market

Traditional trading place

The name Denpasar translates as 'beside the market' and **Pasar Badung** (Badung Market), the largest traditional trading place on the island, is a market that never sleeps. In and around the imposing three-storey building there's always something being traded, and while shopping is serious business for those who work here, it's a fun and lively place to visit. The market is distinctly different on each level: there are spices on the ground floor; fruits, vegetables and meat on the first floor; and homewares and religious items on the third.

To see the colourful produce section in full swing, aim to be at the market between 8am and 10am. By 4pm trading inside the building has almost come to an end, and it's then that the action moves to the streets outside. The southwest corner of the market has the biggest buzz, and it's here that scores of trucks laden with fresh produce brought in from around the island jostle for parking space and buyers. There are truckloads of leafy greens and heaped baskets of tomatoes and

EATING IN DENPASAR: OUR PICKS

Mie Goreng Makassar Pelita: This popular local eatery has a small menu of Sulawesi dishes. The portions are generous. *10.30am-10pm* $

Bali Buda Renon: Healthy-eating cafe with handmade, sustainable and organic food; think lean salads and 'earth bowls'. *8am-9.30pm* $

Kedai Emak: This contemporary Javanese restaurant serves halal food, buffet style. There's fish, chicken and vegetarian options. *8am-5pm* $

Warung Wardani: This Indonesian restaurant is known for its delicious *nasi campur* (rice with a choice of side dishes) and chicken satay. *8am-5pm* $

Pasar Badung

onions, and piles of dragon fruit, sweet potatoes and oranges lend colour to an already vibrant scene. It's also astounding to watch the *tukang suun* – the women who transport the produce on behalf of the buyers – carry heaped baskets of fruit and vegetables weighing as much as 50kg on their heads.

Shifting Perspectives

Visit an upside-down house

At **Upside Down World** *(facebook.com/upsidedownworld indonesia; adult/child 100,000/50,000Rp)* more than a dozen rooms have been staged as a variety of upside-down scenes. It's all about the photo ops, and the whole family can have fun snapping selfies around the house in settings that can be as strangely vertigo-inducing as they are fun. It's not always an upside-down world, though; sometimes the scenes are sideways too, like the Chinese restaurant where all of the furniture is mounted on the right-hand wall. There are enough props handy – a toilet-cleaning brush in the bathroom, for example, and cooking utensils, plus a banister that is ideally located for (simulated) slides – to keep you coming up with ever more wacky poses for photos. Try to arrive early since around mid-morning tour buses roll in and you might need to line up to snap your photos.

TRADITIONAL-DRESS THURSDAYS

In 2018, the Balinese government passed a regulation that every Thursday – and on the days of every full moon and new moon – all school children, professionals and office workers around Bali should wear *pakaian adat*, the traditional clothing of the island. While the aim was to preserve and protect Bali's heritage, it also initiated a renewed appreciation for Indonesia's beautiful textiles. More than 50 kinds of traditional fabrics are produced around the archipelago, and many are sold in central Denpasar's intriguing fabric stores. **I Gusti Ayu Martiasih** *(instagram.com/canangsari experience.bali)* leads an informative walk through the textiles area; it's a wonderful way to learn about the traditions and techniques used to produce these colourful and intricately decorated fabrics.

DRINKING IN DENPASAR: BEST COFFEE SPOTS

Bhineka Djaja: This historic cafe has been serving traditional Balinese coffee since 1935. Come in for a cup and to buy a bag of beans. *9am-3pm*

Bali Buda Renon: Perfect for health-conscious travellers, Bali Buda has smoothies and juices, as well as milk options for coffee. *8am-9.30pm*

Gula Bali the Joglo: A colourful, characterful restaurant with a lovely garden area. There's lots of juices, teas and coffees (hot and cold) on the menu. *10am-5.30pm*

FUKU: A cosy, contemporary cafe known for its excellent speciality coffees and teas. Try the sea-salt latte for something different. *8am-11pm*

Uluwatu

CLIFFTOP VIEWS | DRAMATIC BEACHES | WORLD-CLASS SURF

GETTING AROUND

The notorious traffic jams (especially around the sunset peak hour) are enough to convince most visitors to travel by motorbike rather than car, and the Gojek and Grab ride-hailing apps are convenient and quick. Walking can be perilous along the peninsula's small, traffic-clogged lanes. Catching a ride is often much safer. Motorbikes and scooters are also widely available. Be cautious and wear a helmet and protective clothing, and be aware that traffic police can be stringent about paperwork.

TOP TIP

The monkeys might seem cute, but they can be malicious and are renowned for stealing food, mobile phones and sunglasses. Keep a safe distance, secure your belongings and be aware that monkey bites can transmit serious diseases.

For many, Uluwatu is more a life choice than a holiday – its laid-back surf luxury comes with a big dose of adventure. In the five decades since the epic wave at Uluwatu was first ridden, the ululating sound of its name has echoed around the world among board riders. Many digital nomads have chosen to work here remotely for a period of time, and enjoy its buzzing cafes, restaurants and dramatic cliffside beaches; one featured in *Eat Pray Love* with Julia Roberts.

It's hard to imagine that the dry Bukit Peninsula was once almost uninhabited and known only for its impressive temple, Pura Luhur Ulu Watu, dating to the 11th century. Uluwatu's tiny lanes and infrastructure can't keep up with the mushrooming population – expect streets clogged by water tankers and scooters. Yet Uluwatu can be a dream beach-holiday spot, for both the health-conscious and party crowd: the former can do early-morning yoga and rejuvenate in Ulu's many massage houses, while the latter can spend all day at the many clifftop beach clubs, drinking in a pool to live beats and watching the main event of the day...sunset.

Surfing Uluwatu

Bali's best-known waves

With its consistent right and left waves, including options for all abilities, Uluwatu is considered one of the best places in the world to surf, and the cliffs here provide exceptional vantage points from which to watch the action. It's hard to beat the view from **Single Fin** (p99; *singlefinbali.com*) and the cluster of cliffside cafes at **Pantai Suluban**.

There are five peaks that comprise what is affectionately referred to as Ulu; none of these are suitable for beginners, but neighbouring **Thomas Beach** and nearby **Padang Padang** at **Baby Padang** *(adult/child 15,000/10,000Rp)* have smaller waves. The former is better for newbies and the latter for

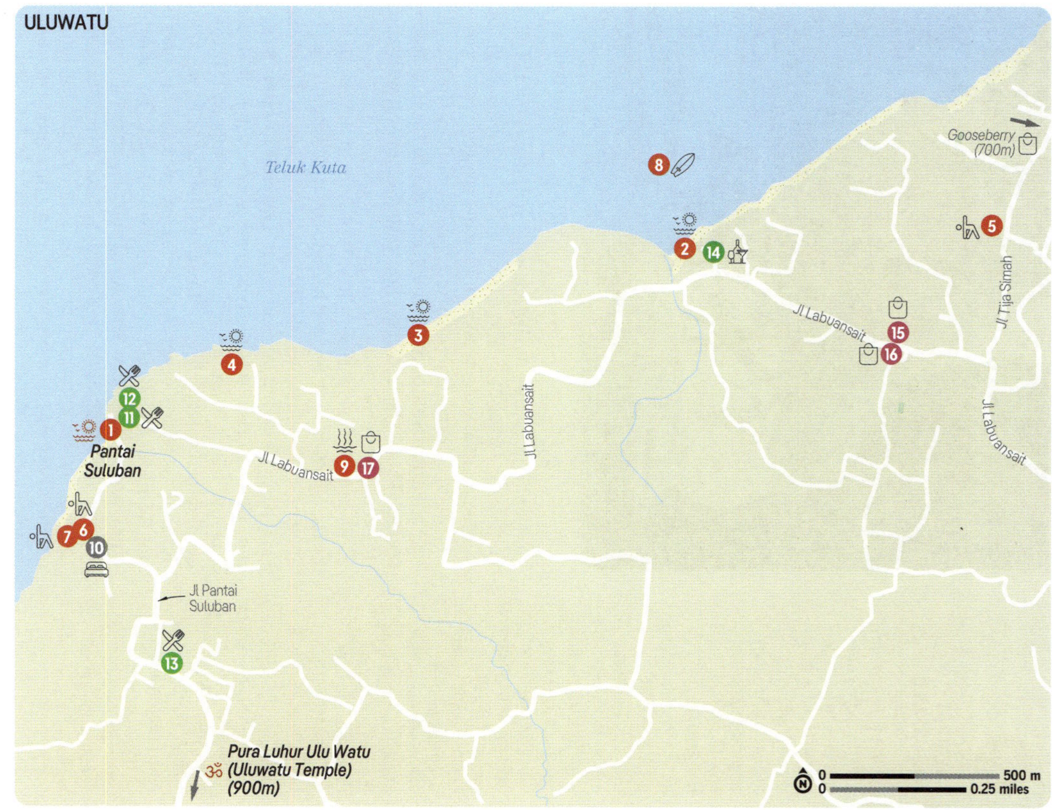

HIGHLIGHTS
1 Pantai Suluban

SIGHTS
2 Pantai Padang Padang
3 Thomas Beach
4 Ulu Cliffhouse

ACTIVITIES
5 Alchemy Yoga and Meditation Center
6 Istana
7 Morning Light Yoga
8 Padang Padang
9 Spring Spa

SLEEPING
10 Uluwatu Surf Villas

EATING
11 By the Cliff
12 Jeffry Warung
13 Land's End Café
see 12 Single Fin

DRINKING & NIGHTLIFE
14 Dugong Lounge & Bar
see 11 La Terrazza
see 11 Uluwatu Sunset Beach Warung

SHOPPING
15 By The Sea Uluwatu
16 Sea Gypsy
see 16 Uma and Leopold
17 Zealous Surf Boutique

THE FIRST TO SURF ULU

In 1971 movie director Albert Falzon's crew was filming footage for the iconic surf movie *Morning of the Earth* when they stumbled upon the now-legendary freight-train left-handers breaking off the cliffs at Uluwatu. That was almost four decades after surfing was first introduced in Kuta (thanks to Bob Koke; see p82) and the other waves of the Bukit Peninsula had barely been discovered yet. Australian surfer Stephen Cooney (just 15 years old at the time, and who later told his story in his book *Unearthed*) was filmed catching the first wave ever ridden at Uluwatu. Within a few years, Wayne 'Rabbit' Bartholomew and Hawaiian legend Gerry Lopez were photographed shooting the barrel at Ulu.

MARIUS DOBILAS/SHUTTERSTOCK

Pantai Suluban

intermediate surfers. Boards can be rented at most beaches for around 150,000Rp, and for around 500,000Rp locals on the beach offer lessons. Expect crowds, always.

If you're an experienced surfer, paddle out from the famous cave at **Pantai Suluban**, the entry point to Ulu, to reach **Racetracks**. This is the fastest section with the steepest walls and the roundest barrels; at mid to lower tides you'll score some of the world's most perfect tubes. Just south of the cave is the **Peak**, which is best avoided around low tide when it can be uncomfortably shallow; it's not for the fainthearted, but the Peak has a forgiving take-off point. **Outside Corner**, where the swell can rise to triple overhead, is where the 'Balinese Pipeline' starts to work some real big-wave magic. It breaks beyond the Peak and fires right across the line of Racetracks. South of Outside Corner (and breaking even further out) is the **Bombie**, which can reach 13m and should be avoided unless you're a big-wave charger of note. If you're looking for a quiet wave, then head for **Temples**, a relatively fickle spot south of the Peak that can break on smaller days; the longer paddle also helps to keep crowds to a minimum. For an excellent guide to the surf breaks around the Bukit Peninsula, see *indonesiansurfguide.com*.

DRINKING AROUND ULUWATU: CLIFFTOP COCKTAILS

Uluwatu Sunset Beach Warung: Bintang, smoothies and coffee served in humble surroundings against killer sunsets and views of the surf below. *8am-10pm*

Dugong: Look out over a curved infinity pool and across the ocean above Pantai Padang Padang. There's a good menu of wines, cocktails and juices. *7.30am-11pm*

Ulu Cliffhouse: There's a relaxed but exclusive atmosphere at this upmarket boutique hotel. Settle into a plush daybed with a cocktail in hand. *8am-10pm*

La Terrazza: Italian food and drinks on the cliff at Uluwatu surf break. Book a seat to nab one of the best sunset views on the peninsula. *8am-9pm Mon-Thu, to 10pm Fri & Sat*

Wellness Scene

Yoga, massage and ice baths

'Recover Hard', read the signs around Uluwatu – a fitting motto for this sun-drenched corner of Bali that's become both a party place and surf epicentre, with a roaring side-trade in wellness. Days here unfold between ocean swims, plant-based cafes and spa rituals steeped in Balinese tradition. Massage houses are cool, minimalist sanctuaries scented with lemongrass, where reflexology and deep-tissue treatments cost little more than a smoothie. One of the newer additions, **Spring Spa** *(spring-spa.com; massages from 150,000Rp)*, has taken the massage house offering up a notch; its treatment rooms, with chic modern island design, could have been plucked straight out of a five-star resort (without the price tag). Its plunge pools and dreamy reflexology sessions relax surf-weary muscles.

Uluwatu is also a chance to try new wellness fads you've probably never heard off – like at **Istana** *(theistana.com; spa sessions from 200,000Rp)*. Here, phones are banned and the relaxation starts with the glorious setting, high above Suluban Beach, where horizons stretch endlessly blue. Classic meditation and yoga happen alongside sensory-deprivation tanks (said to lure participants into a meditative state to reduce stress) or hyperbaric oxygen chambers (believed to speed up recovery in damaged tissue). Or, book into the immersive sound dome to feel the vibration as people chant or sing, before hitting reset in one of the icy cold plunges.

Elsewhere, **Morning Light Yoga** welcomes early risers to a thatched, open-air shala surrounded by tropical greenery and ocean views, while the celebrated **Alchemy Yoga Center** *(alchemyyogacenter.com; classes from 160,000Rp)* grounds each class in the Earth's elements. Post-practice, guests move through saunas and icy plunge pools before refuelling on vibrant plant-based fare at Alchemy's plant-based cafe.

BEST ULUWATU BOUTIQUES

Zealous Surf Boutique: Bali's first women's surf shop, run for women by women selling sustainable and surf-proof swimwear, plus one-of-a-kind streetwear.

Uma and Leopold: Flowing dresses, light playsuits and lots of linen: this Brazilian womenswear brand uses Balinese-inspired craft and design.

By The Sea Uluwatu: Upmarket resort wear with low-impact materials including luxury linens, breathable cottons and high-grade rayon.

Sea Gypsy: Gorgeous jewellery inspired by ocean adventures with unique stones and detailed silverwork.

Gooseberry: Woman-founded independent and sustainable shop for French fashion with the laid-back feel of Bali, for swimwear and beyond.

EATING IN ULUWATU: OUR PICKS

Single Fin: A surfer bar on the cliffs overlooking the surf break. The food is tasty and the vibe is laid-back. Great spot for sunset drinks. *8am-10pm* $$

Land's End Café: This daytime cafe has a good selection of smoothies, smoothie bowls and breakfasts. There are also vegan options. *8am-3.30pm* $$

Jeffry Warung: A good budget option on the cliff overlooking the Ulu epic surf point. Sandwiches here are under 50,000Rp. *7am-7pm* $

By the Cliff: Popular post-surf, with a board rack and healthy eats, from acai bowls and avo-on-toast brekkies to good salads and bowls. *8am-8pm* $$

NYANEWS/SHUTTERSTOCK

Kecak performance

TOP EXPERIENCE

Pura Luhur Ulu Watu

According to ancient Balinese scripts, the Pura Luhur Ulu Watu, or Uluwatu Temple, is a magical portal that has the potential to transport those who set eyes on it directly to heaven. Dating to the 11th century, it is absolutely spectacular, and even the casual observer can feel its significance: the architecture, landscape, sculpted gardens and, above all, the dramatic location atop 70m-high cliffs rising from the ocean.

DON'T MISS

- Inner temple
- Kumba Karna Kerebut Statue
- Dang Hyang Nirartha Statue
- Kecak Dance
- Cliffside paths at sunset

Temple Grounds

Exploring the temple takes roughly 30 minutes to an hour, depending on how much time you spend admiring the architecture, views, gardens and statues. After paying for the entrance ticket, a guide will likely approach. There are no info boards, so guides are useful for interpreting what you're about to see (expect to pay around 150,000Rp for an hour).

Uluwatu Temple is one of Bali's six holiest temples, which are placed around the island to maintain spiritual balance,

PRACTICALITIES

- kecakdancebali.com
- adult/child 50,000/30,000Rp
- open to non-worshippers 7am-7pm

and this temple is dedicated to Shiva Rudra. Statues of deities and notable figures include the striking **Kumba Karna Kerebut Statue**, depicting warrior Kumbakarna, and the **Dang Hyang Nirartha Statue** high above the cliff, honouring an esteemed Hindu priest who shaped Balinese Hinduism. An **inner temple** is guarded by statues of Ganesha, the deity with an elephant head and human body. The prayer courtyard has a three-tiered pagoda at its southern end. Only Hindu worshippers can enter the prayer courtyard, but it's possible to peer in and admire the intricately carved bricks.

Hypnotic Dance

As the sun begins to slip below the Indian Ocean, the air around Pura Luhur Ulu Watu reverberates with the hypnotising *chak-chak-chak* chant and **Kecak** (pronounced kechak) performers mesmerise an audience that's gathered to watch what has become one of the most iconic displays of Balinese culture. With the majestic Uluwatu cliffs as a backdrop, the dancers enact tales from the Ramayana (one of the great Hindu holy books), and their traditional attire, the flickering flames, and rhythmic sounds and movements create a true spectacle. While the Kecak dance is performed in various locations around the island, it's the one at Uluwatu that is the most popular; its clifftop setting is hard to beat, particularly at sunset. The onomatopoeic name *kecak* imitates the chattering sounds produced by the 100 or so bare-chested male performers who form the dance's core; they wear black-and-white *poleng* sarongs and chatter and sway in a circle around an oil lamp or fire.

Queue before the show from 4.30pm for tickets for both the 5.45pm *(150,000Rp)* show and the second 7pm show. Or you can also avoid the queues and buy your ticket online at least 24 hours in advance *(kecakdancebali.com; 200,000Rp)*. There is a maximum of 1000 tickets available for each show.

Views & Monkeys

A long, fortified **concrete pathway** runs along the cliffside to gorgeous viewpoints of the temple with the Indian Ocean below. The Pura Tanah Lot is a favourite location at sunset; however, the route runs along dense forest at its western edge, and an estimated 400 to 800 long-tailed macaque monkeys live in the area, in troops of up to 40. Always on the path, monkeys may be perched on the walls or hanging from the trees waiting for the opportunity to pounce. The monkeys in these parts have learned how to snatch food, phones, jewellery and sunglasses from tourists. They may attempt to barter for food with your stolen belongings, or they may just break your phone in front of you. The danger is if visitors are scratched during the stealing process – although many monkeys are vaccinated, scratches can transmit nasty diseases. Guides are helpful in clearing the path of monkeys.

WHY AREN'T MONKEYS KEPT OUT?

These animals have a spiritual significance, as Hindus believe they guard the temple against bad influences. Their habitat is conserved and they are regularly fed and immunised. Plus every six months, during the Tumpek Kandang celebration, they are offered a platter of fruits by caretakers. Spy one albino monkey safely in its cage at the centre of the temple – it was rescued after being attacked by other monkeys due to its rare white fur.

TOP TIPS

- It's respectful to wear long sleeves and cover your legs. If legs aren't covered, you'll be given a sarong at the entrance (likely pre-worn).
- Temple tickets are valid for re-entry. Grab a bite or a drink outside at the many roadside vendors while waiting for the show to start.
- Don't have sunglasses, jewellery or phones on show, as dozens are stolen daily by the monkeys.
- Don't bring food or drink onto the grounds.
- Arrive before 5pm to avoid sunset crowds or at 7am to have the place almost to yourself.
- Nervous of monkeys? Ask at the gates for a guide who is good at shooing them away.

HELP ME PICK

Beaches on the Bukit Peninsula

Dramatic coves beneath soaring cliffs and golden, sandy bays lie all along Bukit's coastline, and almost every beach is entirely different from the others, from empty to glam to local or ideal for watersports. Generally, the beaches get busier throughout the day as party people wake, or if there's surf to watch, but the most popular time to be at the west-facing beaches is sunset. Expect crowds at the weekends. Most beaches have an entry fee, usually less than 17,000Rp or US$1.

Where to Go If You Want To...

Swim

Guning Payung (p105) A reef keeps the waves off this small, secluded beach quite calm. There is a lifeguard, and you can rent a canoe, umbrella or sun bed.

Jimbaran (p103) With an almost 4km-long beach, it's easy to find a spot here to relax. The water is calm and great for a paddle.

Relax

Thomas Beach (p96) Lush vegetation shrouds its steep sides. There are some warungs and you can swim or surf (the waves are always smaller here than at neighbouring Pantai Suluban). Access via 130 stairs.

Balangan Stilted bars hover high over the sand and rocks are covered in emerald seaweed to the south. Good seafood and surfing too.

Nunggalan Find solitude after a 30-minute hike to the almost-2km-long deserted beach, along a steep, rocky trail.

Green Bowl Beautiful, wild and secluded, Green Bowl is loved by surfers. There's not much beach at high tide; low tide reveals rock pools and two caves.

Hang Out With Family

Melasti Near Bali's southernmost point, a reef forms natural pools at low tide. Kecak is performed at an amphitheatre at sunset.

Nusa Dua (pictured below) For manicured lawns, high-end resorts and restaurants along the beachfront. The water is typically calm at low tide and the beach sandy.

MONTICELLO/SHUTTERSTOCK

Do Some People-Watching

Pandawa Well developed, with canoes and bicycles for rent, and an array of restaurants and shops.

Padang Padang Tiny popular beach, with swimming, tanning, surfing and surf lessons. In a small picturesque cove.

Dreamland A lively crowd-puller for both tourists and expats (in fact everyone...and their dogs). There's even more of a show when the surf's big.

Take Photographs

Suluban (p98) The spot for advanced surfers. After weaving past cliffside cafes, you'll emerge into a limestone cove.

Gunung Payung (p105) Walk through a cave, through an amphitheatre and down a cliff to get to this gorgeous hidden little cove with a cave at its western end at low tide.

NOKURO/SHUTTERSTOCK

Padang Padang

HOW TO

Bay watch
Keep an eye on the tides - some beaches are inaccessible when the tide is high, so be careful you don't get stranded.

Be aware
Monkeys are a real menace on the Bukit. Watch your belongings and don't coax the monkeys closer.

Budget
Keep small notes easily accessible as you'll need to pay 2000Rp or 5000Rp to access some of the beaches.

Go prepared
The walk to some of the beaches can be hot and strenuous. Drinks aren't always available, so take your own bottled water.

Eating Seafood at Jimbaran

Pantai Jimbaran is famous for the scores of seafood restaurants that line the bay and spill out onto the golden sand, and an evening spent here will give you the chance to indulge in exceptionally fresh locally caught fish that's barbecued while you soak up the laid-back tropical ambience. As evening falls and strings of lights begin to twinkle, aromatic smoke from the restaurants' grills swirls through the air, and meandering musicians serenade diners seated at tables on the sand. Along Jimbaran's sweeping 4km beach there are three groups of restaurants. The ones on **Pantai Muaya**, in the south, are midrange in terms of pricing and atmosphere. The cluster of 10 eateries at **Queen Beach**, the smallest section, is more basic and very rustic and this is reflected in the cheaper prices. **Pantai Kedonganan**, on the airport end, is the largest and busiest section; expect more neon lights and higher prices. There are around 40 restaurants in total. They're all relatively similar in that they have ice boxes and tanks of seafood at their entrance, and they sell the fish by weight (snapper is around 150,000Rp per kilogram at Pantai Muaya). The price includes rice and vegetables, and platters and set menus are available, too. While many restaurants open from late morning and take the last order at around 10pm, sunset is prime time to be here and the restaurants are all but empty by about 8pm.

Beyond Uluwatu

The hot and arid Bukit Peninsula is revered for its sunset views, languorous beaches, famous surf breaks and clifftop hotels.

Places

Central Bukit p104
Gunung Payung p105
Jimbaran p105
Nusa Dua p107

GETTING AROUND

Even the main roads in the central part of the Bukit Peninsula are winding country lanes (often covered in potholes). Roads in Nusa Dua are newer, wider and much better quality, and its sprawling lawny areas offer a break from the chaotic traffic noises in other parts of the peninsula. At busy times (particularly around sunset) it can take a long time to travel by car. It's often quicker (and cheaper if you're travelling with friends) to hire individual Gojek or Grab motorbikes. Some riders will, for a small additional fee, allow two passengers on a bike, but beware of the safety implications of this.

It's a bizarre fact that the wider Bukit Peninsula, which hangs off the southern tip of Bali, is markedly less well-known than Uluwatu, its furthest point. On early Dutch maps the peninsula was marked as Tafelhoek (Table Corner) and Bukit (pronounced *book*-it), which translates simply as 'hill', was barely inhabited thanks to its lack of permanent rivers. These days, the Bukit coastline and its luxury-resort enclave of Nusa Dua host some seriously dreamy beach clubs and hotels. You'll find accommodation to suit every budget (from US$10 dorms to Raffles' US$3500-a-night villas) and beaches are incredibly varied; every kind of traveller will find their ideal piece of paradise here.

Central Bukit

TIME FROM ULUWATU: **25MIN**

Indonesia's tallest statue

One of the first things you'll see as you fly into Bali is the **Garuda Wisnu Kencana** statue in GWK Cultural Park, which depicts the Hindu god Vishnu riding the mythical bird Garuda. It towers over the Bukit Peninsula, standing almost 120m high, and is among the tallest statues in the world, rising higher than the Statue of Liberty. It was designed by renowned Balinese sculptor Nyoman Nuarta and comprises 3000 tonnes of copper and bronze. It is a feat of art, science and engineering, and if you're going to the **GWK Cultural Park** *(gwkbali.com; entrance only/with statue tour 150,000/350,000Rp),* it's well worth paying the extra fee for the tour inside the statue to see the far-reaching views of Bukit. There's also a glass-bottomed walkway and excellent displays sharing details on the design, engineering and construction of the statue.

Tours take 45 minutes, and it takes at least an hour to simply view the statue from below – the large surrounding park is vast, with impressive, towering limestone cliffs and gardens, plus a lotus pond, restaurants and kids activities, which are reached by a shuttle bus service from the car park. Park-entrance tickets include 15 free cultural performances, excluding the Barong dance show (a story about the battle between good and evil), which costs 50,000Rp extra.

Garuda Wisnu Kencana

Gunung Payung

TIME FROM ULUWATU: **35MIN**

Paragliding off the coastline

The tall cliffs above **Gunung Payung** have become a hot spot for paragliders due to the area's consistent sea winds, and most days the sky is dotted with coloured fabric wings, gracefully gliding through the sky. **Bali Paragliding Tours** *(baliparaglidingtour.com; 15min flights from 1,200,000Rp)* has a launch site right next to the quiet temple complex of **Pura Dhang Kahyangan Gunung Payung**.

Taking a tandem flight along the coastline is an exhilarating experience, as the glider swoops along the coastline with views of reefs through the crystal-clear waters, over golden sandy coves and above the temple. Included in the price of each flight is the option to hold an action camera and shoot videos as a memento of the experience. For extra thrills, ask your instructor to dip and swoop below and above the cliffs.

Jimbaran

TIME FROM ULUWATU: **35MIN**

Buy seafood at Jimbaran's market

In years gone by **Jimbaran** was predominantly a fishing village, and the tradition still lives on in this seaside town. Every morning from around 7am the **Kedongan Fish Market** (some call it the Jimbaran Fish Market), on the airport end of

BYE-BYE BINGIN

With its lovely strip of white sand framed by steep limestone cliffs, Bingin was one of Bali's most beautiful beaches. Hanging out in its cliffside cafes and watching the surf has been a quintessential Bukit Peninsula experience for decades, so it came as a shock to tourists and locals when local government officials descended on Bingin in July 2025 with an army of demolition workers and began tearing down more than 35 'illegal' buildings on the cliff face, effectively reducing Bingin to rubble. The cleanup is expected to continue through 2026, with a redevelopment plan set to include a stage for cultural performances. You can still surf here, but the Bingin you may have been lucky enough to know has gone.

DRINKING ON THE BUKIT PENINSULA: OUR PICKS

Cliff Bar at Six Senses Uluwatu: Unbelievable ocean views and fab cocktails – try the chipotle margarita. The kombucha is good, too. *11am-9pm*

Rock Bar: Decks jut out over the rocks, and it's spectacular for sunset drinks. Rock Bar is incredibly popular, so book a table in advance. *4pm-midnight*

El Kabron: An adults-only clifftop beach club with a Mediterranean vibe and stunning Indian Ocean views. There's an extensive drinks menu. *11am-midnight*

White Rabbit Lounge: A sultry speakeasy with late-night bites. Order from the extensive cocktail menu or build your own martini. *8pm-late*

TOP EXPERIENCE

Saka Museum

Effigies of the monsters and demons from Balinese mythology, called ogoh-ogoh, are paraded through the streets at the beginning of the Balinese new year. Then the Nyepi, the Balinese Day of Silence, follows and the entire island comes to a complete pause. This fascinating museum, complete with full-sized monsters, delves into this cultural phenomenon.

CATWALKPHOTOS/SHUTTERSTOCK

Ogoh-ogoh parade, Sukawati (p153)

TOP TIPS

- Save time for the 3rd floor's Saka Auditorium, which shows 360-degree movies of Bali scenes in a tented dome theatre.
- A small cafe on the 1st floor serves teas and coffees.
- Tickets are available in advance on the museum website.
- Scan the QR codes around the museum for audio guides.

PRACTICALITIES

- sakamuseum.org
- open 10am-6pm
- entry adult/child/child under 5yr 200,000/100,000Rp/free

The Saka Calendar

The Saka calendar is a lunisolar calendar derived from Hindu calendars. The Saka Museum holds old examples of this Balinese calendar carved in wooden boards, plus cultural relics (from silk scarves and carved wooden doors to intricate jewellery) relating to the five elements connected with the solar and lunar calendars.

Day of Silence

Nyepi is when everything comes to a standstill and the island descends into silence. Roads are closed, lights are turned off and no fires can be made. Even the airspace over Bali is shut. **Pengrupukan**, the night before Nyepi, however, is absolute pandemonium with enormous effigies of monsters paraded around, as musical instruments ring out. Photos in exhibition halls document this remarkable tradition in the Saka calendar.

Walking Among Giants

Visitors can wander the giant-sized permanent ogoh-ogoh figures created as effigies. These astounding pieces are made from bamboo and papier-mâché, often standing more than 3m tall. These fearsome monsters are paraded through the streets to get rid of evil spirits, as percussion instruments are banged, clattered and beaten. Kids and grown-ups alike will love staring up at the menacing depictions of characters from the Hindu stories, with their bulbous eyes, sharp teeth and long tongues.

Pantai Jimbaran (p103), swings into full gear as just-caught fish fresh off the boats is sold to shoppers, chefs and restauranteurs. It's as frenetic as it is fascinating, and the colours, shapes and sizes of the fish and shellfish on sale are mesmerising. The market is open all day, and if you buy anything the seller will scale and gut the fish, which you can then take to a warung just outside the market and, for around 20,000Rp per kilogram, have someone cook it for you.

Nusa Dua

TIME FROM ULUWATU: **45MIN**

Witness the ocean's power

The exclusive resort enclave of **Nusa Dua**, with its manicured lawns, pristine beach and luxury hotels, flanks the northeastern corner of the Bukit. And it has its own little peninsula, **Nusa Gede Island** (sometimes called Peninsula Island), which has been tamed into a park called the **Garden of Hope**, fringed by dramatic, ragged limestone edges that provide a stark contrast to its manicured surroundings. On the east side of this peninsula is the natural phenomenon of water blow – where powerful waves crash against a slab of dangerously jagged rocks, and the water is forced up through steep, tight gaps in the limestone, creating dramatic water eruptions up to 10m high.

For years, this natural phenomenon was obscured by vegetation and the jagged limestone made it difficult (and dangerous) to get closer for a good view. For safety, a concrete walkway and viewing points have now been built, and the path will take you safely over the rocks and close to the **blow hole** *(entry 25,000Rp)*. The gate only opens at 9am; a pity as sunrise here would be epic. This is a picturesque sunrise spot, though, and there's another little outcrop just north of Nusa Gede Island – while you won't see the water blow here, watching the sunrise is well worth waking up for.

THE BUKIT'S WATER WOES

If you get stuck in traffic on the Bukit Peninsula, it's quite likely that a water tanker is slowing things down; they can be an annoyance, but these vehicles have become a very necessary part of life on this arid peninsula. The Bukit has no permanent rivers and no freshwater sources of its own, and as the limestone that comprises this land is extremely porous, rainwater disappears quickly as it drains into the cracks and fissures. With all the development on the Bukit, the existing infrastructure battles to sustain the increasing demands, particularly in the dry season, so it's worth being mindful of your water consumption when you stay in the area.

Try the loaded fresh-fruit açai bowls and avocado toasts.

EATING ON THE BUKIT PENINSULA

Warung Local: This super-popular local-style eatery has an array of delicious Indonesian dishes on offer. *8am-10pm* $

Bali Buda Bukit: A health-food staple on the island, Bali Buda has an eclectic menu featuring organic and locally sourced ingredients. *7.30am-9.30pm* $$

Bukit Cafe: Australian-style brunch composed of fresh local ingredients: think smoothie bowls and smashed avocado. Live music in the evenings. *8am-10pm* $$

Cashew Tree: In a small lane off Bingin Beach, serving awesome local curries, plus health food on tap. *7.30am-10pm* $

Le Bleu by K Club: Chic spot on Nusa Dua Beach with an impressive raised weaved roof, chilled beats and fine international cuisine. *10am-11pm* $$$

Seed: Chilled spot in Bingin for beautifully presented French-Asian food. Creative small plates have bodacious flavour combinations. Live mellow jazz, too. *7.30am-11pm* $$

Arwana: The seafood brunch is a firm favourite at this beachfront grill restaurant, which serves fresh oysters, lobsters and premium fish. *10am-11pm* $$$

Rumari: Indulge in a fine-dining experience at Raffles, where the seven-course menu is inspired by the Indonesian archipelago. *6-10pm* $$$

ART & ARCHITECTURE OF THE BUKIT PENINSULA

Wind through the Bukit Peninsula's buzzing small lanes on a scooter, stopping at awe-inspiring geographical features, architecture and cultural attractions.

START	END	LENGTH
Nusa Gede Island	Saka Museum	40km; 10–12hr

Start early at the Garden of Hope at **1 Nusa Gede Island** (p107) along the Nusa Dua enclave, where the **2 blow hole** (p107) is impressive during big swells. The next stop is **3 Museum Pasifika**, about 1km away, which has a permanent exhibition of art from around the Asia Pacific region. The roads from here are tangled, so use Google Maps to plot your route southwest to **4 Pura Dhang Kahyangan Gunung Payung** (p105), a spacious, quiet temple complex with interesting architecture and lovely ocean views. You'll then need to skirt around a golf course to reach **5 Pantai Pandawa** (p102). It's popular for its beach, but what's remarkable are the large sculptures of characters from Hindu mythology set into cliffside enclaves on the steep road down. Pull into the view-site parking to appreciate them.

Continue east to **6 Pura Luhur Ulu Watu** (p100), renowned for its spectacular architecture and clifftop location. You'll have seen the imposing Garuda statue from various spots around the Bukit; that's your next stop. Jl Raya Uluwatu Pecatu will take you almost to the **7 GWK Cultural Park** (p104), an old illegal quarry that now has sculptures set between walls of cut limestone. It's worth paying the fee for the tour inside the Garuda statue. The final stop is the **8 Saka Museum** (p106), which has an outstanding display of ogoh-ogoh effigies made by some of Bali's most revered artists.

Attempt paragliding over the cliffs next to Pura Dhang Kahyangan Gunung Payung for a bird's-eye view with **Bali Paragliding Tours** (p105).

Stop at outdoor retail complex the **Bali Collection** for coffee or breakfast in one of the many restaurants.

Nusa Lembongan

LESS-CROWDED SURF | WORLD-CLASS DIVING | MANGROVE FORESTS

Easily reachable from Bali by fast boat in 40 minutes, but a world away from the mainland, Nusa Lembongan offers a step back in pace from the often-hectic beach towns of South Bali. The car-free island (aside from mini taxis) is rich with Hindu culture and dramatic landscapes of wave-pounded cliffs, plus quiet mangrove forests, but most visit for its superb and relatively uncrowded surf spots and vibrant marine life.

Off the 2km stretch of white sand of Pantai Jungutbatu must be one of the few beaches where you can snorkel over a coral reef just 100m from surfers who are riding perfectly formed waves. Numerous surf shops and dive centres offer easy access to its ocean bounty. The island is also the launch pad for Nusa Ceningan and Nusa Penida, but for an island of its size, around 8 sq km, it has more variety and activities than your typical beach holiday.

GETTING AROUND

Boats to Nusa Lembongan leave from Sanur, Benoa or Serangan harbours, and a variety of companies offer fast-boat services, which take about 40 minutes, depending on weather and ocean conditions. Find and compare prices at *baliferries.com*. Public boats leave at irregular times from the beach at Sanur. Grab and Gojek apps don't operate in Nusa Lembongan, but 'taxis' (in the form of canopied pickups) ply the streets. Most visitors tend to hire a scooter (available from ferry stations) since distances are minimal. Beware, though, that maintenance might be lax (compared with the mainland) and many lanes are badly potholed.

Underwater World

Dive or snorkel around the islands

Nusa Lembongan (along with neighbours Nusa Ceningan and Nusa Penida) falls within the **Coral Triangle**, a marine region revered for its exceptional biodiversity, and the diving and snorkelling here is absolutely sublime. There are 15 dive sites on the rocky shorelines, with healthy reefs and beautiful coral gardens home to an abundance of marine life. Don a mask and snorkel and you'll likely see schools of colourful reef fish, curious turtles and majestic manta rays gliding with the currents. Between July to October, it's also possible to spot *Mola mola,* known as ocean sunfish, here. These can grow up to 3m long and weigh 2 tonnes. The water around Lembongan, Ceningan and Penida was declared a marine protected area in 2010, and there are said to be around 300 species of coral and 575 species of fish here – it really is an underwater wonderland.

The visibility for diving is good year-round (it averages on 20m, although often it can be up to 30m) and the warm water

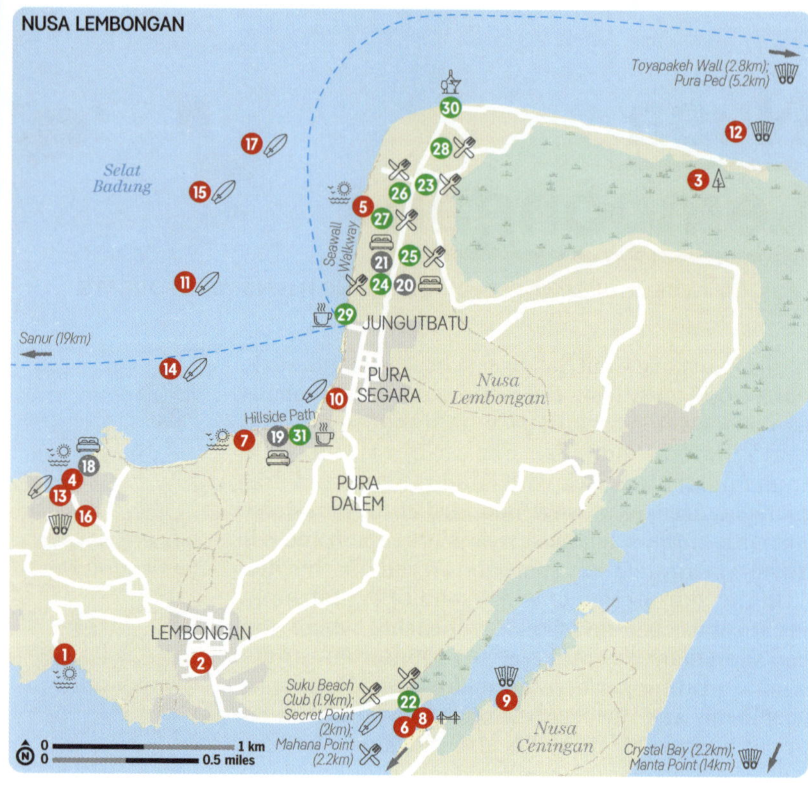

SIGHTS
1 Dream Beach
2 Gala-Gala Underground House
3 Mangroves
4 Mushroom Bay
5 Pantai Jungutbatu
6 Seaweed plantations
7 Song Lambung Beach
8 Yellow Bridge

ACTIVITIES
see 18 Bali Hai
9 Ceningan Divers
10 Eddy Surfboard Hire
11 Lacerations
12 Mangrove Point
13 Nusa Islands Surf School
14 Playgrounds
15 Razors
16 Scuba Center Asia
17 Shipwrecks

SLEEPING
18 Bali Hai Villa
19 Batu Karang
20 Isla Indah Retreat
21 Pondok Jenggala

EATING
22 Alponte Ristorante
23 Curry Traders
24 Fin Island
see 20 Indah Oasis
25 Kayu Lembongan
26 Koa Donuts
27 Ohana's
28 Sampan
see 28 The Coconut Hut

DRINKING & NIGHTLIFE
29 Beach Shack
30 Captain Bar and Grill
31 The Deck Café and Bar

TOP TIP

While departures from mainland Bali will be via jetty, most fast boats and ferries moor off the beach at Nusa Lembongan, meaning you have to wade through the shallows and carry your luggage a short distance across the beach.

makes for pleasant snorkelling. There are more than 15 dive sites around the three islands (**Manta Point** in Nusa Pedina, with its cleaning station, is a highlight for many), with trips leaving directly from Nusa Lembongan. Many sites are accessible for snorkellers, too. If you don't want to head out on a boat, then scoot around to **Mangrove Point** at the northeast of Lembongan. You can hire snorkelling gear here and swim out from the beach (at high tide is best) to explore the pretty coral gardens, or jump in a kayak – the water is so clear you'll likely see marine life from above the water. These can be rented for around 150,000Rp per half-hour from roadside vendors next to the mangroves. Be aware that the currents can be very strong at Mangrove Point and around the island; let others know when you plan to swim out and return, and don't venture far out on your own. Less confident swimmers may find it safest to swim with a guide.

Setting up a boat-based snorkelling or diving trip from Lembongan is easy. Dive shops abound, and most homestays and guesthouses also sell trips; expect to pay from around 200,000Rp for a three-stop snorkelling trip.

For diving, **Bali Hai** *(balihaicruises.com; 2 dives incl equipment from 1,800,000Rp)* and **Scuba Center Asia** *(scubacenterasia.com; 2 dives incl equipment from 1,700,000Rp)* will arrange everything including boat transfers and a basic lunch. If you're interested in learning even more about marine life, then book a diving or snorkelling trip with eco-friendly **Ceningan Divers** *(ceningandivers.com; 2 dives incl equipment & lunch 2,400,000Rp),* who take care to explain the role and significance of conservation for the creatures spotted underwater.

Ride Uncrowded Waves

Surf the breaks off Nusa Lembongan

Crashing waves are not typically conducive to the conditions that make for great diving, but Lembongan offers excellent surfing and outstanding diving off the same stretch of coastline.

Spectacular **Pantai Jungutbatu**, a 2km-long west-facing stretch of Lembongan's coast, has three offshore reefs that catch good, consistent surf on a daily basis – and, on rare occasions, you will see barrelling overhead waves. **Playgrounds** is the southernmost – and most popular – surf spot accessible from **Song Lambung Beach** *(board rental per hr 150,000Rp).* **Lacerations** is just a 150m paddle to the north and **Razors** is another 150m north again with a lovely left-hand peeling wave suited to longboarders in smaller swells. Although some surf schools do bring their students to Lacerations, it might be the intimidating name that keeps the crowds away. But here beautifully peeling waves break both left and right, allowing for an easy paddle with the current back around the edge of the reef. You will sometimes see turtles and, with any luck, manta rays. In larger swells Lacerations is not safe for beginners. Beware of surfing these breaks and the more fickle **Shipwrecks** further to the north at lower tides, as the reef can become very shallow.

THE ISLANDS' BEST DIVE SPOTS

Divemaster **Kadek Gama**, who has worked for Bali Hai *(balihaicruises.com)* since 1999, shares his favourite dive sites.

Manta Point: Throughout the year you'll find at least four or five manta rays here at the cleaning station.

Crystal Bay: In the cold-water season between July and October you'll see *Mola mola* at depths of 18m to 40m.

Mangrove Point: This is great for snorkelling; it's shallow and safe, the coral is beautiful and there are often turtles. If you're lucky you might see dolphins.

Toyapakeh Wall: The coral here is the best in the area but it gets very busy with boats.

Pura Ped: You can usually see turtles, sunfish, pufferfish and sometimes beautiful thresher sharks.

EATING IN NUSA LEMBONGAN: OUR PICKS

Kayu Lembongan: Relaxed setting in a lush tropical garden, serving sustainable, organic healthy eats, including colourful brekkies and salads. *7am-10pm* **$$**

Fin Island: A popular cafe serving everything from soups and variations of avo toast to Mexican options, pizzas, sandwiches and rice bowls. *7am-10pm* **$$**

Curry Traders: Quite unexpected, this dreamy restaurant is as much a feast for the eyes as it is for the taste buds. *5-11pm* **$$**

Alponte Ristorante: With gorgeous views of the Yellow Bridge and Nusa Ceningan, this alfresco-style restaurant serves the Italian faves. *8am-10pm* **$$**

THE OCEAN'S DAY OF SILENCE

Every year on the fourth full moon of the Balinese calendar (usually around October) the ocean surrounding Nusa Lembongan, Nusa Ceningan and Nusa Penida goes quiet. There are no ferries darting between the islands, and no fishers casting their lines. All boats remain moored for 24 hours.

The bays are also empty of surfers, snorkellers and divers, and farmers refrain from collecting seaweed. The day of stillness – **Nyepi Laut** (sometimes also called Nyepi Segara) – is in honour of Dewa Baruna, the god of the sea. It is observed around these three islands only, and it happens about six months after Nyepi, the 'other' day of silence celebrated on Bali to mark the new lunar year (see p106).

ANNA ZHELUDKOVA/SHUTTERSTOCK

Secret Point

You can paddle to these spots from the beach, or for 150,000Rp a boat operator will take you out and pick you up at an arranged time. **Eddy Surfboard Hire** at the southern end of Pantai Jungutbatu has a good selection of boards for all conditions, and **Nusa Islands Surf School** *(nusaislandsbali.com; 2hr lessons from 450,000Rp)* on Mushroom Beach runs well-prepared classes for all levels.

Secret Point is the only surf spot on neighbouring **Nusa Ceningan**. It's a real gem for experienced surfers and is reached through a sort of cellar room under the terrace of the **Mahana Point Bar & Grill**, which has phenomenal views and two high-tide cliff-jump boards, or the break can be reached from the beach below **Suku Beach Club**.

Mangrove Kayaking

Glide through brackish waters

The northeastern corner of Lembongan is wrapped in an immense tangle of **mangroves**, and exploring the waterways here is probably the most peaceful way to experience the island. Shady tunnels that wind through trees offer respite from the sun and – despite the shrill sounds from cicadas – the world here feels quiet, still and cool. For an extremely serene mangrove experience, hire a boat operator to pole you through the waterways *(30min around 150,000Rp)*. If you're

DRINKING IN NUSA LEMBONGAN: OUR PICKS

Deck Café and Bar: Set above Pantai Jungutbatu, the views are a big drawcard. Beer on tap, a good gin selection and interesting cocktails. *7.30am-10pm*

Tigerlillys Beach Shack: Lounge on the sand at Pantai Jungutbatu and sip on cocktails, local wines, fresh-pressed juices or coffees. *8am-10pm*

Captain Bar and Grill: An on-the-beach restaurant near the mangroves serving cocktails, mocktails, juices and beers. *8am-11pm*

Indah Oasis: Great coffee, smoothies and fresh juices at this healthy-eating cafe, shop and yoga studio. *7am-9.30pm*

up for a paddle, rent a kayak and explore on your own, or go on a guided kayak tour *(1hr around 175,000Rp)*.

Mangroves are exceptionally important and diverse ecosystems, and the dense forest plays a vital role in protecting land from erosion and the wrath of the waves. It's a nursery for coral reefs, with many other species thriving; it's here that fish like snappers and tarpons come to spawn. The early mornings and late afternoons are particularly rewarding if you're into birding. The metallic-blue cerulean kingfisher is quite common here, as is the striated heron and the little lemon-bellied white-eye.

The mangroves cover a significant portion of Lembongan, and while most kayak and boat trips run from the northeastern stretch of the island (simply arrive and book your trip from one of the numerous small-scale roadside operators), a handful are based on the southwestern arc of the mangroves near the **Yellow Bridge** (p114). The road that skirts the mangroves, Jl Raya Lembongan, makes for a peaceful drive and is worth travelling simply to experience Lembongan's wilder, quieter side.

Seaweed Farming

Nusa Lembongan's fields of green

Much of Nusa Lembongan's coastline is dominated by a beguiling submarine patchwork of **seaweed plantations**, and while the grid-like pattern can be discerned on many reefs (and even on the fringe of the mangrove forests), it is most noticeable in the shallow, 600m-wide channel between Lembongan and Ceningan islands. This patchwork of plots (most of which measure around 6m by 40m) make for intriguing photos. A trip to the farms will also give you an opportunity to learn about the incredibly hard work of planting, harvesting and drying that's involved in farming this submarine crop, which sustains a large proportion of the island's population.

You can visit the seaweed farms at any stage of the tide, but you will get a better understanding of the complexities of this crop when the water is lower, and, unless you have a working command of Bahasa Indonesia, if you visit with a guide. Most hotels and homestays can arrange this, with tours running from around 200,000Rp per person.

The seaweed industry is relatively new to Lembongan; it was introduced by a businessman from Surabaya in 1984 and almost immediately became a major earner as the lucrative crop was used chiefly in the cosmetics and ice-cream industries.

SPECIES TO SPOT ON NUSA LEMBONGAN

Asian water monitors: These large lizards swim around the island's mangrove forests, and live off a diet of fish, frogs, crabs, birds and rodents.

Crab-eating frogs: The *Fejervarya cancrivora* (or crab-eating frog) loves the brackish freshwater ponds near beaches.

Fiddler crabs: These come in many fascinating colours and sizes, and you'll see them scuttling around everywhere in the mangroves.

Asian vine snakes: A green slender reptile can be up to 1.8m in length and camouflages itself as vines. It's only mildly venomous.

Monkeys: Long-tailed macaques do live in Nusa Lembongan, but they're more chilled-out than in other areas of Bali, such as Ubud and Uluwatu Temple.

EATING IN NUSA LEMBONGAN: FOR FAMILIES

Koa Donuts: A takeaway for when only something sweet will do – homemade flavours include tiramisu, Nutella, and custard. *9.30am-5pm* $

Coconut Hut: While the tacos, smoothie bowls and salads at this casual eatery are fantastic (good kids menu, too), the mini-golf is the big draw. *8am-11pm* $$

Sampan: Kids have a ball at the small playground with a slide and climbing ropes. This seafood restaurant and grill also serves breakfast. *6am-10pm* $$

Ohana's: Slightly swanky, very family-friendly beach club with a kids menu and small pool. It's right on the beach for sand play. *7am-11pm* $$

GIVE BACK AS YOU TRAVEL

The density of rubbish on Indonesia's beaches – Nusa Lembongan's included – often correlates with the seasons and tides, and the rainy season (usually November through February) can be a particularly upsetting time to be on the beaches, in the surf or exploring the region's underwater world. Throughout the year, Lembongan's community regularly holds beach clean-ups. **Lembongan Surf Team** *(instagram.com/lembongansurfteam)* leads a clean-up every Thursday; **French Kiss Divers** *(instagram.com/frenchkissdiverslembongan)* arranges one every Tuesday, and **Ceningan Divers** *(instagram.com/ceningandivers)* holds village clean-ups every Monday. To get involved, check their social media pages for updates. Over on Nusa Penida, **Penida Colada beach bar** *(penidacolada.com)* gives one free fresh coconut for every bag of trash collected.

PETERI16/SHUTTERSTOCK

Yellow Bridge

During the tourism slump of the COVID-19 pandemic, however, prices plummeted when many islanders turned their attention from hospitality to seaweed and, due to increased production, profits dropped by about 75%. Towards the end of 2023, dried seaweed was netting only about 10,000Rp per kilogram.

E-Bike Adventure

Pedal-tour Lembongan

Diving, snorkelling and surfing might be Lembongan's biggest drawcards, but there are some intriguing places to visit on the island too. **Bali E-Bike Tours** *(baliebiketours.com; 4hr tours per person 600,000Rp)* has strung together a 23km route that takes in some of these spots and makes for a fun way to get to know the island.

The tour starts at **Mushroom Bay**; the first stop is **Dream Beach** and the rugged wave-pounded chasm known as Devil's Tears; you'll then visit the unusual **Gala-Gala Underground House** (p37), which was hand-dug into the limestone by one man in the 1960s and '70s – visitors can climb in and emerge through a separate entrance. A cycle over the iconic (if heart-stoppingly narrow) **Yellow Bridge** will put you on Nusa Ceningan to meet with a family of seaweed farmers. The shallow water that stretches half a kilometre between Lembongan and Ceningan is almost entirely patchworked by seaweed farms, and it's insightful to learn more about the gruelling work that goes into maintaining these.

Other stops on the tour include one of the oldest and most beautiful traditional family compounds on Lembongan, a death temple (where you'll learn about the intricacies of temple architecture), and the mangroves (p112). Lembongan is not big; it measures just 5km at its widest part. While it rises to only 50m above sea level there are some steep hills; however, the Indonesian-made Polygon e-bikes make for almost effortless cruising, for any level of fitness.

Beyond Nusa Lembongan

Nusa Penida and the little sliver of 4km-long Nusa Ceningan have crowd-free beaches and an even more laid-back and local feel.

Barely 1km wide, the coral outcrop that is Nusa Ceningan (sandwiched in between Nusa Lembongan and Nusa Penida) offers surprisingly varied landscapes with forested hilltops, sprawling mangrove forests, dramatic cliff views and gorgeous beaches. Nusa Ceningan is connected to Nusa Lembongan via the iconic and narrow Yellow Bridge, which is accessible to scooters, bike and foot only from Nusa Lembongan.

A short boat ride away is Nusa Penida, by far the largest of the three islands (it's 25 times the size and has 12 times the population of Nusa Lembongan). Here a series of steeply forested ridges and ravines rise to an elevation of 524m. It's dry and arid (at least in comparison with Bali), but Penida has remained relatively undeveloped in terms of tourism. However, that doesn't mean hordes of tourists don't come on organised day trips to snap photos of its gorgeous views. At times the traffic of slow-moving tour cars on narrow lanes is unbearable. Those who stay longer can avoid the popular day-trip sites, find remote views and settle into the wonderfully slow island pace.

Nusa Penida

TIME FROM NUSA LEMBONGAN: **15MIN** 

Temple beneath the earth

Deep within a beachside hill in Nusa Penida's Suana district there is a rather unusual temple. **Pura Goa Giri Putri** *(entry free, but expected donation around 20,000Rp)* is located in a cave, and to reach it is an adventure in itself. After wrapping a sarong around you *(rental from shop 10,000Rp)*, you will need to climb 110 steps from the car park before you are blessed by a Hindu priest in a short purification ritual.

The temple is entered by crouching and wiggling through a narrow gap (which larger people will struggle with) between boulders that form its gateway. The entrance can be claustrophobic, but once inside there's no more squeezing – the ceiling reaches the size of a triple-storey house in places, and the cave's size is astounding, with several chambers connected in a natural cave system. Electric lighting has

Places

Nusa Penida p115
Nusa Ceningan p117

GETTING AROUND

On Ceningan you can rent a scooter or walk around. Boats from Nusa Penida run from the Yellow Bridge *(per person from 50,000Rp)* and have no fixed departures; they leave between 6.30am and 5pm when there are more than 10 passengers. The same applies at beach port Toya Pakeh in Pedina (expect to wade a little to get on and off the boat). From Bali you can take a boat from Sanur *(baliferries.com; fares vary)*. On Penida there's no care rental or public transport; book a local driver or rent a scooter *(per day from 100,000Rp)*. Roads are particularly bad in the southwest and there can be a lot of traffic.

SECRET VIEWPOINTS ON NUSA PENIDA

Saren Cliff Point: The rough road means walking the last half-kilometre, but you'll get views of Penida's craggy coastline and churning turquoise bays.

Pura Gunung Cemeng: Off-the-radar temple with unadulterated views of Penida's ragged coastline. Walk 1km from Sebuluh village.

Pantai Tembeling: Where tropical rainforest meets the sea, with a cave and refreshing spring water pools. Hire a local for the perilous drive down.

Pantai Lumangan: Mantas can often be seen here from above. Steps were recently cut so you can now access the beach – it's worth the walk.

Teletubbies Hill: For something entirely different, Teletubbies Hill has rolling green pastures and lovely quiet walking paths.

GANGOO/SHUTTERSTOCK

Kelingking

been fitted here, but it can still be dark and spooky in parts while you walk past atmospheric stations of prayer, which echo around the cave.

This is an important place of pilgrimage for Balinese Hindus, and there are almost always worshippers at the shrines; while you should respect their prayers and speak quietly, you will be more than welcome to pass through. Around the cave you are likely to see swiftlets, bats, spiders, cave crickets and, if you are very fortunate, you might catch sight of a rare orange-pincered Giri Putri cave crab. Unknown to science until 1993, this critically endangered species is found nowhere else on Earth.

Epic views, beaches and hills

Dozens cross the channel between Nusa Lembongan and Nusa Pedina (or come direct from Sanur) to spend a day posing next to the island's breathtaking scenic spots. Among these is **Kelingking** on the west coast, a picture-perfect rock covered in greenery that looks like a T-rex jutting off the mainland. It's offset by turquoise waters and pristine ivory sands. To get to the beach, there's a walk down around 1000 steep steps (don't underestimate the climb back up – it takes roughly two hours to do the whole round-trip hike). Come at mid-tide or high tide for a good stretch of sand.

EATING ON NUSA PENIDA & NUSA CENINGAN

Three Island Bar: Enjoy budget Indonesian classics like *sate ayam* (chicken satay) and *nasi goreng* with gorgeous views over Nusa Ceningan coast. *9am-7pm* **$**

Suku Beach Club (p112): The most chic spot in the area, with a large pool and cliff-edge views, fancy cocktails and imported steaks. *8am-9pm* **$$$**

Penida Colada (p114): A very eco-conscious Nusa Pedina beachfront cafe with a broad menu of healthy foods and excellent cocktails. *8am-11pm* **$$**

Cactus Beach Club: In Nusa Penida, chill beside the pool or in the breezy chic cafe, and feast on Asian-influenced Mediterranean dishes. *11am-10pm* **$$**

NUSA CENINGAN SCOOTER TOUR

Cruise this mini-island on two wheels.

START	END	LENGTH
Yellow Bridge	Mahana Point	6.5km; 1–2hr

Experience the laid-back vibe of tiny Nusa Ceningan by visiting some of the viewpoints around this deceptively hilly 6.5-sq-km island. Start at the iconic 1 **Yellow Bridge** (p114) that connects Nusa Lembongan and Nusa Ceningan, and head for 2 **Three Island Bar** (p116) on the crest of Ceningan. The view of Nusa Penida from its infinity pool is fantastic. Ignore Google Maps, which will guide you up a particularly steep lane, and instead turn right from the bridge and then drive 750m to where the road forks and take the sharp left. This road leads up Ceningan's spine to Three Island Bar. It's good in some places, decidedly rough in others, but nothing a scooter can't handle. Head back down the way you came, then turn right at the fork. The 3 **Island Beach Bar**, just 120m back along this road, has a pool and beach-club vibe, and views of the seaweed farms and Nusa Lembongan. Next stop is 4 **Twilight** (p118) near the southwest tip of the island. It's also a small restaurant with a pool, but it has a very different view as it faces west towards Bali; this is a good spot for a lazy afternoon coffee. Backtrack 200m, then wind your way towards Insta-famous 5 **Blue Lagoon**. Some of the cliffs have been wrapped in concrete pillars to protect the resort built atop them, so for something more spectacular follow the signs to 6 **Arna Ocean Lounge** (p119) for chilled beats and an infinity pool overlooking the cliff edge. Final stop – exceptional for sunsets – is 7 **Mahana Point** (p112), a warung and bar perched dramatically on a clifftop. There are brilliant views of the surf point below.

TRADITIONAL WEAVERS AT WORK

In the hills of remote southeast Nusa Penida is the village of **Tanglad**, which is revered for its weaving traditions. The skills and knowledge have been passed down through generations, and textiles made here end up in clothes worn by many politicians and celebrities.

Tanglad resident Ngurah Hendrawan is an acclaimed dyer who uses only natural ingredients to colour his threads. He makes red from the root bark of his *mengkudu* trees *(Morinda citrifolia)*, and browns from mahogany bark. His wife weaves textiles on a backstrap loom next to their **Ngurah Gallery shop** *(instagram.com/ngurahcepuk tenunalami)* in the village, where you can buy their wares. If you'd like to see his dying process, Ngurah will gladly show you.

GUITAR PHOTOGRAPHER/SHUTTERSTOCK

Diamond Beach

On the east, **Diamond Beach** *(45,000Rp)* offers a similarly dramatic view with two diamond-shaped rocks off the coast, but is far less crowded. It's more of a viewpoint than a beach to enjoy, but for sunbathing and swimming, you can head to the next-door **Atuh Beach**. For marine-life spotting, popular dive and snorkelling spot **Crystal Bay** is loved by Bali day-trippers, who come for the opaque waters, vibrant marine life and the chance to catch a glimpse of *Mola mola*. You can also often see them swimming in the depths from **Pantai Lumangan**, overlooking Manta Bay. **Broken Beach**, meanwhile, has a big natural archway that wraps around the bay; at high tide it's possible to avoid the heavy local traffic and charter-cruise a boat to it (ask at any of the harbours).

It's even better when the sun is setting.

DRINKING ON NUSA CENINGAN: OUR PICKS

Twilight: The cocktails here are excellent value, and you can sip on them with a view across the ocean to Bali. *10am-10pm*

Park Cave Ceningan: A scenic spot for a Bintang beer or fruit juice. It's up on Ceningan's hill, overlooking Nusa Penida. *7am-7pm*

Mahana Point (p112): Grab a beer on a terrace overlooking the surf break and cliff-jumping spot below. *7am-8.30pm*

Sea Breeze: It's rustic vibes and affordable cocktails at this casual tropical-style bar. Good regular happy-hour deals. *7.30am-11pm*

Places We Love to Stay

$ Budget $$ Midrange $$$ Top End

Sanur
MAP p89

Kubu di Kayla $ Sanur's best-value budget rooms offer no frills but easy access to the beach, an eight-minute walk away.

Puri Mesari $$ Spacious, cosy rooms surround a pool and gardens with walkways intersected by fish ponds. It's a five-minute walk from Mertasari Beach and has a casual restaurant.

Laghawa Beach Inn Hotel $$ An old Bali-style hotel with large rooms (each with a verandah) and gorgeous garden. While there is one step onto the verandah, the hotel is popular with those who have mobility issues.

Villa Ivaya 8 $$ Stylish villa with architectural design, tropical gardens and a pool at its centre and a handful of immaculate rooms with terraces. Great value.

Tandjung Sari Hotel $$$ Family-owned boutique hotel built in the 1960s by an Indonesian-Dutch artist. It's on the beach, and comprised of cottages surrounded by a verdant garden. (p90)

Segara Village Hotel $$$ A spacious, luxury beachfront resort surrounded by large trees and a plush garden.

Denpasar
MAP p93

Bali Inna Heritage Hotel $ Dating to 1927, has hosted celebrities and royalty. Past its prime, but still retains some of its charm. Good, clean option in the capital. (p93)

Uluwatu
MAP p97

Uluwatu Surf Villas $$$ Loved by families, this clifftop resort comprising modern villas has soaring ocean views. A skate park and yoga shala add to the appeal.

Bingin

Temple Lodge $$ Dreamy, eclectic suites with a surf-and-yoga vibe, and sea views from Uluwatu to Kuta.

Mû Bungalows Boutique Resort $$$ This laid-back boutique-style resort is perched atop a cliff. There's a bohemian feel here, and stunning views from the pool and restaurant.

Anantara Uluwatu $$$ Incredible views abound from this luxury resort. It's built on the edge of Uluwatu's cliffs; some suites have infinity pools and spa baths with ocean views.

Jimbaran

Bali Bobo Hostel $ Clean, characterful hostel for a budget community feel; mixed dorm rooms and a pool. Not much around, so scooter or Grab are needed.

Open House $$$ This neat, contemporary hotel has a laid-back beach-house vibe. It's 100m from a cluster of seafood restaurants.

Nusa Dua

Laguna $$$ A big, beachfront resort built around seven pools. Perfect for a chilled luxury holiday.

Nusa Lembongan
MAP p110

Pondok Jenggala $ Offering excellent value, this small guesthouse has large, simple rooms set around a deep pool.

Isla Indah Retreat $$ A tropical, mid-range boutique just off Pantai Jungutbatu. There's a yoga space, surf shop and good cafe on-site.

Bali Hai Villa $$$ The luxurious two-bedroom open-air villas have a swimming pool and lounge area. The best face Mushroom Beach.

Batu Karang $$$ This peaceful, sustainable boutique hotel has gorgeous views over Pantai Jungutbatu and Bali's Gunung Agung.

Nusa Penida

Deep Roots Dive & Yoga Resort $$$ A peaceful getaway just 15 minutes from Penida's coastline. Tasteful airy rooms with natural features.

Nusa Ceningan

Tatak Bunut Private Villa $$ Five wooden bungalows dotted around a pool at the top of Nusa Ceningan's tranquil hills.

Ceningan Divers $$ This sustainable dive centre has six cosy bungalows in a peaceful, waterside setting, surrounded by mangroves.

Aurora Beach View $$ The simple rooms, restaurant and pool have gorgeous views over the bay to Nusa Lembongan.

Arna Suites and Ocean Lounge $$$ Boutique luxury camping in air-conditioned tents on a cliff edge.

For places to stay in the Ubud Region, see p155

ALIONA_25/SHUTTERSTOCK

Above: Ceking Rice Terraces (p144); Right: Monkey Forest (p134)

Researched by
Marco Ferrarese

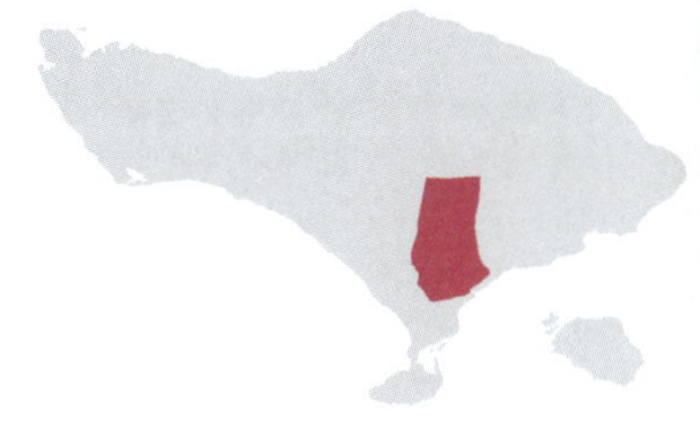

Ubud Region

TEMPLES, ARTS AND INDULGENCE

One of Bali's most popular regions, Ubud has transformed from a rice field and jungle-hemmed village into a busy hub for expats, yogis and digital nomads.

High chances are that if one is Bali-bound, Ubud is going to feature on the itinerary. Welcome to the famed town where all that is magical about Bali comes together in one very popular package – maybe a tad too much, judging from the never-ending gridlock of fume-belching cars stuck along Jl Raya in Ubud town. It is on this central street that temples and traditional buildings rub walls with an endless parade of cafes, restaurants and bars touting menus spanning almost every colour of the world's dining palette.

ROBERT HARDING VIDEO/SHUTTERSTOCK

Breathe in. There's certainly much to love about Ubud's centre: from nightly cultural performances of some of Bali's most entrancing dances to museums celebrating the works of artists whose creativity flowered here, to the impossibly green rice fields that – beyond impossibly overdeveloped alleys – spill down lush hillsides to rushing rivers below. Breathe out. This is also where you'll witness firsthand how the effects of overtourism have changed the authentic Balinese essence of this place to accommodate international travellers' *Eat Pray Love* fantasies.

There's nothing wrong with satisfying some personal cravings by diving into Ubud's ample choice of delicious dining, shopping, spas, yoga shalas and more. But its full charm, attested by the size of Ubud's expat community, may be hard to detect on a quick visit to the town – look north and south of Ubud, where quieter backroads lead to famed ancient temples, archaeological sites, traditional artisans' studios ... and fewer tourists.

THE MAIN AREAS

UBUD
Intoxicating mix of sacred and profane. p124

BEYOND UBUD (NORTH)
Ancient sites, water temples and rice terraces. p144

BEYOND UBUD (SOUTH)
Former kingdoms and masters of handicrafts. p149

Find Your Way

The Ubud region stretches from near the coast to the north, up Gunung Batur. Main roads become steeper as one approaches the mountain. After at least a day in Ubud, take day trips or find a quieter place to lay low.

ON FOOT

Ubud and the surrounding countryside are easily covered on foot. Villages such as Pejeng, Bedulu, Tampaksiring and Taro can be explored on walks. Longer distances are more of a challenge owing to busy roads.

MOTORBIKE & CAR

The region is best explored with the freedom of your own wheels, whether you or someone else does the driving. Motorbikes are particularly handy to weave through traffic and park in Ubud's very narrow streets.

Ubud, p124
The Bali destination for (too) many. A hub for accommodation, activities, personal growth and masterfully choreographed cultural performances.

TOSE/SHUTTERSTOCK

Pura Gunung Kawi Sebatu (p147)

Plan Your Time

Time in Ubud proper may become an enjoyable blur, but save some days to take in the many sights north and south of the town.

Only One Day

Stroll the streets of Ubud, starting with its **palace** (p124) complex and the **Monkey Forest** (p134). Pause at a cafe and browse the shops on Jl Dewi Sita and Jl Hanoman. Make time for a **museum** (p127) filled with the art for which Ubud is famous. Then venture into verdant **rice fields** (p127). Enjoy an evening meal followed by a **dance performance** (p130).

A Week or More

Get in tune with Ubud's rhythm: nap, read, wander about. Take long walks in the countryside in the morning and visit art museums in the afternoon. Try a **course** (p135) in Balinese culture. Head north to ancient sites like **Gunung Kawi** (p147), and explore the wonders of **Pejeng** (p149) and **Bedulu** (p150). Look for handicrafts in villages like **Mas** (p151) and **Sukawati** (p153).

SEASONAL HIGHLIGHTS

DECEMBER–FEBRUARY

School holidays bring many visitors. Lodgings, restaurants and many activities are booked solid. Rain is common.

MARCH–MAY

Mountain breezes make air-con unnecessary at night – enjoy a symphony of frogs, bugs and distant gamelan echoing across rice fields.

JUNE–AUGUST

Temperatures average 30°C by day and 20°C at night; extremes are possible. July and August are peak tourism months.

SEPTEMBER–NOVEMBER

October to April, it's cooler and wetter than in the south. October's Ubud Writers & Readers Festival (p136) is popular.

Ubud

ART & CULTURE | NATURE | CAFES & DINING

GETTING AROUND

From South Bali, Ubud is reached by various routes via Denpasar or Sanur. Expect the trip from the airport to take anything from 90 minutes to two hours or more, depending on traffic. Other than the odd tourist bus, most visitors arrive in a rented car.

Much of central Ubud is walkable. For trips further afield, you will see local taxi drivers holding up signs, but negotiations can be a costly hassle and rides are not metered. The ubiquitous Gojek and Grab apps provide easy access to rides.

TOP TIP

To avoid the worst of the traffic from Denpasar, drive to Ubud via Canggu's Pererenan using the back road Jl Raya Tangeb to Mengwi. Continue east on Jl Raya Puspa Resti and north on Jl Raya Mambal Semana to access Ubud's western side.

Ubud is one of those places where a few days can easily turn into a stay of weeks, months – even years for some. Carefully developed over the decades, the town's reputation for art and culture is well deserved. This is a place where Balinese traditions imbue every waking moment, where colourful offerings adorn the streets, and where the hypnotic strains of gamelan are an ever-present soundtrack to everyday life. It's also somewhere that is relentlessly on trend – a showcase of sustainable design, mindfulness, culinary inventiveness and personal development, be it through yoga or a more esoteric pursuit.

Ubud is also very popular – suffocatingly so. Ubud draws people with creative visions from across Bali and the world. But there's always an escape into a gallery, a hidden cafe or along a rice-field path. Come here for relaxation, rejuvenation and self-fulfilment, and revel in all Ubud has to offer.

Visit Ubud's Palace

MAP p128

Wander amid glitter and sculpture

The modest **Ubud Palace** and **Puri Saren Agung** *(free)* temple share a compound in the heart of Ubud. Most of the structures were built after the 1917 earthquake and the local royal family still lives here. Despite the name, this sprawling compound is not palatial or excessively ornate. Rather, it's a warren of courtyards and traditional Balinese buildings that extend well beyond the limited area open to visitors.

Stone carvings are a highlight. Many are by notable Ubud artists such as I Gusti Nyoman Lempad (1862–1978) and can be easily appreciated on a brief visit. At night, the palace's main courtyard is a popular and evocative venue for dance performances. One way to gain access to the inner sanctum is to stay in one of two midrange guest rooms hidden inside (search for 'Istana Saren Kauh Ubud' on Airbnb). This way, you can rise with the roosters in the morning, feel the rhythms of the royal compound and observe traditional Balinese life.

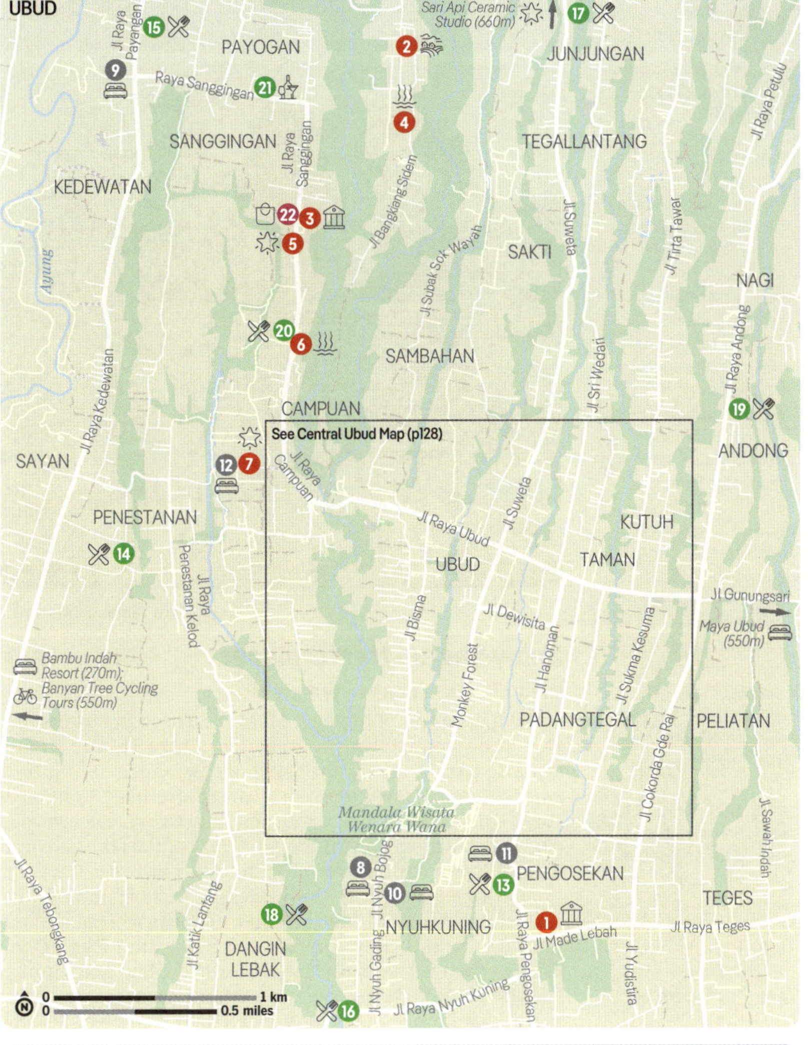

SIGHTS
1 Agung Rai Museum of Art
2 Bangkiang Sidem
3 Neka Art Museum

ACTIVITIES
see 1 ARMA
4 Karsa Spa
5 Powder Room
6 Rob Peetom's Hair Spa
7 Wayan Karja

SLEEPING
8 Alam Indah Ubud
9 Mandapa
10 Swasti Eco Cottages
11 Tegal Sari
12 Villa Nirvana

EATING
13 Merlin's
14 Moksa
15 Nasi Ayam Kedewatan Ibu Mangku
16 Outpost Ubud Coworking
17 Raw Temple
18 The Hidden Space Ubud Cafe
19 Ubud Co-Working
20 Warung Pulau Kelapa

DRINKING & NIGHTLIFE
21 Kawi

ENTERTAINMENT
see 1 ARMA Museum & Resort
see 1 Ubud Village Jazz Festival

SHOPPING
22 Biasa Ubud

UBUD'S ARTFUL HISTORY

Late in the 19th century, Cokorda Gede Agung Sukawati established a branch of the Sukawati royal family in Ubud and began a series of alliances and confrontations with neighbouring kingdoms. In 1900, with the kingdom of Gianyar, Ubud became (at its own request) a Dutch protectorate and was able to concentrate on its religious and cultural life. The Cokorda descendants encouraged Western artists and intellectuals to visit the area in the 1930s, most notably Walter Spies, Colin McPhee and Rudolf Bonnet. They provided an enormous stimulus to local art, introduced new ideas and began promoting Balinese culture worldwide. As mass tourism arrived in Bali, Ubud became an attraction not for beaches or bars, but for the arts.

SEAN HSU/SHUTTERSTOCK

Pura Taman Saraswati

Enjoy Sacred Masterpieces

MAP p128

Visit Ubud's evocative temples

Ubud has dozens of temples. Most are closed to visitors, but there are some noteworthy exceptions. **Pura Taman Saraswati** *(Ubud Water Palace; ubudwaterpalace.com; adult/child 35,000/25,000Rp)* is the most picturesque. Right off Jl Raya Ubud, it provides a welcome relief from the crowded sidewalks. Waters flowing from the rear of the large site feed a pond in front, overflowing with lotus blossoms. Carvings honour Dewi Saraswati, the goddess of wisdom and the arts who clearly blesses Ubud. Regular dance performances are staged at night. Only 100m to the east, quiet **Pura Desa Ubud** *(free)* is the main temple for the Ubud community. It's often closed, but it comes alive for the extravagant ceremonies and processions for which Ubud is known. Stop by to see if something is on.

From Pura Desa Ubud it's a 10-minute walk west along Jl Raya Ubud and the start of Jl Raya Campuan to **Pura Gunung Lebah** *(free)*, which sits on a jutting rock at the confluence of two tributaries of Sungai Cerik (*campuan* means 'two rivers'). One of Ubud's oldest temples, it's thought to date to the 8th century. The setting, far below street level in a lush gorge, is magical: listen to rushing waters while admiring the impressive *meru* (multi-tiered shrine) and a wealth of elaborate carvings. You can easily spend an hour or more wandering paths around the temple, its flowing waters and surrounding hillsides.

Try Ubud's Quintessential Hike

Strike out on the Campuhan Ridge Walk

Walking green hills, lush river valleys and rolling rice fields is a top Ubud activity. Surprises abound, from finding idiosyncratic artists at work in a trailside hut, to a sensational little juice stand where everything's organic.

A classic Ubud walking route is the **Campuhan Ridge Walk** *(campuhanridgewalk.com; free)*, which is easy and gives a good taste of what you'll enjoy on future perambulations. Following this paved trail along a ridge between two rivers is a popular sunrise and sunset activity, but it can be enjoyed at any time of the day. Pick up the trail by the driveway of the **Ibah** (p155) hotel and follow walk signs, bearing left where the walkway crosses the Sungai Wos (Wos River), and passing the tranquil Pura Gunung Lebah. Continue north on the concrete path, climbing up onto the Campuhan Ridge between the Wos and Cerik rivers. Fields of elephant grass, traditionally used for thatched roofs, slope away on either side of the path and you'll be able to see the rice fields above Ubud in all of their lush green majesty. Continue uphill past rice fields to the village of **Bangkiang Sidem**, passing little warungs (food stalls) and low-key vendors and artists along the way. Avoid retracing your steps or braving the narrow road by summoning a ride with the Grab or Gojek apps.

TIPS FOR A GOOD WALK

With its endless beauty and delightful discoveries, walking in the Ubud region is a great idea. Consider the following to better enjoy your walk.

Bring water Outlets for snacks and drinks are common, but don't risk dehydration between stops.

Gear up Bring sunscreen, a good hat, decent shoes and wet-weather gear.

Start early Try to begin at daybreak, before it gets too hot.

Freelance Head down any path that catches your eye; you can't get lost, as helpful locals abound.

Quit while ahead Should you tire, don't worry. The point is to enjoy your walk. Locals on motorbikes will give you a ride, or you can summon one with the Gojek and Grab apps.

See an Overview of Balinese Art

MAP p128

Art amid gardens at Museum Puri Lukisan

The modern Balinese art movement started in Ubud when artists abandoned religious and royal themes for scenes of everyday life. Of the various local art museums, **Museum Puri Lukisan** *(purilukisanmuseum.com; adult/child 95,000Rp/free)* is the most enjoyable, even if your interest in art is limited. Its tiered gardens, replete with water features, are lovely.

Four buildings display works from all schools and periods of Balinese art, with a strong focus on modern masters including I Gusti Nyoman Lempad, Ida Bagus Made Poleng and I Gusti Made Kwandji (1936–2013). Artworks are labelled in English, and QR codes link to excellent additional info. You can easily spend an hour or two here. Immediately east, a river path takes you to rice fields behind the museum.

The **East Building** has a collection of early works from Ubud and surrounding villages. These include examples of classical *wayang*-style paintings (art influenced by shadow puppetry)

continued on p132

EATING IN UBUD: BEST WARUNGS

In Da Compound Warung: Behind a family guesthouse on Jl Goutama. Bargain-priced dishes burst with flavour, and bunnies hop about the garden. *11am-10pm* $

Mama's Warung: Expect spicy Indo classics redolent with garlic. Cheery Mama's peanut sauce is silky smooth and the fried sambal is superb. *8am-10pm* $

Nasi Ayam Kedewatan Ibu Mangku: The star of this Bali version of a roadhouse is *sate lilit* (spiced minced chicken, grilled on skewers). *7am-9pm* $

Warung Pulau Kelapa: Huge menu of Indonesian dishes. Sensational sambals. For real spiciness, ask for dishes 'local style'. *10am-11pm* $$

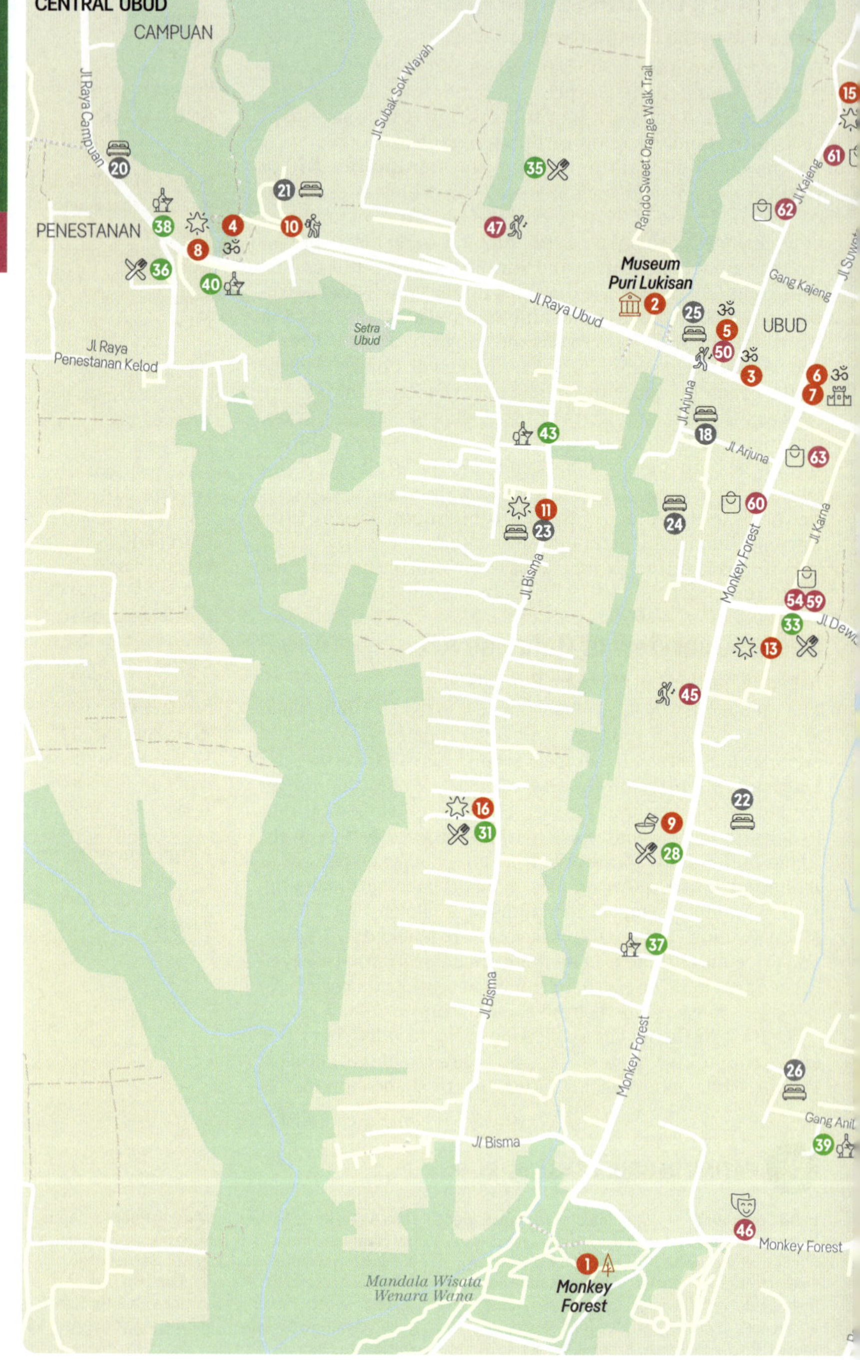
CENTRAL UBUD
CAMPUAN
PENESTANAN
Jl Raya Campuan
Jl Subak Sok Wayah
Rando Sweet Orange Walk Trail
Jl Kajeng
Jl Suweta
Gang Kajeng
UBUD
Museum Puri Lukisan
Jl Raya Ubud
Setra Ubud
Jl Raya Penestanan Kelod
Jl Arjuna
Jl Bisma
Jl Karna
Monkey Forest
Jl Dewi
Gang Anil
Mandala Wisata Wenara Wana
Monkey Forest

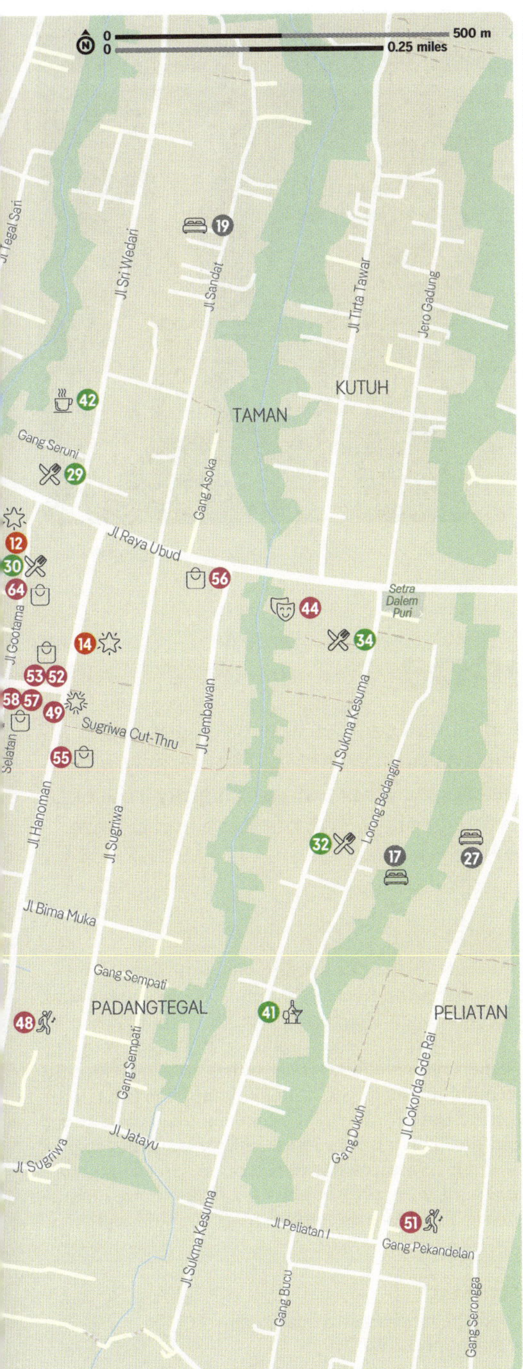

HIGHLIGHTS
1 Monkey Forest
2 Museum Puri Lukisan

SIGHTS
3 Pura Desa Ubud
4 Pura Gunung Lebah
5 Pura Taman Saraswati
6 Puri Saren Agung
7 Ubud Palace

ACTIVITIES
8 Bali Bird Walks
9 Cafe Wayan Cooking Class
10 Campuhan Ridge Walk
11 Casa Luna Cooking School
12 Nirvana Batik Course
13 Pondok Pekak Library & Learning Centre
14 Studio Perak
15 Ubud Botany Interactive
16 Ubud Story Walks

SLEEPING
17 Aji Lodge
18 Arjuna Homestay
19 Capung Cottages
20 Hotel Tjampuhan
21 Ibah
22 Komaneka at Monkey Forest
23 Nick's Pension
24 Okawati Boutique Bungalows
25 Puri Saraswati Dijiwa Bungalows
26 Three Win Homestay
27 Yasa Backpackers House

EATING
28 Honey & Smoke Open Fire Bistro
29 Hujan Locale
30 In Da Compound Warung
31 Littletalks Ubud
32 Mama's Warung
33 Nusantara
34 Sayuri Healing Food Cafe & Academy
35 Ubud.Space Coworking & Coffee
36 Zest

DRINKING & NIGHTLIFE
37 Blue Door
38 Boliche Bar
39 Ibu Susu Bar & Kitchen
40 Lair
41 Lovin Bar
see 37 No Màs
42 Seniman Coffee Studio
43 Why Not

ENTERTAINMENT
44 Bali Culture Workshop
45 Kerta Art
46 Pondok Bamboo Music Shop
47 Pura Dalem Ubud
48 Pura Padang Kerta
49 Pura Penataran Kloncing
50 Pura Taman Saraswati
51 Puri Agung Peliatan
see 7 Ubud Palace

SHOPPING
52 Above the Clouds Natural Wear
53 Ananda Soul
54 Blue Stone Botanicals
55 Curative
56 Ganesha Bookshop
57 Kado by Saraswati Paper
58 Kevala Home
59 Kou
60 Sensatia Botanicals
61 Threads of Life
62 Toko Elami
63 Ubud Art Market
64 Ubud Raw Chocolate

AGP_DREAMS/SHUTTERSTOCK

Legong dance

TOP EXPERIENCE

Balinese Dance

The highlight of an Ubud visit, Balinese dances like the Legong and Kecak flow with a hypnotic grace as performers tell stories rich with the essence of Hindu lore. Multiple shows are staged nightly in Ubud, in a variety of styles. Gamelan music played on bamboo and bronze instruments is an integral part of many.

DON'T MISS

- Semara Ratih
- Gunung Sari
- Semara Madya
- Tirta Sari
- Gamelan performance by Cudamani at Museum Puri Lukisan (p123)

Kecak Dance

Probably the best-known dance for its spellbinding, hair-raising atmosphere, the Kecak features a 'choir' of men and boys who sit in concentric circles and slip into a trance as they chant and sing 'chak-a-chak-a-chak', imitating a troupe of monkeys. Sometimes called the vocal gamelan, this is the only music to accompany the dance re-enactment from the Hindu epic Ramayana, the familiar love story about Prince Rama and Princess Sita. The tourist version of Kecak was developed in the 1960s. The **Semara Madya** troupe *(facebook.com/kecaksemaramadya)* is very famous for its hypnotic chants and performs at **Puri Agung Peliatan** on Thursdays at 7pm.

PRACTICALITIES

- Ubud Palace performances start around 7pm
- General admission price 100,000Rp

Barong & Rangda

The Barong and Rangda dance rivals the Kecak as Bali's most popular performance for tourists. Again, it's a battle between good (the Barong) and bad (the Rangda).

The Barong is a good but mischievous and fun-loving shaggy dog-lion, with huge eyes and a mouth that clacks away. Because this character is the good protector of a village, the actors playing the Barong (who are utterly lost under layers of fur-clad costume) will emote a variety of winsome antics. The Barong is a very sacred character and you'll often see one in processions and rituals.

There's nothing sacred about the Barong's buddies – monkeys who often steal the show. Actors are given free rein, the best aiming a lot of high jinks at the audience. Meanwhile, widow-witch Rangda is bad through and through. The performance of the Queen of Black Magic, the character's monstrous persona, can include flames shooting out of her ears.

The story features a duel between the Rangda and the Barong, whose supporters draw their kris (traditional dagger) and rush in to help. The long-tongued, sharp-fanged Rangda throws them into a trance, making them stab themselves. It's quite a spectacle. Thankfully, the Barong casts a spell that neutralises the power of the kris so it cannot harm them.

Legong Dance

Characterised by flashing eyes and quivering hands, this most graceful of Balinese dances was traditionally performed by young girls (though these days performers are all ages). The dancers' talent is so revered that in old age, a classic dancer will be remembered as a 'great Legong'. The stylised and symbolic story involves two Legong performers dancing in mirror image. They are elaborately made up and dressed in gold brocade, relating a story about a king who takes a maiden captive and consequently starts a war, in which he dies.

Some noteworthy Legong dance troupes include **Semara Ratih** *(semararatih.org)*, which also has great gamelan musicians; pioneer **Gunung Sari** *(peliatan.com/gunungsari)*, founded in 1926; and **Tirta Sari**, performers of both Legong and Barong dance. Catch Gunung Sari at **Puri Agung Peliatan Palace** on Saturdays at 7.30pm.

Kecak Fire Dance

This dance was developed to drive out evil spirits from a village. A male dancer or boy in a trance dances around and through a fire of coconut husks, riding a coconut palm 'hobby horse'. There are many variations of this dance, which are often included as a dramatic, flaming add-on at the end of other performances.

TOP VENUES

Ubud Palace Magical setting with a glittering, ornate backdrop.

Pura Dalem Ubud A temple compound with a flame-lit, carved-stone backdrop.

Pura Taman Saraswati Beautiful temple setting with water features.

ARMA Open Stage (p135) Hosts top troupes.

Puri Agung Peliatan Village hosting serious troupes.

Pura Padang Kerta and **Pura Penataran Kloncing** Convenient venues on Jl Hanoman.

TOP TIPS

- Arrive at least 20 minutes before showtime to get a good seat. Performances last about 90 minutes.
- Snacks, water and beer are often sold inside the venue.
- Be wary of troupes with dirty costumes, disinterested orchestras, performers that break character to tell stale jokes and other hallmarks of a mediocre performance.
- Holding up a bright phone screen to take photographs is very distracting to spectators sitting behind you.
- Leaving in the middle of a performance is extremely rude and an insult to the performers.

UBUD'S FAMOUS PAINTERS

I Gusti Nyoman Lempad (1862–1978) Giant of Balinese art, known for ink drawings conveying movement in a *wayang* style suggestive of shadow puppets.

Ida Bagus Made Poleng (1915–99) Won international competitions in the 1930s. Renowned for his softly coloured depictions of everyday life.

Murni (1966–2006) Famed for her stark, even whimsical depictions of serious issues facing local women.

Walter Spies (1895–1942) This German painter played an important role in promoting Bali's artistic culture in the 1930s.

Arie Smit (1916–2016) Ubud's best-known Western artist. He came to Bali in 1956 and influenced the 1060s Young Artists school of painting in Penestanan.

BELEN SANMA/SHUTTERSTOCK

Agung Rai Museum of Art

continued from p127

from the 10th to 15th centuries. These ancient works have a palette limited to only five colours of pigment that could be produced at the time. Among the impressive 20th-century works is *The Death of Karna* (1935) by I Wayan Tutur. Fine ink drawings by I Gusti Nyoman Lempad and paintings by artists of the Pita Maha school, such as Walter Spies, are displayed in the **North Building**. Don't miss *Temple Festival* (1938) by I Gusti Ketut Kobot (1917–99). Another intricately detailed masterpiece is *The Idiot Who Became King* (1932) by Ida Bagus Made Togog (1913–89), telling the tale of a simple but honest man who became a ruler thanks to divine intervention. Balinese paintings from the 20th century fill the **West Building**. Look for *Barong Dance* (1970) by I Gusti Made Kwandji. Special exhibitions take place in the **South Building**.

Visit an Indonesian Arts Cultural Hub

MAP p125

Admire Ubud's finest masterpieces at ARMA

Agung Rai Museum of Art *(ARMA; armabali.com/museum; adult/child 150,000/free)* is a must-see museum next to the resort of the same name. Founder Agung Rai built his fortune selling Balinese artwork to foreigners in the 1970s, and during his time as a dealer he acquired one of Indonesia's most impressive private collections of art. Highlights displayed include

DRINKING IN UBUD: BEST LIVE MUSIC

Why Not: Feel-good beer bar with live rock, blues and reggae daily, craft beers, cocktails and happy travellers. *3pm-midnight*

Lovin Bar: Tasty food and cocktails in a cosy atmosphere, with live music, open mic and jam sessions in the evening. *8pm-late*

Blue Door: Sports bar with wall-to-ceiling windows, a speakeasy, and bands rocking on the bar-level platform by the entrance. *11am-3am*

No Màs: Upstairs from Liap Liap restaurant, this funky bar has live music daily from 8pm, beer, cocktails and late-night eats. *5pm-1am*

the wonderful 19th-century *Portrait of a Javanese Nobleman and His Wife* by Javanese artist Raden Saleh (1807–80).

Classical Kamasan paintings and Batuan-style works from the 1930s and 1940s are also displayed. Among the artists represented are I Gusti Nyoman Lempad and Ida Bagus Made Poleng, Anak Agung Gede Sobrat (1912–92) and I Gusti Made Deblog (1906–86). In the modern gallery seek out *Green Rice Paddies* (1987) by Nasjah Djamin (1924–99) and *Wild Orchids* (1988) by Widaya (1923–2002).

In the traditional gallery, look for *The Dance Drama Arja* (1990) by I Ketut Kasta (b 1945), *Cremation Ceremony* (1994) by I Ketut Sepi (b 1941) and the extraordinarily detailed *Wali 'Ekadesa Rudra'* (2015) by I Wayan Mardiana (b 1970). The traditional art gallery is also home to a collection of works by expat artist Walter Spies who played a significant role in promoting Ubud's international artistic reputation.

During a visit of an hour or two, you might see local children learning Balinese dance or hear a gamelan practice. The complex also has a hotel and cafe and is a venue for dance performances.

Marvel at a Balinese Art Enthusiast's Collection

MAP p125

Sculptures and paintings at Neka Art Museum

Tucked 2km north along Jl Raya Campuan, the **Neka Art Museum** *(nekaartmuseum.com; adult/child 150,000/75,000Rp)* offers an excellent introduction to Balinese art, with a top-notch collection displayed in a series of pavilions and halls. During your one-hour visit, don't miss the multi-room **Balinese Painting Hall** showcasing *wayang* style and European-influenced Ubud and Batuan styles introduced in the 1920s and 1930s. Also notable are works by the master I Gusti Nyoman Lempad in the **Lempad Pavilion**, and the **East-West Art Annexe** where the artistic prowess of Affandi (1907–90) and Widayat (1919–2002) impress.

The museum is the creation of Suteja Neka, a private collector and dealer in Balinese art. His collection is huge. As well as works by Balinese and Indonesian artists, there are plenty by foreign artists who have called the island home, including Arie Smit, Johan Rudolf Bonnet, Theo Meier, Louise Garrett Koke, Donald Friend and Tay Moh-Leong. The museum's gift shop offers quality local handicrafts and has a good range of books devoted to Balinese art.

TODAY'S TOP BALINESE ARTISTS

Nyoman Masriadi (b 1973) Born in Gianyar, Bali's current painter superstar is renowned for his sharp-eyed observations of Indonesian society.

Made Djirna (b 1957) Ubud's Djirna critiques the relationship between ostentatious money and modern Balinese religious ceremonies.

Agung Mangu Putra (b 1963) His works decry the impact of Bali's tourist boom and its unequal spread of benefits.

Wayan Sudarna Putra (b 1976) Ubud native Putra uses satire to question the absurdities of contemporary Indonesian life.

Gede Suanda Sayur (b 1980) Sayur questions the pillaging of Bali's environment. He helped create an installation in a rice field that spelt out 'Not for sale'.

Go for the char-grilled lamb skewer.

EATING IN UBUD: TOP-END RESTAURANTS

Nusantara: Boldly flavoured, highly spiced dishes by the legendary Locavore team. *noon-2.30pm & 6-9.30pm Tue-Sun, 6-9.30pm Mon* **$$$**

Hujan Locale: Chef Will Meyrick serves creative Indonesian in an open-air dining room. Passion fruit cocktails are addictive. *noon-3pm & 5.30-10pm* **$$$**

Merlin's: Immersive dining experience paired with magic: draw tarot cards to find which food 'chooses you'. Reserve. *2-11pm* **$$$**

Honey & Smoke Open Fire Bistro: From flatbread to veggies, everything is flame-grilled using ancient Ottoman fire-smoke techniques. *noon-11pm* **$$$**

TOP EXPERIENCE

Monkey Forest

A top destination for day-trippers from across Bali, the Sacred Monkey Forest Sanctuary was once a shady expanse, home to three temples and a troop of over 1000 well-fed and light-fingered monkeys. Today, its flashy theme-park-like entrance awaits tour buses at the south end of the eponymous road – you'll be hard-pressed to realise that this is a sacred place.

ADWO/SHUTTERSTOCK

TOP TIPS

- Escape the worst of the crowds by visiting early or late in the day.
- Monkeys smell food. If you have any, don't hide it. In case of an 'attack', surrender it.
- Avoid visiting with children who may not understand the dangers.

PRACTICALITIES

- monkeyforestubud.com
- adult/child 100,000/80,000rp
- 9am-6pm, last entry 5pm

Stick to the Essentials

Ignore stunts like the 'mysterious' tunnel at the entrance and follow the paths to the holiest of the temples, **Pura Dalem Agung**, where the entrance to the inner temple features Rangda figures devouring children. Trails lead down a ravine to a cool and serene river valley.

Although heavily promoted at the entrance, the attraction's app offers little to enhance a visit. Expect to spend about an hour visiting.

Beware of the Monkeys

You can't miss the grey-haired and greedy long-tailed Balinese macaques who are nothing like the innocent-looking, doe-eyed primates in social media shots. They can bite, so be careful – the best course of action is a full rabies treatment. Watch all your belongings carefully, including glasses, phones, bags and anything sticking out of your pockets. Never feed the monkeys, lest you set off a frenzy. If a monkey climbs on your bag or back, don't panic – assuming you aren't carrying any food, it will leave soon enough.

Paper and plastic bags are a big no-no near monkeys, as is running, screaming or staring at them directly in the eyes – they consider it a sign of challenge and may attack.

Wayang kulit

Check Out a Shadow Puppet Show

MAP p128

An evening of Indonesian light artistry

Look for *wayang kulit* (shadow puppet) performances in Ubud, attenuated to a manageable 90 minutes or less. Watching this low-tech artistry in action makes for an enthralling evening. **Bali Culture Workshop** *(balicultureworkshop.com; 100,000Rp)*, inside the very central Oka Kartini BnB, stages popular evening shows at 8pm on Wednesday, Friday and Sunday. Reserve tickets in advance. Short programmes are also performed on Monday and Thursday at 8pm at **Pondok Bamboo Music Shop** *(WhatsApp +62 361 974 807; 100,000Rp)*, in the southern end of town.

Learn Something New

MAP p125, p128

Courses in art, dance and culture

Ubud is the perfect place to develop your creative skills, discover your inner artist and plunge into the wonders of Balinese culture. The range of courses offered could keep you busy for a year.

ARMA Museum & Resort *(armabali.com/cultural-workshops; from 100,000Rp)* is a veritable college of Balinese culture and creativity. Classes include painting, silver jewellery, woodcarving, gamelan and batik as well as Balinese dance and offering-making. **Museum Puri Lukisan** *(purilukisanmuseum.com/museum-puri-lukisan-workshop.html; from 100,000Rp)* and **Neka Art Museum** (p133; *from 100,000Rp*) offer similar courses.

Threads of Life *(threadsoflife.com; from 670,000Rp)* transports students from its exquisite Jl Kajeng shop to its nearby studio to learn the traditional techniques of creating batik with natural dyes. The non-profit is renowned for its work preserving age-old textile skills from across Indonesia. Personalised

INDONESIA'S TRADITIONAL SHADOW PLAYS

Much more than sheer entertainment, *wayang kulit* has been Bali's candlelit village cinema for centuries. Embodying the sacred seriousness of classical Greek drama, traditional performances were long and intense, lasting six hours or more and often not finishing before sunrise. Originally used to bring ancestors back to this world, shows feature painted buffalo-hide puppets believed to have great spiritual power. The *dalang* (puppet master and storyteller) is an almost mystical figure, sitting behind a screen and manipulating the puppets while telling the story, often in dialects. Stories are chiefly derived from Hindu epics like the Ramayana. Find shortened performances nightly in Ubud.

UBUD'S BEST EVENTS

Ubud Writers & Readers Festival: Southeast Asia's major literary event draws writers and readers from around the world for a five-day celebration in October. *ubud writersfestival.com*

Ubud Open Studios: Two-day celebration in March, with over 70 local artists opening their studios to visitors. Many special events. *ubudopenstudios.com*

BaliSpirit Festival: A popular yoga, dance and music festival in May, with hundreds of workshops, concerts and more. *balispiritfestival.com*

Ubud Village Jazz Festival: Annual two-day jazz festival in late July featuring an international line-up of performers. *ubudvillagejazz festival.com*

Ubud Food Festival: Diverse and delicious Indonesian cuisine takes centre stage at this three-day festival in late June or July. *ubudfoodfestival.com*

OKA DIANA/SHUTTERSTOCK

Silversmithing class

training in ceramics at an open-air workshop and kiln is offered at the long-running **Sari Api Ceramic Studio** *(sariapi.com/classes; 15hr intensive course 4,500,000Rp)* offers, while **Studio Perak** *(WhatsApp +62 081 2365 1809; 3hr lesson 250,000Rp)* specialises in Balinese-style silversmithing courses. During a three-hour lesson, expect to make at least one finished piece; classes can be geared to children.

Learn how to combine and refine locally grown plants and herbs into healthful potions and lotions during a botanical workshop at **Ubud Botany Interactive** *(ubudbotany.com; from 300,000Rp)*. It also offers tours exploring Ubud's flora.

A community treasure (and great place to refill your waterbottle), **Pondok Pekak Library & Learning Centre** *(pondokpekak.com/ubud-art-classes; from 200,000Rp)*, on the far side of the football field, offers a shady refuge from the tourist scrum. Its group and individual courses cover Balinese dance, gamelan, carving and offering-making. No matter your age, **Kerta Art** *(Ayu +62 822 3629 4995; 150,000Rp per class)* offers an in-depth Balinese classic-dance class on Friday and contemporary Balinese dance on Saturday. Classes at **Bali Culture Workshop** (p135; *balicultureworkshop.com; from 200,000Rp)* cover shadow puppets, offering-making and dance.

Some of Ubud's most rewarding classes are taught by resident experts in their own homes. Abstract artist **Wayan Karja** *(wayankarja.com)* offers intensive painting and drawing classes in his studio behind Penestanan's Santra Putra guesthouse. The long-running **Nirvana Batik Course** *(nirvanaku.com/batik.html; from 450,000Rp)* combines design skills with the personal discipline needed to craft intricate textiles in the family home of Ubud-born Nyoman.

Cultivate Culinary Creations

MAP p125, p128

Learn how to recreate Balinese flavours

Ubud cooking classes often start at the local produce morning market, set deep within the modern **Ubud Art Market** (p141). You'll learn about the huge range of fruits, vegetables and other foods that are part of the Balinese diet.

The famous **Casa Luna Cooking School** *(casalunacooking school.com; from 450,000Rp)* has a full menu of classes. Half-day courses have a different theme each day of the week and cover a range of dishes.

The basics of Balinese spices and cuisine are the focus of two-hour courses at long-running **Cafe Wayan Cooking Class** *(cafewayan.com/cooking-classes; 450,000Rp)*. The lesson plan varies each day and you get to eat your work for lunch – an inducement to excel.

Or learn from master Balinese chef Wayan Manis in her home kitchen, preparing iconic dishes for a dinner feast using traditional ingredients and a wood stove. Book through travelingspoon.com. For the sweet-toothed, fun and idiosyncratic sweets vendor **Powder Room** *(room4dessert.com/r4d-academy; from 6,265,0000Rp or $400 per person without accommodation)* offers weekly and monthly sweet-making courses.

For coffee lovers, caffeine fanatics at **Seniman Coffee Studio** *(senimancoffee.com/workshop; 450,000Rp)* teach about all things Java (and Bali) in in-depth classes on espresso-making, latte art, manual brewing methods and cupping (the art of tasting and rating coffee).

Embrace a Guided Adventure

MAP p125, p128

Join an Ubud walking or biking tour

Spending a few hours exploring with a local expert is a fabulous way to savour Ubud and its region. Specialised tours in Ubud include thematic walks and cultural adventures.

Perhaps the best two to three hours you'll spend locally is on a remarkably detailed and entertaining tour covering Balinese culture and history with **Ubud Story Walks** *(ubud storywalks.com; from 350,000Rp)*. Learn about Ubud's past and present, the unsung wonders of temples in Pejeng, the works of legendary artist I Gusti Nyoman Lempad, and more.

You could also spend the early morning exploring old villages and landscapes before sunrise with Agung Rai,

BEST COWORKING CAFES

Meet and greet other digital nomads at these Ubud hotspots.

Outpost Ubud Coworking: Three-storey villas with a cafe, pool and private call booths. Hosted lunches Wed and Fri are good for networking. *24hr*

Littletalks Ubud: Small, peaceful library cafe near Campuhan Ridge with fast internet and a good setup for focused work. *7am-10pm*

Ubud.Space Coworking & Coffee: Quiet yet super central, with wooden tables and luminous windows hemmed by greenery. *9am-11.30pm*

Ubud Co-Working: Spacious, with private working spaces, high-speed internet and rice-field views. *8am-11pm*

The Hidden Space Ubud Cafe: Not a nomadic space per se, but a quiet cafe with good food and cosy area to work. *9am-6pm Mon-Sat*

DRINKING IN UBUD: BEST COCKTAILS

Boliche Bar: On the site of Cantina Rooftop, this stylish, top-end cocktail bar draws on local flavours for offbeat drinks. *8pm-2am Thu-Sat*

Kawi ('Poet' in Sanskrit): Inventive drinks, using local ingredients like *arak* infused with dried bananas. Narrow bar, chill garden. *7pm-midnight Mon-Sat*

Lair: Look for the boho sign pointing down at Campuhan Bridge. Within earshot of the flowing river, with primitive decor, sophisticated drinks and snacks. *7pm-midnight*

Ibu Susu Bar & Kitchen: Excellent, well-presented cocktails like pomelo negroni, fusing Southeast Asian tastes with international mixology. *noon-midnight*

A PERFECT DAY IN UBUD

Janet DeNeefe, director of Ubud Writers & Readers Festival *@janetdeneefe*

I love to stroll along the Tjampuhan Ridge for some village life, lush greenery and remnants of old Bali. Starting in Tjampuhan, descend alongside **Pura Gunung Lebah** (p126) and onto **Bangkiang Sidem** (p127).

I usually stop at **Karsa Spa** (p142), where I enjoy a fruit salad and Bali coffee by their glorious lotus pond.

Continue through Lungsiakan, heading towards Jl Raya and eventually to Sanggingan, where the **Neka Art Museum** (p133) is.

Sanggingan is becoming Ubud's Art District, an exciting mix of creativity, style and sophistication. Check out chic designer boutiques like **Biasa Ubud** and maybe pamper yourself at **Rob Peetom's Hair Spa** salon.

SSTK 4K/SHUTTERSTOCK

founder of his namesake art museum ARMA, on a three-hour **Golden Hour Tour** *(armabali.com/product/golden-hour; 1,340,000Rp)*. It usually starts at 5.45am when guests set off in Agung Rai's car to some of his favourite spots: rice paddies, quiet villages, streams and temples bathed in ethereal morning light provide a choreographic backdrop for the art collector's explanations of Balinese cultural nuances.

Ubud native Dewa Rai of **Bali Nature Walks** *(balinature walks.net; from 400,000Rp)* conducts three- to four-hour nature walks through jungle and rice fields around Ubud. Tours start with a hotel pick-up at 8am and a half-hour drive to the starting point in the countryside outside Ubud (which Mr Dewa keeps secret to avoid disrupting the quiet village surroundings).

Whizz downhill on day-long tours led by the popular **Banyan Tree Cycling Tours** *(banyantreebiketours.com; from adult/child 920,000/580,000Rp)* to remote villages near Ubud and interact with villagers.

One of Ubud's first tourist businesses, **Bali Bird Walks** *(balibirdwalk.com; 620,000Rp)*, was founded by the legendary Victor Mason more than 30 years ago. Mason has since gone on to the big nest in the sky, but his legacy lives on. Bird-watching tours include the use of binoculars; expect to spot 30 to 100 species.

Ubud's Fashionable Heart

MAP p128

Shop for stylish wares made in Bali

Within a few hundred metres of where Jl Dewi Sita meets Jl Hanoman you'll find some of Ubud's most interesting and stylish shops. Barely wider than a bolt of fabric, **Above the Clouds Natural Wear** *(abovetheclouds.store)* sells casual linen and cotton clothes designed and sewn in villages around

Cycle tour, Ubud

Ubud; quality and service are both top-notch. Proceeds from locally designed and produced jewellery and a small line of resort wear sold at **Ananda Soul** *(anandasoul.com)*, a store with a heart, support disadvantaged Balinese.

Kado by Saraswati Paper *(saraswatipapers.com)* sells journals, cards, prints and other high-end goods for creative pursuits. Everything is made from recycled paper and produced in Bali. Right next door, slick **Kevala Home** *(kevalaceramics.com)* sells stylish, locally made ceramic and porcelain. At **Curative** *(instagram.com/curativebali)* you can browse the work of more than 30 Balinese and Indonesian jewellery, accessories and clothing designers. Prices are aimed at the local market, meaning bargains abound.

Sample Treats, Potions & Lotions

MAP p128

Shop for Bali-grown and produced

Boutique producers who use ingredients from the Ubud region sell a wide range of foods, drinks, cosmetics and bodycare products. Inside its turquoise confines, **Ubud Raw Chocolate** *(ubudraw.com)* is an uncompromising producer of treats made with locally grown cacao. Cooling packs are available so you can keep your purchases pristine (unless you just want to eat them all immediately).

Sniff your way to a better you at **Blue Stone Botanicals** *(bluestonebotanicals.com)*, an aromatherapy store selling oils made in Bali and Java. Founded in East Bali in 2000, **Sensatia Botanicals** *(sensatia.com)* is a polished cosmetics vendor; packaging is made from cassava starch. **Kou** *(facebook.com/koubali.naturalsoap)* sells evocatively scented handmade soaps redolent of frangipani, tuberose, jasmine, orange and lemon.

BOOKISH UBUD

Art-rich Ubud is also renowned as one of Southeast Asia's top literary towns. For starters, it is the home of Bali's best place for the printed word: **Ganesha Bookshop** *(ganeshabooksbali.com)*, founded in 1986, sells an impressive selection of Indonesia- and Bali-focused titles, plus a well-curated selection of new and used books.

Since 2004 the town has hosted the **Ubud Writers & Readers Festival** (p136) in October, now one of Southeast Asia's (and possibly the world's) largest and most significant literary events. Founded by Australian Janet DeNeefe and her Balinese husband as a healing cultural response to the 2002 Bali bombings, the festival hosts up to 170 international writers, readings and workshops each year.

KAJENG RICE FIELDS ON FOOT

Leave the crowds behind and enjoy a walk with deep forests, lush rice fields and waterfalls just north of central Ubud.

START	END	LENGTH
Jl Kajeng	Jl Raya Ubud	7km; 2–3hr

Head north up Jl Kajeng, passing 1 **vendor stalls**. Just past the 2 **Bale Banjar Ubud Kaja**, head uphill as the road becomes a path, opening to rice-field vistas. Follow north: cement gives way to dirt and eventually becomes the top of a narrow concrete wall along a 3 **subak (irrigation) channel** on one side and small river on the other. Walk carefully until you come to a 4 **tiny footbridge** over the river, followed by a narrow path up an embankment. Continue north for about 1.5km along the footpath through rice fields dotted with the odd villa, drink vendor and artist studio. When you reach a 5 **road wide enough for cars**, turn east and walk down past 6 **Cafe Bintang** – an Indonesian-Japanese restaurant with an affable owner and good food – to a bridge straddling surging waterfalls. Immediately east, take the 7 **small lane** that runs south through the river gorge. Fenced yards filled with ducks give way to more rice as the path rises up out of the gorge and curves south. About 750m after the waterfall, turn east and follow the 8 **car-capable road**, over a bridge and back up to Jl Suweta. Walk south for 1km, past many small cafes perfect for a pause. Cross the 9 **bridge** to Jl Sri Wedari and walk downhill past little warungs and shops back to 10 **Jalan Raya Ubud**.

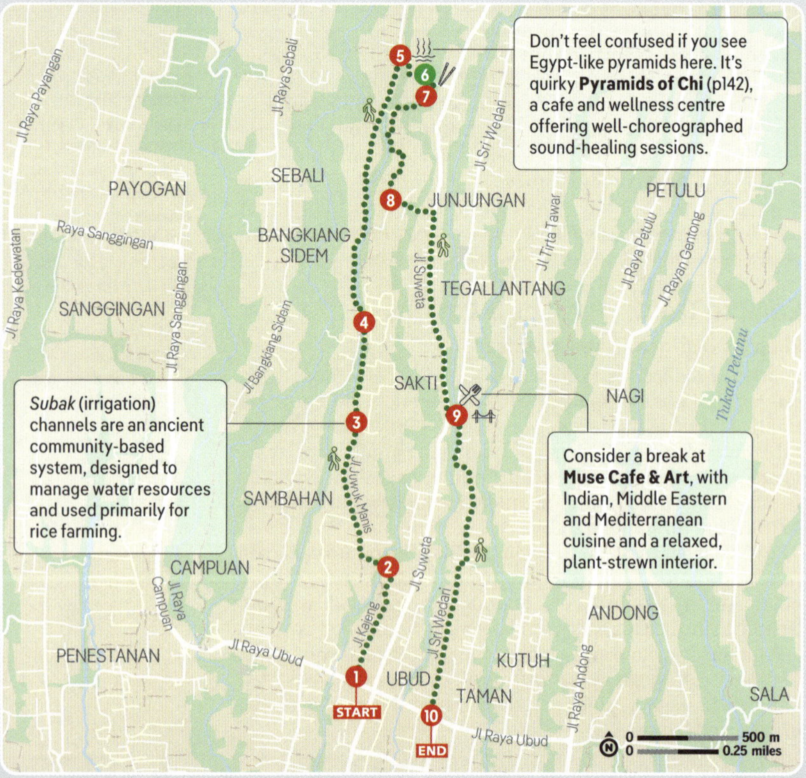

Don't feel confused if you see Egypt-like pyramids here. It's quirky **Pyramids of Chi** (p142), a cafe and wellness centre offering well-choreographed sound-healing sessions.

Subak (irrigation) channels are an ancient community-based system, designed to manage water resources and used primarily for rice farming.

Consider a break at **Muse Cafe & Art**, with Indian, Middle Eastern and Mediterranean cuisine and a relaxed, plant-strewn interior.

DAVID HERLIANTO/SHUTTERSTOCK

Ubud Art Market

Shop Until You Drop

MAP p128

From schlock to high-end

The latest iteration of **Ubud Art Market**, completed in 2023, is the fourth-generation complex to house the vast collection of shops and stalls selling a variety of handmade Balinese crafts – think rattan bags, handcrafted jewellery, woodcarvings and paintings. Occupying a prime corner plot across from Ubud Palace, the market is thronged with Ubud day-trippers all day and feels quite commercialised.

Fortunately, alternatives abound. A short stroll northeast, **Jalan Kajeng** is lined with vendors selling polyester sarongs, Bintang singlets, carved wooden bowls, cheesy masks and every other bit of tourist tat. It's an open-air carnival of consumerism that echoes with come-ons and the promise of bargains.

Look behind the stalls on Jl Pejang to find little boutiques selling more classy goods. Typical is **Toko Elami** *(elami.shop)*, selling the creations of over 20 local artisans, including out-of-the-ordinary T-shirts, prints, games, bags and stickers. Just north is **Threads of Life** (p135), Ubud's famous purveyor of traditional textiles.

UBUD'S NEIGHBOURHOODS

Central Ubud The original heart of Ubud is easily walkable and flush with businesses and attractions.

Padangtegal & Tebesaya Conveniently located, these two areas blend into central Ubud to the west.

Sambahan & Sakti North of Jl Raya Ubud, with rolling rice terraces and expat villas.

Nyuhkuning A popular and quiet area just south of the Monkey Forest.

Pengosekan South of the centre and an extension of Jl Hanoman.

Campuan & Sanggingan Two communities strung out along a namesake road west of the centre.

Penestanan Sitting on a plateau above Campuan, this area of cafes, guesthouses and rice fields can be a long walk to the centre.

EATING IN UBUD: VEGETARIAN & VEGAN

Sayuri Healing Food Cafe & Academy: Restaurant and cooking academy. Japanese chef Sayuri Tanaka promotes raw-vegan food culture. *8am-11pm* $$

Zest: Peaceful bohemian cafe with a delightful forest view serving global foods made from farm-to-table fine plants. *8am-10pm* $$

Has weekly music and transformative experiences.

Raw Temple: Self-proclaimed raw vegan sanctuary serving inventive, uncooked dishes – from pizzas to burritos – and detox juices. *9am-11pm* $$

Moksa: In a bucolic setting on a permaculture farm, Moksa creates extraordinary meals with simple vegetables. Many dishes are raw. *10am-9pm* $$

Wellness, Spas & Yoga

Arts and culture aside, Ubud is well known for its holistic and spiritual side, and enjoying a massage, wellness treatment or yoga course is at the top of most visitors' lists. This popularity is a double-edged sword, however: the plenitude of wellness centres, spas and yoga shalas in all price ranges, that have mushroomed everywhere from the busy town centre to Ubud's furthest forested edge, can make it hard to choose.

Where to Go If You Love...

Balinese Healing Rituals

Karsa Spa *(karsaspa.com)* Therapists certified in energy work start treatments with chakra-opening Reiki, and offer Balinese massages with long strokes and light acupressure.

Fivelements Retreat *(fivelementsbali.com)* Treatments use plant healing powers and village remedies. You might step into a river for a blessing with holy water, or have your skin polished with volcanic clay before a coconut oil massage.

Flower Baths and Scenic Rituals

Mekar Ubud Jungle Spa *(kclubgroup.com/mekar)* Enjoy a soak that feels like a rite in a stone tub filled with layered petals (marigolds, orchids, jasmine) and set on a deck overlooking terraced valleys just east of Tegallalang. Despite being in tourist territory, it's still quiet and scenic.

Tjampuhan Spa *(tjampuhan-bali.com/spa)* The namesake hotel and former home of artist Walter Spies, carved into the rock above the Oos River, also has special vibes. Treatments combine flower baths with plunging in hot and cold spring-fed pools in a cave-like grotto.

Pyramids of Chi *(ubud.pyramidsofchi.com)* Nothing beats the quirky exuberance of this wellness centre and cafe with three life-sized pyramids set by paddies. Come here for dramatic, highly choreographed sound-healing sessions.

Budget-Friendly Massages

Golden Hands Therapeutic Massage *(instagram.com/ubudspa.goldenhands)* Quality without breaking the bank on Jl Kajeng. Skilled deep-pressure sessions often take place with no music or notable decor to distract.

Jaens Spa Center *(jaensspashanti.com)* More polished, offering long, relaxing treatments. Promos and 'happy hour' spa deals are some of the best value in Ubud.

Yoga Shalas

Yoga Barn *(theyogabarn.com)* For a vast range of classes in various yoga practices, the Barn is scenically set near a river valley and also offers upper and whole body treatments at its Kush Spa. It was established in 2007.

Radiantly Alive *(samyama.com)* Another well-known and central shala appealing to students looking for a mix of drop-in and long-term yoga classes in various disciplines.

Bali Swasthya Yoga Centre *(instagram.com/baliswasthyayoga)* The place to go for Balinese-born instructors who eschew trends and style for substance and authenticity.

Intuitive Flow *(intuitiveflow.com)* If you're interested in healing arts workshops, try Intuitive Flow, even even though it's inconveniently located at the top of concrete stairs from Campuhan.

Alchemy Yoga & Meditation Center (*alchemyyogacenter.com*; pictured right) This is a popular Penestanan choice, also thanks to its vegan-friendly restaurant, for those keen to delve into meditation or ecstatic dance classes.

HOW TO

Book early
Ubud gets busy, even if there are thousands of spas. Some like Karsa fill up days in advance, especially on weekends.

Pick your time
Evenings offer cooler air and softer light – perfect if your spa has rice-field views, or for relaxing over yoga after a long day out exploring.

Know the price range
A solid 60-minute Balinese massage costs around 120,000Rp at budget shops and over one million rupiah at high-end resorts.

Double-check
Confirm what is included in each package, especially when you're booking a flower bath or scrub, to avoid a nasty surprise at checkout.

Going Independently or Not?

For flexibility, try handpicking spas and yoga studios across town. For example, have a 120,000Rp massage in a family-run shop, then try a 150,000Rp to 200,000Rp drop-in yoga class, or mix and match treatments across town. The trade-off to this carefree approach is planning – popular spas and yoga classes fill fast. Booking is usually done via WhatsApp and should be done a few days ahead.

At the other end of the spectrum, resort-based wellness packages provide all-inclusive programs: think sunrise yoga, daily spa treatments and plant-based meals. Packages are ideal for short stays, but cost significantly more and can feel less personal. They are also especially hard to cancel or change once you've booked.

If your goal is to take a yoga course, Ubud has everything from daily drop-ins – **Yoga Barn** and **Radiantly Alive** offer single-visit or multi-day passes – to fully scheduled, rigorous yoga teacher-training programs offering 200 hours for foundation courses and 300 hours for advanced courses. Check out centres like **Bali Yoga School** *(baliyogaschool.com)*, **Shades of Yoga** *(shadesofyoga.com)* and **House of Om** *(houseofom.com)*. If you plan to focus on yoga, consider staying near Penestanan or Jl Nyuh Kuning where many studios are clustered. Booking ahead is essential.

CEIRADUNT/SHUTTERSTOCK

Beyond Ubud (North)

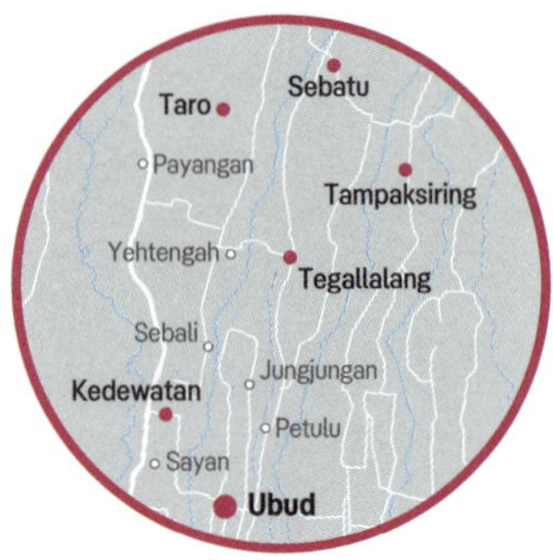

The action of the south melts away as you move upslope from Ubud. It's a lush land with ancient sites.

Places

Tegallalang p144
Kedewatan p145
Tampaksiring p146
Sebatu p147
Taro p148

GETTING AROUND

Having your own wheels is the only way to explore north of Ubud. The relentless uphill climbs make it a challenge for all but the most dedicated cyclists – rent a scooter. Otherwise, given returning to Ubud is all downhill, you can get a ride one-way and cycle back downhill. Use apps for taxi rides and consider hiring a car and driver for a day out to the top sights.

North of Ubud, Bali becomes cooler and greener. Fascinating sights and natural beauty abound in this hilly countryside where the north–south striations of river valleys abound. One easy route from Ubud, northeast towards Gunung Batur, passes through Tegallalang (home to the touristy Ceking Rice Terraces) and continues via Tampaksiring, passing the ancient sites of Gunung Kawi Sebatu, Gunung Kawi and Tirta Empul. The scenery on this route is verdantly picturesque – you'll see farmers working in their fields, colourful flags fluttering in the wind and plenty of rice terraces and roadside shrines. Hillside villages such as Taro remain good spots to observe Balinese life. Closer to Ubud, excellent handicraft shopping can be found.

Tegallalang

TIME FROM UBUD: **30MIN**

Busy terrace views

Heading north from Ubud, the stupendous views of the **Ceking Rice Terraces** from Tegallalang's main road are marred by the vast tourist circus, replete with competing Instagram swings and a barrage of cafes whose viewing terraces now obscure most of the views from the cliffside.

Still, this is one of Bali's most scenic rice terrace panoramas so the continuous frenzy of selfie-hungry tourists is not surprising. Taking it all in from somewhere like coffee plantation **Alas Harum** *(alasharum.com/en; admission 50,000Rp, adult-only swimming pool 200,000Rp)* is not a bad idea for enjoying a sizeable chunk of Tegallalang's dramatic rice fields without too much hassle, particularly if you have kids in tow. For sure, it's posh and geared to the many package-holiday tourists who come here to lounge and swim in its large, cliff-hanging, panoramic pools. There's also a restaurant, ubiquitous swings and a zipline, each with additional fees.

If that's not your scene, to access the Ceking Rice Terraces from the trails that descend into the lush valley, you'll be charged 25,000Rp, plus an occasional toll levied by some farmers.

Cycle to Ceking Rice Terraces

Narrow busy roads in Ubud town are a cyclist's nightmare. Up north, dramatically more peaceful roads wind through

NURLINDA AMIN/SHUTTERSTOCK

Alas Harum

lush and beautiful countryside. They are rarely steep, and often coast gently downhill.

A classic route leaves the town on Jl Raya Ubud and heads north along Jl Suweta and then Jl Sri Wedari to the **Ceking Rice Terraces** in Tegallalang. This is a moderate 17km ride along paved roads that become quieter the further you head north; expect a 244m ascent over the first 9km. Once at the terraces, it's possible to make a 7km detour east to Tampaksiring and then loop back west and south towards Ubud town. En route you pass the villages of **Tangkas Kenderan**, **Kepitu** and **Gentong**. This is a less-busy road embracing lovely scenery and small-town life. You'll know you've reached the surroundings of Jl Raya Ubud again when you hit lines of cars waiting in traffic.

To do this cycle tour on your own, you'll have to either pedal uphill from town (be cautious) or arrange a ride to transport you and your bike to a starting point out of town. It's easy enough to find decent mountain-bike rentals (including helmets) in Ubud.

Options abound for cyclists who prefer the convenience of an organised, supported tour. **Jegeg Bali Cycling** *(jegegbalicycling.com; adult/child 400,000/300,000Rp)* and **Love Bali Bike Tours** *(lovebalibiketours.com; adult/child 500,000/350,000Rp)* are recommended tour operators transporting groups to northern villages for a guided 2- to 5-hour bike ride back to Ubud. **Mason Adventures** *(850,000 Rp)*, another trusted operator, offers a 20km-long guided trip with lunch, starting on the flanks of Gunung Batur in the highlands and winding down through forest trails, rice fields and villages.

BEST WATERFALLS NORTH OF UBUD

Suwat Waterfall: Slightly northeast of Ubud town, this 15m-tall waterfall is peaceful and has a perfect pool for bathing.

Manuaba Waterfall: These two beautiful falls east of Tegallalang can be reached by hiking through the jungle. A short walk in the water allows for a whole loop.

Ulu Petanu Waterfall: A lovely, well-maintained waterfall area for swimming and relaxing in nature – aim for the morning before the crowds arrive.

Tangkup Waterfall: Also called Lateng Kayu, there are three waterfalls here, none too large. The short hike winds through serene paddy scenery.

Pengempu Waterfall: Hidden west of Kedewatan, this small waterfall has a majestic forest backdrop. It's a five-minute walk down the road and has toilet facilities.

Kedewatan

TIME FROM UBUD: **30MIN**

Take to Ubud's rushing river

The Sungai Ayung (Ayung River) is Bali's most popular river for white-water rafting. Depending on rainfall, the river can range from sedate to thrilling. Of the numerous companies offering

COFFEE LUWAK CONCERNS

Coffee luwak *(kopi luwak)* is ubiquitous and over-hyped in tourist areas north of Ubud. It's named after the cat-like civet *(luwak)* indigenous to Sulawesi, Sumatra and Java, which eats ripe coffee cherries. Entrepreneurs initially collected the intact beans found in the nocturnal civet's droppings and processed them to produce a supposedly extra-piquant brew. However, once the profit potential of exploiting coffee luwak was realised, outlets proliferated. With interest in coffee luwak exceeding all reason, trouble abounds. There is *no* certification that your expensive cup of coffee was brewed from beans that passed through the gut of a civet. Reports of mistreatment of caged civets on factory farms are common.

trips – all similar – pioneering operator **Mason Adventure Rafting** *(masonadventures.com/white-water-rafting; from 795,000Rp without transport)* still offers the longest rafting trip, 12km long. It was the first rafting company here three decades ago. Transport is usually provided from hotels and resorts in Ubud and South Bali (the departure from Nusa Dua can be very early) to a starting point off the road north to Kintamani. Protective gear and beverages are provided. Some rafting packages include lunch at tourist-group-oriented restaurants, and additional options include short treks in the lush river valley, or ecologically damaging ATV rides.

Tampaksiring

TIME FROM UBUD: **40MIN**

Experience echoes of Sukarno

Located in the Pakerisan Valley, 18km northeast of Ubud, the tidy town of **Tampaksiring** was the base of one of the major kingdoms during Bali's pre-colonial period. It's cleaved by the Pakerisan River, which flows through a revered valley that's home to both Pura Tirta Empul, an ancient and important water temple, and Gunung Kawi, one of the most impressive ancient sites in Bali. Terraced rice fields striate the hillsides that run down to the river and streams.

Tampaksiring is also notable for its connections to Sukarno (1901–70), the legendary first president of Indonesia, who led the nation from its independence from the Dutch in 1945 until he was deposed in 1967. About 1km south of town, the privately run **Sukarno Center** *(free; donations welcome)* is a cross between a shrine and a museum to his legacy. The walls show the fruits of Sukarno's leadership of the non-aligned movement during the Cold War. Both Soviet and Western leaders regularly called on Sukarno, hoping to curry allegiance; note the 1961 photo of JFK glad-handing the Indonesian president.

Sukarno had a deep affection for Bali and had a presidential palace, **Istana Kepresidenan Tampaksiring** *(isturatampaksiring.istanapresiden.go.id; free)*, built in the centre of town. It's still used for functions today and was a favourite refuge for his daughter Megawati Sukarnoputri when she served as president (2001–04).

Visit Bali's iconic water temple

In the shadow of the presidential palace, immediately east, **Pura Tirta Empul** *(tirtaempultemple.com; adult/child 75,000/50,000Rp)* dates to 962 CE (although little remains from then). This water temple is believed to have magical powers, and the holy springs bubble up into a large pool and gush out through waterspouts into a *petirtaan* (bathing area). The site is always thronged with Balinese and other visitors performing *melukat* (ritual cleansing), to assure a better future.

For a more serene setting, go downstream about 500m and take a long flight of steps down to **Pura Mengening** *(free)*, a temple with a freestanding *candi* (shrine), similar in design to those at Gunung Kawi. This towering stone structure is thought to be over 1000 years old.

MIKECPHOTO/SHUTTERSTOCK

Pura Tirta Empul

Explore a remarkable ancient site

One of Bali's oldest, holiest and most important monuments, the stunning river-valley complex of **Gunung Kawi** *(adult/child 75,000/50,000Rp)* consists of 10 huge, 8m-high *candi* cut out of rock faces. Each is believed to be a memorial to a member of 11th-century Balinese royalty. Legends relate that the whole group was carved out of the rock in one hard-working night by the mighty fingernails of Kebo Iwa.

Groups of *candi* and monks' cells carved into cliff faces are found throughout this area that was once encompassed by the ancient Pejeng kingdom; it stretched south along the Pakerisan River to **Goa Garba** and beyond.

Arrive in Gunung Kawi as early as possible for the best experience. Start making your way down the 250 steps by 7.30am to avoid some of the persistent vendors and observe residents going about their morning ablutions and cleaning of ceremonial offerings in the streams. You'll also still have cool air when you start the hike back up the steep staircase.

MYSTERIOUS GUNUNG KAWI

Uncertainty and myth surround the founding of Gunung Kawi, believed to have been built in 1080 CE by King Anak Wungsu, the third son of Bali's landmark historical figure, King Udayana. The five *candi* on the eastern riverbank are probably dedicated to King Udayana, Queen Mahendradatta and their sons Airlangga, founder Anak Wungsu and Marakata. While Airlangga ruled eastern Java, Anak Wungsu ruled Bali. The four *candi* on the western side are, by this theory, dedicated to Anak Wungsu's chief concubines. Another theory is that the whole complex is dedicated to Anak Wungsu, his wives, concubines and, in the case of the remote tenth *candi*, to a royal minister.

Sebatu

TIME FROM UBUD: **45MIN**

Purification at a temple to Vishnu

Coming from the west by the hilly road, you'll literally plunge above **Pura Gunung Kawi Sebatu** *(gunungkawisebatu.com; adult/child 50,000/25,000Rp)*, a slightly off-the-beaten-track water temple set in a lush gorge. Seen from above, the ensemble of quiet pools, gardens and inner mandalas is much

EATING NORTH OF UBUD: OUR PICKS

Heliostar: Tropical concept cafe in a quiet villa outside Petulu, with hearty well-curated food and a working space upstairs. *8am-8pm* $

Mimpi Manis: Boho-chic cosy restaurant in Sebatu offering a range of flavourful beef and fish steaks, Indonesian mains and live music. *8am-11pm* $$

Warung Umah Bali: Hearty servings of mains like Balinese *nasi goreng* and *sate* in a relaxing garden setting, west of Tagalalang's scrum. *10am-10pm* $$

Semara Ratih Delodsema Village: The viewing platforms above the jungle make this Western and Indonesian forest restaurant in Taro stand out. *8am-6.30pm* $$

ELEPHANT TOURISM IN TARO

Since 1997 the **Mason Elephant Park** near Taro has rescued 25 critically endangered Sumatran elephants from dire government camps. Self-funded by pioneering rafting operator Nigel Mason, the park offers elephant rides on light rattan chairs with no protrusions and bathing with the animals to cover the high costs of their welfare and upkeep. Deciding whether to go is polarising: Mason holds a Gold Accreditation from the animal welfare organisation Asian Captive Elephant Standards (ACES), which promotes conservation through ethical elephant tourism, including elephant rides. However, NGOs like World Animal Protection have criticised the ACES system and condemned Mason Elephant Park for using endangered animals for entertainment.

LEMARET PIERRICK/SHUTTERSTOCK

Pura Gunung Kawi Sebatu

more striking than the perspective you'll see after paying the entrance fee. The temple is dedicated to Vishnu, the supreme Hindu god, who protects the cosmic order, and is used for purification rituals. Inside, spring-fed pools are set against a lush green backdrop. Behind an ornate wall, you'll find two ritual bathing pools fed by water spouting from carved heads, where you can take a dip in the cool, clear water.

In the surrounding small village of **Sebatu**, look for shops run by woodcarvers who create intricate decorative items from fine-grained, light albesia wood.

Taro

TIME FROM UBUD: **1HR**

Tranquil village life

The air is noticeably cooler in the hillside village of **Taro**, 18km north of Ubud. It's compact, easily visited on foot, and the local community runs a useful website *(desawisatataro.com)* filled with info about the village (including homestay options).

Start at **Pura Agung Gunung Raung** *(free)*, the large temple in the centre with statues of *lembu putih* (white cows, a local icon) at its entrance. The temple dates to the 17th century and is named for Gunung Raung, the active volcano in East Java where its founding priests hailed from.

About 300m north, look for signs for **Yeh Pikat Waterfall**. The waterfall is not high (6m), but it is in a lovely spot at the confluence of two rivers and a natural spring. There's a small cafe at the top of the privately maintained trail down into the deep valley and sweeping views of the dense tropical forest.

Learn Balinese cooking on a farm

Spend a day in the untrammelled countryside just north of Taro and learn how to cook Balinese food at **Pemulan Bali Farm Cooking School** *(pemulanbali.com; from 450,000Rp)*, run by villagers passionate about organic farming. Morning courses include a visit to the local market and students learn about local produce and foods. Vegan, vegetarian and omnivore courses are available.

Beyond Ubud (South)

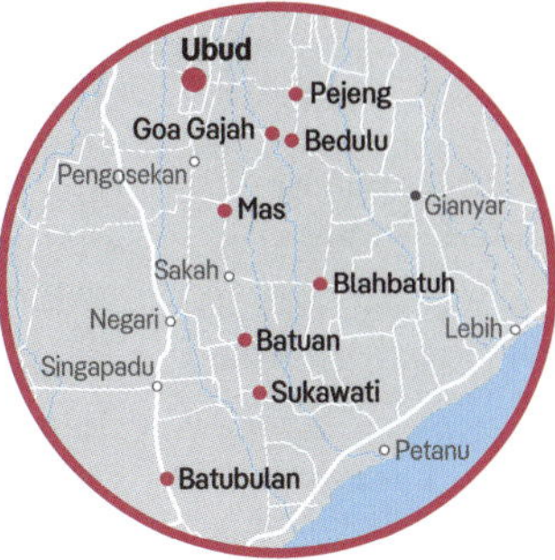

Villages of artisans, astonishing ancient sites and plenty of places to shop for handicrafts dot the lands south of Ubud.

A remarkable artefact more than 2000 years old is but one of the highlights of the adjacent villages of Pejeng and Bedulu, once the centres of a great kingdom. The legendary Dalem Bedaulu ruled the Pejeng dynasty from here, and was the last Balinese king to withstand the onslaught of the powerful Majapahit from Java in the 14th century. These are two of the many villages dotting the drier and flatter countryside running to the coast. The roads are lined with little shops that make and sell handicrafts. Many visitors shop here as they head to and from Ubud. Places like Mas, Blahbatuh, Sukawati and Batubulan are renowned for the quality and craftsmanship of their goods.

Places

Pejeng p149
Bedulu p150
Mas p151
Goa Gajah p152
Blahbatuh p153
Batuan p153
Sukawati p153
Batubulan p154

Pejeng

TIME FROM UBUD: **15MIN**

See an astounding relic

The village of **Pejeng**, just 5km east of central Ubud, was the capital of the Balinese Pejeng kingdom for a short period between Javanese invasions. It collapsed in 1343 when the Majapahits defeated King Dalem Bedaulu. Today, it is home to one of the region's most extraordinary but least-visited sights.

Founded in 1266, **Pura Penataran Sasih** *(donations welcome)* was once the state temple of the Pejeng kingdom. In the inner courtyard is a more remarkable treasure: a huge bronze drum known as the **Moon of Pejeng**, thought to date back as far as 300 BCE. The hourglass-shaped drum is 186cm high and is the largest single-piece cast drum in the world. The bronze alloy and casting technique have been traced back to the Dong Son people of ancient Vietnam, revealing a previously unknown trade route.

Visit intriguing temples

There are three other fascinating sites near Pura Penataran Sasih. **Pura Pusering Jagat** *(donations welcome)* was built in 1329 and is popular with young couples who pray at the stone lingam and yoni – Hindu symbols of the male and female sexual organs, life force of the universe – in hopes of fertility. **Pura Kebo Edan** *(admission 20,000Rp)* translates as 'Crazy Buffalo Temple' and although it's not an imposing structure, it is well-known for its much-weathered 3m-high Giant of Pejeng statue. Across two rivers further east, lesser-known **Goa Garba** *(adult/child 30,000/15,000Rp)* is an ancient rock-hewn

GETTING AROUND

The towns and villages south of Ubud lie along roads that get ever busier the further south you go. Cycling here is tough (even if it's relatively flat) as you dodge traffic along the narrow roads. Having your own motorbike or car (with or without a driver) is the way to go, as it allows for greater flexibility. Pejeng and Bedulu are easily reached by taxi from Ubud.

THE LEGEND OF DALEM BEDAULU

As the legend goes, the powerful Pejeng dynasty ruler Dalem Bedaulu possessed magical powers that allowed him to have his head removed and then put back on during meditation (Bedaulu means 'he who changed heads').

On one occasion, the king attempted to perform this unique party trick but a servant botched it, lopping off the head and accidentally dropping it in a river. As it floated away, the servant panicked and grabbed a pig, cut off its head and popped it on the king's shoulders. Thereafter, the king sat on a soaring throne and forbade his subjects to look up at his curious face.

meditation enclave set deep into a ravine on the banks of the Pakerisan River. Niches in the cliffs known as 'hermit's alcoves' are thought to date to the 11th century.

Many of the region's oldest treasures have been unearthed by farmers while ploughing their fields. Admire a range of artefacts at the **Museum Gedung Arca** *(free; donations welcome for guided tour)*. Exhibits in several small buildings at the archaeological museum include sarcophagi dating from as early as 300 BCE and some of Bali's first pottery from near Gilimanuk. **Ubud Story Walks** *(ubudstorywalks.com/the-myth-of-pejeng; 300,000Rp)* runs an excellent tour of the main Pejeng sites.

Bedulu

TIME FROM UBUD: **20MIN**

Explore a foundational temple

Bedulu was once the capital of a great kingdom. The legendary Dalem Bedaulu ruled the Pejeng dynasty from here and was the last Balinese king to withstand the onslaught of the powerful Majapahit from Java. He was defeated by Gajah Mada in 1343. The capital shifted several times after this, first to Gelgel and then later to Klungkung (Semarapura). You can easily use a bike to visit the sights of Bedulu and nearby Pejeng.

The majestic and tranquil **Pura Samuan Tiga** *(Temple of the Meeting of the Three; admission incl sarong 15000Rp)* is on a small lane, about 200m east of the Bedulu junction. The name probably refers to meetings held here in the 10th century that established that each Balinese village would have temples honouring the three Hindu deities: Pura Desa (village temple for daily worship) for Brahma, Pura Puseh (temple honouring the village's heritage) for Vishnu and Pura Dalem (temple of the dead) for Shiva. This tradition has continued ever since. What you see here today was rebuilt after the 1917 earthquake.

Visit a hidden Hindu hermitage

Set amid rice terraces, under-appreciated **Yeh Pulu** *(adult/child 30,000/15,000Rp)* is a 25m-long carved cliff face next to the Pakerisan and Petanu Rivers. It is believed to be the remnants of a 14th-century hermitage. Even if your interest in carved Hindu art is minor, the site is compelling and you're likely to have it all to yourself. Apart from the figure of Ganesha, the nine scenes depict everyday life 600 years ago. There are good walks here through the surrounding rice fields. Ask for directions to Goa Gajah (p152).

EATING SOUTH OF UBUD: OUR PICKS

Warung Makan Teges: North of Mas, this warung serves one dish – *nasi campur* – and it gets every element just right. *8am-5pm* $

Tonyraka Art Lounge (p151): When in Mas, have a meal of Balinese-infused international dishes inside the namesake art gallery. *9am-10pm* $$

Ni Sarti's Tofu Rice: Local vegetarian *nasi campur*-style place set within a home's courtyard behind Sukawati's market. The handmade tofu is bliss. *7am-1pm* $

Sayan Night Market: Southwest of Ubud, dozens of stalls sell fresh, authentic and cheap meals nightly. *6-11pm* $

JOSHUA GAO/SHUTTERSTOCK

Pura Samuan Tiga

Mas

TIME FROM UBUD: **20MIN**

Discover art and commerce

Woodcarving is the principal craft in the village of **Mas**. Stores and galleries line the main road, JI Raya Mas, and workshops are located both here and alongside the streets. West of the village, dramatic and modern gallery **Ubud Diary** *(ubuddiary.com; free)* is a labour of love by a collector of Indonesian art, with an emphasis on celebrating the Ubud school of painting.

A world of serious make-believe

One of the best museums in the Ubud area, **Setia Darma House of Masks & Puppets** *(maskandpuppets.com; free but donations welcome)* is home to more than 7000 ceremonial masks and puppets from Bali, other parts of Indonesia, Asia and beyond. All are beautifully displayed in a series of renovated historic buildings in a rural compound. Among the many treasures, look for the amazing Barong Landung puppets and the Kamasan paintings.

Visit some artsy spots

One of the premier galleries in the Ubud area, **Tonyraka Art Lounge** *(tonyraka.com)* shows top-notch Balinese tribal and contemporary art. Come to browse, buy and enjoy the cafe.

Or learn how to make your own stencils and prints at **Black Hand Gang** *(bhgstudio.id)*, a creative compound that also features the Toko Hands shop. Recalling the hip Japanese outpost Tokyu Hands, it's filled with irreverent T-shirts designed by local artists.

Create a Balinese mask

Led by master woodcarver **Ida Bagus Anom** *(balimaskmaking.com; 4hr class 500,000Rp per person)*, three generations of Bali's best mask carvers will show you their secrets in the family's Astina Mask Gallery, opposite the football field. Students can complete a simple mask or a puppet in three to four days.

VILLAGE ARTISANS

In small villages throughout the Ubud region, especially in the south, you'll see signs – often near the local temple – for artists and craftspeople. As one resident told us, 'our village is only as rich as our art'. It is for this reason that the creators behind the ceremonial costumes, masks, kris (traditional daggers), musical instruments and other beautiful aspects of Balinese life and religion are accorded great honour.

It's a symbiotic relationship, with the artist never charging the village for the work and the village, in turn, seeing to the welfare of the artist. Many artists are often in residence because of the shame entailed in needing to procure a sacred object from another village.

TOP EXPERIENCE

Goa Gajah

The demonic mouth of the incense-wafting 11th-century Goa Gajah (Elephant Cave) is one of Ubud's most recognisable sights. Its origins are uncertain: myth says that legendary giant Kebo Iwa sculpted it with his fingernail. It likely dates back to the Majapahit era, probably named after the nearby Petanu River, once known as Elephant River – Bali never had the pachyderms.

TRAVEL-FR/SHUTTERSTOCK

TOP TIPS

- Visit before 10am to avoid tour groups.
- Don't buy a sarong from the touts in the parking lot – it's a tourist scam. The ticket price includes one for rent.
- Guides may offer their services – 100,000Rp is a reasonable price per group, but remember that their services are optional.

Getting to the Site

Goa Gajah has a large free parking area. It's about a five-minute walk down the 50-odd steps to the temple's upper section, where you'll find the Elephant Cave. From this level, more stairs lead into the ravine where the oldest section of the complex lies. The full visit takes about an hour.

Into the Cave

Goa Gajah's main sight is the cave you access through the cavernous mouth of a demon – Bhoma or Rangda, according to Balinese lore. Visiting the cave's tiny inside is quick: you'll see the fragmentary remains of a *lingam*, the phallic symbol of the Hindu god Shiva, and its female counterpart, the *yoni*, as well as a statue of Shiva's son, the elephant-headed god Ganesha.

Don't Miss the Rest of the Complex

Outside, a giant sacred *kapok* tree soars next to a square bathing pool with water spouts held by six female figures (doubling as fountains for the *melukat* water purification ceremony). Descending into the ravine is the Tukad Pangkung area, where older Buddhist ruins reclaimed by nature and cloaked in chequered cloths coexist with photo-worthy spots like the moody, tangled ceiba tree by a lotus pond.

PRACTICALITIES

- adult/child 50,000/25,000Rp
- 8am-6pm
- tickets at gianyartourismticket.com/en/

Blahbatuh

TIME FROM UBUD: **30MIN**

Visit vital temples

Blahbatuh is known for its association with Kebo Iwa, the legendary strongman and minister to the last king of the Bedulu kingdom. A massive statue depicting him in full warrior mode adorns a roundabout on the main road between Blahbatuh and Gianyar. An 11th-century carved head of Iwa can be admired in the village's major temple, **Pura Puseh Desa Blahbatuh** *(donations welcome)*. Just north, **Pura Kahyangan Jagat** *(donations welcome)* has **Bukit Dharma** (Dharma Hill) as a backdrop. Climb the hill to reach a shrine featuring a stone statue of the six-armed goddess of death and destruction, Durga, killing a demon-possessed water buffalo.

Learn about traditional textile art

A symphony of click-clacking looms greets visitors to **Pertenunan Putri Ayu** *(tenunputriayu.com)*, which produces colourful batik and woven ikat fabrics (including Bali's much-prized *endek* style) using age-old methods. Staff will show you through the workshop and explain the process. Fabric and clothes are for sale.

Bathe in rushing waters

Community-driven development of waterfall tourism is sweeping Bali. Dozens of sites across the island now have trails, amenities and admission fees. Near Blahbatuh, in the tiny village of **Kemenuh**, residents lead visitors on a five-minute walk shaded by bamboo down a steep set of steps into a gorge misted by the pounding water of **Air Uma Anyar** *(admission 20,000Rp)*. There's swimming and sun loungers.

Batuan

TIME FROM UBUD: **50MIN**

Pray at thousand-year-old temples

Batuan's recorded history goes back 1000 years. In the 17th century, its royal family controlled most of southern Bali. The decline of its power is attributed to a priest's curse, which scattered the royal family to different parts of the island. The twin temples of **Pura Puseh Batuan** and **Pura Dasar Batuan** *(free, donations welcome)* are among Bali's oldest. They're accessible studies in classic Balinese temple architecture. The former is renowned for the quality of its sculptures and its Javanese-influenced water garden.

Sukawati

TIME FROM UBUD: **1HR**

A village of arts and crafts

Once a royal capital, **Sukawati** is now known for its sprawling street and **Art Market** where specialised artisans busily work in small workshops lining the roads. Look for ones marked '*tukang prada*', where you'll find temple umbrellas beautifully decorated with stencilled gold paint.

To the west, artisans in the villages of **Puaya** and **Singapadu** specialise in high-quality leather shadow puppets and masks for Topeng and Barong dances. On the main street,

EXPLORING SOUTH OF UBUD

Khana Putri Pertiwi, tour guide and archaeology major, shares her tips for visiting the area south of Ubud.

Don't skip **Batuan** village, just 30 minutes away from Ubud. This historically rich village holds great significance as it's where the renowned American anthropologist Margaret Mead conducted most of her research on Balinese culture. On Sundays, guests can visit **Studio Gelombang** and watch the local artist Made Griyawan conducting a traditional art class for neighbourhood kids.

Nature lovers can take a refreshing dip in either of the nearby , s, **Air Sumampan** or **Air Uma Anyar**. In the late afternoon, it's fun to walk along Sukawati's new **'jogging track'** through the rice fields, where residents watch the sunset from a wide open space.

SHOPPING FOR WOODCARVINGS

Woodcarving was a traditional art of the priestly Brahmana caste, with the skills said to be a gift from the gods. Historically, carving was limited to temple decorations, dance masks and musical instruments, but in the 1930s carvers began depicting people and animals. Today, Bali's woodcarvers also turn their skills to furniture making and traditional handicrafts. Many moonlight carving the island's top-selling souvenir, the penis-shaped bottle opener.

You'll find carvers plying their trade across the Ubud region. Mas is a big player in Bali's furniture industry, producing chairs, tables and antiques, mainly from teak imported from other Indonesian islands. Check the wood's authenticity if you're purchasing something in sandalwood.

Bali Bird Park

look for workshops where local artisans both make and sell ceremonial items for dance performances. **Nyoman Ruka** *(@nyoman_rukaartshop)* runs a studio famous for its Barong masks.

Batubulan

TIME FROM UBUD: **75MIN**

Explore a village of stone carvers

Stone carving is **Batubulan**'s main craft. Workshops are found right along the road to **Tegaltamu**, with another batch further north around **Silakarang**. The village is the source of the stunning temple-gate guardians seen all over Bali, made with *paras*, a porous grey volcanic rock resembling pumice. Soft and surprisingly light, it also ages quickly, meaning 'ancient' artworks may be years rather than centuries old. By night, the village is a hub of Balinese dance, making it an attractive option for visitors from the south who don't want to go all the way north to Ubud. Depending on the night, Kecak, Barong and fire dances are performed in the village's large **Sahadewa**.

Family fun with birds and reptiles

More than 1000 birds from 250 species and seven regions of the world flit about **Bali Bird Park** *(balibirdpark.com; adult/child 385,000/265,000Rp)*, including the rare *cendrawasih* (bird of paradise) from Papua and the iconic Bali starling. Daily free-flight bird shows are staged. The park is popular with kids; allow at least two hours. **Bali Reptile Park** *(balireptilepark.id; 250,000Rp)* has snakes and lizards galore. Try to time your visit with the daily feedings of the park's huge, prehistoric-like Komodo dragons (11am and 2.30pm).

Places We Love to Stay

$ Budget $$ Midrange $$$ Top End

Ubud

MAP p125

Arjuna Homestay $ Basic rooms in a super-central house with its own temple in the courtyard, perfect for budget backpackers.

Three Win Homestay $ Off Jl Hanoman, the family here offers five modern guest rooms in their compound. Get one with a spacious balcony.

Aji Lodge $ Off Jl Sukma and run by local painter Aji, a quiet homestay next to a river with rooms with terraces.

Yasa Backpackers House $ Greenery abounds at this squeaky-clean flashpacker option with dorms and spacious private rooms, well-equipped common spaces and a curated breakfast.

Hotel Tjampuhan $$ Overlooks two rivers. The artist Walter Spies lived here in the 1930s, and his former home is part of the hotel.

Puri Saraswati Dijiwa Bungalows $$ Centrally located, with lovely gardens that open onto beautiful Pura Taman Saraswati and attractive bungalow-style rooms.

Villa Nirvana $$ Serene retreat designed by local architect Awan Sukhro Edhi, by a river in Penestanan. Modern villas set in garden surrounds, many with pools.

Capung Cottages $$ Comfortable compound just north of the centre on a quiet street. A variety of appealing rooms surround a large pool.

Swasti Eco Cottages $$ A five-minute walk south of the Monkey Forest, featuring an organic garden, pool, yoga shala and traditional houses.

Okawati Boutique Bungalows $$ Rooms have terraces or balconies and there's always a thermos of tea available; older bungalows are the most atmospheric.

Komaneka at Monkey Forest $$ Hidden in lush gardens overlooking a rice field and remarkably tranquil. Comfortable suites and villas have elegant decor.

Alam Indah Ubud $$ South of the Monkey Forest, this spacious and tranquil resort has traditionally designed rooms with views.

Tegal Sari $$ Amid rice fields, the huge rooms and suites with chic contemporary decor are set in modern brick buildings. Well-located south of the centre.

Mandapa $$$ Set in the spectacular Sungai Valley and enclosed by rice fields, this stunning Ritz-Carlton resort is the size of a small village.

Bambu Indah Resort $$$ From famed entrepreneurs John and Cynthia Hardy, this eco-resort near the Ayung Valley has 100-year-old Javanese wooden houses and extraordinary bamboo structures.

Ibah $$$ Overlooking rushing waters and rice-clad hills in Campuhan, these suites and villas combine ancient and modern details. All could feature in an interior-design magazine.

Maya Ubud $$$ East of the centre in a river valley amid rice fields in Peliatan, the riverside spa and swimming pool here are major draws.

Nick's Pension $$$ Sprawling complex with large bamboo-furnished rooms, and a pool in well-tended gardens. Smack in the town's centre.

Beyond Ubud (North)

Mason Elephant Lodge $$$ Stylish cabins at the back of the Elephant Park, with large balconies facing the elephants' feeding and resting area for quiet, prolonged observation. Staying here contributes to their welfare.

Mirah Guesthouse $$ A great find in Sebatu, with a temple-like feel and central pool surrounded by greenery. Tasty breakfast included.

K Club Ubud $$$ Opulent jungle villas, some with their own infinity pools, set in a quiet sliver of nature near the Ceking Rice Terraces. Free shuttles to Ubud town.

Beyond Ubud (South)

Ubud Diary Villa $$ Part of the art gallery Ubud Diary, these villas combine unpainted, natural stones with reclaimed wood and high-end fittings for a literal artful stay.

Telaga Wana Villa $$ In Batubulan, each house is different and sumptuously furnished and designed. Enjoy a floating breakfast in the cosy, intimate central pool.

Batuan Village $$ Good-value, clean and spacious rooms arranged in a two-storey building around a central pool and within walking distance of Sukawati Art Market.

Researched by
Narina Exelby

East Bali

ICONIC TEMPLES, EXHILARATING HIKES AND SPECTACULAR DIVING

Flanked by dramatic beaches and a beautiful coastline, East Bali rises to the island's highest point on Gunung Agung.

Exploring the back roads of East Bali is one of the island's great pleasures. Rice terraces spill down hillsides under swaying palms, wild beaches are washed by pounding surf and age-old villages soldier on with barely a trace of modernity. Watching over it all is Gunung Agung, the active volcano known to the Balinese Hindus as the place where their gods reside. Throughout this region waterfalls, temples, palaces and water gardens are dotted throughout the landscape. Two of the temples – Pura Besakih and Pura Lempuyang – are among the island's most important pilgrimage sites.

You can find Bali's past amid evocative ruins in the former royal city of Klungkung. Follow the rivers coursing down the slopes around Sidemen to find rice-terrace vistas and valleys that could have inspired Shangri-la. Down along the coast, a string of easily accessible black-sand beaches offer surfing, seclusion and seaside temples. Further east still is the ferry hub of Padangbai (gateway to the Gilis) and relaxed Candidasa.

Resorts and hidden beaches dot the seashore and cluster on the Amed coast. Just north of there, Tulamben is all about external exploration: the entire town is geared for diving, especially at the iconic local shipwreck. On the northeast coast, surprises await in an evocative region of Bali where tourism is barely known.

DATUAHE/SHUTTERSTOCK

THE MAIN AREAS

KLUNGKUNG
Centre of historic, scenic Bali. **p160**

SIDEMEN
Stunning rural landscapes, with Agung views. **p166**

PADANGBAI
Port town on the varied coast. **p172**

AMED
Chilled coastal vibes and diving hotspots. **p180**

For places to stay in East Bali, see p187

MONTICELLO/SHUTTERSTOCK

Left: Freediving, Amed (p182); Above: Pura Besakih (p171)

Find Your Way

Shaped like a reverse crescent, East Bali's coastline is backed by mountains. Soaring Gunung Agung dominates the centre, and much of the region is on its sloping hillsides, cleaved by rivers and punctuated by waterfalls.

Sidemen, p166

This stunning agricultural area, with gorgeous views of Gunung Agung, is a haven for hikers and peace-seekers.

Klungkung, p160

The old royal palace anchors a region of beaches, temples and rice terraces stretching up the side of Gunung Agung.

Amed, p180

A favourite with divers, snorkellers and freedivers, this laid-back strip of coastline is the sort of place that's hard to leave.

Padangbai, p172

A ferry hub, Padangbai is at the heart of a coastline peppered with relaxed resorts, sacred sites and top beaches.

MOTORBIKE & CAR

East Bali is all about exploring. Having your own wheels is essential in order to have the freedom to discover untrodden beaches, pristine waterfalls, remote sacred temples and timeless villages.

ON FOOT

Walkers and hikers are spoiled for choice, from beachside strolls to rice-field jaunts to the formidable climb up Gunung Agung. Sidemen in particular is a fantastic base from which you can explore the virescent countryside.

DANVIEWFINDER/SHUTTERSTOCK

Bat-cave statue, Goa Lawah (p175)

Plan Your Time

Much of East Bali can be explored on looping day trips from Ubud and the south, but staying in the region lets you get into the groove of its relaxed rhythms.

Pressed for Time

Pick your theme. For Balinese culture visit **Klungkung** (p160), **Bangli** (p164) and **Gianyar** (p164). For Hindu sites, visit Bali's most sacred temple **Pura Besakih** (p171). For traditional life journey to **Penglipuran** (p165), **Tenganan** (p176) and the **Samsara Living Museum** (p179). For royal life, visit **Amlapura** (p176). For underwater adventure, hit **Amed** (p180).

Five Days or More

With the luxury of more time, **Candidasa** (p175) is a good base for exploring the southern parts of East Bali, while **Amed** (p180) is convenient for the northern parts. Get a room with a rice-terrace view in **Sidemen** (p166) and do some walking. To really escape the crowds, indulge in a few days of peace in **Tejakula** (p185).

SEASONAL HIGHLIGHTS

MARCH–MAY

The dry season from April is the best time to visit. On the coast, there's no one single best month.

JUNE–AUGUST

Top-end resorts and the coast get crowded. The region remains more mellow than South Bali and Ubud.

SEPTEMBER–NOVEMBER

The dry season ends around September – prime walking weather. October ushers in top surf.

DECEMBER–FEBRUARY

Great surfing continues to March, even as rains fall across the region. Resorts fill for Christmas and New Year.

Klungkung

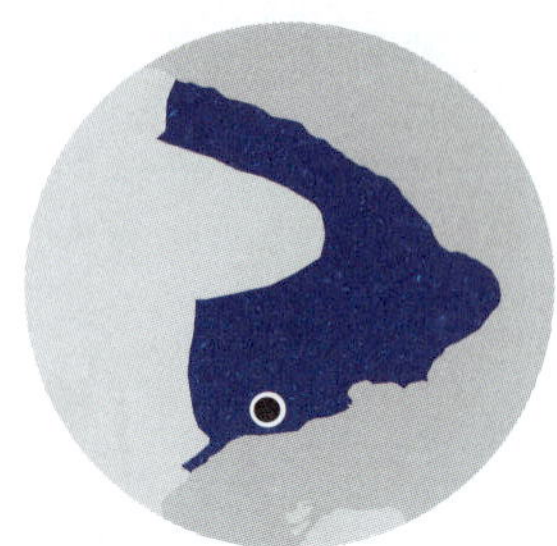

ROYAL RESIDENCES | HISTORIC ARCHITECTURE | MARKETS

GETTING AROUND

Klungkung is best reached with your own wheels. The main road along the east coast runs only 4km south of the centre, so it's an easy detour. It's also convenient to Gianyar, Bangli, Pura Besakih and Sidemen. Klungkung is compact, so it's convenient to walk everywhere. Stashing a car or motorbike is not hard; street attendants will collect a small fee. The town can be reached in an hour or less from both Ubud (via Gianyar) and Sanur (via the coast road).

TOP TIP

Despite its sights, Klungkung is not a tourist town so don't expect to find many eating and drinking options. However, the market is great for fruit, especially before noon.

Officially called Semarapura but commonly known by its traditional name Klungkung, this district capital is home to the historically significant Puri Agung Semarapura or Klungkung Palace, a relic of the days of Klungkung's *rajas* (lords or princes), the Dewa Agungs. Once the centre of Bali's most important kingdom, the busy town retains the palace compound from its royal past, with a market opposite and streets lined with popular shops. Just east of the palace, the main road crosses one of Bali's largest rivers, Sungai Unda. Throughout the area there are also large temples and mosques.

You could spend an hour or two here exploring the remains of the palace and the market. Klungkung is a hub of roads, so it's easy to visit other parts of the south from here or stop off en route during a larger itinerary.

Honouring Ritual Suicide

A monument to sacrifice

Klungkung was the last Balinese kingdom to succumb to the Dutch (in 1908). The sacrifice of its royal family, who died by *puputan* (ritual suicide) rather than surrender, is commemorated in the towering **Puputan Monument** *(Semarapura City Tour ticket adult/child 50,000/25,000Rp)*. In its base are 16 reliefs that showcase important historic events, including a battle led (unusually) by a woman (p165). There's also a sculpture of Ida I Dewa Agung Jambe, who founded the Klungkung kingdom in 1686. Count on 10 minutes to look around. The monument is the logical starting point for exploring Klungkung as the same ticket gets you into the Puri Agung Semarapura complex across the road.

The Puputan Monument is on the northeastern side of the **Patung Kanda Pat** monument, honouring the four 'spiritual siblings' that the Balinese believe accompany us through our lifetime. It stands at the intersection of Jl Untung Suropati and the road to Besakih.

Step Back in Time

Visit Klungkung's historic palace

Stroll around the **Puri Agung Semarapura** *(admission incl in Semarapura City Tour ticket)* compound and you'll catch a glimpse of the Klungkung palace as it was in 1710 when it was completed for the Dewa Agung dynasty. At that time, this was the most powerful of Bali's royal families. The original compound was laid out in a square and featured courtyards, gardens, pavilions and moats. Most of it was destroyed during the Dutch attacks in 1908, and all that remains is the carved **Pemedal Agung** (the impressive gateway on the south side) and two pavilions.

The open-sided **Kertha Gosa** pavilion was the supreme court of the Klungkung kingdom, where disputes and cases that couldn't be settled at village level were brought. A superb example of Klungkung architecture, its ceiling is covered with 20th-century paintings in the local Kamasan style that depict the Garuda story among scenes related to karma. The ceiling of the **Bale Kambang** 'floating pavilion' in the centre of the compound also features Kamasan paintings: the first row is based on the astrological calendar, the second on the folktale of Pan and Men Brayut and their 18 children, and the upper rows on the adventures of hero Sutasona.

On the compound's western side, a colonial-era building houses the **Museum Semarajaya**, also included in the palace admission price. Displays include traditional weapons, costumes and cherished ceremonial items alongside old photos of the royal court. Scan QR codes for information in English.

KLUNGKUNG'S BLOODY HISTORY

In 1849 the rulers of Klungkung and Gianyar defeated a Dutch invasion force at Kusamba (p165), and a peace settlement was brokered. For the next 50 years the South Bali kingdoms jostled for supremacy until the raja (king) of Gianyar petitioned the Dutch for support.

When the Dutch invaded in 1908, the king of Klungkung had to choose between a *puputan* or ignominious surrender. He chose the first option. On 28 April, as the Dutch surrounded his palace, the king led hundreds out to certain death from Dutch gunfire or the blades of their own kris (traditional daggers).

LOVE & DEATH IN BALI

Vicki Baum's novel *Love and Death in Bali* is far more than a beach-blanket love story; it's rooted in historic events.

Set in the old fishing village of Sanur (p88), this haunting tale (first published in 1937) offers insight into life in feudal Bali and the period of colonial history leading up to the *puputan* of the Balinese royals in the face of Dutch oppression.

The fast-moving plot draws you in, and there's something timeless about the central character, the rice farmer known only as Pak, that will resonate with any traveller who explores Bali's rural hinterland.

Endek

From Fresh Fruit to Textiles

East Bali's best market

Nowadays more mall than market, **Pasar Semarapura** (often still called **Klungkung Market**) is a fantastic place to shop for *endek*, the fabric that originated in the Klungkung area. The old market has been transformed into a collection of enormous modern buildings, and the fabrics are opposite the main entrance. Trawl through the buildings and you'll come across everything from gold stores (upstairs from the fabric section) to ceremonial attire, household implements and fresh produce.

The daily market is a vibrant hub of commerce and a meeting place for people of the region. You can easily spend an hour wandering about the warren of stalls on three levels and in the surrounding streets. It's grimy, yes, but also fascinating. Huge straw baskets of fresh produce are islands of colour amid the chaos, and there's plenty of jewellery and ikat (the latter sells for a fraction of what you'll pay elsewhere). It's best visited in the morning.

Beyond Klungkung

From wild beaches to one of Bali's oldest villages, the lands around Klungkung combine beauty, sacred meaning and cultural interest.

Places

East Coast p163
Gianyar p164
Bangli p164

You'll be spoiled for day trips and adventures around Klungkung: look for scenic surprises along the lovely roads linking towns like Bangli and Gianyar, and further on around the hills towards Sidemen. This region presents a very authentic introduction to Indonesia's textile heritage, and you can pop into a decades-old *endek* workshop in Gianyar to watch weavers at work, or stop at the Masa Masa cultural centre to admire beautiful antique fabrics and other cultural artefacts. For a peek at a traditional Balinese village, visit Penglipuran. The coastline beyond Klungkung is lined with moody black-sand beaches, known for pounding surf and few crowds.

GETTING AROUND

This is a good area to rent a scooter and set off on a random adventure: you can never get too lost and there's always a waterfall, view, temple or village around the corner to surprise. Ubud and Sanur are easy day trips by taxi; negotiate with the driver to stick around for your return trip given picking up another ride via one of the ride-hailing apps can be a challenge.

East Coast

TIME FROM KLUNGKUNG: **30MIN**

Connect with Indonesia's cultural heritage

For a very peaceful introduction to Indonesia's cultural heritage, pay a visit to **Masa Masa** *(instagram.com/masamasabali)*. It has a beautifully curated gallery of Indonesian antiques – handwoven fabrics mostly, as well as jewellery, *kebaya* (the elegant tops that Balinese women wear) and other artefacts. There's also a store selling batik fabrics, clothing and handmade goods. At the centre of the airy space, a restaurant features a range of heritage dishes from around the archipelago. Film screenings, music, dance and other cultural events are regularly held in the evenings. See Instagram for details.

Explore the beaches

The coastal highway between Sanur and Kusamba runs alongside a swath of black-sand beaches for over 20km – almost every road heading towards the coastline ends up at a beach. The shoreline is striking if somewhat sombre, with beaches in various shades of volcanic grey pounded relentlessly by waves; at high tide, the beach is swallowed up and waves pummel the breakwater. The entire coast has great religious significance: there are oodles of temples scattered along it, and on the many small coastal village beaches, ashes are consigned to the sea as cremation formalities reach their conclusion.

EAST COAST BEACHES

Pantai Ketewel is a surf spot demanding advanced skills. For a more transcendent experience, **Pantai Purnama** sands sparkle in the sunlight. There's an increasing number of hotels and villas around **Pantai Selukat**, adjacent to **Pantai Keramas**, which has beach cafes, consistent surf and sweeping views to Nusa Lembongan. **Pantai Masceti** feels quite forlorn (workers toil here, sorting stones for use in gardens and paving tiles), but nearby **Pantai Lebih** has glittering mica-infused sand and popular seafood warungs (a good lunch stop). **Pantai Lepang** is fronted by Jivva Beach Club, while **Pantai Klotok** just long the coast is where sacred statues from Pura Besakih are taken for ritual cleansing.

Some beaches have warungs (food stalls) and cafes – others have nothing at all. Few are crowded. **Pantai Keramas** and **Pantai Ketewel** are known for their surf breaks (you can night-surf at Keramas for a fee – book at **Hotel Komune** *(komuneresorts.com)*. Keep in mind that swimming along this stretch of coastline is dangerous.

Go wine or beer tasting

Right off the coastal highway, **Sababay Winery** *(sababaywinery.com; tasting 484,000Rp)* produces wine that hits above its weight given many consider winemaking and tropical climates to be mutually exclusive. Grapes are grown on Bali's north coast, but the wine is produced close to Pantai Keramas, and it's here that you can indulge in a wine-and-cheese tasting experience. There are a few on offer, but the 'Wine Down in the Garden' experience pairs wine with local cheese. If beer's more your thing, **Breman Brewery** *(bremanbrewery.com)*, on the road down to Pantai Keramas, produces lagers and offers a brewery tour with beer tasting.

Gianyar

TIME FROM KLUNGKUNG: **20MIN**

Watch *endek* being produced

Gianyar was once known for its factories producing the vibrantly patterned *weft ikat* – which is called *endek* and originated in Bali in the Klungkung regency. Although many have closed in recent years, two notable holdouts remain. **Pertenunan Setia Cap Cili** *(instagram.com/setiacapcili)*, said to be Gianyar's oldest weaving factory, was founded by a couple in 1948 and at one point employed 200 people from surrounding villages. These days it's run by the third generation and is vastly smaller (the number of employees is in the single figures), but there's still a large showroom where you can buy exquisite fabric and find women weaving out back. You'll have a similar experience about 500m west at **Cap Togog** *(instagram.com/gallerytogog)*. Founded in 1953, you can see how the entire *endek* production process works, beginning with the dyeing of the thread.

Bangli

TIME FROM KLUNGKUNG: **45MIN**

Visit Bangli's Pura Kehen

State temple of the Bangli kingdom, **Pura Kehen** *(50,000Rp)* is considered to be a miniature version of Pura Besakih (p171), Bali's most important temple. Pura Kehen is terraced up the hillside, with a steep flight of steps leading to its beautifully decorated entrance. The first courtyard has an enormous banyan tree with a *kulkul* (hollow tree-trunk drum used to sound warnings) entwined in its upper branches; the inner courtyard has an 11-roof *meru* (multi-tiered shrine). Other shrines have thrones for the Hindu trinity: Brahma, Shiva and Vishnu. No guides or information are available here, so you will get a lot more from your visit if you're with someone who can explain the temple complex to you.

MICHAELBALLERONI/SHUTTERSTOCK

Pura Kehen

Stay in a traditional village

Settled in the 14th century, the village layout of **Penglipuran** *(penglipuran.com; adult/child 50,000/30,000Rp)* is very traditional. It's organised into family compounds branching off a long, grass-lined pedestrian avenue. Visitors are welcome to step through gateways into most of the compounds where many buildings are still made from bamboo – scan the QR code near its entrance for information. Near the top end of the village, don't miss the 500m-long boardwalk running through bamboo forest.

Penglipuran is now a popular tourist attraction, welcoming thousands of visitors each day. If you prefer an experience that goes beyond the crowds, book into a village homestay. Privately run, you will find them on booking sites and the village's website.

STATUE OF A HEROINE

On Bali's east coast, where Jl Rama (from Klungkung) intersects with the coastal highway, there is a statue of a woman facing east. She is standing defiantly, with a *lontar* (traditional palm-frond book; see p177) in her left hand and her right hand pointing upwards in command. The woman depicted is **Ida I Dewa Agung Istri Kanya**, a Balinese heroine celebrated for leading the Klungkung army to victory in the battle against the Dutch at Kusamba in 1849. It was in battle that General AV Michiel, who was leading the temporary commander of the Royal Dutch East Indies Army at the time, was killed.

EATING IN KERAMAS: OUR PICKS

Locas Waroeng: Find inspiration in this cafe's multitude of motivational slogans – or indulge in a hearty, happy beachfront meal. *7am-9pm* $

Keramas Surf Camp Restaurant: Fuel up on post-surf pizza or check out the waves while tucking into a generous serving of *nasi campur*. *8am-10pm* $

Swan Restaurant: Gorgeous ocean views and a menu covering standard Western dishes to Middle Eastern, Indian and Balinese faves. *7am-10pm* $$

Hotel Komune Beach Club: Feast on pizza, pasta and salads or tuck into seafood or a curry. There's an excellent health-juice menu, too. *7am-11pm* $$$

Sidemen

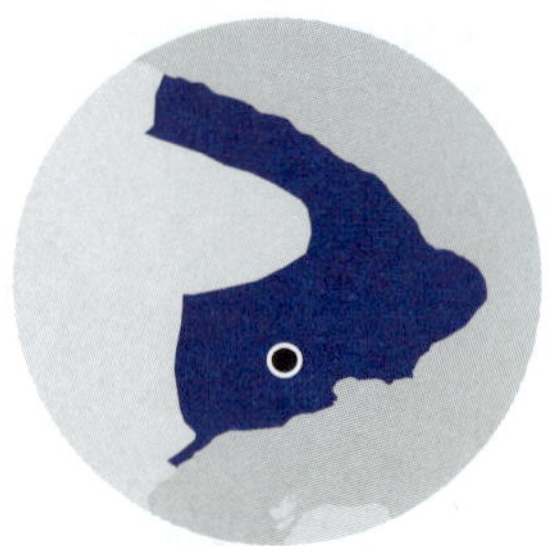

PADDY WALKS | EXTRAORDINARY VIEWS | TRADITIONAL ARTISANS

GETTING AROUND

You'll need to find your own way to Sidemen and, once here, you'll be on your own regarding transport – ride-hailing apps don't cover this area. However, it's very easy to source a scooter to rent, and you'll likely enjoy having your own wheels to explore the area: the rural roads here are a delight. Walking is always an option, but cafes and restaurants are quite spread out.

In Sidemen (pronounced si-da-men), a walk in any direction is a communion with nature. Winding through one of Bali's most beautiful river valleys, the road to this village offers marvellous rice-terrace scenery, a delightful rural character and, when the clouds over the mountain clear, extraordinary views of Gunung Agung, which looms large to the northeast.

People looking for a sense of space flock to Sidemen for day walks through the paddies and to revel in the lush, luxuriant countryside while relaxing in quiet homestays, low-key guesthouses and boutique hotels. There are some delightful cafes too, many of which use fresh produce sourced from the fields around Sidemen.

Travellers who've known Bali for decades sometimes compare Sidemen with Ubud as it was 30 years ago. While tourism is developing and new hotels are vying for those sought-after paddy views it seems, for the time being at least, to be moving forward in a manageable way.

TOP TIP

Sidemen's weather can be quite unstable in the afternoons, so it's best to trek in the mornings. Evenings can be unexpectedly chilly.

Paddies, Forests & Volcano Views

Trek through rural Sidemen

Sidemen's rural charm is its biggest drawcard – many happy hours can be spent exploring paddies, gardens and forests surrounding the town. Every hotel, homestay and guesthouse can hook you up with a local guide to lead you on a trail through valley gardens, and share insights into Bali's farming traditions and UNESCO-listed *subak* system (p72). For a greater physical challenge, ask your guide to take you to **Pura Bukit Tageh** *(free)*, the shrine at the highest point of the hill rising up on Sidemen's west side. The four-hour return hike rewards you with gorgeous views of Agung and the ocean on clear days (as the crow flies, Sidemen is just 10km from the coast).

On Sidemen's western fringe, over the Sungai Telaga Waja, is **Sidemen Rice Terrace** *(instagram.com/sidemenriceterrace; 25,000Rp)*. This circular, well-signposted, 3km-long trail is

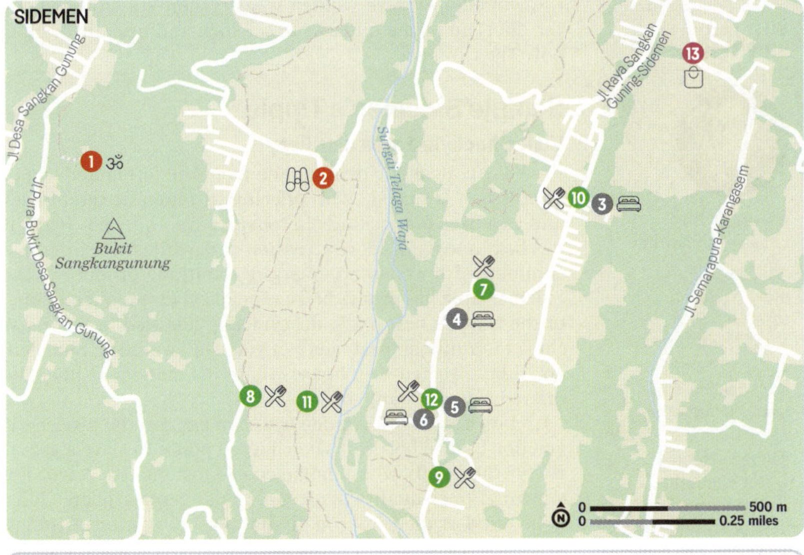

SIGHTS
1 Pura Bukit Tageh
2 Sidemen Rice Terrace

SLEEPING
3 Pondok Indah Homestay
4 Samanvaya
5 Uma Agung Villa
6 Wapa di Ume

EATING
7 Giri Carik
8 Panorama Sidemen
9 Warung Cepik
10 Warung Gunge
11 Warung Made
12 Warung Wisma Bojana

SHOPPING
13 Pelangi Traditional Weaving

managed by a community organisation and can easily be walked on your own; guides *(100,000Rp per hr)* are available if you're keen to learn more about the area. The trail is paved to start with, but soon transitions into a regular paddy path running along the narrow walls of irrigation channels. Farmers in the Sidemen area only plant one rice crop a year. After that's been harvested, they plant chilli, maize, other crops and various flowers. While walking the trail, you're likely to see farmers at work. About 800m from the start point is **Panorama Sidemen** *(instagram.com/panoramasidemen)*, a restaurant with lovely valley views. About 500m further is **Warung Made**, a simple trail-side shelter well worth a stop where young Made sells delicious locally harvested coconuts.

Watch Weavers at Work

Support traditional artisans

Sidemen is renowned for the beautiful handwoven textiles produced in the area, particularly *endek* (a single-ikat fabric) and *songket* (a type of brocade, often with silver and gold threads woven in). This makes it an ideal place to shop for fabric. It can be a bit hit-and-miss finding workshops where you can watch weavers at work, but one reliable place to head to is **Pelangi Traditional Weaving** *(instagram.com/cedut_pelangi)*, at the entrance to Sidemen village from the Karangasem road. You're welcome to take a look around

WHISTLING PIGEONS

Pay attention in the late afternoons or early mornings and you might just hear an eerie whistling coming from the sky. Look for a small flock of birds circling overhead. These are homing pigeons; the sound is made by the *sawangan* (like a whistle) tied around their necks. Keeping homing pigeons was a popular pastime in the Karangasem regency, and a few people around Sidemen still have flocks. If the weather is good, they will fly them twice a day for up to two hours.

WHY I LOVE SIDEMEN

Narina Exelby, Lonely Planet writer

A trip to Sidemen brings a chance to exhale. Time slows down here and, particularly after dealing with traffic in the south of the island, you're presented with a wonderful opportunity to live days at walking pace and explore on foot. The area's known for its rice-terrace trails (an absolute must), but the village itself is a treat to explore too; with every twist and turn in the road there's a different view to be had. Gunung Agung, so often hidden by cloud, also makes unexpected appearances – you could sit down at a rooftop cafe and before you've finished your coffee, the clouds might have cleared and the majestic mountain returned to take centre stage.

the workshop where women weave (there's a tip box near the door) and peep upstairs to see men and boys tie designs onto the threads.

Sample Sidemen's Tipple

Visit a backyard *arak* distillery

Arak is an alcoholic drink made from the fermented sap of palm trees. It's used as an offering in religious ceremonies and as a base for cocktails in tourist bars. In recent years, it has begun to enjoy more attention and, while there are some commercial brands and emerging boutique producers, the Sidemen area has always had a reputation for producing some of the island's best *arak*. It's typically distilled in a *pondok* (hut) in family homesteads – if you ask around in Sidemen, you'll be directed to a house where it's made and likely be offered some to sample.

It's best to go with a guide who can explain the process. If you don't buy a bottle, it's considered polite to leave a gratuity for the family whose home you've just visited. A word of warning: poor-quality *arak* can be dangerous (people have gone blind or died from methanol poisoning after drinking *arak*) so be sure to only drink *arak* from a reputable producer vouched for by your guide.

Craft Your Own Jewellery

Enrol in a silversmithing class

Tap into your creative side and craft your own Bali memento in a silversmithing class. The craft is not one that Sidemen has historically been known for but, as tourism has grown in the village, so too have studios offering visitors the opportunity to create their own jewellery. Generally speaking, look for a studio on the outskirts of the village if you're wanting a view while you work or, for a more artisanal vibe, head to a studio in the village. Classes are very hands-on, and you'll be guided through the process of melting and shaping the silver, as well as various jewellery-making techniques.

Inspiration might strike as you're working, but it helps to arrive with an idea of what you'd like to make. Expect to pay around 300,000Rp for a one- to two-hour class; the price includes a set weight of silver and you'll be charged for every additional gram you might use. Advance booking is not usually required.

EATING IN SIDEMEN: OUR PICKS

Warung Gunge: This small eatery has three tables on a quiet street-side terrace. Dishes are Indonesian, with a good vegetarian selection. *8am-10pm* $

Giri Carik: For Agung views, this rooftop resto is hard to beat. Coffee, beer, wine and Balinese specials like *babi kecap* (pork with sweet soy sauce). *9am-9pm* $

Warung Cepik: Find a four-page vegan menu at this restaurant, serving meaty meals too. Tables enjoy a relaxing paddy view. *7am-8.30pm* $$

Warung Wisma Bojana: Choose from pizza, pasta, Indonesian or Balinese dishes and indulge in lovely paddy and mountain views. *8am-10pm* $$

Beyond Sidemen

Sidemen's enchanting surrounds present beautifully peaceful views and spiritual places, plus exhilarating opportunities to get active.

The quiet hills and verdant valleys around Sidemen have been carefully tended by farmers for centuries; they are absolutely exquisite, particularly when explored in the early-morning light and the sun's rays filter through trees. Tucked into forested valleys are hidden waterfalls and tumbling rivers.

Always in the distance, brooding over the landscape, is mighty Gunung Agung (3142m). This is the most holy of Bali's mountains and also the island's highest. The imposing volcano can be seen from most of south and east Bali when clear of cloud and mist. Traditional houses are laid out on an axis in line with Agung and many locals always know where they are in relation to the peak, which is thought to house ancestral spirits. It's on the southeastern slopes of Agung that you'll find Pura Besakih, Bali's 'mother temple', also a start point for a challenging trek to the summit of the volcano.

Places

Rendang p169
Gembleng Waterfall p170
Besakih p170
Pura Besakih p171

GETTING AROUND

You can't rely on public transport or ride-hailing apps to explore around Sidemen: you'll need to have your own set of wheels. Your accommodation in Sidemen will almost certainly be able to assist with setting something up, be it a private driver or scooter rental. If you're driving yourself, be aware that bigger roads are frequented by large trucks transporting rocks and sand down towards the coastline.

Rendang

TIME FROM SIDEMEN: **20MIN**

Raft the Telaga Waja River

Whoop and cheer your way through East Bali on an exhilarating journey down the **Sungai Telaga Waja**. While rafting the Sungai Ayung (Ayung River; p145) near Ubud will have you slipping between the walls of a canyon flanked with jungle, rafting the Telaga Waja takes you through a more open landscape, past paddies, towering trees and waterfalls gushing tributaries into the river. You'll also shoot down invigorating rapids and weirs – this fast-flowing river is graded Class III+.

The Telaga Waja can be rafted all year, but the best time is usually the dry season (April to October) when the rapids are at their most exciting. Various companies offer rafting trips: **Bali Sobek** *(balisobek.com; adult/child 1,200,000/800,000Rp)*, established in 1989, pioneered rafting in Bali, and **BCR** *(Bukit Cilli Rafting; bcrrafting.com; adult/child from 1,200,000Rp)* also has a good reputation. Two- to three-hour trips often include lunch. The end point is usually about 20 minutes north of Sidemen.

LOCAL KNOWLEDGE

Wayan Tegteg has worked as a trekking guide since 2000 and has summited Gunung Agung more than 1000 times. *@tegtegwayan*

My preferred starting point for an Agung trek is the Pasar Agung temple. It's at a higher altitude than Pura Besakih and while on that route you can choose the ending: either a lower point at 3000m or, if conditions allow, the more challenging route to the peak of Agung (3142m). If you leave from Pura Besakih you can only reach the highest peak, and that route is very long.

Anyone wanting to trek Agung needs to come prepared with long trousers, good hiking shoes, wind-protection layers and gloves. The other equipment needed – like headlamps and trekking poles – is often provided by guides.

Gembleng Waterfall

TIME FROM SIDEMEN: **25MIN**

Frolick in a cascading waterfall

There are many spectacular waterfalls around Bali, but when it comes to a view *from* rather than *of* the cascading water, **Gembleng Waterfall** *(instagram.com/gemblengwaterfall; admission by donation)* tops the charts.

A steep five-minute walk up 130 well-maintained steps leads you to Gembleng's biggest drawcard: a collection of terraced rock pools with a view through palm trees onto a fertile, farmed valley. There are some picture-worthy (but less-spectacular) rock pools on the way up, and you'll know you've reached *the* ones when the path crosses the stream – or when you bump into the queue of people waiting their turn to slip into the pool and pose. Continue a short way up the steps from these pools and you'll reach **Gembleng Waterfall Restaurant**, with impressive views. Prices are surprisingly reasonable given its location.

It'll take about 25 minutes to reach the parking area from Sidemen; it's a stunning drive through farmlands and clusters of homesteads, and is particularly evocative in the early-morning light. Access to the waterfall trail opens at 7am; if you're looking for a peaceful experience, the earlier you arrive the better.

Besakih

TIME FROM SIDEMEN: **35MIN**

Summit Bali's highest mountain

Bali's highest and most revered mountain, the spiritual centre of the island, is **Gunung Agung** (Mt Agung; 3142m). Scaling the imposing volcano is one of Bali's most physically challenging adventures – but watching sunrise from up here is an extremely profound experience.

The two most popular routes are from Pura Pasar Agung Sebudi, on Agung's southern slope, and Pura Besakih on the southwest. The Pura Pasar Agung Sebudi route is the shortest and most direct; count about four or five hours to ascend to the summit from here. It will take six or seven hours on the much tougher Pura Besakih route. While the majority of hikers set off before midnight to summit in time for sunrise, some choose to leave from Besakih in the afternoon and camp on Agung for the night – sunsets up here are gorgeous – before departing to reach the top before dawn; **Raja Rimba Adventure** *(instagram.com/rajarimba_adventure; from 1,600,000Rp)* offers this option. Whichever option and route you go for, be prepared for cold temperatures and a tough climb that's very steep in parts.

Most of the places to stay in the region can recommend climbing guides (you cannot climb Agung without one). Two experienced guides are Wayan Tegteg *(WhatsApp +62 0813 3852 5677; instagram.com/tegtegwayan)* and I Ketut Uriada *(WhatsApp +62 0812 364 6426; ketut.uriada@gmail.com).*

TOP EXPERIENCE

Pura Besakih

Bali's most important temple, Pura Besakih, stands on the southwestern slope of Gunung Agung. It is a vast complex of 23 temples that form a landing complex for the gods on Bali (*besakih* is derived from the Sanskrit word for 'sanctuary'). Constant processions of village groups arrive for ceremonies and blessings, and to take holy water back to their own temples.

GALINA SAVINA/SHUTTERSTOCK

Find the Best Views

Bali's oldest and most important temple, **Pura Penataran Agung Besakih**, stands in the middle of the Besakih complex. Although you can see into the temple area from various angles, it is not always open to visitors. For an exquisite view of scores of jet-black *meru* soaring towards the sky – a dramatic sight on misty mornings – follow the path behind **Pura Penataran Pande Besakih** (the clan temple for the island's blacksmiths, goldsmiths and silversmiths) to the back of Pura Besakih. For a fantastic view over Bali head up to **Pura Gelap**, surrounded by intricately carved walls.

Make an Offering

You can enter some of the temples if you wish to pray – but you must take offerings with you. Women sell these throughout the complex; a notice board at the ticket desk details the prices *(20,000-70,000Rp)*.

Get the Most from Your Visit

The quality of local guides included with entry varies greatly. Get more from your visit by asking lots of questions, and ask them to take you to Pura Gelap. You will invariably be asked for a tip at the end.

TOP TIPS

- You may receive offers to 'come pray with me'. Visitors who seize this chance to enter a closed temple risk facing extortionate demands.
- If you accept offerings from someone, you'll be expected to pay for them. A sign in the ticketing area lists prices.

PRACTICALITIES

- besakih.org
- adult/child 150,000Rp
- 7am-6pm

Padangbai

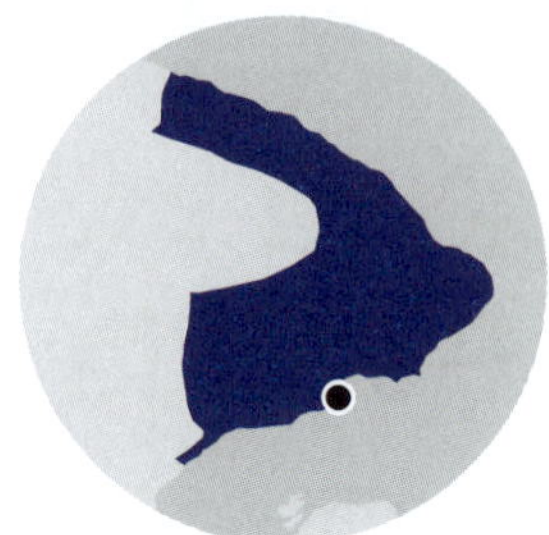

BEACH TOWN | DIVING & SNORKELLING | FERRIES

GETTING AROUND

Padangbai town is small and easily walkable. Its port is a hub for ferries fast, slow and otherwise. Government-run ferries for Lombok and Nusa Penida leave from **Pelabuhan Padangbai**; these are the ones for people who want to take their motorbikes. Fast boats to Lombok and the Gilis depart from the **Fast Boat Pier**, a separate, crowded pier to the east. Buy tickets at pier entrances. For more see p174.

TOP TIP

Need a beach read? **Wayan Bookstore** *(9am-6pm)* has an excellent selection of second-hand novels in English and books in other languages. It's set just off the road opposite the Bamboo Paradise guesthouse – follow the signs.

While there are a few dive spots in the area, most travellers head to Padangbai to get away: the town's busy commercial port connects Bali with Lombok, the Gilis and Nusa Penida. Late in the day, when the boat traffic diminishes, Padangbai takes on a more mellow mood, with visitors wandering the waterfront and hanging out at backpacker cafes and simple restaurants, many fronting the beach. When the moon reflects off the bay, it's almost romantic.

Accommodation ranges from hostels and guesthouses to a few diving-focused resorts. By day, avoid the transiting mobs by hitting nearby beaches to dive and snorkel. Take a short walk around the headland to Pura Silayukti, the place where Empu Kuturan – who introduced the caste system to Bali in the 11th century – is said to have lived.

Accessible Underwater Adventures

Dive into East Bali's underwater delights

Padangbai is one of Bali's main centres for diving and snorkelling. There's good diving on the coral reefs around Padangbai, but the most popular local spots are **Blue Lagoon** and **Jepun**, with a range of soft and hard corals and varied marine life, including sharks, turtles and wrasse. Blue Lagoon boasts a 23m wall.

If you're wanting to snorkel, keep in mind that currents here can be strong: instead of snorkelling from **Blue Lagoon Beach** (which some people do, but it's not recommended), head out to sea with one of the former fishing boats that ferry tourists to snorkelling spots from **Padangbai beach**. You can also ask dive operators if they have room for snorkellers on their boats.

Find Padangbai's dive centres, including well-respected **OK Divers** *(okdiversbali.com)*, on Jl Silayukti, past the fast-ferry pier. Many also offer trips to nearby **Gili Tepekong** and **Gili Biaha**, two islets just off Teluk Amuk, as well as Tulamben (p185) and Nusa Penida (p115).

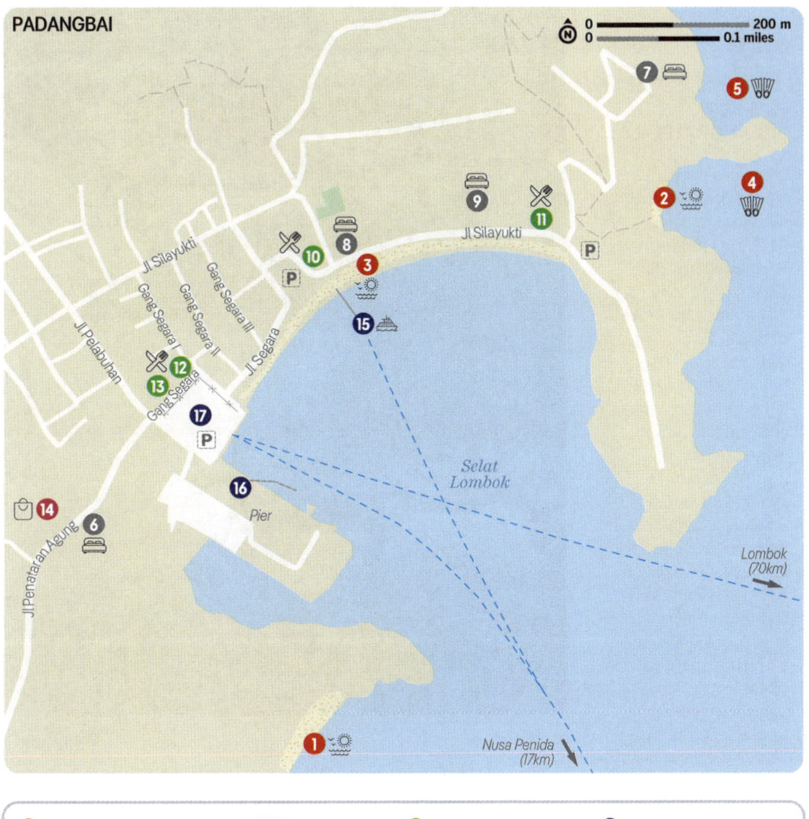

SIGHTS
1 Bias Tugal
2 Blue Lagoon Beach
3 Padangbai beach

ACTIVITIES
4 Blue Lagoon
5 Jepun
see 8 OK Divers

SLEEPING
6 Alola Inn
7 Bloo Lagoon
8 OK Divers Resort & Spa
9 Padang Bai Beach Homestay

EATING
10 Martinis
11 Topi Inn
12 Warung Bu Jero
13 Zen Inn

SHOPPING
14 Wayan Bookstore

TRANSPORT
15 Fast Boat Pier
16 Pelabuhan Padangbai
17 Ticket Office

Hit the Beach

Chill beside the sea

The dive shops and guesthouses at the east end of town along Jl Silayukti are fronted by a long strip of beach that harbours fishing boats. But there are two beaches nearby that you can head to for some delightful R&R.

On the far side of Padangbai's eastern headland, about a 500m walk from the town centre (turn left as you begin to climb uphill), is **Blue Lagoon Beach**. Tucked in a small bay, its has a few warungs and sun loungers, which you can rent for 25,000Rp per day.

TIPS FOR PADANGBAI PORT

Slow government-owned passenger and vehicle ferries run 24/7 from **Pelabuhan Padangbai** (p172). Tickets are cheap; buy them at the **ticket office** in the ferry terminal.

Fast boats usually leave between 8am and 1pm and return in the afternoon. If you have time to spare, shop around for a fast-boat ticket from one of the many offices around the **Fast Boat Pier** (p172). Or buy your ticket online – 12go.asia is a reliable platform to use.

Piers can get manic, so try to travel light. Anyone who carries your luggage on/off a boat will expect to be paid. Agree on the price first; expect to pay from 20,000Rp (it's luggage-dependent) and remember: a little extra from you can make a big difference to a porter.

FEBRIANA SUWARNINGSIH/SHUTTERSTOCK

Bias Tugal

The other (more appealing) option is to walk southwest from the ferry terminal to **Bias Tugal**, a lovely cove with idyllic powder-white sand and warungs, making it a very pleasant base for a day. Be careful in the water as it's subject to strong currents. Access the beach on foot via the rough pathway adjacent to the Bamboo Paradise guesthouse (it's an eight-minute walk from the Wayan Bookstore sign) or, if you're on a scooter, continue up the hill and follow signs to Bias Tugal (also known as Pantai Kecil or 'Little Beach'). You can't drive all the way to the beach, but it's a short walk from the parking.

EATING IN PADANGBAI: OUR PICKS

Martinis: This three-table warung at the fast-boat pier serves large portions of Indonesian dishes (plus seafood and jaffles) at affordable prices. *7am-10pm* $

Warung Bu Jero: Super-affordable seafood and Indonesian fare. You'll be dreaming of its succulent prawns long after you leave Bali. *9am-10pm* $

Zen Inn: Come here for the pasta or playlist – both are well worth it. The menu includes Indonesian and Western staples. *7am-10pm* $

Topi Inn: Meals use chemical-free ingredients whenever possible. The overwhelmingly large menu includes apple crumble and brownies. *7am-10pm* $$

Beyond Padangbai

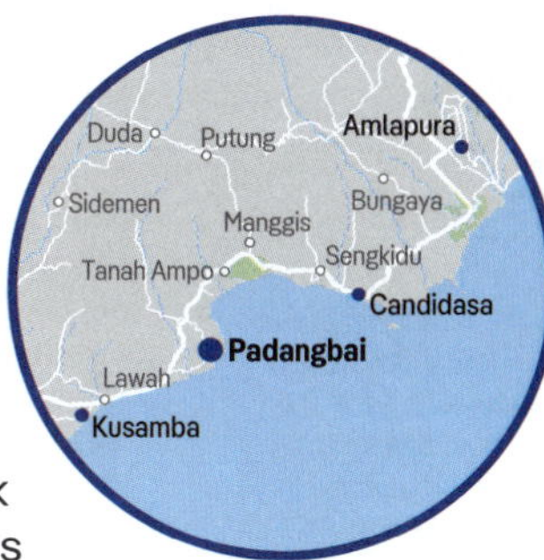

Uncover beautiful water gardens, laid-back beach towns and, in quiet villages, surprises for travellers with a penchant for food.

The coastline around Padangbai is a green, rocky ribbon backed by steep hills, and the narrow roads that wind their way up here through farmlands and forests are a delight to explore. Kusamba is the last of the flatlands to the west and mixes traditional work with the sacred. Around Amlapura you'll find striking temples, gorgeous water gardens and quiet royal residences, while seaside Candidasa charms with mellow waterfront stays in a quiet strip of hotels. The beach at Pantai Pasir Putih makes up for the lack of sand elsewhere in the area with a long, brilliant white strand that's the envy of other Balinese beaches.

Places

Kusamba p175
Candidasa p175
Amlapura p176

GETTING AROUND

The main coast road east and west of Padangbai is traffic-busy; if you're a nervous driver, your accommodation can hook you up with a driver (scooter or car). If you're heading away from the coast (and you must – it's beautiful in the hills), you'll need a scooter with sufficient power to get you up the steep hills, and reliable brakes to get you safely down.

Kusamba

TIME FROM PADANGBAI: **20MIN**

Discover the 'Bat Cave Temple'

One of Bali's small but striking, directional temples is **Pura Goa Lawah** *(instagram.com/penataran_goa_lawah; 30,000Rp)*, established in the 11th century. An unconfirmed legend says the cave leads all the way to Pura Besakih (p171), some 19km away. Set against an oceanside cliff, the temple is full of fruit bats (said to be guardians of the temple) and tour groups. These bats provide sustenance for the legendary giant snake, the deity Naga Basuki, also believed to live in the cave. Across the road from Pura Goa Lawah, there is an impressive bat-cave statue in the rest area. There are some warungs around here too.

Candidasa

TIME FROM PADANGBAI: **25MIN**

Chill out in Candidasa

Candidasa's vast **lotus pond** – larger than two soccer fields – is an underrated delight, especially before mid-morning, when the flowers are open. A wide paved 540m-long walkway surrounds the pond, and the view across the water changes as you walk around: from palm trees and the sea to a densely vegetated hill. Ocean side, boat operators in a small bay offer fishing, snorkelling and sightseeing trips.

Candidasa itself is a low-key town with oceanfront guesthouses and hotels. It's a good place to pause and chill or to head out on a hike. **Trekking Candidasa** *(trekkingcandidasa.com; from 250,000Rp)* offers a range of walks through the verdant rice fields and hills nearby.

BALI AGA

The Bali Aga are the descendants of the original Balinese who inhabited the island before the Majapahit arrival in the 11th century. Bali Aga villages – which include Tenganan and Trunyan (p200) – are mostly in the mountains around East Bali and tend to be very traditional, with strict social rules and unique traditions. Ancient customs include an unusual, old-fashioned version of the gamelan known as the *gamelan selunding*. Girls dance an equally ancient dance known as the *rejang;* a good time to see this is during the **Usaba Sambah Festival**, honouring gods and ancestors. The festival is famous for its contest of *perang pandan* (ritual combat using thorny stalks made of pandan leaves), usually held in June or July.

Visit historic Bali Aga villages

A 10-minute drive from Candidasa, **Tenganan** is home to the Bali Aga. Often spoken of as one village, there are two in fact: Tenganan Pegringsingan (east) and Tenganan Dauh Tukad (west), separated by a small valley. A visit to either is a chance to learn about Bali Aga traditions. Both are car-free and laid out as they have been for centuries, with homes leading off a central walkway.

The two villages offer quite different visitor experiences. **Tenganan Pegringsingan** *(admission by donation)* has a small pavilion at its entrance displaying beautiful photographs. Many residents erect tables outside their homes and demonstrate *prasi* (the art of decorating *lontar*; p177) or display *kamben gringsing*, the double-ikat cloth traditionally woven in Tenganan. Scan the QR code at the front office beside the pavilion for a PDF detailing village food, traditions and crafts.

In smaller **Tenganan Dauh Tukad** *(admission by donation)*, you'll be greeted by someone from the village at the entrance who will show you around and accompany you to a homestead where *kamben gringsing* are made and sold. You can also buy a *lontar* calendar with your name written on.

Amlapura

TIME FROM PADANGBAI: **1HR**

Step into a royal palace

The very tranquil **Puri Agung Karangasem** *(instagram.com/puriagungkarangasem; 30,000Rp)* is still home to descendants of the royal family, but visitors are welcome to wander around a lovingly kept part of it. Entry to the royal palace is past beautifully sculpted panels and an impressive multi-tiered gate. Inside, admire architectural influences from Bali, Europe and China. The main building in the 19th-century compound is **Maskerdam**, the raja's residence, built as a gift by the Dutch as a reward for the Karangasem kingdom's acquiescence to Dutch rule. It houses furniture and photos from that time. A highlight of the lovely, manicured grounds is the **Bale Kambang**, an ornate floating pavilion surrounded by a large pond.

A captivating water garden

Wander between pretty ponds dotted with stone statues and home to hundreds of koi fish at **Tirta Gangga** *(instagram.com/tirtagangga.bali; adult/child 90,000/45,000Rp)*, an exquisite water palace north of Amlapura. Built in 1946 for the last raja of Karangasem, there are fountains and flowers, bridges, stepping stones and even a small pool that you can bathe in. The garden's ponds, fed by a natural spring, are considered to be holy, hence the garden's name 'Sacred Water of the Ganges'. A small museum in the southeast corner of the property displays a collection of the royal family's heirloom *keris* (sacred blades) and in the upstairs pavilion is a statue of the king, with lovely views of the garden and neighbouring rice paddies. Tirta Gangga gets incredibly busy – arrive early (gates open at 6am) to enjoy the peace here.

TANYA JONES/SHUTTERSTOCK

Taman Ujung

Stroll the grounds of Taman Ujung

On the coast, a 20-minute drive from Tirta Gangga, water palace **Taman Ujung** *(instagram.com/tamansoekasadaujung; 100,000Rp)* was built by the last king of Karangasem and dates to 1919. Compared with the more popular Tirta Gangga, Taman Ujung is far more simple in overall design. It's the geometry of the design here that makes it so striking, particularly when the water of its three large ponds is still, perfectly reflecting the garden's bridges and pavilions. Taman Ujung was largely destroyed by an earthquake in 1979. It's mostly been restored, but on the western side of the complex, evocative ruins of Bale Kapal (an old pavilion) remain. From here you have a view over the water palace to the sea.

See Bali's 'gates of heaven'

Pura Lempuyang is the place to get *that* iconic photo – with a mirror reflection of the *candi bentar* (split gates) in front of majestic Gunung Agung. The scene makes a striking photo, but there's far more to this sought-after picture than a clever illusion. The *candi bentar,* which serve as a spiritual threshold between the outside world and a sacred space, mark the entrance to one of Bali's important directional temples.

Pura Lempuyang *(70,000Rp)* is a complex of seven temples perched on the steep slopes of Gunung Lempuyang (1058m), a 'twin' of neighbouring Gunung Seraya. The largest and most easily accessed temple is **Pura Penataran Lempuyang**, where visitors queue for hours to be photographed. From a second temple, 2km uphill, the calf-punishing stair climb begins: it's 1700 steps from here to the highest temple, **Pura Lempuyang Luhur**. Visiting all seven temples takes at least four hours and involves a breathtaking 2900 steps.

Pura Lempuyang is open to visitors from 5am. In the parking lot, you'll need to pay 50,000Rp for the shuttle that takes around eight minutes to transport you up the steep, winding hill to the entrance. Upon paying the admission fee, you'll be given a ticket number to have your pic taken between the gates.

PALM-FROND BOOKS

Lontar (traditional palm-frond books) are made from the fan-shaped leaves of the lontar (or rontal) palm. The leaf is dried, soaked in water, cleaned, steamed, dried again, then flattened and cut into strips. Words and pictures are inscribed onto the strips using a sharp blade or point, then coated with a black stain from candlenut. The *lontar* strips are then threaded onto a string, with a carved bamboo 'cover' at each end. Lontar palms are easily spotted by their shorn tops; fronds are harvested as fast as they grow to satisfy the demand for both *lontar* books and *arak* (fronds are part of the distillation process). **Museum Pustaka Lontar** *(instagram.com/museumpostakarlontar)*, a 10-minute drive north of Puri Agung Karangasem, explains more.

ROAD TRIP

East Bali for Foodies

Set off on a culinary journey that takes you from beach to factory, to market, farm and kitchen. This driving route celebrates artisans who have honed their craft of perfecting a kitchen staple, and chefs who use carefully sourced ingredients to create food supporting small-scale farmers and respecting the environment. Drive it in a day or, to dive into the experiences, take two days.

1 Kusamba Salt Farmers

Salt farmers in Kusamba produce some of Bali's most delicious *garam* (salt) and a stop at a beachside *pondok* is an opportunity to see how it is made and buy some. Several of Bali's top chefs shop here. Keep a lookout for small handmade 'salt maker' signs on the side of the road.

The Drive: You'll have parked on the side of the coastal road. Be patient and take care when you pull out back onto this road (which takes you to Jasri) – heavy trucks often whizz past.

2 Sorga Chocolate

Tucked between the palms of the Jasri neighbourhood is **Sorga** *(sorgachocolate.com)*, a small chocolate factory with cafe that makes artisanal dark chocolate from ethically sourced cacao beans grown in Bali. Come here for a 45-minute factory tour to learn how chocolate is made and taste 15 different chocolates *(adult/child 200,000/150,000Rp)*. Book in advance for a three-hour chocolate-making class.

YUSNIZAM YUSOF/SHUTTERSTOCK

Salt farmer, Kusamba

The Drive: Before winding up to Bali Asli, you drive through Amlapura – be aware of one-way roads.

3 Bali Asli

A meal at **Bali Asli** *(baliasli.com.au)* might well be the best you have in Bali. The restaurant, with gorgeous views of Gunung Agung, has long been revered for its traditional Balinese dishes made from locally produced, organic ingredients. It's worth booking ahead to embark on one of Bali Asli's 'culinary adventures', ranging from street-food tours in Amlapura to mountaintop sunrise breakfast feasts and 'a day in the village' cooking classes.

The Drive: Leaving Amlapura you join lovely tree-lined roads. Arriving by car, park at the Raya Honey Sibetan sign roadside, then follow the signposted scooter track on foot to the homestead.

4 Raya Honey Sibetan

Sibetan village is known for its abundant *salak* (snakefruit) palms. Down a winding lane between trees, at remarkable homestead **Raya Honey Sibetan** *(instagram.com/raya_honey_sibetan)*, apiarist I Kadek Swanjaya keeps seven species of bees, producing seven different honeys. Visitors can taste (delicious!) and buy. Kadek is deaf and his wife has partial hearing; when you arrive you might need to find them instead of calling out.

The Drive: The road twists and turns from Sibetan to Jungutan. You're in for a treat – it's stunning around here!

5 Samsara Living Museum

End with a cooking class at **Samsara Living Museum** *(samsarabali.com; 900,000Rp)*, a community-run centre in the village of Jungutan. Cook Balinese dishes in a traditional kitchen and help make *arak*, a Balinese alcoholic drink.

Amed

UNDERWATER ADVENTURES | DRAMATIC VIEWS | COASTAL SCENERY

GETTING AROUND

There's a lot packed into a small area here. To make the most of your time, rent a scooter (your accommodation will point you in the right direction for hiring one) to explore the coastline. Roadworks are ongoing as the coastal road is upgraded. Motorists should check before booking accommodation that parking is available – space for four-wheel vehicles can be hard to find here.

Stretching from Amed village to Bali's easternmost tip near Kusambi, the semi-arid coast generically called 'Amed' draws visitors with its succession of small scalloped bays. Fishing boats lined up like multi-hued sardines colour grey-sand beaches, and the area revels in its relaxed atmosphere, boho vibe and very enjoyable diving and snorkelling. Resorts, flush cafes and open-air restaurants dot 15km-long coastline and overnight options cover most price points, tastes and interests: find dive resorts, health and meditation retreats, plus dozens of hotels, guesthouses and homestays. Amed village and Jemeluk are dining hotspots – vegetarian and vegan options are as common as offers to head out to sea on a *jukung* (traditional outrigger boat). Many people come to Amed for a day or two and end up staying for much, much longer.

Explore a Striking Coastline

Go beach-hopping around Amed

For such a compact area, the beaches and bays along the Amed coastline are surprisingly different in character – beach-hopping makes for an interesting break from time spent underwater. Some, like **Pantai Lean** and **Pantai Bunutan**, are predominantly working beaches, more practical than pretty, that tend to be a hive of activity around 8am when fishing boats return to shore. Others, such as **Pantai Selang** and **Pantai Lipah**, are good options for snorkelling, despite the fair number of fishing boats lining the sand. Tucked in a well-protected bay, **Pantai Jemeluk** sports many beachfront restaurants, and is popular for snorkelling and swimming. At more than 2km long, **Pantai Amed** is popular for walking and, with its striking black sand, makes for dramatic sunrise and sunset photos.

Actually getting to beaches along this stretch of coastline can be quite exasperating as much of the development here has severely restricted access to the shoreline. Using Google

TOP TIP

At time of research plans were apparently under way to build a pier servicing fast boats to Lombok and the Gili Islands. Do some research into this if your travel plans include a trip to these other islands.

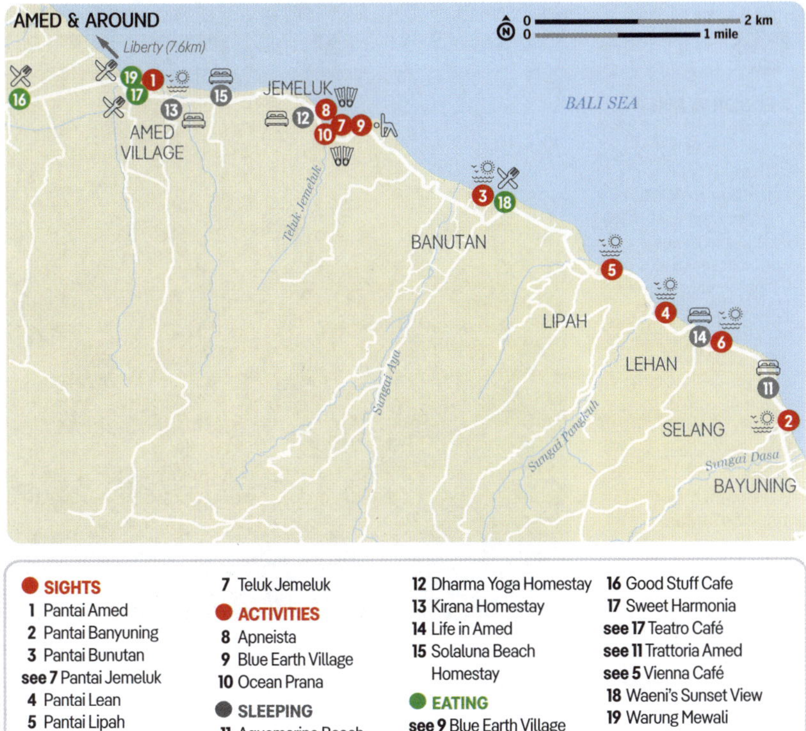

SIGHTS
1 Pantai Amed
2 Pantai Banyuning
3 Pantai Bunutan
see 7 Pantai Jemeluk
4 Pantai Lean
5 Pantai Lipah
6 Pantai Selang
7 Teluk Jemeluk

ACTIVITIES
8 Apneista
9 Blue Earth Village
10 Ocean Prana

SLEEPING
11 Aquamarine Beach Villas
12 Dharma Yoga Homestay
13 Kirana Homestay
14 Life in Amed
15 Solaluna Beach Homestay

EATING
see 9 Blue Earth Village Restaurant
16 Good Stuff Cafe
17 Sweet Harmonia
see 17 Teatro Café
see 11 Trattoria Amed
see 5 Vienna Café
18 Waeni's Sunset View
19 Warung Mewali

Maps doesn't help much: the easiest way to find a route in is to look for places where scooters are parked up together.

Experience Amed's Underwater Paradise

Dive and snorkel the east coast

The Amed area is revered for its clear water and abundant marine life – the reason so many travellers linger here. Snorkelling is excellent: **Teluk Jemeluk** (Jemeluk Bay) is a protected area where you can admire live coral and plentiful fish within 100m of the beach, while the coral gardens and colourful marine life at **Pantai Selang** are highlights. The much-hyped sunken Japanese fishing boat off **Pantai Banyuning** is little more than a few bits of wooden debris, but it's still a popular spot for snorkellers.

Diving is obviously excellent too, and there are many dive shops and centres along this stretch of coastline. Dive sites off beaches Pantai Jemeluk, Pantai Selang and Pantai Lipah feature slopes and drop-offs with soft and hard corals, and abundant fish; some are accessible from the beach, while some require a short boat ride. Tulamben's *Liberty* (p185) wreck is 13km north of Amed; count on 20 minutes by car or scooter.

DECODING AMED

Called 'Amed' by both tourists and marketing-minded residents, tourist development here began at Amed village. It soon spread to three nearby bays with fishing villages: Jemeluk, which has a buzzy travellers strip; Banutan, with both a beach and headlands; and Lipah, which has a lively mix of cafes. Development has marched onward through Lehan, Selang, Banyuning, Aas and on to Kusambi, each a minor oasis at the base of arid hills.

For accommodation, you'll need to choose between the villages and the sunny headlands in between. The former put you right on the sand and offer a small amount of community life, while the latter give you sweeping vistas and isolation.

PURWANTO NUGROHO/SHUTTERSTOCK

Diving, Amed

Underwater in One Breath

Enrol in a freediving course

Breath-hold enthusiasts from around the world are drawn to Amed. The exceptional diving area has also earned a reputation as Bali's freediving capital thanks to its clear waters, minimal currents and drop-offs close to the coastline that create ideal conditions for both beginners and advanced freedivers.

There are numerous freediving schools around Amed. Two of the most established are Bali's first freediving school **Apneista** *(apneista.com; 1-day level 1 course 3,900,000Rp)* and freediving village **Ocean Prana** *(oceanprana.com; 2-day introductory course $190)*, created by champion freediver Yoram Zekri. Courses include theory, pool and ocean sessions.

EATING IN AMED: OUR PICKS

Sweet Harmonia: Come here for plate-licking-good Asian fare. The menu also covers vegetarian and vegan options. *11am-10pm* $

Good Stuff Cafe: Smoothie bowls, cold-pressed juices, kombuchas, mouth-watering burgers, steaks and more – all eco-sourced. *7.30am-10pm* $$

Teatro Café: Build your own salad or tuck into tasty Italian dishes at this locally owned eatery with Europe-inspired menu. Excellent coffee. *7am-9pm* $$

Warung Mewali: A chilled family-run warung right on Amed beach. Peer through fishing boats to the ocean while enjoying *arak* cocktails, seafood and burritos. *10am-9pm* $

Watch Sunset from the Sea

Take a late-afternoon boat ride

While there are some spectacular sunset spots along Amed's coastline, it's hard to beat the late-afternoon view you have of Gunung Agung from the ocean. As the sun lowers towards the horizon, it brings the outline of both Bali's tallest peak and smaller Gunung Batur (1717m) into sharp view. With the sea in the foreground and the gentle motion of the boat, the sunset experience hits next level.

The beaches and bays around Amed are jam-packed with *jukung* and you'll easily find someone willing to take you out for a sunset jaunt. Many guesthouses and restaurants have at least one boat operator they work with, and can set up your trip as little as an hour or two in advance. Expect to pay around 300,000Rp for two people for a 90-minute sunset trip, or around 700,000Rp for a 5am fishing trip.

Climb Gunung Seraya

Follow a trail up a volcano

Trekking up the slopes of **Gunung Seraya** (1175m) is both a good workout and a fascinating look at this side of Bali. Note that there is sparse vegetation and it gets hot. Ask your hotel if it's safe to walk (staff are sure to be monitoring volcano warnings) and, if it's OK to set off, allow a good three hours to get to the top of Seraya, starting from the rocky ridge just east of Jemeluk Bay. Most trails are well-defined, so guides aren't required. Sunrises are spectacular but will require hiking in the dark, so you will need a guide for this. Inquire at your lodging.

YOGA STUDIOS AROUND AMED

Blue Earth Village: Two dreamy yoga spaces in a hillside resort overlooking Jemeluk Bay. Daily classes at 8am and 5pm include yin, vinyasa and medicinal yoga. Book a day in advance. *blueearthvillage.com*

Ocean Prana: This 'freedivers' village' in Jemeluk offers daily classes in a poolside yoga space at 5pm. Classes are popular with freedivers who use the disciplines to regulate their breathing. Book before 3pm. *yogaprana.com*

Life in Amed: This beachfront boutique hotel in Lehan sports a lovely elevated yoga shala with a garden and ocean view – for multi-day retreats and also classes most days (drop-ins welcome). Contact reception for class schedule. *lifebali.com*

EATING IN AMED: RESTAURANTS WITH A VIEW

Blue Earth Village Restaurant: Begin a day in Jemeluk with coffee, juice, a healthy breakfast and peaceful view of Gunung Anung and the ocean. *7.30am-10pm* $

Waeni's Sunset View: Affordable option for a sunset drink (the view's better than the food), overlooking Bunutan Beach and Gunung Agung. *7am-9pm* $$

Vienna Café: Tropical-style cafe on Lipah Beach with seafood, Asian and continental options; gluten-free and allergy-friendly dishes. *7.30am-10pm* $$

Trattoria Amed: Italian on Ibus Beach (near the Japanese shipwreck), with pizzas and a wine list even better than its palms-and-ocean view. *7.30am-10.30pm* $$

Beyond Amed

Definitely roads less travelled, this region is perfect for those with a sense of adventure and a yearning for peace.

Places

Seraya p184
Budakeling p185
Tulamben p185
Tejakula p185

GETTING AROUND

This part of Bali remains off the tourist track (so far), meaning you'll need to set transport up yourself. Rent a scooter through your accommodation or arrange a private driver and you'll have the benefit of exploring this quiet area on your own terms. If you prefer the convenience of staying in Amed, this area can easily be explored on a day trip.

The further you travel along the coastal road from Amed – whether it be up towards North Bali or down and around the bulge of the island – the more you venture into an area that's completely off the regular tourist trail. And that is precisely its charm.

The coastal road towards Candidasa is especially dramatic, and while the churning currents of the Lombok Strait look violent and foreboding, the water is calm around the coast at Tulamben. This is where you'll find one of Bali's most popular dive sites. Head further west and a string of quiet villages beads the route to the Tejakula area, home to a waterfall, unassuming beaches and idyllic beachfront retreats inviting stillness and relaxation.

Seraya

TIME FROM AMED: **1HR**

To Amed, the long winding way around

The usual route that travellers take to reach Amed is island via Tirta Gangga (p176), but there is another longer, twistier and far less-travelled road that will delight those who prefer to get off the beaten track. This route runs from Taman Ujung (p177) near Amlapura to the Amed region; without stops it's a 1½-hour drive. The undulating road twists and turns as it follows the coastline around the far eastern bulge of Bali, between mountains and sea. Ocean views are astounding – as are views of distant Gunung Rinjani (3726m) the closer you get to Amed.

En route you'll pass hidden bays with tiny villages and beaches tightly packed with *jukung*. Access to these villages is usually by scooter path; if you're travelling by car, safely pull off the road and park on the headland after the **Gili Selang lighthouse** (closed to visitors). If you're into textiles be sure to stop at **Kerijinan Tenun** *(instagram.com/wastro_bebali)* in Seraya, 12km from Taman Ujung. Threads here are coloured with natural dyes made from leaves, roots and flowers, and woven into *rangrang*, a beautiful fabric native to Nusa Penida.

Budakeling

TIME FROM AMED: 1HR

A sunset cycle to Amed

Breeze down the southeastern slopes of Gunung Agung as you wind your way along palm-lined roads, between rice paddies and from village to village en route to Amed – by bicycle. **East Bali Bike Tour** *(eastbalibike.com; tours from 600,000Rp)* arranges small-group trips that begin at an altitude of 1000m near Budakeling and descend to the coast. Tour leaders collect you at your hotel. Stops are made at traditional Balinese homes along the way, and you'll get to witness daily life in the villages. See how coffee is roasted up here, or, if you are lucky, watch women weaving or carvers carving. You will most likely pass farmers tending their paddies. The ride is through the late afternoon, and you'll finish with gorgeous sunset views. The route is mostly along gravel and asphalt roads, and not particularly challenging. Other routes are available if you'd prefer to cycle in the morning and finish up at popular **Virgin Beach**.

Tulamben

TIME FROM AMED: 25MIN

Dive a wreck

Tulamben's big attraction is the wreck of the **Liberty**, a US cargo ship that sunk over 80 years ago. It is among the most popular dive sites in Bali and has transformed what was once a simple fishing village into a resort town based on diving. Coral reefs lining this coast are also a draw.

Even snorkellers can easily swim the 50m out and explore the wreck. The stern rears up visibly from the depths, 5m below the surface, and the coral-encrusted wreck swarms with dozens of colourful fish species – and scuba divers most days. The ship's hull is broken into sections: the most interesting parts are between 15m and 30m deep. Entry to the site from the road is 25,000Rp per person; bring extra cash if you'd like to buy a T-shirt or shell necklace.

Tejakula

TIME FROM AMED: 1HR

Cool off beside a waterfall

Tucked in a small valley just up from the coastline of Les village in the Tejakula district is 40m-high **Air Terjun Yeh Mampeh** *(Les Waterfall; 30,000Rp)*. A walk up here presents a refreshing opportunity to cool off in a small pool at the base of one of Bali's quieter falls. Count around 15 minutes to walk

THE WRECK OF THE LIBERTY

In January 1942 the US military cargo ship USAT *Liberty* was torpedoed by a Japanese submarine near Lombok while sailing from Australia to the Philippines. It was beached at Tulamben so that its cargo of rubber and railway parts could be saved. The Japanese invasion prevented this and the ship sat on the beach until the 1963 eruption of Gunung Agung, when it broke in two and sunk just off the shoreline – much to the delight of divers and snorkellers. The *Liberty* was built in 1918 for service during WWI. Over 125m long, it had a globe-spanning career before WWII. (And for the record, it was not a WWII Liberty-class freighter.)

EATING BEYOND AMED: OUR PICKS

Warung Seni Tejakula: An absolute delight, this creative cafe in Tejakula takes as much care preparing healthy food as it does with its garden and decor. *9am-8pm* $

Tropikal Bar: Delicious pizza is the focus of this Tejakula bar. There's a small cocktail menu (try the spicy mango) and a pool table. *5-10pm* $$

Slice & Brew: The menu at this Tulamben cafe covers almost everything: coffees, juices, cocktails, cakes and pastries, ramen, pizzas and salads. *8am-9.30pm* $$

Dapur Bali Mula: Delicious traditional Balinese lunches and dinners are available in this renowned restaurant in Les. By reservation only. $$

THE WALLACE LINE

Take the scenic route to Amed – the road that wraps around the eastern bulge of Bali – and you'll notice white peaks on waves signalling the turbulent currents that churn between Lombok and Bali. These currents form part of what naturalists now refer to as the Wallace Line. More than 170 years ago, when British naturalist Alfred Russell Wallace explored the Indonesian archipelago, he noticed that there seemed to be an imaginary line slicing between Borneo and Sulawesi and between Bali and Lombok. It divided the types of flora and fauna found on the islands. On the east, he noted, the plants and animals seemed to be more Australian than Asian, which characterised the west.

MOCHAMMAD ABDUL AZIS/SHUTTERSTOCK

Tejakula

the 1km trail from the parking area to the waterfall; the path is concrete and well-shaded most of the way.

To add something special to your visit, a few hours before your arrival call Ibu Made *(WhatsApp +62 813 3821 2635)*, who lives along the trail and can prepare offerings and facilitate a blessing at the waterfall *(250,000Rp)*. About 300m from the parking area along the trail, you'll find a handful of soulful warungs. They make for a very peaceful stop on the way back from the waterfall.

Retreat in Tejakula

As you drive the main road towards Lovina there's not much that will distinguish the Tejakula district from the rest of this coast-road area. But keep an eye on Google Maps for the turn-off into the lanes of **Les**, **Tejakula** or **Bondalem**. These lovely villages in the Tejakula district are well worth an overnight stop at least. Tucked between banana and palm trees fringing lanes to beaches and hills, you'll find enticing boutique resorts, retreats and creative cafes. Add the opportunity to book a cooking class at **Dapur Bali Mula** (p185; *instagram.com/dapurbalimula; 450,000Rp per person*), to go diving or snorkelling without any crowds, and watch fishing boats launching at sunset, and you've reasons to linger here for days.

Places We Love to Stay

$ Budget $$ Midrange $$$ Top End

Keramas

Nirmala Guest House Surf $$ With spacious rooms and bungalows surrounded by a garden, this is a good option for those who enjoy a sense of space. It's a short walk to the beach.

Hotel Komune $$$ Absolute heaven for health and fitness enthusiasts. Komune's gyms, steam rooms, Pilates and yoga studios, ice baths and healthy menus have some guests booking in for weeks. (p164)

Sidemen

MAP p167

Pondok Indah Homestay $ Two rooms in a family compound with a lovely garden. The host family is very helpful with organising activities and transport.

Uma Agung Villa $$ Beautiful views, spacious rooms with balconies, and there's a glistening pool too – you get a lot more than you pay for here.

Samanvaya $$$ This adults-only retreat is absolutely dreamy. Think: stunning stone or bamboo villas, gorgeous paddy and mountain views, infinity pools and swinging chairs.

Wapa di Ume $$$ For a real treat upgrade to the resort's luxury tent or pool-fronted villa. The restaurant's excellent, and yoga is offered too.

Padangbai

MAP p173

Padang Bai Beach Homestay $ This peaceful homestay, close to the fast-ferry pier, has simple rooms set around a garden with swimming pool. Great value.

Alola Inn $$ Just a short walk from the port, you're paying more for convenience than style – but this colourful guesthouse is comfortable. Breakfast included.

OK Divers Resort & Spa $$ Built around a pool shrouded with palms, this small hotel feels very boutique-y. It's beside the fast-ferry pier.

Bloo Lagoon $$$ Set atop a headland with gorgeous ocean views, this eco-village ticks every responsible-travel box. The 25 villas are individually decorated.

Candidasa

Ida's Homestay $ Thatched bamboo bungalows are dotted between palm trees on a beachfront property. It's peaceful, old-school Bali; stay here and time slows down.

The Forty Eight Resort $$ Large bungalows surround a lovely pool; it's excellent value for money. The good restaurant overlooks the lotus pond.

Candi Beach Resort & Spa $$$ A superbly comfortable beachfront resort with gorgeous gardens and a dive shop too. Come here to escape the world.

Amankila Manggis $$$ With infinity pools and marble slabs an integral part of the terraced design, this ultra-luxurious resort is nothing short of grand.

Amed

MAP p181

Kirana Homestay $ Large rooms here are actually cottages with their own small kitchen and verandah with daybed. Excellent value.

Dharma Yoga Homestay $ This conveniently located homestay has double rooms and a mixed dorm. Right across the road from Jeluk Bay, and surrounded by restaurants and cafes.

Solaluna Beach Homestay $$ Enjoy direct access to Amed Beach (and views of Agung) from the guesthouse. It has a wonderful pool. For a treat, book a beachfront room.

Aquamarine Beach Villas $$$ Each large villa has its own kitchenette and a deep verandah with comfy couches and idyllic sea views.

Tejakula

Alam Kowang $ The large pool makes this budget stay feel quite luxurious. Rooms have a verandah and outdoor bathroom. It's a five-minute drive to the beach.

Villa Selina $$ Well-priced bungalows are tucked in a lush, established garden that fronts a secluded beach. It's incredibly peaceful here.

The Kirana Tembok $$ Come here for a quiet escape. The beachfront pool, surrounded by a deck and palm trees, is idyllic.

For places to stay in the Central Highlands, see p201

GATHOT SUBROTO/SHUTTERSTOCK

Above: Temple, Danau Tamblingan (p195); Right: Gunung Abang (p198)

Researched by
Mark Eveleigh

Central Highlands

VOLCANOES, FORESTS AND BEAUTIFUL MOUNTAIN VIEWS

The Central Highlands, lush with forests and sculpted by volcanoes, feel a world away from the island's tropical coastline.

Hikers, bird-watchers, mountaineers and nature lovers are drawn to Bali's Central Highlands, where tangled forests, towering plantations and stark volcanic landscapes form the backdrop for a variety of adventures. The old town of Munduk – filled with Dutch colonial history – is the ideal base from which hikers and waterfall seekers can explore terraced hillside paddies and spice-scented plantations, while the sacred crater lakes of Danau Tamblingan and Danau Buyan shimmer amid surprisingly vast tracts of virgin jungle. It's the best place to experience the floral wealth of the world's second-most-biodiverse country, and winding mountain roads make for colourful journeys where every hairpin reveals a different view. This is a land of water and fire, and from the rim of a smouldering caldera you can look down on, or hike to, both the sacred Danau Batur (with the open-air cemetery of the 'Hindus of the Wind' beside the lake) and to the 1717m peak of Gunung Batur. Every morning this active volcano draws hundreds of trekkers seeking unforgettable sunrise views, but Gunung Abang (p198) offers a more pristine and wilder option. Bali's central mountains are rich in culture and it's here that you'll find astounding temples like Pura Ulun Danu Bratan and Pura Luhur Batukau. In the lower region, hillside slopes have been carved into the picturesque terraces that form Jatiluwih, a traditional rice-growing area that is protected by UNESCO.

NH.NUGROHOHERU/SHUTTERSTOCK

THE MAIN AREAS

MUNDUK
Hike through forests and ancient rice terraces.
p192

BEYOND MUNDUK
Gunung Batur: a geological marvel.
p198

Find Your Way

Stay close to Munduk town and you'll find enough walking trails to keep you inspired for a week without even needing transport. To explore more widely you'll need private transport or an organised tour.

CAR

Self-driving is the ideal way to get around if you're confident on winding mountain roads that are frequented by heavy trucks. For guests who prefer to hire a driver, many hotels have separate (basic) driver accommodation.

MOTORBIKE

While the highland traffic is a breeze compared to the coastal towns, motorcycling up here comes with its own complications as roads are steep and frequently potholed. Rent a more powerful scooter, especially if travelling as a pair.

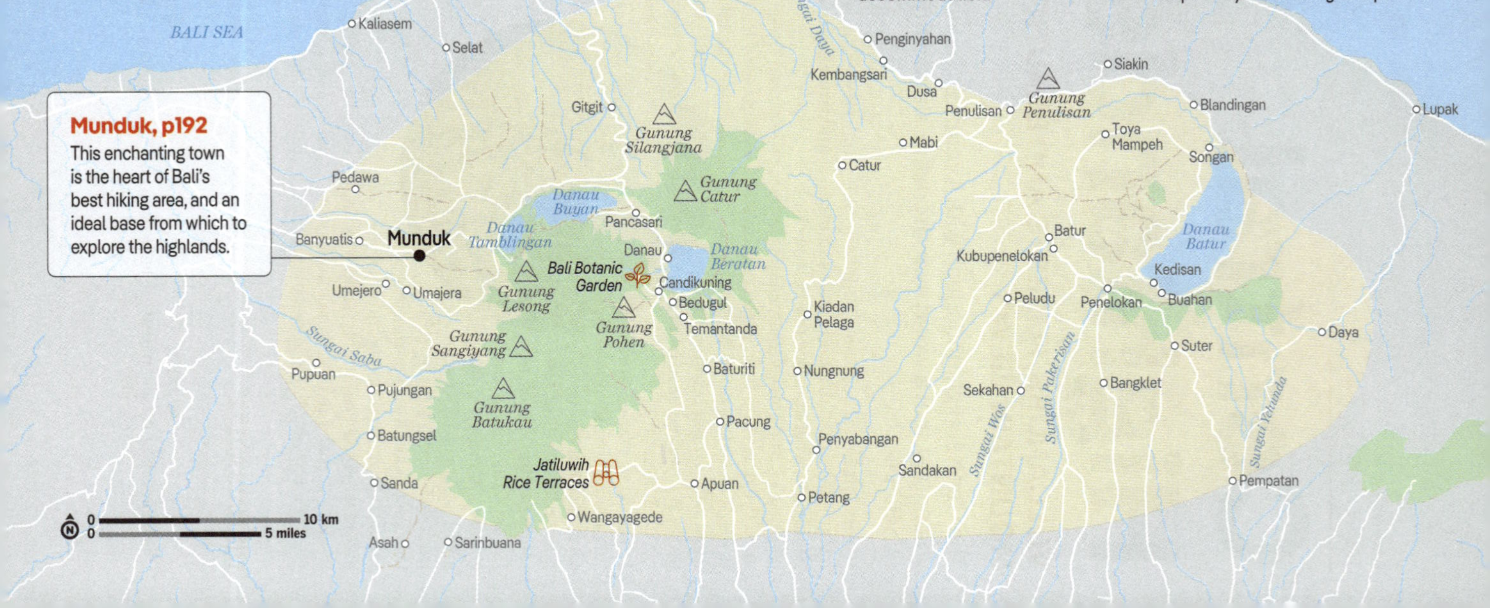

Munduk, p192
This enchanting town is the heart of Bali's best hiking area, and an ideal base from which to explore the highlands.

STEPHANE BIDOUZE/SHUTTERSTOCK

Melanting waterfall (p195)

Plan Your Time

Distances are small; less than 40km separates Munduk town (in the west of the Central Highlands) from Gunung Batur (in the east), but allow at least two hours for the incredibly scenic drive.

Pressed for Time

For blissful mountain solitude head to **Munduk** (p192). Spend the morning hiking to the spectacular **waterfalls** (p195) and an afternoon exploring the **nutmeg and clove forests** (p194) with one of Munduk's excellent guides. The next day head to **Danau Tamblingan** (p195) for a walk through the protected primary jungle and a boat ride across the crater lake.

Five Days to Roam

Stop at **Pura Luhur Batukau** (p196) and spend the next day hiking from **Danau Tamblingan** (p195) to the famous **Jatiluwih rice terraces** (p196). Take a slow drive east, stopping at the **Bali Botanic Garden** (p195) and the **Batur Geopark Museum** (p198). Watch the sunset from the crater rim and catch sunrise the following day from **Gunung Abang** (p198).

SEASONAL HIGHLIGHTS

JANUARY

The wettest month is a tough time for jungle trekking but expect fewer tourists, lower prices and dramatic waterfalls.

APRIL

The end of the rains is a great time time to be in the highlands, with the forests thick with birds and butterflies.

JUNE

Clove season is fascinating and deliciously aromatic; the dramatic harvesting is done on 10m-long bamboo ladders.

OCTOBER

With orchids in rioting bloom this is the best time for jungle treks, but pack warm layers for sunrise treks.

Munduk

SPECTACULAR HIKING | ICONIC TEMPLES | EXCEPTIONAL VIEWS

GETTING AROUND

Munduk town and the surrounding hillsides are best explored on foot. Motorbikes are available for rent if you want to explore further afield (you can get to the north coast from here in a little over half an hour). Cars with drivers are easily organised through any hotel, and the best drivers will also serve as informative guides.

Long before the Dutch took advantage of Munduk's blissful climate to establish a hill station here around 130 years ago, these pretty highlands had been settled by the early Balinese (some say the Bali Aga) who, according to legend, were escaping a plague of ants. Whatever the case, Munduk and the exquisite surrounding highlands make for an idyllic escape, even today.

The views across hillsides of plantations of clove, nutmeg, coffee and cacao trees – all the way to the ocean – are astounding, and there are some special lodges and homestays tucked in between the trees. The hills and UNESCO-protected terraces of this quiet region are laced with tracks and walking trails, and while it's possible to explore some solo, Munduk has an established network of experienced guides who share anecdotes, legends and the enthralling culinary and medicinal traditions that are still an integral part of the unique highland culture.

TOP TIP

People who dress for the beach are often surprised – night-time temperatures in the highlands can drop to 12°C. Pack warm layers, especially if you plan on getting up for a sunrise hike. July to September are the coldest months.

The Road Least Travelled

Take the scenic route to Munduk

The journey up to Munduk is as much part of the adventure as time spent actually hiking in the Central Highlands. A stunning introduction to the area is to take the Antosari road – leading from Pantai Soka on the West Bali coast up to Pupuan – sweeping you past spectacular rice terraces, palm trees and tumbling bougainvilleas. For an even more memorable route, turn right in the village of **Punjungan** onto the Jl Gunung Batukaru, and follow the winding lanes to Munduk. It's a magnificent journey along small rural roads that will have you ogling spice plantations, fruit orchards, jungle ravines and countless flower-decked temples.

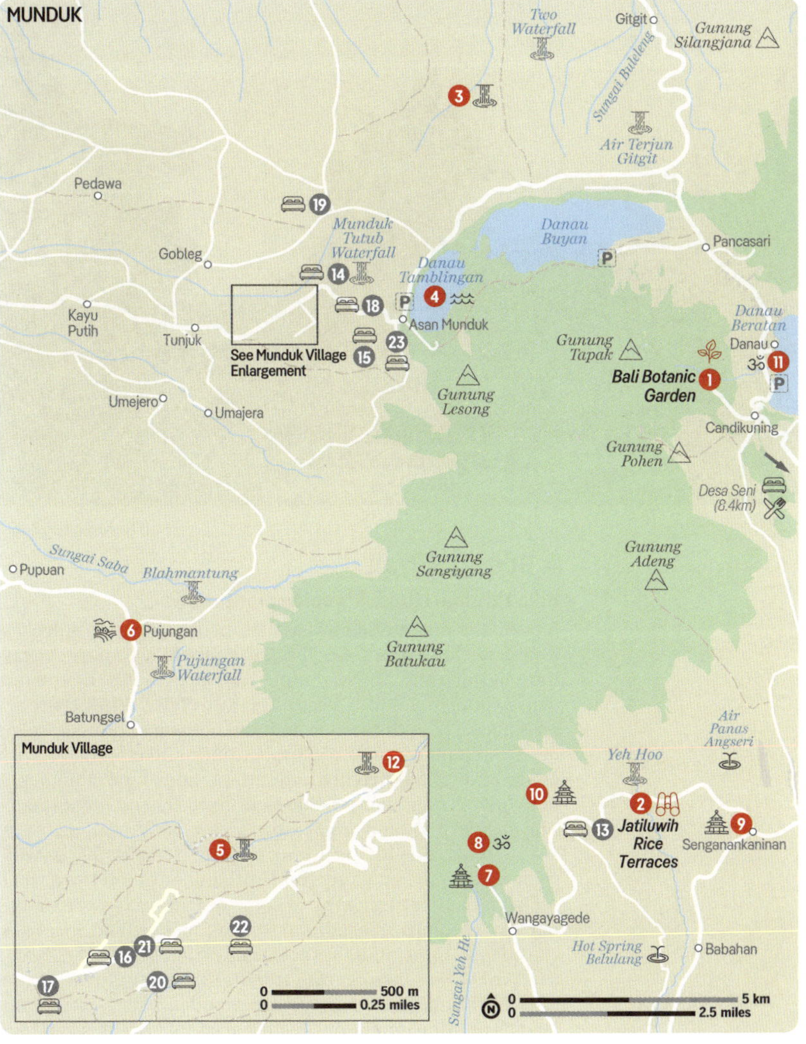

HIGHLIGHTS

1 Bali Botanic Garden
2 Jatiluwih Rice Terraces

SIGHTS

3 Banyumala Twin Waterfalls
4 Danau Tamblingan
5 Melanting Waterfall
6 Punjungan
7 Pura Jero Taksu
8 Pura Luhur Batukau
9 Pura Luhur Besikalung
10 Pura Luhur Pucak Petali
11 Pura Ulun Danu Bratan
12 Red Coral Waterfall

SLEEPING

13 Adhi Jaya Suites
14 Desa Eko Glamping
15 Elevate Bali
16 Made Oka Homestay
17 Meme Surung Homestay
18 Munduk Farm House
19 Munduk Moding Plantation
20 Nadya Homestay
21 Puri Lumbung Cottages
22 Puri Sunny Guesthouse
23 Terrasse du Lac Munduk

EATING

see 14 Botanist
see 13 Jatiluwih Resto
see 18 Munduk Farm House
see 19 Munduk Moding Plantation

JAY WU/SHUTTERSTOCK

Bali Botanic Garden

A Scented Trail

Hike through Munduk's spice plantations

Munduk is surrounded by paddies, plantations and spice forests. Travellers who are seeking to connect with nature gravitate to this small town in order to hike through the region's densely forested hills to cascading waterfalls. While there are virgin forests in the area, woodland here more often consists of working plantations of clove, nutmeg and cinnamon, with coffee and cacao thriving under the shade of the canopies. A network of trails connects hamlets, markets and homesteads. The blissful highland temperatures – typically around 20°C to 25°C – make this idyllic hiking country. It's possible to walk some trails independently from Munduk – around town you'll see signs indicating paths to some of the area's waterfalls – but for fascinating insights into local history and lifestyles, consider hiring a guide. Ketut Darma *(WhatsApp +62 822 3657 6149; walking tours per day 700,000Rp)* is highly respected.

To an uninitiated observer, the wooded valleys might appear as pristine jungle, but you'll learn that almost everything seems to be either edible, medicinal or of folkloric spiritual value. A guide can add interest to your walk by telling you about the intricacies of ancient spice crops, as well as the

EATING AROUND MUNDUK: RESTAURANTS WITH VIEWS

Munduk Moding Plantation: Tuck into locally grown produce and homegrown coffee while gazing over the infinity pool all the way to Java. *10am-9pm* $$

Desa Seni: Irresistible offerings on a changing menu that invariably features organic local vegetables and delicious regional produce. *10am-8pm* $$$

Munduk Farm House: Enjoy cosy evenings in front of the log-fire, dining on the best beef rendang and sipping perfectly crafted Irish coffee. *8am-9pm* $$

Botanist: Seasonal veg, smoothies and chilled playlists – plus beer, wine and excellent burgers – overlooking a jungle-clad ravine at Desa Eko Glamping. *8am-10pm* $$

complicated methods of preparing staples like cassava, taro, palm sugar and *arak* (distilled palm spirit). You can learn about the cultivation of coffee, cacao and vanilla (which is pollinated here entirely by hand). There are set routes you can walk, but guides (easily arranged through any hotel) can also tailor treks to suit your interests.

Explore a Sacred Forest

Trek around Danau Tamblingan

Shrouding the rim of the caldera that forms **Danau Tamblingan** (Tamblingan Lake) is an ancient, sacred rainforest that for centuries has been a source of plants for traditional medicine. It's an enchanting place, with towering nettle trees and magnificently tangled ficus trees (some older than 600 years) growing as pillars of a lush ecosystem entangled with ferns, orchids and vines.

Walking trails here vary from a short hourlong stroll to extended hikes through the forest, returning across the lake by motorised canoe. Since it's a community project a guide is obligatory, and you'll be assigned one when you arrive at the ranger office at Danau Tamblingan. Entrance to the protected forest is 100,000Rp per person, plus the rate for the walk (which varies depending on the length of the trail you do). There are also tents for rent for those who wish to sleep on the lakeshore, an experience that's equally unforgettable for the star-studded nights as for the moody mist that rises off the lake at dawn. Kadek Sandiana *(WhatsApp +62 877 8436 7848)* is an experienced and highly knowledgeable guide.

Discover Indonesia's Botanical Riches

Visit Bali's beautiful botanical garden

Indonesia is the world's second-most-biodiverse country (after Brazil), and **Bali Botanic Garden** *(kebunraya.id/bali; weekday/weekend 15,500/25,500Rp)*, known locally as Kebun Raya Bali, showcases some of its most spectacular floral riches. You could spend an entire day wandering around the collection of themed gardens, but if time is short, hire an e-scooter, electric moped, e-bike or bicycle *(10,000Rp-100,000Rp)* from the ticket office at the entrance. These vehicles are rented out in half-hour blocks, but to do justice to the extensive gardens will take at least an hour...and that's just to scratch the surface. Highlights include the **Cactus Greenhouse**, featuring a collection of 68 species, and the **Rhododendron Garden**, with over 100 varieties. The **Orchid Garden** – at its most colourful when many specimens are flowering around July and August – is mind-blowing, and **Taman Usada** has more than 300 plants that are used by traditional healers.

Sprawling across almost 160 hectares, Bali Botanic Garden boasts 2400 species of plants in total. Bird-watchers are also drawn here by an estimated 79 resident and migrant bird species.

MUNDUK'S WONDERFUL WATERFALLS

Divemaster **Ketut Darma**, a senior trekking guide and traditional healer *(WhatsApp +62 822 3657 6149)*, describes some of his favourite waterfalls.

Red Coral Waterfall is very easy to access, so it's a good one to visit for older people and those travelling with small children. You'll walk through plantations of coffee, cloves, avocados and vanilla to get there.

Melanting Waterfall is one that not many people go to; it's one of Bali's tallest and is really pretty. There are about 500 steps that you'll need to go down, and it can be slippery in the wet season.

Banyumala Waterfall – the twin waterfall – is a great option if you want to swim; there is a wonderful clear pool at the bottom and it's never too crowded.

THE MYSTERIOUS TEMPLES OF BATUKARU

Established in the 11th century, **Pura Luhur Batukau** (often written Batukaru) stands at the end of a lonely road on the slopes of Gunung Batukau. Hindu worshippers will invariably stop first at **Pura Jero Taksu**, which serves as a spiritual and literal gateway to Batukau – it's believed that only if you pray there first will your Batukau prayers reach the gods. Batukau was historically said to be a lair for bandits, and 2km from the old temple is the almost-forgotten **Pura Luhur Pucak Petali**. Dedicated to Sang Hyang Maling ('God of Thieves'), this temple, along with **Pura Luhur Besikalung** nearby, is said to have been the place to pray at if you wanted to become adept at 'the thieving business'!

Fingerprints of the Gods

Walk among terraced rice fields

With elegantly stepped terraces curving like enormous fingerprints, the paddy landscapes of **Jatiluwih** are postcard perfect. This 195-sq-km area is protected by UNESCO, and it's here that the island's *subak* tradition – a complex irrigation system that dates back to the 9th century – remains deeply rooted. It's easy to explore the area on your own, and a good starting point is **Jatiluwih Resto**, the small restaurant that faces a paved track with a signboard listing marked trails (ranging from 1.5km to 5.5km).

Jatiluwih was recognised as one of the Best Tourism Villages of 2024 by UN Tourism and the trails are busy from about mid-morning (despite a 75,000Rp fee for every international tourist to enter the area). For a more sedate paddy experience, arrive in the afternoon, enjoy sunset from a cafe terrace and stay overnight. This way you can enjoy the spellbinding solitude of a sunrise walk through the paddies when this beautiful landscape is saturated with colours: the vibrant neon green of young rice shoots; the mirror-like, sky-blue sheen of flooded paddies; and the swaying golden sheaves of the harvest.

Cloud Forest Adventures

A long trek across jungle highlands

Near the centre of an island that's often described as 'overcrowded and overdeveloped' it's unimaginable that you can hike for more than five hours across virgin rainforest without meeting a single person.

You should allow at least seven hours to complete the 16km **jungle route** from Tamblingan's sacred forest to Jatiluwih's UNESCO-protected rice paddies, and during the five-hour crossing of the jungle you won't see a single human habitation. The route changes frequently thanks to falling trees, so this trek should not be attempted without a guide, who will surely ask to pause to make offerings at the three remote temples you'll pass.

The forest is home to barking deer, porcupine, mongoose, flying foxes, monkeys (lutungs and macaques) and civets. But it's the rioting vegetation that's really astonishing, with towering fig trees and tree ferns and tangled lianas. Orchids and bromeliads hang from every tree.

Carry at least 1.5L of water and wear long trousers (protection against leeches) and long sleeves to guard against itchy nettles and thorny *tunggu sebentar* (wait-awhile) bushes. Tamblingan-based jungle guide Kadek Sandiana *(WhatsApp +62 877 8436 7848)* has walked this route countless times and charges 800,000Rp per person, including a substantial picnic lunch in a jungle clearing. Guides can also be found at Tamblingan ranger station, but ask for confirmation that they've walked the route recently since fallen trees often mean complex detours.

THE GODDESS OF RICE

The paddy fields of Jatiluwih are decorated with intricately sculpted shrines. According to Balinese farmers, water and the fertile volcanic soil are only two of the facets that make up this rich agricultural system – without the all-important offerings to Dewi Sri, the goddess of fertility, the harvest would assuredly fail. Bali can achieve up to three rice harvests a year (a rarity elsewhere), but then Balinese *petani* (farmers) point out that other areas fall short because nowhere else is Dewi Sri worshipped. These are intensely sacred landscapes and signs have recently been placed along Jatiluwih's paddy-field trails requesting that visitors respect these shrines and don't encroach closer than 1 metre in their hunger for holiday happy snaps.

Jatiluwih

SENNARELAX/SHUTTERSTOCK

Beyond Munduk

With its lake, smouldering peak and extensive black lava fields, Gunung Batur is one of Indonesia's geological wonders.

Places

Gunung Batur Area p198
Trunyan p200

GETTING AROUND

To trek Gunung Batur or Gunung Abang you'll need a guide. Most hotels and homestays will be able to help, and guides will usually arrange transport to and from your accommodation. Most people come here for the sunrise Batur walk only, and tour companies include in their price an early-morning pickup (often around 1am or 2am) from most tourist centres on the island. If you're staying longer, explore the surrounding area by renting a scooter, but if you're going to be carrying a pillion passenger, opt for a more powerful bike (an N-Max or similar).

The Gunung Batur area is a geological marvel, and the volcano you see today rises from within a caldera formed during an eruption some 30,000 years ago. The town of Kintamani spreads around the southern rim, overlooking a crater lake and barren black lava fields, and onto the lower slopes of the relatively 'new' (still spectacularly active) volcano. It's here that hundreds of visitors arrive in the early hours of each morning, eager to climb its slopes and catch a view of the sunrise with mighty Gunung Agung in the distance. This area is as captivatingly stark as Munduk is lush, and the atmosphere here – possibly fuelled by the Earth's fiery forces – is instilled with a rugged sense of adventure.

Gunung Batur Area

TIME FROM MUNDUK: **2HR 20MIN**

Understanding the connection between geology and spirituality

Gunung Batur stands as the centrepiece of the **Batur UNESCO Global Geopark**, a 370-sq-km area renowned for its geological and cultural significance. It is encircled by a vast caldera, the remains of a 3000m-high volcano that erupted 30,000 years ago, and within it the rugged lava fields from various eruptions are flanked by a lake, clustered with houses, and tamed pockets of farmlands. Just off the southern rim of the caldera is the imposing **Batur Geopark Museum** *(adult/child 50,000/30,000Rp; 8am-4pm)*, which serves as a portal to the geological and spiritual heritage of the area. Its exhibits showcase the fascinating history of volcanic eruptions, the evolution of the landscape and, in the upstairs section, the deep-rooted relationship between regional culture and the fiery surroundings. An hour at the museum will add a rich layer of understanding to the time you spend exploring this dramatic landscape.

A volcano sunrise trek

A sunrise trek up Gunung Batur (1717m) has long been one of Bali's most popular excursions, with up to 300 people setting off every morning for a dawn rendezvous. Spectacular as the view might be, it is hardly a spiritual experience. Neighbouring **Gunung Abang** (2151m) is Bali's third-highest mountain,

JOSEPH CHRISTANTO/SHUTTERSTOCK

Gunung Batur

reaching just below the level of Gunung Batukau and almost 1000m below mighty Gunung Agung. Abang offers exceptional sunrise views all of its own, and a poignant solitude that is at odds with the crowds on Batur.

As with Batur, the Abang hike typically starts at 2am if you want to catch sunrise at the summit, although a daylight hike through the gorgeous cloud forest has a thrill all of its own. You need a local guide, and **Bali Sunrise Trekking and Tour** *(balisunrisetrekkingandtour.com; per person from 900,000Rp)* can arrange the entire package, including transfers from your hotel. Even relatively fit hikers will take up to three hours to reach Abang's summit, and it's a challenging trek, particularly after heavy rain. Once on the peak – with just a handful of other hikers – you'll have unspoiled sunrise views to the summit of Agung to the east, and to the west a view of Batur across the mirror-like expanse of the crater lake. In the distance you'll see Rinjani (Lombok), Batukau (Bali) and even Arjuna on distant Java.

Watch the sunrise from the roof of a 4WD

Every morning hundreds of travellers converge on the slopes of Gunung Batur to shoot selfies while the sun rises. While most walk to the summit, a more accessible – and, for some, more exciting – option is a 4WD excursion. The photographs you can get, with the rugged 4WD playing a star role and Gunung Abang and Gunung Agung in the background, will capture the essence of fun, freedom and adventure. This is not an experience wrapped in wild solitude, however. In low season about 100 colourful 4WDs park bumper to bumper on terraced sections of Batur's lower slopes, but in July and August numbers rise closer to 300 and the entire valley seems to reverberate with 4WD revving from around 3am.

ONE OF BALI'S MOST ICONIC TEMPLES

Beautiful lakeside **Pura Ulun Danu Bratan**, which was built around 1634 CE, is one of the most important place of worship for Balinese Hindus. It honours Dewi Danu, the goddess of water, and ceremonies are held here to ensure a sufficient supply of water in the *subak* (irrigation) system for the island's rice farmers. Images of the temple – with its striking *merus* (multi-roofed shrines), formally landscaped garden and stunning backdrop mountain reflected in the still water of the lake – have become iconic of Bali, and the temple attracts busloads of tourists every day. While it remains a functioning temple, tourism here is big business, so expect souvenir stalls lining the parking area, ATMs, a children's playground and lakeside restaurants.

BALI'S OWN DOG BREED

Bali's highlands are home to the island's very own internationally recognised dog breed: the Kintamani. The dogs, which are rarely found outside of Bali, are most often white but can also be black or brindle; they stand about half a metre tall and have a medium-length coat, a fluffy curved tail and soft, thick ears that always look alert. They're known to be intelligent, loyal and obedient dogs who also have a good sense of smell and are excellent hunters and guards. The fact that they are one of only two breeds with blue (or partially blue) tongues has led to the hypothesis that they are descended from chow chows that were introduced by Chinese traders. Some Balinese believe that a lick from a blue-tongued Kintamani can cure wounds.

The vehicles are modified short-wheelbase Suzukis (despite the propensity for 'Jeep' stickers), fitted with roof racks that are sturdy enough to hold the weight of several people (crucial for those photos). The drive is only 1.3km up a rough road, but you'll need to reach the viewpoint at least an hour before sunrise to secure a good parking space; take warm clothes and some cash for a coffee or hot chocolate for you and your driver. A 4WD tour can be arranged through any hotel and some operators, like **Mount Batur Bali Trekking** *(mountbaturbalitrekking.com; per person 675,000Rp)*, offer the option to visit the black lava fields afterwards. This is an exciting opportunity to explore the vast hillside of lava left behind after Batur's devastating 1963 eruption.

Trunyan

TIME FROM MUNDUK: **3HR**

Witness the sky burials of Trunyan village

Trunyan is the only community in Bali to use what are sometimes referred to as 'sky burials' for their dead. This cemetery, isolated from the outside world on the eastern shore of Danau Batur, is accessible only by boat. Eleven bodies at a time are laid to rest here, covered only by slatted bamboo frames, known as *ancak-saji*. When new bodies arrive the oldest of the eleven is relegated to the heap of bones and collection of skulls piled under the sacred *taru menyan* tree, which apparently neutralises the odour so that there's absolutely no discernible smell from the decomposing bodies. (Kintamani is perpetually plagued by flies, yet this is the only spot that's relatively fly-free.)

Pak Donal *(WhatsApp +62 812 3879 5153; tours up to 6 people from 450,000Rp)* is one of several reliable local guides who can arrange boat trips to the cemetery. While it was once a location that was far off the tourist radar, Trunyan's special cemetery has become one of the highland's most popular sites and is bringing much-needed revenue into this formerly very under-privileged area.

The authentic beef rendang has become famous among locals.

EATING IN KINTAMANI: OUR PICKS

Toteme Restaurant: A very chic, open-sided restaurant that's charmingly laid out. Grab a comfy armchair and enjoy excellent coffee and cakes. *7am-11pm* **$$$**

O Club By Oculus: This avant-garde restaurant has a rooftop terrace with spectacular views of Batur, the lake and lava fields. *5am-10pm* **$$**

Ritatkala Cafe: The best among a parade of chic cafes offering views towards Batur, serving everything from fish and chips to Massaman curry. *6am-6pm* **$$**

Rumah Makan Pitopang Jaya: Kintamani's newest, best and most affordable warung serves excellent buffet-style Masakan Padang. *10am-6pm* **$**

Places We Love to Stay

$ Budget $$ Midrange $$$ Top End

Munduk

MAP p193

Terrasse du Lac Munduk $ Only four rooms and – thanks in part to the romantic log fires – they book up fast. Also an appealing dining room overlooking Danau Tamblingan.

Puri Sunny Guesthouse $ Centrally located in Munduk, this is an opportunity to stay in the building that the owners claim functioned as a 'dak' hostel (government accommodation) from 1908. Rooms 1 and 2 have outstanding views.

Meme Surung Homestay $ An atmospheric property with a long verandah, two old Dutch houses and a gorgeous garden, with typically spectacular Munduk views.

Made Oka Homestay $ A million-dollar view for a budget-friendly price and a great little restaurant make this homestay a very affordable base for exploring the area.

Puri Lumbung Cottages $$ A lovely mountaintop resort with a variety of rooms. An ideal base for a range of activities from hiking to medicinal-plant workshops and dance classes.

Nadya Homestay $$ The view over North Bali from this comfortable homestay is worth paying triple for. Enjoy rooftop breakfasts and lazy afternoons in the infinity pool.

Munduk Farm House $$ Lovely bungalows set around charming gardens. A cosy spot with a lounge that features roaring log fires.

Munduk Moding Plantation $$$ A luxury property with good eco-credentials set on an organic coffee plantation and with an infinity pool that looks like it's at the edge of the world.

Elevate Bali $$$ A sinuously curving layout, perfectly mimicking the lines of the rice terraces, runs through what is probably the region's most chic and stylish resort.

Desa Eko Glamping $$$ Cosy highland nights under canvas, in what might be Bali's most appealing designer tents, make this an unforgettable experience.

Jatiluwih Area

Adhi Jaya Suites $ Attracts return guests time and again for its breathtaking views over Jatiluwih rice terraces. For the best outlook ask for room 5 or 7.

Desa Seni $$$ A blissful retreat featuring a collection of antique timber *joglo* houses set across the edge of a jungle valley in Bali's secluded rural heartland.

Kintamani

Tamalia House $ While the farmlands around the western shore of Danau Batur are perpetually plagued by flies, this friendly family-run property makes an affordable highland escape.

Bali Cottages Lake View $ This collection of four *lumbung* (rice barn)-style rooms has a fantastic view of the lake. It's well worth staying here for sunrise, instead of hiking up the peaks.

Lakeview Hotel $$ This solid old hotel has a range of rooms. The standard ones are very basic, while the more luxurious deluxe rooms are worth the upgrade.

Toteme Glamping $$$ The perfect location if you plan a sunrise rendezvous on Batur's summit (although less ideal if you hope to sleep after the 4WD engines start revving at 4am).

Desa Oculus $$$ Spacious suites and unbelievable views – especially from Kintamani's best and biggest infinity pool – make this an unbeatable choice.

Researched by
Sarah Reid

North Bali

ADVENTURE AND NATURE ALONG THE COAST

Diving, hiking, waterfall-gazing and relaxing by the sea are the best ways to fill your North Bali days.

The land on the other side of the mountains, that's North Bali. Although nearly one-fifth of the island's population lives here, this vast region is overlooked by many visitors who stay in the South Bali–Ubud axis. The big draw is the incredible diving and snorkelling at Pulau Menjangan, which is in West Bali National Park – a nature wonderland, with surprisingly good wildlife spotting.

Arcing around a nearby bay, Pemuteran may be Bali's best beach town: a relaxed oasis with superb snorkelling just steps from the sand. To the east is Lovina, a sleepy beach strip with cheap hotels and even cheaper sunset beer specials. All along the north coast are outcrops of quiet hotels and villas, set on the reef-protected shore.

Inland, North Bali thrums to the roar of dozens of waterfalls cascading down from impossibly green hillsides thick with wild fruit trees and laced with hiking trails. Museums and history await in Bali's second city, Singaraja, which was once the gateway to the entire island.

Getting to North Bali lives up to the cliché: it's half the fun. Routes follow the thinly populated coastlines east and west, or you can go up and over the mountains by any number of routes, marvelling at crater lakes and maybe stopping for a misty hike on the way.

MYMODENA/SHUTTERSTOCK

THE MAIN AREAS

LOVINA
Handy seaside base for exploring. **p206**

PEMUTERAN
Beaches, nature and superb diving. **p215**

For places to stay in North Bali, see p223

POELZER WOLFGANG/ALAMY

Left: Dolphin, Lovina (p206); Above: Diving, Pulau Menjangan (p220)

Find Your Way

North Bali is just that, the island-spanning swath that starts in the chain of central highlands and flows down to the minimal surf at the shore. A busy main road hugs the coast.

ON FOOT

Hiking in waterfall-punctuated hillsides or across the wildlife-filled expanses of West Bali National Park are highlights, but you can also explore Lovina, Singaraja and Pemuteran on foot.

MOTORBIKE & CAR

A motorbike is handy for exploring beyond central Lovina and Pemuteran. A car and driver is easily arranged through your accommodation.

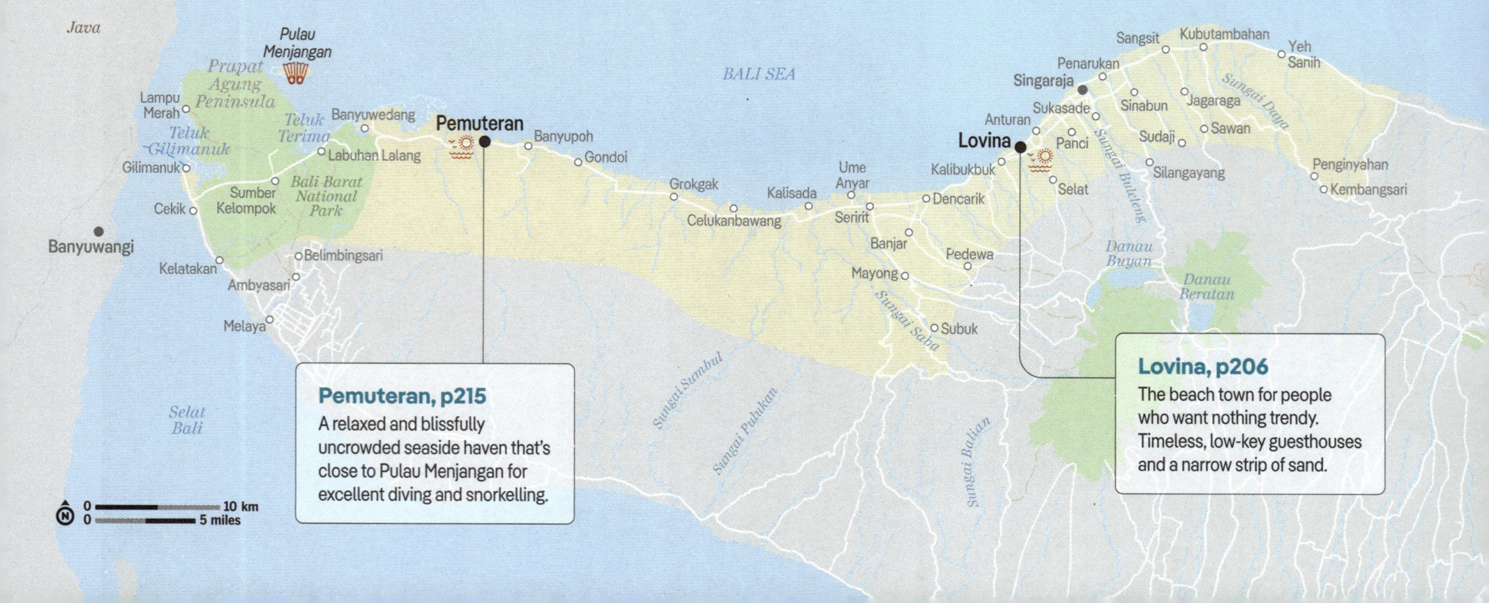

Pemuteran, p215

A relaxed and blissfully uncrowded seaside haven that's close to Pulau Menjangan for excellent diving and snorkelling.

Lovina, p206

The beach town for people who want nothing trendy. Timeless, low-key guesthouses and a narrow strip of sand.

ELIZAVETA GALITCKAIA/SHUTTERSTOCK

Brahma Vihara Arama (p211)

Plan Your Time

In general, North Bali is a brilliant antidote to the throngs of the south and Ubud. During rainy season it's wonderfully lush.

Pressed for Time

With only a couple of days, choose your delight. Getting to the north from South Bali takes a few hours, so make your time count. There is world-class diving and snorkelling at **Pulau Menjangan** (p220), which is most easily accessed from **Pemuteran** (p215). Or you can opt for the workaday charms of **Lovina** (p206) and its proximity to waterfalls.

A Week to Work With

Start in the east, coming north on the coast from Amed. See the temples near **Yeh Sanih** (p214) and then delve into **Singaraja** (p209), Bali's historic second city. Use **Lovina** (p206) as a base for exploring the hinterland and visiting waterfalls like **Sekumpul** (p213). Continue west, landing in **Pemuteran** (p215) for snorkelling, diving, hiking and bird-watching.

SEASONAL HIGHLIGHTS

MARCH–MAY

Waterfalls in the lush hills are at their thundering best as the rainy season nears its end.

JUNE–AUGUST

Pemuteran and Pulau Menjangan get busy as holidaymakers flock to Bali from around the world.

SEPTEMBER–NOVEMBER

West Bali National Park is at its driest and the sparse vegetation makes for easier wildlife spotting.

DECEMBER–FEBRUARY

Christmas is busy at Pemuteran. Rain brings lush beauty to the nearby verdant hillsides and rice terraces.

Lovina

QUIET DAYS | QUIET NIGHTS | MELLOW BEACHES

GETTING AROUND

Depending on the traffic gods and your route, the trip to Lovina can take three to five hours over the central mountains from South Bali. Descending the fertile hillsides of North Bali brings alluring virescent scenery and opportunities to stop at waterfalls. Most people use their own wheels or line up a ride through their accommodation at either end of the trip.

Alternatively, you can reach Lovina from the coasts to the east or west, which takes considerably longer than from the south, but which also allows for stops along the way. There are a few tourist shuttles from the south.

Lovina is at its best when the setting sun nears the horizon, heralding a brilliant display of fiery colours. Otherwise, 'relaxed' is how most people describe this strip of fishing villages and rather dated beachside development. Low-key, low-rise, low-priced Lovina is the antithesis of Canggu. The waves are calm, the beach is thin and Insta-ready poseurs are few and far between.

A highlight every afternoon at fishing villages such as Anturan is watching *prahu* (traditional outrigger canoes) being prepared for night fishing. When sunset reddens the sky, the boats flicker to life as dozens of points of light moving across the horizon. Lovina is not overstocked with sights, but it's close to various temples, soaring waterfalls and the urban charms of Singaraja about 10km to the east.

Hit the Beaches

Grey sand and calm water

The beaches are made up of grey and black volcanic sand, and while they're mostly clean near the hotel areas, they're not spectacular. Reefs protect the shore, reducing the waves to ripples most of the time.

A paved but run-down footpath follows the seashore in **Kalibukbuk** and is possibly Lovina's best feature. Enjoy the postcard view to the west of the mountainous North Bali coast.

The best beach areas include the main beach east of Kalibukbuk's **Dolphin Monument**, as well as the curving stretch a bit west. Look for pickup volleyball games on the sand; they get heated.

Dolphin Watching

Early-morning aquatic adventure

Sunrise (6am) boat trips to observe and 'swim' with **dolphins** (typically spinner dolphins) are Lovina's much-hyped tourist attraction, with prices for the two-hour excursions

SIGHTS
1 Dolphin Monument
2 Pier

SLEEPING
3 Frangipani Beach Hotel
4 Funky Place
5 Lovina Beachhouse Villas
6 Mandhara Chico Bungalow

EATING
7 Akar Cafe
8 Buda Bakery & Resto
9 Global Village Kafe
10 Tanda Pizza

DRINKING & NIGHTLIFE
11 Drinks Vendors Zone

fixed by the boat-owners *(viewing only/with swimming 100,000/225,000Rp)*. The swimming part sees you don a snorkel and hang onto a bar dangling from the curved boom of the small outrigger as it moves. For an extra 75,000Rp you can add a snorkelling session at Lovina's reef on the way back, making it a three-hour excursion.

The ocean can get pretty crowded with dozens of roaring motorised outriggers chasing the dolphins around, and there's debate about how this impacts the animals, which, amazingly, continue to cruise Lovina in huge pods. Maybe it's the fish, which are plentiful here. There are generally fewer boats on the later (7am) tour, but for us it was still too many.

TOP TIP

Touts are more active in Lovina than in other areas of Bali and can be pushy. Beware that hotel prices they quote include a kickback.

Diving & Snorkelling

Explore Lovina's reefs

With most of Lovina's reefs damaged by dynamite fishing, the snorkelling and diving here isn't spectacular. The best spot for snorkelling is 1.3km west of the centre, a few hundred metres offshore, which most people visit as part of a dolphin-watching tour. Even though the reef isn't in great shape, there are still plenty of tropical fish to admire. Local dive centres take most divers to **Pulau Menjangan** (p220); with the boat dock 62km (about 1½ hours) west, it's a long day out.

DECODING LOVINA

The Lovina tourist area stretches over 8km, and one fishing village seems to blend into the next. **Kalibukbuk** is the centre of the action, particularly along Jl Bina Ria and Jl Mawar. Going east, Jl Pantai Banyualit is an area dense with modest rental villas.

Some 3km northeast of the centre, a few tiny side tracks and Jl Kubu Gembong lead to lively little **Anturan**, which is a real travellers' hang-out. Further along, quiet **Tukad Mungga** feels removed from the rest of Lovina. To the west, **Kaliasem** is good for simple warungs and older waterfront lodging. Most Lovina hotels are budget-focused, as are the no-frills cafes and restaurants.

JUAN CARLOS HERRERA/SHUTTERSTOCK

Lovina sunset

Spectacular Sunsets

Lovina's free show

Don't miss **sunsets** from the waterfront when the western sky becomes a beautiful show of orange and crimson. The best place for viewing is the **drinks vendors zone** about 150m northeast of the Dolphin Monument. Shaded by trees, there is a mixed bag of chairs, loungers and reclining pillows on the sand where you can enjoy cheap beer and drinks sold by charming vendors. Nearby, there's a crumbling **pier** popular with residents for sunset-watching at the end of Jl Mawar.

Top-shelf salami makes the Diavola pizza simply belissimo.

EATING IN LOVINA: OUR PICKS

Global Village Kafe: Deaf staff don't miss a beat at this sweet charity cafe on the main road serving up great-value pan-Asian dishes. *noon-9pm* $

Akar Cafe: Many shades of green set the mood at this vegetarian cafe. Great falafel pockets and house-made gelato. *7am-10pm* $$

Tanda Pizza: Hot contender for Bali's best Italian-style pizzas, served in an Italian-kitsch dining room with a checkerboard floor. *noon-10pm* $$

Buda Bakery & Resto: Behind Kalibukbuk, a great bakery (try the cinnamon scrolls) with an upstairs cafe serving superlative Indonesian and Western fare. *8am-9pm* $$

Beyond Lovina

Hike through luxuriant landscapes and discover urban culture in Singaraja, plus explore intriguing temples, waterfalls and natural springs.

Waterfalls, waterfalls, everywhere! That's the glorious truth about the lands south of Lovina. Impossibly green mountainsides are cleaved by gorges and sprayed by pounding cascades of water. Hiking here is a delight, with evocative scents in the air, ripe fruit hanging from trees and magical vistas in every direction.

The city of Singaraja embodies Balinese history in its museums and architecture – in particular, at the old port. Throughout the region there are temples that are core to Balinese beliefs, and many have surprising features in their ornamentations. The Bali Sea laps this reef-protected coast, with a natural spring bubbling to the surface at Yeh Sanih.

Places

Singaraja & Around p209
Sekumpul p213
Yeh Sanih p214

GETTING AROUND

Singaraja is served by long-distance buses from Java and via Gilimanuk, as well as occasional large buses from Denpasar. Generally, it's best to have your own wheels as the lands around Lovina reward free exploration. Taxis are not common, but you can arrange rides (and motorbike hire) through accommodation. Expect to pay 400,000Rp for a lift to Pemuteran and 9000Rp per day for a motorbike. Guides usually provide transport for days out.

Singaraja & Around

TIME FROM LOVINA: **20-40MIN**

Historic waterfront

Singaraja (which means 'lion king') is Bali's second-largest city and the capital of Buleleng Regency, which covers much of the north. It's worth exploring the tree-lined streets for a couple of hours; most people stay in nearby Lovina.

At the charmingly sleepy waterfront north of Jl Erlangga, you'll find the atmospheric old harbour, once Bali's main port before WWII. A modern pier juts out over the water with a couple of simple warungs, and elderly men play chess in a shady waterfront park.

Across the car park, look for some old Dutch shipping company buildings. One has been restored and now houses the small but interesting **Museum Soenda Ketjil** *(12,000Rp; 10am-4pm Mon to Fri)*. It covers the colonial era of Buleleng with displays in English. Other exhibits include early European contact, the role of the royal family and the multicultural mix (Balinese, ethnic groups from across the archipelago, Chinese, Indians, Arabs and Europeans).

Nearby is the vibrantly red Chinese temple **Ling Gwan Kiong** *(by donation)*, which dates to 1873, and a few old canals. Walk up Jl Erlangga to see the Art Deco lines of late-colonial Dutch buildings.

ROAD TRIP

Lovina Hinterland Drive

Lovina makes a great base for exploring the many attractions hidden in the lush foothills of the mountains rising up from the coast. You can hire a driver to take you around, but it's more fun exploring on a motorbike. Hire one in Lovina and embark on a leisurely day exploring the winding roads west of town, where local life plays out much as it has for decades.

1 Seririt Market

Follow the main coast road 12km west of Lovina to Seririt. From here, one road runs south and on to Munduk (p192) and beyond; another leads to West Bali near Pantai Balian (p234) via the beautiful Antosari Rd (p192) and the equally scenic road via Pulukan to Medewi (p235). The traditional **market** in the centre of Seririt is renowned for its stalls selling supplies for offerings, and if you're looking for a wide range of dried fish or chillies, you've come to the right place.

The Drive: Avoid the busy main roads and instead wind up through the backstreets to your next destination, about 5km southeast. Urban development gives way to lush greenery as you go.

2 Air Panas Banjar

Hot springs percolate amid lush tropical plants at **Air Panas Banjar** *(45,000Rp)*.

JUDITH LIENERT/SHUTTERSTOCK

Air Panas Banjar

Eight fierce-faced carved stone *naga* (mythical snake-like creatures) pour water from a natural hot spring into the first bath, which then overflows (via the mouths of five more *naga*) into a larger pool. In a third pool, water pours from 3m-high spouts to give you a pummelling massage. The water is slightly sulphurous and pleasantly steamy (about 35°C). You must wear a swimsuit.

The Drive: Slow down and observe local life unfolding alongside the narrow streets. We rode past one local lovingly bathing his rooster.

3 Brahma Vihara Arama

Bali's only Buddhist monastery, **Brahma Vihara Arama** *(35,000Rp)* is a fascinating place to explore, with a lofty location that affords great views down across the rice fields to the north coast and manicured gardens brimming with frangipani and bougainvillea. Highlights include a miniature version of Borobudur, the famous Buddhist temple and UNESCO site in Java. Statues of Buddha and lotus ponds abound. There are daily meditation programmes in prayer pavilions. Just down the road, Lotus Cafe makes a good lunch or snack stop.

The Drive: It's a 20-minute ride to your last stop on a mixture of backstreets and the main coast road.

4 Air Terjun Singsing

Just 5km from Lovina, **Air Terjun Singsing** (Daybreak Waterfalls) is reached by a 200m path to the lower of two sets of falls. Though not very high, the main waterfall flows into a large pool that's good for swimming, though not crystal clear. Clamber up the stairs to the left of the falls to reach another set of falls, which cascade into a deep pool. There was no entrance or parking fee when we visited. From here it's an easy 10-minute drive back to Kalibukbuk in Lovina.

THE HISTORIC GATEWAY TO BALI

In the 18th century, the colonial Dutch became the main purchasers of enslaved Balinese people. In the 1840s, the Dutch tried to make treaties with Balinese rajas to assert their control over the island before other colonial powers arrived. But, ultimately, the Dutch resorted to force and seized control of much of the island in 1849. Singaraja became the centre of Dutch power in Bali and remained the administrative centre for the Lesser Sunda Islands (Bali through to Timor) until 1953. Until Denpasar airport in South Bali became the main means of arrival after WWII, most visitors arrived on steamships at Singaraja.

Tour royal museums

Singaraja's royal family maintains a compound with two decent museums. Most compelling is the **Gedong Kirtya Library** *(10,000Rp)*, a historical centre established in 1928 by Dutch colonialists and named after the Sanskrit for 'to try'. It has a superb collection of over 2000 *lontar* (dried-palm-leaf) books, the traditional form of printed text on Bali going back for many centuries. Curators give intriguing demonstrations of how these books are created. Displays cover some of the more notable works preserved here, including manuscripts written on copper plates *(prasasti)*.

Nearby, the **Museum Buleleng** *(10,000Rp)* recalls the life of the last *radja* (raja or prince) of Buleleng, Pandji Tisna, who is credited with developing tourism in Lovina in the 1970s. It's a bit like an uncurated attic of artefacts. Both museums close for the weekend from 1pm on Friday.

Splash around in a natural waterpark

North Bali's answer to Kuta's Waterbom (p76), Aling-Aling is a natural waterpark made for adrenaline junkies. Thundering down through the jungle, **Air Terjun Aling-Aling** is the tallest of four waterfalls you can view on a loop trail *(20,000Rp)* that takes about 30 minutes from the ticket booth; factor in some steep stairs. Like Sekumpul there are also 'trekking' options. Short trekking *(1½-2hr 125,000Rp)* includes a chance to swim, slide and jump into three of the four waterfalls of various heights on the main trail and a local guide to show you the safest way to do so (note that this activity is not without risk, so it is important to have a guide). Visits to a picturesque local rice terrace and the **Blue Lagoon**, a natural pool with an idyllic turquoise hue, are added to the medium trekking package *(3-4hr 250,000Rp)*. Long trekking *(5-6hr 500,000Rp)* also includes lunch and visits two additional waterfalls upriver. With a restaurant next to the **ticket office**, and several other warungs nearby, you can make a whole day of it up here in the lush hills above Singaraja.

Easy waterfall walks

Powerful **Air Terjun Gitgit** *(45,000Rp)* is on the main road to South Bali, around 12km south of Singaraja's waterfront. An 800m path from the parking area leads to impressive 40m-high falls that produce refreshing mists. With more time, you can lose the crowds 2km further up the hill, where the multitiered **Air Terjun Bertingkat** *(20,000Rp)* waterfall is about 600m off the western side of the main road.

EATING IN SINGARAJA: OUR PICKS

Royal Sunset Resto: The best of the Indonesian restaurants on the pier, with sublime sunset views. *10.30am-9pm Mon-Fri, to 10pm Sat & Sun* $

Bali Intan Cafe: Modern cafe serving local and international staples, including a good burger and Dutch *bitterballen* (bite-sized croquettes). *7am-9pm* $

VB Bakery & Pastry: Cakes and sweet and savoury pastries galore, from chocolate doughnuts to red-bean twists. On the Jl A Yani commercial strip. *7am-9pm* $

Warung Kita: Simple *nasi campur* (rice with a choice of side dishes) joint with a good variety of dishes to choose from. *8am-6pm Mon-Sat* $

KESTRELOCULUS/SHUTTERSTOCK

Sekumpul Waterfalls

Sekumpul

TIME FROM LOVINA: **1HR**

Marvel at the Sekumpul cascades

If you only see one waterfall in Bali, make it this one. Collectively known as the **Sekumpul Waterfalls**, the group of cascades that pour over cliffs in a verdant valley is up to 80m high and ascends a green gorge that's almost mystical in its beauty. Trees including clove, cacao, jackfruit and mangosteen scent the air. Trails wind through the valley from one cascade to another and it's easy to spend a day here revelling in the splendour.

Approaching from the north coast road, there's a car park and a ticket booth at the intersection of Jl Air Tejun and Jl Lemukih. There are three main entrance options: viewing only from a scenic **lookout** *(20,000Rp)*, medium trekking *(150,000Rp)* and long trekking *(250,000Rp)*. A guide is included in trekking prices along with a plastic bottle of water; it's best to bring your own reusable bottle instead.

If you opt for trekking, an *ojek* (passenger motorcycle) ride to the lookout is included. Otherwise, it's a 20- to 30-minute walk to the lookout point, or you can ride your own motorbike (turn left at **Spice Warung** and follow the gorgeous but steep and winding path).

Facing Sekumpul's main **Twin Waterfalls**, with **Fiji Waterfall** visible to the right, the view from the lookout is magical, with several simple warungs perched on the cliffside offering an opportunity to linger. From here trekkers follow steep stairs down to **Hidden Waterfall** (not visible from the lookout) then onto Twin Waterfalls. The 'long' trek continues to the base of Fiji Waterfall. Allow at least 30 minutes for the medium trek, and an hour for the long trek.

FRUITS OF THE FOREST

On hikes in the lush hills of the north, look for the following fruits growing both wild and on farms.

Jackfruit *(nangka):* Can be huge, with a spiky green exterior. The fruit forms into sweet, bite-sized nodules that combine many tropical flavours.

Mangosteen *(manggis):* Despite its name, not related to the mango. Its white centre has a peach-like flavour and texture; often called 'queen of fruit'.

Passion fruit *(markisa):* Popular whether eaten raw or used as the base of a drink or dessert; have a spoon ready to scoop out the jelly-like interior.

Snake fruit *(salak):* Named after its brown scaly skin, with firm orbs inside that are like a cross between segments of apple and pear.

LESSER-KNOWN TEMPLES

Pura Ponjok Batu: Legend holds that it was built to provide spiritual balance to all the temples in the south; it's 7km east of Yeh Sanih.

Pura Beji Sangsit: Temple for the *subak* (association of rice-growers), dedicated to the goddess Dewi Sri. Sculptured panels feature demons; in Sangsit.

Pura Dalem Sangsit: This temple of the dead 500m from Pura Beji shows scenes of punishment in the afterlife.

Pura Dalem Jagaraga: Small temple with sculptured panels. Look for a vintage car, a steamer at sea and an aerial dogfight; in Jagaraga.

Pura Melanting: Dedicated to good fortune in business. Look for the dragon statue bearing a lotus blossom; 2km inland from Pemuteran's Pura Pulaki (p217).

Pura Maduwe Karang

Wear your swimwear if you plan to take a dip at the base of any of the three main waterfalls, as there are no change rooms. Expect to get soaked by the spray even if you don't swim; water shoes are advisable.

It's also possible to access the falls from **Warung Fiji** in Lemukih Village to the south. Access to the trails to the bottom of the falls is 20,000Rp, but a guide isn't currently required. Beware of scam ticket booths along the approach to Sekumpul from South Bali.

Yeh Sanih

TIME FROM LOVINA: **30-45MINS**

Temple and a cool pool

A number of attractions lie on the coast road that runs from Singaraja to East Bali. Worth a pause is the unkempt but intriguing **Pura Maduwe Karang** (Temple of the Landowner) in **Kubutambahan**. Dedicated to agricultural spirits looking after non-irrigated land, the frangipani-scented temple's walls are decorated with detailed panels including a famous relief that depicts a man in Balinese clothes riding a bicycle with a lotus flower serving as the back wheel. The cyclist may be WOJ Nieuwenkamp, a Dutch artist who, in 1904, brought with him what was probably the first bicycle in Bali. Outside the walls are 34 carved figures from the Ramayana. Kubutambahan is 5km east of Pura Beji Sangsit on the main road. Entrance is by donation, and like most temples in North Bali, it's open from sunrise to sunset.

Another 4km east, the freshwater springs of **Air Sanih** *(adult/child 10,000/5000Rp)* are channelled into large swimming pools before flowing into the sea. The refreshingly cool, azure pools are open daily and have a shallow children's area complete with slides.

Pemuteran

UNDERWATER ADVENTURES | RELAXATION | CHEAP EATS

One of Bali's most delightful beach towns, Pemuteran is northwestern Bali's tourism hub, but it's still refreshingly relaxed. Peaceful resorts mix with welcoming homestays, all set back from a black-sand bay. The beach is calm, thanks to its location protected by coral reefs. Most people spend at least some time viewing the undersea wonders offshore and at nearby Pulau Menjangan, while others delight in days of relaxation on a sunlounger under a shady tree.

The busy Singaraja–Gilimanuk road is the town's spine and many businesses aimed at visitors can be found along it. While noise can be distracting along the main road, numerous good cafes and restaurants line it. Despite its increasing popularity, Pemuteran's community and tourism businesses have forged a sustainable vision for development that could be a model for the rest of Bali.

GETTING AROUND

Pemuteran is a four-to five-hour drive from South Bali, either over the central mountains or around the west coast. Hotels at either end of the journey can arrange a car and driver; expect to pay about 1,000,000Rp to and from Canggu. Lovina is about an hour's drive to the east. Pemuteran is on the Gilimanuk-Lovina-Singaraja public bus run; just flag one down. Tourist buses generally do not serve the area. You can get around all of Pemuteran by walking. Expect to pay 50,000Rp to 150,000Rp per day for motorbike rental to explore further afield.

Under the Sea

Reefs and human-made surprises

Strap on a snorkel and head straight out from the beach in front of the BioRock Indonesia info booth (p217) to explore more than 100 metal structures (including a long, twisting dragon) adorned with corals and anemones and swarming with fish. Most structures lie between the shallows and a pontoon anchored about 100m off the beach.

Pemuteran's reefs, accessed by boat, aren't nearly as spectacular as those of Pulau Menjangan, but the macro life makes them worth a dive, particularly **Napoleon Reef**, where we saw a good variety of anemone shrimp and nudibranch on our visit. Beginners typically do their first Open Water dives in Pemuteran before graduating to Pulau Menjangan.

Also accessed by boat is the **BioWreck**, featuring an artificial ship and turtle that's a popular dive site for beginners and night dives. Erected on the seafloor about 400m off the beach in front of the **Reef Seen** dive centre, the **Garden of the Gods** dive site is not as popular, owing to the lack of coral growth.

SIGHTS
1 BioRock Indonesia Info Booth
2 Pemuteran Beach
3 Proyek Penyu hatchery

ACTIVITIES
4 Dimpil Spa
5 Garden of the Gods
6 Java Spa
7 Juvenex Spa & Salon
8 Putri Massage
9 Reef Seen
10 Tirta Sari Spa

SLEEPING
11 Arjuna Homestay
12 Kubuku Eco Divelodge
13 Mango Tree Inn
14 Pondok Shindu Guest House
15 Taman Sari
16 Tirta Sari

EATING
17 Dimpil Beachbar & Resto
18 Eco Taste
19 Lakawi
20 Mantra Sari
21 Quarry
22 Sage Bali
23 Warung Bukit
24 Warung D'Bucu

TOP TIP

With the exception of live music in the early evening at beachfront Dimpil, and the odd Balinese dance performance at Pondok Sari resort, Pemuteran doesn't have a nightlife scene to speak of. If you want to party, head elsewhere.

Pemuteran's Sandy Idyll

Life's a beach

Pemuteran's **beach** is wonderfully relaxed. It's a fun scene at sunset, with village children playing football amid smiling visitors and couples strolling the charcoal-hued sand. At the western end, where the hotels are concentrated, you can rent sun loungers and enjoy refreshments. And there's excellent snorkelling just metres offshore, where the BioRock Indonesia community initiative has successfully grown a new reef. You can walk east along the sand for over 4km to Pura Pulaki.

The gado gado is a refreshing lunch option.

EATING IN PEMUTERAN: OUR PICKS

Warung D'Bucu: This no-frills family warung gets our vote for Pemuteran's most flavoursome *ikan bakar* (grilled fish). *11am-10pm* $

Warung Bukit: South of the main road on a narrow lane, this simple, peaceful warung makes an excellent Balinese chicken curry. *7am-10pm* $

Quarry: Rice and noodle classics are available alongside curries, pastas, soups and sandwiches at this cute laneway warung. *11am-10pm* $

Lakawi: Bali's best burgers? Served with homemade fries, they sure hit the spot after a day's diving. *noon-10pm* $$

Support Baby Turtles

Visit Pemuteran's turtle hatchery

Run by the beachfront Reef Seen Divers' Resort since 1992, the nonprofit **Proyek Penyu** purchases turtle eggs found by locals and looks after them here until they're ready for ocean release. You can visit its small **hatchery** *(reefseenbali.com; 40,000Rp)* to see eggs incubating and adorable hatchlings (green, hawksbill and/or olive ridley) in small pools, which are typically full during the nesting season (January to May). Another pool holds Buddy, a 25-year-old hawksbill turtle surrendered to the hatchery in 2010 by village children who had raised it in a tank. Time your visit for the 4.30pm feeding time, when the baby-turtle tanks come alive with tiny flapping flippers. If there are juveniles available for release, it happens locally between 10am and 11am. Entrance fees directly support Proyek Penyu's conservation and community-education initiatives.

The Other Monkey Temple

See Pemuteran's sea temples

Flanked by a pair of tiger sculptures, **Pura Pulaki** *(by donation)* at the east end of Pemuteran is home to a large (and intimidating) troop of monkeys. Dating to at least the 16th century, this is one of Bali's auspicious sea temples, part of a chain of sacred places that protect the island from waterborne evil spirits, but the hulking metal cage built around the inner sanctum to keep the monkeys out somewhat detracts from the ambience. About 150m across the busy road, a subsidiary temple, **Pura Pabean** *(by donation)*, has a lovely location on a waterfront knoll that's also popular with monkeys. Its unusual Chinese-accented architecture is a legacy of traders who once lived here.

Indulge in a Massage or Spa Visit

Enjoy a lazy afternoon

A tranquil setting and skilled therapists make the **Java Spa** a delightful place to spend a lazy afternoon – its signature massage is good value *(1hr 210,000Rp)*. Alternatively, the **Dimpil Spa** and **Juvenex Spa & Salon** both offer massages, facials, manis and more at reasonable prices.

In a bungalow in the garden of a Balinese home, Putri, the owner of **Putri Massage** does great Balinese massages *(1hr 120,000Rp)*. Or for even more of a bargain, the price is right at the simple but sweet **Tirta Sari Spa** on the main road *(1hr 100,000Rp plus tax)*.

GROWING A NEW REEF

By the early 1990s, dynamite and cyanide fishing, along with a warming ocean, had bleached and damaged large parts of Pemuteran's reef. Facing this threat to the area's growing tourism, a group of local hotels, diving operators and community leaders hit upon a novel solution: grow a new reef using electricity. The idea had already been floated by scientists internationally, but Pemuteran was the first place to implement it on a wide – and hugely successful – scale. Three decades on, the project, called **BioRock Indonesia** *(biorock-indonesia.com)*, is being adopted across the archipelago. Learn more at an **info booth** (generally open 9am to 3pm) on the beach by Pondok Sari.

Mantra Sari: Dishes including a standout *nasi campur* are beautifully presented on miniature *jukungs* (Balinese outriggers). *11am-10pm* $$

Dimpil Beachbar & Resto: Come for a sundowner and stay for tasty seafood and Indo mains. *11am-10pm* $$

Eco Taste: An excellent brunch option, with air-con and a wholesome international menu including great salad bowls. *8am-9pm* $$

Sage Bali: Flavoursome bowls, burgers, curries, baguettes and more with plenty of veg and vegan options. *9am-9pm* $$

Beyond Pemuteran

Bali's best snorkelling, diving and bird-watching draw visitors to the island's only national park to the west. But wait, there's more...

Places

Sanggalangit p218
West Bali National Park p218
Pulau Menjangan p220
Banyuwedang p222

GETTING AROUND

West Bali National Park can be reached from North Bali or via the busy road to the Java ferries in Gilimanuk, which runs west from South Bali. The closest tourist centre is Pemuteran. You can either arrange rides with your accommodation or use your own wheels. Walking and trekking are major reasons to visit the park, but be aware that most excursions require the services of a park guide.

Occupying the island's western tip, West Bali National Park is the main attraction – a place where you can enjoy Bali's best diving at Pulau Menjangan, hike, bike or drive through forests in search of birds and wildlife, explore coastal mangroves by kayak and discover untrodden white-sand beaches. The mangrove-lined cove of Banyuwedang, east of West Bali National Park, offers both easy access to the park and a pleasant hot spring, though many use Pemuteran as a base for exploring the park.

East of Pemuteran is a clutch of vineyards forming part of Bali's first winery, complete with cellar-door tours and tastings.

Sanggalangit

TIME FROM PEMUTERAN: **25MIN**

Taste Bali wine

You can't miss the vineyards east of Pemuteran, a surprise for those lulled by the rice fields that cover so much of Bali. Yet the island has a burgeoning wine scene that has been developing for two decades. One of the pioneering vineyards is **Hatten Wines**, which like East Bali's Sababay Winery (p164), creates white, rosé, red, sparkling and fortified wines. Sample its wares with a tour and tasting at **Hatten Wines Vineyard Visitor Centre** (*hattenwines.com; 100,000Rp; 9am-4.30pm Mon-Fri, to noon Sat*).

West Bali National Park

TIME FROM PEMUTERAN: **30-60MIN**

Lace your boots

Most visitors to **West Bali National Park** *(Taman Nasional Bali Barat; 200,000Rp)* are struck by the mellifluous sounds emanating from the birds darting among the rustling trees. The park covers 190 sq km of the western tip of Bali, including almost 70 sq km of coral reef and coastal waters. Together, this represents a significant commitment to conservation on a densely populated island.

From a trail west of the **Labuhan Lalang park entrance** (the main access point to Pulau Menjangin), a two- to three-hour hike exploring the fringe of **Teluk Terima** (Terima Bay) begins at the mangroves and monsoon forest. Another two- to

West Bali National Park

three-hour hike will allow you to explore the savannah area at the heart of the park. There are many more hiking options, including a longer hike up **Gunung Kelatakan** (Mt Kelatakan; 698m). Note seasonal variations: in the dry season vegetation is brown and sparse, which aids animal-spotting. In the wet season, the park gets green and lush, but animals also have plenty of cover.

Guides, who can be found at the various park gates and who are required for tours, are of variable quality. Recommended guides include Ketut Suliastra *(WhatsApp +62 813 3778 4500)*, Komang Mastika *(WhatsApp +62 852 5371 5022)* and Muhamad Idriss *(WhatsApp +62 823 4018 5768)*. Hiking prices are more or less set (there's a rate sheet in the run-down information centre at the Labuhan Lalang gate) and aren't cheap, with the standard monsoon forest hike costing 850,000Rp for one or two people. At 300,000Rp for every extra person, it's more affordable if you split the cost between a group.

WHY I LOVE NORTH BALI

Sarah Reid, Lonely Planet writer

North Bali flies under the radar, and this is exactly why I love it. Hidden behind a mountain range, the region's isolation has helped places like Pemuteran retain a wonderfully relaxed Balinese beach-town vibe now rare on the island. And the wall diving at Pulau Menjangan? Wow. And I've dived all over the world. Then there's the waterfalls – the first time I set eyes on Sekumpul, it seemed too beautiful to be real. And you could spend months visiting the many temples in this region.

People often ask me why I return to Bali, year after year. Sure, I'm partial to a fancy Canggu restaurant meal. But North Bali feeds my soul.

EATING & DRINKING BEYOND PEMUTERAN: OUR PICKS

Warung Makan Sri Ayu: Simple, great-value warung near Banyuwedang Hot Spring with *nasi goreng* (fried rice) for 30,000Rp. *2-11pm* $

Mangroove Bay Cafe: Great selection of Indo and Western dishes (including house-made ravioli for dinner) in a serene, modern setting. *7.30am-10pm* $$

Sunset Beach Restaurant: On the water in Banyuwedang, with a good range of Asian dishes and the usual pizzas and pastas. *7am-11pm* $$

Bali Tower Bistro: Buy a drink to enjoy superb views over West Bali National Park from a 5th-floor tower at the Mengangin. *7.30am-3pm, to 11pm May-Oct*

The sunset views from here are magnificent.

NOVRIZAL HERDANANTO/SHUTTERSTOCK

TOP EXPERIENCE

Pulau Menjangan

The home of Bali's best diving and snorkelling, uninhabited Pulau Menjangan is ringed by more than a dozen superb dive sites. The experience is excellent – iconic tropical fish, vibrant hard and soft corals, great visibility (usually), caves and spectacular drop-offs. Huge gorgonians (branching soft corals) provide both texture and hiding spots for small fish that form a colour chart for the sea.

DON'T MISS

- Eel Garden
- Bat Cave
- Dream Wall
- Anchor Wreck
- POS 2
- Coral Garden
- Pura Gili Kencana

Diving Menjangan

Most of Menjangan's dive sites are walls that meet the sandy bottom at various depths and are suitable for Open Water–certified divers; advanced divers can explore deeper, more challenging sites. If conditions allow, operators typically aim for a dive at **Eel Garden**. After exploring a coral-encrusted wall, you'll pass a sandy patch dotted with garden eels. Other popular sites include **Bat Cave**, **Dream Wall**, **POS 2** and **Anchor Wreck**, named for the rusting anchor of a

PRACTICALITIES

- The West Bali National Park entrance fee *(per day 200,000Rp)* is applicable to divers and snorkellers.

mysterious 19th-century boat that lies about 7m below the surface. The remains of the wreck lie on the sandy bottom beside the reef at about 30m; you can get a good look from about 25m (advanced divers only).

The highlight of diving in Menjangan is its splendid walls covered in soft, hard and whip corals and lacey gorgonian fans. Keep your eyes peeled for anemone shrimp, frogfish, crocodile fish, pygmy seahorse, electric clams, nudibranch and lionfish. Among the 'big stuff' you might see are turtles, eagle rays, grouper, barracuda, giant trevally, dogtooth tuna, reef sharks and even the odd whale shark.

A standard dive trip from Pemuteran includes two dives and lunch, and gets you back to town about 4pm. Most boats dock at a jetty at the southwestern end of the island for a lunch break between dives; there are shaded sitting areas, toilets, curious rusa deer and a small beach. Some operators use a smaller jetty at the southeastern end of the island instead, near Pura Gili Kencana.

Snorkelling Menjangan

There's good snorkelling all around the island. Depending on the conditions, operators typically take you to several spots along the southern side of the island (including **Mangrove Point**) to admire colourful corals, anemones and myriad reef fish in the shallows, or to snorkel along the edges of the drop-offs that extend along the southern side of the island for better chances of spotting 'big stuff'. You might see bubbles rising up from divers below.

If conditions allow, you'll also get a chance to snorkel on the northern side of the island; **Coral Garden** is a fine spot. Snorkelling boats also utilise both of the island's jetties for lunch breaks.

Exploring the Island

Pulau Menjangan has what is thought to be Bali's oldest temple, **Pura Gili Kencana**, dating from the 14th century and about 300m from the pier of the southwestern jetty. It has a huge Ganesha (the elephant-headed Hindu deity) carved from brilliant white stone at the soaring arched entrance.

An easy trail circles the low island. It's 6km in length and a circuit takes about 90 minutes (divers won't have enough time to reach the temple during a lunch break). On the way you'll pass small temples, mangroves and some thin but lovely beaches on the northwest side. Having a picnic lunch here is one of the good reasons to arrange for your own boat with a skipper amenable to a flexible schedule.

GETTING THERE

Most dive operators (which also run snorkelling trips) are based in Pemuteran; dive trips include transport to the boat dock at Labuhan Lalang. Dive centres in Banyuwedang also accommodate snorkellers.

Independent snorkellers can arrange trips at the Labuhan Lalang boat dock for about 650,000Rp per person including gear, depending on the number of people.

TOP TIPS

- Factor in a one-hour return boat trip to Palau Menjangan.
- Arranging a snorkelling trip ad hoc at the Labuhan Lalang boat dock is more cost-effective for larger groups. Trips take three to four hours, including transit time.
- If your guide adds to your experience, tip accordingly.
- The Biosphere Foundation *(biosphere foundation.org)* undertakes stewardship projects in the national park; support its work with a donation.
- Leave no trace on the island, including food scraps (don't feed them to the deer), and consider bringing a rubbish bag to collect marine debris you encounter.
- Wear reef-safe sunscreen to help protect the coral.

BALI-BASED READS

***Snowing in Bali* by Kathryn Bonella (2012):** Excellent true-crime bio lifting the lid on Bali's drug world.

***Paon* by Tjok Maya Kerthyasa and I Wayan Kresna Yasa (2022):** Chef Wayan (p66) and writer Tjok take readers on a Balinese food journey, with 80 recipes to try.

***A House in Bali* by Colin McPhee (1947):** The writer and composer's fascination with Balinese life continues to inspire.

***Bali: Sekala & Niskala* by Fred B Eiseman Jr (1989):** A deep dive into Balinese religion, ritual and performing arts.

***Eat, Pray, Love* by Elizabeth Gilbert (2006):** The memoir that brought Balinese spirituality to the masses.

Spot Bali starlings

Previously tightly guarded, the **Bali Starling Centre** *(by donation)* is home to scores of the critically endangered Bali starling, a brilliant white bird with cobalt highlights around the eyes. Once collected to the point of extinction, the starling has made an incredible comeback, largely thanks to breeding programmes here and elsewhere in Bali. On a half-hour visit, staff explain the facility and talk about the birds. It's 200m from a park entry gate near Sumber Kelompok; you will need to pay the park admission.

An easy place to see wild Bali starlings is at a starling feeding station directly left of the Labuhan Lalang park entrance (p218). You don't need a guide, and you typically don't need to pay the park entry fee, either.

A temple to Bali's Romeo

Jayaprana, the foster son of a 17th-century king, planned to marry Leyonsari, a girl of humble origins. The king, however, also fell in love with Leyonsari and had Jayaprana killed. Leyonsari learned the truth of Jayaprana's death in a dream and killed herself rather than marry the king. This *Romeo and Juliet* story is a common theme in Balinese folklore, and Jayaprana's grave is regarded as sacred. A 10-minute walk up stone stairs will bring you to the monkey-filled temple built atop the grave, **Pura Jayaprana**. There are fine views to Pulau Menjangan. It's just southwest of Labuhan Lalang and has no entrance fee, nor do you need to pay the national park entrance fee to visit.

Flora and fauna in the park

Most of the natural vegetation in West Bali National Park is not tropical rainforest, which requires year-round rain, but coastal savannah, with deciduous trees that become bare in the dry season. The southern slopes receive more rainfall, and so have more tropical vegetation, while the coastal lowlands have extensive mangroves.

There are more than 200 species of plants growing in the park. Local fauna includes leaf monkeys and macaques; rusa and barking deer; and wild pigs, squirrels, buffalo, iguanas, pythons and green snakes. There were once tigers, but the last confirmed sighting was in 1937 – and that one was shot. The birdlife is prolific, with many of Bali's 300-odd species found here.

Banyuwedang

TIME FROM PEMUTERAN: **15MIN**

Get some pool time

The mangrove-fringed cove east of West Bali National Park is a convenient base for exploring the park, including Pulau Menjangan, with several excellent resorts dotting the shore. With its own white-sand beach and an airy, modern restaurant, the **Pasir Putih Beach Club** at the end of a diabolically bad road is a nice place to relax for a day. At the eastern end of the cove, the well-kept **Banyuwedang Hot Spring** *(45,000Rp; 7am-9pm)* is a toasty 41°C. It's a nice spot to relax after a day's diving, and there's a good little warung on-site.

Places We Love to Stay

$ Budget $$ Midrange $$$ Top End

Lovina

MAP p207

Funky Place $ In Kalibukbuk; a rollicking hostel with dorms and a treehouse, and proximity to the beach.

Mandhara Chico Bungalow $ In Anturan; family-run guesthouse on a small strip of charcoal-sand beach lined with fishing boats. Rooms are basic but tidy.

Frangipani Beach Hotel $$ A clutch of spacious, traditional rooms face off in a lush garden. Direct beach access, with pool and restaurant. In Anturan.

Damai $$$ Set on a hillside behind Lovina, with sweeping views from luxury villas that mix antiques and a modern style. Great infinity pool and restaurant.

Lovina Beachhouse Villas $$$ Near Frangipani Beach Hotel, atmospheric villas here are historic wooden structures brought from Java and have private pools.

Sekumpul

Ananda Homestay $ Basic homestay with simple rooms south of the Sekumpul Waterfalls. Lovely family owners and many opportunities for hiking in the surrounding rainforest.

Villa Manuk $$ In the hills near the Sekumpul Waterfalls is this small villa complex with rice-field views. It has its own natural-spring-fed pool.

Yeh Sanih

Cilik's Beach Garden $$$ Three kilometres east of Yeh Sanih, Cilik's offers large oceanfront villas and extensive private gardens.

Air Sanih Beach Villa $$$ Luxury villa sleeping eight in four rooms, with waterfront frontage, gardens and a pool behind a seawall.

Seririt

Nalika Beach Resort $$ Just west of Seririt is one of Bali's newest swaths of beach development. This lovely small hotel is right on narrow Pantai Nalika.

Mayo Resort $$ At Pantai Umeanyar is this small waterfront resort with large units; each has a big terrace. Right on the beach near seafood warungs.

Pemuteran

MAP p216

Mango Tree Inn $ One of Pemuteran's best budget stays, with canopy beds and alfresco showers. Set in a lush garden.

Pondok Shindu Guest House $ Family-run guesthouse near the beach. Rooms have traditional-style open-air bathrooms. Good breakfasts.

Arjuna Homestay $$ Also the home of Dive Concepts, this lovely hotel's 2nd-floor rooms offer more privacy, with balconies overlooking the leafy pool. Great breakfast and an all-day restaurant.

Taman Sari $$ Traditional-style bungalows with intricate carvings and traditional artwork. Right on Pemuteran's beach.

Tirta Sari $$ Just 100m from the beach, with pleasant traditional-style bungalow rooms and a large pool in a lush garden.

Kubuku Eco Divelodge $$ Modern rooms and pool in a mountainside compound off the main road. Yoga and diving.

Puri Ganesha Villas $$$ Two-storey villas on sweeping waterfront grounds, each with an individual style that mixes antiques with relaxed comfort and a pool.

Banyuwedang Area

Mangroove Bay Hostel $ Just east of Banyuwedang, this stylish modern hostel also has nice double rooms. Offers loads of activities.

NusaBay Menjangan by WHM $$$ Secluded in West Bali National Park on a beautiful white-sand beach reached by private boat. Comfortable rooms, plus glamping.

Plataran Menjangan Resort $$$ Northeast of the Labuan Lalang boat dock is this luxe resort with beach villas set on 382 hectares.

Mimpi Resort Menjangan $$$ Stylish resort on Banyuwedang's lovely inlet with its own dive centre.

For places to stay in West Bali, see p239

GUITAR PHOTOGRAPHER/SHUTTERSTOCK

Above: Pura Taman Ayun (p228); Right: *Selerek* boats, Perancak (p237)

Researched by
Marco Ferrarese

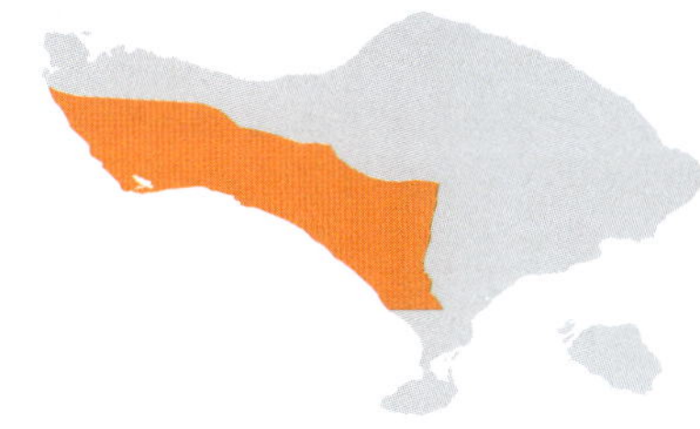

West Bali

SURF BREAKS, BALINESE CULTURE AND FISHING BOATS

Going west, South Bali's overtourism thaws into endless rice paddies and lonesome black coasts – one of Bali's least-visited and most multicultural regions.

Never-ending development from South Bali has already encroached beyond sacred Pura Tanah Lot, one of Bali's most iconic temples, laying its first bricks on Pantai Kedungu. But along the remaining 113km of highway to Gilimanuk and Java, Bali's west offers more sedate, less touristed and authentic experiences.

Those in the know come here to spend quiet weeks hopping between wild charcoal-coloured surf beaches, waterfalls, rice fields and – of course – temples. Tucked in the tidy town of Tabanan, the region's northeastern corner, Pura Taman Ayun is as marvellous as Bali's UNESCO-listed *subak*, the system of irrigation that ensures everybody gets a fair share of the water, which originated here.

DENIS MOSKVINOV/SHUTTERSTOCK

Further west along the coast are a couple of established beachside surfing communities like Pantai Balian and Medewi, one of the region's best point breaks. A burgeoning collection of guesthouses, resorts and some superb places to eat offer comfort, pleasure and relaxation – but drive north right across the highway, and solitary mountains draped with traditional villages and lush jungle beckon.

Few foreigners go further west past the sea-hugging Pura Rambut Siwi temple to Negara and Perancak, the heart of the Jembrana Regency. Here Bali's Hinduism coexists with the Islam of Javanese migrants, rare pink buffaloes graze, and the *perahu selerek*, one of the world's most colourful fishing fleets, still hauls its daily catch the hard way.

THE MAIN AREAS

TABANAN & MENGWI
Glorious temples and quiet countryside. p228

JEMBRANA REGENCY
Surf breaks, culture and paddy fields. p235

Find Your Way

West Bali is hemmed by mountains to the north and dark sands to the south. It's about a nine-hour drive from Bali's Ngurah Rai airport to Gilimanuk and back, but you should stay longer to enjoy the sights.

ON FOOT

All those beaches are made for walking, and you don't need boots; bare feet will do. Elsewhere, following a small lane through rice fields can be sublime.

MOTORBIKE & CAR

Your own wheels are the secret to unleashing West Bali adventure – just stay off the infamous Jalur Tengkorak (Skull Track) highway between Gilimanuk and Denpasar, and enjoy the tiny roads that crisscross the agricultural hinterland.

Jembrana Regency, p235

This long strip of black coast crowned by misty hills holds some of Bali's quieter surf breaks, authentic nooks and multicultural villages.

Tabanan & Mengwi, p228

Beyond sacred Pura Taman Ayun, this is where one can get lost amid verdant countryside and little-visited villages.

MATHILDE.LR/SHUTTERSTOCK

Pura Rambut Siwi (p238)

Plan Your Time

With at least three days, you can savour most of what West Bali has to offer and still have the freedom to make decisions on the fly.

Pressed for Time

You can see most highlights even if you are zipping through West Bali, as most of them are easy to reach. From the south or Ubud, stop first at **Pura Taman Ayun** (p228), one of Bali's most rewarding temples. Next, cruise to the waterfront at **Pantai Balian** (p234) for lunch. Then stop at **Pura Rambut Siwi** (p238) and see *selerek* fishing boats bathed in sunset at Ujung Muara in **Perancak** (p237).

Five Days to Explore

Besides the one-day highlights, spend a morning at **Pura Tanah Lot** (p233) before checking out how futuristic art blends with nature at **Nuanu Creative City** (p232). Head west, stopping at beaches like **Yeh Gangga** (p234) before considering a longer pause at **Pantai Balian** (p234). Use **Medewi** (p235) as a base to rent a scooter and explore temples, waterfalls and hills, and then end with views and culture in **Perancak** (p237).

SEASONAL HIGHLIGHTS

MARCH–MAY

The dry season offers the best weather for outdoor activities and self-driving around the region.

JUNE–AUGUST

Even when South Bali is overrun during the peak months of July and August, West Bali remains quiet.

SEPTEMBER–NOVEMBER

With the rainy season comes moody days, good for watching storms in beach towns and waterfront resorts.

DECEMBER–FEBRUARY

December holidays mean that Cemagi villas and towns such as Pantai Balian and Medewi can book up.

Tabanan & Mengwi

UNMISSABLE TEMPLE | UNIQUE STAYS | RICE FIELDS

GETTING AROUND

Useful public transit is non-existent. For stays in the scattered guesthouses, hotels, retreats and resorts, either make arrangements through your lodging or use a ride-hailing app. From Seminyak, it can take 90 minutes or more to drive here.

Self-driving is the quickest and most rewarding way to explore Tabanan and its surrounding sights. You can get around the heart of the town and the temple on foot, but otherwise, you'll want your own wheels to head north and south of the traffic-choked main road.

TOP TIP

To avoid traffic, stay off the main Gilimanuk–Denpasar road and use the well-paved back roads connecting Pererenan Beach to the west of Ubud. Secondary roads will always be more scenic and less jammed up.

Making up the best part of the less-travelled hinterland between Ubud and northern Canggu, rural Tabanan and Mengwi see little tourist traffic beside a trickle of van-hopping day-trippers. Like most regional capitals in Bali, Tabanan is a large, well-organised place with a central temple next to a huge banyan tree. The verdant surrounding fields are emblematic of Bali's rice-growing traditions and are part of its UNESCO recognition of the *subak* system of irrigation. The magnificent Pura Taman Ayun temple celebrates this, together with the renovated Tabanan's Mandala Mathika Subak (Subak Museum).

You'll need your own transport to drive the fecund back roads north of Tabanan, with chances to experience idiosyncratic and interesting places to stay while passing rice-field vistas around almost every turn.

The southern part of the Tabanan district takes you past vigorously growing rice shoots, revered by many as the most productive in Bali, and charming villages like Pejaten and Kediri, important centres of ceramic production.

Visit an Alluring Temple

Beautiful Pura Taman Ayun

One of the most rewarding temples on Bali to visit, **Pura Taman Ayun** *(30,000Rp)* is a beautiful place of enveloping calm. This huge royal water temple, northeast of Tabanan in Mengwi, is surrounded by a wide, elegant moat. It was the main temple of the Mengwi kingdom, which survived until 1891, when it was conquered by neighbouring kingdoms. The complex was built in 1634 and extensively renovated in 1937.

The first courtyard is an open, grassy expanse. The *jeroan* (inner courtyard) is screened by a low wall, which, unusually for Bali, allows easy viewing of the thicket of evocative *meru* (multitiered shrines) within. The canal-bordered walk around the perimeter of the *jeroan* is a sublime treat.

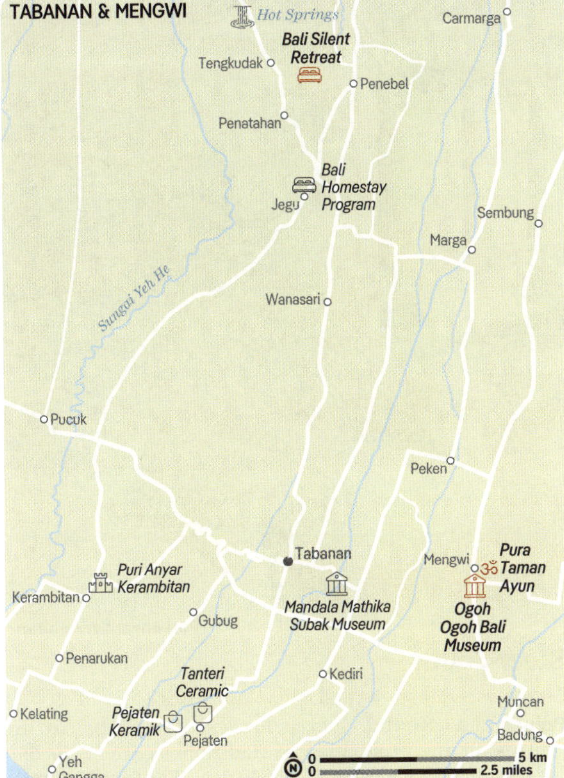

Lotus blossoms fill the temple's frangipani-shaded pools; the temple is part of the *subak* system (rice-field irrigation) recognised by UNESCO. Fittingly, canals and water features are found throughout. A small museum and an excellent video presentation are included in admission.

Just west of the temple complex, the **Ogoh Ogoh Bali Museum** *(20,000Rp)* celebrates the huge and outlandish papier-mâché monsters that have become a part of Nyepi celebrations. The market area immediately east of the temple has good warungs for lunch.

MONSTROUS OGOH-OGOH

In the weeks prior to Nyepi (usually in March), huge and elaborate papier-mâché monsters called ogoh-ogoh are built in villages across the island, with everybody in the community getting involved. Construction sites buzz with fevered activity around the clock. It's a recent tradition, beloved by village youth.

On Nyepi eve, large ceremonies across Bali lure out the demons. The whole island erupts in mock 'anarchy', with people banging drums, setting off firecrackers and yelling *'megedi megedi!'* (get out!) to expel the demons. For the grand finale, the ogoh-ogoh all go up in flames. Any demons that survive this wild scene are believed to evacuate the village when confronted with the boring silence on the morrow.

Learn About Bali's Ancient Irrigation System

Visit the Mandala Mathika Subak Museum

To learn about UNESCO-inscribed *subak*, a social-agrarian institution deeply tied to Balinese culture since the 9th century, head to the **Mandala Mathika Subak Museum** *(adult/child 15,000/10,000 Rp)*, also known as the Water Museum, located approximately 8km west of Pura Taman Ayun.

It was renovated and reopened in 2024, expanding its scope beyond the traditional Balinese irrigation system to include water management from other parts of Indonesia and the world, all explained with decent English-language placards.

STAY SOMEWHERE DIFFERENT

Set amid gorgeous scenery 18km northwest of Tabanan, **Bali Silent Retreat** *(balisilentretreat.com)* is an ashram-style retreat for spiritual folks – all in total silence. Visitors can self-explore water meditation, get lost in the walking labyrinth or stroll the Medicine Garden to learn about the centre's 'living pharmacy'. Daily events and programmes (included in a day pass option) include movement and meditation classes, hot-spring soaks and sunset music sessions.

You can also experience village life as part of the innovative **Bali Homestay Program** *(bali-homestay.com)*, which places travellers in the homes of residents of the rice-growing village of Jegu, 9km north of Tabanan. The recommended full two-night package includes activities such as making offerings, village visits and cultural tours, plus all meals.

DAVID SOUTH/ALAMY

Puri Anyar Kerambitan

Steer South

Ceramics, workshops and a timeless palace

Pejaten and **Kediri** villages, 10km south of Tabanan, are centres for the production of traditional pottery, including elaborate ornamental roof tiles. **Tanteri Ceramic** *(instagram.com/tanteribali)* is part showroom and part factory; nearby, **Pejaten Keramik** *(WhatsApp +62 831 1431 9000)* manufactures trademark pale-green pieces. You can spend a couple of hours browsing both shops.

Closer to the main road to Gilimanuk, **Kerambitan** village is noted for its dance troupe and musicians who perform in Ubud. Banyan trees shade the 17th-century **Puri Anyar Kerambitan** *(instagram.com/purianyarkerambitan_bali; by donation)*, a palace that's quietly mouldering away after having been a prominent 'social club' throughout the 1970s and '80s, with guests of the calibre of David Bowie, King Hussein of Jordan, Dewi Sukarno and Rolling Stones' frontman Mick Jagger, who reportedly came here three times to learn the *tektekan* dance. On a visit, which should last about half an hour, you can get a sense of Balinese royal life in days gone by.

Beyond Tabanan & Mengwi

South of Tabanan, Canggu's ever-growing sprawl starts to thin out, and one of Bali's most sacred (and touristed) temples marks the way to the 'wild west'.

The sticky fingers of Canggu's westward development have already grabbed Cemagi and Pantai Seseh and spilled into southeastern Tabanan Regency, where Nuanu Creative City blends futuristic art with AI-powered nature. Right to the west is Pura Tanah Lot, one of Bali's most sacred and visited temples – avoid the conga lines of sunset-seeking tourists and find your peace at other times of the day. A few kilometres away, Pantai Kedungu is becoming South Bali's next real-estate battleground.

It's when one gets to Pantai Yeh Gangga that South Bali's ominous villas and eco-earnest, green-juice-slinging cafes finally trade place with empty black beaches. You enter West Bali proper at Soka Beach: from here, crowds seem to be another island's problem. Things even out a little at Pantai Balian and Medewi, two low-key spots for surfing and hanging out.

Places

Cemagi p231
Pantai Nyanyi p232
Pantai Kedungu p232
Pura Tanah Lot p233
Pantai Balian p234

GETTING AROUND

It's possible and practical to use ride-hailing services to Cemagi, Pura Tanah Lot and Nuanu Creative City, but beyond that, a rental scooter or car is the way to go. If you have your own wheels, set your GPS from Canggu to Pantai Kelecung, and enjoy a beautiful ride. Be aware, though, that at the end of this route you re-join the infamous Gilimanuk-Denpasar Bypass to Pantai Balian, which locals dub the Jalur Tengkorak, or 'Skull Track', due to the high rate of deadly accidents. Beware of bus drivers, who overtake at full speed.

Cemagi

TIME FROM TABANAN: **30-45MIN**

Beach development and a sea-cliff temple

The area between Canggu's western fringes at Pererenan Beach and Pura Tanah Lot (p233) has generically picked up the name of Cemagi, where you could easily spend a day checking out beachside bars and visiting a waterfront temple.

Closest to Canggu, **Pantai Seseh** is a wide grey-sand beach good for watching the surf and sunsets, if you can cope with crossing the barrage of villas and waterfront cafes that practically shelter it from view. At the time of research, the construction site for the huge, snake-shaped Anantara Dragon Seseh Bali Resort, scheduled to open in 2027, was a particular eyesore.

About 1km west of less-developed Pantai Cemagi is the temple **Pura Gede Luhur Batu Ngaus**, sitting atop a dramatic outcrop of black lava rock jutting out into the pounding waves like a mini version of Tanah Lot, which is a further 3km northwest. To the immediate southeast, simple warungs serve drinks and snacks at cliffside tables. Just north of the temple is the black-sand **Pantai Mengening**, a fine place to while away an afternoon.

SEEING SEA TEMPLES

The legendary 16th-century priest Nirartha is credited with introducing many of the complexities of Balinese religion to the island, as well as establishing its chain of *pura segara* (sea temples). These sacred coastal spots both honour the sea gods and protect Bali from sea demons. Each was intended to be within sight of the next, and several have dramatic locations.

In addition to the famous, such as Pura Luhur Ulu Watu (p100) on the island's southwest tip, and the lesser-known, including Pura Pulaki (p217) near Pemuteran on the north coast, the sea temples are most heavily concentrated in West Bali. Notable examples include Pura Tanah Lot, Pura Rambut Siwi (p238) and Pura Gede Perancak (p237).

Pantai Nyanyi

TIME FROM TABANAN: **30MIN**

See the future at Nuanu Creative City

Imagine a place where towering sculptures that wouldn't look out of place at Nevada's Burning Man Festival coexist with an art gallery, Bali's only **alpaca park**, a **Magic Garden** featuring butterflies and orchids, and interactive spaces where AI-powered projections blend futurism with nature.

Bordering Tanah Lot, Pantai Nyanyi and science fiction, the 44 hectares of **Nuanu Creative City** *(nuanu.com; adult 50,000/20,000Rp online, children free; additional ticketing for activities)*, opened in early 2025, celebrate the intersection of art, technology and nature – with a promise to keep 70% of the area entirely undeveloped and green.

From the Balinese word *nu-anu*, meaning 'in the process', this theme park for creative minds is good to visit during the day, when you can try cutting-edge wellness activities such as those on offer at **Lumeira** *(lumeirawellness.com)*, self-defined as a 'social wellness complex' featuring the world's largest wood-fire dome sauna, thermal walking circuits and a pool with sound treatments.

But Nuanu literally shines at night, when its centrepiece sculpture, *The Earth Sentinels* by South African artist Daniel Popper – a mix of human heads and fossilised trees facing each other across the main walking path – fires up nightly at 6.30pm for an immersive AI-assisted multimedia light experience. After that, take a night walk through **Aurora Media Park** *(aurora.nuanu.com)*, where the open-air installations take on unique, dream-like impressions.

End the night or catch the sunset over Pantai Nyanyi at **Luna Beach Club** *(lunabeachclubbali.com; entry morning/afternoon/VIP daybed free/250,000/1,700,000Rp)*, one of Bali's most creative dance clubs, featuring gravity-defying bamboo architecture inside the **369 Restaurant**. Closer to the shore, underground **Utopia Cave Club** has a throwback swim-up bar and annexed water slide (kids are allowed during the day) sitting next to an outdoor dance floor topped by another of Nuanu's symbolic artworks: the steel rod, pregnant mother-goddess *Luna* by Ukrainian sculptor Alexander Milov.

Pantai Kedungu

TIME FROM TABANAN: **30MIN**

Step onto an up-and-coming coastline

Ask those in the known, and they'd tell you that **Pantai Kedungu** *(entry with bike 3000Rp)* is where foreign money is being invested in Bali right now. When we visited, it was still low-key, with a timid surfing crowd catching waves and two temples closed to visitors. **Kedungu Surf Shack** *(instagram.com/kedungu_surf__shack)* rents surfboards and sits next to a row of simple warungs spilling tables onto a patch of grass. On the eastern side of the beach, concrete steps lead to the statue of Bali's mythical minstrel **I Ketut Garing**, where black boulders soar above a scenic, less wavy part of the bay that attracts swimmers.

TOP EXPERIENCE

Pura Tanah Lot

A hugely popular tourist destination, the sea temple Pura Tanah Lot, closely associated with the Majapahit priest Nirartha, has great spiritual significance to the Balinese. Because of its floating illusion at high tide, when the rock on which the temple stands seems to be drifting on the waves, Tanah Lot is also one of Bali's most visited and photographed temples, especially for the overhyped sunsets.

MARIUS DOBILAS/SHUTTERSTOCK

Getting There

Most people arrive at Pura Tanah Lot on a tour for the much-touted sunset rush – try to avoid it. From the ticket gate, you normally follow walkways from the vast car parks through a mind-boggling sideshow of tatty souvenir shops, animal attractions and other schlock down to the sea.

Visiting the Site

You can walk over to the temple at low tide, but non-Balinese people are not allowed to enter. Two sacred snakes are said to live in the innermost sanctum. Follow the pathways in the gardens along the overlooking clifftop to escape the crowds and enjoy a somewhat more contemplative atmosphere. **Pura Batu Bolong** is connected to land by a natural bridge of stone over the surf.

Is It Worth Visiting?

It's up to you to decide: Pura Tanah Lot is an important spiritual place and the site has an innate beauty, but it can be hard to discern amid the crowds, clamour and chaos. The place also has all the authenticity of a stage set – even the tower of rock that the photogenic temple sits upon is an artful reconstruction, and more than one-third of the rock is artificial.

TOP TIPS

- Avoid the pre- and post-sunset rush, when traffic stretches for many kilometres.
- Arrive before noon: you'll beat the crowds and the vendors will still be elsewhere.
- Get dropped off and picked up just north at the small Pura Batu Mejan to avoid the worst of the scrum.

PRACTICALITIES

- tanahlot.id
- adult/child 75,000/30,000Rp; motorcycle/car parking 3000/5000Rp
- 6am-8pm

LESSER-KNOWN BEACHES IN WEST BALI

Pantai Yeh Gangga: West of Tanah Lot, the coast here is still secluded and has some luxe lodging options and dramatic rock formations.

Pantai Rahasya: Aka 'Hidden Beach'. Enjoy a sandy escape less than an hour from Canggu before it becomes too unhidden.

Pantai Tibubiyu: About 5km from southern Kerambitan is this small beachside village. The sand is hard-packed and at low tide you can cycle for great distances.

Pantai Bonian: Vast tidal flats of black sand bookended by rivers make this beach a moody stop.

Pantai Melaya: In the far west, this is a beach with natural shade and no development. A few fishing boats and stunning sunsets.

ANOM HARYA/SHUTTERSTOCK

Pantai Kedungu (p232)

Pantai Balian

TIME FROM TABANAN: **50MIN**

Surfing and crocodiles

Ever more popular, **Pantai Balian** (Balian Beach) is a rolling area of dunes and knolls that overlooks pounding surf. It attracts both surfers and those looking to escape the bustle of South Bali. The sand is right at the mouth of the wide Sungai Balian (Balian River); it's 800m south of the town of **Lalang-Linggah**.

Behind the beach, there's a small village of cafes, tourist businesses and guesthouses where travellers band together for drinks, talk surf or watch the sunset. The surf break is a reliable walled-up clean left shoulder; other activities include yoga and bodysurfing. Many try to snag photos of the crocodiles that inhabit the river.

EATING IN PANTAI BALIAN: OUR PICKS

Tekor Bali: Airy cafe set under a breezy awning, with coffee, homemade pastries and international food, plus good wi-fi to sit and work. *7am-10pm* $$

Mojo Balian: Coworking space and cafe facing a wall of greenery. All-day breakfast, good coffee and healthy food like smoothie bowls. *7am-9.30pm* $$

Deki's Warung: Breakfast, burgers, pizzas and less expensive Indonesian dishes at this warung with impressive beach views. *7am-9pm* $$

Secret Bay: Beautifully choreographed beachside seafood restaurant on a cape overlooking secluded Mejan Beach. *7.30am-10.30pm* $$

Jembrana Regency

RICE FIELDS | FISHING BOATS | SEASIDE TEMPLES

The Jembrana Regency, Bali's most sparsely populated district, is also one of the largest, with mountains to the north and a long coast of nearly empty, dark-sand beaches to the south. Most travellers come here for Medewi Point, home to a popular left-hand point break, but also razor-sharp rocks. Right to the east are Pulukan Beach and Pekutatan village, where one can experience local culture in the form of sunset walks with the region's rare pink buffalo.

Less-experienced surfers can try their hand further west at paddy-field-backed Pantai Yeh Sumbul, which offers a more forgiving sandbank and a laid-back, village-like atmosphere. Further west, the lonesome cliff-hanging sea temple Pura Rambut Siwi is a mandatory stop on the way to the inlet of Perancak, just south of the regional capital Negara, where beautiful *selerek* fishing boats, one of the world's most extravagant fleets, await keen photographers on the way to the port of Gilimanuk and ferries to Java.

GETTING AROUND

The region is best toured with your own wheels or by hiring a driver. Distances are far; don't expect to walk much. Whether transiting to Java or taking the coastal route to North Bali and West Bali National Park, you'll have to negotiate the main Gilimanuk–Denpasar road with its impatient strings of jockeying cars and trucks. You could hop on and off any of the buses plying the distance between the ferry port and Denpasar, but it's often a long and sweaty walk to any of the accommodation where you can rent a scooter.

Catch Waves at All Levels

Surfing at Medewi Point and Pantai Yeh Sumbul

The Jembrana Regency's main tourist draw is a top surf break, **Medewi Point**, with a much-vaunted long left-hand wave that makes rides of 200m to 500m common. Spectators view the action out on the water from the point, most likely seated at either **Bombora Medewi Wave Lodge** or **Umadewi Surf & Retreat**, two plush beachside resorts with restaurants, coffee and loungers. The immediate beach, **Pantai Medewi**, feels less touristy and has a stretch of huge, smooth grey rocks interspersed among round black pebbles – think of it as free reflexology.

Just west, **Pantai Yeh Sumbul** is another long swath of grey-sand beach with less dangerous rocks, more suitable

TOP TIP

Base yourself midway along the coast, either in Medewi or Pantai Yeh Sumbul, and take day trips to the surrounding sites. A rental scooter gives you the freedom to explore.

HIGHLIGHTS
1 Medewi Point

SIGHTS
2 Kurma Asih Sea Turtle Conservation Center
3 Pantai Medewi
4 Pantai Yeh Sumbul
see 2 Pura Gede Perancak
5 Pura Gereja
6 Pura Rambut Siwi
7 Sacred Heart Catholic Church
see 2 Ujung Muara Perancak

ACTIVITIES
8 Pekutatan Pink Buffalos Tour

SLEEPING
9 Alen's Stay & Surf
10 Anara Surf Camp
11 Asri Villas
12 Hotel Arda Bali
13 Jembrana Bali Homestay
14 Puri Dajuma Cottages
15 Riverside Medewi
16 Wide Sands Beach Retreat

EATING
17 Bombora Medewi Wave Lodge
18 Holy Tree Kitchen
see 2 Lesehan Ikan Bakar New Muara Indah
19 Rasta Cafe
see 17 Umadewi Surf & Retreat
20 Warung Negaora Ikan Bakar & Nyatnyat

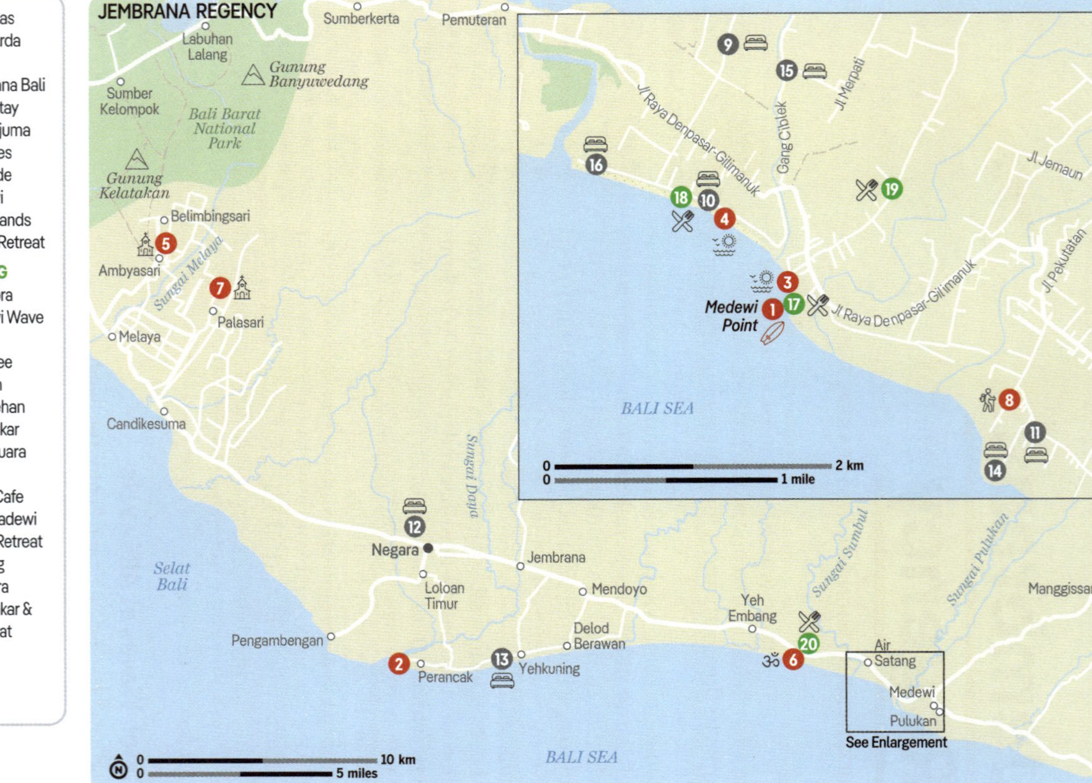

for less-experienced surfers. There's a sufficient number of guesthouses and cafes here, and yet it feels much more like its own secluded village. At sunset, the rice fields just beyond the beach get washed in ethereal shades of light.

Walk with Bali's Rare Pink Buffalo

Bovine encounters in Pekutatan

West Bali's rare pink buffaloes are endangered because of sacrifices and *makepung*, the brutal buffalo chariot races held in the paddies south of Negara. In **Pekutatan** village, farmer Pak Saudana tailors a two-hour conservation-driven **walking tour** *(westbali.net/experience-medewi; adult/child under 8 yr 200,000Rp/free)*, taking guests along as he herds his three animals along the beach. Saudana's son, Komang, speaks good English and assists with translations.

Stop by a Kaleidoscopic Cape

Turtles, temples and fishing culture in Perancak

Some 10km south of the regional centre of Negara, the fishing village of **Perancak** is the site of Nirartha's arrival in Bali in 1546, commemorated by the limestone sea temple **Pura Gede Perancak**. It's on a wide river inlet, between mangroves and the ocean, at the end of which is the lettering sign **Ujung Muara**. Look for the multihued, elaborate fishing boats called *perahu selerek*. They are always moored in pairs, believed to be husband and wife. A string of humble cafes near the oceanfront point has sunset drinks, fresh seafood and boat operators happy to take you out for a closer look at the boats. At sunset, the wide black beach to the south fills with locals flying kites.

Midway east along the cape, **Kurma Asih Sea Turtle Conservation Centre** *(kurmaasih.com; by donation)* and restaurant has been incubating turtle eggs for over 25 years, releasing thousands of turtles back into the sea. Learn about its work and the turtles on a 30-minute tour.

CHRISTIAN BALI

Discouraged by the secular Dutch, Christian evangelism via sporadic missionary activity in Bali resulted in few converts, many of whom were subsequently rejected by their own communities. In 1939 they were encouraged to resettle here in the wilds of West Bali. The two communities they established are examples of the hidden multiculturalism of the island.

Palasari boasts the huge **Sacred Heart Catholic Church**, largely made from white stone and set on a large town square. It's a peaceful, off-the-beaten-path spot with gently waving palms. Nearby **Belimbingsari** was established as a Protestant community, and now has the largest Protestant church, **Pura Gereja**, on the island. It has Balinese details such as a *kulkul* (hollow tree-trunk drum) instead of a bell.

EATING IN MEDEWI & PERANCAK: OUR PICKS

Rasta Cafe: This beloved vegan-focused Medewi cafe has a range of curated curries and rice-based dishes. *noon-10pm* $

Holy Tree Kitchen: Right on Pantai Yeh Sumbul, with good coffee, healthy breakfasts, tasty lunches and addictive views. *7am-9.30pm* $$

Warung Negaora Ikan Bakar & Nyatnyat: Near Rambut Siri Temple, excellent *mujair* fish or chicken served grilled or in sweet-sour *nyatnyat* sauce. *10am-8pm* $$

Lesehan Ikan Bakar New Muara Indah: Eat grilled fish in a relaxing seaside garden looking over the *selerek*. *8am-10pm* $

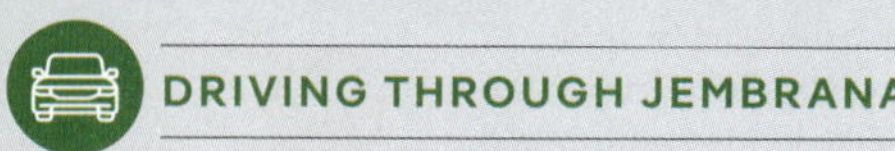

DRIVING THROUGH JEMBRANA

Zoom from Jembrana's black-sand coast to its lush hills, taking in beaches, waterfalls, sacred sites and local culture.

START	END	LENGTH
Pantai Yeh Leh	Pelabuhan Perikanan Nusantara Pengambengan	82km; 2½hr

Start on the Jalur Tengkorak at ❶ **Pantai Yeh Leh** *(entry 3000Rp)*, a local tourist beach with warungs and a palm-strewn field to sit in the shade by the sea. You'll leave the highway madness 7km further west, steering north past traditional villages to ❷ **Juwuk Manis Waterfall**. It takes about 15 minutes to descend the 800 steps to these twin falls and a clear, swimmable pond. Loop back west on the scenic Antosari Rd and pass through the majestic ❸ **Bunut Bolong**, a tunnel formed by two enormous trees (*bunut* is a type of ficus and *bolong* means 'hole'). It's 13km more to the coast, where ❹ **Yeh Sumbul Fishermen Port**, backed by a mosque shrouded in palm trees, offers a first taste of the traditional *selerek* (fishing boats), which are sometimes pushed into the sea over long poles arranged like rails. Six kilometres west is the superb 16th-century ❺ **Pura Rambut Siwi**, picturesquely situated on a clifftop overlooking a wide stretch of grey-sand beach.

If you overnight in Perancak or Negara after catching sunset and more *selerek* at ❻ **Ujung Muara** (p237), the next day, go to ❼ **Pelabuhan Perikanan Nusantara Pengambengan** before 8am, where men with rattan baskets on their shoulders enter the water to meet flocks of returning boats to haul their catch to weighing stations.

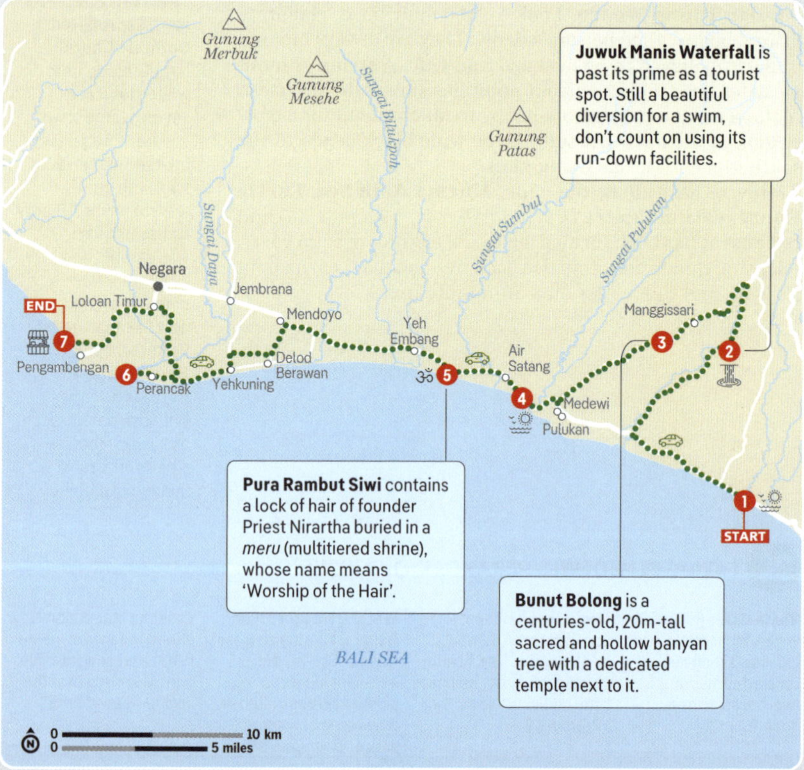

Juwuk Manis Waterfall is past its prime as a tourist spot. Still a beautiful diversion for a swim, don't count on using its run-down facilities.

Pura Rambut Siwi contains a lock of hair of founder Priest Nirartha buried in a *meru* (multitiered shrine), whose name means 'Worship of the Hair'.

Bunut Bolong is a centuries-old, 20m-tall sacred and hollow banyan tree with a dedicated temple next to it.

Places We Love to Stay

$ Budget $$ Midrange $$$ Top End

Cemagi, Pantai Nyanyi & Kedungu Area

KD Suites $$ Big balconies with rice-field views are the top feature of this newish hotel with a pool; not far from beaches.

Little Ripper Bali $$ Six rooms and three loft-like apartments at this Kedungu boutique hotel that's part hipster shop, part community space and part cafe with housemade sourdough bread and pastries.

Udara Bali $$$ Yoga classes with sea views and many more new-agey programmes, like sonic baths, feature here. It's right near the waterfront; opt for an all-inclusive health package.

Oshom Bali $$$ Beautiful boutique hotel inside Nuanu Creative City, furnished with upcycled materials and featuring tree houses in a mangrove forest or villas with dramatic ocean views over Pantai Nyanyi.

Yeh Gangga

WakaGangga $$$ On a black-sand beach, a small villa compound with multiple private pools amid rice terraces. It's a quiet area.

Soori Villas $$$ A luxury villa compound in Kelating, on a quiet stretch of Bali's west coast. Each villa has its own plunge pool. Expect modern minimalism in a secluded setting.

Pantai Balian

Surya Homestay $ One of a dozen excellent homestays at Pantai Balian. The owners are charming; the basic rooms are close to the surf break.

Pondok Pitaya $$ Beachfront property with cottage fronted by a swimming pool by the main beach, a popular restaurant, spa and a yoga shala.

Gajah Mina $$ Slightly aged clifftop villas spread around a wild garden, manicured yard and a freeform swimming pool. The hotel has a private, secluded beach facing its restaurant; a perfect sunset spot.

Medewi

Asri Villas $ A comfy, welcoming budget guesthouse that you won't want to leave. Features large bungalow-style rooms, a shared kitchen and a pool. It's southeast of the surf break.

Anara Surf Camp $ A surf camp and modern guesthouse near the sea and rice fields, at Pantai Yeh Sumbul. Attractive hardwood motifs.

Riverside Medewi $ Very clean and simple rooms with large bathrooms, cosy outside verandahs by a river, and located a five-minute drive from the beach. There's a common kitchen and an upstairs deck with lounge pillows.

Alen's Stay & Surf $ Peaceful, spacious rooms with verandahs facing verdant slopes hemmed by rice fields, and about five minutes by scooter from Medewi's point break.

Puri Dajuma Cottages $$ Suites, cottages and villas have private gardens, hammocks and walled outdoor baths. Most have ocean views too.

Wide Sands Beach Retreat $$$ Barefoot luxury resort on the western end of Pantai Yeh Sumbul, with two swimming pools, including one metres from the sand, and a range of attractive rooms.

Negara & Perancak

Jembrana Bali Homestay $ The seaside accommodation of choice in Perancak, featuring clean en-suite rooms with wooden accents and a good breakfast.

Hotel Arda Bali $ Set within rice fields and greenery off the main highway in Negara, this simple hotel has decent rooms, parking space and an enthusiastic owner. It's a 20-minute drive from Ujung Muara Perancak.

Researched by
Leyla Rose

Lombok

BALI'S LESS-TRAVELLED NEIGHBOUR

With sweeping coastlines, lust-worthy surf and one of Indonesia's most sought-after mountain treks – calling Lombok diverse would be an understatement.

It's hard to play favourites when it comes to islands in Indonesia, but Lombok's fan base of travellers just keeps growing. Equipped with impressive bays, the archipelago's second-highest peak and an ever-increasing number of enticing places to stay and dine – this island continues to attract the masses. Surfers flock to the southern half of the island for highly lauded waves, while trekking enthusiasts traverse the north-central region to Gunung Rinjani, an active volcano clocking in at 3726m high. Those with less intensive hobbies find themselves somewhere in between, typically with their toes in powdery-soft sand.

Unlike Bali, Lombok's indigenous community – the Sasak – are predominantly Muslim. Across the varied landscape, you'll see ornately designed mosques and hear the call to prayer five times a day. The island's cultural makeup remains diverse, but with lasting remnants of Balinese rule during the 1800s, when the Dutch and Balinese entered into a joint power-sharing agreement. By 1894, the Dutch eliminated Balinese rule, fully colonising the island on their own. This continued until the Indonesian National Revolution in 1945, marking the end of three centuries of Dutch colonial rule.

Well-paved main roads make it easy to get around the island, whether you opt to rent a motorbike or take private or public transport. Thankfully, traffic is seldom a gripe in Lombok, compared to the often choked streets of South Bali.

HARIADI MAHSYAR/SHUTTERSTOCK

THE MAIN AREAS

KUTA
Fast-growing town near popular beaches. p244

SENGGIGI
Longstanding resorts and quieter shores. p251

SENARU
Mountains and trekking. p257

SOUTHWESTERN PENINSULA & THE SECRET GILIS
Snorkelling and surfing. p264

For places to stay in Lombok, see p268

MUHD FUAD ABD RAHIM/SHUTTERSTOCK

Left: Surfing, Gerupuk (p248); Above: Gunung Rinjani (p262)

Find Your Way

Lombok's 4739 sq km encompass a variety of terrain: mountains, seaside cliffs, tobacco and rice fields, plus shimmering shoreline in all directions. When hopping from one destination to the next, expect the journey to last between one and three hours.

CAR

Private car rides start at around 200,000Rp for a 30-minute ride, such as from Lombok international airport to Kuta. Car rentals start at around 350,000Rp per day.

MOTORBIKE

Scooter rentals start at around 80,000Rp per day. Longer rentals often have cheaper rates. You can hop on a bemo (minibus) for a fraction of the price.

Senaru, p257
Gear up for Gunung Rinjani trekking, swim in a waterfall, and learn about traditional Sasak practices in this nature-shrouded town.

Senggigi, p251
Lombok's original resort town is quieter these days, but the palm-fringed beaches along the entire western coast maintain their allure.

Kuta, p244
This fast-growing town is popular among travellers and expats, just a half-hour's drive from some of Lombok's most loved beaches.

Southwestern Peninsula & the Secret Gilis, p264
Far from any noise, Lombok's Southwestern Peninsula is a prime pick when it comes to surfing, snorkelling and diving.

HARIADI MAHSYAR/SHUTTERSTOCK

Tetebatu (p249)

Plan Your Time

You can meander Lombok's finest beaches in a weekend, but the island is not one to be underestimated. It's easy to spend an entire week (or longer) checking out all the best spots.

One-Week Sampler

With just one week, you can experience the duality of Lombok's stunning coastlines and impressive mountainous region. Using **Kuta** (p244) as your base for the first four days, surf, swim and snorkel – including the **Southwestern Peninsula** (p264) if you're feeling adventurous. Head up to **Gunung Rinjani** (p262) and the **Sembalun Valley** (p261) when you're ready for something different.

The Big Loop

Bask in the joy of completing a giant loop in two weeks. Start by travelling from **Senggigi** (p251) to **Mataram** (p255), the capital city. Base up in **Kuta** (p244) for several days to explore the beaches and the **Southwestern Peninsula** (p264). Spend your remaining time taking in the rice fields in **Tetebatu** (p249) and the lofty heights of **Gunung Rinjani** (p262) before concluding in **Senaru** (p257).

SEASONAL HIGHLIGHTS

JANUARY–MARCH

Keep a raincoat handy, and don't plan treks – Gunung Rinjani is closed from 1 January to 31 March. Ramadan begins in February.

APRIL–JUNE

The occasional rain shower lingers. High season begins late June, and trekking starts up once again as the seasons shift.

JULY–SEPTEMBER

Dry season begins. The land is considerably less green, but dazzling against the ocean nonetheless.

OCTOBER–DECEMBER

There's still plenty of sun in October. Be aware of downpours mid-November to December.

Kuta

STUNNING BEACHES | FAMOUS SURF | CAFES & SHOPS

GETTING AROUND

Kuta itself is walkable. It takes 15 minutes to stroll the main strip, Jl Raya Kuta. The main streets have footpaths. As the best natural sights are just outside of Kuta, it makes sense to rent a car or scooter for the duration of your stay. If you don't drive, you'll have no trouble finding a driver – signs with ride rates for frequented destinations can be found around town, or arranged with most accommodation places. The coast makes for a beautiful journey.

TOP TIP

Since Kuta is a popular weekend getaway, accommodation can get booked up on the weekend. If swinging by Friday to Sunday, consider booking in advance if you want the full gamut of places to choose from, especially during July and August.

Fast-growing and increasingly popular, Lombok's Kuta is often confused with Bali's Kuta, despite vast differences. With close proximity to many of Lombok's most acclaimed beaches, Kuta has become a hotspot for surfers and beachgoers. The most fantastic sandy stretches are within just a half-hour's drive of the town's centre. Development has boomed in recent years, from the large-scale Mandalika resort area to the outcrop of trendy restaurants catered towards visitors. Regardless of the seemingly constant stream of new business, crowds and traffic aren't really a thing here.

You'll see surf shops up and down the town's main streets, with Jl Raya Kuta running from north to south, and Jl Mawun running west to east. While there's no shortage of places to grab a beer on an evening out, the nightlife is far more relaxed, with most people waking up early to head out for explorations rather than partying the night away.

Get the Lay of the Land

Swims and sunsets

Drive 20 minutes east of Kuta to **Tanjung Aan**: a horseshoe-shaped bay that definitely deserves to be your first beach experience in Lombok. Set up shop for the afternoon, grab a coconut and take cooling dips in the sandy-bottomed sea.

When the sun starts to hang low in the sky, hop a few minutes over to **Bukit Merese**: a hill just above Tanjung Aan, locally known for being one of the best places to watch the sunset. Roughly a 15-minute ride from the centre of Kuta, it's a prime spot for views of the south coast in both directions, giving you a taste of what to expect as you plan adventures to more far-flung beaches. You'll have to pay 10,000Rp to enter before you can park and walk to the top of the hill and those 360-degree views. Expect a crowd before sundown, though you'll have plenty of open space to roam.

SIGHTS
1 Bukit Merese
2 Pantai Kuta
3 Pantai Lancing
4 Pantai Mawi
5 Pantai Mawun
6 Pantai Seger
7 Pantai Semeti
8 Tanjung Aan

ACTIVITIES
9 Adventure Divers Kuta
10 Blue Marlin Dive Kuta Lombok
11 Scuba Froggy

SLEEPING
12 Kumbara Villas
13 Lara Homestay
14 LMBK Surf House
15 Origin Lombok
16 Porter Lombok Hotel
17 Sikara Lombok
18 Villa Homey Lombok

EATING
19 Jiang Nan
20 Munchies
21 Terra
see 9 Warung Flora

ENTERTAINMENT
22 Bau Nyale Festival

INFORMATION
23 Project Hiu

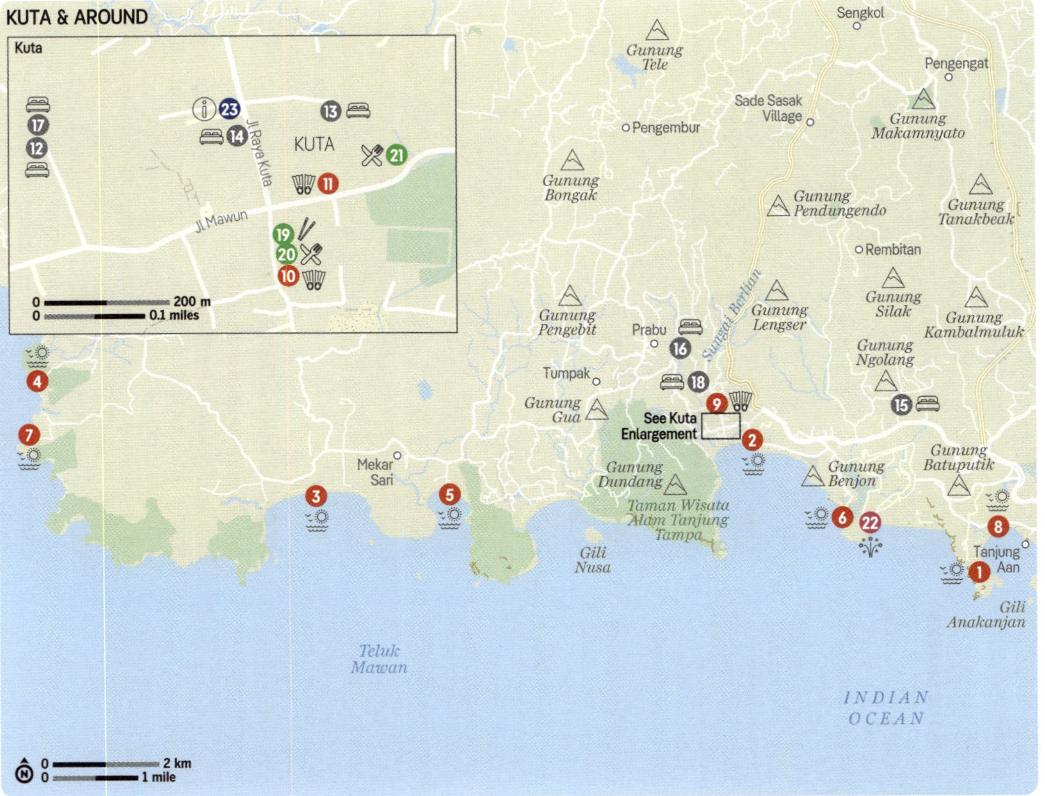

SAVE THE SHARKS

As the world's number one nation for shark fishing, Indonesia has historically been a dangerous place for sharks. **Project Hiu** *(projecthiu.com)* is a Kuta-based initiative working against this by providing alternative incomes to shark fishers through eco-friendly tourism. Join a crew of former shark fishers to explore Lombok's south coast by boat, learning about the reefs and marine life off the coast. Day trips start at 1,200,000Rp, all of which goes directly towards the shark-fishing crew as an alternative source of income. If you're not up for a day trip, the Project Hiu shop right in the heart of Kuta has both dive gear and locally made goods.

DENIS MOSKVINOV/SHUTTERSTOCK

Pantai Mawun

Explore Sun-Soaked Beaches

Revel in the turquoise coastline

The word *pantai* means beach, and you'll find a lot of them around here. For starters, the logical first pick is **Pantai Kuta**. You'll likely notice the giant Mandalika sign before your toes hit the sand, as the area has been rapidly developed in the last few years. This bay-shaped stretch of sand is gorgeous, but you'd be remiss to visit Kuta without checking out other nearby spots that are the pinnacle of tranquillity. You can essentially hop from one glittering bay to another half-moon-shaped cove all the way down the south coast – plenty of the coastline's magic lies beyond Kuta.

Drive 20 minutes from Kuta's centre to **Pantai Mawun**, a small cove flanked by rolling hills. Apart from a few beachside warungs with sunbeds and coconuts, there's not much else here, and that's what makes it lovely. With little reef, it's also ideal for swimming. Venture seven minutes further west to **Pantai Lancing**, a lengthy strip of white sand backed by grasslands, most frequented by doting groups of cattle. These westward roads have been gorgeously paved, presumably in anticipation of more developments, but the area remains rustic and fairly sparse. There are a couple of beach shacks here selling snacks and local dishes.

If you're up for a more intrepid adventure, **Pantai Semeti** is a 45-minute drive west of Kuta. Part of the fun is getting there – from the main road, you'll need to then drive down a dirt path with some steep sections and large potholes. It's a rewarding drive, though, as the beach is rarely visited and you'll most likely get it all to yourself. There are also some striking volcanic rock formations at one end of the beach that you can climb, which make for epic photos.

Surfing for All Skill Levels

Surf solo or learn from experts

Whether you're a seasoned pro or hopping on a board for the first time, there are plenty of surf spots to accommodate all skill levels. Kuta is a year-round surfing destination, with consistent swell and a variety of different breaks. You'll find it less crowded during the rainy season (roughly from November through March), which can sometimes provide 'cleaner' waves as there's less chop from the wind.

Just 20 minutes' drive from Kuta, the waves at **Pantai Seger** are suitable for all levels, with both lefts and rights. East of Kuta, surf schools such as **Heartbeach Lombok Surf Academy** *(heartbeachlombok.com; sessions from 500,000Rp)* dot the shorelines of Tanjung Aan (p244), as well as surfboard rental shacks. A 35-minute drive west of Kuta lies **Pantai Mawi** (not to be confused with Mawun), one of Kuta's most famous surf spots, with strong currents suited for intermediate and advanced surfers. Beware of the semi-treacherous 10-minute ride leading to the beach with its many potholes and loose rocks. The end views are worth it.

For fewer crowds, **Are Guling** is a 20-minute drive west from the centre of Kuta. This quiet bay offers left- and right-hand breaks that are ideal for intermediate and advanced surfers. You can paddle out from the beach, but be mindful of the currents around the left-hander and the sharp reef at low tide.

BAU NYALE FESTIVAL

Once a year in February, people flock to the shoreline of Pantai Seger, right by the Pertamina Mandalika International Circuit (a racetrack) with a unique quest: capturing *nyale*, a surprisingly colourful species of sea worm. Crowds and ceremonies fill the area as part of the **Bau Nyale Festival** – an age-old tradition that is believed to bring good fortune. These are regarded as no ordinary worms – the colourful, yarn-like sea creatures are thought to bring prosperity to those who catch them. The exact date depends on the year, but expect crowds if you happen to be in town for the festival. During the other 364 days of the year, Pantai Seger is frequented by swimmers, sunbathers and surfers.

EATING IN KUTA: OUR PICKS

Munchies: Spacious cafe on the main intersection with all-day breakfasts, lunch and pizzas, plus healthy drinks and wines. *7.30am-11pm* **$$**

Terra: Fully vegan and gluten-free restaurant with a focus on wellness. The healthy desserts make a visit worth it. *8am-10pm* **$$**

Jiang Nan: Chinese sharing dishes with all the classics like won tons, bao buns and soup dumplings. Perfect for a casual date night. *1-10pm* **$$**

Warung Flora: Indonesian favourites right on the main road, including all the *nasi* (rice) and *mie* (noodles) classics, plus soups and curries. *5-10pm* **$**

Beyond Kuta

Outside of Kuta lie sleepy fishing towns, empty white-sand beaches, rice fields with mountain views and plenty of traditional Sasak culture.

Places

Selong Belanak p248
Gerupuk p248
Tetebatu p249
Ekas p250
Sekaroh p250

GETTING AROUND

The main east and west roads along Lombok's southern coast are well-paved. When heading westbound, expect steep hills and sharper turns – the area is hilly. Previous riding experience is advised for those who plan to take a scooter. Northbound towards the mountains, the land is fairly flat. You'll find plenty of amenities along the way, such as minimarts and larger gas stations. Arranging transport with a driver is generally quick and easy.

It's easy to get into the swing of life in Kuta, but venturing further along Lombok's southern coast and up north into the foothills of Gunung Rinjani offers wow-worthy scenery and a true escape from it all. West of Kuta, developments dwindle, whereas the twinkling ocean's glow only seems to strengthen. In Lombok's remote southeastern corner, the rugged landscape replete with seaside cliffs remains silent, apart from the occasional small-town hum. Drive an hour and a half north of Kuta to Tetebatu, a charming Sasak village, and you'll be immersed in a verdant landscape of rice fields and farmland. Waterfalls, cultural experiences and fantastic Indonesian food make the decision to visit Tetebatu a no-brainer – this village is worth adding to your list.

Selong Belanak

TIME FROM KUTA: **30MIN**

Surf and swim in clear waters

The picture-perfect bay of **Selong Belanak** is one of the most talked-about beaches of the coast, drawing both locals and visitors to its lengthy, powdery shoreline. Upon arrival, expect to pay around 10,000Rp for parking before a narrow sandy path takes you through a gap in between two beach warungs. The view becomes panoramic – an elongated beachfront framed by rolling hills on either side. It's certainly not an empty beach, but there's plenty of room to spread out – especially at low tide. Take a stroll, grab a fresh coconut or go for a surf, it's a popular spot for beginners. You can post up with your own beach towel, or opt for a lounge chair in front of one of the warungs, so long as you make a purchase while you sunbathe. Come around 5pm, and you might see the local farmers herding their water buffalo after they've grazed in the nearby fields. It's quite a sight.

Gerupuk

TIME FROM KUTA: **20MIN**

Surf the breaks near a traditional fishing village

The coastal fishing village of **Gerupuk** is frequented by surfers and overlooks a bay with five different surf breaks that can only be accessed by boat. Simply head to the beach and you'll be met with plenty of locals offering to take you out on their boat. This costs 150,000Rp for three or fewer people, or 50,000Rp per person for more than three people.

The area remains considerably untouched by foreign influence, with just a few fishing boats lining the shore and a handful of small surf shops, homestays and warungs. If arriving from Kuta, you'll pass through the massive Mandalika development's shiny new gate on the way to Gerupuk, though the contrast between the two areas remains stark. Stop by for a quick surf and a roam through the area. Either bring your own board or rent from a nearby surf shop, such as **Rasta Surfshop & Surfschool** *(instagram.com/rasta_surf_shop)* or **Insider Surf** *(insidersurflombok.com)*. Rentals range from 100,000Rp to 300,000Rp per day, depending on the size of the board.

Tetebatu

TIME FROM KUTA: 1½HR

Learn about Sasak culture in a beautiful setting

Backed by a postcard-like view of Gunung Rinjani, the small village of **Tetebatu** exemplifies traditional Sasak charm. Here, bright-green rice and tobacco fields form most of the landscape, and the air has a lovely lightness to it, thanks to nearby mountain mist and slightly lower temperatures. Several *air terjun* (waterfalls), gushing springwater and flowing over eroded volcanic rock formations, are found around the area. **Tetebatu Waterfall** in the heart of town is the most frequently visited.

Here, traditional architecture is neighboured by tropical flowers of all shades, and the palm-fringed streets have never seen traffic. You'll find homestays and restaurants catering to tourists, but the overwhelming majority of businesses are locally owned, making it a much more authentic experience compared to more completely gentrified areas. Apart from cruising the serene streets of Tetebatu via scooter, the best way to explore the area is by walking tour. Most homestays can connect you with a local guide, often including experiences such as Lombok coffee production, spice markets and the Sasak arts, including weaving and pottery: stop by **Aqila Warung** *(WhatsApp +62 877 5503 0317; cooking class/tour 150,000/300,000Rp)* to book some locally led tours of the area and cooking classes. While you're there, enjoy a traditional meal.

You can easily take a day trip out to Tetebatu since it's only a short drive from Kuta, but it's also a great place to wake

PACKING FOR DAY TRIPS

Some things can be harder to come by once you leave Kuta, like ATMs and sunscreen. Whether you're planning an all-day excursion to the Southwestern Peninsula (p264) or going to a beach 30 minutes away, packing your day bag accordingly can save some headache (or rather, heatstroke) down the line.
Most of the further beaches have plenty of small beachside warungs, but keeping a water bottle handy, plus some cash and sunscreen, is advantageous. When in smaller towns, cash payments are the norm – and that includes getting petrol for your scooter everywhere you go.

EATING IN TETEBATU: OUR LOCAL PICKS

Warung Monkey Forest: Classic Indonesian plates with a Sasak lens. The curries and vegetable dishes are particularly tasty. Also offers local tours. *7am-10pm* $

Zaeni Warung: Family-run favourite offering Indonesian plates, including rice, noodles, curries and more, along with plenty of fresh juices. *7am-11pm* $

Oktavia Warung: Sasak dishes such as *urap-urap* (vegetables with coconut) and a long list of chicken plates. *7am-10pm* $

Aqila Warung: Delicious Indonesian eats in a restaurant that also offers cooking classes and local tours. *7am-10.30pm* $

DIVING & SNORKELLING TIPS

You can slap on some flippers and a mask at any beach that you please, but some of the best marine life experiences are further afield. The lesser-visited **Southwestern Gilis** (p266) – Gili Gede, Gili Asahan and Gili Layar – are fairly sparse when it comes to human activity, yet are teeming with coral and marine life. From Kuta, it takes about 1½ to two hours to ride up to Tembowong Harbour in Sekotong, where you can organise a private boat for around 400,000Rp. Accommodation places offer day-trip packages for snorkelling and diving, but be advised: you'll likely end up paying more than average if your hotel is a fancy one. Shop around a bit.

up in the morning. If you have extra time on your hands, spending a night or two in the area can be a deeply relaxing experience, especially if you're either preparing for or resting after a mountain trek up Rinjani.

Ekas

TIME FROM KUTA: **1HR 10MIN**

Unspoiled beach and surf along a tranquil bay

Yet another surfer's paradise on southern Lombok's broad coast, the small seaside village of **Ekas** is contrastingly tiny in comparison to the massive **Awang Bay** on its doorstep. Surfers of all skill levels ride out here year-round for two well-loved waves – **Ekas Outside** and **Ekas Inside**. If you're keen on sticking around for a night or two (or even longer), **Ekas Surf Resort** (p268; *ekassurfresort.com; surf boat per person 50,000Rp*) has affordably priced rooms and a surf boat to get you out to the breaks.

There's plenty of beautifully mindless lazing under the sun to be had, too. **Ekas Beach** is decorated with fishing boats and tonnes of open space. Drive just a few minutes south to discover its surrounding area, adorned with spectacular shorelines, some of which are bordered by towering cliffs. **Paradise Beach** and **Pantai Kura Kura** are more remote picks nearby, where you won't hear too much beyond the waves.

Sekaroh

TIME FROM KUTA: **1½HR**

Stroll on pink beaches in a remote area

Lombok's southeasternmost corner, **Sekaroh**, might very well be the definition of 'out there'. The coastline here is where it's at, with naturally pink beaches along the northern shores of the region. A quick web search reveals several images with dramatically boosted saturation, but it's true: the sand really *is* a light shade of pink. This phenomenon occurs thanks to the delightful mixture of red reef particles and white sand. You'll find several 'Pink Beach' markers on the map near **Tanjung Sabui**, some of which have irked reviewers expressing ire over discrepancies from the internet's dubious imagery. Expect company and likely an entrance fee of 15,000Rp per scooter and 20,000Rp per car.

While pink-ish sand can be an enticing lure, there are plenty more lesser-visited beaches along the south shore featuring pristine waters lapping on sand without a single footprint. Rocky outcroppings flank the shores of **Pantai Tanjung Bloam**, next to the gorgeous **Jeeva Beloam Beach Camp**, a rustic off-grid experience. Further south, **Pantai Antak-Antak**'s staggering cliffs are heavenly. Make your way down to the thin strip of land that's home to **Pantai Lemerang**: this sweeping beach is remote as can be.

While Sekaroh is only 1½ hours from Kuta, don't underestimate the exhaustion that can come with smaller roads in remote areas, especially if you're on a scooter. Plan a day trip.

Senggigi

FANCY RESORTS | QUIET BEACHES | MOUNTAINOUS BACKDROP

Like something out of a 1990s holiday time-capsule, Senggigi rose to fame decades ago as Lombok's premier tourist destination. The scenery is a treat: mountains, doused in junglescape, bordering the deep-blue ocean. This combination is particularly spectacular when viewed from elevated areas on the main road, giving unparralleled views of the entire landscape for vast stretches. Groves of coconut palms provide generous shade close to the water, where people gather for sunset views overlooking Gunung Agung – Bali's mighty volcano – in the distance.

These days, Senggigi is quieter than it used to be. Longstanding resorts remain on bays up and down the town's coastal stretch, some of which appear empty. There's a low hum of activity, but you're unlikely to encounter anywhere particularly busy. The waters are prime for snorkelling, and you can easily line up a day trip to the Gilis – so if you're looking for a quiet seaside spot, this might be the one for you.

GETTING AROUND

Senggigi is essentially one main road along the coast with short offshoots leading inland and to the beach. The town spans roughly 2.5km from north to south, but the central area is walkable. Some accommodation is closer to Mangsit on the northern end of Senggigi, where the tourist zone begins. The hotels and resorts are fairly spread out, so you may want to rent your own vehicle or save a taxi driver's number for daily outings – unless, of course, you plan to just laze beachside.

Cruise to Pura Batu Bolong

A serene temple on the water

Not to be confused with the famed Batu Bolong of Canggu, **Pura Batu Bolong** *(by donation)* is a Hindu temple perched on a rocky outcrop looking over the sea. Ornately crafted pagodas and statues stand tall above crashing waves, with small offerings placed around the grounds daily. There's a low hum of activity throughout the day, picking up around sunset when people gather to watch the sky turn hues of sherbet orange and pastel pink. Expect to pay around 5000Rp for parking, plus a donation amount of your choice for entry to the grounds. Come prepared with covered legs, or rent a sarong on arrival *(5000Rp)*. Getting to Pura Batu Bolong takes about three minutes via scooter or car from central Senggigi.

TOP TIP

Accommodation is spread out in Senggigi, so check before booking to see that you'll be within walking distance of things. Many homestays, hotels and resorts are labelled 'Senggigi', but are actually several kilometres from the town's centre.

SIGHTS
1 Coconut Beach
2 Pantai Klui
3 Pantai Senggigi
4 Pura Batu Bolong

ACTIVITIES
see 2 Surf School Lombok Wave

SLEEPING
5 Central Inn Senggigi
6 Holiday Resort Lombok
7 Katamaran Resort
8 Sammy Cottage

EATING
9 Asmara Restaurant & Lounge
10 Begibung Beach & Sunset View Resto
11 Coco Beach Restaurant
12 Pasta Pojok
13 Warung Ijo

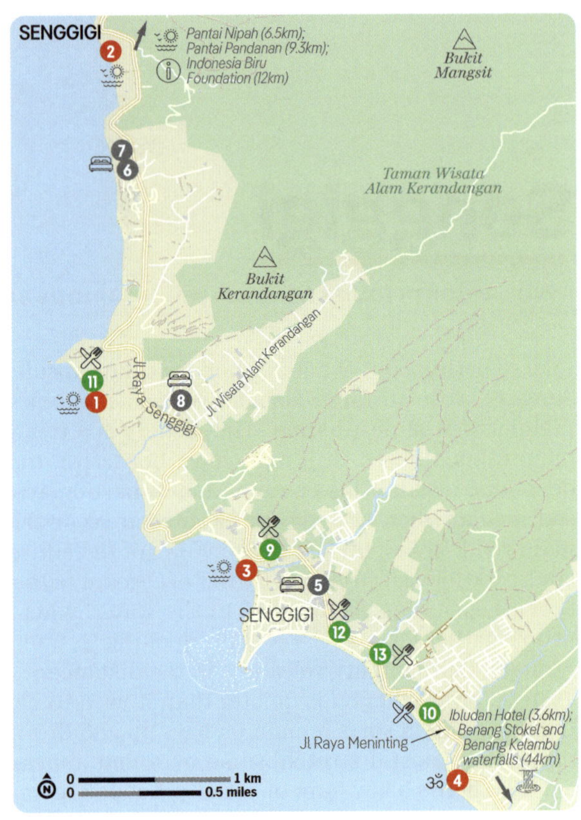

Beach-Hop Around the Coast

Soak up Senggigi's laid-back coastline

Walk far enough west anywhere in Senggigi, and you'll eventually hit the beach. Consider Jl Raya Senggigi your serpentine route to the surrounding region's best beaches – there's a lot more than what's within the town's limits. For starters, the aptly named **Pantai Senggigi** is the closest beach to the main tourist area, an elongated bay fit for swimming or just hanging out in the shade of a palm tree. Minutes north, **Coconut Beach** is accessible through dusty pathways that weave through a field of sky-high coconut palms. Both locals and tourists gather around the beachside **Coco Beach Restaurant** at sunset, sipping on Bintangs and fresh coconuts. The vibe is family-friendly, and you'll see groups of vacationers young and old kicking back.

For a more secluded experience, a short drive up the coast is a must. **Pantai Nipah** is a 20-minute drive from central Senggigi – a scenic route that'll have you doing double-takes at the wondrous views. This white-sand stretch is bordered

QUIET WEEKDAYS, BUSY WEEKENDS

Senggigi sees a lot of domestic tourism, especially on the weekends when local families come from other parts of Lombok to hit the beach. While, overall, the area is far less busy than it used to be in years past, there's definitely an uptick in activity on the weekends – typically along the shoreline, right around when the sunset turns the sky a dreamy shade of pastel orange and candy pink. Regardless of when you go, there won't be nearly as much of a touristy buzz as in Kuta, which has continued to draw more and more attention in the last decade or so.

by a quintessentially tropical palm-tree forest, and its shores are decorated with more beached fishing boats than tourists. Around the next bend a few minutes north, **Pantai Pandanan** is equally as quiet, commanding attention from anyone who catches a view of it. A few local vendors operate, selling snacks and drinks.

Hop on a Surfboard

Ride the waves with local experts

Most surfers flock to the southern coast of Lombok, but Senggigi has surf, too, and it's generally uncrowded. The reef break at **Pantai Klui** is suitable for beginners, and you can take lessons at **Surf School Lombok Wave** *(WhatsApp +62 831 2962 4531),* located right on the beach. If you're already established when it comes to waves, rent a board from them and do your own thing. Sip on fresh coconuts in between lessons and stay for sunset to make a full day of it.

Wander Waterfalls Shrouded in the Jungle

Visit Benang Stokel and Benang Kelambu

Swim in crisp mountain waters tumbling down from a lush canopy of jungle vegetation. The waterfalls **Benang Stokel** and **Benang Kelambu** are nestled near the foothills of Gunung Rinjani's western side. You'll have to drive around an hour and 20 minutes from Senggigi, but it's worth a day trip, especially if you need a break from the muggy heat of the coastal air. Expect to pay for a guide *(per person around 90,000Rp)* – you're required to have one.

CORAL RESTORATION

Marine pollution, coral bleaching caused by a warming ocean and overfishing are just some of the threats to Lombok's coral reefs. Based in Pantai Kecinan, a 25-minute drive north from Senggigi, the **Indonesia Biru Foundation** *(indonesiabiru.id)* is an NGO dedicated to protecting Lombok's marine habitats via initiatives including reef restoration, community engagement and education programmes. Travellers can support its work by joining a reef restoration dive *(from 550,000Rp)* or a snorkelling session to see its ocean-based coral nurseries. The NGO also hosts regular mangrove-planting events and beach clean-ups, and volunteering opportunities are available.

EATING IN SENGGIGI: OUR PICKS

Pasta Pojok: Highly popular spot serving authentic handmade pasta and wood-fired pizza. *11am-10pm* $$

Begibung Beach & Sunset View Resto: Beachside restaurant with Lombok dishes served under thatched umbrellas with benches and beanbags. *4-10pm* $

Warung Ijo: Simple eatery with Indonesian food, both à la carte and a buffet-style spread with a huge choice of dishes. *8am-10pm* $

Asmara Restaurant & Lounge: Both Indonesian and international cuisine with alfresco tables in a leafy setting right in the centre of town. *4-11pm Mon-Sat* $$

Beyond Senggigi

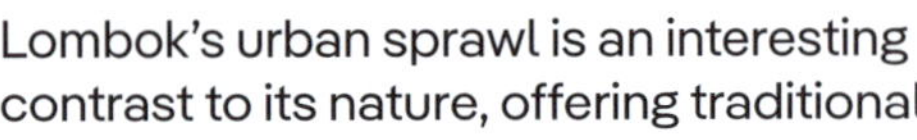

Lombok's urban sprawl is an interesting contrast to its nature, offering traditional markets, historic buildings, street food and cultural experiences.

Places

Meninting p254
Ampenan p255
Mataram p255

GETTING AROUND

Although it's pretty easy to get around the city area, you'll need your own set of wheels. Motorbikes are king here, although there are sidewalks for covering short distances. The roads are in good condition, and while there can be traffic, the wide lanes of the main avenues assuage the worst of it. Newbie motorbike riders may be intimidated by the broad streets – you should come prepared with riding experience if you're planning to ride anywhere in Indonesia.

Lombok's capital city, Mataram, feels like a big town – perhaps because it's the culmination of what was once several villages. Mataram has some unique experiences that provide context to the fabric of Lombok's culture, plus practical city amenities that aren't found in the island's smaller communities. Lively Indonesian markets, fascinating architecture and multi-denominational temples with centuries of history make this city rich in heritage. While the majority of people are Sasak Muslim, relics of Hindu culture are found throughout the city. Multi-storey malls coexist with traditional markets on motorbike-filled avenues.

Ampenan, Mataram and Cakranegara – once villages that blended to form today's Mataram – still differentiate the city's areas. Ampenan borders the sea, and it's a port area with remnants of Dutch colonial architecture. Mataram both was and is the government centre, where you'll find administrative buildings and hotels. Cakranegara, the business district, spans the eastern side of the city. It's a commercial area with malls and shops.

Meninting

TIME FROM SENGGIGI: **15MIN**

Join a cooking class with Anggrek Putih Lombok

Food offers an insight into a country's people, culture and history. Whether you're a keen chef or just enjoy tasting new dishes, a cooking class is a fun way to connect with and learn more about the local culture in Lombok. **Anggrek Putih Lombok** *(anggrekputih.com; per person 400,000Rp)* is a family-run cookery school in **Meninting**, on the outskirts of Mataram. There's an organic garden on-site where most of the ingredients are grown. Friendly and knowledgeable local cooks talk you through the variety of fruit, vegetables and herbs, and you even get to pick fresh ingredients to use in the class (you can choose to join a lunch or dinner session). They'll guide you through various Indonesian and Lombok dishes, including curries, satay and vegetarian dishes. There is on-site accommodation, but if you're staying elsewhere, the school also offer free transport to and from class.

Ampenan

TIME FROM SENGGIGI: **20MIN**

Wander Ampenan's historic streets

Ampenan, the western district of Mataram, is an ageing port town that was once used by Dutch colonisers. The port was used heavily for spice trade, and a roam around the area reveals countless weathered buildings with Dutch-style architecture. Today, it's frequented by local foodies and families looking for fresh grilled seafood and other Indonesian plates. Local food vendors post up along the **waterfront** to neighbour established warungs and markets. **Pasar Kebon Roek**, a traditional market, has just about everything when it comes to groceries. From succulent tropical fruit, vegetables, meat and seafood to coffee and sweets – it's a grand selection. You won't find many tourists around here. Pro tip: go first thing in the morning before the heat of the day kicks in.

Mataram

TIME FROM SENGGIGI: **30MIN**

Shop at Mataram's malls and markets

Whether you need warmer clothes to hit the mountains, a rogue item you forgot to pack, or you simply want to browse local handicrafts – **Mataram** is definitely *the* place in Lombok for shopping. **Lombok Epicentrum Mall** *(lombokepicentrum.com)* is the largest of the lot, with four floors of shops, plus a cinema and plenty of food options. A close second goes to **Mataram Mall**, less than 10 minutes east. Clothing, electronics, restaurants and a supermarket can all be found here with ease. As for traditional markets, they're scattered throughout Mataram and vary in size. **Pasar Cakranegara** is one of the more well-known markets, with items ranging from traditional batik fabrics (a classic Indonesian design) to household items and trinkets; these are authentic souvenirs, compared with those found in many more gentrified and touristy areas of Indonesia.

VISA EXTENSIONS

If you need to extend your Indonesian visa (some visas can be extended online) while in Lombok, Mataram is the place to do it. **Kantor Imigrasi Mataram**, the immigration office, is located in the heart of Mataram, at the intersection of the main streets of Jl Udayana and Jl Mahoni. If you entered the country on a 30-day visa on arrival (VOA), you can extend it for 30 days. From drop-off to pickup, budget between five and seven days for the entire process. You'll find it a far less crowded experience compared to Bali's immigration offices. Expect to pay around 500,000Rp for a 30-day extension for your VOA. The phone number is 37-063 2520.

EATING IN MATARAM: LOCAL FOOD

Sukma Rasa Ayam Panggang: Traditional Sasak fare with a menu full of local delights in a comfortable setting outside the busy area. *8am-11pm* $

Sate Rembiga Ibu Sinnaseh: No-frills eatery serving grilled satay, vegetable dishes and other Lombok-style delights. *9am-10pm* $

Rumah Makan Asano: Arguably the best Padang restaurant in town, serving Minang-style rice with various side dishes. *8am-9pm* $

Seafood and Grilled Fish 99: A seemingly endless array of fresh-caught seafood smothered in a variety of different sauces. Arrive hungry. *11am-9.30pm* $

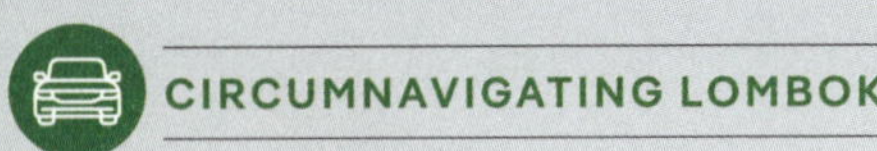

CIRCUMNAVIGATING LOMBOK

Explore Lombok with this driving tour that takes in villages, beaches, highlands and cities.

START	END	LENGTH
Kuta	Kuta	334km; minimum 1 week

Set off from 1 **Kuta** (p244) and drive east along the bumpy coastal road, all the way to 2 **Sekaroh** (p250), Lombok's easternmost 'leg'. Here, the peach-hued sands of the pink beaches are a great spot for a break.

Head north, driving inland to 3 **Tetebatu** (p249). Take a walk among its rice paddies and rainforest, followed by a swim in the waterfalls. This is a great spot to stay a night or two. Drive north to 4 **Sembalun** (p261), where cooler temperatures, hiking trails and views of Gunung Rinjani await. Spend at least two days here.

Carry on to 5 **Senaru**, where you can swim at **Sendang Gile** (p257) and **Tiu Kelep** (p257) waterfalls. Stay the night, before dropping back down to the west coast where the winding coastal road offers brilliant views at every turn. Around an hour and 20 minutes later, stop at 6 **Pantai Nipah** (p252) for a coconut and a swim.

As you drive further south, you'll pass villages and towns that gradually morph into Lombok's urban sprawl. 7 **Senggigi** (p251) is worth a stop for its restaurants and souvenir stores, but skip if you're keen for a more local experience.

Once you get to the main city area, check out the goods at 8 **Pasar Kebon Roek** (p255) market in Ampenan, or drive to 9 **Pasar Cakranegara** (p255) for a larger selection of local handicrafts. From here, the hour's drive back to Kuta is easy thanks to the wide roads.

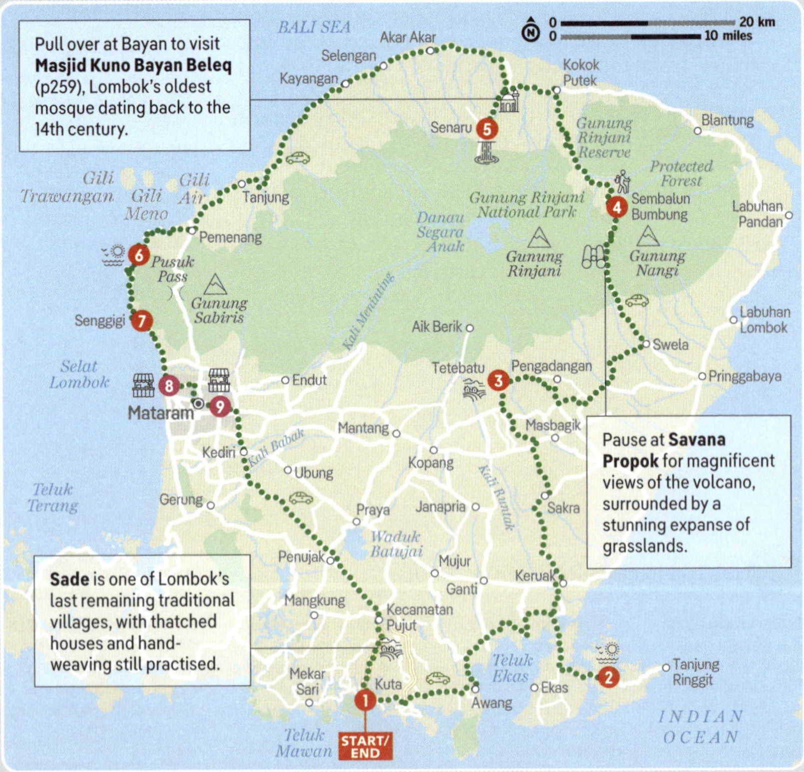

Pull over at Bayan to visit **Masjid Kuno Bayan Beleq** (p259), Lombok's oldest mosque dating back to the 14th century.

Pause at **Savana Propok** for magnificent views of the volcano, surrounded by a stunning expanse of grasslands.

Sade is one of Lombok's last remaining traditional villages, with thatched houses and hand-weaving still practised.

Senaru

RINJANI TREKKING | LUSH WATERFALLS | RICE TERRACES

Senaru is known as the gateway to Gunung Rinjani, Indonesia's second-tallest mountain. While that in itself is a significant enough lure for most, the small village is also home to misty waterfalls, cultural riches and a labyrinth of lush rice fields. It's far from the buzz, providing a different experience to its coastal counterparts. Although the region faced significant damages with the 2018 earthquake, many homes and businesses have since been rebuilt, and homestays, warungs and trekking organisers are once again abundant. A steady stream of trekking enthusiasts continues to fuel tourism in the area, but it remains untouched by mass commercialisation.

Even if you're not fixing for a multiday trek up into some of Indonesia's highest territory, visiting the area is still worthwhile, especially if you're already making a round through the island. The land is lush, and the backdrop couldn't be better, all thanks to the mighty mountainscape that borders the village.

GETTING AROUND

Most things are within walking distance. Exploring on foot is common – whether heading out to organise a trek, grabbing a bite or taking a stroll to one of the waterfalls. You can explore via motorbike and zip around the whole area in a matter of minutes. Some walks to the nature areas around town can take anywhere from 30 minutes to an hour. Either way, it's easy to stroll compared to Lombok's busier towns.

Surrender to Cascading Falls in the Forest

Discover thundering Sendang Gile and Tiu Kelep

Sendang Gile, a waterfall enveloped in a tropical thicket, isn't far off Senaru's main road. This two-tiered fountain has impressive height with water roaring down atop black volcanic rock, and cool waters that are believed to have healing properties. Further down the same trail is the beautiful **Tiu Kelep** with its wide curtain of smaller streams and thundering cascade tumbling down the middle. The pools are too shallow for swimming, but the mist of the falls is enough to get you damp. Plus, you'll have to walk across a small river to get there.

The walk from the main road takes around 15 minutes down to Sendang Gile, with stairs most of the way, and an extra 35 minutes to Tiu Kelep. While you'll likely be asked about a tour upon arrival, you can easily walk the trail sans guide. Expect to be followed by a gaggle of local children offering to guide you or carry your belongings – if you don't want to

TOP TIP

Get to know the locals by staying at a homestay. The hospitality is warm, and most family-run options can set you up with information on trekking, local guides and other up-to-date know-how. Many of the surrounding sights don't require a guide, but Gunung Rinjani (p262) does.

SIGHTS
1 Sendang Gile
2 Tiu Kelep

SLEEPING
3 Dragonfly Senaru Lodge
4 ILA Homestay
5 Rinjani Lighthouse Cottages
6 Rinjani Lodge
7 Rudy Trekker

EATING
8 Cafe Rifka
9 Cafe Rinjani Dawn
see 3 Dragonfly Senaru Bar & Resto

INFORMATION
10 Rinjani Women Adventure

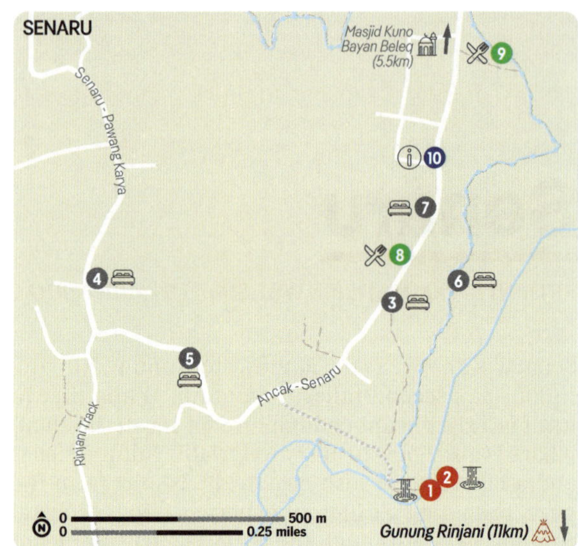

pay for their services, politely say 'no thank you' and they'll likely leave you to it. The entrance fee is around 20,000Rp, but beware of profiteers attempting to charge foreign tourists five times this price.

A Tour Through Rinjani's Foothills

Stroll the Senaru Panorama Walk

Guided walking tours throughout Senaru and the foothills of Gunung Rinjani (p262) offer a deeper insight into the region's flora, fauna and local community traditions, including Sasak cooking and farming. **Rinjani Women Adventure** *(rinjaniwomenadventure.com)* is a local women-owned and operated trek and tour company that shows travellers around the area. Its **Senaru Panorama Walk** *(per person 450,000Rp)*, led by local women, is a half-day excursion that meanders through small villages and rice terraces. You'll traverse irrigation channels bordered by bamboo groves, ending up at Sendang Gile, the oh-so gorgeous waterfall nestled in the jungle. Most, if not all, homestays in the area can also connect you with a local guide for tours around the area.

EATING IN SENARU: OUR PICKS

Rinjani Lodge: Western and Indonesian dishes with jungle and valley views and free use of the pool with purchase of food. *7am-10pm* $$

Cafe Rinjani Dawn: Pizzas, burgers, ample vegan options and great coffee, tucked down a little pathway. *7.30am-10pm* $

Cafe Rifka: Family-run spot with fresh, homemade Indonesian and local Lombok dishes, with a wide range of fresh juices. *hours vary* $

Dragonfly Senaru Bar & Resto: Rice, noodles and curries in a friendly little joint, often with live music, and always backed by beautiful views. *9am-10pm* $

LOMBOK'S OLDEST MOSQUE

Denda Sukatniwati, trekking guide and founder of **Rinjani Women Adventure** (p258), shares her knowledge on Lombok's oldest mosque.

Bayan (the region around Senaru) is home to the oldest mosque in Lombok, **Masjid Kuno Bayan Beleq**.

Islam in Lombok began here in the 14th century. Bayan first adopted Wetu Telu culture, which combines Islam with the original Sasak religion. In the surrounding area, you can learn about culture, religion and traditional life, including the weaving of *sarung tenun* (traditional fabric).

Masjid Kuno Bayan Beleq

SUNETRI/SHUTTERSTOCK

Beyond Senaru

When leaving Senaru, you're presented with two vastly different options: the wild northwest coast or the vast mountains of the north and central region.

Places

Bukit Selong p260
Sajang p260
Sembalun Valley p261
Gunung Rinjani p262

GETTING AROUND

The mountain roads throughout the north and central region of Lombok are wonderfully paved – necessary for some of the steep inclines and sharp switchbacks that come with increasing elevation. If travelling with two people on one bike, beware of your collective weight against the strength of the bike on some of the steep inclines. Motorbikes with lower cubic capacity may struggle when overloaded on intense sections of the route. In contrast, the northwest coast is easy cruising.

While there's an overwhelming amount of ground to cover (on foot, mostly) in Senaru, there is even more beyond it – most notably, Gunung Rinjani. Head south from Senaru for an evolving mountainous landscape dotted by valley towns and striking views of Indonesia's second-highest mountain. Serpentine roads loop through the varied terrain, with majestic views at countless turnoffs. Due north of Senaru lies the northwest coast of Lombok, a comparatively untravelled strip. Here, the main road snakes in and out of the ocean's view, passing numerous tranquil small towns. Further west in the Sire Peninsula, a small handful of high-end, luxury resorts take up prime beachfront real estate. Apart from the honeymooner vibes, you won't find much else here.

Bukit Selong

TIME FROM SENARU: **1HR**

Hike to gorgeous views from a small hill

A vibrant patchwork of varied shades of green makes the view from **Bukit Selong** a stunning, utterly photogenic panorama. This viewpoint overlooks a vast stretch of fields, backed by a mountain to the east, and the town of Sembalun and Gunung Rinjani to the west. A small parking area leads to an unassuming dirt path, where you'll pay an entry fee of around 10,000Rp before continuing. Less than 10 minutes later, the uphill path leads you to the top. A wooden star-shaped platform beckons photo enthusiasts, but the attraction remains fairly quiet. Note that Google Maps might lead you astray. Should you end up at what appears to be a dead end, ask someone to point you in the right direction – it's quite close to the map marker.

Sajang

TIME FROM SENARU: **40MIN**

Swim in Mangku Sakti Waterfall

Sajang is a village that most people just drive through on their way to Sembalun. However, it's worth stopping here for a few hours to splash about in **Air Terjun Mangku Sakti**. This stunning waterfall features milky-blue waters that rush through the limestone rapids. Despite this, not many tourists come here, so don't be surprised if you're the only one around.

Pergasingan Hill

From the main road, you'll have to drive down a dirt road to the parking area, from which a 15-minute walk will lead you to the waterfall. Depending on when you're visiting (high season or a weekend), you'll sometimes find local guides at the main road offering to guide you to the parking area for around 100,000Rp – this is worth paying for an easier experience.

Sembalun Valley

TIME FROM SENARU: **1HR**

A hillside hike to Pergasingan Hill

If Bukit Selong was the appetiser, consider **Pergasingan Hill** the main course. The ascent is often done at sunrise, leading to skyward views of the entire **Sembalun Valley**, plus the entirety of Gunung Rinjani in the distance. It provides an impressive perspective of the landscape and can be done at a fairly steady pace in around two hours, depending on how much time you spend oohing and ahhing at the views on the way. While the soft morning light and mist make for an ethereal sight, it's also lovely at sunset. Entrance to the trailhead costs 50,000Rp. If you arrive before sunrise, expect to pay on your way back down.

SEMBALUN'S SUNNY STRAWBERRIES

Sembalun Valley's mountainous climate is a perfect setting for growing strawberries: something local farmers have leveraged for sweet benefit. The rich volcanic soil and cooler temperatures mean that these juicy berries are all over the place, a source of income for the community, and a source of delight for anyone picking up a pack. You'll see farms dotted throughout the sprawling valley.

Contrary to what you might imagine, strawberry fields don't produce a sea of red colour. The ornate lines of these green plants are organised into rows, with most of the fruit hanging below. Whether you want to pick them yourself at a local farm or sample from a vendor, they're pretty much everywhere.

EATING IN SEMBALUN: OUR PICKS

Kedai Sawah Sembalun: Chow down on Indonesian dishes in this popular open-air cafe in the middle of flower fields and farmland. *8am-9pm* $

Mahakala: Sembalun's best restaurant serving tasty Western and Indonesian dishes, plus high-quality coffee, with amazing views across the valley. *8am-8pm* $$

Sembalun Clasik Cafe: Simple and straightforward menu with home-cooked rice and noodle dishes, and a selection of local coffees. *8am-11.30pm* $

Kebon Kupi Sembalun: Away from the main road, enjoy fried rice, soups, fried snacks, coffee and juices with a side of mountain views. *9am-7pm* $

VENCAII/SHUTTERSTOCK

TOP EXPERIENCE

Gunung Rinjani

Clocking in at an impressive 3726m high, Indonesia's second-highest mountain is both mighty and revered. The breathtaking Gunung Rinjani is sacred for both the Sasak and Hindu people, and is a frequent pilgrimage site. The volcano's summit makes for a strenuous hike that isn't for the fainthearted, but the incredible views are among some of Indonesia's most lauded.

DON'T MISS

- Gunung Rinjani National Park
- Danau Segara Anak
- Senaru Crater Rim
- Surya Sakti Waterfall
- Rinjani Hot Springs
- Mountainside camping

Gunung Rinjani National Park

The entirety of **Gunung Rinjani National Park** spans some 413 sq km, including the greater radius of Gunung Rinjani itself. The volcano's elevation places it in a biogeographical crossroads, where the land differs from what is typical of Southeast Asian terrain, evolving into arid landscape instead. If you're not keen on lacing up your boots and hiking it, the foothills of Gunung Rinjani alone reveal a distinctly different and mesmerising ecosystem.

A Sacred & Cherished Landscape

Each year, the Balinese perform ceremonies atop Rinjani to honour the gods and spirits. It's one of three peaks they consider

PRACTICALITIES

- rinjaninationalpark.com
- per day entrance fee 250,000Rp
- open to climb Apr-Dec

sacred, along with Gunung Bromo in Java and Gunung Agung in Bali. The Sasaks ascend the slopes to pray when the moon is full. Their faith, Wetu Telu, is a melange of Hindu and Islamic beliefs, as well as ancestral worship and animism.

Planning Your Hike

Climbing Gunung Rinjani is not permitted from 1 January to 31 March. While that sounds like a big chunk of time, you don't want to climb it in bad or dangerous weather. If you're planning to hike, make sure your trip isn't during rainy season (mid-November to March). April through November are typically favourable months. Finding a guide is quite easy, as tourism in the area accounts for a large part of the economy – you'll be able to join a trek fairly last-minute. Check out an independent trekking agency such as **Rudy Trekker** *(rudytrekker.com)* or ask a homestay; nearly all of them are well-connected with local guides.

The Hike

After departing from either Senaru (p257) or Sembalun (p261), trails ascend through rainforest teeming with wildlife. The route is challenging, but frequented by many people – plenty of whom aren't experienced hikers. That said, it's not exactly cruisey – this is a real trek.

The Crater Rim

Once the landscape shifts from lush to arid, the crater rim reveals a panoramic view of the skyline and summit. For less-experienced hikers, it's possible to hike for two days and one night to reach – and finish at – the crater rim.

The Summit

Expect loose rocks, soft ground and a steep gradient on the final gruelling stretch to the summit. The topside views are nothing short of staggering, revealing the crater below and the landscape beyond. This prized peak takes a minimum of three days and two nights to reach, with the first night spent camping along the crater rim. Most hiking groups begin their second day before sunrise. Longer trips of three nights are also available.

Danau Segara Anak

Crescent-shaped and deeply blue, **Danau Segara Anak** is a volcanic lake west of Gunung Rinjani's attention-commanding massif, just below the crater rim. The word *danau* means 'lake', and *segara anak* is 'child of the sea' – alluding to the lake's similarities to the ocean.

Rinjani Hot Springs

If you decide to do the three-day, two-night hike, you can continue to the summit or head down from the crater rim to experience the natural **hot springs** beside Danau Segara Anak. It takes two hours to reach these natural pools – an airy downhill hike that floats through low-hanging clouds. The hot thermal waters flowing from **Surya Sakti Waterfall** make for a picturesque scene.

ALTERNATIVE TREKKING ROUTES

The overwhelming majority of treks begin from either Senaru or Sembalun, but you can also start from Tetebatu (p249) on the mountain's southern slope. You'll meet far fewer hikers on the way up, and you can reach the summit in a two-day, one-night ascent. If you've flown in, this also cuts travel time to and from your starting point, as Tetebatu is just an hour away from Lombok international airport (p242).

TOP TIPS

- A local guide is required; don't try to hike without one.
- Read up on Senaru, Sembalun and Tetebatu to decide where you want to start from.
- Research trekking companies thoroughly before booking.
- Spend more time hiking the same distance if you're less experienced.
- Phone service is available in most of the park, but spotty inside the crater.
- Bring much warmer clothes than you think you'll need on a tropical island.
- Don't try to break in brand-new boots.
- Pack swimwear if you fancy a dip in the hot springs.
- There's not a lot of shade. Wear sunscreen like it's your job.

Southwestern Peninsula & the Secret Gilis

SECLUDED ISLANDS | DESERTED BEACHES | LEGENDARY SURF

GETTING AROUND

The main road of the Southwestern Peninsula, Jl Raya Sekotong, runs from Lembar to the westernmost point of Lombok, changing its name to Jl Raya Pelangan and Jl Raya Siung along the way. It's a smooth road, with hills and bends after Lembar. Further west, the road hugs the coast and flattens out. Smaller roads in the area are often dirt and gravel, which can be tricky, especially on approach to Desert Point. A few bemos run between Lembar and Pelangan.

TOP TIP

There are some lodgings on the northern coast, but the Southwest Gilis – 10 minutes by boat – have the best beaches and lodgings. You could day-trip to the Southwestern Peninsula from Kuta, Senggigi or Mataram, but it's a one- to two-hour journey there and back.

Rustic and mellow, Lombok's Southwestern Peninsula is full of deserted beaches, world-class surf and undisturbed local life – the type of place where passersby smile and wave at each other. The peninsula's one large road meanders along its northern shore, weaving through small villages. This ribbon-like route ascends in a circuitous nature over arid-looking hills, playing peek-a-boo with views of the aqua coastline.

While there is a handful of accommodation options, ranging from chilled-out beachside bungalows to upmarket boutique hotels, most are offshore, on the Southwest Gilis. For a long time, this series of blissfully low-key islands, often dubbed 'the Secret Gilis', was something of a word-of-mouth phenomenon – the type of place you only heard about from locals or backpacking aficionados. However, they're quickly earning a reputation for their gorgeous waters and landscape, and are seeing an increase in visitors, especially among day-trippers from Kuta.

Explore a Tranquil Chain of Islands

Visit Gili Nanggu, Tangkong, Sudak and Kedis

While the Gili Islands (p271) have become a much-discussed experience of Southeast Asia's traveller trail, this tiny chain of partially inhabited islands epitomises off-grid at its finest. A bountiful array of marine life, including intricate corals and multihued fish of all sizes, surrounds each island's rim. **Gili Nanggu** – the westernmost island of the group, where most tours go – is known for its prime snorkelling spots. The neighbouring islands, **Gili Tangkong** and **Gili Sudak**, are also fantastic places to snorkel. **Gili Kedis** might be the tiniest island to actually make it on a map – a whimsical patch of sand emerging from the sea with only a scruff of vegetation. These islands don't offer accommodation, but it's possible to camp overnight – ask your tour operator for more details as they can provide camping gear and food.

SIGHTS
1 Desert Point
2 Gili Asahan
3 Gili Gede
4 Gili Kedis
5 Gili Layar
6 Gili Nanggu
7 Gili Rengit
8 Gili Sudak
9 Gili Tangkong

ACTIVITIES
10 Blow Bubbles Divers
11 Oceanway

SLEEPING
12 Bleu Mathis Gili Asahan
13 Catappa Village
14 High Dive Gili Gede Resort
15 Yellow Coco Gili Gede

TRANSPORT
see 17 Sekotong Boat Transport & SSBT Tour Agent
16 Tawun Harbour
17 Tembowong Harbour

Many tours leaving from Kuta (p244) and labelled as 'the Secret Gilis' will take you around Gili Nanggu and its neighbours. If you're looking to venture onward to the Gilis out west (yes, there are even more – Gili Gede and its neighbours) then be sure to mention this before booking. If you're already slowly roaming the Southwest Peninsula, you can organise a tour from either **Tembowong Harbour** (close to Gili Gede, Asahan, Layar and Rengit) or **Tawun Harbour** (close to Gili Nanggu, Tangkong, Sudak and Kedis), where a few tour agencies operate. One of the most highly rated is **Sekotong Boat Transport & SSBT Tour Agent** *(WhatsApp +62 821 4554 6823)* based in Tembowong Harbour, which offers boat charters, snorkelling tours and island-hopping adventures.

There are no public boats or taxi boats in this area, but you'll find several independent boat operators who offer their local expertise in the form of private tours. Getting a ride to any of these islands is typically priced per boat, starting around 400,000Rp. The price will depend on how many people you're with, so booking a boat with a group is your best bet. Should you go it solo, you'll pay more, but will have the peace of a boat all to yourself.

STICK FIGHTING

Stick fighting, a martial art of the Sasak people, is a local tradition. Two fighters armed with rattan sticks and a leather shield face off while traditional music plays. The performance is carried out to ask for better rainfall for the season ahead. Stick fighting happens all over Lombok and also on the Gilis. The fighting usually starts in July and lasts up until the rain arrives – typically in November or December. Ask your homestay or local guide about stick-fighting events.

PORT OF LEMBAR

If you're already in the Southwestern Peninsula and are heading to Bali next, consider taking the slow ferry. **Pelabuhan Lembar** is Lombok's main port for car ferries to Bali, which run every 1½ to three hours, for almost 24 hours a day. It takes four to five hours to sail to Padang Bai in Bali, and costs 65,000Rp per person. It's also the best option if you're hiring a scooter or car and want to take your vehicle with you, costing 169,400Rp per scooter, while cars start from 1,184,100Rp depending on the size. Tickets are available to purchase on ferizy.com, or at the ticket office at the port.

79 SURF PHOTOGRAPHY/ALAMY

Snorkel in Paradise

The best of Gili Gede, Asahan, Layar and Rengit

Closer to Lombok's westernmost edge lies another collection of gorgeous isles. **Gili Gede**, the largest, is also the most developed. This interestingly shaped island is ringed by dazzling reefs and white-sand beaches, only some of which appear to be touched by human influence. To the west, the beautiful **Gili Asahan** offers an undisturbed getaway with not much to do besides unwind on palm-shaded beaches and explore the colourful reefs around the island. **Gili Layar** and **Gili Rengit** border some of the area's best offshore snorkelling spots, where massive coral formations dominate the ocean's floor. It couldn't get more serene. Again, the best places to organise a snorkelling trip around these islands are at Tembowong Harbour (p265) and Tawun Harbour (p265), although accommodation on Gili Gede and Gili Asahan will often include a pickup service from the mainland.

Even fewer travellers seem to make it out here, although there's a greater selection of salty beachfront stays and boutique hotels across Gili Gede and Gili Asahan. Gili Layar and Gili Rengit don't offer accommodation. The quintessential beach bungalows at **Yellow Coco Gili Gede** are the perfect, simple place to unplug and have a rustic digital detox. Those looking for a sumptuous, 'treat yourself' type of experience will find it at **Bleu Mathis Gili Asahan**, where personal plunge pools overlook the serene shoreline. If you're coming to snorkel, gear is typically provided on tours or can be rented from your accommodation. It's definitely the go-to activity around here.

Desert Point

Surf Desert Point's Famous Waves

Catch Lombok's most iconic wave

It's as far west as it gets on the Southwestern Peninsula: **Desert Point** is a famous break, albeit a temperamental one. Roughly a 15-minute drive from the fishing village of **Bangko Bangko**, this landscape is mostly desolate without much around (you know, besides arguably some of the world's best surf, but no big deal). Expect much better conditions during the dry season (from May to September), when offshore winds from the north create longer barrels. Even during this period, it can be an arduous waiting game when conditions suddenly go calm and leave everyone hanging for more.

Desert Point requires an advanced skill level when it comes to surfing and navigation. Getting here is a bit of a mission, but that's part of what makes it so special. While the main road along the coast (Jl Raya Siung) is in pretty good condition, once you turn off left at the fork in the road leading away from Bangko Bangko, it transforms into more of a treacherous dusty gravel path that can have even the most experienced motorbike drivers wincing over surprise potholes for 3km. So prepare for a proper road trip. There is only a handful of simple accommodation here, and no surf schools or rental shops, so make sure to bring your own gear.

THE PENINSULA'S BEST SNORKELLING & SCUBA-DIVING OPERATORS

Many Kuta-based scuba and snorkelling trips head over to the Southwest Peninsula, as well as operators closer to the Secret Gilis.

Scuba Froggy: Dive courses, plus daily dive and snorkelling trips. *(scubafroggy.com)*

Blue Marlin Dive Kuta Lombok: Dive classes and day trips to reefs. *(bluemarlindive.com)*

Adventure Divers Kuta: Dive and snorkelling excursions, plus PADI courses. *(adventuredivers lombok.com)*

The High Dive Gili Gede Resort and PADI Scuba Dive Centre: Beachfront villas on Gili Gede, combined with a dive centre. *(thehighdiveindonesia.com)*

Blow Bubbles Divers South Gilis: Dive centre close to the Southwestern Gilis. *(blowbubblesdivers.com)*

Oceanway: Dive centre on Gili Asahan, with courses and accommodation. *(oceanwaydive.com)*

Places We Love to Stay

$** Budget **$$** Midrange **$$$ Top end

Kuta

MAP p245

Lara Homestay $ Family-run homestay just off the main stretch, with bright and airy en-suite rooms, some with balconies.

Sikara Lombok $$ Modern rooms overlooking a spacious garden and pool deck, just off Kuta's main street.

Porter Lombok Hotel $$ Hillside boutique hotel with spacious rooms, a restaurant with a varied menu and a yoga shala.

Origin Lombok $$ Modern rooms with a serene feel just outside Kuta, close to the popular beach of Tanjung Aan.

Villa Homey Lombok $$ Spacious rooms in a garden setting with a pool, tucked down a quiet street but close to Kuta's centre.

LMBK Surf House $$ Centrally located surf-focused accommodation with both private and dorm rooms.

Kumbara Villas $$$ Clifftop resort with prime views of the south shore, impressive architecture and an upscale clubhouse-style restaurant.

Selong Belanak

Singon Lombok Homestay $ Updated, modern rooms with mountain views, slightly inland from Selong Belanak beach.

Tropik Resort $$ A range of wooden bungalows and modern one- to three-bedroom villas, with a huge pool and lush garden.

Mango Lodge $$ Large rooms overlooking a long pool, with tranquil views of coconut groves from the rooftop restaurant.

Amber Lombok $$ Contemporary beachside retreat with a lounge and restaurant, as well as suites, lofts and eco-friendly amenities.

Selong Selo Resort & Residences $$$ Remote hillside resort with chic and modern designs, overlooking nearby mountains and the sea.

Gerupuk

Anto Guesthouse $ Simple, clean rooms with air-con and private bathrooms, just a few steps from the beach.

Dome Lombok $$ Nine uniquely designed dome-shaped structures in a lush setting, with healthy cuisine and hilltop views.

Roots Surf & Yoga Retreat $$$ Cheerful surf-camp-and-yoga-retreat combo with an emphasis on wellness during its weeklong package stays.

Tetebatu

WinaWani Bungalow $ Cosy wooden cottages overlooking rice terraces and gardens, and offering walking tours and cooking classes.

Mu Homestay $ Family-run homestay surrounded by greenery, with friendly hospitality, comfy rooms and a waterfall just up the road.

Alam Tetebatu $ Double and family-sized wooden cabins with incredible rice terrace views in quiet surroundings.

Les Rizieres $$ Charming decor, views of Gunung Rinjani and a rice field as a backyard at this homestay with a cafe.

Ekas & Sekaroh

Ekas Surf Resort $$ Chilled-out surf accommodation with surf camps, kitesurfing and snorkelling for enthusiasts of all levels.

Jeeva Beloam Beach Camp $$$ A series of A-frame bungalows in a secluded and rustic setting, right on a private beach. (p250)

Innit Lombok $$$ Minimalist luxury on Ekas Bay with seven beach houses sitting on a relatively undiscovered part of the south coast.

Senggigi

MAP p252

Sammy Cottage $ Friendly guesthouse with private rooms (breakfast included), in close proximity to Coconut Beach.

Central Inn $ Simple digs for good value close to Senggigi Beach and the largest supermarket in town.

Ibludan Hotel $$ Eco-friendly rooms in a tropical garden setting with a pool, close to Senggigi's main area.

Holiday Resort Lombok $$ Longstanding beachside resort with poolside cabanas, lots of palm-tree shade, and a mountainous backdrop.

Katamaran Resort $$$ A glass infinity pool, private beach and a wide gamut of wellness amenities in a classy beachside resort.

Mataram

Dewi Sri Guesthouse $ Dorms and private rooms close to the heart of Mataram, with plenty of shared common space and a pool.

Prime Park Hotel $$ Upscale yet laid-back hotel featuring a rooftop pool with city and mountain views, close to Mataram's centre.

Lombok Astoria $$ Large hotel with a traditionally fancy feel, featuring a rooftop garden, spa, lounge and restaurant.

Aston Inn Mataram $$ Modern hotel, part of a popular chain, on Mataram's main road, close to Mataram Mall and Mayura Park.

Senaru

MAP p258

Dragonfly Senaru Lodge $ Volcano views, simple rooms and home-cooked meals in a guesthouse right by Senaru's waterfalls.

ILA Homestay $ Family-run homestay with home-cooked meals, basic rooms with small terraces and trek-planning support.

Rudy Trekker $ Eco-tours and guided trekking services in a guesthouse used as a base for hiking the lofty heights of Gunung Rinjani.

Rinjani Lighthouse Cottages $$ Eco-friendly guesthouse right in front of Gunung Rinjani National Park with an in-house coffee shop and bungalows amid a garden.

Rinjani Lodge $$ Large rooms with outdoor bathrooms, a pool with jungle and valley views and a popular restaurant. (p258)

Sembalun Valley

Sembalun Kita Cottages $ Cosy rooms in a beautiful garden with mountain views, set back from the main road.

Bukit Tiga Lima Boutique Hotel $$ A-frame cabins right on the main road leading into the village of Sembalun, surrounded by mountain views.

Bobocabin Gunung Rinjani $$ Modern and minimalist tiny cabins with views of Gunung Rinjani and Pergasingan Hill.

Rautani Guesthouse $$ Spacious and updated cabins with small terraces and picturesque views in an open area near the foothills of Rinjani.

Southwestern Peninsula

MAP p265

Yellow Coco Gili Gede $ Easy-going and unpretentious cabins with mosquito nets, on the beach facing mainland Lombok. (p266)

High Dive Gili Gede Resort $$ Beachfront resort offering scuba diving and other watersport activities, plus tours of the surrounding islands. (p267)

Catappa Village $$$ Bamboo bungalows right on the beach, with outdoor bathrooms, pool and restaurant.

Bleu Mathis Gili Asahan $$$ Remote and idyllic boutique resort at the end of the only road on Gili Asahan. (p266)

Katamaran Resort, Senggigi

For places to stay in the Gili Islands, see p285

WONDERFUL NATURE/SHUTTERSTOCK

Above: Nest (p278), Gili Meno; Right: Gili Air (p281)

Researched by
Leyla Rose

Gili Islands

CRYSTAL-CLEAR WATERS AND LAID-BACK LIVING

You'll have to zoom in on the map to find the Gilis, but this tiny archipelago is anything but small when it comes to nature and activities.

Reminiscent of somebody's tropical desktop wallpaper, the Gili Islands are a trio of paradise-like islands stocked with low-hanging palms and crystal-clear waters. While the outer perimeter of each island is the place for tourist-catered offerings, a quick walk down the dusty inland roads leads to traditional Sasak living. There's plenty to do onshore, but a top draw of the Gilis is the marine life in surrounding waters, where sea turtles and colourful fish twirl around the reefs.

The only wheels on the Gilis belong to bicycles and *cidomo* (horse-drawn carts; see p274 for concerns about their use); motorbikes and cars are not allowed. While Gili Trawangan has earned a reputation for having quite the social scene, it can be thought of as a 'choose your own adventure' novel, where each page leads to something completely different. Despite the heaving parties, it's easy to slink away into the background, which, typically, includes panoramic views of both Lombok and Bali off in the distance.

Gili Meno, the middle island, remains the quietest of the three, maintaining plenty of local character and tradition. To the east, Gili Air feels like a fusion of the two – a place where you can grab a beer somewhere with a vibe, or bliss out in silence with a coconut. It's tricky to advise visiting one Gili over the other when each brings its own unique personality – far better is to see for yourself and sample each of them.

NITISH WAILA/SHUTTERSTOCK

THE MAIN AREAS

GILI TRAWANGAN
All-night parties and ample hangout spots. **p274**

GILI MENO
Tranquil escape with traditional charm. **p278**

GILI AIR
Yoga, wellness and laid-back living. **p281**

Find Your Way

A mere 15 sq km makes the collective landmass of the Gilis comparatively petite. But factor in surrounding turquoise waters, with a generous handful of top-notch dive and snorkel spots, and the breadth of adventure here belies the islands' small size.

ON FOOT

For zero dollars, the perimeter of Gili Trawangan can be walked in less than two hours – even less for Gili Meno and Gili Air. The topography of the land is flat, and you'll see people walking everywhere.

BICYCLE

At the time of research, the price of 50,000Rp for a daily bicycle rental was the standard. Some may offer half-day prices at a slight discount. Expect to dodge a few carts on the way.

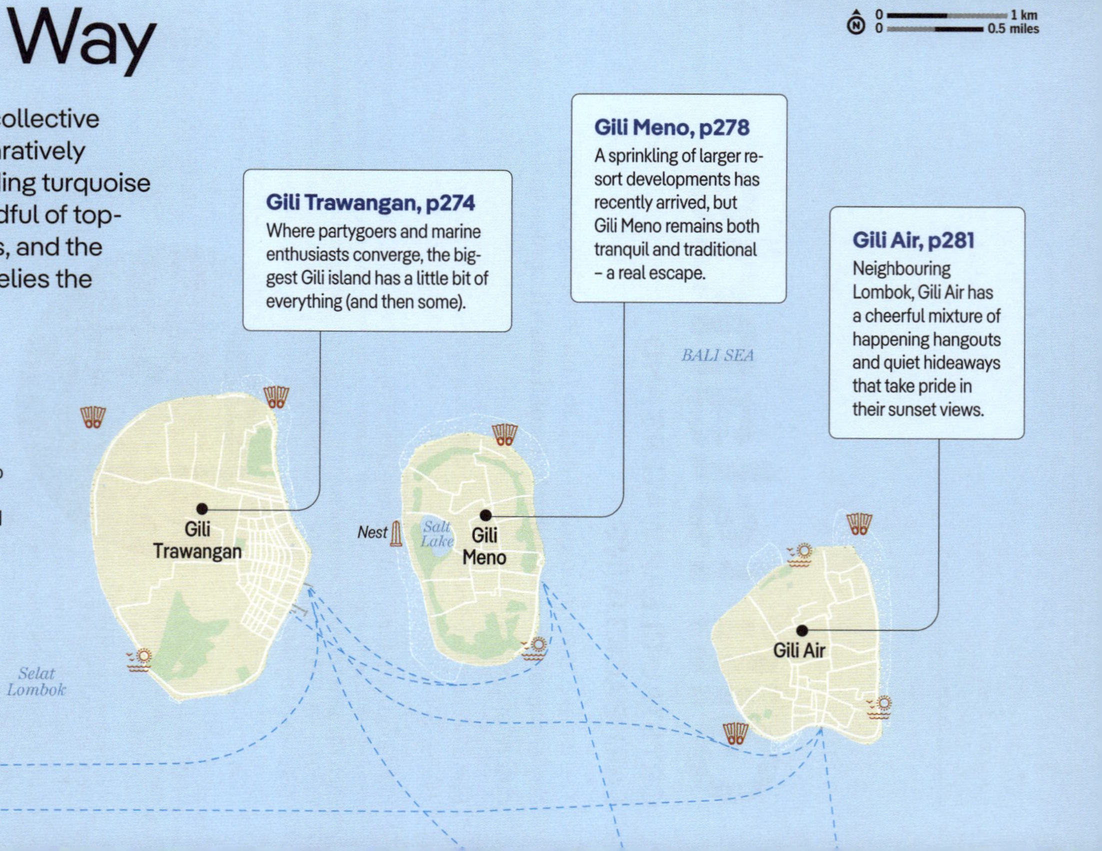
0 1 km
0 0.5 miles
Gili Trawangan, p274
Where partygoers and marine enthusiasts converge, the biggest Gili island has a little bit of everything (and then some).
Gili Meno, p278
A sprinkling of larger resort developments has recently arrived, but Gili Meno remains both tranquil and traditional – a real escape.
Gili Air, p281
Neighbouring Lombok, Gili Air has a cheerful mixture of happening hangouts and quiet hideaways that take pride in their sunset views.
BALI SEA
Gili Trawangan
Nest
Salt Lake
Gili Meno
Gili Air
Selat Lombok

LEMARET PIERRICK/SHUTTERSTOCK

Gili Trawangan (p274)

Plan Your Time

Zip through the Gilis like a true island-hopper, or turn down the velocity and revel in the laid-back way of living for an extended stay. For either option, start with a swim.

Three-Day Getaway

Boat services make it easy to hop between the islands, even on a shorter timeframe. Arrive at the main port on Gili Trawangan and plan a **snorkelling or scuba trip** (p276) to visit the underwater sculptures, such as **Nest** (p278), just off Gili Meno. Hit up the nightlife, then recover beachside. Spend the last day relaxing on Gili Air. **Island View Bar & Bungalow** (p283) is perfect for prime sunset views.

Weeklong Escape

Spend three days on Gili Trawangan, **diving or snorkelling** (p276) by day and sampling the **nightlife** (p274) after sundown. Next, spend two days recharging on quieter Gili Meno, where you can **snorkel** (p278) with the marine life. Conclude your trip with two relaxing days on Gili Air, soaking up the vibes at the many **beach hangouts** (p283) after some well-earned **yoga and wellness** (p283) activities.

SEASONAL HIGHLIGHTS

JANUARY–MARCH

It's rainy season. Nyepi, a Balinese 'Day of Silence' in March, causes many tourists to flock to the Gilis, where things remain open.

APRIL–JUNE

Right before high season, the waters are less crowded for scuba diving and snorkelling. Rainfall diminishes as the seasons shuffle.

JULY–SEPTEMBER

Dry season grants consistent sunshine. Tourism is bustling in July and August and only begins to slow by September.

OCTOBER–DECEMBER

Holidays pick up the visitor count, but rainy season is looming. You can expect showers to start mid-November.

Gili Trawangan

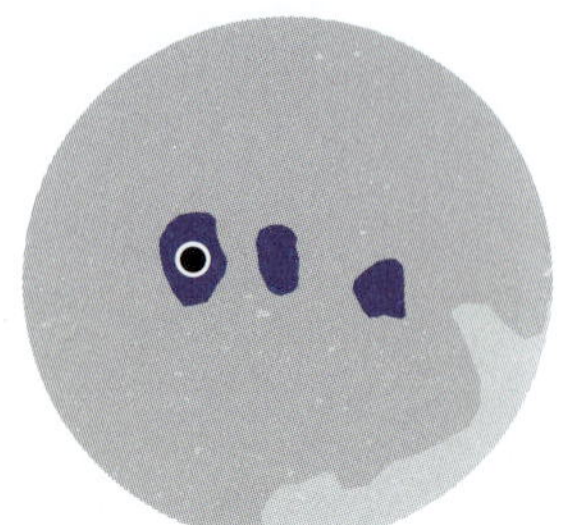

SUN & SAND | WILD PARTIES | GREAT DIVING

GETTING AROUND

A ban on motorised vehicles is one of the Gilis' many pros. Explore on foot or rent a bicycle – the entire island is walkable. The *cidomo* operate like taxis, but we can't recommend them due to concerns over how the horses are treated. Nowadays, local organisations such as **Horses of Gili** *(horsesofgili.com)* provide supplies and support to the horses through veterinary care and education, but there's still a way to go.

TOP TIP

Ramadan, the Muslim fasting month, varies each year, moving back by ten days a year (February to March in 2027). This brings a quieter Gili T, with music being turned off early at bars and restaurants. You won't find any big parties during this time.

Arriving at Gili Trawangan's port, you might wonder what you've let yourself in for, with crowds of people waiting to get on the boat you just got off. The main strip has quite a pace: bicyclists and *cidomo* (horse-drawn carts) share a dusty lane with meandering pedestrians. The first few minutes on Gili Trawangan might feel less than tranquil, but venture beyond the beachfront bars and hotels to an easy-going, beautiful coastline. Affectionately called 'Gili T', this island exudes friendliness and couldn't be more laid-back if it tried. Coastal views of Lombok's rugged shoreline and Bali's towering Gunung Agung in the distance are simply a chef's kiss.

If you're looking for a great party, you'll find it here. But it's also easy to escape the noise. Roam the criss-crossed pathways of the island's centre over to the west coast, where serene sands remain between looming developments. Inland, the call to prayer echoes five times a day.

Join in the Famous Party Scene

Hit the nightlife 'til sunrise

Whether you want to throw back a questionable volume of Bintangs with your toes in the sand or join a full-on pub crawl, Gili T's nightlife accommodates. Known for getting rowdy, Trawangan's social scene ranges from beachfront shacks to fancy resort bars and worn-in backpacker staples. Partying is an all-night affair here, with things starting to get busy at around 11pm and lasting all the way through to 5am.

Casa Vintage *(instagram.com/casavintagebeach)*, a beachside bar and restaurant that gets buzzy, is popular for sunset libations. **Lava Bar** *(instagram.com/lavabargilit)* always draws a crowd with cheap drinks and Friday bingo. Midweek festivities are a staple at **Tír na nÓg** *(tirnanogbar.com)*, an Irish sports bar with a particular knack for throwing Wednesday bangers. Reggae music colours the scene at

SIGHTS

1 Gili Trawangan Beach
2 Gili Trawangan Sunset Beach

ACTIVITIES

3 Blue Marlin Dive
4 Compass Divers
5 DPM Diving Gili Trawangan
6 Glenn Nusa Wreck
7 Manta Dive
8 Shark Point
9 Trawangan Stingray Divers

SLEEPING

10 Atlas Gili Trawangan
11 Gili Teak Resort
12 Kuno Villas
13 La Cocoteraie Ecolodge
14 Mad Monkey Hostel
15 Pearl of Trawangan
16 Pesona Beach Resort & Spa
17 PinkCoco Gili Trawangan
18 Radika House

EATING

19 Banyan Tree
20 Casa Vintage
see 7 Coffee & Thyme
21 Jali Kitchen
22 La Cala Beach Club
23 My House
24 Taste Cafe & Restaurant
25 The Shack Restaurant & Bar
26 Warung Jaman Now

DRINKING & NIGHTLIFE

see 19 Lava Bar
see 7 Sama Sama
27 Tír na nÓg
28 Window Sports Bar

Sama Sama *(samasamareggaebar)*, a two-storey reggae bar full of both locals and travellers nearly every night of the week – especially Saturdays.

Most of these nightlife spots are located within a few minutes of each other along the island's southeast coast where the harbour is, so it's easy to hop (or stumble) from one spot to another. There are also several beach bars along the west coast, such as **Window Sports Bar** *(instagram.com/windowsportsbar)*, which offer a more relaxed night out.

ILLEGAL SUBSTANCES

On notoriously rowdy Gili Trawangan, you'll spot some beachside cafes openly advertising the sale of magic mushrooms, and it's not uncommon to get offers of drugs while walking on the street. This is despite Indonesia's strong anti-drug stance. It's worth keeping in mind that Indonesia has extremely strict laws against illicit substances, and intoxication and/ or possession is punishable by lengthy imprisonment, or worse. While the island has earned a party reputation over the years, Indonesia remains firmly anti-drugs, and it's important to remember this to avoid trouble.

DANIEL WILHELM NILSSON/SHUTTERSTOCK

Discover the Quieter Side of Gili T

Quiet snorkelling

Primo spots to swim and snorkel are found in droves throughout the island's quieter areas: the south, north and entire west coast. Seeing as the shoreline spans the entire perimeter, picking a specific beach isn't entirely necessary – but **Gili Trawangan Sunset Beach** lives up to its name, with sundowner views and lots of open space. Keep heading north for **Gili Trawangan Beach**, a long stretch of quiet sand with much less activity than the busy eastern coast. That said, you're not going to have a hard time finding a good place to swim around here. There aren't any public bathrooms, but you'll find little shops along the beaches selling snacks and drinks, and you're never too far from a cafe or restaurant. Do check the tides; swimming at high tide is better when the rocky coral formations are submerged.

Scuba-Dive the Gilis

Discover a wealth of marine life

Roughly 25 different dive sites are located in the Gilis' greater Marine Protected Area. Tiny creatures – pygmy seahorses,

EATING ON GILI T: OUR PICKS

Taste Cafe & Restaurant: Fresh and healthy dishes with plenty of seafood options, ideal for light lunches on the beach. *7.30am-9.30pm* $$

Warung Jaman Now: Indonesian fare, plus burgers, pasta and smoothie bowls, dished-up in super chilled-out surroundings. *8am-11pm* $

Coffee & Thyme: Sandwiches, pastas, salads and homemade cakes, plus fruit juices and coffee. *7am-9pm* $

The Shack Restaurant & Bar: A mix of Western and Indonesian dishes, from breakfast to all-day snacks and mains. *7.30am-10pm* $$

Green sea turtle, Gili Trawangan

mantis shrimp, pipefish – flutter about the corals. There are also plenty of large species, including whitetip and blacktip sharks.

Dive sites are found all over the Gili map. **Shark Point** lies west of Gili T, living up to its moniker, with sharks (and turtles) gliding around. **Turtle Heaven** is another aptly named, turtle-filled site on the east side of Meno. **Manta Point** (also referred to as Sunset Reef) is just south of Gili T, with mantas and plenty of smaller fish flitting between the corals. Experienced divers can venture down 45m to the **Japanese Wreck**, a shipwreck of a Japanese patrol boat off the southern coast of Gili Air.

You're spoilt for choice when it comes to dive centres and schools in the Gilis, especially on Gili T where dive centres are found all along the east coast. Take your time reading reviews and comparing prices before committing to one. It's also worth popping in and getting a feel for the place and the people. One of the best-known dive schools is **Blue Marlin Dive** *(bluemarlindive.com; PADI Open Water course 6,400,000Rp)*.

GILI T'S BEST DIVING SCHOOLS

Blue Marlin Dive: The Gili T branch of a popular diving school. They're in Senggigi and Kuta, too. *(bluemarlindive.com)*

DPM Diving Gili Trawangan: Scuba courses and day trips for beginners and advanced divers, located steps from the east shore. *(dpmdiving.com)*

Manta Dive: Dive centre and resort combo with training facilities on both Gili T and Gili Air. *(manta-dive.com)*

Compass Divers: Dive courses and accommodation, with both private and hostel dorm rooms, just steps from Gili T's ferry port. *(compassdiving.com)*

Trawangan Stingray Divers: Courses ranging from beginner to divemaster in the northeast corner of the island. *(trawanganstingraydivers.com)*

The chocolate mousse is highly rated.

Jali Kitchen: Asian-fusion cuisine with Indonesian-, Thai- and Vietnamese-influenced plates, all served in a leafy setting. *noon-10pm* $$

My House: Authentic Italian cuisine in a courtyard garden setting. *noon-9.30pm* $$

Banyan Tree: Small bites, soups, sandwiches and heartier mains, plus a full menu of quality coffee, juices and health drinks, on the beach. *7am-8pm* $$

La Cala Beach Club: BBQ meat and seafood, salads, sandwiches and a long cocktail list, with seats right on the sand. *8.30am-11pm* $$

Gili Meno

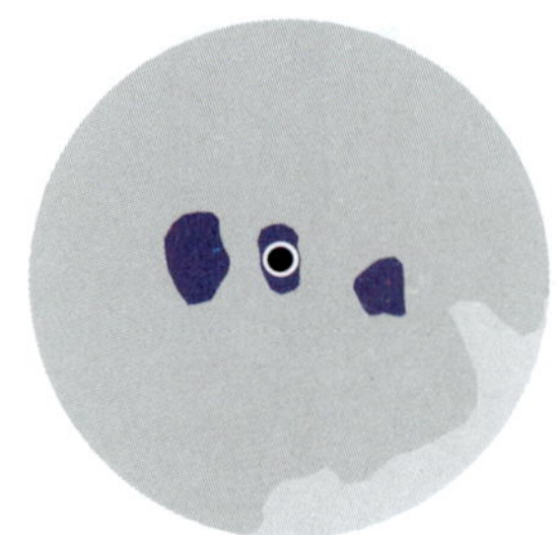

PEACE & QUIET | SASAK CULTURE | SNORKELLING SPOTS

GETTING AROUND

Walking and cycling are the ways to get around Gili Meno. You might see a rogue electric scooter – but they're silent (and typically privately owned, not for rent). It's an arduous workout to ride a bicycle around the island's sandy outer edge. If you try, be prepared for an upper-body workout as you walk your bike. It's better to walk the coast and save cycling for inland.

TOP TIP

If you're heading from Trawangan to accommodation on Meno's west coast (the opposite side of the island's public port), organise a private ride right to the shore. Ask some of the boat operators near the port if they'll take you, ideally with another stray traveller or two to split the cost. A private boat costs around 300,000Rp – fairly economical, and highly convenient for a group.

Stunningly calm and undisturbed, little Gili Meno is by far the most chill of the trio. If you're after a true escape, you'll find it here. This tiny, oval-shaped island is also the most traditional of the three Gilis, where the lovely hum of local Sasak life continues on without as much tourist-catered development. Meno has all the same natural delights as the others: alabaster sand in all directions and translucent water that glows aqua under the sun's strong rays. The small port lies on the eastern coast, where a handful of low-key accommodation options and places to grab a bite dot the sand. On the west coast, a few glitzy stays change up the vibe, luring honeymooners and luxury-lovers to revel in stylish solitude. Inland, coconut groves give shade to traditional Sasak homes. There's a big saltwater lake adorned with mangroves, too – and you might just have its boardwalk all to yourself.

Snorkel Around the Gilis

Underwater sculptures and intricate corals

Most snorkelling excursions sample different spots across all three Gilis. You have two options: join a snorkelling trip or rent the gear on your own. Snorkelling can be enjoyed from any Gili beach, but some of the best spots are off the northern and western coasts of Meno, where colourful tropical fish dart in and around the reef. Off Meno's west coast lies **Nest**, an underwater sculpture made famous on social media by photography-loving visitors on their snorkel sojourns. Sculpted from environmental-grade concrete, 48 human figures stand in a circle and are slowly becoming a part of the oceanscape. You'll find tour boats hovering around the area for much of the day, mostly full of people from Gili T and Gili Air. Pro tip: you can DIY and swim right up to it from **Bask** (p280) on Meno's shore in just a few minutes. Be aware that this spot can get very busy – visit first thing in the morning or right before sunset to avoid the crowds.

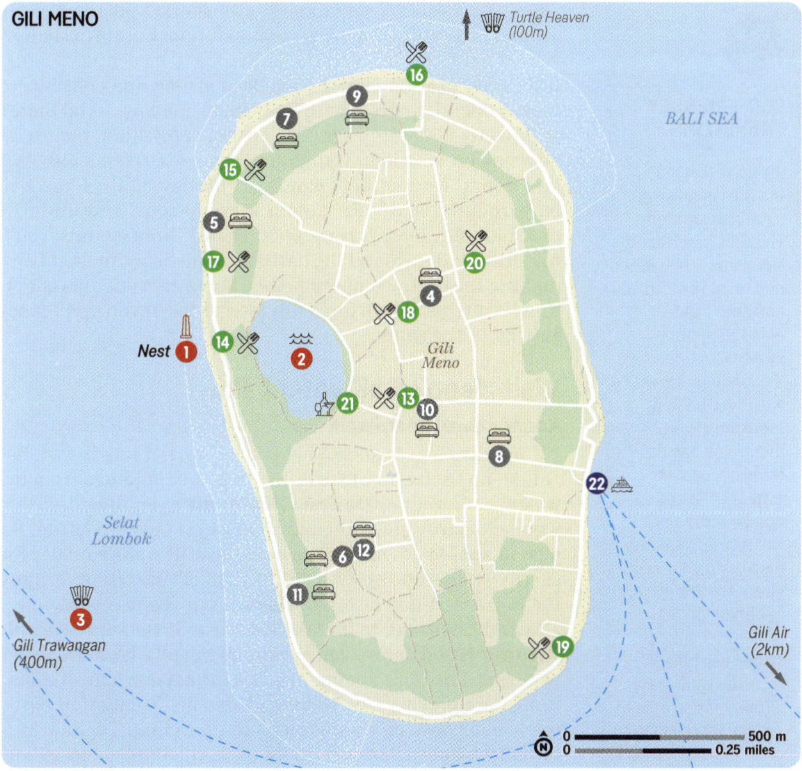

GILI MENO

Turtle Heaven (100m)
BALI SEA
Gili Meno
Nest
Selat Lombok
Gili Trawangan (400m)
Gili Air (2km)
0 500 m
0 0.25 miles

HIGHLIGHTS
1 Nest

SIGHTS
2 Danau Gili Meno

ACTIVITIES
3 Bounty Wreck

SLEEPING
4 Gili Meno Escape
5 Mahamaya
6 Meno Dream Resort
7 Meno House
8 Meno Smile Cottages
9 Mimpi Bungalows
10 Rabbit Tree
11 Two Brothers Bungalows
12 United Colors of Gili

EATING
13 Backyard Island Cafe
14 Bask
15 Bubbles Bar & Restaurant
16 Easy Warung & Bar
17 Malfina Beach Bar & Resto
18 Tip of the Tongue Warung
19 Umar Resto
20 Warung Licung Bamboo

DRINKING & NIGHTLIFE
21 Brother Hood

TRANSPORT
22 Public Boat Landing

EATING ON GILI MENO: INDONESIAN FOOD

Backyard Island Cafe: Simple place for pizza, seafood and grilled dishes, as well as curries and Indonesian classics. *noon-11pm* **$$**

Tip of the Tongue Warung: Local dishes and lots of fresh seafood, in a quiet spot in the centre of the island. *6.30am-10pm* **$**

Warung Licung Bamboo: Huge selection of local dishes, including plenty of vegetarian options. *10am-10pm* **$**

Easy Warung & Bar: Waterside warung with prime sunset views, plus grilled fish and fruity cocktails. *10am-10pm* **$**

ECO-FRIENDLY TRAVELLING

It's no secret that the Gili Islands have a rubbish problem. The Gilis have faced significant challenges due to mass tourism and poor waste-management systems. To minimise the amount of waste you leave behind, there are several things you can do. Bring a reusable water bottle and pop by the many water-refill stations. Also bring your own straw, toothbrush and hairbrush, as many hotels still provide single-use plastic toiletries and straws.

There has also been significant damage to the reefs of the Gilis in the last two decades. **Gili Eco Trust** *(giliecotrust.com)* was founded in 2002 to protect the reefs from illegal and damaging fishing. Some businesses on Gili T might ask if you're interested in making a reef donation for 50,000Rp, which goes directly to reef restoration and protective patrolling.

Renting a snorkel set (a mask with snorkel plus fins) costs around 50,000Rp at most accommodation. Corals in shallow waters have seen better days, sadly, due to bleaching. Thankfully, regeneration efforts have been strong and continue to make hopeful progress with BioRock technology – and there's still plenty of coral to see. The cost of snorkelling boat trips depends on how long you go for. Some excursions only last two hours, while others can be a full-day affair. Expect to pay around 200,000Rp to join a group tour, and upwards of 700,000Rp for a private boat. On all three islands, you'll find little stalls around the harbour advertising snorkel trips, making it easy to compare prices. Some also offer glass-bottom boat trips, which are a fun alternative if you don't fancy getting in the water.

Visit Meno's Saltwater Lake

Roam a quiet boardwalk

It's puzzling to see such a big lake on such a tiny island, but Gili Meno's saltwater lake is just that. Just minutes from the western shoreline, **Danau Gili Meno** is equipped with a wooden boardwalk, although some parts need updating. It's a good spot for the sunset, where the still waters reflect the sherbet-coloured sky with a thin strip of vegetation forming the horizon. A quick stop to check it out is worthwhile.

Near the entrance to the lake's boardwalk, the super-friendly **Brother Hood** bar welcomes visitors warmly. It's more than a watering hole. This community hub organises rubbish collections for a greener Gili Meno and also hosts donation-based workshops centred around art and upcycling. The best way to learn what's currently going on is to simply stop by and say hello – you'll be greeted with warmth. So, come for the lake, but stay for the inevitable good vibes and post-sunset reggae jam-sesh next door.

EATING BEACHSIDE ON GILI MENO: OUR PICKS

Malfina Beach Bar & Resto: Fabulously located beach bar on the west coast, with a mix of Western and Indonesian food. *8am-10pm* $

Umar Resto: Simple, homemade Western and Indonesian dishes with tables, beanbags and loungers on the sand. *8am-9pm* $

Bubbles Bar & Restaurant: Good for vegetarians and meat eaters, with beanbags to lounge on, lovingly shaded by beach umbrellas. *7.30am-9pm* $$

Bask: The ultimate fancy experience with artfully crafted plates and thoughtful details in a sleek, minimalist setting. *7am-10pm* $$

Gili Air

LAID-BACK VIBES | POWDERY BEACHES | DIVING & SNORKELLING

Mellow yet upbeat Gili Air is the best of both worlds – fusing a bit of Trawangan's social energy with Meno's pleasant lull, the island's perimeter is full of bright and inviting beach bars, longstanding dive centres and a range of accommodation, from simple and homey to barefoot luxury. It's hard to pick favourites when it comes to beaches in the Gilis, but the overall vibe and scenery of Meno's shoreline is something special. Hushed in some corners and animated in others, you can recharge in peace but engage in tropical merriment whenever the mood arrives.

The heart of Gili Air has paved streets, unlike its neighbouring islands. While the central area is lined with tourist-catered shops and a sprinkling of Western-looking restaurants, a short walk off the main path reveals quiet palm-tree groves dotted with Sasak architecture, grazing livestock and children playing games, often with their *ibu* (mothers) working nearby.

GETTING AROUND

You can walk from the top to the bottom of Gili Air in 20 minutes – strolling is easy here. Mostly paved main streets connect to smaller sandy offshoots, which comprise most of the north. Gili Air has the best conditions of all three islands for cycling, but you'll still find some beachside sections that are too sandy for riding. Gili Air is only about a 15-minute ride from Bangsal Port. Take the public boat or negotiate a private ride from one of the portside companies.

Wander the Cheerful Streets of Gili Air

Charming shops and inviting warungs

After stepping off the boat at Gili Air's southward-facing **port**, jovial streets entice. There's a bit of a buzz along Jl Mojo, a lane leading to the island's centre. You'll find everything from tour agencies to gelato shops, shops filled with handmade trinkets and a smattering of little cafes serving both Indonesian and Western cuisine. Here, warungs with savoury Indonesian buffets border Aussie-style breakfast joints and Italian restos. Take as long as you like wandering down the street – a good 45-minute stroll will allow plenty of time to shop and drink.

Steps from the port, **Il Gelato Damonte** *(instagram.com/ilgelatodamonte)* beckons with fresh waffle cones and countless sweet flavours (there's also a branch on the west coast). **Warung Parida**'s buffet-style Indonesian food is always ready, serving generous portions for as low as 25,000Rp per plate. **JUJU Zero Waste Store & Vegan Cafe** *(instagram.*

TOP TIP

Lock your bike whenever it's not in sight. Rather than fastening the lock around a stationary object every time, you can simply loop it around the wheel so it renders the bike immobile until you're ready to roll again. This goes for all three of the Gili Islands.

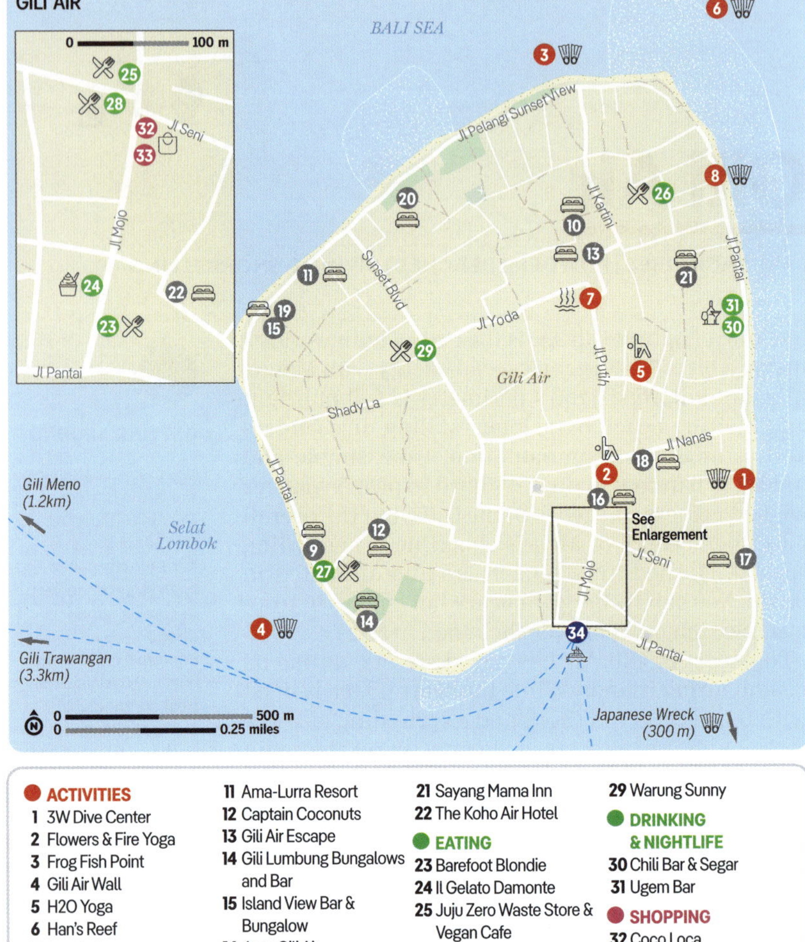

ACTIVITIES
1 3W Dive Center
2 Flowers & Fire Yoga
3 Frog Fish Point
4 Gili Air Wall
5 H2O Yoga
6 Han's Reef
7 Lovely Spa
8 Next Level Scuba

SLEEPING
9 Adinda Bungalows
10 Akasia Villas
11 Ama-Lurra Resort
12 Captain Coconuts
13 Gili Air Escape
14 Gili Lumbung Bungalows and Bar
15 Island View Bar & Bungalow
16 Jago Gili Air
17 Manta Dive Resort
18 Nanas Homestay
19 PinkCoco Gili Air
20 Puri Air Beach Resort
21 Sayang Mama Inn
22 The Koho Air Hotel

EATING
23 Barefoot Blondie
24 Il Gelato Damonte
25 Juju Zero Waste Store & Vegan Cafe
26 Pachamama Cafe & Cantina
27 Papaya Restaurant & Beach Club
28 Warung Parida
29 Warung Sunny

DRINKING & NIGHTLIFE
30 Chili Bar & Segar
31 Ugem Bar

SHOPPING
32 Coco Loca
33 Mojo Boutique
see 33 Sunkissed

TRANSPORT
34 Port

com/juju.zerowaste) has a little gift shop with handmade goods, plus a menu of fresh juices, smoothies and healthy eats. For more retail therapy, **Mojo Boutique** *(instagram.com/mojogiliair)*, **Sunkissed** *(instagram.com/sunkissed.boutiques)* and **Coco Loca** *(instagram.com/cocoloca_gili)* sell island-essential clothing such as tropical shirts, swimwear and accessories like hats and sunglasses. These shops also stock a great selection of gifts and local, Lombok-made products such as handwoven baskets, textiles and toiletries made from natural ingredients, all of which make for lovely souvenirs.

Kick Back on Gorgeous Beaches

Gili Air's beach hangouts

Like the rest of the Gilis, Gili Air is gifted with a ring of white-sand beach met by azure waters. It's arguably some of the archipelago's best shoreline, both for its condition and the lovely establishments that line the shore. The sunset views from the north coast are a point of local pride, and there's no shortage of beanbags shaded by fringed umbrellas to post up under. The east coast, lined with eateries and dive shops, is popular during the day. Later on, everyone heads north and west as the sky descends into a swirly canvas of soft pink and deep orange.

On the eastern coast, **Ugem Bar** *(instagram.com/@ugembar)* and neighbouring **Chili Bar & Segar** *(instagram.com/chilibar_giliair)* draw a loyal customer base with their bamboo loungers and cabanas on the sand. A handful of cheerful beach cafes surround **Puri Air Beach Resort** *(puriairbeachresort.com)* on the north coast, all with lovely views of the neighbouring islands. Further west, you can find swings in the water at both **Gili Lumbung** *(instagram.com/gili.lumbung_giliair)* and **Island View Bar & Bungalow** *(WhatsApp +62 878 6588 0103)*. Expect a queue for the Instagrammable swings at sunset.

In the Gilis, swimwear is fully accepted on the beach and at the pool, but anywhere else is disrespectful. Throw on a cover-up if you're leaving the shoreline.

Dive & Snorkel Gili Air's Coast

Enviable waters and excellent spots

Snorkelling and scuba-diving conditions are blissful around Gili Air, with coral reefs just off the eastern shore. **Han's Reef** is home to sea turtles and magnificent corals. Slightly north, there's **Frog Fish Point**, where sea critters such as ghost pipefish and scorpionfish flutter about. The **Gili Air Wall** lies southwest, with a solid drop-off that extends about 30m deep. If you're swimming out with snorkel gear from the shore, don't be surprised if you swim back to a different spot; the current causes some drift, which is potentially hazardous for weaker swimmers. You should be aware of the tides and the changes these bring.

You can also join a boat trip around the Gilis with a local provider such as **Manta Dive** *(manta-dive.com; Open Water courses 5,500,000Rp)*, **3W Dive Center** *(3wdivegili.com; fun dive 600,000Rp)* or **Next Level Scuba** *(next-level-scuba.com; fun dive 600,000Rp)*, all on Air's east coast. They offer various courses but if you're already qualified, you can also do fun dives around the islands. The price for fun dives includes all equipment rental and guides, and the more fun dives you do, the cheaper it is per dive.

Slow Down with Yoga & Wellness

Unwind, stretch and relax

We often don't realise how much noise there is in our lives until we find ourselves somewhere totally tranquil, away from the fast-paced rhythm of everyday life. Gili Air is the ideal place

SHIPWRECKS AROUND THE GILIS

A small trio of once-bouyant ships are scattered around the Gili Islands, all with different stories. The **Japanese Wreck** (p277) lies at a depth of 45m underwater, between Gili Air and Lombok, and dates back to the 1940s. Theories as to why the wreck sank are murky – some say it was abandoned, others assert it was struck by a torpedo. **Bounty Wreck** – the result of a storm 15 years ago – is off Meno's southwest coast. The last of the lot, the **Glenn Nusa Wreck**, was actually intentional: this former tugboat was cleaned and sunk in 2016 to form an artifical reef and a new dive site.

ISLAND-HOPPING

Many people choose to visit all three islands, spending a night or two on each one. Day trips are also possible, but you'll want to limit a trip to just one other island in a day to allow time to sightsee. The best option is the public speedboats that run between the islands, usually hourly between 9am and 4pm – these cost 85,000Rp per person. For more flexibility, organise a private speedboat, which typically costs 300,000Rp. They take up to ten people, so this often works out cheaper if you're with a large group. The best way to organise an island-hopping trip is to visit the various boat companies at the harbour on each island. The currents in between the islands are notoriously strong, so don't attempt to swim between them.

SOLARISYS/SHUTTERSTOCK

Snorkelling, Gili Air

to take a break and slow down, listening to the waves lapping the shore and the sea breeze rustling through the trees. And what better surroundings to ground yourself with some yoga and self-care? There's a real sense of relaxation on Gili Air, evident from the number of yoga studios and spas on the island.

Get into a chill groove at **Flowers & Fire Yoga Garden** *(flowersandfire.yoga)*, a treehouse yoga studio shrouded in verdant foliage near Gili Air's heart. It also has a healthy cafe and cosy accommodation. A few minutes north, **H2O Yoga and Meditation Center** *(h2oyogaandmeditation.com; yoga class 150,000Rp)* offers vinyasa flow, traditional hatha and various yin classes in a spacious shala.

Spa-seekers can find plenty of small spas throughout the island, with a one-hour massage ranging from 150,000Rp to over 300,000Rp (at fancier spots). The spa at **PinkCoco Gili Air** *(instagram.com/pinkhotels)* is in a colourful setting fit for pampering, with floral decor and a long list of treatments. Further north, **Lovely Spa** *(WhatsApp +62 878 1669 2236)* offers great-value Balinese massage in a simple, open-air setting.

EATING ON GILI AIR: OUR PICKS

Warung Sunny: Indonesian classics for both veggie and meat eaters and freshly grilled seafood. Also offers cooking classes. *10am-10pm* $

Barefoot Blondie: Western-style brunches and snacks, plus excellent coffees and baked treats, right by the harbour. *7.30am-5pm* $$

Papaya Restaurant & Beach Club: Popular spot for barbecue and cocktails on the west coast, particularly busy at sunset. *10.30am-11pm* $$

Pachamama Cafe & Cantina: Mainly healthy, plant-based dishes, plus guilt-free desserts, smoothies and coffee. *11am-10pm* $$

Places We Love to Stay

$** Budget **$$** Midrange **$$$ Top end

Gili Trawangan

MAP p275

Radika House $ Simple but spacious rooms with friendly vibes, close to the action yet still quiet.

Compass Divers $ Dive centre plus accommodation with private and dorm rooms, providing dive courses at different levels. (p277)

Mad Monkey Hostel $ Backpacker haven on the northwest coast with shared dorms, bungalows and even tents with AC.

Atlas Gili Trawangan $ Social hostel with daily activities for those who want to stay in the main area's action.

Pearl of Trawangan $$ Ocean-view rooms and cottages with bamboo roofs, right on the southeast coast.

La Cocoteraie Ecolodge $$ Luxury glamping tents with a pool, surrounded by tropical gardens on the west coast.

Pesona Beach Resort & Spa $$ A range of seaview and poolside rooms right on the beach, plus an on-site spa and dive centre.

Kuno Villas $$ Charming poolside *joglos* (traditional Javanese houses) and private villas with thoughtful details, just steps from the island's north shore.

PinkCoco $$$ Stylish adults-only hotel by the beach, living up to its namesake with rose-coloured decor in 27 all-pink rooms.

Gili Teak Resort $$$ Laid-back boutique resort on the quieter western shore with poolside gardens and a beachfront bar.

Gili Meno

MAP p279

Meno Smile Cottages $ Comfy rooms in a flower-filled garden within walking distance of the pier.

Rabbit Tree $ Whimsically designed hostel quite literally in the island's middle, with individualised furnishings including a boat-shaped room.

Mimpi Bungalows $ Bungalows with hammocks on the northern shore, close to a few beachside restaurants and bars.

Two Brothers Bungalows $ Spacious guesthouse nestled on the edge of Meno's southwest shore, not far from the port.

Meno Dream Resort $ Rooms and traditional bungalows with outdoor bathrooms, just a couple of minutes' walk from the beach.

Mahamaya Gili Meno $$ Eco-inspired resort with beachfront villas, one- and two-bedroom suites, and family rooms that mix modern with traditional.

Gili Meno Escape $$ Cosy adults-only stay with six pool-facing bungalows, less than a 10-minute walk from the beach.

United Colors of Gili $$ Slightly inland, seven bungalows of traditional Indonesian craft accompanied by a pool and gardens.

Bask $$$ The definition of splurge and modern luxury, providing arguably the most 'treat yourself' resort experience around. (p280)

Meno House $$$ Beachfront resort with sumptuous design and an infinity pool, situated on the quiet northwest shore.

Gili Air

MAP p282

Sayang Mama Inn $ Beautifully designed rooms with verandahs, in a quiet spot just a two-minute walk to the beach.

Adinda Bungalows $ Bright and airy rooms with an on-site restaurant right on the beach.

Captain Coconuts $$ Resort-style hostel with an open-air bamboo lodge, on-site cafe and eco-friendly details.

Jago Gili Air $$ Modern rooms overlooking a pool, a few minutes' walk up the island's central street.

Nanas Homestay $$ Thatched-roof bungalows with terraces and hammocks, close to the central road and beach.

The Koho Air $$ Charming boutique hotel just steps from the port, with an eco-friendly focus.

Gili Air Escape $$ Single-level and two-storey bungalows inland towards the northern shore, tucked away from the main drag.

Manta Dive Resort $$ Scuba-centric accommodation offering myriad dive courses in a prime beachfront location. (p283)

Akasia Villas $$$ Serene and spacious villas on a quiet road, plus hanging swings and floating breakfasts.

Ama-Lurra Resort $$$ Private pool villas on the island's quiet north coast, with an eco-friendly focus.

Researched by
Leyla Rose

Nusa Tenggara

TIMELESS CULTURE, EPIC NATURE AND BIG WAVES

Welcome to the more remote part of Indonesia, home to rumbling volcanoes, limitless surf breaks, Komodo dragons and animist culture.

Spreading west from the Wallace Line dividing Asia from Australasia, the Nusa Tenggara archipelago is an Indonesia less trodden: a verdant, volcano-studded, mountainous land of technicolour volcanic lakes, pink-sand beaches, limitless surf breaks and barrels, and traditional villages that continue to resist Balification.

On Flores, far away from crowds bristling with selfie sticks poised to capture an Insta-ready sunset, you'll encounter Komodo dragons, unspoiled underwater worlds teeming with creatures of the deep, waterfalls and hot springs hidden in the jungle, and steep volcanic slopes that throw down a gauntlet to intrepid hikers, challenging them to race to the top to watch the sun rise.

XIAOYUN NEO/SHUTTERSTOCK

West Timor, Sumba and the smaller islands will make you forgo creature comforts as you leave the main towns, the bass-pumping buses, the minarets and the evening bustle of the night markets behind and venture inland to explore traditional villages with soaring thatched roofs, where the spirits of the ancestors reside side-by-side with the living, animist rituals that rule daily life, splatters of blood on totem poles and carvings speak of recent animal sacrifice, and Bahasa Indonesia – the lingua franca – is little spoken. You'll find yourself stepping out of your comfort zone and coming away with experiences that leave an indelible mark on your memory. But as everywhere, change is on the way, so step into this unique world while you still can.

THE MAIN AREAS

FLORES
Volcanoes, rice terraces, traditional villages and diving. p290

WEST TIMOR
Traditional villages and ikat-weaving. p306

SUMBA
Indigenous culture, ikat and epic surf. p318

For places to stay in Nusa Tenggara, see p330

MARCELO JOHAN OGATA/SHUTTERSTOCK

Left: Komodo dragon, Komodo National Park (p302); Above: Gunung Kelimutu (p300)

Find Your Way

Nusa Tenggara comprises over 550 islands and accounts for a substantial chunk of Indonesia. We've picked the places that best capture the region's history, culture and natural landscapes. Flores, West Timor and Sumba make for good bases.

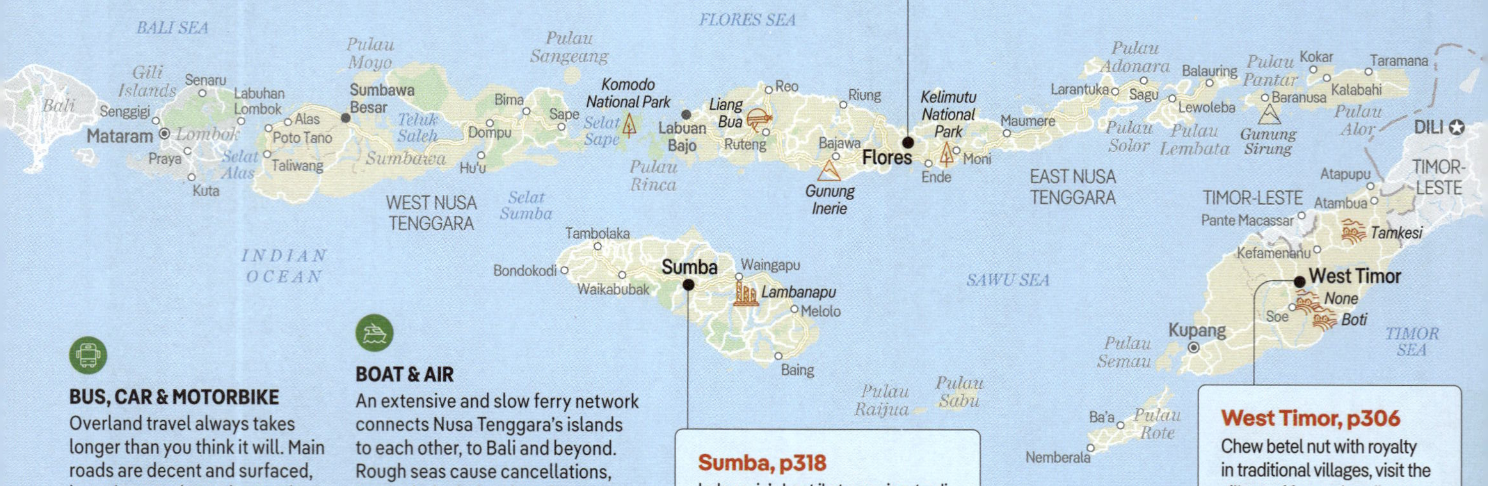

Flores, p290

Hike up volcanoes, explore rice terraces and visit traditional villages before going island-hopping, diving and snorkelling from this all-rounder island.

West Timor, p306

Chew betel nut with royalty in traditional villages, visit the village of former headhunters and seek out intricately woven ikat cloth.

Sumba, p318

Indonesia's best ikat-weaving, traditional culture and terrific year-round surfing draw independent-minded travellers to this hilly island.

BUS, CAR & MOTORBIKE

Overland travel always takes longer than you think it will. Main roads are decent and surfaced, but minor roads can be rough. Trucks and buses connect main towns, and for everything else, rent a car or motorbike.

BOAT & AIR

An extensive and slow ferry network connects Nusa Tenggara's islands to each other, to Bali and beyond. Rough seas cause cancellations, particularly during the rainy season. Several airlines cover inter-island routes, many of which start in Denpasar, Bali.

KRISTINA ISMULYANI/SHUTTERSTOCK

Weaver, Tamkesi (p309)

Plan Your Time

For Komodo-dragon encounters, diving, snorkelling, volcano treks and beaches, prioritise Flores. If you're more into weaving, animist culture and overnighting in traditional villages, head for Sumba or West Timor.

Pressed for Time

If you're a diver, head for **Komodo National Park** (p302). Is Komodo dragon spotting a deal breaker? Spot the legendary lizards on a speedboat day trip that includes bouts of snorkelling. For immersion in indigenous culture, fly to Tambolaka in **Sumba** (p318), then spend a couple of days visiting the traditional villages around **Wanokaka** (p322) and **Waikabubak** (p324).

Two Weeks to Travel

After two days of **Komodo dragons** (p302) and snorkelling from **Labuan Bajo** (p290), head into the mountains to visit the traditional villages of **Wae Rebo** (p295) and **Bena** (p296) before ascending **Gunung Kelimutu** (p300). Fly to **Kupang** (p306), spend two days visiting **Tamkesi** (p309) and **Boti** (p312). Then journey between **Waingapu** (p318) and **Tambolaka** (p327), with ikat-shopping and culture immersion en route.

SEASONAL HIGHLIGHTS

MARCH–JUNE

As rains abate, trek up the volcanoes in Flores. Surf in Rote and Sumbawa, and search for Komodo dragons on Komodo Island.

JULY–AUGUST

Dry season is ideal for exploring Komodo NP on day trips from Labuan Bajo, or the Alor Archipelago on a liveaboard.

SEPTEMBER–OCTOBER

Surf in southwest Sumba, Rote and Sumbawa. Experience Nusa Tenggara's charm between downpours.

NOVEMBER–MARCH

Rainy season makes the islands lush and green. Watch warriors on horseback engage in combat during Sumba's Pasola Festival (p323).

Flores

SPECTACULAR NATURE | TRADITIONAL VILLAGES | SUPERB DIVING

GETTING AROUND

The Trans-Flores Hwy is a beautiful drive that'll always take longer than Google Maps estimates. Secondary roads range from narrow and paved to shocking, with the latter accessible by 4WD or motorbike. Most hotels rent motorbikes and scooters *(per day 80,000-100,000Rp)*. Car rental is available in Labuan Bajo and Ende. Many travellers hire a car and driver *(per day 800,000-1,200,000Rp)*. Regular buses run between Labuan Bajo and Maumere. More comfortable air-con public minibuses link major towns.

TOP TIP

Visit traditional villages with a local guide to bypass the language barrier, learn about indigenous beliefs and avoid making embarrassing faux pas. Visitors must sign the guestbook in each village and make a donation.

Pass through a succession of diverse topographies as you follow the serpentine, 670km-long Trans-Flores Hwy, which follows the spine of Nusa Tenggara's longest, equally sinuous island (whose original name appropriately references snakes rather than the flowery title bestowed upon it by 16th-century Portuguese colonists).

In the west, buzzy, coastal Labuan Bajo is the destination du jour of divers and dragon-seekers, and the gateway to the pink-sand beaches and gin-clear waters of Komodo National Park. Heading into the jungle-covered mountains, you pass through the highland towns of Ruteng and Bajawa, fringed by rice terraces, volcanic cones, hot springs and traditional villages, some seemingly unchanged for millennia. Further north, Riung and its offshore archipelago are another draw for divers, while east of Bajawa, rainforest gives way to verdant, vertiginous hills, white sand, beaches and busy ports. There is also the mountain town of Moni, from where you summit Gunung Kelimutu with its emerald lake, and seek out ikat (woven textiles) and Lio culture in nearby villages.

Lounge Around Labuan Bajo

Explore Labuan Bajo's terrestrial attractions

Its glossy marina and ever-expanding number of restaurants aside, **Labuan Bajo** – the jumping-off point for Komodo National Park (p302) and its famous dragons – is a smidgen short on sights. Everything you need is on one-way Jl Soekarno Hatta, from Western restaurants and local *rumah makans* (eating houses) to coffee shops, accommodation, travel agents, ATMs and dive shops.

Head up to a centrally located spot on Jl Ande Bole, a block from the waterfront, for terrific sunsets. If you want to explore further afield, rent a motorbike or scooter *(per day 100,000Rp)* from numerous outlets along Jl Soekarno Hatta, and head

ANDY PASH/SHUTTERSTOCK

Liang Bua

south of Labuan Bajo to **Gua Batu Cermin** *(Mirror Stone Cave; entry/plus guide 50,000/100,000Rp)*, 5km east of town. You'll need a torch to check out the large grotto with stalactites and stalagmites, while squeezing through tight spaces lets you see a fossilised turtle. To get to the more popular **Gua Rangko** *(50,000Rp)*, an oceanic cave famed for its sunlit turquoise water (visit in the afternoon for the best light), drive 12km northeast from Labuan Bajo to Rangko village, then pay around 350,000Rp for a boat to take you there. An hour or two should be plenty of time to explore each cave.

Hang with Hobbits

Encounter tiny human remains

The Manggarai have long-told folk tales of *ebo gogo* – hairy little people with flat foreheads who once roamed the jungle. Then, in September 2003, archaeologists made a stunning find.

Excavating the limestone cave at **Liang Bua** *(30,000Rp)*, archaeologists unearthed a skeleton the size of a three-year-old child but with the worn-down teeth and bone structure of an adult. Six more remains confirmed that the team had unearthed an entirely new species of human, who reached around 1m in height. The species was named *Homo floresiensis* and nicknamed 'hobbit'.

Commandeering an *ojek* (motorbike taxi) in Ruteng, you can travel 12km north, past flooded rice paddies, and visit the vast stalactite-hung overhang looming above a small vegetable garden. Local guides, whose service is included in your entry fee, will meet you at the cave's entrance, explain why Liang Bua is considered sacred and point out the excavation site where the bones of at least eight more 'hobbits' were found. The small adjacent **museum** tells the story of the findings (in English and Bahasa Indonesia), displays a replica 'hobbit' skeleton, explains the theories of *Homo floresiensis* evolution and, of course, quotes Tolkien.

THE MYSTERIOUS ORIGINS OF THE FLORES 'HOBBIT'

New research into the *Homo floresiensis* has raised new questions. An Australian study in 2017 supposedly disproved the prevailing theory that the 'hobbits' were descendants of *Homo erectus* (who spread from Africa to Asia around two million years ago). After analysing *Homo*-related bones and dental samples from multiple countries, the research found the two had vastly different structures.

Homo floresiensis could be even more ancient than *Homo erectus*, most likely evolving from a common African ancestor. Rival anthropologists suggest that the Flores find could represent *Homo sapiens* (who travelled between Australia and New Guinea 35,000 years ago) that suffered from microcephaly – a form of dwarfism. But a 2018 study refuted any link between the 'hobbit' and *Homo sapiens*.

FLORES

HIGHLIGHTS
1 Gunung Inerie
2 Kelimutu National Park
3 Liang Bua

SIGHTS
4 Bena
see 2 Inspiration Point
5 Koanara
6 Luba
7 Pulau Bakau
8 Pulau Laingjawa
see 7 Pulau Ontoloe
9 Pulau Rutong
see 9 Pulau Tembang
see 8 Pulau Tiga
10 Sa'o Ria
11 Sopi Lontar Aimere
12 Spider Web Rice Fields
13 Tololela
14 Wae Rebo
15 Wae Rebo trailhead
16 Wolotopo

ACTIVITIES
17 Air Panas Malanage
18 Air Panas Soa
19 Gua Batu Cermin
20 Gua Rangko
21 Komodo Kayaking
22 Seventeen Islands Marine Park

SLEEPING
23 Arnolds Family Homestay
24 Bintang by Tobias Lodge
25 Blasius Monta Homestay
26 Café Del Mar
27 D-Rima Homestay
28 Kelimutu Crater Lakes Ecolodge
29 La Boheme Bajo Hostel
see 27 Mama's Homestay Ruteng
30 Manulalu B&B
31 Manulalu Jungle

32 Pu'u Pau Hostel
33 Scuba Junkie Komodo Beach Resort
34 Seaesta Komodo Hostel
see 27 Spring Hill Bungalows
35 Wae Rebo Lodge

EATING
36 Alma
37 Buso Izakaya
see 27 Café Agape
see 26 Café Rico Rico
38 Copper Bonnet Bistro
see 24 Good Moni
see 42 Istana Sehat
see 23 Kartini Restaurant
39 Komodough Artisan Bakery & Coffee
see 39 La Cucina
see 37 Le Bajo Flores
see 23 Milonari Restaurant
see 24 Mopi's Place
40 Pari Koro Resto
41 Pasar Malam
see 26 Pato Resto
see 26 Rutong Café
see 27 Spring Hill Restaurant
see 36 Taman Laut Handayani

SHOPPING
42 Ikat Market

FLORES ROAD TRIP FROM TIP TO TOE

Discover the best of Flores' villages, highlands and coastal scenery.

START	END	LENGTH
Labuan Bajo	Larantuka	787km; 1 week

This island-wide road trip follows the scenic Trans-Flores Hwy and takes in diverse sights. Begin in ❶ **Labuan Bajo**, a harbour town from which you can launch explorations of Komodo National Park. A four-hour drive along a picturesquely winding road through jungled hills bring you to ❷ **Ruteng**, a highland market town ideal for visiting the Liang Bua Cave (p291) and detouring to Nikengto to hike Wae Rebo (p295). Heading east, you pass a scenic viewpoint overlooking terraced rice fields before the road skirts the coast at ❸ **Aimere**, home to several *arak* distilleries, while the volcanic cone of Gunung Inerie (2245m; p295) comes into view. Ignore the hairpin bends leading directly to Bajawa, and skirt the volcano along the occasionally bumpy coastal road, via the village of ❹ **Bena** (p296), to approach ❺ **Bajawa**. Detour north from Bajawa to ❻ **Riung** to snorkel and island-hop in the Seventeen Islands Marine Park (p298) before driving along the northern coast and back down south through banana plantations. The scenic coastal road brings you to ❼ **Ende** (p299), a muggy port, market town and regional transport hub, with the cones of Gunung Meja and Gunung Iya looming over it. Head up forested hills to reach ❽ **Moni**, gateway to Gunung Kelimutu (p300) and ikat-weaving villages. Passing a string of beautiful white-sand beaches at ❾ **Paga**, detour to ❿ **Sikka**, one of Flores's first Portuguese settlements, before proceeding to ⓫ **Maumere**, an urban hub backed by layered hills, with some decent off-coast diving. A three-hour drive brings you to the port of ⓬ **Larantuka**, from which you can sail to West Timor or the Alor Archipelago.

Larantuka also has a small airport with flights to West Timor.

Take a 45-minute drive from Aimere to **Kampung Adat Belaraghi** for a wonderful, non-touristy traditional village.

Get incredible sunrise and sunset views of Gunung Inerie from **Wolo Bobo** peak, a half-hour drive south from Bajawa.

Wander to Wae Rebo

Visit a traditional Manggarai village

The most intact of traditional Manggarai villages, **Wae Rebo** is only accessed on foot, via a 5km hike from the **trailhead** at the end of a cratered narrow road leading north from the village of **Denge**. The footpath climbs relentlessly up the jungle-covered mountain slope for around 3km before the greenery opens up and you catch a glimpse of the valley, Denge's tin roofs and the blue of the Savu Sea. Shortly thereafter, past the lookout tower from which you glimpse the cone-shaped houses of your destination, the trail flattens out and you descend gently to the clearing, with robusta coffee thickets, banana trees and taro plants signifying human habitation, before the much-photographed clearing with its horseshoe of conical houses comes into view.

Sitting on the woven mat of the main house, you take in the hearth in the centre, the smoke from the cooking permeating the interior; the curtained-off living quarters – one room per each of the eight families that live here – and the ceremonial gongs. You're welcome to wander around, taking in village life: children playing amid darting chickens, women pounding husks of rice in giant pestles, men returning from their plots of land come sundown. The only place that's off-limits is the raised ceremonial ground in the centre, where ritual sacrifices are made.

The hike is best made early in the morning before the heat; simple meals of rice, cassava, tempeh and vegetables can be arranged through your guide, and you can stay overnight on a mattress on the floor in the *mbaru tembong* (traditional house) turned guesthouse *(per night incl meals 500,000Rp)*, or retrace your steps before sunset. Hire guides via guesthouses in Denge or bring them with you from Labuan Bajo or Ruteng.

SPIDERWEB RICE FIELDS

Scramble to the viewpoint *(25,000Rp)* up the hill near Cara village, 20km west of Ruteng, and an extraordinary sight awaits: vast rice fields in the shape of spiderwebs. This is the last surviving vestige on Flores of the traditional communal agriculture of the Manggarai, whereby the *lingko* (land) is divided by the village headman among the village's families. During the allocation of each segment, a buffalo sacrifice takes place at the *lodok* (ceremonial ground) in the centre of the web. The more resources the family has, the bigger its slice of the web, with choice sections owned by the headman's family. When the head of a family dies, the land segment is re-allocated.

Summit Gunung Inerie

Tackle Flores' highest volcano

A breathtakingly beautiful, spectacularly jagged cone of a volcano looming above Bajawa, **Gunung Inerie** (2245m), 10km south of town, throws down the gauntlet to intrepid would-be climbers. The ascent is relentless but not quite as daunting as the steep sides suggest. Guided ascents are possible outside the wetter months; with an English-speaking guide and transport from Bajawa, expect to pay about 1,000,000Rp for one person and 1,200,000Rp for two people. Bring plenty of water and

EATING IN LABUAN BAJO: OUR PICKS

La Cucina: Popular Italian-owned spot reminiscent of an authentic trattoria, with handmade pasta and a long list of pizzas. *7am-11pm* **$$**

Buso Izakaya: Authentic Japanese food and creative cocktails in gorgeous interiors that open up onto a jetty. *5-11pm* **$$**

Pasar Malam: From sunset, smoky, lamp-lit waterfront stalls cook up fresh fish, prawns, squid and crab. Wash it down with BYO Bintang. *6-11pm* **$$**

Taman Laut Handayani: Fish steamed in banana leaf and seafood dishes served with a side of sunset views await at this lofty outdoor restaurant. *10am-10pm* **$$**

CACI WHIP FIGHTS

Every November, as part of the Penti harvest festival, Manggarai villages such as Wae Rebo stage **Caci** – a ritual whip fight between pairs of men. One man plays the role of aggressor and the other, the defender. The aggressor tries to hit the defender's bare upper body with a rattan whip while the defender blocks with a buffalo-hide shield.

At the beginning, the participants run towards each other to raise the tension. If the defender is struck on the back, it's considered a good sign, with the blood anointing the earth and promising bounteous harvest. The aggressor and defender switch roles after every whip lash, with a new pair stepping up after four whip strikes.

a sun hat, since beyond the sparce eucalyptus forest at the volcano's base, the cone is shadeless. Beyond the treeline, you zigzag up its north flank to the summit; many guides prefer to do the ascent in the predawn dark, starting around 3am and arriving in time for sunrise. Depending on your fitness levels, the round-trip hike takes roughly seven hours.

Explore Bajawa's Traditional Villages

Immerse yourself in Ngada culture

Perched at 1100m above sea level, framed by forested volcanoes and blessed with a cooler climate, **Bajawa** is a laid-back, predominantly Catholic hill town, and a great base from which to explore dozens of surrounding Ngada villages.

One of the most traditional is **Bena**, resting on the flank of Gunung Inerie, 19km south of Bajawa *(return trip by ojek 120,000Rp)*. Though all villagers are now officially Catholic, traditional beliefs and customs endure. Sacrifices are held three times each year, and village elders still talk about a rigidly enforced caste system that prevented 'mixed' relationships, with those defying the *adat* (traditional law) facing serious consequences.

Bena is home to nine clans, and its houses with high, thatched roofs line up in two rows on a ridge. They're interspersed with ancestral totems, including megalithic tombs, *ngadhu* (thatched parasol-like structures) – the bases of which are splattered with animal blood from sacrifices – *bhaga* (miniature thatched-roof houses), and small sacred houses where significant relics are kept. Most houses have male or female figurines on the roofs, while doorways are decorated with buffalo horns and pig jawbones – more remnants of ritual sacrifice. Look out for woodcarvings at the base of each house: roosters symbolise greatness; horses, hard work and abundant harvest; while serpents protect the inhabitants from evil powers.

After paying the entrance fee *(25,000Rp)* you're given a purple scarf to wear for the duration of your visit, and as you walk around, you'll see cash crops of cloves, vanilla pods and candlenut drying on the ground. It's possible to stay the night for 150,000Rp per person, which includes meals of boiled cassava and banana, but if you want a more intimate experience, walk several hundred metres uphill to the village of **Luba**.

A baker's dozen of houses and a handful of Catholic graves silhouetted against Gunung Inerie, Luba is home to four welcoming clans. You'll see four *ngadhu* and *bhaga*, and houses

EATING IN LABUAN BAJO: OUR PICKS

Copper Bonnet Bistro: Come for the meze, noodle bowls, Cobb salad and BBQ ribs and linger over craft beer on the terrace. *8am-11pm* **$$**

Komodough Artisan Bakery & Coffee: A cosy bakery serving a range of pastries, cakes and hot and cold drinks, perfect for breakfast or a light lunch. *6am-10pm* **$$**

Alma: Mediterranean fare with tapas and plenty of fresh seafood options, with harbour views. *8am-11pm* **$$**

Le Bajo Flores: Grilled meats and seafood, burgers and pasta in this all-day eating spot right on the jetty. *11am-11pm* **$$**

KARITING PICAH/SHUTTERSTOCK

Air Panas Malanage

decorated with depictions of symbolic horses, buffalo and snakes. Leave a donation of 25,000Rp.

Alternatively, a mere 4km trek from Bena, or a short drive south via Gurusina, brings you to **Tololela** *(donation per person 25,000Rp)*, a seldom-visited Ngada settlement consisting of three linked traditional villages.

Soak in the Hot Springs

Bajawa's mineral waters

Unofficially staffed by friendly locals and featuring basic changing rooms, the natural **Air Panas Malanage** *(20,000Rp)* hot springs are 6km south of Bena. At the base of one of the many volcanoes in the area, two streams – one hot (up to 50°C), one cold – mix together in a temperate stream. Soak amid the greenery-covered boulders and flitting dragonflies, and don't be surprised if you're joined by locals who take the opportunity to wash their clothes while they bathe.

If you're making the journey from Bajawa to Riung along the rough road northeast of town, **Air Panas Soa** *(10,000Rp)* is another option. The most-serviced hot springs in the region consist of two manufactured pools (one a scintillating 45°C, the other a more pedestrian 35°C to 40°C) and one natural pool (25°C to 30°C), and can get rather busy, particularly on weekends.

THE NGADA PEOPLE

More than 60,000 Ngada people inhabit the upland Bajawa plateau and the slopes around Gunung Inerie. Most practise a fusion of animism and Christianity, worshipping Gae Dewa, a god who unites Dewa Zeta (the heavens) and Nitu Sale (the earth). The Ngada are matrilineal, meaning that kinship passes through the female line.

The most evident symbols of Ngada traditions are the pairs of *ngadhu* (male) and *bhaga* (female) structures, each associated with a particular family within a village. Some structures were built over 100 years ago to commemorate ancestors killed in battle. The *ngadhu* is a parasol-like structure about 3m high, consisting of a carved wooden pole and thatched 'roof', while the *bhaga* is a miniature thatched-roof house.

EATING IN RUTENG & BAJAWA: OUR PICKS

Café Agape: Simple but homey place in Ruteng selling a mix of Western and Indonesian meals, snacks and desserts. *8am-9pm* $

Spring Hill Restaurant: Indonesian classics with vegetarian options, set among landscaped gardens in Ruteng. *11.30am-9pm Mon-Sat, 8.30am-9pm Sun* $$

Milonari Restaurant: Tempeh and tofu dishes alongside chicken and rice combos, sweet-and-sour fish, good coffee and pancakes. In Bajawa. *9am-10pm Mon-Sat* $

Kartini Restaurant: Extensive menu of Western and Indonesian dishes with generous portions and outdoor seating, next to a park in Bajawa. *10am-10pm* $$

IKAT TEXTILES

Ikat textiles are not just for aesthetic appeal – they hold cultural significance across Flores and other islands in Nusa Tenggara. These fabrics are used in everyday life, always present at births, weddings and funerals. They're often used as dowry, with exclusive types of ikat such as *kikir kobar* priced at the same amount as a horse. In the past, the motifs indicated status and social ranking. The *patola* ikat (introduced to Flores by Gujarati traders) were only allowed to be worn by nobility or community leaders. It's common for old and sacred ikat cloths to be passed down as family heirlooms through generations. The women of the village are responsible for creating ikat textiles – girls start learning as young as 10 years old.

DANAAN/SHUTTERSTOCK

Seventeen Islands Marine Park

Snorkel the Seventeen Islands

Boat-tripping off Flores' north coast

Lapped at by turquoise waters and fringed with white-sand beaches, the 23 islands that make up the misnamed **Seventeen Islands Marine Park** (government authorities decided on the number 17 as a convenient tie-in with Indonesia's Independence Day, 17 August) are a worthwhile detour. The park is accessed via a three-hour bumpy drive from Boawae, a four-hour bone-shaking bus ride via a bumpy (but improving) road from Bajawa, or a four-hour bus journey along an arid coastal road from Ende to the laid-back, coconut-fringed little fishing town of Riung – the islands' gateway.

Standard day trips tend to include lunch, snorkelling and four island stops, the first almost always being the mangrove-fringed **Pulau Ontoloe**, home to a massive colony of fruit bats and a few Komodo dragons. This is typically followed by snorkelling over the shallow reef near **Pulau Tiga**, **Pulau Laingjawa** and **Pulau Bakau**. The park's coral was impacted by the El Niño bleaching of 2002, so there are patches where the reef hasn't recovered. However, the visibility is up to 15m, and you're likely to spot a variety of reef denizens, from parrotfish and clownfish to the venomous lionfish. Stops on **Pulau Rutong** (for the viewpoint) and **Pulau Tembang** (for picture-perfect white sand) are also popular.

EATING IN RIUNG: OUR PICKS

Café Rico Rico: Grilled fish with punchy tomato sambal is the standout at this casual pier-side spot. Live music some nights, and snorkelling trips arranged. *8am-10pm* $

Pato Resto: Hoover up fried noodles with vegetables, aubergine with tomato sauce and fried squid washed down with banana juice. *7am-midnight* $

Café del Mar: Dine on grilled catch-of-the-day with *cah kangkung* (garlicky water spinach); stay overnight and arrange your snorkelling trips. *6am-11pm* $

Rutong Café: Barbecued fish, chicken satay and an array of vegetable and noodle dishes really shine when complemented by Simeon's special sambal. *8am-midnight* $$

To arrange your boat trip, hang out by the boat dock, where in high season you're likely to find fellow travellers to split day-trip fares with. Prices depend on how many people you're with, but the going rate is between 600,000Rp and 800,000Rp for a boat, which includes a guide, snorkelling gear and lunch. Alternatively, organise a guide via your guesthouse; Al Itchan, owner of **Café Del Mar**, comes recommended. Before going to the islands, sign in and pay 100,000Rp per person entrance fee at a separate booth by the dock.

Take the Ikat Trail to Moni & Ende

Go in search of fine textiles

The mountain villages east (around Jopu) and northeast (around Lio) of the gritty port town of **Ende** – and around the appealing mountain town of **Moni**, which is fringed by rice fields and greenery-clad volcanic peaks – are still renowned for their ikat and sarong weavings, with distinctive regional patterns of triangular motifs made of continuous lines. In Ende, a block inland from the waterfront, visit the daily **ikat market**, where there's a good selection of ikat from the region and beyond; bargaining is acceptable. Alternatively, catch an *ojek* up the rough road from Ende to the village of **Wolotopo** to observe the weaving process right in front of weavers' houses and buy directly from the source.

Accessed from Moni, weaving is practised in the villages of **Koanara**, **Jopu** and, further afield, in **Wolonjita** and **Nggela**. A 10-minute drive through the rice paddies south of Moni gets you to **Koanara**, with the vivid purples, oranges and electric blues of ikat cloths hanging by the roadside and weavers working their looms.

Visit Sa'o Ria

Delve into Lio culture

A mere 10 minutes' drive south of Moni is the village of **Sa'o Ria**, just up from the bend in the road overhung by a giant ficus tree. There, you'll be able to see its thatched *rumah adat* (traditional house). If you're lucky, the headman's effusive wife, Maria, will welcome you inside the house; only other Lio headmen, their wives and visitors from outside the Lio culture are granted entry (a 20,000Rp donation is appropriate). You'll step inside the tiny doorway, decorated with intricate carvings, and sit on the springy bamboo floor inside the smoky interior while your guide translates stories of local traditions.

THE ART OF ARAK DISTILLATION

Approaching Aimere from the west, you'll pass **Sopi Lontar Aimere**, an *arak* distillery, marked by a display of plastic bottles containing different-coloured liquid – not to be confused with other displays of plastic bottles sold by the roadside (petrol = '*arak* for motorbike'). Coastal *arak* is made from the sap of a particular palm tree, with men scaling the tree and attaching a bucket for five days. On day six, the bucket is retrieved and stored in plastic vats to ferment.

The resulting juice is distilled over a wood fire, with the clear liquid slowly dripping through a bamboo pipe. The first dripping is the most potent (up to 50%) while the second and third go from 30% to 20%.

EATING IN MONI & ENDE: OUR PICKS

Mopi's Place: Start the day in Moni with local coffee, then come back for live reggae, *tapa kolo* (coconut rice) and *arak* cocktails. *hours vary* $$

Good Moni: With a friendly chef-owner and misty hill views, this open-air restaurant does Indonesian staples and the Moni potato croquette. *8am-9pm* $

Istana Sehat: Fresh and healthy local and Indonesian dishes, plus freshly caught seafood, with views of the beach in Ende. *6am-10pm* $

Pari Koro Resto: Free-range chicken rubs shoulders with sauteed pumpkin shoots and water spinach with papaya flower. In Ende. *10am-10pm Mon-Sat, to 11pm Sun* $$

BIRD-WATCHING IN FLORES & BEYOND

Clichéd as it may be to say this, the Lesser Sunda Islands are a bird-watcher's paradise, with hundreds of feathered species spotted across varied habitats, including over 70 endemics – some very rare.

Yovie Jehabut *(jagarimba.id)* is a well-regarded Flores-based bird-watching guide who specialises in custom-made trips in the Wallacea bioregion (Lesser Sunda Islands, Sulawesi and Maluku). He can arrange itineraries to suit you, whether you want to scour the Flores lowlands for the Flores crow, the Flores green pigeon and the critically endangered Flores hawk eagle, hunt for the Timor friarbird and Timor figbird in woodlands near Kupang, or spot Sumba's apricot-breasted sunbird and the greater Sumba boobook by night in Langgiliru National Park.

The Gavi ceremony, which accompanies the beginning of planting season in October, sees 1000 Lio from other villages come to Sa'o Ria. There are four days of dancing, imbibing of *arak* (colourless, distilled palm wine), and buffalo sacrifice. The hearts of the buffalo are cooked in the *rumah adat* and placed onto a sacred woven platform as an offering to the spirits. After the four days, the hearts mysteriously disappear. After the harvest in April, there's a two-day thanksgiving ceremony, accompanied by a pig sacrifice and the consumption of yellow rice.

Marvel at Multicoloured Lakes

Summit Indonesia's unique volcano

Waking up at 4am, you either hop on the motorbike for the solo hour-long ride from Moni to the car park near the top of **Gunung Kelimutu** (1639m), or you're driven there by your guide, which can be arranged through your accommodation in Moni. Pay the entrance fee at the ticket booth at the **Kelimutu National Park** *(weekdays/weekends 150,000/225,000Rp)* entrance. A gentle 15-minute ramble along the pine-fringed slope followed by a climb up some steps brings you to **Inspiration Point** at the summit. This is the most common route, but if you're hiking the full loop it can take up to 8½ hours.

As the first rays of the sun crest Kelimutu's western rim, filtering mist into the sky and revealing three deep volcanic lakes, there's a collective gasp of wonder from the shivering crowd.

A sacred and extinct volcano, Kelimutu is the centrepiece of the mountainous, jungle-clad Kelimutu National Park. It is sacred to the local Lio people, who believe the souls of the dead migrate here. Young people's souls go to the warmth of **Tiwu Koo Fai Nuwa Muri** (Teal Lake); old people's to the cold of **Tiwu Ata Bupu** (Royal Blue Lake); and those of the wicked to **Tiwu Ata Polo** (Black Lake). If you happen to be up the volcano on 14 August, you'll witness the exuberant dancing on Lio ceremonial grounds en route to the summit – part of the annual 'Feed the Spirits of the Forefathers' ceremony, after which pork, betel nuts, rice and other valuable offerings will be left on ceremonial rocks beside the lakes. Alert your guide if you have dreams about the sacred lakes prior to your ascent – apparently, siren-like spirits have lured people to their demise, which can be avoided if the right prayers and offerings are made. Resist temptation from these will-o'-the-wisps, and don't stray beyond the two official lookouts. Several hikers have perished after slipping on the loose scree.

A pre-dawn visit to Kelimutu is not the meditative, tranquil experience you may hope for, since it's when you'll encounter the biggest crowds. There's a risk of clouds pulling in later on, but on a fine day, you'll find Kelimutu's summit empty and peaceful, and when the sun is high, the lakes really sparkle.

On the way down, take the shortcut (you'll need to ask locals for directions) down to **Moni** through steep, scenic copses of eucalyptus, and through farmland rich in banana, taro and vanilla, until you reach a gorgeous waterfall and dipping pool right below the road running through Moni. Budget half a day for the 15-minute ramble up, or a full day for the full loop.

Beyond Flores

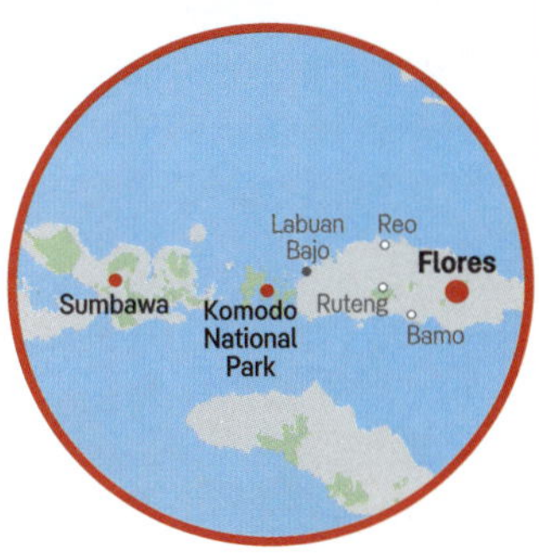

Head west of Labuan Bajo for primeval monster encounters or further west to Sumbawa for monster waves.

Arguably the single biggest reason to come to Labuan Bajo is the chance to visit Komodo National Park, centred on Komodo Island and the main home of the fearsome *ora* (Komodo dragon), the world's largest monitor lizard. Dragon sightings are also common on the smaller Rinca Island, though since Rinca has been 'tamed' in recent times for cruise-ship visitors, it has become far less popular with Labuan Bajo crowds. West of Flores, the large, conservative island of Sumbawa is full of natural beauty with untouched beaches and desert islands. It's never been a great tourist destination, and continues to fly under the radar, save for in-the-know surfers who come for the island's powerful breaks and uncrowded waves.

Places

Sumbawa p301
Komodo National Park p302

GETTING AROUND

There's fierce competition among Labuan Bajo's boat operators and diving outfits for day and multiday trips to Komodo National Park. Group day trips by speedboat cost from 1,350,000Rp per person and allow for more time at each location than the cheaper slow boats. Multiday liveaboards cater to divers and explorers. Rinca Island is accessible by private boat only *(from 1,500,000Rp)*. Fly to Bima, Sumbawa to catch a bus to Hu'u, or take a taxi from Bima *(1,000,000Rp)* directly to Pantai Lakey.

Sumbawa

TIME FROM FLORES: **1HR**

Ride the waves in Sumbawa

Hollow tubes break on the reefs of the white-sand **Pantai Lakey**, attracting international championship surfers year-round with its surf – the most consistent swell is between June and August. Lakey Peak and Lakey Pipe are hallowed names, both within easy paddling distance of Lakey's string of modest beach guesthouses, all linked by a sandy path studded with bars. From August to October, the wind gusts, which turns Pantai Lakey into Indonesia's best kitesurfing destination. Firman *(WhatsApp +62 823 4125 6400; group/private lessons 500,000/750,000Rp)* is a great surf instructor who offers group and private lessons.

Grounded by reef, the A-frame **Lakey Peak** is the wave here, right in front of the famous tower; it's for experienced surfers only. Next to it, **Lakey Pipe** is a nice left-hander, best at mid-to-high tide. A five-minute drive from Lakey, less crowded **Cobblestones** is a left- and right-hander break; the gentler right-hander is good for beginners.

A short paddle from the shore, 15 minutes from Lakey, **Periscope** is a steep right-hander barrel reef-break. A similar distance away, left- and right-hander **Nangadoro** is worth seeking out at high tide, while **Nungas**, a long left-hander reef break near Lakey, is gentler than Peak or Pipe and best at low- to mid-tide, with killer sunsets from the beach.

THRITOTH/SHUTTERSTOCK

Pulau Padar

TOP EXPERIENCE

Komodo National Park

Most visitors to Labuan Bajo have dragons on their mind. To see the world's largest lizards in their most spectacular setting, the Komodo National Park is a bucket-list destination. The best way of getting around the park is a boat trip, with most Labuan Bajo operators running a standard day trip to Komodo, either via speedboat or slow boat, and stopping in the same six locations.

DON'T MISS

- Pulau Rinca
- Pulau Komodo
- Pulau Padar
- Snorkelling
- Scuba diving
- Kayaking

Pulau Padar

The first stop on a boat trip around the park is typically the compact, vertiginous **Pulau Padar**. A steep 15-minute hike brings you to the highest of a series of viewpoints, from which you can admire the volcanic island's scalloped bays fringed with white sand, the island's mountainous spine and the surrounding marine panorama. Next up is swimming and sunbathing on one of the national park's pink-sand beaches, on the far side of Pulau Padar.

PRACTICALITIES

● komodonp.com ● park entrance per day 350,000Rp; drone permit per day 2,000,000Rp ● 6am-6pm

ANDY CROCKER/SHUTTERSTOCK

Komodo dragon

Pulau Komodo

A short boat ride away, **Pulau Komodo** awaits, its steep hillsides lush with greenery in the short wet season (December to March) and frazzled by sun to a rusty tan that makes its crystal waters pop the rest of the year. Ashore, you are paired with a ranger armed with a forked staff for keeping dragons at bay. The 1,355,000Rp entrance fee includes a choice of three walks: the short walk (1.5km, 45 minutes), which includes a stop at an artificial waterhole that attracts diminutive local deer, wild boar and, of course, *ora* (Komodo dragons); the medium walk (2km, 1½ hours), which includes a hill with sweeping views and a chance to see colourful cockatoos; and the long walk (4km, two hours), which includes the features of the shorter hikes and distances you from peak-season crowds.

Pulau Rinca

After sailing past dramatically hilly, sparsely forested islets and islands, you'll arrive at the arid **Pulau Rinca**, where you're greeted with a larger-than-life statue of two Komodo dragons engaged in mortal combat.

A five-minute stroll along the wheelchair-accessible wooden boardwalk with a mandatory ranger accompaniment brings you to the excellent museum, with its detailed information on Komodo dragons, and the terrestrial and marine fauna of the national park. Directly behind the museum, you're likely to find Komodo dragons resting under the trees in the daytime heat. Get here early in the day to observe them at their most active. Besides dragons, you may see tiny Timor deer, snakes, monkeys, wild boar and birds.

Long walks or overnight stays on Rinca are no longer permitted. On request, the ranger can lead you through the

FUN FACTS ABOUT KOMODO DRAGONS

Believed to have originated in Australia four million years ago, Komodo dragons reside on Komodo and Rinca, and parts of North and West Flores. One toxin-loaded bite from these dragons promotes bleeding that slowly kills its prey. Komodos can eat up to 80% of their body weight in a single sitting, before retiring for up to a month to digest. An estimated 5000 dragons live in the wild today, but only a few hundred or so are egg-laying females.

TOP TIPS

- Avoid visiting the dragons during menstruation, as they can smell blood from 8km away.
- Stick to designated safe zones and don't go wandering by yourself – always stay with your group.
- Don't make any loud noises or sudden movements when near the dragons.
- There's not a lot of shade on the islands, so bring sun protection.
- The terrain can be uneven, so wear sturdy shoes and comfortable clothing.
- Bring cash as there are souvenir stands on the islands.
- Do not touch or step on the corals when snorkelling and scuba diving.

DRAGON-SPOTTING

At Komodo and Rinca, your odds of seeing dragons are very good, with the exception of mating season on Komodo (June and July), when females go into hiding and males spread out on the vast island trying to find them. Peak months for sightings are September to December, when both sexes are out and about. Mating season is less of a problem at Rinca, where the dragons hang around near the museum.

mangroves and up a steep, barren slope for spectacular panoramic views of the bay.

Snorkelling

After lunch, the boat makes a snorkelling stop at the spectacular **Taka Makassar** with its diversity of healthy coral, vast shoals of reef fish and frequent sightings of sea turtles and other pelagic life. Next, you head to **Karang Makassar** (Manta Point) in search of manta rays – often reliably present. The final stop is the rather anticlimactic **Pulau Kanawa** for more snorkelling. If you have more time, a rewarding way of experiencing Komodo National Park is via three-day, two-night liveaboard boat trips, offered by some operators such as **Kanha Liveaboard** *(kanhaliveaboard.com; from 3,750,000Rp)*. Most dive companies have liveaboard options, too. A three-day trip takes in all the day trip's highlights, and less-visited spots, such as the small, uninhabited **Siaba**, **Kalong** and **Bidadari** islands – all excellent for snorkelling. It also means beating the crowds to Padar's viewpoint in the morning, and visiting Komodo Island earlier, when the dragons are more active.

HEIKO JETZKOWITZ/SHUTTERSTOCK

Manta ray

Kayaking

Komodo Kayaking *(komodokayaking.com; 2/3 day US$590/890)* – the only Indonesian kayaking operator in Labuan Bajo – offers an active, eco-friendly way of exploring the park that includes dining in beachside safari tents in the evening and paddling along the coastlines of various islands during the day, stopping to snorkel and occasionally catching a glimpse of the dragons – excellent swimmers – in the water.

Scuba Diving

With its submerged seamounts haunted by manta rays, reef sharks and turtles; its vibrant, exceptionally diverse reefs that teem with life; and its excellent underwater visibility, Komodo makes for an incredible diving experience, with several dozen dive sites dotted around the national park's islands. The challenging underwater topography, combined with strong, unpredictable currents, means that some of the top diving sites are for experienced divers only, though there are calmer spots for beginners. There's tremendous competition for divers in Labuan Bajo, with dozens of scuba-diving operators based there; you can also opt for a multiday liveaboard for a more tranquil experience away from diving day-trippers. Look out for the 'DOCK' (Dive Operators Community Komodo) sticker in the windows of the most conservation-minded of the diving outfits; they actively combat dynamite fishing and other harmful practices. Some also have programmes that hire and train locals and turn them into conservation ambassadors.

The best place to see Komodo's manta rays is **Karang Makassar** (Manta Point), a shallow (12m max) drift dive along a sloping rubble reed. It's a manta cleaning station and a popular feeding spot when the water is plankton-rich.

Off Pulau Komodo's northern side, **Castle Rock** is a submerged seamount, well known for its intense currents and encounters with grey, whitetip and blacktip reef sharks, as well as schooling jacks, giant trevally, tuna and huge schools of fusiliers. Another terrific site for huge shoals of fish is **Batu Bolong** (for experienced divers only due to the currents), with the shallows on the lee side of the pinnacle thick with damselfish, fairy basslets, Moorish idols, large sweetlips and sheltering lionfish, while the deep blue teems with Spanish mackerel, surgeonfish and red-toothed triggerfish.

Near Pulau Seraya Besar, **Sabolan Kecil** is great for macro diving and for beginners, with batfish, seahorses, scorpion fish and blue-spotted stingrays spotted among the gorgonian fans and barrel sponges of the sloping coral reef and sand below. The white-sand bottom of the reef on the north side of **Pulau Sebayur** (halfway between Komodo and Flores) attracts eagle rays, while the reef's ledges and overhangs house cleaner shrimp and glassfish, with hairy squat lobsters spotted between the sponge and barrel corals, and emperor fish and groupers cruising by.

LABUAN BAJO'S BEST DIVING OPERATORS

Wunderpus Liveaboard Diving and snorkelling liveaboard operator offering three- to seven-day trips, focusing on small groups, environmentally conscious tours and uncrowded dive sites. *(wunderpusliveaboard.com)*

Manta Rhei Specialises in themed day trips and PADI courses. Nitrox dives and liveaboards also available. *(mantarhei.com)*

Uber Scuba Komodo Offers a range of day and multiday dives, liveaboard trips and SSI courses. Also offers trips combining diving and Komodo dragon visits. *(uberscubakomodo.com)*

Neren Diving Komodo Dive centre with a focus on conservation, offering courses, daily fun dive trips plus dragon spotting on Rinca. *(nerendivingkomodo.net)*

Scuba Junkie Komodo Excellent range of diving and snorkelling outings, liveaboard experiences and PADI courses. *(scubajunkiekomodo.com)*

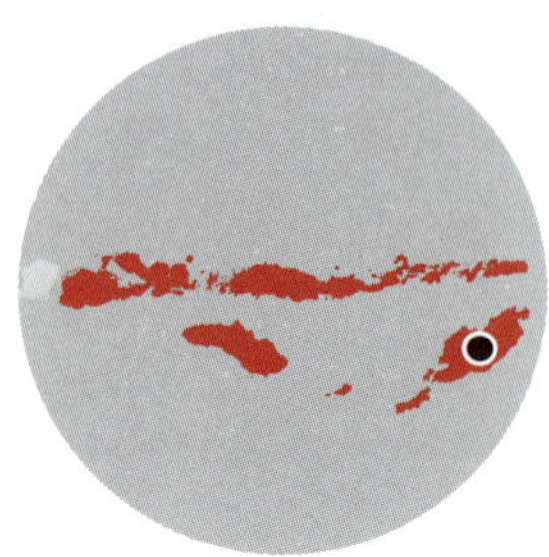

West Timor

TRADITIONAL CULTURE | IKAT | CAVE DIVING

GETTING AROUND

Bemos reach most of Kupang's spread-out attractions. A ride costs 5000Rp; clap loudly when you want to stop. Useful routes include 1 & 2 Kuanino-Oepura (past popular hotels), 5 Oebobo-Airnona-Bakunase (past the main post office), and 10 Kelapa Lima-Walikota (Terminal Kota, the Oebobo bus terminal and the Museum Nusa Tenggara Timur). Hotels rent motorbikes and scooters for 100,000Rp per day. Buses from **Terminal Oebobo** (bus terminal), 7km from the airport, run to Soe (three hours), Kefamenanu (5½ hours) and Atambua (12 hours). You can rent a car and driver from 800,000Rp to 1,000,000Rp per day.

Fringed by vast, rice-growing plains and white-sand beaches, the greenery-clad hills and deep valleys of West Timor are as beguiling as the island's inhabitants. Smile at someone, and you're likely to get a smile in return, often with teeth stained red from betel nut – an integral part of indigenous culture here.

It was the island's natural wealth – sandalwood – that brought the Portuguese here in the early 1500s, followed by the Dutch, as well as missionaries from both countries, who introduced Christianity. Nonetheless, West Timor's ruggedly mountainous, *lontar*-palm-studded topography and centuries-old division into independent, warring kingdoms have made it possible for animist traditions to persist, alongside 14 different languages and tribal dialects. After leaving the music-thumping bemos of Kupang, the capital, you enter the less-visited world of beehive-hut villages, whose chiefs preserve *adat* and whose artisans produce exquisite ikat.

Revel in the Sweet Sounds of Sasando

Mastering a Rotinese string instrument

Heading towards Soe, pull up outside **Tempat Pembuatan Sasando** in Oebelo and step inside. A young man clad in a *ti'i langga* (*lontar*-leaf hat with a centre plume) – traditional headgear from the island of Rote – will treat you to an unforgettable musical repertoire as his hands fly deftly over the strings of the *sasando*, Rote's traditional 32-string zither that sounds alternately like a cross between a harp, a piano and steel pans. Used by the Rote islanders since the 17th century (though the original had bamboo or civet-gut strings rather than metal ones), the *sasando* is crafted from bamboo and teak, with a foldable palm leaf 'sail' for resonance. After the son of locally renowned Rotinese musician Pak Pah finishes serenading you, you can choose to take lessons at

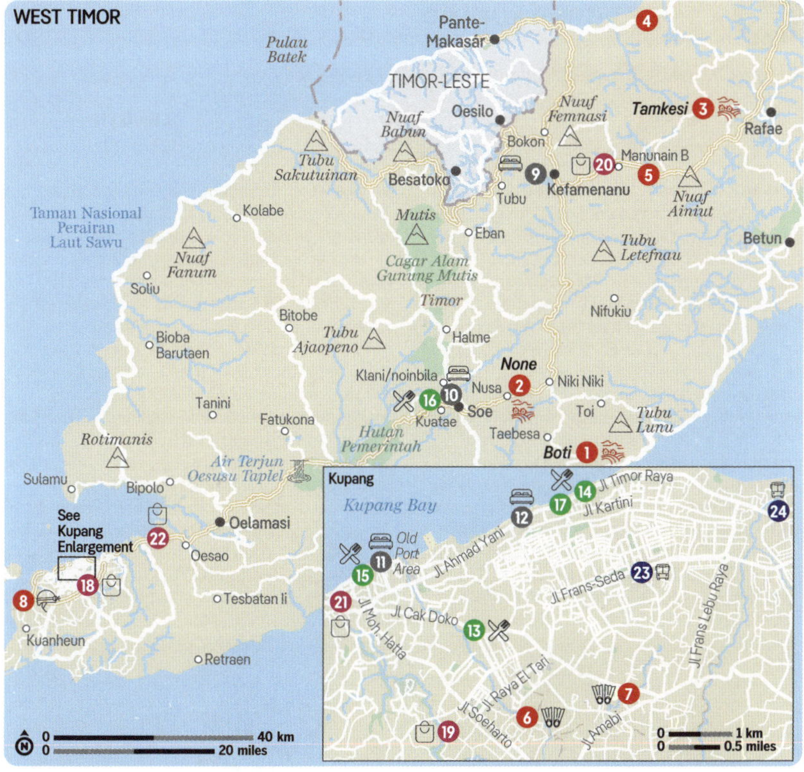

HIGHLIGHTS
1 Boti
2 None
3 Tamkesi

SIGHTS
4 Oepuah
5 Tapenpah

ACTIVITIES
6 Cendana Dive
7 Dive Kupang Dive
8 Goa Kristal
see 8 Goa Uihani

SLEEPING
9 Comfort Inn
10 Dena Hotel
11 Lavalon Hostel
12 Sotis Hotel

EATING
see 9 Bekhaus
13 Depot Se'i Babi Aroma
14 Kelapa Restaurant & Sky Lounge
15 Pasar Malam Seafood
see 10 RM Sari Bundo II
16 Rumah Makan Depot Remaja
see 9 Sisterhood Coffee & Eatery
17 Subasuka Paradise

SHOPPING
18 Edon Sasando Musik
see 10 Galeri Alekot
19 Ina Ndao
20 Kain Tenun Tradisional
see 20 Maubesi Market
21 Pak Haji Noer
22 Tempat Pembuatan Sasando

TRANSPORT
23 Terminal Oebobo
24 Timor Tour & Travel

Edon Sasando Musik, on the outskirts of Kupang, if you're feeling inspired. *Sasando* virtuoso Aby Edon claims that if you have a modicum of musical talent, he'll have you coaxing out a tune within a couple of hours. Not content with playing the instrument, he also designs and builds his own, from the traditional acoustic *(from 4,000,000Rp)* to electric *(8,000,000Rp)* to hybrid *(10,000,000Rp)*, just in case you'd like to take one home with you.

TOP TIP

Local guides are essential for visiting traditional villages, in some of which Bahasa Indonesia isn't widely spoken. They can explain local traditions and customs.

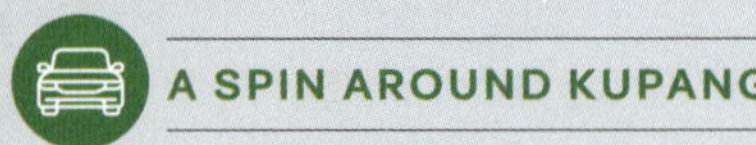

A SPIN AROUND KUPANG

Explore Kupang's top sights with this easy driving tour.

START	END	LENGTH
Pasar Oeba	Pantai Tablolong	54km; 8hr

Despite Kupang's scruffy waterfront, heavy traffic (you have to be a confident driver to join in) and a lack of endearing architectural elements, there is a certain chaotic charm to West Timor's capital and regional hub. If travelling to the interior of Alor or Rote, you'll be spending time here and may discover that it grows on you. England's Captain Bligh had a similar epiphany when he spent 47 days here after that emasculating mutiny on the HMS *Bounty* in 1789. This day tour takes in Kupang's disparate sights. Start the morning by absorbing the clamour and pungency of **1 Pasar Oeba** produce market and the adjacent fish market. Head east along the coast, then cut south to the fantastic **2 Museum Nusa Tenggara Timur**, a wonderful introduction to West Timor's history and cultural heritage. Amid displays of ceramics and kris (traditional daggers), you'll find ritual masks, warrior wear from Timor, elaborate woodcarvings of statues used to ward off disease and natural disasters, and superb examples of ikat. Displays on the Pasola festival (p323), traditional music and natural history add context. Proceed to the rambling **3 Pasar Inpres** to browse fresh produce and buy a *ti'i langga* (*lontar*-leaf hat with a centre plume) from Rote. Head north, then follow the coastal road to the west, past the well-signposted **4 Monkey Cave**, with macaques hanging around outside. Proceed past the port to **5 Goa Kristal** (p311; Crystal Cave), where locals swim in turquoise water and partake in photoshoots. Nearby, **6 Goa Uilebahan** is another cave with an aquamarine pool and interesting rock formations. Duck inland to frolic at the **7 Air Terjun Oenesu** before finishing with sunset-watching at the white-sand **8 Pantai Tablolong**, 25km southwest of Kupang.

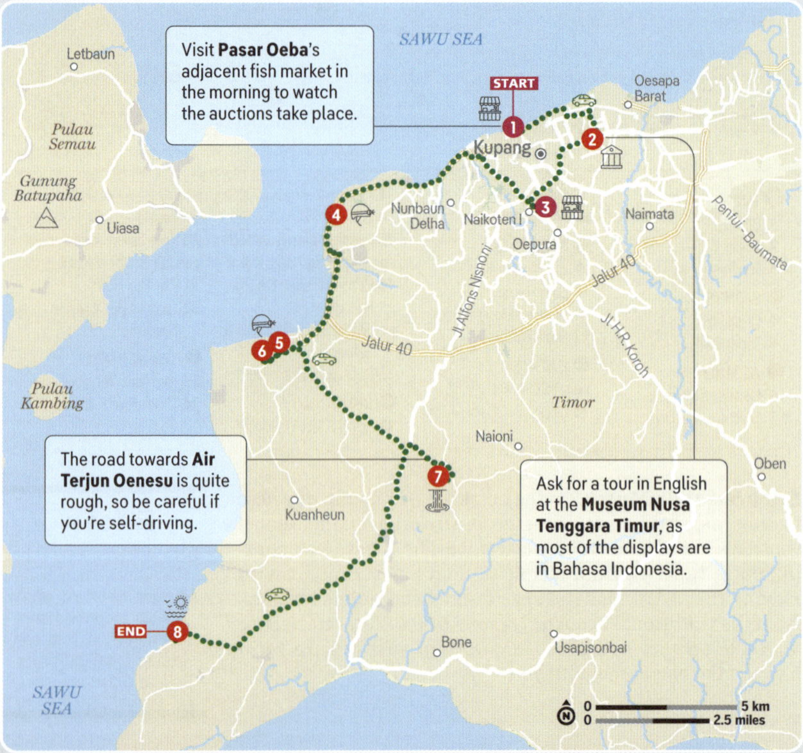

Visit **Pasar Oeba**'s adjacent fish market in the morning to watch the auctions take place.

The road towards **Air Terjun Oenesu** is quite rough, so be careful if you're self-driving.

Ask for a tour in English at the **Museum Nusa Tenggara Timur**, as most of the displays are in Bahasa Indonesia.

SAWU SEA
START
END
Letbaun
Pulau Semau
Gunung Batupaha
Uiasa
Kupang
Oesapa Barat
Nunbaun Delha
Naikoten I
Oepura
Naimata
Penfui - Baumata
Jalur 40
Jl Alfons Nisnoni
Jl H.R. Koroh
Pulau Kambing
Timor
Naioni
Oben
Kuanheun
Bone
Usapisonbai
SAWU SEA
0 5 km
0 2.5 miles

Hang Out with (Former) Headhunters

Visit a traditional village

Near the market town of Niki-Niki, a gravel road runs for 1km past corn, pumpkin and bean fields to the village of **None**, one of the area's most compelling attractions. You'll stop by one of the *ume bubu* (beehive-shaped huts) at the roadside to greet the village chief. In some ways, this appears to be a typical Dawan village, its cramped and smoky *ume bubu* without windows and its 1m-high doorways sitting alongside modern concrete houses. At the end of the road, you reach the ceremonial grounds that end abruptly in the vine-covered sheer cliff that made the village easy to defend from enemies. It's so peaceful here that it's hard to believe they were hunting heads just two generations ago – the last conflict was in 1944.

If you have a local guide with you, they'll point out the *lopo* (village meeting place) and explain that None has a proud population of 56 families who have lived here for 10 generations and who still adhere to traditional practices.

At the cliff's edge, you'll find a 300-year-old banyan tree and totem pole where shamans once met with warriors before they left on headhunting expeditions. Nearby is a stone platform where enemy heads were once displayed. Proceed to the *ote naus*, an awning beneath which guns and spears were stored. It is here that elders consulted chicken eggs and a wooden staff before predicting if the warriors would prevail. If there was a speck of blood in the egg, a sign of poor fortune, they'd delay their attack. The village women may bring out their looms as you're leaving, with weaving demonstrations upon request (a 50,000Rp donation is appropriate) and a decent selection of ikat cloth for sale.

WEST TIMOR'S FORMER HEADHUNTERS

The village of None is home to the animist Dawan people who have lived here for at least 250 years. Set atop a high promontory, its strategic location came in handy for fighting off attackers during a time when tribal wars were rife. Headhunting among the men of the village was commonplace in this area, a way of intimidating and asserting power over other tribes. Although it's now a thing of the past (the practice was banned in 1942), there's still a strong sense of pride among the residents of None that the village has never been conquered by rival tribes.

Drop in on Highland Royalty

Not just cats may look at a king

Some 50km northeast of Kefa, accessible via a two-hour drive along a periodically rough road and across windswept ridges, **Tamkesi** is one of West Timor's most isolated and best-preserved villages. Balancing on a jagged rock path, you pass through a keyhole between jutting limestone cliffs to find yourself in the middle of it all. There are two entrances: one is reserved for royalty but often used by travellers; the correct entrance has a sign reading 'Eno Fatnai Naimnune' on a stone platform, from which it's a short uphill walk along a cobblestone pathway under a canopy of trees.

EATING IN SOE & KEFAMENANU: OUR PICKS

Rumah Makan Depot Remaja: Succulent *se'i babi* (Rotinese smoked pork) and *jantung pisang* (banana-flower salad) are standouts at this spot in Soe. *10am-10pm* $$

RM Sari Bundo II: A typical Padang (West Sumatran cuisine) place in Soe where you can choose various sides to go with your rice. *8am-10pm* $

Sisterhood Coffee & Eatery: This Fata Morgana of a city cafe in Kefa serves bona fide espresso coffees, katsu sandwiches and fried rice. *11am-11pm Mon-Sat, 1-11pm Sun* $$

Bekhaus: A bakery cafe in Kefa with hot and iced coffees and teas, plus snacks like fries and chicken wings. *hours vary* $

Maubesi Market

RHADEX/SHUTTERSTOCK

BEST IKAT SHOPPING

West Timor is renowned for its ikat, whether sarong decorated with complex geometric patterns or antique *kelim* (tapestries). Quality varies, as do the dyes and yarn: pricier pieces use local cotton; others use imports from China.

Maubesi Market: Sells some quality ikat that a keen eye may spot.

Kain Tenun Tradisional: Stocks some truly excellent pieces that take a year to make.

Galeri Alekot: Options for all budgets; in Soe.

Ina Ndao: Sources ikat, as well as patterned espadrilles, shirts and ties; in Kupang.

Pak Haji Noer: A Kupang-based ikat expert who stocks collectors' pieces from across Nusa Tenggara, including antiques woven using ancient techniques no longer practised.

The house of the raja (king) overlooks the village, with the east and west pillars representing the male and female, respectively. Clamber up the stone steps to meet the turbaned raja and his family, where you'll offer betel nut (buy it in Manufui, the last village off the main road before turning off for Tamkesi) and make a donation *(per person 50,000Rp)*. After the obligatory respectful chewing (p312), you can shoot pictures of the low-slung beehive huts built into the bedrock and connected by red-clay paths that ramble to the edge of a precipice. Just don't take pictures of the conical hut where the village's sacred objects are stored, lest bad luck befall you. The same applies if you drop something; don't pick it up immediately, instead alert local villagers, who will first pray to the ancestors for forgiveness.

You can't miss the soaring, craggy limestone cliff. At least once every seven years, the king and the village elders climb the face of **Tapenpah**, sans rope, with a goat, rooster, branches of betel nut, bamboo, coconut, sugar cane and cotton. Depending on the size of the offering, this is done in multiples of seven. Other members of the community also ascend in multiples of seven. They slaughter the goat (but not the rooster), chew betel nut and only come down once everything has been eaten. This **Natamamausa** ritual is performed to give thanks for a good harvest, or to stop (or start) the rain.

If you want to climb the other notable rock face, **Oepuah**, enlist the help of a young villager, but only attempt it if you're a keen scrambler. The view over the village from the top, not to mention the 360-degree views, is invigorating. Tip your adventurous leader 20,000Rp.

Very little Bahasa Indonesia is spoken here, so a guide is essential. The overall mood is warm and welcoming.

TIMOR-LESTE VISA RUN

Crossing the border to Timor-Leste is no longer complicated. It's cheapest to cross at Napan, 20km north of Kefamenanu; or Atapupu, which costs just 60,000Rp by *ojek* from Atambua.

You can also make the 12-hour, one-way journey to Dili, Timor-Leste, for 250,000Rp; arrange 4am pickup with **Timor Tour & Travel** via your lodgings.

Short on time? Catch the 45-minute morning Wings Air flight from Kupang to Atambua, cross the border, and fly back to Kupang.

Europeans from the Schengen Area may visit Timor-Leste visa-free for 30 days. Visitors from other countries are issued a visa on arrival at the border, once they pay US$30 and present proof of onward journey.

Kupang's Underwater World

Indonesia's only freshwater cave diving

While West Timor's dive sites cannot compete with Alor, its lack of currents do make them beginner-friendly. Kupang is also the only place in Indonesia to offer freshwater cave dives, with up to 50m visibility, limestone tunnels, narrow swim-throughs and stalactite formations. With its fossilised, shell-encrusted walls, a 75m-long channel, a submerged chamber and an air chamber, **Goa Kristal** is the easier dive of the two. **Goa Uihani** – a 500m-long sinkhole with three air chambers – is best suited to experienced cave divers, due to

EATING IN KUPANG & AROUND: OUR PICKS

Subasuka Paradise: Seafood restaurant right by the sea with a huge menu and Indonesian noodles and rice dishes. *10am-10pm* $$

Depot Se'i Babi Aroma: Contemporary Kupang chain specialising in *se'i babi*, *sate babi* (pork satay) and other porky bites. *9am-8.30pm* $

Kelapa Restaurant & Sky Lounge: Seaview restaurant serving steaks and Indonesian dishes, plus a swimming pool and live music. *8.30am-11pm* $$

Pasar Malam Seafood: Come evening, head for this lamplit seafood market for *ikan* (fish), *cumi* (squid), *kepiting* (crab) and *udang* (prawns). *5pm-midnight* $

THE ART OF BETEL-NUT CHEWING

Before visiting a Dawan village, purchase a generous amount of *pinang* (dried or fresh betel nut) and *sirih* (betel nut leaves and flowers) at any market or roadside stall. It's customary to offer betel nut to the leader or king of a village as a goodwill gesture. It is avidly chewed by many in West Timor in conjunction with lime powder, which lessens the bitterness but can burn if it touches your gums. After acceptance, your host will probably offer you a chew: it's supposed to generate a warm buzz similar to a cigarette head-spin, but most first-timers will find it a bitter experience, their mouths numb and flooded with crimson saliva. Spitting is okay.

JHON ELIASS/SHUTTERSTOCK

Goa Kristal (p311)

difficult access and narrow tunnels. Kupang's dive operators are **Dive Kupang** *(divekupangdive.com; freshwater cave dive 2,000,000Rp)* and **Cendana Dive** *(WhatsApp +62 821 4750 4428; dives from 2,000,000Rp).*

Visit the Last King in West Timor

Explore the traditional village of Boti

A two-hour ride into the mountains from Soe via an undulating, unpaved road, you'll find the traditional village of **Boti**. Here, Ama Namah Benu, the charismatic *kepala suku* (chief), often referred to as the 'last king in West Timor', maintains the strict laws of *adat*.

Bring a guide conversant with local *adat* and the language spoken in the village. On arrival, you'll be led to the king's house, where you will offer betel nut as a gift. You'll then enjoy sweet coffee with steamed cassava cakes, served by the king's sister.

Day-trippers are expected to contribute a donation *(50,000Rp);* staying overnight (or longer) in the simple thatched guesthouse allows you to delve deeper into the life of a village that has resisted Christianisation, whose 300 or so inhabitants still follow ancient animist rituals, and whose king has only recently allowed just one child from each family to attend primary and middle school (but not high school, to avoid the clash between mainstream education and ancestral lore). Boti's autonomy is partially due to Dutch colonial powers failing to find the village in times past.

Boti children are named after elements in their natural surroundings. The men grow their hair long after marriage, symbolising their connection to nature. Conversely, when a woman is pregnant, a hair-cutting ceremony is held for the woman's youngest child: a sign for the community to help

THE GRAND TOUR OF WEST TIMOR

Drive through West Timor's interiors and around its coastline to take it all in.

START	END	LENGTH
Kupang	Kupang	625km; 5 days

This loop of West Timor covers market towns, traditional villages and stunning beaches. Begin in ❶ **Kupang**, West Timor's bustling capital. Pause in ❷ **Oebelo**, a small salt-mining town 22km from Kupang on the Soe road, to visit the *sasando* workshop (p306), then proceed to the cool, leafy market town of ❸ **Soe**, the gateway to some of the fascinating traditional villages of the interior. Seventeen kilometres east of Soe, take the turnoff for ❹ **None** (p309), a former headhunting village, before passing through the market town of ❺ **Niki-Niki** – market day is Wednesday. The winding road continues through the lush interior to ❻ **Kefamenanu**, a visually unimpressive former Portuguese stronghold that's nonetheless a decent overnighter. Just 3.5km from Kefa is ❼ **Maslete Village**, a traditional village with a thatch-roofed *sonaf* (palace), made from wood carved with mythical birds. Nineteen kilometres east of Kefa, ❽ **Maubesi** is home to the Kefa Regency's best textile market. Market day is Thursday, when, along with produce, animals and pottery, ikat is displayed beneath tamarind trees. If you're not passing by on a Thursday, Maubesi Art Shop, on the eastern outskirts, has a terrific selection of local ikat. Turn north 11km east to visit ❾ **Tamkesi** (p309), a traditional village in a lofty setting, before retracing your steps to just north of Niki-Niki. If it's Thursday, consider making the bone-shaking detour to ❿ **Ayotupas** to check out the clamour of the weekly produce market. Just south of Niki-Niki, take the minor road east into the mountains to the animist village of ⓫ **Boti** (p312). From Boti, descend to the stunning white-sand ⓬ **Pantai Kolbano**, then return to Kupang, past the dune-backed ⓭ **Pantai Oetune** and through West Timor's vast rice-growing plains.

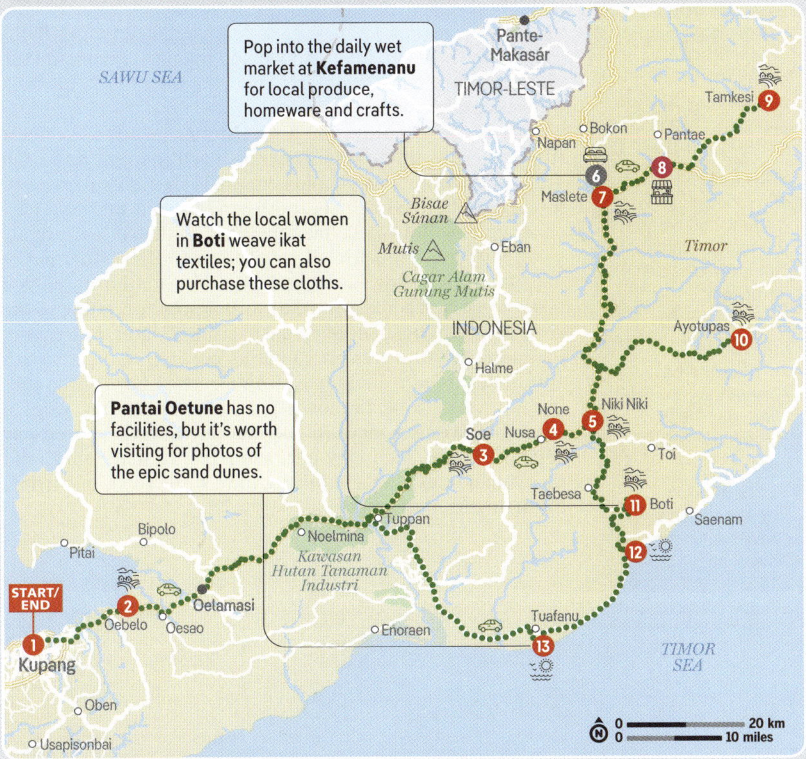

Pop into the daily wet market at **Kefamenanu** for local produce, homeware and crafts.

Watch the local women in **Boti** weave ikat textiles; you can also purchase these cloths.

Pantai Oetune has no facilities, but it's worth visiting for photos of the epic sand dunes.

WEST TIMOR'S BEST GUIDES

West Timor's traditional villages are a minefield of cultural dos and don'ts. A local guide is essential; some charge 2,000,000Rp per day.

Edwin Lerrick: The irrepressible owner of Kupang's Lavalon Hostel (p330) has deep regional knowledge and connections throughout West Timor. *(lavalonbar@gmail.com)*

Ony Meda: A guide with over two decades of experience organising anthropological tours and treks. *(WhatsApp +62 8133 940 4204)*

Willy Kadati: Willy specialises in cultural, botanic and ikat tours of West Timor. *(willdk678@gmail.com)*

Aka Nahak: Enthusiastic, Kefamenanu-based Aka has been touring Timor since 1988. *(timorguide@gmail.com)*

Yabes Olbata: Soe-based guide conversant in the Dawan language, charging 1,200,000Rp per day. *(WhatsApp +62 8133 894 9694)*

LEONARDUS NYOMAN/SHUTTERSTOCK

Boti

out where they can. Men and women may marry outside the village, but women are expected to bring their husbands back to live with them.

Early in the morning, you'll see the men go off to the fields to grow crops, including bananas, corn, papaya and cash crops of peanuts. The people here are incredibly self-reliant, having in the past refused both government and NGO assistance. The Boti week has nine days, with every ninth day devoted to rest, music and spiritual activities. During the day, you'll be followed around by curious children as you observe women cooking at the outdoor kitchen, going to the river to bring back bamboo buckets full of water, or weaving ikat sarongs. Children as young as six help out: girls with spinning thread from locally grown cotton, boys with tending animals. Come sundown, the men return, and women serve the evening meal in coconut-shell bowls. If you pay 100,000Rp, the men may perform a traditional dance, and the women may sing a haunting tune while the king strums his stringed instrument.

Beyond West Timor

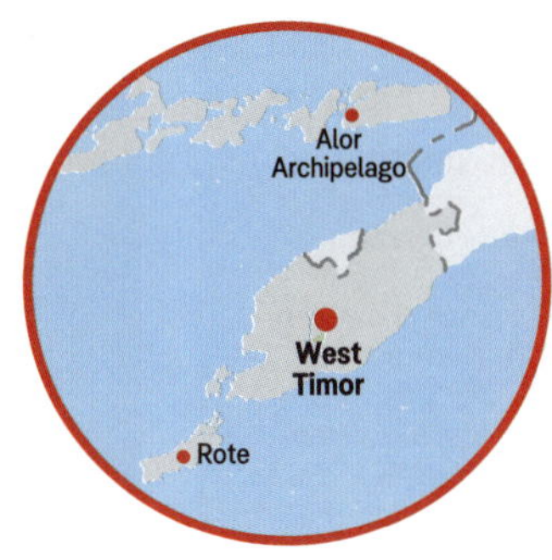

Incomparable underwater worlds, a world-renowned surf break and tiny, seldom-visited islands await, a mere short plane or ferry hop from Kupang.

If you're a diver, you will have heard of the Alor Archipelago, north of West Timor, and its epic dive sites such as Fish Bowl and Mike's Delight. Odds are, you're heading there right now aboard a liveaboard, all set for underwater exploration, or else staying in a diving lodge on one of its islands. But there's so much more to this tiny, isolated cluster of islands, whose 134 tribes speak 18 languages and 52 dialects, and where animist practices still thrive in fortress-like, hilltop villages. Southwest of West Timor, the parched limestone speck that is Rote draws surfers with its legendary T-Land break, relaxed vibe and white-sand beaches.

Places

Alor Archipelago p315
Rote p316

GETTING AROUND

Public minibuses ply the Bo'a–Nemberala route on Rote *(with/without surfboard 120,000/70,000Rp)*; alternatively, arrange pickup with your accommodation for 450,000Rp or direct transfers from Kupang for US$100 and up. Homestays and hotels can arrange motorbike or scooter rental for around 100,000Rp per day. A daily fast ferry (9am) connects Kupang to Bo'a (two hours) and Kalabahi (15 to 18 hours, Tuesday and Saturday). Daily flights link Kupang with Alor.

Alor Archipelago

TIME FROM WEST TIMOR: **50MIN**

Alor Archipelago beneath the waves

One of Indonesia's most astonishing underwater archipelagos, the **Alor Archipelago** has it all: tremendous visibility, a vast array of dive sites, world-class coral reefs abuzz with shoals of reef fish, stunning walls, and frequent sightings of reef sharks, rays and turtles, as well as the occasional dolphin pod and whale. Best of all, you'll have it all pretty much to yourself. Strong, unpredictable currents mean that many sites are best suited to experienced divers, although correct timings open up parts of this world to novices and intermediate divers. Day dives from **Pulau Pantar** and **Pulau Kepa** aside, the Alor Archipelago is best experienced aboard a liveaboard. There are a handful of liveaboard companies sailing around Eastern Indonesia that include Alor in their itineraries, such as **Coralia Liveaboard** *(coralia-liveaboard.com; from 11,300,000Rp)*.

One of Alor's most exhilarating drift dives is the aptly named **Fish Bowl**, in the channel between Alor and Kepa. As you float along the sloping reef covered in soft corals, look out for scorpionfish, lone titan triggerfish and midnight snappers as schools of neon-blue fusiliers stream around you and Moorish idols flit by. On the east coast of Pulau Pura, **Mike's**

ARRANGE YOUR BEST ALOR ADVENTURE

Alor Divers: Operated by a French-Slovenian couple on Pulau Timur's eastern shore, Alor caters exclusively to divers, with a range of sites and courses. *(alor-divers.com)*

Lazy Turtle Dive Alor: This Alor Kecil-Pulau Kepa-based French-UK operation runs daily dives and offers accommodation packages. Book in advance as their six dive spaces fill up quickly. *(lazyturtledive.com)*

Mila Salim: Mila Salim is a local guide who can arrange cultural excursions across Alor. She runs Kalabahi's first souvenir shop, supporting local craftspeople. *(milasalim619@gmail.com)*

Gabriel Tang: Kalabahi-based guide who can arrange cultural itineraries of Alor, including visits to traditional houses and dugong trips. *(gabriellobangtang@gmail.com)*

Alor Dream Trip: Kalabahi-based local guides who can take you around the islands for snorkelling, wildlife and land-based adventures. *(alordreamtrip.com)*

VONNY I/SHUTTERSTOCK

Delight is another excellent reef drift dive with visibility up to 40m and an abundance of hard and soft corals that are alive with parrotfish, damselfish, angelfish and Napoleon wrasse; schools of jacks, passing reef sharks and dolphin pods can be spotted in the deep blue. A stunning slope reef suitable for beginners, combined with a challenging wall dive, **Symphony No 9** off Pulau Pantar offers tremendous coral diversity and density, along with seemingly endless schools of damselfish and basslets, and the opportunity to be suspended beneath the overhang at 15m, scanning the fathomless depths for pelagic life. **Kal's Dream**, a seamount between Pura and Kepa, is also wonderful for passing large pelagics, barracuda, Spanish mackerel, giant trevallies and schooling jacks, with octopus, morays and shrimp hiding in the 12m-deep plateau. Strong currents sweeping over the top of the pinnacle warrant a quick descent.

Rote

TIME FROM WEST TIMOR: **2HR** 

Hanging ten in Nemberala

Between March and November, the consistent southwest swell brings reliable waves to the white-sand beach of the chilled-out fishing village of **Nemberala** on the west coast of **Rote** island, along with a contingent of surfers.

Unlike some other Indonesian surfing hotspots, Nemberala is a friendly place, without locals guarding their favourite surf spots. Breaking at all tides, the main wave here is the legendary **T-Land**, one of Indonesia's longest left-handers, divided into the Peak, the Pyramid and the Mountain (accessible to surfers of different abilities). Nearby is **The Bommie**,

Alor Archipelago (p315)

a short right-hander reef break, particularly fun at low tide with big swells. If you prefer a heavier, hollow, intense right-hander with few others in the lineup, head for **Sucky Mama's**, 3km north of Nemberala, accessed only via a 10-minute boat ride. Another hollow right, **Do'o**, breaks off an uninhabited island a 20-minute boat ride from Nemberala and is perfect for intermediate and expert surfers. Beginners take note: just north of the Nemberala fishing-boat harbour is **Squealers**, a right- and left-hander thus named for the screeches made by novices catching their first wave. About 8km south of Nemberala, **Bo'a** has a spectacular white-sand beach and a mid-tide right-hander with a good tube section, accessed either by paddling out or a 10-minute boat ride. The local surf resorts such as **Manduna Resort** *(mandunaresort.com)* can take you out to other world-class waves that fluctuate according to the wind and tide. Many resorts rent high-quality boards from about 100,000Rp per day.

THE WONDROUS LONTAR PALM

Rote remains dependent on the drought-resistant *lontar* palm. The palm is extremely versatile; its tough yet flexible leaves are woven to make sacks and bags, hats and sandals, roofs and dividing walls. *Lontar* wood is fashioned into furniture and floorboards. But what nourishes the islanders is the milky, frothy *nirah* (sap) tapped from the *tankai* (orange-stemmed inflorescences) that grow from the crown of the *lontar*. Drunk straight from the tree, the *nirah* is refreshing, nutritious and energising. If left to ferment for hours, it becomes *laru* (palm wine), which is hawked around the lanes of Rote. With further distillation, the juice is distilled into gin-like *sopi* – the power behind many a wild Rote night.

EATING IN NEMBERALA: OUR PICKS

Blu Oceano: Authentic Italian dishes, homemade bread and pastries, plus desserts, made with ingredients from their garden. *7am-11pm* $$

Luwababa The Cave: Fresh seafood cooked in a Western Asian fusion style, plus pastas, sandwiches and salads, all under a giant thatched roof. *hours vary* $$

The Pasar: Enjoy excellent coffee, sandwiches, couscous and feta salads and other international dishes at this open-sided, breezy spot. *hours vary.* $$

Sagarika: Heritage Indonesian dishes cooked in a stunning open-air kitchen with seats among coconut palms. *8am-9pm* $$

Sumba

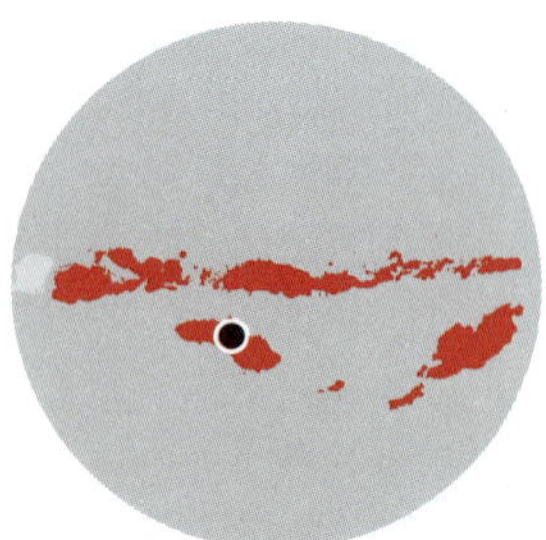

TRADITIONAL VILLAGES | MEMORABLE FESTIVALS | UNTAMED NATURE

GETTING AROUND

Buses connect Waingapu with Kalala and with Tambolaka (five hours) via Waikabubak. Most hotels arrange motorbike and scooter rental *(per day 200,000Rp)*. Car rental is around 1,000,000Rp per day including the driver's pay; it's hard to rent a car without a driver.

There are daily flights from Waingapu to Ende (Flores), Denpasar (Bali), Praya (Lombok) and Kupang (West Timor). Ferries run to Ende and Kupang. There are daily flights from Tambolaka to Denpasar, Praya and Kupang, and ferries to Sape in Sumbawa (three weekly, nine hours).

TOP TIP

You need a guide to visit traditional villages. Some will not accept visitors if their guide has no contacts within the community. A set donation and signing the visitor book are part of village visits.

There's something truly enchanting about Sumba. Its intricately woven ikat textiles are displayed in museums worldwide as exemplars of their kind; its verdant, hilly interior – so unlike Indonesia's northern volcanic isles – is populated by roaming horses and dotted with traditional hilltop villages of tall grass roofs clustered around megalithic tombs. Its Christian villagers still adhere to indigenous *marapu* (spiritual force) practices, and animal sacrifice is common. In February and March, warriors on horseback clash en masse while wielding blunt spears during the annual Pasola festival.

Culturally fascinating, Sumba is no slouch when it comes to natural attractions, either. It's encircled by pristine white-sand beaches and pounded by relentless breaks that have been drawing surfers for years, while secret swimming holes, waterfalls and caves beckon further inland. Friendly and low-key, this part of Nusa Tenggara is particularly vulnerable to change. Developers have their eye on Sumba, so go without delay.

A Perfect Day Around Waingapu

Traditional villages, historic sites and viewpoint

East Sumba's transport hub, **Waingapu**, is a laid-back town with a leafy, dusty centre interspersed with accommodation and small *toko* (shops). It also has a busy produce market, a harbour that becomes redolent with grilled fish after sundown, and villages in the middle of it all. From Waingapu, you can launch trips along the north coast and into the interior, seeing traditional villages and archaeological sites all in one day.

Near the Praikundu Ikat Centre (p326), 6km south of Waingapu, an awning protects the small archaeological site of **Lambanapu**, whose compact size belies its considerable importance. Extensive archaeological excavations (between 2016 and 2022) have taken place here. It's the burial site of an ancient civilisation of East Sumba's prehistoric people.

JOEYMONO/SHUTTERSTOCK

Tanau Hills

The physical remains of 45 individuals have been unearthed, along with weaponry, household items and jewellery. The jar burials, no longer practised on Sumba, are thought to date back to the earliest presence of humans in Sumba, and it is hoped that the discovery will shed light on the arrival of Austronesian speakers.

For lunch, head southeast along the coast to grab some hot and sour fish soup at the thatched **Amu Dahi** in Melolo village, then proceed to **Praiyawang**, a traditional Sumbanese village near Melolo. It has an imposing line-up of nine stone tombs, the largest being that of the chief of this former kingdom. Shaped like a buffalo, it consists of four stone pillars (2m high) supporting a monstrous slab (about 5m long and 2.5m wide). Two stone tablets stand atop the main slab, carved with figures. A massive Sumbanese house with concrete pillars faces the tombs, along with a number of *rumah adat* and an uninhabited ceremonial house. Within the tombs, it's permitted to bury siblings, grandchildren and grandparents together, but the deceased can't be buried alongside their parents. Crocodile statues represent the king; turtles are only seen on women's tombs; and the cockatoos and horses symbolise democracy.

On your way back to Waingapu, take the bumpy track to the **Tanau Hills** for exceptional panoramic views of Sumba's unique topography.

SUMBANESE IKAT

Displayed in museums around the world as examples of the highest-quality textile, Sumbanese ikat is recognised as the best in Indonesia. East Sumbanese ikat depicts village scenes, mythological creatures, Pasola tournaments and tribal wars. West Sumbanese ikat does not adhere to the complex ikat-making process and is much simpler, featuring geometric patterns. The most authentic ikat is still made with natural dyes, with each strand of yarn dyed individually before being affixed to the loom. The bark and roots of the mengkudu tree produce red dye; indigo plants produce blue dye; and a mix of indigo and mengkudu produces brown and purple dyes. The ikat-weaving process is now partially mechanised, which is why vintage ikat pieces fetch collector's prices.

EATING IN WAINGAPU: OUR PICKS

Kopi Dari Hati Sumba: A coffee shop with a selection of mains, snacks and desserts, with live music every evening. *hours vary* $

PC Corner: Killer views, selfie-worthy murals, live music and dishes such as papaya flower with *kangkung* (water spinach) are big draws here. *9am-10pm Mon-Sat* $$

La Paranda: Order chicken, prawns or squid in various guises, along with garlicky *kangkung* at this breezy restaurant. *10am-10pm Mon-Sat, 4-10pm Sun* $$

Kedai Sei Babi Karunia: Buy *se'i babi* (Rotinese smoked pork) by weight, or opt for other porky dishes. *9am-8pm Mon-Sat* $

SUMBA

Taman Nasional Perairan Laut Sawu
Selat Sumba
Waikelo
Tambolaka
Radamata
Mananca
Wanuuka
MEMBORO
Lenang
KODI
Kori
Waimangura
WEJEWA BARAT
Bondowoeg
Maderi
WEST SUMBA
Tanareu
Waibanca
Pasunga
Weeleo
Praigege
Waikabubak
LOLI
Gallu Bakul
Taman Nasinal Tana Daro
Wainyapu
Denduka
Dikira
GAURA
LEMBOYA
Padede Weri
Makatakeri
ANAKALANG
Panenggoede
Taramanu
Gunung Watumandeta
Gaura
Patiala
WANOKAKA
Taman Nasional Manupeu Tana Daru
See Wanokaka Area Enlargement
Konda
Watumbelar
INDIAN OCEAN
Tidas

Wanokaka Area

Kadenga
Praigoli
Waigalli
Pedede Watu
Kabukarudi
Waihura
Rua
Nihiwatu
Kadolu
Kebun Warga
0 2 km
0 1 mile

HIGHLIGHTS
1 Lambanapu

SIGHTS
2 Air Terjun Tanggedu
3 Air Terjun Wai Marang
4 Kampung Praigoli
5 Kampung Waigalli
6 Laipopu Waterfall
7 Pantai Dassang
8 Pantai Kalala
9 Pantai Kerewe
10 Pantai Marosi
11 Pantai Nihiwatu
12 Pantai Pahiri
13 Pantai Pero
14 Pantai Rua
15 Pantai Tarimbang
16 Pantai Wainyapu
17 Prailiu
18 Praiyawang
19 Sodana
20 Tanau Hills
21 Waihura

ACTIVITIES
22 Explore Sumba
see 15 Miller's Rights
23 Occy's Left
see 8 Racetrack
24 Sumba Adventure Tours & Travel
see 8 The Office
see 24 Tour Sumba
see 22 Yuliana Leda Tara

SLEEPING
25 Amuya Homestay
see 15 Camp Tarimbang
26 Casa Kandara
27 Lambo Homestay
28 Maringi Sumba
29 Nihi Sumba
30 Oro Beach Houses
see 17 Praikamarru Guest House
31 Sumba Sunset Surf Camp
see 9 Sumba Surf Camp
32 Wajonata Sumba

EATING
33 Alamayah
34 Amu Dahi
35 Dapur Sumba
see 22 D'Sumba Ate
36 Kedai Sei Babi Karunia
37 Kopi Dari Hati Sumba
38 La Paranda
see 24 Makan Dulu
39 PC Corner
40 Resto Ne'neru Loco
see 22 Soemba Coffee & Resto
41 Talasi Estate at Weetabula
see 35 Warung Gula Garam

ENTERTAINMENT
42 Pasola

SHOPPING
43 Praikundu Ikat Centre

KAMPUNG ADAT

Sumbanese villages were traditionally built on hillsides (to see approaching enemies) and consist of two rows of houses with their thatched roofs, or are arranged in a rough circle surrounding the tombs and *kateda* (sacrificial altars) in the centre. Villages typically have several clans living there, and each clan has its own *rumah adat*, where sacred objects are kept and ancestral spirits dwell.

Houses are constructed from bamboo tied together with vines and finished with tall traditional roofs, their bamboo scaffolding covered with dried alang-alang grass. The main struts represent different elements, while the hearth in the centre represents the sun. The underfloor section is for animals; the ground floor, for humans.

Do Go Chasing Waterfalls

Explore waterfalls near Waingapu

A couple of hours' drive (60km) northwest of Waingapu, along rough roads, and a further 20-minute trek through savannah or grasslands, depending on the time of year, is **Air Terjun Tanggedu**, arguably Sumba's best waterfall. What awaits will blow you away: two rivers run between time-layered limestone cliffs and converge into waterfall terraces that feed into multiple pools; there are dipping pools nearby.

Alternatively, get an early start and follow the north coast southeastwards in the direction of Kalala to the town of **Melolo** (where you sometimes see sunbathing crocodiles on the riverbanks), near Praiyawang (p319). Take the smooth, unpeopled road inland for 8km to the parking area overlooking a verdant valley, pay the entrance fee *(50,000Rp)* and descend for around 15 minutes along some concrete steps, followed by a steep trail, to reach **Air Terjun Wai Marang**, a startlingly blue dipping pool in the middle of the jungle, surrounded by limestone walls and fed by a waterfall.

Wander Wanokaka's Villages & Beaches

Traditional culture and slivers of sand

South of Waikabubak, you'll encounter some of Sumba's most striking scenery, the oldest megalithic tombs, pristine beaches and world-class surfing. Taking the main road south, turn off after 8km and follow the narrower paved road west. Passing some Pasola grandstands, with rice-paddy vistas opening up and locals swimming in the river, you'll reach **Hapumada**, where the road forks. The rougher, partially paved northward fork leads towards the jungly trailhead to **Laipopu waterfall**. South and downhill from Hapumada is **Waigalli**, a traditional village on a promontory above the sea; further south is the fishing village of **Waihura**, at the western end of the vast, wave-battered, white-sand **Pantai Pahiri**, where the village youth practise bareback horse riding.

A shortcut up a bumpy, unpaved road from Waigalli brings you to **Praigoli**, home to Sumba's most famous megalithic statue – the fleur-de-lis *Lakaruka Jiwa Tada Bita Laka*. If you happen to be in one of the traditional villages while a roof is being repaired, you may come across a roof-fixing ceremony involving a dog sacrifice and the playing of gongs, or all of the village men partaking in the fixing while the women cook for everyone in an outdoor kitchen. From Praigoli, take a bumpy,

EATING IN WAIKABUBAK & WANOKAKA: OUR PICKS

Soemba Coffee & Resto: Score a proper espresso at this modern spot, or settle in for a meal of chicken sate or *nasi goreng* (fried rice). *10am-10pm* $$

D'Sumba Ate: Waikabubak Wood-fired pizzas, seafood, noodles and rice dishes under an open-air, thatched bamboo roof. *noon-10pm* $$

Alamayah: Strong cocktails, good coffee and a mix of Aussie and Indonesian dishes in refined surroundings. Open to non-guests through bookings only. *6am-10pm* $$

Resto Ne'neru Loco: Chow down on stir-fried sweet and sour dishes with a side of rice-paddy views. *10am-10pm* $

DESTINAZONES/SHUTTERSTOCK

Air Terjun Tanggedu

steep shortcut up a particularly scenic road with great views of Pantai Pahiri, passing the turnoff to **Pantai Rua**, a white-sand beach with a resort and some calmer spots for bathing. Further along, you pass the turnoff for the exclusive resort of **NIHI Sumba** (p331) before rejoining the main road towards Kerewe Beach and the Lamboya district. On your right, you'll spy the traditional roofs of the village of **Sodana** atop a steep hill (reachable by rough 4WD track). You may only visit if your guide has contacts in Sodana, as the locals prioritise preserving their traditional culture. Shortly after, a turnoff south brings you to the surfing hotspot of **Pantai Kerewe** (p325) and Sumba's most touristy part.

Witness a Ritual Horseback Tournament

Let the battle commence

Pasola (from *pa* meaning 'game' and *sola* meaning 'wooden spear') has to be one of the most extravagant (and bloody) harvest festivals in Asia. Held annually in February and March in West Sumba, it takes the form of a ritual battle between two teams of blunt-spear-wielding, ikat-clad horsemen. The bloodier the proceedings, the better the harvest, as the blood is believed to please the spirits. Although the festival is considerably less bloody than it used to be, and blunt spears are now used, it's still a dangerous sport. Spectators should be aware of any potential animal welfare issues, including animal sacrifices.

Pasola takes place in Lamboya and Kodi villages in February and in Kodi Bangedo, Lamboya Barat and Wanokaka villages in March. A *rato* (priest) decides the exact timing based on the arrival of a sea worm called *nyale* on nearby coasts, but these days, tourism comes first, and eager fans are now given up to a month's warning. Dressed in full ceremonial garb, the *rato* wades into the ocean to examine the worms at dawn; they're usually found on the eighth or ninth day after a full moon.

SUMBA'S BEST GUIDES

Erwin Pah: Waingapu-based guide who seems to know everyone in Sumba. Can arrange caving, rock-climbing and village tours. *(erwinpah9@gmail.com)*

Sumba Adventure Tours & Travel: Experienced guide Pilipus Renggi and his team lead trips into seldom-explored villages, arranges itineraries, sets you up for Pasola, rents cars and more. *(sumbaislandtours.com)*

Yuliana Leda Tara: Expert Tarung-based English- and French-speaking guide, in demand from anthropologists and filmmakers; organises West Sumba village tours. *(yuli.sumba@gmail.com)*

Tour Sumba: Hugo and his team of Sumbanese guides offer tour packages across the island, including waterfalls, beaches, villages, caves and more. *(tour-sumba.com)*

Explore Sumba: Well-established tour company who can arrange day trips, honeymoon packages, tailor-made trips, car rentals and hotel bookings. *(exploresumba.com)*

TOUR TRADITIONAL VILLAGES

Take a drive around west Sumba to soak up the culture and magnificent views.

START	END	LENGTH
Waibakul	Kampung Manola	70km; 6hr

Those interested in traditional Sumbanese culture will find numerous traditional villages clustered around Waikabubak and Waibakul, some with exceptional stone tombs. It's best to visit with a guide. Starting in ❶ **Waibakul**, take the paved road 2.5km south through the rice fields to ❷ **Kampung Gallubakul**, home to Sumba's heaviest tomb (70 tonnes). Allegedly, 6000 workers took three years to chisel the Umbu Sawola tomb out of a hillside and drag it 3km, using vines and banana-tree rollers.

Returning to Waibakul, proceed to tin-roofed ❸ **Kampung Pasunga**. Visible from the main road is a particularly impressive tomb with images of a chief and his wife dating from 1926. Take the main Waikabubak road, then turn south up a steep road to ❹ **Kampung Bondo Maroto**, a friendly, somewhat steep, village whose thatched roofs have been restored after a recent fire; overnight stays are possible.

Take a different turnoff from the Waikabubak road to ❺ **Kampung Praijing**. Popular with visitors from Java, it has a lofty viewpoint to admire the rows of thatched houses. Proceed to ❻ **Waikabubak**, a compact market town. Several villages are walkable from Waikabubak: ❼ **Kampung Tambelar**, just off Jl Sudirman, features very impressive *kubur batu* (stone graves).

Uphill, beneath a giant ficus tree, ❽ **Kampung Tarung** is known for its intricately woven palm-containers and is home to a famous male model; homestays possible. Some 17km northwest of Waikabubak, a rough road leads to ❾ **Kampung Manola**, a village so traditional it eschews electricity; it's populated by elders and children, whose parents live elsewhere.

Only in Wanokaka, two days before the main event, opposing 'armies' drawn from coastal and inland villages meet on deserted beaches at night for no-holds-barred, brutal boxing matches called *pajura,* with the combatants' fists bound in thorn-edged palm leaves. Teeth are lost and noses broken, but when dawn breaks, everyone sits on the sand and sings ancestral songs of peace.

The night before the Pasola tournament, participant riders sacrifice chickens to the *rato* in the relevant village, who then consecrates the tournament ground. Early in the morning of the event, spectators gather around the Pasola stadiums, dressed in their best. There's no entrance fee; just get there on time to claim a good vantage point.

Two rows of riders of up to 50 men each, in traditional headgear and their mounts splendidly adorned, charge at each other at breakneck speed, like knights in the Middle Ages. Just when collision feels inevitable and you find yourself holding your breath, they rein in their steeds and hurl the blunt spears at one another. You'll see the most skilled riders not only evade the projectiles with ease but also pluck them out of the air, flinging them back at their opponents. In spite of the violence, the underlying purpose of Pasola battles is peace, with all interclan conflicts considered resolved – until the following year.

MARAPU BELIEFS

The basis of traditional Sumbanese religion is *marapu*, a collective term for Sumba's spiritual forces, including gods, spirits and ancestors. At death, the deceased join the invisible world of spirits, *praing marapu*, from where they can influence the world of the living. *Marapu mameti* is the collective name for all dead people. The living can appeal to *marapu mameti* for help, especially their own relatives, though the dead can be harmful if irritated. The *marapu maluri* are the original people placed on Earth by God, and their power is concentrated in certain places or objects, which are often kept safe in the family's thatched loft. Offerings to the spirits involve betel nut and/or animal sacrifice.

Catch the Surf in Sumba

Surf's up

The beaches on West Sumba's south coast are on their way to being discovered, and not just by surfers (who've been coming here for years). In **Pantai Kerewe**, while the waves are surfable year-round, the best time is March to November, when longboarders come to ride the long, mellow right-hander out front for up to 600m. A 15-minute speedboat ride out to sea, and you have access to a dozen empty left- and right-hander reef breaks for most abilities, including some heavy barrels. North up the coast, **Pantai Pero** has nice lefts and rights on opposite sides of the river mouth, while **Pantai Wainyapu** is good for consistent and clean lefts.

A 30-minute walk from Pantai Kerewe, the white-sand **Pantai Marosi** has a nice beach break, suitable for rookies. At **Pantai Dassang**, a wide sweep of white sand fronted by a resort, there's more beachside action; drive up to the north end of the beach using a public road unless staying at the resort.

EATING IN TAMBOLAKA: OUR PICKS

Talasi Estate at Weetabula: A cashew farm with delicious coffee grown on-site, served with homemade cashew milk. *8am-6pm Mon-Fri, 9am-6pm Sat-Sun* $

Warung Gula Garam: Run by expat Frenchman Louis, this open-air cafe near the airport plays R&B tunes and serves good wood-fired pizza. *10am-9pm* $$

Makan Dulu: Braised lamb in coconut milk and Sumbanese cassava leaf and rice cream soup are standouts at this bamboo-roofed restaurant. *11am-9.30pm Mon-Sat* $$

Dapur Sumba: Clean, air-conditioned eatery serving Indonesian and Sumbanese dishes with huge portions. *9am-9pm Mon-Sat, 10am-9.30pm Sun* $$

SUMBA'S MEGALITHIC TOMBS

Megalithic culture on the island of Sumba goes back some 4500 years, and in numerous Sumbanese villages, you'll come across megalithic tombs, many of them highly elaborate in appearance. The tombs are rectangular and the grave is covered with a stone plate to resemble an altar or table, with the stone weighing many tonnes. The erection of these cover stones has traditionally required the sacrifice of buffalo, cows and pigs, with the stones pulled over long distances using tree trunks and lianas to the tune of rhythmic song. Today, trucks are often used to transport the cover stones, but the ceremonies and singing still take place. Once the cover stone is in place, the grave is engraved with scenes from the life of the deceased.

CALLAGHAN WALSH/GETTY IMAGES

Surfing, Pantai Nihiwatu

The region's legendary, world-class surf spot is **Occy's Left**, featured in the film *The Green Iguana*, off the achingly stunning **Pantai Nihiwatu**, but unless you have deep pockets and are staying at **NIHI Sumba** (p331), it'll remain a dream.

On Pantai Kerewe, the best digs for surfers are **Sumba Sunset Surf Camp** *(WhatsApp +62 821 4754 6538)*, run by Petu, locally known as 'Raja di Laut' ('King of the Sea'); he spent eight years working as a lifeguard at NIHI Sumba and can sort out boat transport to the best breaks. Arnaud of **Sumba Surf Camp** *(sumbasurfcamp.com)* is another expert surfer who knows the local breaks; lessons for beginners can be arranged.

Further south along the coast is **Miller's Rights** – a series of rights breaking off **Pantai Tarimbang** and arguably Sumba's most popular wave; the lineup gets busy from May to October.

On Sumba's east coast, **The Office** is a fun wave at the western end of the reef off **Pantai Kalala** – for intermediates and up – while nearby **Racetrack** is a faster, more intense ride.

Shop for Ikat in East Sumba

Seek out Sumba's best textiles

While in the past, only high-ranking members of Sumbanese society were able to afford ikat, today it's much more affordable. Near Waingapu, **Prailiu** village has numerous weavers, and prices start from 200,000Rp for small pieces; if you buy direct, the weavers get 100% of the profits. Run by English-speaking Kornelis Ndapakamang, **Praikundu Ikat Centre** *(WhatsApp +62 812 3758 4629; from 1,500,000Rp)* on the outskirts of Waingapu is hung with some of Sumba's most prized ikat, all naturally dyed with detailed motifs. Kornelis is renowned for some of the island's finest pieces, the largest of which go for millions of rupiah. Lengthier ikat workshops are available upon request with the help of Erwin Pah (p323).

TAMBOLAKA TO KEREWE BEACH – THE SLOW WAY

Visit Sumba's villages and natural wonders with this driving tour.

START	END	LENGTH
Tambolaka	Pantai Kerewe	127km; 8hr

This day-long road trip follows the route less travelled from Tambolaka to Kerewe, taking in the west coast's diverse sites. On the outskirts of 1 **Tambolaka**, Sumba's second city, 2 **Rumah Budaya Sumba** is a cultural museum that's an excellent introduction to traditional Sumbanese culture, spiritual beliefs and ikat.

Next door, enjoy a cashew-milk coffee at the 3 **Talasi Estate** (p325) before taking the narrow road along Sumba's west coast. An hour's drive brings you to 4 **Weekuri Lagoon**, where the Indian Ocean rages against the cliffs and bursts through blowholes, and you can swim in the cerulean waters of the sheltered lagoon.

Further south, in Karoso village, the paved road becomes unpaved and bumpy, acting as a shortcut to the main road and the large village of 5 **Bondokodi**, the gateway to Sumba's Kodi district, renowned for its traditional houses. The best-known is nearby 6 **Ratenggaro**, with a breathtaking view along the palm-fringed shoreline and elaborately decorated tombs at the village entrance. A fee will be expected, and some goods-sellers can be aggressive, but treating the residents with respect earns respect in turn.

Following the bumpy main road eastwards, you pass 7 **Paranobaroro**; the house of the Raja of Kodi features Sumba's tallest (30m) roof. In 8 **Wainyapu** – a Pasola (p323) site – take the bridge across the crocodile-infested river and follow the shockingly rutted road past turnoffs to traditional waterside villages – Bwanna, WatuMalando; then the gorgeous Rita, Katobo and Mambang beaches, and past a cacao plantation. At 9 **Wetana**, the paved road reappears, leading you a further 29km to 10 **Pantai Kerewe** (p325).

0 — 10 km
0 — 5 miles

Tambolaka
START
Hutan Lindung/ Hutan Jati
KODI
Kori
Waimangura
Bukabani
Wudi
Tanareu
Sumba
WEJEWA BARAT
Tosi
Bondokodi
Weeleo
Ratenggaro
Wainyapu
Weha
Denduka
INDIAN OCEAN
Paneggoede
GAURA
LEMBOYA
Kahale
Gaura
Kadenga
Gunung Watumandeta
END

Talasi Estate has a little cafe serving coffee and snacks made with the cashews grown on the farm.

Wainyapu is home to around 1400 megaliths, one of the highest concentrations in Sumba.

When the tide goes out at **Pantai Kerewe**, you'll spot the elephant-like Watu Gajah Cecek rock formation.

Nusa Tenggara Islands

Stretching east of Bali and Lombok, Nusa Tenggara comprises over 550 islands. It's dominated by three main ones: Flores, studded with volcanoes, forests and beaches; Sumba, rich in indigenous culture and covered in hills, caves and waterfalls; and West Timor, thronged with traditional villages vying for your attention alongside the brash capital. The smaller islands, some inhabited, others not, have their own appeal, from surfable waves and incredible underwater landscapes to the world's largest monitor lizard.

Where to Go If You Love...

Traditional Villages

Boti A picturesque Dawa village reachable from Timor's Kefamenanu, strictly practising only animist beliefs. Little electricity, and traditional dance.

Bena Bajawa-adjacent Ngada village, with a scenic ridge location, megalithic tombs and ancestral totems.

Tamkesi Thrillingly located hilltop Dawa village; scale a nearby cliff for tremendous views.

Wae Rebo Traditional Manggarai village reachable via a scenic hike; stay overnight and hike to a nearby waterfall.

Manola Take a rough track to this friendly, electricity-free Sumbanese village, populated by elders and children.

Fantastic Waves

Pantai Kerewe Good surfing year-round in Sumba, with a beach break out front, and half a dozen waves easily reachable by boat, including the legendary Occy's Left.

Nemberala Hit the consistent off-season beach break on Rote's Bo'a; ride the heavy, hollow tube at Suckie Mama's or hit the big T-Land wave.

Pantai Lakey In Sumbawa, Lakey Peak and Lakey Pipe are within paddling distance; alternatively, ride to Nungas, Cobblestone, Nangadoro and Periscope. Lakey Pipe and Nungas are top kiting destinations from August to October.

Epic Volcanoes

Gunung Inerie Sweat your way up this spectacularly jagged cone (2245m), starting from Bajawa at 3am to catch the sunrise from the top. A six- to eight-hour round-trip.

Kelimutu Watch the sun's first rays illuminate the three multicoloured lakes from the summit of this volcano, then hike down to Moni through scenic farmland.

Komodo Dragons

Pulau Komodo The main home of the world's largest monitor lizard; if you're lucky, your guide will spot some handsome specimens near the beach.

Pulau Rinca Komodo dragon sightings practically guaranteed, since they often hang out next to the nature museum.

Underwater Landscapes

Komodo National Park Drift with manta rays at Karang Makassar, encounter reef sharks, turtles, tuna and giant trevally at Castle Rock, and brave the strong currents of the Cauldron to 'fly' over the reef.

Alor Archipelago (p315) Moorish idols, angelfish and fairy basslets await at the Fish Bowl reef, while Kal's Dream means barracuda and shark encounters amid schools of jacks and fusiliers.

Goa Kristal and Goa Uihani (p311) In West Timor, these are among Indonesia's very few freshwater cave dives, with fossil-encrusted walls, mysterious chambers and flooded tunnels to explore.

IRYNA SHPULAK/SHUTTERSTOCK

Pulau Rinca

HOW TO

Choose when to go
Hiking and diving are best April to October (dry season); Komodo dragons are hardest to spot in June and July. Islands are greenest November to March.

Book ahead
If visiting traditional villages, contact guides ahead of time. Book liveaboards and diving trips in advance, especially in summer.

Prepare before you go
Make sure your vaccinations are up to date. Research the dive sites and traditional villages you want to explore.

Budget
A guide and car will cost around 1.2 to 2 million rupiah per day, depending on the island and the guide. For liveaboards, budget from US$280 per day.

DIY or Guided Tour

Flores is easiest to explore under your own steam, with public transport connecting the main towns; it's also easy to rent a car, motorbike or scooter in the main towns, and to pootle around on your own, particularly along the Trans-Flores Hwy. Hotels and guesthouses in Ruteng, Bajawa, Moni and elsewhere can help arrange local guides if you want to visit traditional villages nearby.

West Timor is logistically trickier: car and scooter rental is possible to arrange in Kupang, but the main places of interest are inland, and you really need to have knowledge of the island's interior, since minor roads are often in bad condition and unlabelled. You also have to be a very good driver.

In Sumba, while cars with drivers are easy to negotiate, few individuals will rent you a car without a driver. Though most hotels can arrange scooter or motorbike rental, and you may see some of the sights off the island's main road independently, minor roads in the interior are often rough and unlabelled.

To visit traditional villages in Flores, West Timor and Sumba, you need to go with a knowledgeable local guide – both to overcome the language barrier (since there are places where Bahasa Indonesia is barely spoken) and to explain the local traditions and customs so that you don't inadvertently break the many unspoken rules.

Places We Love to Stay

$** Budget **$$** Midrange **$$$ Top end

Flores

MAP p292

Arnolds Family Homestay $ Run by super-helpful owner Arnold, this Bajawa homestay is clean, comfortable and comes with home-cooked meals. Arnold can help with information and arranging tours and transport.

Wae Rebo Lodge $ A lodge comprising four fan-cooled rooms and two air-con rooms sits serenely amid rice fields in Denge. Owner Martin cooks up delicious meals and offers pickup from Labuan Bajo.

Bintang by Tobias Lodge $ Owner Tobias is a fount of local information for Moni; simple tiled rooms come with hot water, and the cafe serves a Western/Indonesian mashup.

D-Rima Homestay $ Cosy, three-room homestay in Ruteng run by a beautiful family brimming with information about the local area; home-cooked vegetarian dinners available.

Cafe Del Mar $ Off the main road heading to the pier in Riung, these 12 air-conditioned rooms with timber furniture and private bathrooms are overseen by Riung's loveliest family. (p298)

Blasius Monta Homestay $ Wae Rebo–expert owner Blasius runs this friendly 15-room spot, right by the trailhead. If the phone signal is patchy, send him a message *(WhatsApp +62 813 3935 0775)*.

Mama's Homestay Ruteng $$ One of the nicer accommodation options in Ruteng, with bright and spacious rooms, and a peaceful garden; owners Faldi and Nina are knowledgeable on the local area.

Scuba Junkie Komodo Beach Resort $$ Stay in breezy beach bales or seaview rooms at this fantastic dive resort in an isolated bay, an hour's boat ride south of Bajo.

Seaesta Komodo Hostel $$ All-round crowd-pleaser with cheery blue-and-white rooms, seriously comfy dorms, a full social calendar and rooftop bar catering to backpackers and divers.

La Boheme Bajo Hostel $$ Labuan Bajo's best hostel has simple but cosy dorms with eight beds, plus private double rooms, and social spaces with games.

Spring Hill Bungalows $$ Two storeys of deluxe rooms with plush bedding and filtered drinking water overlook a lily pond in Ruteng. Good restaurant on-site.

Manulalu B&B $$ Manulalu Jungle's more wallet-friendly sister accommodation, comprising a clutch of comfortable en suites, complimentary breakfasts and access to Heaven's Door restaurant.

Pu'u Pau Hostel $$ Spotless air-conditioned rooms in the thick of Labuan Bajo's Jl Soekarno action, friendly staff and a great on-site cafe.

Kelimutu Crater Lakes Ecolodge $$$ Nestled by the riverside east of town in Moni are 21 rooms and villas, with solar power, outdoor sitting areas and restaurant.

Manulalu Jungle $$$ Off a scenic road 20km south of Bajawa, glassed-in bungalows feature day beds on wooden decks, perfect for admiring one of Flores' most spectacular outlooks.

Sumbawa

Lakey Peak Haven $$ Hilltop Bali-style 'haven' with two-storey surf shacks overlooking a chequered pool deck and distant breaks. Reserve in advance, as walk-ups aren't accepted.

Lakey Peak B&B $$ Friendly, family-run place featuring spacious rooms with terraces, en-suite bathrooms and air-con. There's a huge rooftop with views of the Nungas surf break.

Peak Surf House $$ Oceanfront spot right by the legendary A-frame break, right in the heart of Lakey Peak. Modern rooms feature all the home comforts, plus terraces and a large garden.

West Timor

MAP p307

Lavalon Hostel $ A dorm and two air-con doubles, run by living Nusa Tenggara encyclopedia and former Indonesian film star Edwin Lerrick in Kepang. Guides and transport arranged.

Dena Hotel $ Unremarkable yet clean rooms in Soe with air-con and wi-fi, across the road from the market. Soe's best digs.

Comfort Inn $ Clean, homey digs in Kefamenanu with air-con, TV and hot water. Friendly owner who can arrange day trips and tours.

Sotis Hotel $$ This Kupang waterfront mid-rise features stylish rooms with pops of colour, two pools, a spa, a decent restaurant and bar.

Alor

La P'tite Kepa $$ This French-owned, solar-powered dive resort consists of 11 bungalows with sea and island views, outdoor bathrooms, memorable meals and snorkelling and diving outings.

Rote

Mulia Bungalows Nemberala Beach $$ Air-con bungalows just steps away from Pantai Nemberala, with outdoor bathrooms. Just a short scooter ride into the centre of town.

Villa Santai $$$ Waterfront villa with spacious bungalows surrounded by tropical gardens, plus a beachfront bar, swimming pool and fresh meals cooked with ingredients grown in the garden.

Sumba

MAP p320

Wajonata Sumba $ This secluded resort 2km east of Kalala Beach consists of basic bamboo huts with porches looking out onto the garden and beach. Owners Shirley and Marcel are great hosts and cook up delicious local food.

Sumba Sunset Surf Camp $$ Four traditional bungalows with mosquito nets, set up to accommodate couples, friends or families. Owner Petu is familiar with nearby surf breaks; in Kerewe. (p326)

Praikamarru Guest House $$ Sumbanese-style thatched cottages on the outskirts of Waingapu. Simple but clean and comfortable rooms; owner Eddy is super helpful and full of local knowledge.

Amuya Homestay $$ Run by affable Luci, this cosy central homestay in Waingapu consists of en-suite rooms fanning out around a lovely garden and pool. Indonesian breakfasts included.

Lambo Homestay $$ Four beautifully decorated rooms inside a traditional (tin-roofed) house in Wanokakaare presided over by effusive English- and Russian-speaking Azerbaijani Nailya. Meals arranged on request.

Casa Kandara $$ Excellent, newish hotel on Waingapu's outskirts. Stylish air-con rooms with terraces, rice-paddy views from the large pool and decent restaurant.

Oro Beach Houses $$ Circular thatched bungalows overlooking a white-sand beach in Tambolaka, with mosquito-netted beds and outdoor bathrooms. Meals, mountain bikes and snorkelling arranged. Occasional wildlife in rooms.

Camp Tarimbang $$$ A jungle glampsite near Pantai Tarimbang with ten tents, each with a porch and double or twin beds. There's a kitchen tent and a fire pit for barbecues, and surf packages are available.

Maringi Sumba $$$ Beautifully designed bamboo pavilions with oval glass doors and outdoor bathrooms, powered by solar energy and run by a not-for-profit NGO that teaches hospitality; in Tambolaka.

Sumba Surf Camp $$$ Rates for four solar-powered rooms and three private bungalows in Kerewe include boat transport to a dozen surf breaks. Family-style meals use produce from the organic garden. (p326)

NIHI Sumba $$$ Celebrity-favoured resort in Wanokaka with exclusive access to the beach out front, myriad amenities and multi-day stays in stunning beachfront villas.

ADHI_WIBOWO/SHUTTERSTOCK

NIHI Sumba

DK 4893 ZR

Galungan decorations (p369)

NOKURO/SHUTTERSTOCK

TOOLKIT

The chapters in this section cover the most important topics you'll need to know about in Bali, Lombok and Nusa Tenggara. They're full of nuts-and-bolts information and valuable insights to help you understand and navigate the region and get the most out of your trip.

Arriving p334

Getting Around p335

How to Hire a Car & Driver p336

Money p337

Accommodation p338

Family Travel p339

Health & Safe Travel p340

How to Travel Safely by Boat p341

Food, Drink & Nightlife p342

Responsible Travel p344

LGBTIQ+ Travellers p346

Accessible Travel p347

Bali's Temple Architecture p348

Women Travellers p350

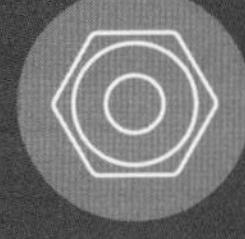

Nuts & Bolts p351

Language p352

Arriving

Most visitors to this part of Indonesia will arrive by air in Bali, but Lombok and Nusa Tenggara also have regional airports. Island-hoppers catch frequent ferries between eastern Java and Bali, between Bali and Lombok, and between many destinations in Nusa Tenggara.

Arrival Card

Indonesia introduced a new arrival card system in 2025, which must be completed online within three days of arrival *(allindonesia.imigrasi.go.id)*. Make certain your passport will be valid for six months after arrival.

Visas

A visa on arrival (VOA) is good for 30 days and can be extended once. Apply in advance online for a 60-day visa *(imigrasi.go.id)*, which can be extended twice. E-gates at Bali's airport have replaced visa stickers.

Tourism Tax

Bali's tourism levy costs 150,000Rp *(lovebali.baliprov.go.id)*. There is currently no system for checking if visitors have paid, but the provincial government has warned that non-payers may be fined in future.

Money

There are ATMs at the airports and many more of them across Bali. Most have a withdrawal limit of 1,250,000Rp to 2,500,000Rp. Electronic payments are widely accepted at tourism businesses.

From Airports to Popular Destinations

FROM		TO	DURATION
BALI	car >	SEMINYAK	30–90MIN
BALI	car >	CANGGU	1½–2HR
BALI	car >	ULUWATU	55MIN–1¼HR
BALI	car >	NUSA DUA	20–30MIN
BALI	car >	SANUR	30–45MIN
BALI	car >	UBUD	1½–2HR
LOMBOK	car >	KUTA	20MIN
LOMBOK	car, boat >	GILIS	3HR
LABUAN BAJO	car >	TOWN CENTRE	10MIN
LABUAN BAJO	car >	RUTENG	5HR
MAUMERE	car >	MONI	3HR
KUPANG	car >	TOWN CENTRE	15MIN
TAMBOLAKA	car >	WAIKABUBAK	1HR

Getting Around

Gett ing around requires many modes of transit. In Bali most people use cars with drivers or rent motorbikes. Elsewhere, shared transport is more common; ferries and aeroplanes are inescapable between islands.

TRAVEL COSTS

Motorbike rental
75,000Rp+/day

Petrol
Approx 12,000Rp/litre

Ferry
80,000Rp+

Flight
US$70+

Plane

There are regular flights between Bali's airport and airports in Nusa Tenggara and across Indonesia. Many regional flights link Lombok, Labuan Bajo, Kupang etc. Airlines include Lion Air, Batik Air, Wings Air, Air Asia, Garuda and others. Flight delays are common, so avoid tight connections. Consider staying in Bali before an international flight.

Boat

Fast boats link Bali with Lombok and the Gilis. Slow car ferries link the region's major islands. Journey times vary greatly. Liveaboards are a popular way to get from Lombok to Labuan Bajo (Flores). Shipping company Pelni *(pelni.co.id)* provides infrequent, long-distance shipping services, but these trips are for the very adventurous.

TIP

The one reliable taxi company in Bali and Lombok is **Bluebird**. Look for blue cabs clearly branded 'Bluebird' (ersatz blue taxis abound). Drivers speak English and always use the meter.

BALI'S PUBLIC BUS

Trans-Sarbagita *(@trans_sarbagita)* runs air-con commuter buses, more suited to residents due to its complex route network. It is handy for the following routes: the bypass linking Sanur to Jimbaran; Denpasar to Jimbaran; or Ubud to points south to Denpasar. Other routes require transfers; airport service is inconvenient. The cheap fares require Indonesian e-payment apps.

Car & Motorbike

Renting a car or motorbike can open up the region for exploration – and also leave you counting the minutes until you return it. Driving conditions can be harrowing and Bali's main roads are often clogged with traffic. Motorbike rental is popular, but there are many road-safety issues and the matter of theft.

Taxi & Ojek

Metered taxis are common in South Bali and parts of Lombok. Elsewhere, a taxi ride will require negotiating a fare in advance – an opaque process. *Ojeks* (motorbike taxis) are common, and you'll find them available from dedicated drivers as well as on an ad hoc basis, particularly out in the countryside.

Ride Apps

The widespread adoption of ride apps has been a boon to transport in Bali. Operating just like Uber (which was banned), the apps allow you to summon a driver and then reach your destination for a set fare that is usually cheaper than a negotiated fare. The main apps are **Grab** and **Gojek**. Both offer cars and *ojeks*.

DRIVING ESSENTIALS

Drive on the left.

An international driving permit valid for a car and/or motorbike is essential, along with your home country licence.

Motorbike riders must use a helmet (although many residents flaunt this law).

WILLIAM'S PHOTO/SHUTTERSTOCK

HOW TO... Hire a Car & Driver

A popular and convenient way to travel around Bali and Nusa Tenggara is by a hired vehicle with a driver. This provides maximum convenience and comfort. Day trips in Bali and longer-distance transport are common reasons for having your own vehicle. There's no better way to make the fabulous multi-day trek across Flores, for instance.

A local driver will be most versed in local driving conditions, whether it's finding something that's otherwise elusive on your mapping app, taking a hidden shortcut or advising on the best times to visit sights to avoid crowds and traffic.

Multi-day trips allow you and the driver to become familiar with your desires and styles.

Selecting a Driver

It's easy to arrange for a vehicle and driver. Consider the following:

- Ask at your hotel, which is often a good method because it increases accountability. The person who picked you up at the airport may also be available to drive you around.
- Consult other travellers for their recommendations.
- Meet the driver to check out your chemistry. Make sure that their English is sufficient for you to communicate your wishes.
- Most vehicles used to transport tourists are some type of minivan that seats four to seven. Make certain your driver's is modern and clean.
- If you're visiting several islands, ask your driver to recommend other drivers further along your itinerary.
- Agree on the journey and the price beforehand; know that changes may increase your cost.

Budget Considerations

If you're part of a group, it can make economic sense to hire a car and driver. Talk to other travellers at your guesthouse, hotel or cafes popular with travellers in hubs such as Labuan Bajo.

Large public buses link the islands and go right across islands like Flores. However, there are also vans and minivans plying popular routes. These offer comfort more akin to hiring your own minivan and can be convenient with pickup and dropoff at your hotel.

WHILE ON THE ROAD

Make it clear if you want to avoid tourist-trap restaurants and shops, which offer large parking areas and possible driver kickbacks (smart drivers understand that tips depend on following your wishes).

Buy your driver lunch (they'll want to eat elsewhere to get a break from work and your company). Offer snacks and drinks.

Feel free to make requests about your driver's driving style – you're the boss. However, never ask your driver to go faster, as they normally go at the speed they are comfortable driving.

Many drivers find ways to make your day delightful in unexpected ways. Tip accordingly (10% is fair).

 TOP RIGHT: BITHOGRAPHY/SHUTTERSTOCK; BOTTOM RIGHT: ANDRI YASI/SHUTTERSTOCK

Money

CURRENCY: RUPIAH (IDR/RP)

ATMs

There are ATMs in Bali, Lombok and larger towns in Nusa Tenggara. For small, isolated places such as Lombok's Gili Gede – and in case ATM networks go down – always carry plenty of cash. ATMs are fussy about the cards they accept, so you may need to try a few different ones.

Credit Cards

Credit and debit cards are accepted at midrange and upscale hotels and resorts. More expensive restaurants and shops will also accept them; there is often a surcharge of around 3%. Visa and Mastercard are the most commonly accepted, American Express not so much.

E-payments

Paying with phones is popular in Indonesia, as is tapping your card. From trendy cafes in Canggu to busy convenience stores, residents and visitors alike go cash-free. One wrinkle is that you may need to have an Indonesian digital wallet app on your phone; try Gopay.

HOW MUCH FOR...

Beaches
Usually free

A Bintang
40,000Rp

Warung lunch
50,000Rp

Car and driver
US$40–80

HOW TO... Avoid Ripoffs

- ATM exchange rates are usually good.
- Currency exchanges are rife with problems. Anyone approaching you on the street to change money is a scammer.
- With ATMs and credit card payments, never accept the option for conversion to your home currency; it's a ripoff.
- ATMs return your card after dispensing cash, so it's easy to forget your card.
- Card skimming is widespread – protect your PIN and look for attached skimming devices.

TIPPING

With average wages in Bali hovering around 3,000,000Rp a month, all tips are appreciated.

Restaurants Tipping a set percentage is not expected, but if service is good, 10% or more is appropriate.

Services Hand cash directly to individuals (drivers, porters, masseuses, people bringing you beer at the beach etc); 10% to 20% of the total is generous.

Hotels Most midrange and all top-end hotels add 21% to the bill for tax and service.

Spas Not mandatory, though 5% to 10% is appreciated.

LOCAL TIP

In shops, change in small coins of 100Rp or less is often not given or is replaced with a small piece of candy.

Accommodation

Homestays & Guesthouses

Bali's family-run accommodation can be a delightful part of your visit. Ubud is a centre for these cheery lodgings. Rooms usually have air-con, wi-fi and some sort of terrace. You can enjoy the rhythms of the compound's life as you come and go. Best of all, prices are very cheap. Guesthouses are found across the region, but check quality as it varies.

Hostels

Found across South Bali, Ubud, the Gilis and beyond, hostels are a recent addition to Indonesia's lodging scene. Aimed at international travellers, they tend towards the flashpacker end of the scale. Look for stylish decor and amenities. Many have private rooms and organise tours and activities. Hostels are usually close to the action and can arrange transport further afield.

Hotels

Bali has hundreds of hotels in all styles, shapes and sizes. Lombok also has many, as do towns and areas across Nusa Tenggara that are popular with tourists. International budget and midrange chains are found by the score in South Bali. Older midrange hotels are often constructed in bungalow style or in two-storey blocks and are set on spacious grounds with a pool.

Resorts

Bali has some of the world's best resorts, often at prices less than you'd pay elsewhere. You can stay on the beach or be nestled in a lush mountain valley. Service is refined and you can expect decor that astounds. Resorts such as those at Nusa Dua have hundreds of rooms. Across the region, boutique properties may have as few as two.

HOW MUCH FOR A NIGHT IN A...

Homestay
200,000–400,000Rp

Hotel
400,000–1,000,000Rp

Resort
1,000,000Rp+

Villas

Enjoy a luxurious villa escape, private pool and even your own staff, often in a walled compound. Multiroom villas are good for groups and can become your holiday party HQ. They are found across Bali, with huge concentrations built atop the lost rice fields of Canggu and Ubud. The villa boom is controversial for environmental, aesthetic and economic reasons.

HOW TO RENT A VILLA

Airbnb and Vrbo are popular sources of rentals. There are also many agents; some are excellent, others not. It is essential to be as clear as possible about what you want when arranging a rental. Some considerations are:

- How far is the villa from the beach, nightlife and shops?
- Is a driver or car service included?
- If there is a cook, is food included?
- Is there an electricity surcharge?
- Are there extra cleaning fees?
- What refunds apply on a standard 50% deposit?

Family Travel

Travelling with children in this part of the world is an enriching experience. Residents consider kids part of the community, and everyone has a responsibility towards them. Children of all ages will enjoy both the attention and the many diversions that will make their holiday special too. The many outdoor activities are a plus.

Staying Safe

The sorts of facilities, safeguards and services that many visiting parents regard as basic may not be present. For example, places with great views might not have proper railings. The main danger to kids – and adults – is traffic and bad footpaths in busy areas. Rabies is present in Bali, so keep away from stray dogs and cats, and be wary of monkeys.

What to Pack

Supermarkets are stocked with almost everything you'd hope to find, including international foods (at higher prices). Nappies (diapers), baby food, UHT milk, infant formula and other supplies are easily purchased in Bali, but can be harder to find in Nusa Tenggara. Items to bring include a portable changing mat, car seats, favourite foods and a front or back sling or other baby carrier.

Dining with Kids

Dining as a family is one of the joys of travelling. Bali is so relaxed that kids can just be kids. At many eateries, kids romp nearby while their parents enjoy a meal. Kitchens will usually cater to fussy palates.

Breastfeeding

Breastfeeding in public is generally accepted in Bali and Nusa Tenggara, as many local women do so, but a discreet approach is still recommended. Keep a lightweight shawl on-hand.

BEST REGIONS FOR KIDS

Kuta & Legian, Bali Surf lessons and souvenirs entice kids and teens, though it can be crowded, crazy and sometimes sleazy.

Sanur, Bali Beachside resorts, a reef-protected beach and many kid-friendly activities.

Nusa Dua, Bali Huge resorts with kids' programmes and a reef-protected beach.

Ubud, Bali There are many things to see and do (walks, monkeys, markets, dance performances).

Gili Air, Gili Islands Gentle surf, many amenities and activities such as snorkelling.

CULTURED JOY

The obvious drawcards for kids are the outdoor adventures available across the region. But there are also cultural treats that kids will love.

Dance Check out an evening of Barong dance at the Ubud Palace or Pura Dalem Ubud, two venues that look like sets from *Tomb Raider,* right down to the flaming torches. Barong has monkeys, monsters and a witch.

Markets Vendors are charmed by kids enthusiastically shopping for oddball souvenirs.

Temples Goa Gajah in Bedulu has a deep cavern where hermits lived and which you enter through a monster's mouth. Pura Luhur Batukau is in dense jungle.

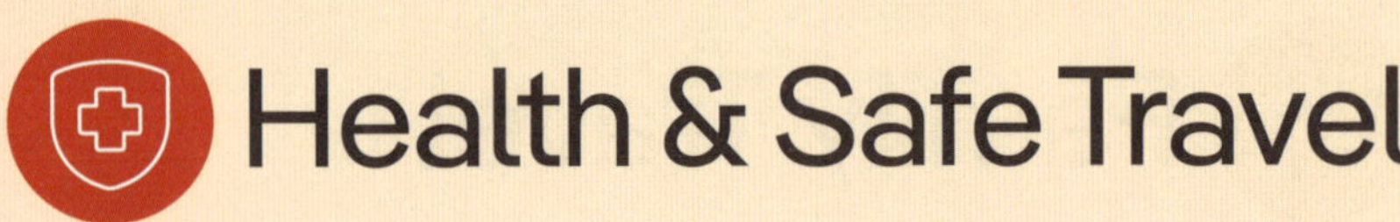

Health & Safe Travel

SWIMMING

Beaches in Bali and Nusa Tenggara are subject to heavy surf and strong currents, so swim between safety flags (if present). Lifeguards are on duty only at Kuta, Legian, Seminyak, Nusa Dua and Sanur. Other hazards include sharp coral and water pollution – stay away from any open streams flowing into the surf.

Scams

Scams occur, beyond dodgy money-changers and blatant overcharging.

- Fake orphanages extract money from tourists (research online before donating).
- Scammers charge an outrageous sum to 'fix' a fake problem with your car or motorbike.
- Unofficial guides charge a fee to allow you to take a selfie at a public site.
- You get the wrong change and are hurried along.

Drugs

High-profile drug cases in Indonesia should be enough to dissuade anyone from being involved with illicit drugs. As little as two ecstasy tabs or a bit of pot have resulted in huge fines and long jail sentences (Google the 'Bali Nine'). Cops pose as dealers, and busting a foreigner for drugs, whether in a club or a private villa, is an easy bust.

SAFETY ON THE WATER

Ferries, ships and boats in Indonesia have a mixed safety record. Never assume any voyage will be safe.

TSUNAMI EVACUATION SIGNS

In tsunami-prone coastal areas of Indonesia, look for orange signs, which point the way to high ground.

NATURAL DISASTER AWARENESS

Gunung Agung on Bali erupted as recently as 2019. Lombok had a significant earthquake in 2018. Volcanoes continuously smoke on Flores. Over 170,000 died in the 2004 tsunami. Remember: Indonesia is prone to natural disasters. While you can't prevent these types of tragedies, you can protect yourself with a few simple precautions.

Staying Safe from Disasters

Be aware of your surroundings. Note if residents are worried about a volcano erupting or other incident. Check your hotel for hazards (eg heavy objects near your bed) and locate fire escapes. Check whether you're in a tsunami zone. Keep bottled water and your phone handy. You may be able to call for help, and extra water can be crucial for survival.

WAKEBALI/SHUTTERSTOCK

Nusa Lembongan (p109)

HOW TO... Travel Safely by Boat

With 17,000 islands, Indonesia relies on ocean travel to link the archipelago together. Small boats with outriggers, fast boats powered by huge outboards, smoking car ferries and well-travelled ships are part of what is all too often a shambolic fleet. Safety regulations are more theory than practice and accidents happen regularly. In 2025, there were several fatal accidents on boats linking Nusa Penida and Bali, and a ferry from East Java sank on its trip across the Bali Strait and Gilimanuk, leaving more than 20 dead. Yet, it is possible to improve your odds on an Indonesian boat with some simple precautions.

Many Dangers

Boating standards are low. Crews may have little or no training. In one accident, the skipper admitted that he panicked and had no recollection of what happened to his passengers. And rescue is far from assured: a volunteer rescue group in East Bali reported that they had no radio. Conditions are often rough in the waters off Bali and east through Nusa Tenggara. Although many islands are close to each other, the channels can get more turbulent than is safe for boats trying to cross.

Seeking Safety

With these facts in mind, you must take responsibility for your safety, because no one else will. Two worthwhile points:

Bigger can be better It may add half an hour or more to your journey, but a larger boat deals with the open ocean better than a small, overpowered speedboat. Also, trips on small boats can be unpleasant because of the ceaseless pounding through the waves and the fumes coming from the screaming outboard motors. Still, the large – and often rust-streaked – car ferries linking Bali, Lombok and other islands have all had high-profile sinkings.

Use common sense There are good operators on Indonesia's waters, but the lineup changes constantly. If a service or boat seems sketchy before you board, go with a different operator. Try to get a refund, but don't risk your safety for the cost of a ticket.

SAFETY ON BOARD

Look for exits Cabins may have only one narrow entrance, making them death traps in an accident.

Don't ride on the roof It looks like fun, but travellers get bounced off when boats hit swells and crews may be inept at rescue.

Avoid overcrowding Some boats leave with more people than seats and with aisles jammed with luggage. Don't use the boat if it's too full of luggage and passengers.

Check for safety equipment Make certain your boat has life preservers and that you can locate and use them. Also check for lifeboats. Don't expect the crew to be any help in an emergency.

TOP LEFT: NEW AFRICA/SHUTTERSTOCK; BOTTOM LEFT: WATCH THE WORLD/SHUTTERSTOCK

Food, Drink & Nightlife

When to Eat

Women go to their local market in the morning to buy fresh produce. Coconut is roasted and spices are painstakingly ground. They cook enough to last all day, as meals are usually grabbed on the run. The dishes are covered for family members to serve themselves when convenient. Visitors can follow local eating habits and enjoy anything at any time.

Ramadan

For Muslims in Bali and across Nusa Tenggara, the largest celebration is Ramadan. Each day of Ramadan, Muslims rise before sunrise to eat their only meal before sunset. At sunset, people joyously break their fasts. The first thing eaten is *kolak* (fruit in coconut milk), a gentle start to the evening's feasting. After Ramadan, much of Indonesia hits the road to go home to their families and celebrate Idul Fitri (Lebaran).

MENU DECODER

Ayam: Chicken

Bakar: Barbecued, roasted

Bakso/ba'so: Meatball soup

Daging sapi: Beef

Es buah: Crushed ice, condensed milk, shaved coconut, syrup, jelly and fruit

Ikan: Fish

Jajanan: Snacks

Kelepon: Green rice-flour balls with a palm-sugar filling

Krupuk: Prawn or fish cracker

Lombok: Chilli

Mie goreng: Fried wheat-flour noodles, served with vegetables or meat

Nasi: Rice

Nasi campur: Steamed rice topped with a little bit of everything

Nasi goreng: Fried rice

Nasi putih: White *(putih)* rice, usually steamed

Nasi uduk: Rice cooked in coconut milk, served with meat, tofu and/or vegetables

Pisang goreng: Banana fritters

Sate: Skewers of grilled meat, served with peanut sauce

Sayur: Vegetables

Soto: Meat and vegetable broth

Telur: Egg

Udang: Prawns

HOW TO... Eat on the Street

As many Indonesians can't afford fine service and surroundings, the most authentic food is found at street level. Everyone dines at stalls or gets their noodle fix from vendors, who carry their victuals in two bundles connected by a stick over their shoulders: a stove and wok on one side, and ready-to-fry ingredients on the other.

Then there are *kaki lima* (roving vendors), whose carts hold a workbench, stove and cabinet. '*Kaki lima*' means 'five legs' – two for the wheels of the cart, one for the stand and two for the legs of the vendor, who sells every type of dish, drink and snack. Some have a permanent spot; others roam the streets, calling out what they are selling or making a signature sound, such as the 'tock' of a wooden *bakso* bell. In some places, *sate* sellers operate from a boat-shaped cart, with bells jingling to attract the hungry.

HOW MUCH FOR A...

Top-end restaurant meal
US$20+

Nasi campur
40,000Rp

Large Bintang at a cafe
60,000Rp

Babi guling (spit-roast pig)
50,000Rp

Coffee
10,000Rp

Cocktail
160,000Rp

Jamu (herbal health drink)
20,000Rp

Fresh coconut water
15,000Rp

HOW TO... Be a Good Dinner Guest

In Indonesia, hospitality is highly regarded. If you're invited to someone's home for a meal, you'll be treated warmly and social miscues will be ignored. Nevertheless, here are some tips to make the experience more enjoyable for everyone.

When food or drink is presented, wait until your host invites you to eat.

Indonesians rarely eat at the table, preferring to sit on a mat or around the lounge room.

Don't be surprised if, when invited to a home, you're the only one eating. This is your host's way of showing you're special, and you should have choice pickings. But don't eat huge amounts as these dishes will feed others later.

While chopsticks are available at Chinese-Indonesian eateries, and a fork and spoon in restaurants, many Indonesians prefer to eat with their hands. Use only your right hand. If you're left-handed, ask for a spoon.

In Islamic areas, be sure not to eat and drink in public during Ramadan. Restaurants do stay open, though they usually cover the door so as not to cause offence. And know that outside of Balinese Hindu areas, pork is never served.

Just Say No

If you're invited to an Indonesian home for a meal, your hosts will no doubt insist you eat more. You may always politely pass on second helpings or refuse food you don't find appealing.

EATING IN NUSA TENGGARA

Once you board the ferry to Sumbawa from Lombok, you enter a different culinary world. Outside larger towns, cities and tourist areas such as Labuan Bajo, there are limited choices for dining out. Warungs are simple, open-air eateries that provide a small range of dishes. *Rumah makan* (eating house) or *restoran* refers to anything that is a step above a warung. Offerings may be as simple as those from a warung, but usually include a wider selection of meat and vegetable dishes and spicy accompaniments.

As Indonesia's middle class grows, the warung is also going upmarket. In urban areas, a restaurant by any other name advertises itself as a 'warung' and serves good local dishes to customers. Markets *(pasar)* have no refrigeration, so freshness is dependent on quick turnover. You'll also find a huge range of sweet and savoury snacks. Supermarkets and convenience stores are becoming more common.

In East Nusa Tenggara, you'll eat less rice (although much is imported) and more sago, corn, cassava and taro. Fish is popular, and one local dish is Sumbawa's *sepat* (shredded fish in coconut and mango sauce). Also recommended is *sate pusut* (minced meat or fish satay, mixed with coconut and grilled on sugar-cane skewers). Look for *se'i babi* (pork smoked over kesambi wood) in non-Muslim eateries in West Timor. Non-meat dishes include *kelor* (soup with vegetables) and *timun urap* (cucumber with coconut, onion and garlic).

LEFT: ARY PRANGGAWAN/SHUTTERSTOCK; FROM TOP: MONTELLOOO/SHUTTERSTOCK, LOTUS IMAGES/SHUTTERSTOCK

Responsible Travel

Climate Change & Travel

It's impossible to ignore the impact we have when travelling; Lonely Planet urges all travellers to engage with their travel carbon footprint, which will mainly come from air travel. While there often isn't an alternative, travellers can look to minimise the number of flights they take, opt for newer aircrafts and use cleaner ground transport, such as trains. One proposed solution – purchasing carbon offsets – unfortunately does not cancel out the impact of individual flights. While most destinations will depend on air travel for the foreseeable future, for now, pursuing ground-based travel where possible is the best course of action.

The **UN Carbon Offset Calculator** shows how flying impacts a household's emissions:

The **ICAO's carbon emissions calculator** allows visitors to analyse the CO_2 generated by point-to-point journeys:

Threads of Life *(threadsoflife.com)* teaches about and sells traditional textiles, including beautiful works from Nusa Penida. It's one of many shops in Ubud featuring locally produced products and their designers.

The **Muntigunung** *(@muntigunungcse)* community organisation works to improve lives through activities aimed at tourists in and around its namesake village in East Bali and a village-made products shop in Sanur.

REFILL YOUR WATER BOTTLE

Reliance on bottled water puts tens of thousands of empty plastic bottles into landfills daily. Do your part by using a refillable water bottle. Many cafes offer free or cheap refills.

Saving Sea Turtles

Several turtle hatcheries work to protect eggs from poachers and predators: **Kuta Beach Sea Turtle Conservation Center** (p78), **Turtle Conservation and Education Centre** (p92), Serangan, and **Kurma Asih Sea Turtle Conservation Center** (p237), Perancak.

Regenerative Rice

The **Astungkara Way** (p60) provides farmers with free training and support to transition to sustainable rice farming. Farm experiences and multi-day hikes support its work.

SAVING LOMBOK'S SHARKS

Southeast Lombok has long been a centre for poaching and harvesting shark fins. **Project Hiu** *(projecthiu.com)* gives shark harvesters new income protecting sharks and guiding tourists. It offers tours and you can sponsor a boat.

Cleaning Rivers

Sungai Watch *(sungai.watch)* has identified over 350 illegal landfills in Bali and organises river clean-ups to keep plastic off the beaches. It's expanding its work across Indonesia and you can help out.

Cleaning Nusa Lembongan's Beaches

Throughout the year, Nusa Lembongan's community holds weekly beach and town clean-ups (p114). You can join in with **French Kiss Divers** *(@frenchkissdiverslembongan)*, Tuesday; **Trash Hero Ceningan** *(@trashhero.ceningan)*, Monday; and **Trash Hero Lembongan** *(@trashherolembongan)*.

Supporting Sumba Communities

Nihi Sumba (p331) in Wanokaka pays fair wages to staff, contributes to educational programmes and supports anti-malaria efforts. **Maringi Sumba** (p331) in Tambolaka is run by an NGO that teaches hospitality to Indonesian students.

Learning Village Life

JED *(jed.or.id)* organises highly regarded tours of small villages, some overnight. Working with villages off the tourist routes of Bali, the group reveals rural life, culture, farming and food. Proceeds are returned to the communities.

Rainy Season Blight

The density of rubbish on Indonesia's beaches correlates with the seasons and tides, and the rainy season (which peaks November through February) sends torrents of water through rubbish-filled river valleys, resulting in headline-grabbing scenes.

LEAVE THE ANIMALS BE

Reconsider swimming with captive dolphins, riding elephants and patronising attractions where wild animals are made to perform for crowds. These interactions have been identified by animal welfare experts as harmful to the animals.

Seminyak's legendary **Desa Potato Head** (p66) details how every aspect of its functioning is dedicated to sustainability.

The **Penida Colada** (*@penidacolada*; p114) beach bar gives one free coconut for every bag of rubbish collected.

RESOURCES

refillmybottle.com
Find places to refill water bottles in Bali.

keepbalibeautiful.com
Donate to community recycling programmes.

ecotourismbali.com
Search for sustainability-certified hotels and operators.

CLOCKWISE FROM TOP LEFT: JIANGDI/SHUTTERSTOCK, WOOPICS/SHUTTERSTOCK, VERA LARINA/SHUTTERSTOCK, KUNGFU01/SHUTTERSTOCK

LGBTIQ+ Travellers

LGBTIQ+ travellers in Indonesia should follow the same precautions as straight travellers: no public displays of affection. This is especially important in conservative areas such as Sumba, where residents of the same sex seen hugging have sparked outrage. Bali is a notable exception, but otherwise, travellers should exercise caution in their public behaviour across the region.

Tolerant Bali

Bali is a popular spot for LGBTIQ+ travellers owing to the many ways it caters to a rainbow of visitors. There is a large gay and lesbian expat community and many own businesses that are very queer-friendly. In South Bali and Ubud, couples have few concerns, beyond remembering that the Balinese are quite modest. Otherwise, there's a rollicking strip of very gay-friendly nightclubs in the heart of Seminyak, and there's no part of Bali that any LGBTIQ+ person should avoid.

IMPORTANT CONSIDERATIONS

Islamic groups proscribe homosexuality, but physical harassment is still uncommon.

Morality police – and, increasingly, regular police – are known to patrol guesthouses and hotels outside of tourist centres looking for unmarried couples, including same-sex ones. Two men checking into the same room have led to raids.

Local Groups

GAYa Nusantara *(gayanusantara.or.id)* The national Indonesian LGBTIQ+ community group. Focuses on social issues, government policy, support services, HIV prevention and more.

Yayasan Gaya Dewata (YGD; *@yayasangayadewata*) Bali's oldest community-run LGBTIQ+ organisation works to prevent HIV and provide support services across the island.

LGBTIQ+ LEXICON

Gay men in Indonesia are referred to as *maho*, homo or gay; lesbians are *lesbi*.

Indonesia's community of transgender *waria* – from the words *wanita* (woman) and *pria* (man) – has always had a very public profile; they are also known by the less polite term *banci*.

LGBTIQ+ STATUS IN INDONESIA

Attitudes towards LGBTIQ+ people are changing slowly in Indonesia. A 2020 survey found that only 9% of Indonesians agreed that homosexuality should be accepted, an increase from only 3% in 2013. Though same-sex sexual acts are not criminalised in Indonesian law, they are prohibited in Aceh and South Sumatra.

Avoid PDAs

Avoid public displays of affection. As the nation becomes more religiously conservative, any form of closeness between people of the same sex may be unwise.

 NITO/SHUTTERSTOCK

Accessible Travel

Bali is the favoured destination for travellers with disabilities because it is much easier to find suitable amenities and adapted accommodation. Lombok, the Gilis and Nusa Tenggara are not well set up to cater to those with vision, hearing or mobility impairments.

Accessibility Challenge

Indonesia is a difficult destination for those with issues such as limited mobility or vision or hearing impairment. Few buildings have disabled access, and even international chain hotels may not have fully accessible facilities.

Airports

The airports in Bali, Lombok, Labuan Bajo and Kupang are modern and able to handle passengers with diverse needs. Smaller airports in the region are not as well equipped but should be able to assist all passengers.

Accommodation

Most places to stay across the region are not equipped for people with special accessibility needs. Staff may be very willing to offer assistance, but don't expect ramps, elevators, specially equipped bathrooms etc.

FEW FACILITIES

Expect high kerbs, few kerb cuts, badly maintained and crowded pavements (sidewalks) and steps into many establishments. Help, however, is usually at hand even if it may not be skilled.

Accommodation Listings

Even international chain hotels may not be accessible. UK-based travel agent Disabled Holidays *(disabledholidays.com)* lists accessible hotels and resorts in Indonesia.

Waterpark for All

Waterbom Bali (p76) offers discounted entrance for people with disabilities and medical carers. Not all slides are accessible, but much of the park is wheelchair friendly, with ramps, wide pathways and accessible toilets.

BEACH ROLL

Paved, wheelchair-accessible beach promenades stretching from Kuta to Legian, and along the Sanur foreshore, are pleasant locations for a seaside roll. Go early to beat the sun and crowds.

RESOURCES

Bali Access Travel *(baliaccesstravel.com)* Wheelchair-accessible travel agent providing tours, accommodation, transport, equipment hire and fully licensed nursing services. Arranges diving and snorkelling expeditions.

Accessible Indonesia *(accessibleindonesia.org)* This well-credentialled inbound travel agent welcomes clients with any type of disability, offering tours principally to Bali, Yogyakarta and Sulawesi.

Zero Gravity Diving *(zerogravitydivingbali.com)* Offers dives and courses for qualified disabled divers. Based in Sanur.

Temples & Sights

Stairs abound and are an integral philosophical part of every Hindu temple, so most shrines and religious sites are not accessible. An exception is **Pura Tanah Lot** (p233), which has a wheelchair-accessible viewing path.

Bali's Temple Architecture

Design is part of Bali's spiritual heritage and this heritage contributes to the look of traditional homes, temples and even modern buildings. Yet it's the temples that remain paramount to the very essence of Bali's architectural and design heritage. A temple must conform to the Balinese concept of cosmic order and every aspect of the structure, from the smallest shrine in a family compound to grand complexes at Besakih and Tanah Lot, has deep meaning.

Temple Orientations

Every village in Bali has several temples, and every home has at least a simple house-temple. The Balinese word for temple is *pura*, from the Sanskrit word meaning 'a space surrounded by a wall'.

All temples are built on a mountain–sea orientation, not north–south. The direction towards the mountains, *kaja*, is the end of the temple, where the holiest shrines are found. The temple's entrance is at the *kelod* (side closest to the sea). *Kaja* may be towards a particular mountain – Pura Besakih in East Bali is pointed directly towards Gunung Agung – or towards the mountains in general.

Temple Types

There are three basic temple types found in most villages. The most important is the *pura puseh* (temple of origin), dedicated to the village founders and at the *kaja* end of the village. In the middle of the village is the *pura desa*, for the many spirits that protect the village community in daily life.

At the *kelod* end of the village is the *pura dalem* (temple of the dead). It honours the destructive sides of the gods Shiva and Parvati.

In addition to these 'local' temples (which number in the thousands), there are a smaller number of great temples. Often a kingdom would have three of these temples that sit at the top of the temple pecking order: a main state temple in the heartland of the state (such as **Pura Taman Ayun** in Mengwi, West Bali); a mountain temple (such as **Pura Besakih**, East Bali); and a sea temple (such as **Pura Luhur Ulu Watu**, South Bali).

Building New Temples

The art of temple and shrine construction in Bali is as vibrant as ever. With the island's relative wealth, more than 500 temples in all sizes are built new or renovated every month. Travelling on the backroads of East and West Bali, you'll pass numerous stone-carving sites where all the needed components for a temple are produced with power tools amid clouds of mineral dust. The soft pumice-like stones that are used weather rapidly, which means that last year's new temple looks like this year's ancient monument.

Left: Pura Ulun Danu Bratan (p199); Above: *Candi bentar*

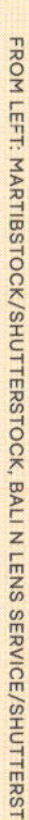

TEMPLE DESIGN ELEMENTS

No two temples on Bali are identical. Variations in style, size, importance, wealth, purpose and much more result in near-infinite variety. But there are common themes and elements. Use this as a guide and see how many design elements you can find in each Balinese temple you visit.

Candi Bentar The intricately sculpted temple gateway, like a tower split down the middle and moved apart, symbolises that you are entering a sanctum (unfortunately, it has become a clichéd selfie shot). It can be grand, with auxiliary entrances on either side for daily use.

Kulkul Tower The warning-drum tower, from which a wooden split drum *(kulkul)* is sounded to announce events at the temple or warn of danger.

Bale A pavilion, usually open-sided, for temporary use or storage. It may include a *bale gong*, where the gamelan orchestra plays at festivals, or a *wantilan*, a stage for dances or cockfights.

Kori Agung or **Paduraksa** The gateway to the inner courtyard is an intricately sculpted stone tower. Entry is through a doorway reached by steps in the middle of the tower.

Raksa or **Dwarapala** Statues of fierce guardian figures who protect the doorway and deter evil spirits. Above the door will be the equally fierce face of a Bhoma, with hands outstretched against unwanted spirits.

Aling Aling If an evil spirit does get in, this low wall behind the entrance will keep it at bay, as evil spirits find it difficult to make sharp turns.

Betelan Most of the time (except during ceremonies), entry to the inner courtyard is through this side gate.

Gedong These small shrines include ones to Ngrurah Alit and Ngrurah Gede, who organise things and ensure the correct offerings are made. At the *kaja* end of the courtyard, *gedong* may include a shrine to the sacred mountain Gunung Batur; a Maospahit shrine to honour Bali's original Hindu settlers (Majapahit); and a shrine to the *taksu*, who acts as an interpreter for the gods.

Padma Stone Throne for the sun god Surya, placed in the most auspicious *kaja-kangin* (sunrise in the direction of the mountains) corner. It rests on the *badawang* (world turtle), which is held by two *naga* (mythical snakelike creatures).

Meru A multiroofed shrine. Usually there is an 11-roofed *meru* to Sanghyang Widi, the supreme Balinese deity, and a three-roofed *meru* to the holy mountain Gunung Agung. However, *meru* can take any odd number of steps in between, depending on where the intended god falls in the pecking order. The black thatching is made from sugar-palm fronds. The number and height of *meru* are an easy way to discern a temple's importance.

Gedong Pesimpangan A stone building dedicated to the village founder or a local deity.

Paruman or **Pepelik** Open pavilion in the inner courtyard, where the gods are supposed to assemble to watch a festival.

Women Travellers

Plenty of women travel in Indonesia either solo or in groups, and most seem to travel through the country without problems, especially in Bali (a popular destination for female travellers). However, women travelling solo or otherwise may receive unwanted attention.

Bali

Generally, Bali is safer for women than many areas of the world, and with the usual care and common sense, women should feel secure travelling alone. Women travelling solo will get attention from Balinese men, but they are, on the whole, more relaxed and non-judgmental towards women compared to many parts of the world. Greater care should be reserved for outsiders on Bali, whether tourists or foreign workers.

In Bali, women may not enter temples if they are menstruating. And remember to behave respectfully in temples: incidents of nude yoga selfies, suggestive poses and other offensive behaviour have outraged even the otherwise mellow Balinese.

Nusa Tenggara

For the most part, Indonesia feels pretty safe as a solo female traveller. Like anywhere, however, there will always be the occasional individual trying to get your attention. Two or more women together are less likely to experience problems, and women accompanied by a man are unlikely to be harassed. There have been a small number of accounts of women being groped or followed by men in recent years, but this is not common. Watch out for touchy-feely guides.

If you're a solo female and you hire a car with a driver for several days, it's not culturally appropriate for a male Muslim driver to be travelling alone with you. A third party should come along as a chaperone. Traditionally, women in Lombok are treated with respect. But would-be guides, boyfriends and gigolos are often persistent in their approaches and can be aggressive when ignored or rejected.

Although it's rare, some foreign women have experienced sexual harassment and even assault while on the Gilis – don't walk home alone in the quieter parts of the islands.

COVER UP

- Nude and topless sunbathing is deeply offensive and may lead to conflict on any beach. Away from the sand, always cover up. Note the number of signs forbidding bikinis and swimming trunks away from the beach on otherwise freewheeling Gili T.
- Dress conservatively in Nusa Tenggara, especially in Sumbawa. Cover your shoulders, wear shorts and skirts that go down to the knees, and avoid showing cleavage.

Women's Health

Birth-control options may be limited, so bring adequate supplies of your own form of contraception. In tourist areas and large cities, basic sanitary napkins and tampons can be purchased. However, this becomes more difficult the more rural you go, including much of Sumbawa, West Timor and Sumba. Even in Bali, the selection may be limited, so bring whatever you need – and prefer – with you.

OPENING HOURS

Banks 8am–2pm Monday to Thursday, 8am–noon Friday, 8am–11am Saturday

Government offices 8am–3pm Monday to Thursday, 8am–noon Friday (although these are not standardised)

Restaurants & cafes 8am–9pm daily

Shops & services catering to visitors 9am–8pm or later daily

Toilets

Toilets are porcelain holes in the floor with footrests on either side, although Western-style toilets are common in tourist areas.

Note: public toilets only exist at some sights.

Tap Water

Never drink tap water in Indonesia. Most ice in restaurants is fine if it is uniform in size and made at a central plant (standard for cities and tourist areas). Avoid ice that is chipped off larger blocks (more common in rural areas).

GOOD TO KNOW

Time zone
Central Indonesian Time (GMT/UTC +8)

Country code
+62

Emergency number
Police 110; Fire 113; Medical 119

Population
4.4 million (Bali)

Weights & Measures

Indonesia uses the metric system.

Wi-Fi & Internet

Wi-fi is easy to access across Bali and Nusa Tenggara.

Electricity

220–230V/50Hz

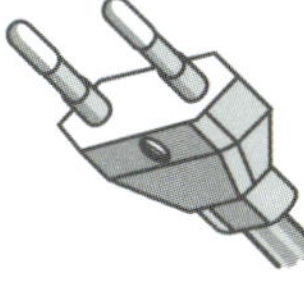

Type C
220V/50Hz

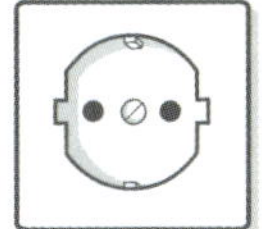

Type F
230V/50Hz

PUBLIC HOLIDAYS

- **Tahun Baru Masehi** (New Year's Day) 1 January
- **Tahun Baru Imlek** (Chinese New Year) Late January to early February
- **Nyepi** (day of silence when the island shuts down completely) February or March
- **Wafat Yesus Kristus** (Good Friday) Late March or early April
- **Hari Buruh** (Labour Day) 1 May
- **Hari Waisak** (Buddha's birth, enlightenment and death) May
- **Kenaikan Yesus Kristus** (Ascension of Christ) May
- **Hari Proklamasi Kemerdekaan** (Independence Day) 17 August
- **Hari Natal** (Christmas Day) 25 December

Islamic holidays:

- **Isra Miraj Nabi Muhammad** (Ascension of the Prophet Muhammad)
- **Idul Fitri** (also known as Lebaran) End of Ramadan
- **Idul Adha** (Islamic feast of the sacrifice)
- **Muharram** (Islamic New Year)
- **Maulud Nabi Muhammad** (Birthday of the Prophet Muhammad) Around December

Language

Bahasa Indonesia is the official language of Indonesia. It has approximately 220 million speakers, although it's the mother tongue for only about 20 million. Most people in Bali and on Lombok also speak their own indigenous languages, Balinese and Sasak, respectively.

Basics

Hello. Salam. *sa·lam*

Goodbye. Selamat jalan. *se·la·mat ja·lan*

Yes. Ya. *ya*

No. Tidak. *ti·dak*

Please. Tolong. *to·long*

Thank you. Terima kasih. *te·ri·ma ka·sih*

Excuse me. Permisi. *per·mi·si*

Sorry. Maaf. *ma·af*

What's your name? Siapa namanya? *si·a·pa na·ma·nya*

My name is ... Nama saya ... *na·ma sa·ya ...*

Do you speak English? Anda bisa Bahasa Inggris? *an·da bi·sa ba·ha·sa ing·gris*

I don't understand. Saya tidak mengerti. *sa·ya ti·dak meng·er·ti*

Directions

Where's (the station)? Di mana (stasiun)? *di ma·na (sta·si·oon)*

What's the address? Apa alamatnya? *a·pa a·la·mat·nya*

Can you show me (on the map)? Bisa tunjukkan kepada saya (di peta)? *bi·sa toon·joo·kan ke·pa·da sa·ya (di pe·ta)*

Signs

Buka Open

Tutup Closed

Dilarang Prohibited

Kamar Kecil Toilets

Keluar Exit

Masuk Entrance

Pria Men

Wanitai Women

Polisi Police

Rumah Sakit Hospital

Time

What time is it? Jam berapa? *jam be·ra·pa*

It's (10) o'clock. Jam (sepuluh). *jam (se·poo·looh)*

Half past (10). Setengah (sebelas). *se·teng·ah (se·be·las)*

morning Pagi *pa·gi*

afternoon Sore *so·re*

evening Malam *ma·lam*

yesterday Kemarin *ke·ma·rin*

today Hari ini *ha·ri i·ni*

tomorrow Besok *be·sok*

Emergencies

Help! Tolong! *to·long*

Go away! Pergi! *per·gi*

Call ...! Panggil...! *pang·gil*

...a doctor dokter. *dok·ter*

...the police polisi. *po·li·si*

Eating & Drinking

What would you recommend? Apa yang Anda rekomendasikan? *a·pa yang an·da re·ko·men·da·si·kan*

Cheers! Bersulang! *ber·soo·lang*

That was delicious. Ini enak sekali. *i·ni e·nak se·ka·li*

NUMBERS

1 **satu** *sa·too*

2 **dua** *doo·a*

3 **tiga** *ti·ga*

4 **empat** *em·pat*

5 **lima** *li·ma*

6 **enam** *e·nam*

7 **tujuh** *too·jooh*

8 **delapan** *de·la·pan*

9 **sembilan** *sem·bi·lan*

10 **sepuluh** *se·poo·looh*

DONATIONS TO ENGLISH

Orangutan, dugong, bamboo, papaya, satay, sarong, gong

PRONUNCIATION

Pronunciation is easy to master in Bahasa Indonesia. Each letter always represents the same sound and most letters are pronounced the same as their English counterparts.

Origins

Bahasa Indonesia, and its closest relative Malay, both developed from Old Malay, an Austronesian language spoken in the kingdom of Srivijaya on the island of Sumatra.

Official Language

With the Declaration of Independence in 1942, Bahasa Indonesia was proclaimed the country's official language.

Street Talk

Blend in with the cool kids with the following sentences.

Alay – Tacky, garish, drama queen
Basian – Hangover
Jijay – Disgusting, grotesque
Kimpoi – Sexual intercourse
Koplak – Silly
Ndakik-ndakik – Words or phrases too hard to understand
Pansi – What the hell?

WHO SPEAKS BAHASA INDONESIA?

Bahasa Indonesia is the official language of the Republic of Indonesia. It's used in administration, education, business and the media, although less than 10 per cent of the population claim it as their mother tongue. For the majority of speakers it's the second language, but it is a uniting force for the hundreds of ethnic groups scattered across the world's largest archipelago.

ERIC ISSELEE/SHUTTERSTOCK

THE BALI, LOMBOK & NUSA TENGGARA

STORYBOOK

Our writers delve deep into different aspects of life in Bali, Lombok & Nusa Tenggara

A History of Bali, Lombok & Nusa Tenggara in 15 Places

From 'hobbits' to a possible second airport on Bali

p356

Meet the Balinese

Learn what's important to the Balinese people

Ni Wayan Murni

p360

Threads of Tradition

Batik fabrics are an integral part of Indonesia's culture and history

Leyla Rose

p362

Saving the 'Last Paradise'

The effects of tourism and nickel extraction threaten Raja Ampat's otherworldly beauty

Tiara Maharani

p364

Balinese Hinduism: A Spiritual Blend

Hinduism in Bali is distinct from Hinduism in India

Christine Gilbert

p366

In Indonesia, Contemporary Art Blooms & Booms

Indonesian artists are producing daring contemporary works

Ian Lloyd Neubauer

p370

Pura Taman Saraswati (p126), Ubud

MUNZIR ROSDI/SHUTTERSTOCK

A HISTORY OF BALI, LOMBOK & NUSA TENGGARA IN 15 PLACES

The Hindu Majapahit kingdom moved to Bali in the 12th century where their culture – like rice – found fertile ground. By the 20th century, the Dutch conquered the island even as the island's unique culture thrived. Westerners celebrated Balinese arts in the 1930s; surfers arrived in the 1970s and tourism has boomed ever since.

ISLAM SWEPT THROUGH Java in the 12th century, compelling Hindu royalty, artisans and priests to move across the narrow channel to Bali. Blessed with prodigious resources, Bali became a thriving centre of arts and faith. The priest Nirartha established landmark temples that helped develop Bali's own unique form of Hinduism. From the initial strand of seaside temples, the numbers multiplied to today's tens of thousands of temples island-wide.

The evolving Balinese culture emphasised collaboration and resourcefulness, qualities embodied in the UNESCO-recognised *subak* system that ensures fair allocation of water to every rice farmer. Various regencies formed around the island. While beneficial for funding artistic pursuits, the royalty also took to squabbling, which gave the colonial Dutch an opening.

By the 20th century, the Dutch formed alliances with some local princes while brutally suppressing others. Meanwhile, foreigners discovered the richness of Balinese arts and began collaborations in Ubud that are still felt today. Mass tourism began in the 1960s and took off in the 1970s as jets began serving the airport. Huge swaths of the island have been transformed, competition for resources like the once abundant water is fierce and material wealth has soared. Even so, Bali's extraordinary culture remains resilient.

1. Liang Bua Cave

THE MYSTERIOUS FLORES HOBBIT

Until recently it was believed that the first humanoids *(Homo erectus)* lived in Central Java around 500,000 years ago – having reached Indonesia across land bridges from Africa – before either dying off or being wiped out by the arrival of *Homo sapiens*. But the 2003 discovery in Flores of *Homo erectus* remains, a tiny islander dubbed *Homo floresiensis* (or 'hobbit'), upended that notion. Found in deep sediment in the limestone Liang Bua Cave near Ruteng, the bones are around 30,000 years old. In Bali, the oldest human remains found date back to about 1000 BCE and are displayed at the Museum Manusia Purba in Gilimanuk.

For more on Liang Bua, see p291.

2. Lambanapu

ANCIENT CIVILISATION ON SUMBA

The small archaeological site of Lambanapu near Waingapu in Sumba hints more at what we don't know than what we do know about the early inhabitants in Indonesia. Just as the 'hobbit' find on Flores has caused a reevaluation of existing theories, this site – which dates to about 1000 BCE – shows that a complex Austronesian civilisation existed on Sumba earlier than previously thought. Investigations begun in 2016 have uncovered the remains of 45 individuals, along with weaponry, household items and jewellery. Evidence of jar burials shows influences from elsewhere in Southeast Asia, which supplanted the local practice of burials in megaliths.

For more on Lambanapu, see p318.

3. Boti

OVER 20 GENERATIONS OF CULTURE

Boti is an animist village in West Timor that has held out against Christianisation and still maintains a more traditional way of life. One of many isolated villages with ancient cultures in the region, Boti's 300 residents can trace their lineage back over 20 generations. Outside influences are kept at bay by tradition-minded *kepala sukus* (chiefs) who have vowed to maintain the strict laws of *adat* (customs). Yet visitors are welcomed and the populace readily shares its lifestyle and artistic creations. The people of Boti are emblematic of surviving ancient cultures found in pockets across Nusa Tenggara, especially in West Timor and Flores.

For more on Boti, see p312.

Lambanapu (p318)

MISBACHUL MUNIR/SHUTTERSTOCK

4. Gunung Kawi

EXTRAORDINARY 11TH-CENTURY MEMORIALS

Java spread its influence to Bali during the reign of King Airlangga (1019–42), one of its greatest rulers. His mother moved to Bali and remarried shortly after his birth, so when Airlangga gained the throne, there was an immediate link between Java and Bali. It was at this time that the courtly Javanese language known as Kawi came into use among the royalty of Bali; cultural and artistic influences followed as well. The 10 towering rock-cut memorials seen at 11th-century Gunung Kawi, north of Ubud, were dedicated to early royalty. They provide a clear link between Bali and 11th-century Java.

For more on Gunung Kawi, see p147.

5. Pura Rambut Siwi

A SCENIC 16TH-CENTURY LANDMARK

In the early 16th century, Java converted entirely to Islam, causing the Hindu intelligentsia on the island to flee to Bali. Notable among them was the priest Nirartha, who is credited with introducing many of the complexities of what became Balinese Hinduism. Among his many lasting legacies are the 'sea temples' that ring the coast and which are meant to protect against evil spirits. Notable examples include Pura Luhur Ulu Watu and Pura Tanah Lot. Locks of Nirartha's hair are said to be buried at Pura Rambut Siwi, the evocative seaside temple he built in West Bali.

For more on Pura Rambut Siwi, see p238.

6. Pura Taman Ayun

THE MAGNIFICENT TEMPLE OF SUBAK

A place of enveloping calm, this vast royal water temple in West Bali is surrounded by an elegant moat. The complex was built in 1634 and extensively renovated in 1937. Amid the lily-pad-dappled beauty, lotus blossoms fill the pools. The many water features symbolise the temple's role in Bali's *subak* irrigation system, which was recognised by UNESCO in 2012. Playing a critical role in rural Bali life, the *subak* is a village association that deals with water, water rights and irrigation. Apportioning a fair share to everyone is a model of mutual cooperation and an insight into the Balinese character.

For more on Pura Taman Ayun, see p228.

7. Masjid Kuno Bayan Beleq

LOMBOK'S OLDEST MOSQUE

Wektu Telu, Lombok's animist-tinted form of Islam, was born in humble thatched mosques nestled in the Rinjani foothills. The best –and oldest – example is Masjid Kuno Bayan Beleq, next to the village of Beleq. Its low-slung roof, dirt floors and bamboo walls reportedly date from the early 1600s. Wektu Telu, a complex mixture of Hindu, Islamic and animist beliefs, has been supplanted by a more traditional form on Islam, as shown by the many new mosques financed with Middle Eastern money across the island. Balinese influence on the island faded after the Dutch victories in the late 1890s.

For more on Masjid Kuno Bayan Beleq, see p259.

8. Kertha Gosa

REMAINS OF A CONQUERED KINGDOM

In 1906, the Dutch mounted a large invasion of Bali to subdue it once and for all. The Dutch forces landed despite Balinese opposition and, four days later, had marched 5km to the outskirts of Denpasar. Thereafter, a string of military victories gave them increasing control of the island. Some of the royal families chose capitulation while others chose *puputan* (ritual suicide). Wearing their best dress and armed with 'show' daggers, the last Balinese royals and warriors in Klungkung marched into Dutch gunfire in a *puputan* in 1908. The ornate remnants of Kertha Gosa, the royal palace, are all that remain.

For more on Kertha Gosa, see p161.

9. Museum Soenda Ketjil

COLONIAL MUSEUM IN FORMER GATEWAY

Singaraja in North Bali is the island's second-largest city. A prosperous settlement, it seems far removed from the tourism frenzy of South Bali. Many are surprised to learn that until airline travel took off in the 1970s, Singaraja was the gateway for visitors to Bali through much of the 20th century. Quiet today, the port was once busy with ships bringing Dutch administrators, tourists and cargo. The small Museum Soenda Ketjil is located in an old Dutch shipping company building and details the colonial era locally and across the island. On Lombok, the area of Ampenan west of Mataram served the same role.

For more on the Museum Soenda Ketjil, see p209.

10. Ubud Palace

ARTISTIC AND CULTURAL

Ubud's royal palace is only a little over 100 years old. While it has many ornate details and a certain grandeur, it is hardly an ostentatious monument to the town's royalty, who continue to live here and exert great influence over local matters large and small. Nevertheless, the palace symbolises what Ubud has become: an internationally renowned tourism destination with a significant cultural reputation. Many of the elaborate stone carvings are the work of I Gusti Nyoman Lempad, one of the artists responsible for Ubud's acclaim. At night, the main courtyard is evocatively lit for one of the town's famous dance performances.

For more on the Ubud Palace, see p124.

11. Uluwatu Surf Break

THE HEART OF BALI'S SURFING FAME

While filming scenes for what became the seminal movie about Bali surfing, *Morning of the Earth* (1972), filmmaker Albert Falzon and his crew were struck by the now legendary freight-train left-handers breaking off the cliffs at Uluwatu, on the Bukit Peninsula. All but unknown at the time, they quickly became one of the most revered surfing spots on the planet. Amid the myriad tourism developments and crowds today, it can be hard to grasp how inaccessible the region once was – even to Balinese surfers, who'd been introduced to the sport by Bob Koke at Kuta Beach in the 1930s.

For more on surfing Uluwatu, see p96.

Surfing, Uluwatu (p96)

Resort, Nusa Dua (p107)

12. Jalan Sugriwa, Ubud

CULTURAL HOMESTAYS

One of several similar streets in the centre of Ubud, Jl Sugriwa is lined with simple guesthouses generically known as family homestays. Each is a traditional Balinese compound that's home to several generations. Rooms have been added for visitors and the revenue this produces has fuelled more comfortable lifestyles for homestay families. The Balinese openness to outsiders and welcoming culture make this a special cultural experience for guests, who are exposed to the daily fabric of life. Once found island-wide, family homestays have been largely supplanted by more commercial operations elsewhere on Bali, but remain a core part of the Ubud experience.

For more on Ubud, see p124.

13. Nusa Dua

RESORTS AND PACKAGED TOURISM

Beginning in the 1970s, Nusa Dua was designed to compete with international beach resorts the world over. A gated compound of huge resorts, it's a vast and manicured place where you leave the chaos of the rest of the island behind as you pass the guards. Balinese 'culture' takes the form of attenuated shows and the odd architectural detail meant to convey a local feel. Resort construction has spread beyond Nusa Dua, marching right around the south coast of the Bukit Peninsula to Uluwatu. Trucks clog the roads, bringing water to a region that has little.

For more on Nusa Dua, see p107.

14. Kuta Memorial Wall

RECALLING THE 2002 TRAGEDY

On 12 October 2002, two bombs exploded on Kuta's bustling Jl Legian. The number of dead, including those unaccounted for, exceeded 200, although the exact number will probably never be known. Many injured Balinese made their way back to their villages, where, for lack of adequate medical treatment, they died. Authorities blamed an Islamic terrorist group; dozens were arrested and many were sentenced to jail, including three who received the death penalty. But most received relatively light sentences, enraging many in Bali and Australia.

For more on the Kuta Memorial Wall, see p77.

15. Ngurah Rai International Airport

BUSY AIRPORT WITH A HEROIC NAMESAKE

Bali's busy airport is named for I Gusti Ngurah Rai, the national hero who died leading the resistance against the Dutch at Marga in West Bali in 1946. The text of a letter he wrote in response to Dutch demands to surrender ended with 'Freedom or death!' He chose the latter, but his *puputan* slayed the Dutch colonial spirit, and soon Indonesia was independent. His namesake airport is ever-expanding as the inexorable increase in visitor numbers fuels traffic. Constrained by a short runway that precludes long-distance flights from Europe and North America, there is constant debate about building a second airport in North Bali.

For more on arriving in Bali, Lombok and Nusa Tenggara, see p334.

MEET THE BALINESE

You might think we're nosy, but we're not. We're just friendly. NI WAYAN MURNI introduces her people.

WHERE ARE YOU going? *Ke mana?* That's the standard opening question when you meet someone in the street. To a stranger, it sounds rather nosy, but no one expects an answer. It's just a greeting in the absence of a word for 'Hello'. *Jalan, jalan* ('Walking, walking') is an acceptable reply.

You'll meet a lot of people with the same name. It's rather confusing. You get your name at birth, and it's preordained, because the name you are given accords to the order in which you and your siblings are born. Everyone's position in the family is immediately clear, meaning we're all a bit pigeonholed at birth! The names are the same, regardless of whether you're a boy or girl. You'll meet an awful lot of Wayans in Bali, but not so many Ketuts. I am a Wayan.

First born: Wayan, Gede or Putu; second born: Made, Nengah or Kadek; third born: Nyoman, Komang or Koming; fourth born: Ketut.

In 2022, the population of Bali amounted to around 4.37 million people. About 83.5% follow Balinese Hinduism. It's evolved separately from Indian Hinduism, and the differences are clear in temple layouts, ceremonies and beliefs. Christianity, Buddhism and Islam are also practised in Bali, mostly by the Chinese community and people from other islands.

Indonesia is the largest Muslim country in the world, with 87% of the population identifying as Muslim. I often get asked why Bali is unique in Indonesia for being predominantly Hindu. The reason is that Islam, which entered Sumatra in the 13th century, made headway along the coasts of Java at the beginning of the 16th century, pressing inland and dealing the great Hindu Majapahit Empire a fatal blow in 1527, when the last king of Majapahit was defeated and died. The aristocracy, priests, jurists, artists, artisans and all others unwilling to convert to Islam moved to the easternmost parts of Java, and to Bali.

Religion is the most important thing in Balinese life. You can see this in the numerous daily offerings – in my restaurant, hotel, shop and spa, we prepare about 200 basic offerings a day. Much of our time is taken up preparing for large religious ceremonies – staged in ornate temples full of elaborate stone carvings.

The Balinese also love food. Most meals revolve around rice. We eat the best dishes on ceremonial occasions. Bali's most famous dish – *bebek betutu* – is duck richly marinated in Balinese spices, stuffed with vegetables, wrapped in banana leaves and cooked underground – often overnight – for at least eight hours. It makes my mouth water just thinking about it!

On reflection, maybe a better answer to the perennial *Ke mana?* is *Makan, makan* ('To eat, to eat').

What's in a Name?

Bali's name reflects its Indian heritage: it's Sanskrit, and much older than the name 'Indonesia'. 'Bali' means 'offering' in Sanskrit, and in High Balinese, 'Bali' is called 'Banten', which also means 'offering' – usually to the gods.

I'M 100% BALINESE

I was born in Penestanan, now a lively suburb of Ubud that's full of yoga studios, healthy restaurants and art galleries. My parents and grandparents are from the same area. As we are Hindu, it's almost certain that our ancestors came from Java, though there are no records – it's only with my generation that birth certificates were issued. As such, many older people have no idea how old they are. It doesn't help that a Balinese year is 210 days!

I opened Ubud's first 'real' restaurant, Murni's Warung, in 1974. It came about by chance. I used to cook lunch for myself and my husband every day in my antiques shop, where I sold textiles, jewellery and other ethnic pieces. Passing tourists asked if they could eat what we were eating. And within a week, I was cooking local food for them! I started with just a couple of chairs and a bamboo table. Now, we can accommodate over a hundred people!

THREADS OF TRADITION

Indonesia's ancient textile art form is still a style staple today. By Leyla Rose.

IT'S ALMOST IMPOSSIBLE to visit Indonesia and not encounter batik fabric, whether being worn as a piece of clothing, used in handicrafts and decorative items such as purses and bags, or furnishings like tablecloths and cushion covers. These intricate, UNESCO-listed fabrics are an integral part of the Indonesian nation's culture and history.

Early examples of batik and wax-resistant dyeing techniques have been found across Central Asia, India and the Middle East, dating back 2000 years. It's thought that the craft was brought to Indonesia via maritime trade routes, and although there are no definitive dates, it really burgeoned between 13 CE and 15 CE in Java during the Majapahit Empire – a Hindu-Buddhist kingdom in which art and culture including literary works, decorated temples, ornate sculptures and batik textiles, all flourished. The word 'batik' itself originates from the Javanese term *ambatik,* a combination of two words meaning 'painting' and 'dots' – a reference to how this particular type of textile is made.

The most traditional batik-making techniques in Indonesia are *batik tulis* and *batik cap. Batik tulis* is where a canting (a type

Batik-making

of copper tool) is dipped in hot wax and traced over the pattern on the cloth. Meanwhile, *batik cap* is where patterned stamps made of copper are dipped into the wax and pressed onto the fabric repeatedly to create a uniform pattern. Once the patterns have been traced or stamped with wax, the fabric is dyed. The waxed areas don't absorb the dye, and these are subsequently removed to reveal the motif underneath. The fabric can be dyed multiple times to create multicoloured, multipatterned pieces. Alternative methods include *batik kombinasi,* a combination of *batik tulis* and *batik cap,* as well as tie-dyeing and digital printing using machines.

The patterns depicted on batik fabrics always have a symbolic meaning, representing prayers, hopes and dreams, noble values and moral lessons passed down from ancestors. While batik was originally reserved for and worn by only the royal courts, it soon became mass produced for the general population.

THE PATTERNS DEPICTED ON BATIK FABRICS ALWAYS HAVE A SYMBOLIC MEANING, REPRESENTING PRAYERS, HOPES AND DREAMS, NOBLE VALUES AND MORAL LESSONS PASSED DOWN FROM ANCESTORS.

Motifs vary depending on the area. Batik from coastal areas such as Cirebon and Pekalongan in North Java are known for their bright blues, reds, yellows and oranges. These cities were once popular ports of call for Indian, Chinese and Arab traders, which meant that a wider choice of dyes and inks was available. Trade with these different cultures also influenced the patterns on the batik made in these areas, such as Chinese-influenced dragons and phoenixes, and Indian-influenced geometric patterns. Meanwhile, batik from inland areas like Yogyakarta and Solo feature more earthy colours such as brown, beige and black. They tend to take on a more spiritual meaning too, often featuring symbols from Javanese-Hindu beliefs, such as *sidomukti* (the hope that the wearer will always be happy) and *truntum* (the wearer will receive endless love).

Batik fabrics are still a large part of everyday life in Indonesia, from slings that mothers use to carry their babies, to the shrouds used to wrap the dead, and everything in between: weddings, ceremonies, even workwear – many offices in Indonesia have a mandatory 'Batik Friday' policy.

And batik is experiencing a new evolution. There's a current movement among Indonesia's youth called *berkain,* or 'to cloth' (*kain* means cloth, and *ber* is an action suffix). It's about celebrating traditional fabrics such as batik and ikat (cloth in which the pattern is produced by dyeing the individual threads before weaving), wearing them in everyday life and not just as formal attire. It's a way for young people to express pride in cultural heritage in their own, creative way by pairing traditional fabrics with modern fashion and accessories. The *berkain* movement is driven by a resurgence of interest in traditional crafts, with young, innovative designers incorporating batik into contemporary styles including T-shirts, chic jumpsuits and trendy culottes. Batik can even be seen hitting the runways in Indonesia and abroad, with high-end designers utilising the textiles in their collections. Despite being over 2000 years old, batik is clearly here to stay.

FROM LEFT: SIHASAKPRACHUM/SHUTTERSTOCK, ARPAN BHATIA/SHUTTERSTOCK

SAVING THE 'LAST PARADISE'

Raja Ampat's deeply interconnected ecosystem faces threats. Here's what locals are doing to preserve its delicate balance. By Tiara Maharani

RAJA AMPAT IS home to more than 1300 species of reef fish and 75% of the world's coral species, making it a true bucket-list destination and paradise for nature lovers. However, the effects of tourism and now nickel extraction threaten its otherworldly beauty, and locals are spearheading efforts to preserve this 'Amazon of the Seas'.

A Biodiversity Hotspot

Located off the northwest coast of Southwest Papua province, the over-1500 islands of the Raja Ampat archipelago are home to critical habitats for a trove of marine biodiversity, from whale sharks to pygmy seahorses.

Designated a UNESCO Global Geopark in 2023 and a Biosphere Reserve in 2025, Raja Ampat draws over 30,000 travellers yearly, with visitors bringing vital income but also the potential to disturb delicate reefs and forests. Research and local experience suggest the ever-increasing visitor numbers are already a third more than what the reefs can sustainably accommodate.

Local Guardians

Thankfully, local residents have played their part in protecting this remote corner of West Papua since long before the arrival of tourism.

Communities are guided in daily life by beliefs that involve deep respect for their environment, and one way they safeguard their home is through *sasi,* a traditional practice that temporarily pauses fishing and harvesting to allow ecosystems to recover.

In 'closed' *sasi,* fishing is completely off limits anywhere from a week to two years, depending on how local elders read the rhythms of nature. When the area reopens ('open' *sasi*), the community is free to harvest the bounty of the sea but with strict conditions in place. Catches must be taken sustainably using traditional tools rather than modern methods.

This has proven effective: when dynamite fishing severely damaged coral reefs and seagrass beds in the waters of Misool in the 1980s and '90s, it was the reinstatement of *sasi* that allowed these ecosystems to heal.

A New Threat

However, Raja Ampat faces a potentially more damaging threat in the form of nickel mining, with more than 22,000 hectares of nickel-mining concessions found within the archipelago.

Large-scale nickel mining commenced here in the late 1960s. Operations continued sporadically, but between 2020 and 2024, land use for mining grew by nearly 500 hectares, triple the pace of the previous five years, according to data from conservation NGO Auriga Nusantara.

This sparked outrage locally and also drew global concern. After mounting public pressure, the Indonesian government revoked four nickel-mining licences, leaving just one operation on Gag Island.

But the damage had been done. Environmental groups have documented at least three major impacts from mining in Raja Ampat: heavy sedimentation, extensive coral breakage and widespread coral bleaching. Of these, only bleaching offers any real chance of recovery, but even then, restoration can take decades.

Local Impact

The deepest wounds are felt by the same local communities that have protected these islands for generations. On Gag Island, contaminated water prevents villagers from swimming, while mangroves and coastal vegetation have been damaged, leaving homes exposed to waves and storms.

As forests are cleared and shores darken with sediment, traditional fishing grounds shrink and the ancient biocultural practices are at risk of extinction. In some places, fish have become scarce, forcing villages that once relied entirely on the ocean to supplement their income with small-scale tourism.

An Uncertain Future

There are also plans to build a nickel smelter, a 500-hectare project inside the Sorong Special Economic Zone that's expected to process up to 160,000 tonnes of nickel each year. The gateway to Raja Ampat, Sorong is just 35km by sea from the Dampier Strait.

The smelter could turn quiet waters into busy shipping lanes. Increased marine traffic brings the risks of oil spills, sediment runoff and noise pollution, which could stress coral reefs and fragile ecosystems, threatening the traditional livelihoods of local fishing communities.

The concern isn't limited to the Sorong project: without clear rules and consistent oversight, new mining operations could pop up elsewhere.

The Local Fight

While these threats loom, communities are taking action to protect their islands' ecosystems. In villages across Southwest Papua, homestays are now more than places to sleep. With training through NGOs and government bodies, homestay owners teach visitors how to protect the ocean through traditional beliefs and practices.

Dive operators also instruct their guests how to avoid damaging corals, and plan trails to avoid damaging mangroves and forest floors. Even small measures, like limiting visitor numbers in sensitive spots or coordinating boat departures, help reduce pressure on the islands' resources.

Locals know that tourism brings many challenges, but they say these issues are manageable and reversible. The extraction industry is not. The tension is no longer framed as development versus conservation. It's about whether Raja Ampat's future will be shaped by decisions made in boardrooms or by the communities who have cared for these ecosystems for generations.

The choices made today will determine whether the next generations inherit thriving eco-tourism economies and intact forests, or the long shadow of industrial scars.

CLOCKWISE FROM TOP LEFT: DIVEIVANOV/SHUTTERSTOCK, UTE WEEREN/SHUTTERSTOCK, TUNATURA/SHUTTERSTOCK, VACLAV SEBEK/SHUTTERSTOCK

GHURU VIDUKA/SHUTTERSTOCK

BALINESE HINDUISM: A SPIRITUAL BLEND

Unique rituals and ceremonies to live in harmony on the Island of the Gods. By Christine Gilbert

NINETY PERCENT OF Bali's population identifies as Hindu, according to Indonesia's Ministry of Religious Affairs. However, Hinduism in Bali has its own history and practices, making it distinctive from Hinduism in India. Elements of Balinese Hinduism incorporate indigenous Balinese paradigms, traditions and rituals. It also has parallels with Buddhism, Shinto and Taoism.

What is Balinese Hinduism?

Balinese Hindus believe in god, the soul, the law of karma, reincarnation and nirvana. To unite with god at the end of life, followers practise different types of yoga. I Made Gunarta, a founder of the BaliSpirit Festival who comes from a long line of Balinese temple and sarcophagus builders, describes the four types in this way: '*Bhakti yoga,* simply you [are a] devotee. Second one is...*kriya yoga,* you use your skill. Third one [is] *jnana yoga,* you use your knowledge...and *raja yoga*...when you [are] leading people with spirituality.'

While these tenets cross over with Indian Hinduism, Balinese Hinduism adds to them by incorporating animism (the indigenous belief that animals, objects and places have their own spirits). The ocean, mountains, rivers and houses all have spirits to be recognised, and one should attempt to live in harmony with them via shrines and offerings.

Bali has its own symbols and stories apart from Indian lore, like the figures of Barong and Rangda, representing good and evil, respectively. The struggle between these two entities is shown in dances with performers wearing ornate masks blessed with holy water. Barong is often depicted as a lion, while Rangda's mask incorporates huge teeth and matted hair.

History of Hinduism in Bali

The beginnings of Hinduism in Bali can be attributed to Indian traders and priests visiting in the 1st century CE, bringing their regional religions with them. Hinduism's spread greatly increased when Java's Majapahit Empire took over Bali in 1343, prompting a huge wave of Javanese Hindus to migrate. At the turn of the 15th century, when Java became increasingly Muslim, even more Javanese Hindus moved to Bali. Yet it wasn't until Indonesia gained independence from the Dutch in the 1940s that some Balinese started to strongly identify as Hindu. They recognised that their type of Hinduism was specific to Bali and by claiming it, they could protect themselves against Dutch influence and proselytisation by both Muslims and Christians.

Important Balinese Religious Days

Bali has two calendar systems that affect significant religious holiday dates. The lunar Saka calendar, made up of 12 months, determines the date on which Nyepi, the annual Day of Silence, falls. The other calendar, Pawukon, runs for 210 days, and is based on rituals, not solar or lunar cycles. Consisting of 10 weeks running concurrently, it determines the date when most of the island's religious festivals will land, as they change yearly.

Nyepi begins the Saka calendar year. To observe it, silence falls throughout the island for 24 hours. The Balinese take time to reflect and observe rituals tied to self-control, release of attachment, stillness and abstaining from entertainment. Everyone stays indoors, and everything closes. Malevolent spirits are believed to roam the island, and its deserted appearance is a strategy to prevent them from bringing harm.

FOR TEMPLE VISITS AND CEREMONIES IN BALI, THE RITUAL DRESS IS THAT OF A SARONG PAIRED WITH A SASH.

This prevention begins prior to Nyepi, when neighbourhood groups make ogoh-ogoh, massive sculptures representing evil spirits or sometimes gods and goddesses. Made of polystyrene and bamboo covered in painted paper, ogoh-ogoh are paraded through the streets the day before Nyepi and then burned.

Another auspicious holiday is Galungan, a celebration of good triumphing over evil, coupled with the visit of ancestral spirits. The origin of Galungan is tied to King Mayadenawa, said to be an ancient king in Bali. He forbade worship of the island's gods and destroyed its temples. Indra (the god of war) began a war against the king, who in turn poisoned the well of Indra's army. Indra responded by creating a new spring to heal those who'd drunk from the poisoned one. Indra's army then defeated the king. Galungan is the anniversary of their victory.

From the beginning of Galungan until Kuningan (the 10th day after Galungan), spirits of deceased ancestors are said to visit Bali. Festivities include feasting, temple visits and streets filled with bamboo poles decorated with offerings for ancestors.

Offerings, Rituals & Blessings

Walk down the streets of Bali and you'll see *canang sari*, a popular offering adorning the entrances to homes, storefronts, temples and even the handlebars of motorbikes. Made of small boxes of banana or coconut leaves, *canang sari* contains flowers, betel and pandan leaves, incense, rice and other tokens of devotion. All parts of the offering symbolise various things: different flower colours for certain gods and rice for prosperity. The incense is thought to usher prayers between the physical and spiritual worlds. *Canang sari* is believed to bring spiritual balance and protection – meaning it can be, and usually is, placed virtually everywhere.

For temple visits and ceremonies in Bali, the ritual dress is that of a sarong paired with a sash. The sarong represents the idea of duality in Balinese Hinduism, known as *rwa bhineda* (literally meaning 'two opposites'). This concept applies not only to good and evil, but to all aspects of life, such as birth and death – states and emotions' opposites are needed to find harmony and balance throughout the universe. The sash symbolises a 'tying off' of emotions to control them in sacred spaces and ceremonies, as well as the desire for purity.

One of the most famous Balinese rituals is *melukat*, a bathing ritual for spiritual and physical purification. The significance of holy water in Hinduism dates back to the Bhagavad Gita, an epic poem in which the Hindu deity Krishna says he accepts water offerings. Holy water features prominently in ceremonies, temples, blessings and household shrines. Holy water's potency depends on several factors: its source, the mantras used to bless it and the type of priest performing the blessing. One of the most accessible ways to experience *melukat* is to go to the Tirta Empul temple, the very one Indra was said to have created in the Galungan origin story.

Penglipuran (p165), during Galungan

ANOM HARYA/SHUTTERSTOCK

Street art, Canggu (p52)

TOM HENTY/SHUTTERSTOCK

IN INDONESIA, CONTEMPORARY ART BLOOMS & BOOMS

Well known for traditional and indigenous art, Indonesian artists are now stepping into the 21st century with daring new contemporary works. By Ian Lloyd Neubauer

TAKE A STROLL through any tourist area in Indonesia and you might think Indonesian art is all about the past: intricate batik fabrics and paintings of bucolic rice fields by colonial-era artists of the Ubud style. But when it comes to modern and contemporary art, Indonesia has traditionally been a laggard – and with good reason.

From Traditional to Modern

From independence in the 1940s through to the late 1990s, the country was mostly under military rule. Critical voices that drive dialogue and debate – one of the cornerstones of contemporary art – were heavily censored. By the time democracy was restored at the turn of the century, Indonesia was a cultural wasteland as far as contemporary art was concerned.

However, the new era of openness that followed let a young, tech-savvy population (around one in four Indonesians are young adults) harness the nation's long tradition of visual culture and apply it to modern styles with such vigour and lack of subtlety that Indonesia is now a Southeast Asian hotspot for contemporary art.

'Indonesia has one of the strongest markets in Southeast Asia because it has a community that gathers together to support the art scene and that is what I see is lacking in many other countries in the region. Economically, it is very strong,' says Joel Harumal, the Singaporean owner of Kotak Art Collective, a gallery in Jakarta. 'The whole world can learn from Indonesia about how to successfully share culture. It's the only country I know of that has a Ministry of Creative Economy.'

Bolthole for Artists

In the capital Jakarta, the opening of MACAN (Museum of Modern and Contemporary Art) in 2017 has led to a proliferation of galleries, artist collectives, collectors groups and nonprofits: a comprehensive art ecosystem rivalling that of Indonesia's cultural capital Yogyakarta.

But it is the neighbouring island of Bali – a bolthole for international artists for more than 100 years and now a global tourism hub flush with cash and crypto – where Indonesia's burgeoning contemporary art scene can be most easily accessed by visitors.

From the ramshackle capital Denpasar to the island's hipster headquarters Canggu, alleyways, breakwaters and sometimes entire buildings have been tagged with graffiti and public murals that mix ancient Balinese culture and contemporary themes. Take, for example, the work of

Slinat, a Balinese artist who spray paints large-scale reproductions of black-and-white photographs of Balinese dancers with biohazard masks juxtaposed across their faces.

'These old photos were the first imagery used to promote tourism in Bali and convey that it is an exotic place. They kick-started tourism in Bali,' Slinat says. 'But then we had too much tourism and it ruined the exoticness of Bali. So I created this parody to express how much things have changed here since those photos were taken.'

Galleries are a dime a dozen in beachfront tourist areas and also in Ubud, a small city in the lush green riverlands of Central Bali. The majority focus on traditional art because it's what tourists come to Bali ready to buy. But contemporary art is gaining ground, particularly in the busy beachside strip running from Kuta to Canggu.

CONTEMPORARY ART IS GAINING GROUND, PARTICULARLY IN THE BUSY BEACHSIDE STRIP RUNNING FROM KUTA TO CANGGU.

The island also boasts a calendar chock-a-block with art and cultural events: the Ubud Writers & Readers Festival, the largest literary event in Southeast Asia; the BaliSpirit Festival, which combines art, yoga, healing and music; and the Bali Art Festival in July, an event dedicated entirely to preserving and promoting traditional handicrafts.

Last year, the island also got its first event dedicated to contemporary art. Art & Bali takes place in September at Nuanu Creative City (p232), a visionary entertainment and residential project on Bali's west coast, featuring a beach club, luxury residential villas, a day school, a hotel, galleries, and an abundance of art, including giant sculptures that resemble those from the Burning Man festival in the US. In fact, they were designed by Daniel Jonathan Poppers, the South African sculptor whose large-scale flammable sculptures define the Burning Man zeitgeist.

Nuanu Creative City (p232)

ARBIWIRATAMA/SHUTTERSTOCK

The Fair Comes to Town

The two-day event features performances, talks, workshops, after-dark celebrations of art and more. However, its epicentre is the Labyrinth Convention Centre where, last year, 17 galleries and collectives representing 150 local and international artists from Indonesia and the region peddled their wares. The contrast in the utility of the works created by these two groups was well pronounced, though not in favour of the international artists as one might imagine.

Contributors, including Ubud-based Australian contemporary artist Rodney Glick and South Korean fashion designer Consteller DL, exhibited works at the event to varying degrees of success and originality.

Things were much more interesting at the Kotak Art Collective booth. The centrepiece here was a statue of a tall, squashed, canary-yellow double-decker bus made from resin, acrylic and automotive paint with playful plastic animal characters in the seats and cartoon-cloud-like smoke belching from the exhaust. Created by Yogyakartan sculptor Sumbul Pranov, it represents 'the way we see things as children, bigger and more colourful as they are', said gallery director Joel Harumal.

At the Laku Art Space booth, I was drawn to three paintings by another heavy hitter from Yogyakarta, Valentino Febri. The second-generation artist paints scenes from his hometown, like a woman patting her dog and lovers sitting by a canal. The fair complexions and plus-size bodies of the models, combined with pastel-coloured backgrounds, make me think the artists borrowed heavily from European impressionists like Claude Monet, who emphasised light and colour, and the famous women of Colombian artist Fernando Botero.

But Febri's inspiration came much closer to home. 'I based the subjects in these paintings on the skinny figures in the *wayang*,' he said, referring to the famous puppetry of Indonesia, the country's most iconic art, which originated in his home island, Java. 'I just gave them rounder faces.'

INDEX

A

- accessible travel 347
- accommodation 36, 338, *see also individual locations*
- activities 32-3, 42-5, **44-5**, *see also individual activities*
- Aimere 294, 299
- air travel 334, 335
- airports 334
- Alor Archipelago 315-16, 328, 331
- Amed 180-3, 187, **181**
- Amlapura 176
- Ampenan 255
- animal welfare 345
- animals 18, 113, 222, 345, *see also individual animals*
- *arak* 67, 168, 299
- archaeological sites
  - Lambanapu 318-19, 356-7
  - Liang Bua 291
  - Pejeng 150
- architecture
  - Ampenan 254
  - Bukit Peninsula 108
  - *candi bentar* 81, 177, 349
  - Denpasar 93-4
  - Klungkung 161
  - Seminyak 67, 70
  - temples 348-9
- art 370-3
  - Bukit Peninsula 108
  - courses 135
  - Denpasar 94
  - Legian 80
  - Mas 151
  - Nuanu Creative City 232
  - Ubud 126, 127, 132-3
- art galleries, *see* museums & galleries
- art markets
  - Legian 80
  - Sukawati 153
  - Ubud 141
- artisans 151
- ATMs 337

B

- *babi guling* 39, 70-1
- Bahasa Indonesia 352-3
- Bali Aga culture 176
- Bali Arts Festival 33, 94
- Bali Belly 78
- Bali Bird Park 154
- Bali bombing 77, 359
- Bali Botanic Garden 195
- Bali itineraries 28-9, 30-1, **29**, **31**
- Bali Kite Festival 91
- Bali Reptile Park 154
- Bali Sea Turtle Society 77-8
- Bali starlings 222
- Balinese compounds 359
- Balinese culture, *see* culture
- Balinese dance 12-13, 101, 130-1
- Balinese Hinduism 366-9
- Balinese names 360
- Balinese traditional clothing 95
- BaliSpirit Festival 33, 136
- Bangli 164
- Banyuwedang 223
- bargaining 19
- Barong dance 104, 131, 153-4
- bathrooms 351
- batik 153, 362-3
- bat cave 175
- bats 175, 298
- Batuan 153
- Batubulan 154
- Baum, Vicki 162
- beach clean-ups 114, 253, 345
- beach clubs 20, 58-9
- beaches 8-9, 26-7, 45
  - Amed 180
  - black-sand beaches 53, 163, 231, 234, 238
  - Bukit Peninsula 102-3
  - Canggu 52-3
  - Cemagi 231
  - East Coast 163-4
  - Ekas 250
  - Gili Air 283
  - Gili Trawangan 276
  - Jimbaran 103
  - Kelingking 116, 118
  - Kuta (Bali) 78-80
  - Kuta (Lombok) 244, 246-7
  - Legian 78-80
  - Lovina 206
  - Padangbai 172-4
  - Pantai Balian 234
  - Pantai Kedungu 232
  - Pemuteran 216
  - pink-sand beaches 302
  - safety 340
  - Sanur 88-9, 90
  - Selong Belanak 248
  - Seminyak 66
  - Senggigi 252-3
  - Sumba 322-3
  - Uluwatu 96, 98
  - West Bali 234
- Bedulu 150
- beer 21, 164
- Berawa 61, 83
- betel nuts 312
- bicycle travel, *see* cycling
- Bingin 105, 119
- birds 154, 222
- bird-watching
  - Bali Botanic Garden 195
  - Flores 300
  - Ubud 138
  - West Bali National Park 222
- Blahbatuh 153
- boat travel 174, 266, 335, 341, *see also* liveaboard trips
- books 35, 162, 222
  - bookshops 139, 172
  - *lontar* books 177, 212
  - Ubud Writers & Readers Festival 33, 136, 139
- Boti 312, 314, 357
- Budakeling 185
- Buddhism 360
- Buddhist temples & monasteries 80-1, 211
- budget 333, 343, 347
- Bukit Peninsula 102-8, **108**
  - accommodation 36
  - drinking & nightlife 105
  - food 107
- Bukit Selong 260
- bus travel 335
- bushwalking, *see* hiking
- business hours 351

C

- Caci 296
- Campuhan Ridge Walk 127
- *canang sari* 369
- *candi bentar* 81, 177, 349
- Candidasa 175-6, 187
- Canggu area 52-62, **54-5**
  - accommodation 36, 83
  - drinking & nightlife 60, 61
  - food 56, 57
  - shopping 62
  - travel within 52
- Canggu & Southwest Beaches 49-83, **50**
  - accommodation 83
  - festivals & events 51
  - itineraries 51
  - navigation 50
  - travel seasons 51
  - travel within 50
  - weather 51
- car & driver hire 336
- car travel 37, 335, 336
- cave diving 311-12
- caves
  - Goa Gajah 152
  - Goa Kristal 308, 311-12, 328
  - Goa Uihani 311-12, 328
  - Goa Uilebahan 308
  - Gua Batu Cermin 290-1
  - Gua Rangko 291
  - Liang Bua 291, 356
  - Monkey Cave 308
- Ceking Rice Terraces 144
- Cemagi 231, 239
- Central Highlands 189-201, **190**
  - accommodation 201

Map Pages **000**

itineraries 191
navigation 190
travel seasons 191
travel within 190
weather 191
ceramics 230
children, travel with, *see* family travel
chocolate 139, 178
Christianity 237, 360
climate 32-3
clothes 34
clubs 20, 58-9, 232, 274-5
coffee 144
coffee luwak 146
cooking classes
East Bali 179
Lombok 254
Meninting 254
Seminyak 63, 66
Taro 148
Tejakula 186
Tetebatu 249
Ubud 137
coral restoration 253
costs 333, 337, 343
country code 351
courses, *see also* cooking classes
art 135-6
batik 135-6
botanical 136
ceramics 136
culture 135-6
dance 135-6
jewellery 62, 135, 168
mask carving 151
printing 151
silversmithing 62, 136, 168
coworking 60, 137
crabs 113
credit cards 337
culture 12-13, 360-1, *see also* Bali Aga culture, Dawan culture, Lio culture, Manggarai culture, Ngada culture, Sasak culture, Sumbanese culture
celebrations 33
Hotel Tugu Bali 57, 60
itineraries 28-9, **29**
cycling 214
Bali Botanic Garden 195
Budakeling 185
Ceking Rice Terraces 144-5
e-bike tours 114
Gili Meno 278
Gunung Agung 185
Nusa Lembongan 114
Sanur 88-9
tours 145, 185
Ubud 137-8, 144-5

D

Dalem Bedaulu 150
Danau Gili Meno 280
Danau Tamblingan 195
dance 12-13, 366
Barong 104, 131, 153-4
Batubulan 154
courses 135-6
Kecak 101, 130-1, 154
Kerambitan 230
Legong 131
Rangda 131
Ubud 130-1
dangers, *see* safe travel
Dawan culture 309
debit cards 337
DeNeefe, Janet 138, 139
Denpasar 92-5, **93**
accommodation 36, 119
air travel 334, 335
food 94
travel within 92, 335
Desa Potato Head 66-7
distilleries 67, 168, 299
diving 14-15, 43, 45, *see also* snorkelling
Alor Archipelago 315-16
Amed 181
cave diving 311, 312
Gili Air 283
Gili Trawangan 276-7
Komodo National Park 305
Lombok 250, 267
Lovina 207
Nusa Lembongan 109-11
Padangbai 172
Pulau Menjangan 220-1
Tulamben 185
USAT *Liberty* 185
West Timor 311, 312
dogs 200
dolphins 206-7, 345
drinks 20, 21, 40, *see also arak*, beer, coffee, coffee luwak, wine
driving tours
Bukit Peninsula 108, **108**
East Bali 178-9, **179**
Flores 294, **294**
Jembrana Regency 238, **238**
Lombok 256, **256**
Lovina 210-11, **211**
Nusa Ceningan 117, **117**
Sumba 324, 327, **324**, **327**
West Timor 308, 313, **308**, **313**
drugs 276, 340
Dutch colony 161, 212, 356, 358

E

earthquakes 340
East Bali 156-87, **158**
accommodation 187
itineraries 159
navigation 158
travel seasons 159
travel within 158
weather 159
east coast 163-4
e-bike tours 114
Ekas 250, 268
electricity 351
Elephant Cave 152
elephants 148
emergencies 352
emergency numbers 351
endek, *see also* ikat
Blahbatuh 153
Gianyar 164
Klungkung 162
Sidemen 167-8
environmental concerns 344-5
etiquette 34, 343
events, *see* festivals & events

F

fabric 362-3, *see also endek*, ikat
family travel 339
activities 43
Bali Bird Park 154
Bali Reptile Park 154
beach clubs 58
beaches 102
Kuta 80
Legian 80
Upside Down World 95
Waterbom 76-7
festivals & events 32-3
art 136, 373
Bali Arts Festival 33, 94
Bali Kite Festival 91
BaliSpirit Festival 33, 136
Bau Nyale Festival 33, 247
Indonesian Independence Day 33
Kuningan 33
music 133
Nyepi 32, 33, 70, 81, 106, 229, 369
Pasola 323, 325
Penti harvest festival 296
Ubud Food Festival 136
Ubud Village Jazz Festival 136

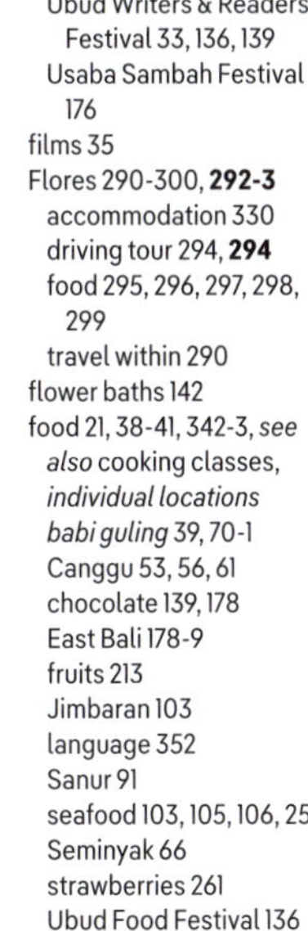

Ubud Writers & Readers Festival 33, 136, 139
Usaba Sambah Festival 176
films 35
Flores 290-300, **292-3**
accommodation 330
driving tour 294, **294**
food 295, 296, 297, 298, 299
travel within 290
flower baths 142
food 21, 38-41, 342-3, *see also* cooking classes, *individual locations*
babi guling 39, 70-1
Canggu 53, 56, 61
chocolate 139, 178
East Bali 178-9
fruits 213
Jimbaran 103
language 352
Sanur 91
seafood 103, 105, 106, 255
Seminyak 66
strawberries 261
Ubud Food Festival 136
freediving 182
frogs 113
fruits 213

G

galleries, *see* museums & galleries
Galungan 33, 369
gardens, *see* parks & gardens
gateways, *see candi bentar*
Gerupuk 248-9, 268
Gili Air 281-4, 285, **282**
Gili Islands 271-85, **272**
accommodation 285
festivals & events 273
itineraries 273
navigation 272
travel seasons 273
travel within 272
weather 273
Gili Kedis 264-5
Gili Meno 278-80, 285, **279**
Gili Nanggu 264-5
Gili Sudak 264-5
Gili Tangkong 264-5
Gili Trawangan 274-7, 285, **275**
Goa Gajah 152
Goa Kristal 308, 311-12, 328
Gojek 335
Grab 335
guesthouses 36, 338, 359

guides
Alor Archipelago 316
Denpasar 94
Flores 300
Gunung Abang 199
Gunung Agung 170
Nusa Tenggara 329
Sumba 323
Tamblingan 196
West Bali National Park 219
West Timor 314
Gunung Agung 170
Gunung Batur 198-9
Gunung Inerie 295
Gunung Kawi 147, 357
Gunung Rinjani 262-3
Gunung Rinjani National Park 262-3
gyms
Canggu 57
Seminyak 70

H

headhunters 309
health 78, 340
highlights 6-7, 8-21
hiking 43, 45, 60-1
Bukit Selong 260
Candidasa 175
Central Highlands 196
Danau Tamblingan 195
Flores 295
Gunung Abang 198-9
Gunung Agung 170
Gunung Batur 198-9
Gunung Rinjani 262-3
Gunung Seraya 183
Komodo National Park 303
Munduk 194-5
Senaru 258
Ubud 127
West Bali National Park 218-19
Hinduism 360, 366-9
history 356-9
colonial 161, 212, 356, 358
Denpasar 93-4
Hinduism 366
Singaraja 209

Map Pages **000**

hobbits 291, 356
holidays 351
homestays 338
Homo floresiensis 291, 356
honey 179
hostels 338
hot springs
Banyuwedang 222
Flores 297
Gunung Rinjani 263
Lovina 210-11
hotels 36, 338

I

ikat 298, *see also endek*
Blahbatuh 153
Flores 299
Sumba 319, 326
West Timor 310
Indonesian art 370-3
Indonesian Independence Day 33
internet 351
irrigation, *see subak*
Islam 259, 342, 351, 356, 358, 360
itineraries 24-31, **24-5**, **27**, **29**, **31**, *see also individual locations*

J

jamu 82
Jatiluwih 196, 201
jazz 136
Jembrana Regency 235-8, **236**
jewellery-making courses 62, 135, 168
Jimbaran 103, 105, 107, 119
jukung 91

K

Kalibukbuk 206
kayaking
Komodo National Park 305
Nusa Lembongan 112-13
Sanur 91
Kecak dance 101, 130-1, 154
Kecak fire dance 131
Kelingking 116
Keramas 165, 187
Kerobokan 36, 71
Kertha Gosa 161, 358
Kintamani 200, 201
kitesurfing 42, 301
Klungkung 160-2, **161**
Koanara 299
Koke, Bob 82, 358
Koke, Louise 82
Komodo dragons 303, 304, 328
Komodo National Park 302-5, 328
Kristal Cave, *see* Goa Kristal
Kuningan 33, 369
Kupang 308
Kusamba 175, 178
Kuta (Bali) 73-82, **74-5**
accommodation 36, 83
drinking & nightlife 77, 78, 82
food 76, 80, 82
shopping 80
travel within 73
walking tour 79, **79**
Kuta (Lombok) 244-7, 268, **245**
Kuta Beach Sea Turtle Conservation Center 78

L

Labuan Bajo 290-1
lakes
Danau Tamblingan 195
Gili Meno 280
Gunung Abang 199
Gunung Batur 198
Gunung Rinjani 263
Kelimutu National Park 300, 328
Lakey Peak 300, 328
Lakey Pipe 300, 328
Lambanapu 318-19, 356-7
language 35, 352-3
Legian 73-82, **74-5**
accommodation 36, 83
drinking & nightlife 77, 78, 82
food 76, 80, 82
shopping 80
travel within 73
walking tour 79, **79**
Legong dance 131
LGBTIQ+ travellers 346
Liang Bua Cave 291, 356
Lio culture 299-300
liveaboard trips 304, 305, 315, 329, 335
Lombok 240-69, **242**
accommodation 268-9
driving tour 256, **256**
itineraries 243
navigation 242
travel seasons 243
travel within 242
weather 243

lontar books 177, 212
lontar palm 317
Lovina 206-8, 223, **207**
Luba 296

M

macaques 113, 134
Manggarai culture 291, 295, 296
manta rays 33, 305
markets 19, 39, *see also* art markets, night markets
Ampenan 255
Denpasar 94-5
Flores 299
Jimbaran 105, 107
Klungkung 162
Kuta 82
Legian 82
Mataram 255
Seririt 210
West Timor 310, 313
Mas 151
Masjid Kuno Bayan Beleq 259, 358
mask carving 151
massages
Canggu 56
Pemuteran 217
Ubud 142-3
Uluwatu 99
Mataram 255, 268
measures 351
Medewi 239
megalithic tombs 326
Melasti ceremonies 70
melukat 369
memorials, *see* statues & monuments
Mengwi 228-30, **229**
Meninting 254
money 334, 337
monitors 113
Monkey Forest 134
monkeys 18, 101, 113, 217
monuments, *see* statues & monuments
mosques 259, 358
motorbike tours, *see* driving tours
motorbike travel 335
mountains, *see* volcanoes
Munduk 192-7, 201, **193**
museums & galleries
Agung Rai Museum of Art 132-3
Batur Geopark Museum 198
Black Hand Gang 151
Gedong Kirtya Library 212
Le Mayeur Museum 90

Mandala Mathika Subak Museum 229
Masa Masa 163
Museum Buleleng 212
Museum Gedung Arca 150
Museum Manusia Purba 356
Museum Negeri Propinsi Bali 93-4
Museum Nusa Tenggara Timur 308
Museum Pasifika 108
Museum Puri Lukisan 127, 130
Museum Pustaka Lontar 177
Museum Semarajaya 161
Museum Soenda Ketjil 209, 358
Neka Art Museum 133
Ngurah Gallery 118
Nuanu Creative City 232, 373
Ogoh Ogoh Bali Museum 229
Rumah Budaya Sumba 327
Saka Museum 106, 108
Samsara Living Museum 179
Setia Darma House of Masks & Puppets 151
Sukarno Center 146
Taman Werdhi Budaya Art Centre 94
Theatre Art Gallery 80
Tonyraka Art Lounge 151
Ubud Diary 151
music 35, 306-7

N

names 360
national parks
Gunung Rinjani National Park 262-3
Kelimutu National Park 300
Komodo National Park 302-5
West Bali National Park 218-22
natural disasters 340
Negara 239
Nest 278
Ngada culture 296-7
Ngurah Rai International Airport 359
night markets
Sanur 91
Sayan 150
nightlife 20, 58-9, 232, 274-5
None 309
North Bali 202-23, **204**
accommodation 223
itineraries 205
navigation 204
travel seasons 205
travel within 204
weather 205
Nusa Ceningan 114, 117, 118, 119, **117**
Nusa Dua 107, 119, 359
Nusa Lembongan 109-14, **110**
accommodation 36, 119
drinking & nightlife 112
food 111, 113
travel within 109
Nusa Penida 115-16, 119
Nusa Tenggara 286-331, **288**
accommodation 330-1
food 343
itineraries 289
navigation 288
travel seasons 289
travel within 288
weather 289
women travellers 350
Nusa Tenggara islands 328-9
Nyepi 32, 33, 70, 81, 106, 229, 369
Nyepi Laut 112

offerings 171, 369
ogoh-ogoh 81, 106, 229
ojek 335
opening hours 351

Padangbai 172-4, 187, **173**
painters 132, 133
pakaian adat 95
palaces, *see also* water palaces
Kertha Gosa 161, 358
Klungkung 161
Puri Agung Karangasem 176
Puri Anyar Kerambitan 230
Ubud Palace 124, 358
Pantai Balian 234, 239
paragliding 105
parks & gardens, *see also* national parks
Bali Botanic Garden 195
GWK Cultural Park 104
Tirta Gangga 176
Pasola 323, 325
Pejeng 149-50
Pekutatan 237
Pemuteran 215-17, 223, **216**
Penglipuran 165
Pengrupukan 106
Perancak 237, 239
Pererenan 53, 83
pigeons 167
pink buffaloes 237
planning 34-5
accommodation 36, 338
budget 336, 343
itineraries 24-31, **24-5**, **27**, **29**, **31**
podcasts 35
population 351
Potato Head Beach Club 66-7
public holidays 351
Pulau Menjangan 220-1
Punjungan 192
puppets 151
puputan 160, 358
Pura Besakih 171
Pura Luhur Ulu Watu 100-1
Pura Rambut Siwi 238, 357
Pura Taman Ayun 228-9, 357
Pura Tanah Lot 233
Pura Tirta Empul 146

rafting 145-6, 169
rainforests 10
Raja Ampat archipelago 364-5
Ramadan 274, 342, 343
Rangda dance 131
reef restoration 217, 253, 280
religion 366
remote work 60, 137
Rendang 169
reptiles 154
resorts 17, 338, 359
responsible travel 344-5
rice fields 10, 72, 140
Ceking Rice Terraces 144-5
Flores 295
Jatiluwih 196, 197
Sidemen 166-7
south of Ubud 153
rice terraces, *see* rice fields
ride apps 335
river clean-ups 76, 345
Rote 316-17, 331
rubbish 76, 114, 280, 344-5

S

safe travel 62, 78, 340-1
Sajang 260-1
Saka calendar 106, 369
Saka Museum 106, 108
sambal 40
Sanggalangit 218
Sanur 88-91, **89**
accommodation 36, 119
drinking & nightlife 91
food 89
travel within 88
walking tour 90, **90**
Sa'o Ria 299-300
Sasak culture 249-50, 265
Sasak food 39
sasando 306-7
scams 337, 340
scooter tours, *see* driving tours
scuba diving, *see* diving
sea temples 232, 357
Pura Gede Perancak 237
Pura Luhur Ulu Watu 100-1
Pura Petitenget 67, 70
Pura Pulaki 217
Pura Rambut Siwi 238, 357
Pura Tanah Lot 233
sea turtles, *see* turtles
seafood 103, 105, 106, 255
seaweed plantations 113-14
Sebatu 147-8
Secret Gilis 264-7, **265**
Sekaroh 250, 268
Sekumpul 223
Selong Belanak 248, 268
Semarapura 160-2
Sembalun Valley 261, 269
Seminyak area 63-72, **64-5**
accommodation 83
drinking & nightlife 67
food 66, 70
shopping 71
travel within 63
Senaru 257-9, 269, **258**
Senggigi 251-3, 268, **252**
Seraya 184
Seririt 223
Seventeen Islands Marine Park 298-9
shadow puppets 135
sharks 246, 305, 345
shopping 19, *see also* markets
Canggu 62
Kuta 80
Legian 80
Seminyak 71
Ubud 138-9
Uluwatu 99

Sidemen 166-8, 187, **167**
silversmithing 62, 136, 168
Singaraja 209, 358
snakes 113
snorkelling 14-15, 43, 45, *see also* diving
  Amed 181
  Flores 298-9
  Gili Air 283
  Gili Meno 278, 280
  Gili Trawangan 276
  Komodo National Park 304
  Lombok 250, 266, 267
  Lovina 207
  Nusa Lembongan 109-11
  Padangbai 172
  Pemuteran 215
  Pulau Menjangan 221
  Tulamben 184
South Bali & the Islands 84-119, **86**
  accommodation 119
  festivals & events 87
  itineraries 87
  navigation 86
  travel seasons 87
  travel within 86
  weather 87
Southwest Beaches, *see* Canggu & Southwest Beaches
Southwestern Peninsula 264-7, 269, **265**
spas
  Gili Air 284
  Pemuteran 217
  Seminyak 68-9
  Ubud 142-3
  Uluwatu 99
stand-up paddleboarding 91
statues & monuments 349
  Bajra Sandhi Monument 93
  Garuda Wisnu Kencana 104
  Gunung Kawi 147, 357
  Ida I Dewa Agung Istri Kanya 165
  Kuta Memorial Wall 77, 359
  Patung Kanda Pat 160
  Puputan Monument 160
  Pura Luhur Ulu Watu 101

Map Pages **000**

stick fighting 265
stone carving 154
strawberries 261
subak 72, 357
Sukawati 153-4
Sumba 318-27, 345, **320-1**
  accommodation 331
  driving tours 324, 327, **324**, **327**
  food 319, 322, 325
  travel within 318
Sumbanese culture 325
Sumbawa 301, 330
sunrise
  Besakih 170
  Gunung Abang 198-9
  Gunung Agung 170
  Gunung Batur 199-200
  Gunung Inerie 328
  Nusa Dua 107
  Pergasingan Hill 261
  Wolo Bobo 294
sunsets
  Amed 183
  Budakeling 185
  Bukit Merese 244
  Bukit Peninsula 102-3
  Canggu 60
  Gili Air 283
  Gili Meno 280
  Gili Trawangan 276
  Kuta (Bali) 78, 79, 80
  Kuta (Lombok) 244
  Legian 78, 79, 80
  Lovina 208
  Mahana Point 117
  Pantai Nyanyi 232
  Pantai Tablolong 308
  Pemuteran 216
  Pura Luhur Ulu Watu 100-1
  Pura Tanah Lot 233
  Southwest Bali 58-9
  Sumbawa 301
  Uluwatu 96, 98, 100-1
  West Bali National Park 219
surfing 11, 32, 42-3, 44
  Canggu 52
  Gerupuk 248
  Jembrana Regency 235, 237
  Kuta (Bali) 76
  Kuta (Lombok) 247
  Lombok 267
  Nusa Lembongan 111-12
  Nusa Tenggara 328
  Pantai Balian 234
  Rote 316-17
  Sanur 91
  Senggigi 253
  Sumba 325-6
  Sumbawa 301
  Uluwatu 96, 98, 358
swimming 340
  Bukit Peninsula 102
  Gili Trawangan 276
  Nusa Lembongan 110-11
  Selong Belanak 248

Tabanan 228-30, **229**
Tamkesi 309-10
Tampaksiring 146
Tanglad 118
tap water 351
Taro 148
taxes 334
taxis 335
Tegallalang 144
Tejakula 185-6, 187
temples 12-13, 348-9, 369, *see also* sea temples, water temples
  architecture 348-9
  Amlapura 177
  around Lovina 214
  Bangli 164
  Bat Cave Temple 175
  Batuan 153
  Batukaru 196
  Bedulu 150
  Blahbatuh 153
  Buddhist 80
  Cemagi 231
  Denpasar 93-4
  Goa Gajah 152
  Gunung Payung 105
  Kubutambahan 214
  Kusamba 175
  Kuta 80-1
  Mengwi 228-9
  Nusa Penida 115-16
  Pejeng 149-50
  Pemuteran 217
  Perancak 237
  Pulau Menjangan 221
  Pura Besakih 171
  Pura Lempuyang 177
  Pura Luhur Ulu Watu 100-1
  Pura Rambut Siwi 238, 357
  Pura Taman Ayun 228-9, 357
  Pura Tanah Lot 233
  Pura Tirta Empul 146
  Pura Ulun Danu Bratan 199
  Sebatu 147-8
  Senggigi 251
  Tampaksiring 146
  Taro 148
  Ubud 124, 126, 134
  Uluwatu Temple 100-1
  West Bali National Park 222
Tetebatu 249-50, 268
textiles 344, *see also endek*, ikat
time zone 351
Timor-Leste 311
tipping 337
toilets 351
tourism tax 334
tours, *see also* driving tours, guides, walking tours
  cycling 138, 145, 185
  Desa Potato Head 66-7
  e-bike 114
  Seminyak 72
traditional clothing 95
traditional villages 345
  Boti 312, 314, 357
  Flores 296-7
  Nusa Tenggara islands 328
  Penglipuran 165
  Sumba 322, 324
  Tenganan 176
  West Timor 309-10, 312-14
traffic 37
travel seasons 32-3, 40, *see also individual locations*
travel to/from Bali, Lombok & Nusa Tenggara 334
travel within Bali, Lombok & Nusa Tenggara 335, *see also* boat travel, bus travel, car travel, cycling, motorbike travel, walking, *individual locations*
  travel within Bali 37, 335
  travel within Lombok 242
  travel within Nusa Tenggara 288, 329
  travel within the Gili Islands 272
travelling with kids, *see* family travel
trekking, *see* hiking
Trunyan 200
tsunamis 340
Tulamben 185
Turtle Conservation & Education Centre 92-3
turtles 18, 77-8, 92-3, 217, 237, 305

U

Ubud 124-43, 359, **125**, **128-9**
  accommodation 155
  drinking & nightlife 132, 137

food 127, 133, 141, 147, 150
shopping 138-9
travel within 124
walking tour 140, **140**
Ubud Monkey Forest 134
Ubud Palace 124, 358
Ubud region 121-55, **122**
accommodation 155
festivals & events 123
itineraries 123
navigation 122
travel seasons 123
travel within 122
weather 123
Ubud Writers & Readers Festival 33, 136, 139
Uluwatu 96-101, 358, **97**
accommodation 36, 119
drinking & nightlife 98
food 99
shopping 99
travel within 96
Uluwatu Temple 100-1
UNESCO sites 72, 196, 228-9, 364-5
Upside Down World 95

vegetarian travellers 39, 141
viewpoints
Bukit Selong 260
Diamond Beach 118
Gunung Batur 199-200
Nusa Penida 116
Sekumpul Waterfalls 213
Tanau Hills 319
villas 338
visas 255, 311, 334
volcanic eruptions 340
volcanoes 10, 44
Gunung Abang 198-9
Gunung Agung 170, 340
Gunung Batur 198-9
Gunung Inerie 295-6
Gunung Kelimutu 300
Gunung Rinjani 262-3
Gunung Seraya 183
Nusa Tenggara islands 328
volunteering 76, 114, 253

Wae Rebo 295
Waingapu 318-19
walking 43, 45, *see also* hiking, walking tours
tips 127
Ubud 127
Sidemen 166-7
walking tours
Candidasa 175
Denpasar 94, 95
Kuta 79, **79**
Legian 79, **79**
Sanur 90, **90**
Senaru 258
Ubud 137-8, 140, **140**
Wallace Line 185
warungs 41
waste management 280
water, drinking 107, 344, 351
water palaces
Pura Taman Saraswati 126
Taman Ujung 177
Tirta Gangga 176
Ubud Water Palace 126
water temples 147-8, 357
Pura Gunung Kawi Sebatu 147-8
Pura Taman Ayun 228-9, 357
Pura Tirta Empul 146
Waterbom Bali 76-7
waterfalls 10
Air Terjun Bertingkat 212
Air Terjun Gitgit 212
Air Terjun Singsing 211
Air Terjun Yeh Mampeh 185-6
Air Uma Anyar 153
Banyumala Waterfall 195
Gembleng 170
Gunung Rinjani 263
Melanting Waterfall 195
north of Ubud 145
Red Coral Waterfall 195
Sajang 260-1
Sekumpul 213-14
Senaru 257-8
Senggigi 253
Sumba 322
waterparks
Kuta 76-7
North Bali 212
wayang kulit 135
weather 32-3, *see also individual regions*
weaving 118, 299, *see also endek*, ikat
weights 351
West Bali 225-39, **226**
accommodation 239
itineraries 227
navigation 226
travel seasons 227
travel within 226
weather 227
West Bali National Park 218-22
West Timor 306-14, **307**
accommodation 330-1
driving tours 308, 313, **308**, **313**
food 309, 311
travel within 306
whip fighting 296
white-water rafting 145-6, 169
wi-fi 351
wildlife 18, 113, 222, 345
wine 164, 218
women travellers 350
woodcarving 151, 154
work spaces 60, 137

Yeh Gangga 239
Yeh Sanih 214, 223
yoga 366
Amed 183
Canggu 57
Gili Air 283-4
Seminyak 70
Ubud 142-3
Uluwatu 99

NOTES

NOTES

'It's surreal to stand at Gunung Rinjani's crater rim (p263) and watch the sunset fill the crater in an orange glow.'

LEYLA ROSE

'Visiting North Bali (p202) always stirs up my nostalgia for the Bali I first visited 20+ years ago.'

SARAH REID

'The coastal road near Seraya (p184) twists and turns dramatically and while the scenery on land is beautiful, it's the ocean outlook that I find most compelling.'

NARINA EXELBY

'Scootering in Bali is both terrifying and brilliant – coastal views, wind in your hair and the delicious smells of street food – but take it slowly, wear a helmet and expect anything.'

JADE BREMNER

FROM LEFT: JR BALI/SHUTTERSTOCK, DANIEL_FERRYANTO/SHUTTERSTOCK

Mapping data sources:
© Lonely Planet
© OpenStreetMap http://openstreetmap.org/copyright

THIS BOOK

Destination Editor James Pham

Production Editor Hannah Cartmel

Image Researcher Megan Cassidy

Cartographer Corey Hutchison

Coordinating Editor Michael Mackenzie

Assisting Editor Nicola Williams

Contributing Writers Anna Kaminski, Sarah Lempa, Ryan Ver Berkmoes

Cover Researcher Giada de Agostinis

Thanks Sofie Foldager Andersen, Kate Chapman, Melanie Dankel, Anne Mulvaney

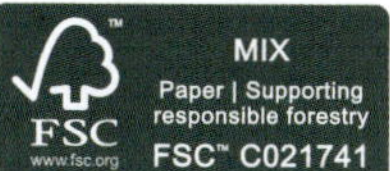

Paper in this book is certified against the Forest Stewardship Council™ standards. FSC™ promotes environmentally responsible, socially beneficial and economically viable management of the world's forests.

Published by Lonely Planet Global Limited
CRN 554153
20th edition – Aug 2026
ISBN 978 1 83758 431 4

10 9 8 7 6 5 4 3 2 1
Printed in China